THE WORLD
OF PHILOSOPHY

THE WORLD OF PHILOSOPHY

An Introductory Reader

EDITED BY
STEVEN M. CAHN

New York   Oxford

OXFORD UNIVERSITY PRESS

Oxford University Press is a department of the University of Oxford.
It furthers the University's objective of excellence in research,
scholarship, and education by publishing worldwide.

Oxford   New York
Auckland   Cape Town   Dar es Salaam   Hong Kong   Karachi
Kuala Lumpur   Madrid   Melbourne   Mexico City   Nairobi
New Delhi   Shanghai   Taipei   Toronto

With offices in
Argentina   Austria   Brazil   Chile   Czech Republic   France   Greece
Guatemala   Hungary   Italy   Japan   Poland   Portugal   Singapore
South Korea   Switzerland   Thailand   Turkey   Ukraine   Vietnam

For titles covered by Section 112 of the US Higher Education
Opportunity Act, please visit www.oup.com/us/he for the
latest information about pricing and alternate formats.

Published in the United States of America by
Oxford University Press
198 Madison Avenue, New York, NY 10016
http://www.oup.com

Library of Congress Cataloging-in-Publication Data
The world of philosophy : an introductory reader / edited by Steven M. Cahn.
    pages cm
  ISBN 978-0-19-023339-6
  1. Philosophy--Introductions. I. Cahn, Steven M.
  BD21.W667   2015
  100--dc23
                                                          2015011377

Printing number: 9 8 7 6 5 4 3 2 1

Printed in the United States of America
on acid-free paper

For my brother,

Victor L. Cahn

Contents

⧖

VI. Moral Theory   237

VII. Moral Problems   311

Preface

This collection of readings offers an introduction to philosophy that includes not only standard analytic materials and Western historical texts but also writings reflecting Chinese, Indian, and other non-Anglo-American sources. Approximately one-quarter of the contemporary selections are authored by women, including work by recent feminist theorists.

While some of the articles are reprinted unabridged, many have been edited to increase their accessibility. None presupposes prior acquaintance with any particular philosophical tradition.

ANCILLARY MATERIALS

An Instructor's Manual, Ancillary Resource Center (ARC), and Companion Website (www.oup.com/us/cahn) accompany *The World of Philosophy*. The Instructor's Manual, located in the password-protected ARC, features PowerPoint lecture outlines, reading summaries, a glossary, and a test bank of objective and essay questions. A link to the ARC can be found on the companion website. The companion website includes student resources such as self-test questions with answers and helpful web links.

ACKNOWLEDGMENTS

I remain grateful to my longtime editor Robert Miller. This book is the fourteenth we have done together, and here the vision was his. As usual, Robert's wise counsel and unwavering support were crucial to the effort. I also wish to express my appreciation to his editorial assistants, Kaitlin Coats and Alyssa Palazzo, who helped in so many ways. Their enthusiasm, sound judgment, and conscientiousness contributed greatly to the project. Thanks also to project editor Marianne Paul and the staff of Oxford University Press for their generous assistance throughout production. My deepest appreciation is to my wife, Marilyn Ross, M.D., to whom I owe more than I would try to express in words.

NOTE

Some of the materials throughout the book were written when the custom was to use the noun "man" and the pronoun "he" to refer to all persons, regardless of sex, and I have retained the author's original wording. With this proviso, let us begin the study of philosophy.

Part I

⊠

The Nature of Philosophy

What Is Philosophy?

MONROE C. BEARDSLEY AND ELIZABETH LANE BEARDSLEY

The study of philosophy is unlike the study of any other subject. No dates, formulas, or rules need be memorized. No field work is necessary, and no technical equipment required. The only prerequisite is an inquiring mind.

About what do philosophers inquire? The word *philosophy* is of Greek origin and literally means "the love of wisdom." But what sort of wisdom do philosophers love?

The answer is provided in our first selection. Its authors are Elizabeth Lane Beardsley (1914–1990), a philosopher who taught at Lincoln University and then at Temple University, and her husband, Monroe C. Beardsley (1915–1985), who taught at Swarthmore College and then at Temple University.

While the best way to understand the nature of philosophical inquiry is to consider some specific philosophical issues, an overview of the subject is helpful, and that is what the Beardsleys provide.

Philosophical questions grow out of a kind of thinking that is familiar to all of us: the thinking that we do when we ask ourselves whether something that we believe is reasonable to believe. "Reasonable" has a broad, but definite, meaning here: a reasonable belief is simply a belief for which a good reason can be given. Reasonable beliefs are logically justifiable. It would seem that a belief that is reasonable stands a better chance of being true than one that is not, so anyone who is interested in the truth of his beliefs should be concerned about their reasonableness.

All of us have known, long before we approached the systematic study of philosophy, what it is like to want to make a belief reasonable, and also what it is like not to care whether a belief is reasonable or not. We have all had the experience of accepting beliefs without worrying about their logical justification, for we have all been children. We absorbed the beliefs of our parents, or the opinions current in our society or culture, without thinking about them very much or looking at them with a critical eye. We may not even have been fully aware that we had them; we may have acted on them without ever having put them into words. As long as our own experience did not seem to conflict with those early beliefs, or those beliefs did not seem to clash with one another, it did not occur to us to question them or to inquire into the reasons that could be given for them.

But a growing individual cannot grow for very long without sometimes wondering whether his most cherished beliefs have any foundation. This experience, too, dates back to childhood. When, for example, a child notices that the Santa Claus on the street corner is about as tall as his father, while the one in the department store is a good deal taller, and is moved to ask questions about Santa's location and stature, he is looking critically at a belief and inquiring into its reasons.

As we emerge from childhood, we continue to have experiences of this kind and to acquire further beliefs. Some beliefs we go on accepting without checking up on their reasonableness; other beliefs we do question, some of them very seriously. But two things happen to many of us. First, the questioned beliefs increase in proportion to the unquestioned beliefs. And second, the questioning process, once begun, is carried on for longer and longer times before it is allowed to end. The child who is told that the department store Santa is "really" Santa Claus, while those in the street are merely trusted helpers, may be satisfied for a time, but at some later stage he will probably ask himself what reason there is for believing *this* to be true, especially if he compares notes with his cousin from another city, who has been provided with a different candidate for the "real Santa Claus." The junior high school student who has been told he should accept what his science teacher says because the latter knows his subject may wonder why the teacher is judged to be a qualified authority in this field. If provided with satisfactory assurances, he will call a halt to his questioning process at that stage; but later on, perhaps in college, he may be moved to ask why we should ever accept anything told us by "authorities," no matter how well qualified. Should we not rely entirely on our own firsthand experience? Is anything else really *knowledge*?

The search for good reasons for our beliefs, and for good reasons for the reasons, can be carried as far as we wish. If it is carried far enough, the searcher finds himself confronted by questions of a peculiar kind: the questions of philosophy. Among these questions you will find some that you have already thought about, as well as others that will be unfamiliar to you. Many of them, however, originally came to be asked because someone undertook a critical examination of his ordinary beliefs.

PHILOSOPHICAL QUESTIONS

As our first example, let us trace the origin of a few philosophical questions that arise out of the moral aspects of life. People sometimes say, "He ought to be put in jail for that." Sometimes this is only an exclamation of anger at some instance of meanness or brutality; sometimes it leads to action, however, for juries do put people in jail because (if the jurors are conscientious) they believe that this punishment is just. Suppose you hear a friend remark, about the recent conviction of someone who has violated the law—a holdup man, a venal judge, an industrialist who has conspired to fix prices, a civil rights demonstrator who has blocked a construction site—that the jail sentence is deserved. After you hear all the relevant details, you may agree with him. But even so, you might still wonder whether you are right, and—not because you plan to do anything about the case, but merely because you would like to be sure you *are* right—you may begin to ask further, more searching, questions.

Why does the man deserve to be sent to jail? Because he committed a crime, of course. Yes, but why should he be sent to jail for committing a crime? Because to disobey the laws of the state is wrong. But *why*? Just because certain people you don't even know, perhaps people who died years before you were born, passed a law against, let us say, spitting in the subway or disorderly conduct, how does that obligate you to obey the law? This line of questioning, as we can foresee, will, if carried far, lead into some perplexing questions about the moral basis of the law, the tests of right and wrong, the purposes of government and society. For example, we may discover that in approving the jail sentence we are assuming that the existence of a government is so important to maintain that governments have the right, under certain conditions, to deprive any citizen of his liberties. This assumption is a philosophical belief. And when we ask whether or not it is true, we are asking a philosophical question.

But consider how the questioning might turn into a different channel. Granted that the act was illegal, there still remains the question whether the man should be punished. Sometimes people do wrong things because they are feeble-minded or mentally ill, and we do not regard them as punishable. Well, in this case, it might be said, the man is responsible for his action. Why responsible? Because he was free when he committed it—free to commit the act or to refrain from committing it. He had, some would say, free will. Indeed, all men have free will—though they do not always exercise it. Then what reason is there to believe that this, in turn, is true? How do we know there is such a thing as free will? Again, we seem to have uncovered an underlying belief that lies deeper than the lawyer's or the juror's immediate problems, something they do not themselves discuss, but (according to one theory) take for granted. We have reached another belief that can be called philosophical, and exposed another philosophical question: do human beings have free will?

Let us see what it is about these questions that makes them philosophical. One of the first things that might be noticed about them is that they are highly *general*. One question is more general than another if it is about a broader class of things: about brown cows rather than about Farmer Jones's brown cow Bessie, or about cows rather than about brown cows, or about animals rather than about cows. A question about everything there is would be the most general of all—we shall be trying in due course to answer such questions. Most philosophical questions are highly general: Are all right actions those that promote human happiness? Is all knowledge based on sense experience? Or—to recall those that turned up in our example—do all human beings have free will? Do all citizens owe certain obligations to their governments? Those who specialize in subjects other than philosophy may be interested in particular things or events, such as individual crimes or criminals. Or they may be interested in things or events of certain limited kinds, such as the psychological or sociological causes of crime. The philosopher goes into action when questions are raised about much larger classes, such as the class of human beings or of

knowledge. Those who limit their investigations are entirely justified in doing so, for human knowledge could scarcely develop otherwise. Courts would never get their work done if every judge felt called upon to solve wide-ranging questions about guilt and responsibility before he could get down to the business of trying a particular case. But somebody, sometime, must ask those broad questions and try to answer them. That is the job of the philosopher.

Some questions count as philosophical because of a second, and even more important, quality: they are highly *fundamental*. The beliefs that a particular person has at a particular time constitute a more or less orderly system, depending on the extent to which they are logically interconnected, some being reasons for others, some of the others being in turn reasons for still others, etc. When you are pressed for your reason for predicting rain, if you reply that you observe dark clouds, then in your thinking at that time the second belief is more fundamental than the first. Of course a belief that is very fundamental in one person's thinking may not be at all fundamental in another's; that is one reason why each person comes at philosophy a little differently from everyone else. But there are some beliefs that are pretty sure to be fundamental in the thinking of anyone who holds them at all, and it is these that we have in mind when we speak of fundamental beliefs and fundamental questions without mentioning any particular believer.

When one belief supports another, but is not itself supported by it, it is logically more fundamental; there is more to it, so to speak, and therefore, in principle at least, it is capable of supporting a wider range of other beliefs. Thus, of two beliefs, the more fundamental one is probably the one that underlies and supports more of your other beliefs. If you should discover that you were mistaken about a particular fact, you would probably not have to revise many of your other beliefs to accommodate this change. But, for example, a belief in the immortality of the soul may be tied up with many other beliefs about morality, religion, education, and science.

A highly fundamental question is a question about the truth of a highly fundamental belief. And such questions are philosophical ones. The more general a question is, the more fundamental it is likely to be, because it will range over a larger area. But this is not necessarily true. For example, the question, "Are all men selfish?" and the question, "Do all men wear shoes?" are equally general, since they are about all men; but they are not equally fundamental, since the former has important consequences for our beliefs about the nature of moral obligation (which includes a host of beliefs about particular obligations), while little seems to depend upon the latter. On the other hand, the philosophical question, "Does God exist?" does not seem to be general at all, for it is about a single being. Nevertheless, this question is fundamental for many people, since many other beliefs about human beings and the physical universe may depend upon the answer to it—and some of these beliefs are themselves highly general.

We do not know how to set up any rules telling exactly how general or how fundamental a question must be in order for it to be considered a philosophical one. Philosophers themselves might not all agree on the proper classification of every question you can think of. But if the demand for good reasons is pressed, beginning with any belief, it will gradually pass beyond the scope of various special fields of knowledge and investigation, and at some point it will bring to light a question that many philosophers would be interested in, and would recognize—perhaps with joy, and perhaps, if it is a very tough one, with uneasiness—as their very own.

PHILOSOPHICAL EXAMINATION

Any thinking that concerns the truth of a philosophical belief is *philosophical thinking*. It may take the form of accepting a belief as true and investigating its logical connections with other beliefs; this may be called *exploring* the belief. Or it may take the form of questioning the belief

and attempting to determine whether it is based on good reasons; this may be called *examining* the belief. Professional philosophers are those who have made philosophical thinking their vocation; but they have no monopoly on that activity. It is pursued by specialists in other fields—by scientists, historians, literary critics— whenever they inquire into the fundamental questions about their own disciplines. And it is pursued by all intelligent human beings who want to understand themselves and their world. Professional philosophers who genuinely respect their subject do not erect "No Trespassing" signs around philosophical questions.

In order to illustrate a little more fully what is involved in the process of examining a belief philosophically, let us take an example from history—let us begin with the belief that such-and-such a culture flourished hundreds of years before the Christian era in Central Africa or Nigeria. When the historian tells us this, we believe him. But if we have some intellectual curiosity, we might wonder how he knows it. Since the culture had no written language, he cannot rely on documents. And since their thatched houses and all the organic materials they once used in their daily life (wood, hide, cloth) would long ago have disintegrated in the tropical climate, the African historian has less to go on than his colleagues in other areas.[1] The usual methods developed by archaeologists are seldom available to him. It is hard to find organic materials on which to use the carbon-14 dating method (based on the constant rate of decay of this isotope in living organisms), though some artifacts have been dated in this way. Because of the rapid decay of dead wood and the eccentricities of seasonal growth, he cannot make much use of dendrochronology (dating by tree rings). But suppose the historian answers our challenge by using another method, thermoluminescence. In pottery there are uranium impurities that radiate naturally, but this radiation is trapped until the pottery is heated to a very high temperature. When the radiation rate for a particular substance is known, it is possible to determine how long ago the pottery was baked by measuring the amount of radiation built up in it.

Now we began with a question asked by the historian, "When did this culture flourish?" and the historian gave his answer. But when we ask him for his reasons he appeals to principles of physics: for example, that the radiation rate of this kind of pottery is always such-and-such. If we ask him, "How do you know this?" he will, of course, conduct us to the physicist and advise us to direct our question to him—he is the expert on radiation. Suppose we do so. Presumably the physicist's answer will be something of this sort: "We have tested various samples in our laboratory under controlled conditions, and found that the radiation rate is constant." Now, "constant" here means that it holds not only for last week's laboratory samples, but for the same substance a thousand years ago and a thousand years hence.

Our historical curiosity is satisfied, and we would ordinarily be content to accept the physicist's conclusion, too. But, however irritating it may be, let us continue to press our question ruthlessly. "Why do you say," we ask the physicist, "that just because the radiation rate was constant all last week, it must have been the same thousands of years ago?" At first he may not quite know what we are after. "Well," he might say, hoping to appease us, "my experiments have shown that the radiation rate is independent of various environmental conditions, such as moisture, and I have reason to believe that the *relevant* conditions were the same in the past as they are now." If we are astute as well as doggedly persistent, we can point out something to him in return: "But you seem to be assuming a general proposition that whenever the same conditions exist, the same effects will occur—'Like causes, like effects,' or something of the sort."

Granted that if this general principle holds true, the physicist's particular law about the constancy of radiation rate can be justified—but again we can ask, "How do we know that like causes produce like effects? How do we know that an event always has certain relevant causal conditions, and that whenever these conditions recur, the effect must recur, too?" Now we have left the physicist behind, too, and crossed over into the mysterious territory of philosophy. For we have asked a highly general question—since it is about all events, without exception, including everything that has happened or ever will happen. And it seems to be a highly fundamental question, since the assumption that every event has a cause, if it is true, must underlie an enormous number of other beliefs, not only in history and physics but in the common affairs of ordinary life.

Indeed, at this point we seem to have left everyone behind but the philosopher. And that is one of the peculiarities of this subject. When Harry Truman was President, he had a sign over his desk that said, "The buck stops here." The philosopher does his intellectual work under a similar sign, for there is no one to whom he can pass on a question with the plea that it is too general or too fundamental for him to deal with. The philosopher—and with him anyone else who is doing philosophical thinking—stands at the end of the line.

Here are two more samples of thinking that begin with a nonphilosophical belief but lead gradually but directly into philosophy. We present them in the form of brief dialogues.

Dialogue I

A: You ought to have written to your parents last Sunday.

B: Why?

A: Because you promised you would write every Sunday.

B: I know I did, but I've been awfully busy. Why was it so important to keep my promise?

A: Not just *that* promise—*any* promise. It's wrong ever to break a promise.

B: Well, I used to think that, but now I'm not sure. What makes you think it's always wrong to break promises?

A: My reason is simply that most people in our society disapprove of it. You know perfectly well that they do.

B: Of course I know that most people in our society disapprove of breaking promises, but does that prove it really is always wrong to do it? The majority opinion in our society could be mistaken, couldn't it? I don't see why it should be taken for granted that what most Americans *think* is wrong and what really *is* wrong should always coincide. What's the connection between the two?

Dialogue II

A: In my paper for political science I had to define "democracy." "Democracy" means "government by the people collectively."

B: What made you choose that definition?

A: I looked up the word in the dictionary, of course.

B: How do you know your dictionary is right? My dictionary doesn't always give the same definitions as yours.

A: Oh, but mine is larger and more recent, so it's bound to be more reliable.

B: Yes, but language is constantly changing, and words like "democracy" are used in lots of different ways. I think one shouldn't feel bound by any dictionary definition. Every writer should feel free to define any word as he wishes.

A: But that would be chaotic. Besides, you wouldn't really have definitions at all, in that case.

B: Why wouldn't you have definitions? There's no such thing as *the* "one true meaning" of a word, is there? Words mean whatever people make them mean, so why shouldn't I select my own meanings and put them in definitions of my own?

Very different topics are discussed in these brief conversations; but they follow a similar pattern. In each case, speaker A makes an opening remark of a fairly specific sort, speaker B asks A to give a good reason for his opening statement, and A does provide what, on the level of ordinary common-sense thinking, would be regarded as a satisfactory reason. Many conversations would end at this stage; but B is disposed to probe more deeply, to uncover the assumptions underlying A's reasons, and to ask whether these more basic assumptions, in turn, are reasonable. Notice how the beliefs being questioned become more general and more fundamental as the questioning goes on. In each of the little dialogues, B pushes A over the brink into philosophy. At the end of each, he raises a question concerning the truth of a philosophical belief—and there the matter is left, for the time being.

But you may not be content to leave it at that. If you feel some frustration or impatience with the way A and B are arguing, you are on the verge of doing some philosophical thinking yourself. Wouldn't you like to ask B some searching questions—for example, about the way in which he is using some of his key words? This would all be a lot clearer, you may have said to yourself while you were reading Dialogue I, if we were sure just what the word "wrong" means here. Maybe it means simply "disapproved by a majority of people in one's own society." In that case, what happens to B's final question? Isn't he confused? But *does* "wrong" mean only this? And take the term "free will," which was used in one of the other examples of philosophical thinking discussed above. How can we decide whether it is reasonable to believe that human beings have this mysterious thing without saying precisely what it is?

If you have been thinking for yourself along these lines, or (even if you haven't) if you can now see the sense in raising these questions about the meaning of key words, you will be able to sympathize with a good deal of what contemporary philosophers have been doing. Philosophers at all periods have been concerned to analyze the meaning of basic philosophical terms, but this task has received more attention from twentieth-century philosophers—or from many of them, at least—than ever before. By "key words" in philosophy we mean simply those words that are used in statements of beliefs that are highly general and fundamental, and in questions about these beliefs. A question about the meaning of such a word, such as the question, "What does 'cause' mean?" is itself highly fundamental, since the notion of causality plays a pervasive part in our thinking, and much might depend upon being clear about it. And we can see how it is that questions about the meaning of particular terms have led philosophers very naturally to still more fundamental questions about meaning itself, along with other basic characteristics of language. This further stage of interest in language is displayed in Dialogue II, in which speaker B is not content to accept A's remarks about the definition of the word "democracy" without questioning his assumptions about the very process of definition itself. Here B reveals a conviction (which we all can share) that we ought to be as clear as possible about the words in which we express our beliefs.

Increased clearness in your own beliefs is, then, one of the three chief benefits you can derive from a study of philosophy—if, as we hope, you are not content merely to learn about the theories and arguments of the great philosophers (interesting and valuable as that is), but will make this study an active exercise in philosophical thinking.

The second benefit, partly dependent on the first, is increased assurance that your beliefs are reasonable. A belief whose reasons have been examined deeply enough to reach the level of philosophical questioning rests on a firmer foundation than one that has been examined less thoroughly. This does not mean that everyone should become a professional philosopher (though we cannot help hoping that some readers of this book will ultimately make that choice). Admittedly, the philosopher's desire to base his beliefs on good reasons is unusually persistent and intense: the philosopher would not only rather be right than President—he would rather be right than anything. But all of us who want assurance that our beliefs are well grounded should do some philosophical thinking about some of them, at least, in order to secure the firmest possible grounds.

The third benefit which the study of philosophy can confer upon our beliefs is increased consistency. For philosophical thinking forces each of us to see whether his fundamental beliefs in different areas of experience form a logically coherent whole. We have already encountered . . . a pair of philosophical beliefs that seem in danger of clashing head-on in a contradiction. You will recall how we found that the philosophical examination of a belief about an African culture seemed to uncover an underlying assumption that every event happens under such conditions that when they are repeated, the same sort of event must happen again—in other words, that every event happens in accordance with a law of nature. And when we examined the assumptions underlying punishment we found that these seem to include the assumption that human beings have free will. To have free will is to be able to act in two different ways under precisely the same conditions. But if it is ever true that a man could have acted differently under the same conditions—i.e., that the conditions did not completely determine his action—then here is *one event* (namely the action) that did *not* happen in accordance with any law of nature. Perhaps further examination would clear things up; but it looks as if we have here a contradiction in beliefs. Philosophical thinking has diagnosed it, and further philosophical thinking is the only thing that will provide a cure.

The three values we have cited—clarity, reasonableness, and consistency—are basic intellectual values. But perhaps you are saying to yourself something like this: "I can see that studying philosophy may help me improve my beliefs, but, after all, there is more to life than thinking and believing. What I most want from my education is to improve my *actions*. How can philosophical thinking help me to *live* better?"

Part of our answer here is that we must beware of drawing too sharp a line between beliefs and actions. Our beliefs—including philosophical beliefs—have a considerable influence on our actions. This influence can be seen most directly in one area of philosophy, where we are concerned with questions of value, but answers to some other basic philosophical questions may also possess some power to affect, however indirectly, the way we live. Although knowledge may be valuable for its own sake, as well as for its practical consequences, it is not wrong to expect philosophy to have its effects. It would be wrong, however, to ask every philosophical belief to show a direct and simple connection with human action. Perhaps the growing appreciation of the importance of basic research in science may foster an appreciation of the quest for answers to other highly fundamental questions, without insistence on immediate practical results.

In saying that beliefs influence actions, we do not mean to lose sight of the effect of emotions on human conduct. Temporary emotions, as well as more enduring emotional attitudes, are often powerful enough to make us behave in ways counter to what we believe intellectually. Philosophical thinking can do a great deal to clarify and harmonize our beliefs at all levels, and to strengthen their foundations. But the philosopher is no substitute for the psychiatrist, or for the parents and teachers of our early years who help create our emotional make-up. Yet many philosophers have claimed that the experience of thinking about philosophical questions can affect our emotional attitudes as well as our beliefs.

When we detach our minds from immediate practical matters and from the limited boundaries of particular fields of specialization, we experience a kind of release from petty and provincial concerns. The experience of thinking as human beings who are trying to understand themselves and their universe may produce a serenity and breadth of mind that can in time become enduring attitudes.

NOTE

1. For this example, and the details concerning it, we are indebted to Harrison M. Wright, "Tropical Africa: The Historian's Dilemma," *Swarthmore Alumni Magazine* (October, 1963).

Study Questions

1. According to the Beardsleys, what is a philosophical question?
2. Construct a brief dialogue of your own, like Dialogues I and II, that illustrates how a philosophical issue can arise in the course of an ordinary conversation.
3. According to the Beardsleys, what three chief benefits can be derived from the study of philosophy?
4. Present an example of a philosophical belief that has influenced action.

The Value of Philosophy

BERTRAND RUSSELL

As we begin the study of philosophy, you may wonder whether the value of the subject can be explained briefly. Here is an insightful, inspirational statement from Bertrand Russell (1872–1970), the English philosopher, mathematician, social activist, winner of the 1950 Nobel Prize for Literature, and one of the most prominent figures of the twentieth century.

... [I]t will be well to consider ... what is the value of philosophy and why it ought to be studied. It is the more necessary to consider this question, in view of the fact that many men, under the influence of science or of practical affairs, are inclined to doubt whether philosophy is anything better than innocent but useless trifling, hair-splitting distinctions, and controversies on matters concerning which knowledge is impossible.

This view of philosophy appears to result, partly from a wrong conception of the ends of life, partly from a wrong conception of the kind of goods which philosophy strives to achieve. Physical science, through the medium of inventions, is useful to innumerable people who are wholly ignorant of it; thus the study of physical science is to be recommended, not only, or primarily, because of the effect on the student, but rather because of the effect on mankind in general. Thus utility does not belong to philosophy. If the study of philosophy has any value at all for others than students of philosophy, it must be only indirectly, through its effects upon the lives of those who study it. It is in these effects, therefore, if anywhere, that the value of philosophy must be primarily sought.

But further, if we are not to fail in our endeavour to determine the value of philosophy, we must first free our minds from the prejudices of what are wrongly called "practical" men. The "practical" man, as this word is often used, is one who recognizes only material needs, who realizes that men must have food for the body, but is oblivious of the necessity of providing food for the mind. If all men were well off, if poverty and disease had been reduced to their lowest possible point, there would still remain much to be done to produce a valuable society; and even in the existing world the goods of the mind are at least as important as the goods of the body. It is exclusively among the goods of the mind that the value of philosophy is to be found; and only those who are not indifferent to these goods can be persuaded that the study of philosophy is not a waste of time.

Philosophy, like all other studies, aims primarily at knowledge. The knowledge it aims at is the kind of knowledge which gives unity and system to the body of the sciences, and the kind which results from a critical examination of the grounds of our convictions, prejudices, and beliefs. But it cannot be maintained that philosophy has had any very great measure of success in its attempts to provide definite answers to its questions. If you ask a mathematician, a mineralogist, a historian, or any other man of learning, what definite body of truths has been ascertained by his science, his answer will last as long as you are willing to listen. But if you put the same question to a philosopher, he will, if he is candid, have to confess that his study has not achieved positive results such as have been achieved by other sciences. It is true that this is partly accounted for by the fact that, as soon as definite knowledge concerning any subject becomes possible, this subject ceases to be called philosophy, and becomes a separate science. The whole study of the heavens, which now belongs to astronomy, was once included in philosophy; Newton's great work was called "the mathematical principles of natural philosophy." Similarly, the study of the human mind, which was a part of philosophy, has now been separated from philosophy and has become the science of psychology. Thus, to a great extent, the uncertainty of philosophy is more apparent than real: those questions which are already capable of definite answers are placed in the sciences, while those only to which, at present, no definite answer can be given, remain to form the residue which is called philosophy.

This is, however, only a part of the truth concerning the uncertainty of philosophy. There are many questions—and among them those that are of the profoundest interest to our spiritual life—which, so far as we can see, must remain insoluble to the human intellect unless its powers become of quite a different order from what they are now. Has the universe any unity of plan or purpose, or is it a fortuitous concourse of atoms? Is consciousness a permanent part of the universe, giving hope of indefinite growth in wisdom, or is it a transitory accident on a small planet on which life must ultimately become impossible? Are good and evil of importance to the universe or only to man? Such questions are asked by philosophy, and variously answered by various philosophers. But it would seem that, whether answers be otherwise discoverable or not, the answers suggested by philosophy are none of them demonstrably true. Yet, however slight may be the hope of discovering an answer, it is part of the business of philosophy to continue the consideration of such questions, to make us aware of their importance, to examine all the approaches to them, and to keep alive that speculative interest in the universe which is apt to be killed by confining ourselves to definitely ascertainable knowledge. . . .

The value of philosophy is, in fact, to be sought largely in its very uncertainty. The man who has no tincture of philosophy goes through life imprisoned in the prejudices derived from common sense, from the habitual beliefs of his age or his nation, and from convictions which have grown up in his mind without the co-operation or consent of his deliberate reason. To such a man the world tends to become definite, finite, obvious; common objects rouse no questions, and unfamiliar possibilities are contemptuously rejected. As soon as we begin to philosophize, on the contrary, we find . . . that even the most everyday things lead to problems to which only very incomplete answers can be given. Philosophy, though unable to tell us with certainty what is the true answer to the doubts which it raises, is able to suggest many possibilities which enlarge our thoughts and free them from the tyranny of custom. Thus, while diminishing our feeling of certainty as to what things are, it greatly increases our knowledge as to what they may be; it removes the somewhat arrogant dogmatism

of those who have never travelled into the region of liberating doubt, and it keeps alive our sense of wonder by showing familiar things in an unfamiliar aspect.

Apart from its utility in showing unsuspected possibilities, philosophy has a value—perhaps its chief value—through the greatness of the objects which it contemplates, and the freedom from narrow and personal aims resulting from this contemplation. The life of the instinctive man is shut up within the circle of his private interests: family and friends may be included, but the outer world is not regarded except as it may help or hinder what comes within the circle of instinctive wishes. In such a life there is something feverish and confined, in comparison with which the philosophic life is calm and free. The private world of instinctive interests is a small one, set in the midst of a great and powerful world which must, sooner or later, lay our private world in ruins. Unless we can so enlarge our interests as to include the whole outer world, we remain like a garrison in a beleaguered fortress, knowing that the enemy prevents escape and that ultimate surrender is inevitable. In such a life there is no peace, but a constant strife between the insistence of desire and the powerlessness of will. In one way or another, if our life is to be great and free, we must escape this prison and this strife. . . .

Thus, to sum up our discussion of the value of philosophy: Philosophy is to be studied, not for the sake of any definite answers to its questions, since no definite answers can, as a rule, be known to be true, but rather for the sake of the questions themselves; because these questions enlarge our conception of what is possible, enrich our intellectual imagination and diminish the dogmatic assurance which closes the mind against speculation; but above all because, through the greatness of the universe which philosophy contemplates, the mind also is rendered great, and becomes capable of that union with the universe which constitutes its highest good.

Study Questions

1. Do you agree with Russell that the goods of the mind are at least as important as the goods of the body?
2. According to Russell, who are wrongly called "practical men"?
3. What value does Russell find in uncertainty?
4. According to Russell, what is the mind's highest good?

Defence of Socrates

PLATO

Philosophers build on the work of their predecessors, and the intellectual links that form the chain of the history of Western philosophy extend back to ancient Greece, more than five centuries before the Christian era. While only tantalizing fragments remain from the writings of the earliest philosophers, three men made such enormous contributions to the development of the subject that their overwhelming impact is widely acknowledged: Socrates (c. 470–399 B.C.E.), Plato (c. 429–347 B.C.E.), and Aristotle (384–322 B.C.E.).

Their relationship is unusual. Socrates wrote nothing, but in conversation was able to befuddle the most powerful minds of his day. Plato, his devoted student, responded to Socratic teaching not, as one might suppose, by being intimidated but by becoming the greatest of philosophical writers, whose *Dialogues*, mostly featuring the character Socrates, form the foundation of all subsequent Western philosophy. Such a towering figure as Plato could have been expected to produce mere disciples, but, after studying with Plato for more than two decades, Aristotle developed his own comprehensive philosophical system, opposed in many respects to that of Plato, and so powerful in its own right that throughout history its impact has rivalled that of Plato. Surely Socrates and Plato were remarkable teachers as well as philosophers.

The *Defence of Socrates* (or *Apology* as it is sometimes titled) is an account of the trial of Socrates, who, after having been found guilty of impiety, was put to death by the Athenian democracy. Socrates' speech to the jury, as related by Plato, has come down through the ages as an eloquent defense of not only Socrates' life but also philosophy itself.

Are the words actually those Socrates spoke? Scholars disagree, but a plausible answer is provided by David Gallop, Professor Emeritus of Philosophy at Trent University in Ontario, Canada, the author of the translation from the Greek that we are using:

> [I]t is inconceivable that any speaker could have improvised before a real court such an artfully structured, nuanced, and polished composition as Plato's *Defence of Socrates*.

That is not to say that the work falsifies any biographical facts about Socrates, still less that its content is wholly invented. For we all know to the contrary, it may even in some places faithfully reproduce what Socrates said in court. But whatever blend of fact and fiction it contains, the speech as a whole is a philosophical memoir, intended to convey a sense of Socrates' mission and the supreme injustice of his conviction. It remains, above all, an exhortation to the practice of philosophy. No less than Plato's dramatic dialogues, it is designed to draw its readers into philosophical reflection, so that they may recover for themselves the truths to which the master had borne witness.

If that is the chief aim of the *Defence*, its fidelity to fact becomes a secondary issue.

To assist you in reading the *Defence*, Notes and an Index of Names prepared by the translator are provided at the end.

I don't know[1] how you, fellow Athenians, have been affected by my accusers, but for my part I felt myself almost transported by them, so persuasively did they speak. And yet hardly a word they have said is true. Among their many falsehoods, one especially astonished me: their warning that you must be careful not to be taken in by me, because I am a clever speaker. It seemed to me the height of impudence on their part not to be embarrassed at being refuted straight away by the facts, once it became apparent that I was not a clever speaker at all—unless indeed they call a "clever" speaker one who speaks the truth. If that is what they mean, then I would admit to being an orator, although not on a par with them.

As I said, then, my accusers have said little or nothing true; whereas from me you shall hear the whole truth, though not, I assure you, fellow Athenians, in language adorned with fine words and phrases or dressed up, as theirs was: you shall hear my points made spontaneously in whatever words occur to me—persuaded as I am that my case is just. None of you should expect anything to be put differently, because it would not, of course, be at all fitting at my age, gentlemen, to come before you with artificial speeches, such as might be composed by a young lad.

One thing, moreover, I would earnestly beg of you, fellow Athenians. If you hear me defending myself with the same arguments I normally use at the bankers' tables in the market-place (where many of you have heard me) and elsewhere, please do not be surprised or protest on that account. You see, here is the reason: this is the first time I have ever appeared before a court of law, although I am over 70; so I am literally a stranger to the diction of this place. And if I really were a foreigner, you would naturally excuse me, were I to speak in the dialect and style in which I had been brought up; so in the present case as well I ask you, in all fairness as I think, to disregard my manner of speaking—it may not be as good, or it may be better—but to consider and attend simply to the question whether or not my case is just; because that is the duty of a judge, as it is an orator's duty to speak the truth.

To begin with, fellow Athenians, it is fair that I should defend myself against the first set of charges falsely brought against me by my first accusers, and then turn to the later charges and the more recent ones. You see, I have been accused before you by many people for a long time now, for many years in fact, by people who spoke not a word of truth. It is those people I fear more than Anytus and his crowd, though they too are dangerous. But those others are more so, gentlemen: they have taken hold of most of you since childhood, and made persuasive accusations against me, yet without an ounce more truth in them. They say that there is one Socrates, a "wise man," who ponders what is above the earth and investigates everything beneath it, and turns the weaker argument into the stronger.[2]

Those accusers who have spread such rumour about me, fellow Athenians, are the dangerous ones, because their audience believes that people who inquire into those matters also fail to acknowledge the gods. Moreover, those accusers are numerous, and have been denouncing me for a long time now, and they also spoke to you at an age at which you would be most likely to believe them, when some of you were children or young lads; and their accusations simply went by default for lack of any defence. But the most absurd thing of all is that one cannot even get to know their names or say who they were—except perhaps one who happens to be a comic playwright.[3] The ones who have persuaded you by malicious slander, and also some who persuade others because they have been persuaded themselves, are all very hard to deal with: one cannot put any of them on the stand here in court, or cross-examine anybody, but one must literally engage in a sort of shadow-boxing to defend oneself, and cross-examine without anyone to answer. You too, then, should allow, as I just said, that I have two sets of accusers: one set who have accused me recently, and the other of long standing to whom I was just referring. And please grant that I need to defend myself against the latter first, since you too heard them accusing me earlier, and you heard far more from them than from these recent critics here.

Very well, then. I must defend myself, fellow Athenians, and in so short a time[4] must try to dispel the slander which you have had so long to absorb. That is the outcome I would wish for, should it be of any benefit to you and to me, and I should like to succeed in my defence—though I believe the task to be a difficult one, and am well aware of its nature. But let that turn out as God wills: I have to obey the law and present my defence.

Let us examine, from the beginning, the charge that has given rise to the slander against me—which was just what Meletus relied upon when he drew up this indictment. Very well then, what were my slanderers actually saying when they slandered me? Let me read out their deposition, as if they were my legal accusers:

"Socrates is guilty of being a busybody, in that he inquires into what is beneath the earth and in the sky, turns the weaker argument into the stronger, and teaches others to do the same."

The charges would run something like that. Indeed, you can see them for yourselves, enacted in Aristophanes' comedy: in that play, a character called "Socrates" swings around, claims to be walking on air,[5] and talks a lot of other nonsense on subjects of which I have no understanding, great or small.

Not that I mean to belittle knowledge of that sort, if anyone really is learned in such matters—no matter how many of Meletus' lawsuits I might have to defend myself against—but the fact is, fellow Athenians, those subjects are not my concern at all. I call most of you to witness yourselves, and I ask you to make that quite clear to one another, if you have ever heard me in discussion (as many of you have). Tell one another, then, whether any of you has ever heard me discussing such subjects, either briefly or at length; and as a result you will realize that the other things said about me by the public are equally baseless.

In any event, there is no truth in those charges. Moreover, if you have heard from anyone that I undertake to educate people and charge fees, there is no truth in that either—though for that matter I do think it also a fine thing if anyone *is* able to educate people, as Gorgias of Leontini, Prodicus of Ceos, and Hippias of Elis profess to. Each of them can visit any city, gentlemen, and persuade its young people, who may associate free of charge with any of their own citizens they wish, to leave those associations, and to join with them instead, paying fees and being grateful into the bargain.

On that topic, there is at present another expert here, a gentleman from Paros; I heard of his visit, because I happened to run into a man who has spent more money on sophists[6] than everyone else put together—Callias, the son of

Hipponicus. So I questioned him, since he has two sons himself.

"Callias," I said, "if your two sons had been born as colts or calves, we could find and engage a tutor who could make them both excel superbly in the required qualities—and he'd be some sort of expert in horse-rearing or agriculture. But seeing that they are actually human, whom do you intend to engage as their tutor? Who has knowledge of the required human and civic qualities? I ask, because I assume you've given thought to the matter, having sons yourself. Is there such a person," I asked, "or not?"

"Certainly," he replied.

"Who is he?" I said; "Where does he come from, and what does he charge for tuition?"

"His name is Evenus, Socrates," he replied; "He comes from Paros, and he charges 5 minas."[7]

I thought Evenus was to be congratulated, if he really did possess that skill and imparted it for such a modest charge. I, at any rate, would certainly be giving myself fine airs and graces if I possessed that knowledge. But the fact is, fellow Athenians, I do not.

Now perhaps one of you will interject: "Well then, Socrates, what is the difficulty in your case? What is the source of these slanders against you? If you are not engaged in something out of the ordinary, why ever has so much rumour and talk arisen about you? It would surely never have arisen, unless you were up to something different from most people. Tell us what it is, then, so that we don't jump to conclusions about you."

That speaker makes a fair point, I think; and so I will try to show you just what it is that has earned me my reputation and notoriety. Please hear me out. Some of you will perhaps think I am joking, but I assure you that I shall be telling you the whole truth.

You see, fellow Athenians, I have gained this reputation on account of nothing but a certain sort of wisdom. And what sort of wisdom is that? It is a human kind of wisdom, perhaps, since it might just be true that I have wisdom of that sort. Maybe the people I just mentioned possess wisdom of a superhuman kind; otherwise I cannot explain it. For my part, I certainly do not possess that knowledge; and whoever says I do is lying and speaking with a view to slandering me—

Now please do not protest, fellow Athenians, even if I should sound to you rather boastful. I am not myself the source of the story I am about to tell you, but I shall refer you to a trustworthy authority. As evidence of my wisdom, if such it actually be, and of its nature, I shall call to witness before you the god at Delphi.[8]

You remember Chaerephon, of course. He was a friend of mine from youth, and also a comrade in your party, who shared your recent exile and restoration.[9] You recall too what sort of man Chaerephon was, how impetuous he was in any undertaking. Well, on one occasion he actually went to the Delphic oracle, and had the audacity to put the following question to it—as I said, please do not make a disturbance, gentlemen— he went and asked if there was anyone wiser than myself; to which the Pythia responded that there was no one. His brother here will testify to the court about that story, since Chaerephon himself is deceased.

Now keep in mind why I have been telling you this: it is because I am going to explain to you the origin of the slander against me. When I heard the story, I thought to myself: "What ever is the god saying? What can his riddle mean? Since I am all too conscious of not being wise in any matter, great or small, what ever can he mean by pronouncing me to be the wisest? Surely he cannot be lying: for him that would be out of the question."

So for a long time I was perplexed about what he could possibly mean. But then, with great reluctance, I proceeded to investigate the matter somewhat as follows. I went to one of the people who had a reputation for wisdom, thinking there, if anywhere, to disprove the oracle's utterance and declare to it: "Here is someone wiser than I am, and yet you said that I was the wisest."

So I interviewed this person—I need not mention his name, but he was someone in public life; and when I examined him, my experience went something like this, fellow Athenians: in conversing with him, I formed the opinion that, although the man was thought to be wise by many other people, and especially by himself, yet in reality he was not. So I then tried to show him that he thought himself wise without being so. I thereby earned his dislike, and that of many people present; but still, as I went away, I thought to myself: "I am wiser than that fellow, anyhow. Because neither of us, I dare say, knows anything of great value; but he thinks he knows a thing when he doesn't; whereas I neither know it in fact, nor think that I do. At any rate, it appears that I am wiser than he in just this one small respect: if I do not know something, I do not think that I do."

Next, I went to someone else, among people thought to be even wiser than the previous man, and I came to the same conclusion again; and so I was disliked by that man too, as well as by many others.

Well, after that I went on to visit one person after another. I realized, with dismay and alarm, that I was making enemies; but even so, I thought it my duty to attach the highest importance to the god's business; and therefore, in seeking the oracle's meaning, I had to go on to examine all those with any reputation for knowledge. And upon my word,[10] fellow Athenians—because I am obliged to speak the truth before the court—I truly did experience something like this: as I pursued the god's inquiry, I found those held in the highest esteem were practically the most defective, whereas men who were supposed to be their inferiors were much better off in respect of understanding.

Let me, then, outline my wanderings for you, the various "labours" I kept undertaking,[11] only to find that the oracle proved completely irrefutable. After I had done with the politicians, I turned to the poets—including tragedians, dithyrambic poets,[12] and the rest—thinking that in their company I would be shown up as more

ignorant than they were. So I picked up the poems over which I thought they had taken the most trouble, and questioned them about their meaning, so that I might also learn something from them in the process.

Now I'm embarrassed to tell you the truth, gentlemen, but it has to be said. Practically everyone else present could speak better than the poets themselves about their very own compositions. And so, once more, I soon realized this truth about them too: it was not from wisdom that they composed their works, but from a certain natural aptitude and inspiration, like that of seers and sooth-sayers—because those people too utter many fine words, yet know nothing of the matters on which they pronounce. It was obvious to me that the poets were in much the same situation; yet at the same time I realized that because of their compositions they thought themselves the wisest people in other matters as well, when they were not. So I left, believing that I was ahead of them in the same way as I was ahead of the politicians.

Then, finally, I went to the craftsmen, because I was conscious of knowing almost nothing myself, but felt sure that amongst them, at least, I would find much valuable knowledge. And in that expectation I was not disappointed: they did have knowledge in fields where I had none, and in that respect they were wiser than I. And yet, fellow Athenians, those able craftsmen seemed to me to suffer from the same failing as the poets: because of their excellence at their own trade, each claimed to be a great expert also on matters of the utmost importance; and this arrogance of theirs seemed to eclipse their wisdom. So I began to ask myself, on the oracle's behalf, whether I should prefer to be as I am, neither wise as they are wise, nor ignorant as they are ignorant, or to possess both their attributes; and in reply, I told myself and the oracle that I was better off as I was.

The effect of this questioning, fellow Athenians, was to earn me much hostility of a very vexing and trying sort, which has given rise to numerous slanders, including this reputation

I have for being "wise"—because those present on each occasion imagine me to be wise regarding the matters on which I examine others. But in fact, gentlemen, it would appear that it is only the god who is truly wise; and that he is saying to us, through this oracle, that human wisdom is worth little or nothing. It seems that when he says "Socrates," he makes use of my name, merely taking me as an example—as if to say, "The wisest amongst you, human beings, is anyone like Socrates who has recognized that with respect to wisdom he is truly worthless."

That is why, even to this day, I still go about seeking out and searching into anyone I believe to be wise, citizen or foreigner, in obedience to the god. Then, as soon as I find that someone is not wise, I assist the god by proving that he is not. Because of this occupation, I have had no time at all for any activity to speak of, either in public affairs or in my family life; indeed, because of my service to the god, I live in extreme poverty.

In addition, the young people who follow me around of their own accord, the ones who have plenty of leisure because their parents are wealthiest, enjoy listening to people being cross-examined. Often, too, they copy my example themselves, and so attempt to cross-examine others. And I imagine that they find a great abundance of people who suppose themselves to possess some knowledge, but really know little or nothing. Consequently, the people they question are angry with me, though not with themselves, and say that there is a nasty pestilence abroad called "Socrates," who is corrupting the young.

Then, when asked just what he is doing or teaching, they have nothing to say, because they have no idea what he does; yet, rather than seem at a loss, they resort to the stock charges against all who pursue intellectual inquiry, trotting out "things in the sky and beneath the earth," "failing to acknowledge the gods," and "turning the weaker argument into the stronger." They would, I imagine, be loath to admit the truth, which is that their pretensions to knowledge have been exposed, and they are totally ignorant. So because these people have reputations to protect, I suppose, and are also both passionate and numerous, and have been speaking about me in a vigorous and persuasive style, they have long been filling your ears with vicious slander. It is on the strength of all this that Meletus, along with Anytus and Lycon, has proceeded against me: Meletus is aggrieved for the poets, Anytus for the craftsmen and politicians, and Lycon for the orators. And so, as I began by saying, I should be surprised if I could rid your minds of this slander in so short a time, when so much of it has accumulated.

There is the truth for you, fellow Athenians. I have spoken it without concealing anything from you, major or minor, and without glossing over anything. And yet I am virtually certain that it is my very candour that makes enemies for me—which goes to show that I am right: the slander against me is to that effect, and such is its explanation. And whether you look for one now or later, that is what you will find.

So much for my defence before you against the charges brought by my first group of accusers. Next, I shall try to defend myself against Meletus, good patriot that he claims to be, and against my more recent critics. So once again, as if they were a fresh set of accusers, let me in turn review their deposition. It runs something like this:

"Socrates is guilty of corrupting the young, and of failing to acknowledge the gods acknowledged by the city, but introducing new spiritual beings instead."

Such is the charge: let us examine each item within it.

Meletus says, then, that I am guilty of corrupting the young. Well I reply, fellow Athenians, that Meletus is guilty of trifling in a serious matter, in that he brings people to trial on frivolous grounds, and professes grave concern about matters for which he has never cared at all. I shall now try to prove to you too that that is so.

Step forward, Meletus, and answer me. It is your chief concern, is it not, that our younger people shall be as good as possible?

—It is.

Very well, will you please tell the judges who influences them for the better—because you must obviously know, seeing that you care? Having discovered me, as you allege, to be the one who is corrupting them, you bring me before the judges here and accuse me. So speak up, and tell the court who has an improving influence.

You see, Meletus, you remain silent, and have no answer. Yet doesn't that strike you as shameful, and as proof in itself of exactly what I say—that you have never cared about these matters at all? Come then, good fellow, tell us who influences them for the better.

—The laws.

Yes, but that is not what I'm asking, excellent fellow. I mean, which *person*, who already knows the laws to begin with?

—These gentlemen, the judges, Socrates.

What are you saying, Meletus? Can these people educate the young, and do they have an improving influence?

—Most certainly.

All of them, or some but not others?

—All of them.

My goodness, what welcome news, and what a generous supply of benefactors you speak of! And how about the audience here in court? Do they too have an improving influence, or not?

—Yes, they do too.

And how about members of the Council?[13]

—Yes, the Councillors too.

But in that case, how about people in the Assembly, its individual members, Meletus? They won't be corrupting their youngers, will they? Won't they all be good influences as well?

—Yes, they will too.

So every person in Athens, it would appear, has an excellent influence on them except for me, whereas I alone am corrupting them. Is that what you're saying?

—That is emphatically what I'm saying.

Then I find myself, if we are to believe you, in a most awkward predicament. Now answer me this. Do you think the same is true of horses? Is it everybody who improves them, while a single person spoils them? Or isn't the opposite true: a single person, or at least very few people, namely the horse-trainers, can improve them; while lay people spoil them, don't they, if they have to do with horses and make use of them? Isn't that true of horses as of all other animals, Meletus? Of course it is, whether you and Anytus deny it or not. In fact, I dare say our young people are extremely lucky if only one person is corrupting them, while everyone else is doing them good.

All right, Meletus. Enough has been said to prove that you never were concerned about the young. You betray your irresponsibility plainly, because you have not cared at all about the charges on which you bring me before this court.

Furthermore, Meletus, tell us, in God's name, whether it is better to live among good fellow citizens or bad ones. Come sir, answer: I am not asking a hard question. Bad people have a harmful impact upon their closest companions at any given time, don't they, whereas good people have a good one?

—Yes.

Well, is there anyone who wants to be harmed by his companions rather than benefited?—Be a good fellow and keep on answering, as the law requires you to. Is there anyone who wants to be harmed?

—Of course not.

Now tell me this. In bringing me here, do you claim that I am corrupting and depraving the young intentionally or unintentionally?

—Intentionally, so I maintain.

Really, Meletus? Are you so much smarter at your age than I at mine as to realize that the bad have a harmful impact upon their closest companions at any given time, whereas the good have a beneficial effect? Am I, by contrast, so far gone in my stupidity as not to realize that if I make one of my companions vicious, I risk incurring harm at his hands? And am I, therefore, as you allege, doing so much damage intentionally?

That I cannot accept from you, Meletus, and neither could anyone else, I imagine. Either I am not corrupting them—or if I am, I am doing so unintentionally;[14] so either way your charge is false. But if I am corrupting them unintentionally, the law does not require me to be brought to court for such mistakes, but rather to be taken aside for private instruction and admonition—since I shall obviously stop doing unintentional damage, if I learn better. But you avoided association with me and were unwilling to instruct me. Instead you bring me to court, where the law requires you to bring people who need punishment rather than enlightenment.

Very well, fellow Athenians. That part of my case is now proven: Meletus never cared about these matters, either a lot or a little. Nevertheless, Meletus, please tell us in what way you claim that I am corrupting our younger people. That is quite obvious, isn't it, from the indictment you drew up? It is by teaching them not to acknowledge the gods acknowledged by the city, but to accept new spiritual beings instead? You mean, don't you, that I am corrupting them by teaching them that?

—I most emphatically do.

Then, Meletus, in the name of those very gods we are now discussing, please clarify the matter further for me, and for the jury here. You see, I cannot make out what you mean. Is it that I am teaching people to acknowledge that some gods exist—in which case it follows that I do acknowledge their existence myself as well, and am not a complete atheist, hence am not guilty on that count—and yet that those gods are not the ones acknowledged by the city, but different ones? Is that your charge against me—namely, that they are different? Or are you saying that I acknowledge no gods at all myself, and teach the same to others?

—I am saying the latter: you acknowledge no gods at all.

What ever makes you say that, Meletus, you strange fellow? Do I not even acknowledge, then, with the rest of mankind, that the sun and the moon are gods?[15]

—By God, he does not, members of the jury, since he claims that the sun is made of rock, and the moon of earth!

My dear Meletus, do you imagine that it is Anaxagoras you are accusing?[16] Do you have such contempt for the jury, and imagine them so illiterate as not to know that books by Anaxagoras of Clazomenae are crammed with such assertions? What's more, are the young learning those things from me when they can acquire them at the bookstalls, now and then, for a drachma at most, and so ridicule Socrates if he claims those ideas for his own, especially when they are so bizarre? In God's name, do you really think me as crazy as that? Do I acknowledge the existence of no god at all?

—By God no, none whatever.

I can't believe you, Meletus—nor, I think, can you believe yourself. To my mind, fellow Athenians, this fellow is an impudent scoundrel who has framed this indictment out of sheer wanton impudence and insolence. He seems to have devised a sort of riddle in order to try me out: "Will Socrates the Wise tumble to my nice self-contradiction?[17] Or shall I fool him along with my other listeners?" You see, he seems to me to be contradicting himself in the indictment. It's as if he were saying: "Socrates is guilty of not acknowledging gods, but of acknowledging gods"; and yet that is sheer tomfoolery.

I ask you to examine with me, gentlemen, just how that appears to be his meaning. Answer for us, Meletus; and the rest of you, please remember my initial request not to protest if I conduct the argument in my usual manner.

Is there anyone in the world, Meletus, who acknowledges that human phenomena exist, yet does not acknowledge human beings?—Require him to answer, gentlemen, and not to raise all kinds of confused objections. Is there anyone who does not acknowledge horses, yet does acknowledge equestrian phenomena? Or who does not acknowledge that musicians exist, yet does acknowledge musical phenomena?

There is no one, excellent fellow: if you don't wish to answer, I must answer for you, and for the jurors here. But at least answer my next question yourself. Is there anyone who acknowledges that spiritual phenomena exist, yet does not acknowledge spirits?

—No.

How good of you to answer—albeit reluctantly and under compulsion from the jury. Well now, you say that I acknowledge spiritual beings and teach others to do so. Whether they actually be new or old is no matter: I do at any rate, by your account, acknowledge spiritual beings, which you have also mentioned in your sworn deposition. But if I acknowledge spiritual beings, then surely it follows quite inevitably that I must acknowledge spirits. Is that not so?—Yes, it is so: I assume your agreement, since you don't answer. But we regard spirits, don't we, as either gods or children of gods? Yes or no?

—Yes.

Then given that I do believe in spirits, as you say, if spirits are gods of some sort, this is precisely what I claim when I say that you are presenting us with a riddle and making fun of us: you are saying that I do not believe in gods, and yet again that I do believe in gods, seeing that I believe in spirits.

On the other hand, if spirits are children of gods,[18] some sort of bastard offspring from nymphs—or from whomever they are traditionally said, in each case, to be born—then who in the world could ever believe that there were children of gods, yet no gods? That would be just as absurd as accepting the existence of children of horses and asses—namely, mules—yet rejecting the existence of horses or asses!

In short, Meletus, you can only have drafted this either by way of trying us out, or because you were at a loss how to charge me with a genuine offense. How could you possibly persuade anyone with even the slightest intelligence that someone who accepts spiritual beings does not also accept divine ones, and again that the same person also accepts neither spirits nor gods nor heroes? There is no conceivable way.

But enough, fellow Athenians. It needs no long defence, I think, to show that I am not guilty of the charges in Meletus' indictment; the foregoing will suffice. You may be sure, though, that what I was saying earlier is true: I have earned great hostility among many people. And that is what will convict me, if I am convicted: not Meletus or Anytus, but the slander and malice of the crowd. They have certainly convicted many other good men as well, and I imagine they will do so again; there is no risk of their stopping with me.

Now someone may perhaps say: "Well then, are you not ashamed, Socrates, to have pursued a way of life which has now put you at risk of death?"

But it may be fair for me to answer him as follows: "You are sadly mistaken, fellow, if you suppose that a man with even a grain of self-respect should reckon up the risks of living or dying, rather than simply consider, whenever he does something, whether his actions are just or unjust, the deeds of a good man or a bad one." By your principles, presumably, all those demigods who died in the plain of Troy[19] were inferior creatures—yes, even the son of Thetis,[20] who showed so much scorn for danger, when the alternative was to endure dishonour. Thus, when he was eager to slay Hector, his mother, goddess that she was, spoke to him—something like this, I fancy:

> My child, if thou dost avenge the murder of thy
>   friend, Patroclus,
> And dost slay Hector, then straightway [so runs
>   the poem]
> Shalt thou die thyself, since doom is prepared
>   for thee
> Next after Hector's.

But though he heard that, he made light of death and danger, since he feared far more to live as a base man, and to fail to avenge his dear ones. The poem goes on:

> Then straightway let me die, once I have given
>   the wrongdoer
> His deserts, lest I remain here by the
>   beak-prowed ships,
> An object of derision, and a burden upon the
>   earth.

Can you suppose that he gave any thought to death or danger?

You see, here is the truth of the matter, fellow Athenians. Wherever a man has taken up a position because he considers it best, or has been posted there by his commander, that is where I believe he should remain, steadfast in danger, taking no account at all of death or of anything else rather than dishonour. I would therefore have been acting absurdly, fellow Athenians, if when assigned to a post at Potidaea, Amphipolis, or Delium[21] by the superiors you had elected to command me, I remained where I was posted on those occasions at the risk of death, if ever any man did; whereas now that the god assigns me, as I became completely convinced, to the duty of leading the philosophical life by examining myself and others, I desert that post from fear of death or anything else. Yes, that would be unthinkable; and then I truly should deserve to be brought to court for failing to acknowledge the gods' existence, in that I was disobedient to the oracle, was afraid of death, and thought I was wise when I was not.

After all, gentlemen, the fear of death amounts simply to thinking one is wise when one is not: it is thinking one knows something one does not know. No one knows, you see, whether death may not in fact prove the greatest of all blessings for mankind; but people fear it as if they knew it for certain to be the greatest of evils. And yet to think that one knows what one does not know must surely be the kind of folly which is reprehensible.

On this matter especially, gentlemen, that may be the nature of my own advantage over most people. If I really were to claim to be wiser than anyone in any respect, it would consist simply in this: just as I do not possess adequate knowledge of life in Hades, so I also realize that I do not possess it; whereas acting unjustly in disobedience to one's betters, whether god or human being, is something I *know* to be evil and shameful. Hence I shall never fear or flee from something which may indeed be a good for all I know, rather than from things I know to be evils.

Suppose, therefore, that you pay no heed to Anytus, but are prepared to let me go. He said I need never have been brought to court in the first place; but that once I had been, your only option was to put me to death. He declared before you that, if I got away from you this time,

your sons would all be utterly corrupted by practising Socrates' teachings. Suppose, in the face of that, you were to say to me:

"Socrates, we will not listen to Anytus this time. We are prepared to let you go—but only on this condition: you are to pursue that quest of yours and practise philosophy no longer; and if you are caught doing it any more, you shall be put to death."

Well, as I just said, if you were prepared to let me go on those terms, I should reply to you as follows:

"I have the greatest fondness and affection for you, fellow Athenians, but I will obey my god rather than you; and so long as I draw breath and am able, I shall never give up practising philosophy, or exhorting and showing the way to any of you whom I ever encounter, by giving my usual sort of message. 'Excellent friend,' I shall say; 'You are an Athenian. Your city is the most important and renowned for its wisdom and power; so are you not ashamed that, while you take care to acquire as much wealth as possible, with honour and glory as well, yet you take no care or thought for understanding or truth, or for the best possible state of your soul?'

"And should any of you dispute that, and claim that he does take such care, I will not let him go straight away nor leave him, but I will question and examine and put him to the test; and if I do not think he has acquired goodness, though he says he has, I shall say, 'Shame on you, for setting the lowest value upon the most precious things, and for rating inferior ones more highly!' That I shall do for anyone I encounter, young or old, alien or fellow citizen; but all the more for the latter, since your kinship with me is closer."

Those are my orders from my god, I do assure you. Indeed, I believe that no greater good has ever befallen you in our city than my service to my god; because all I do is to go about persuading you, young and old alike, not to care for your bodies or for your wealth so intensely as for the greatest possible well-being of your souls.

"It is not wealth," I tell you, "that produces goodness; rather, it is from goodness that wealth, and all other benefits for human beings, accrue to them in their private and public life."

If, in fact, I am corrupting the young by those assertions, you may call them harmful. But if anyone claims that I say anything different, he is talking nonsense. In the face of that I should like to say: "Fellow Athenians, you may listen to Anytus or not, as you please; and you may let me go or not, as you please, because there is no chance of my acting otherwise, even if I have to die many times over—"

Stop protesting, fellow Athenians! Please abide by my request that you not protest against what I say, but hear me out; in fact, it will be in your interest, so I believe, to do so. You see, I am going to say some further things to you which may make you shout out—although I beg you not to.

You may be assured that if you put to death the sort of man I just said I was, you will not harm me more than you harm yourselves. Meletus or Anytus would not harm me at all; nor, in fact, could they do so, since I believe it is out of the question for a better man to be harmed by his inferior. The latter may, of course, inflict death or banishment or disenfranchisement; and my accuser here, along with others no doubt, believes those to be great evils. But I do not. Rather, I believe it a far greater evil to try to kill a man unjustly, as he does now.

At this point, therefore, fellow Athenians, so far from pleading on my own behalf, as might be supposed, I am pleading on yours, in case by condemning me you should mistreat the gift which God has bestowed upon you—because if you put me to death, you will not easily find another like me. The fact is, if I may put the point in a somewhat comical way, that I have been literally attached by God to our city, as if to a horse—a large thoroughbred, which is a bit sluggish because of its size, and needs to be aroused by some sort of gadfly. Yes, in me, I believe, God has attached to our city just such a creature—the kind which is constantly alighting

everywhere on you, all day long, arousing, cajoling, or reproaching each and every one of you. You will not easily acquire another such gadfly, gentlemen; rather, if you take my advice, you will spare my life. I dare say, though, that you will get angry, like people who are awakened from their doze. Perhaps you will heed Anytus, and give me a swat: you could happily finish me off, and then spend the rest of your life asleep—unless God, in his compassion for you, were to send you someone else.

That I am, in fact, just the sort of gift that God would send to our city, you may recognize from this: it would not seem to be in human nature for me to have neglected all my own affairs, and put up with the neglect of my family for all these years, but constantly minded your interests, by visiting each of you in private like a father or an elder brother, urging you to be concerned about goodness. Of course, if I were gaining anything from that, or were being paid to urge that course upon you, my actions could be explained. But in fact you can see for yourselves that my accusers, who so shamelessly level all those other charges against me, could not muster the impudence to call evidence that I ever once obtained payment, or asked for any. It is I who can call evidence sufficient, I think, to show that I am speaking the truth—namely, my poverty.

Now it may perhaps seem peculiar that, as some say, I give this counsel by going around and dealing with others' concerns in private, yet do not venture to appear before the Assembly, and counsel the city about your business in public. But the reason for that is one you have frequently heard me give in many places: it is a certain divine or spiritual sign[22] which comes to me, the very thing to which Meletus made mocking allusion in his indictment. It has been happening to me ever since childhood: a voice of some sort which comes, and which always—whenever it does come—restrains me from what I am about to do, yet never gives positive direction. That is what opposes my engaging in politics—and its opposition is an excellent thing, to my mind; because you may be quite sure, fellow Athenians, that if I had tried to engage in politics, I should have perished long since, and should have been of no use either to you or to myself.

And please do not get angry if I tell you the truth. The fact is that there is no person on earth whose life will be spared by you or by any other majority, if he is genuinely opposed to many injustices and unlawful acts, and tries to prevent their occurrence in our city. Rather, anyone who truly fights for what is just, if he is going to survive for even a short time, must act in a private capacity rather than a public one.

I will offer you conclusive evidence of that— not just words, but the sort of evidence that you respect, namely, actions. Just hear me tell my experiences, so that you may know that I would not submit to a single person for fear of death, contrary to what is just; nor would I do so, even if I were to lose my life on the spot. I shall mention things to you which are vulgar commonplaces of the courts; yet they are true.

Although I have never held any other public office in our city, fellow Athenians, I have served on its Council. My own tribe, Antiochis, happened to be the presiding commission[23] on the occasion when you wanted a collective trial for the ten generals who had failed to rescue the survivors from the naval battle.[24] That was illegal, as you all later recognized. At the time I was the only commissioner opposed to your acting illegally, and I voted against the motion. And though its advocates were prepared to lay information against me and have me arrested, while you were urging them on by shouting, I believed that I should face danger in siding with law and justice, rather than take your side for fear of imprisonment or death, when your proposals were contrary to justice.

Those events took place while our city was still under democratic rule. But on a subsequent occasion, after the oligarchy had come to power, the Thirty summoned me and four others to the round chamber,[25] with orders to arrest Leon the Salaminian, and fetch him from Salamis[26] for execution; they were constantly issuing such orders, of course, to many others, in their wish to implicate as many as possible in their crimes. On that occasion, however, I showed, once again not just by words, but by my actions, that I couldn't care less about death—if that would not be putting it rather crudely—but that my one and only care was to avoid doing anything sinful or unjust. Thus, powerful as it was, that regime did not frighten me into unjust action: when we emerged from the round chamber, the other four went off to Salamis and arrested Leon, whereas I left them and went off home. For that I might easily have been put to death, had the regime not collapsed shortly afterwards. There are many witnesses who will testify before you about those events.

Do you imagine, then, that I would have survived all these years if I had been regularly active in public life, and had championed what was right in a manner worthy of a brave man, and valued that above all else, as was my duty? Far from it, fellow Athenians: I would not, and nor would any other man. But in any public undertaking, that is the sort of person that I, for my part, shall prove to have been throughout my life; and likewise in my private life, because I have never been guilty of unjust association with anyone, including those whom my slanderers allege to have been my students.[27]

I never, in fact, was anyone's instructor[28] at any time. But if a person wanted to hear me talking, while I was engaging in my own business, I never grudged that to anyone, young or old; nor do I hold conversation only when I receive payment, and not otherwise. Rather, I offer myself for questioning to wealthy and poor alike, and to anyone who may wish to answer in response to questions from me. Whether any of those people acquires a good character or not, I cannot fairly be held responsible, when I never at any time promised any of them that they would learn anything from me, nor gave them instruction. And if anyone claims that he ever learnt anything from me, or has heard privately something that everyone else did not hear as well, you may be sure that what he says is untrue.

Why then, you may ask, do some people enjoy spending so much time in my company? You have already heard, fellow Athenians: I have told you the whole truth—which is that my listeners enjoy the examination of those who think themselves wise but are not, since the process is not unamusing. But for me, I must tell you, it is a mission which I have been bidden to undertake by the god, through oracles and dreams,[29] and through every means whereby a divine injunction to perform any task has ever been laid upon a human being.

That is not only true, fellow Athenians, but is easily verified—because if I do corrupt any of our young people, or have corrupted others in the past, then presumably, when they grew older, should any of them have realized that I had at any time given them bad advice in their youth, they ought now to have appeared here themselves to accuse me and obtain redress. Or else, if they were unwilling to come in person, members of their families—fathers, brothers, or other relations—had their relatives suffered any harm at my hands, ought now to put it on record and obtain redress.

In any case, many of those people are present, whom I can see: first there is Crito, my contemporary and fellow demesman, father of Critobulus here; then Lysanias of Sphettus, father of Aeschines here; next, Epigenes' father, Antiphon from Cephisia, is present; then again, there are others here whose brothers have spent time with me in these studies: Nicostratus, son of Theozotides, brother of Theodotus— Theodotus himself, incidentally, is deceased, so Nicostratus could not have come at his brother's urging; and Paralius here, son of Demodocus, whose brother was Theages; also present is Ariston's son, Adimantus, whose brother is Plato here; and Aeantodorus, whose brother is Apollodorus here.

There are many others I could mention to you, from whom Meletus should surely have called some testimony during his own speech. However, if he forgot to do so then, let him call it now—I yield the floor to him—and if he has

any such evidence, let him produce it. But quite the opposite is true, gentlemen: you will find that they are all prepared to support me, their corruptor, the one who is, according to Meletus and Anytus, doing their relatives mischief. Support for me from the actual victims of corruption might perhaps be explained; but what of the uncorrupted—older men by now, and relatives of my victims? What reason would they have to support me, apart from the right and proper one, which is that they know very well that Meletus is lying, whereas I am telling the truth?

There it is, then, gentlemen. That, and perhaps more of the same, is about all I have to say in my defence. But perhaps, among your number, there may be someone who will harbour resentment when he recalls a case of his own: he may have faced a less serious trial than this one, yet begged and implored the jury, weeping copiously, and producing his children here, along with many other relatives and loved ones, to gain as much sympathy as possible. By contrast, I shall do none of those things, even though I am running what might be considered the ultimate risk. Perhaps someone with those thoughts will harden his heart against me; and enraged by those same thoughts, he may cast his vote against me in anger. Well, if any of you are so inclined—not that I expect it of you, but if anyone *should* be— I think it fair to answer him as follows:

"I naturally do have relatives, my excellent friend, because—in Homer's own words—I too was 'not born of oak nor of rock,' but of human parents; and so I do have relatives—including my sons,[30] fellow Athenians. There are three of them: one is now a youth, while two are still children. Nevertheless, I shall not produce any of them here, and then entreat you to vote for my acquittal."

And why, you may ask, will I do no such thing? Not out of contempt or disrespect for you, fellow Athenians—whether or not I am facing death boldly is a different issue. The point is that with our reputations in mind—yours and our whole city's, as well as my own—I believe that any such behaviour would be ignominious, at my age and with the reputation I possess; that reputation may or may not, in fact, be deserved, but at least it is believed that Socrates stands out in some way from the run of human beings. Well, if those of you who are believed to be preeminent in wisdom, courage, or any other form of goodness, are going to behave like that, it would be demeaning.

I have frequently seen such men when they face judgment: they have significant reputations, yet they put on astonishing performances, apparently in the belief that by dying they will suffer something unheard of—as if they would be immune from death, so long as you did not kill them! They seem to me to put our city to shame: they could give any foreigner the impression that men preeminent among Athenians in goodness, whom they select from their own number to govern and hold other positions, are no better than women.[31] I say this, fellow Athenians, because none of us who has even the slightest reputation should behave like that; nor should you put up with us if we try to do so. Rather, you should make one thing clear: you will be far more inclined to convict one who stages those pathetic charades and makes our city an object of derision, than one who keeps his composure.

But leaving reputation aside, gentlemen, I do not think it right to entreat the jury, nor to win acquittal in that way, instead of by informing and persuading them. A juror does not sit to dispense justice as a favour, but to determine where it lies. And he has sworn, not that he will favour whomever he pleases, but that he will try the case according to law. We should not, then, accustom you to transgress your oath, nor should you become accustomed to doing so: neither of us would be showing respect towards the gods. And therefore, fellow Athenians, do not require behaviour from me towards you which I consider neither proper nor right nor pious—more especially now, for God's sake, when I stand charged by Meletus here with impiety: because if I tried to persuade and coerce you with entreaties in spite of your oath, I clearly *would* be teaching you not to believe in gods; and I would

stand literally self-convicted, by my defence, of failing to acknowledge them. But that is far from the truth: I do acknowledge them, fellow Athenians, as none of my accusers do; and I trust to you, and to God, to judge my case as shall be best for me and for yourselves.

For many reasons, fellow Athenians, I am not dismayed by this outcome[32]—your convicting me, I mean—and especially because the outcome has come as no surprise to me. I wonder far more at the number of votes cast on each side, because I did not think the margin would be so narrow. Yet it seems, in fact, that if a mere thirty votes had gone the other way, I should have been acquitted.[33] Or rather, even as things stand, I consider that I have been cleared of Meletus' charges. Not only that, but one thing is obvious to everyone: if Anytus had not come forward with Lycon to accuse me, Meletus would have forfeited 1,000 drachmas, since he would not have gained one-fifth of the votes cast.

But anyhow, this gentleman demands the death penalty for me. Very well, then: what alternative penalty[34] shall I suggest to you, fellow Athenians? Clearly, it must be one I deserve. So what do I deserve to incur or to pay, for having taken it into my head not to lead an inactive life? Instead, I have neglected the things that concern most people—making money, managing an estate, gaining military or civic honours, or other positions of power, or joining political clubs and parties which have formed in our city. I thought myself, in truth, too honest to survive if I engaged in those things. I did not pursue a course, therefore, in which I would be of no use to you or to myself. Instead, by going to each individual privately, I tried to render a service for you which is—so I maintain—the highest service of all. Therefore that was the course I followed: I tried to persuade each of you not to care for any of his possessions rather than care for himself, striving for the utmost excellence and understanding; and not to care for our city's possessions rather than for the city itself; and to care about other things in the same way.

So what treatment do I deserve for being such a benefactor? If I am to make a proposal truly in keeping with my deserts, fellow Athenians, it should be some benefit; and moreover, the sort of benefit that would be fitting for me. Well then, what *is* fitting for a poor man who is a benefactor, and who needs time free for exhorting you? Nothing could be more fitting, fellow Athenians, than to give such a man regular free meals in the Prytaneum;[35] indeed, that is far more fitting for him than for any of you who may have won an Olympic race with a pair or a team of horses: that victory brings you only the appearance of success, whereas I bring you the reality; besides, he is not in want of sustenance, whereas I am. So if, as justice demands, I am to make a proposal in keeping with my deserts, that is what I suggest: free meals in the Prytaneum.

Now, in proposing this, I may seem to you, as when I talked about appeals for sympathy, to be speaking from sheer effrontery. But actually I have no such motive, fellow Athenians. My point is rather this: I am convinced that I do not treat any human being unjustly, at least intentionally—but I cannot make you share that conviction, because we have conversed together so briefly. I say this, because if it were the law here, as in other jurisdictions, that a capital case must not be tried in a single day, but over several,[36] I think you could have been convinced; but as things stand, it is not easy to clear oneself of such grave allegations in a short time.

Since, therefore, I am persuaded, for my part, that I have treated no one unjustly, I have no intention whatever of so treating myself, nor of denouncing myself as deserving ill, or proposing any such treatment for myself. Why should I do that? For fear of the penalty Meletus demands for me, when I say that I don't know if that is a good thing or a bad one? In preference to that, am I then to choose one of the things I know very well to be bad, and demand that instead? Imprisonment, for instance? Why should I live in prison, in servitude to the annually appointed prison commissioners? Well then, a fine, with imprisonment until I pay? That would amount to what I just mentioned, since I haven't the means to pay it.

Well then, should I propose banishment? Perhaps that is what you would propose for me. Yet I must surely be obsessed with survival, fellow Athenians, if I am so illogical as that. You, my fellow citizens, were unable to put up with my discourses and arguments, but they were so irksome and odious to you that you now seek to be rid of them. Could I not draw the inference, in that case, that others will hardly take kindly to them? Far from it, fellow Athenians. A fine life it would be for a person of my age to go into exile, and spend his days continually exchanging one city for another, and being repeatedly expelled—because I know very well that wherever I go, the young will come to hear me speaking, as they do here. And if I repel them, they will expel me themselves, by persuading their elders; while if I do not repel them, their fathers and relatives will expel me on their account.

Now, perhaps someone may say: "Socrates, could you not be so kind as to keep quiet and remain inactive, while living in exile?" This is the hardest point of all of which to convince some of you. Why? Because, if I tell you that that would mean disobeying my god, and that is why I cannot remain inactive, you will disbelieve me and think that I am practising a sly evasion. Again, if I said that it really is the greatest benefit for a person to converse every day about goodness, and about the other subjects you have heard me discussing when examining myself and others—and that an unexamined life is no life for a human being to live—then you would believe me still less when I made those assertions. But the facts, gentlemen, are just as I claim them to be, though it is not easy to convince you of them. At the same time, I am not accustomed to think of myself as deserving anything bad. If I had money, I would have proposed a fine of as much as I could afford: that would have done me no harm at all. But the fact is that I have none—unless you wish to fix the penalty at a sum I could pay. I could afford to pay you 1 mina, I suppose, so I suggest a fine of that amount—

One moment, fellow Athenians. Plato here, along with Crito, Critobulus, and Apollodorus, is urging me to propose 30 minas,[37] and they are saying they will stand surety for that sum. So I propose a fine of that amount, and these people shall be your sufficient guarantors of its payment.

For the sake of a slight gain in time, fellow Athenians, you will incur infamy and blame from those who would denigrate our city, for putting Socrates to death[38]—a "wise man"—because those who wish to malign you will say I am wise, even if I am not; in any case, had you waited only a short time, you would have obtained that outcome automatically. You can see, of course, that I am now well advanced in life, and death is not far off. I address that not to all of you, but to those who condemned me to death; and to those same people I would add something further.

Perhaps you imagine, gentlemen, that I have been convicted for lack of arguments of the sort I could have used to convince you, had I believed that I should do or say anything to gain acquittal. But that is far from true. I have been convicted, not for lack of arguments, but for lack of brazen impudence and willingness to address you in such terms as you would most like to be addressed in—that is to say, by weeping and wailing, and doing and saying much else that I claim to be unworthy of me—the sorts of thing that you are so used to hearing from others. But just as I did not think during my defence that I should do anything unworthy of a free man because I was in danger, so now I have no regrets about defending myself as I did; I should far rather present such a defence and die, than live by defending myself in that other fashion.

In court, as in warfare, neither I nor anyone else should contrive to escape death at any cost. On the battlefield too, it often becomes obvious that one could avoid death by throwing down one's arms and flinging oneself upon the mercy of one's pursuers. And in every sort of danger there are many other means of escaping death, if

one is shameless enough to do or to say anything. I suggest that it is not death that is hard to avoid, gentlemen, but wickedness is far harder, since it is fleeter of foot than death. Thus, slow and elderly as I am, I have now been overtaken by the slower runner; while my accusers, adroit and quick-witted as they are, have been overtaken by the faster, which is wickedness. And so I take my leave, condemned to death by your judgment, whereas they stand for ever condemned to depravity and injustice as judged by Truth. And just as I accept my penalty, so must they. Things were bound to turn out this way, I suppose, and I imagine it is for the best.

In the next place, to those of you who voted against me, I wish to utter a prophecy. Indeed, I have now reached a point at which people are most given to prophesying—that is, when they are on the point of death. I warn you, my executioners, that as soon as I am dead retribution will come upon you—far more severe, I swear, than the sentence you have passed upon me. You have tried to kill me for now, in the belief that you will be relieved from giving an account of your lives. But in fact, I can tell you, you will face just the opposite outcome. There will be more critics to call you to account, people whom I have restrained for the time being though you were unaware of my doing so. They will be all the harder on you since they are younger, and you will rue it all the more—because if you imagine that by putting people to death you will prevent anyone from reviling you for not living rightly, you are badly mistaken. That way of escape is neither feasible nor honourable. Rather, the most honourable and easiest way is not the silencing of others, but striving to make oneself as good a person as possible. So with that prophecy to those of you who voted against me, I take my leave.

As for those who voted for my acquittal, I should like to discuss the outcome of this case while the officials are occupied, and I am not yet on the way to the place where I must die. Please bear with me, gentlemen, just for this short time: there is no reason why we should not have a word with one another while that is still permitted.

Since I regard you as my friends, I am willing to show you the significance of what has just befallen me. You see, gentlemen of the jury—and in applying that term to you, I probably use it correctly—something wonderful has just happened to me. Hitherto, the usual prophetic voice from my spiritual sign was continually active, and frequently opposed me even on trivial matters, if I was about to do anything amiss. But now something has befallen me, as you can see for yourselves, which one certainly might consider—and is generally held—to be the very worst of evils. Yet the sign from God did not oppose me, either when I left home this morning, or when I appeared here in court, or at any point when I was about to say anything during my speech; and yet in other discussions it has very often stopped me in mid-sentence. This time, though, it has not opposed me at any moment in anything I said or did in this whole business.

Now, what do I take to be the explanation for that? I will tell you: I suspect that what has befallen me is a blessing, and that those of us who suppose death to be an evil cannot be making a correct assumption. I have gained every ground for that suspicion, because my usual sign could not have failed to oppose me, unless I were going to incur some good result.

And let us also reflect upon how good a reason there is to hope that death is a good thing. It is, you see, one or other of two things: either to be dead is to be nonexistent, as it were, and a dead person has no awareness whatever of anything at all; or else, as we are told, the soul undergoes some sort of transformation, or exchanging of this present world for another. Now if there is, in fact, no awareness in death, but it is like sleep—the kind in which the sleeper does not even dream at all—then death would be a marvellous gain. Why, imagine that someone had to pick the night in which he slept so soundly that he did not even dream, and to compare all the other nights and days of his life with that one; suppose he had to say, upon consideration, how many days or nights in his life he had spent better and more agreeably than

that night; in that case, I think he would find them easy to count compared with his other days and nights—even if he were the Great King of Persia,[39] let alone an ordinary person. Well, if death is like that, then for my part I call it a gain; because on that assumption the whole of time would seem no longer than a single night.

On the other hand, if death is like taking a trip from here to another place, and if it is true, as we are told, that all of the dead do indeed exist in that other place, why then, gentlemen of the jury, what could be a greater blessing than that? If upon arriving in Hades, and being rid of these people who profess to be "jurors," one is going to find those who are truly judges, and who are also said to sit in judgment there[40]—Minos, Rhadamanthys, Aeacus, Triptolemus, and all other demigods who were righteous in their own lives—would that be a disappointing journey?

Or again, what would any of you not give to share the company of Orpheus and Musaeus, of Hesiod and Homer? I say "you," since I personally would be willing to die many times over, if those tales are true. Why? Because my own sojourn there would be wonderful, if I could meet Palamedes, or Ajax, son of Telamon, or anyone else of old who met their death through an unjust verdict. Whenever I met them, I could compare my own experiences with theirs—which would be not unamusing, I fancy—and best of all, I could spend time questioning and probing people there, just as I do here, to find out who among them is truly wise, and who thinks he is without being so.

What would one not give, gentlemen of the jury, to be able to question the leader of the great expedition against Troy,[41] or Odysseus, or Sisyphus, or countless other men and women one could mention? Would it not be unspeakable good fortune to converse with them there, to mingle with them and question them? At least that isn't a reason, presumably, for people in that world to put you to death—because amongst other ways in which people there are more fortunate than those in our world, they have become immune from death for the rest of time, if what we are told is actually true.

Moreover, you too, gentlemen of the jury, should be of good hope in the face of death, and fix your minds upon this single truth: nothing can harm a good man, either in life or in death; nor are his fortunes neglected by the gods. In fact, what has befallen me has come about by no mere accident; rather, it is clear to me that it was better I should die now and be rid of my troubles. That is also the reason why the divine sign at no point turned me back; and for my part, I bear those who condemned me, and my accusers, no ill will at all—though, to be sure, it was not with that intent that they were condemning and accusing me, but with intent to harm me—and they are culpable for that. Still, this much I ask of them. When my sons come of age, gentlemen, punish them: give them the same sort of trouble that I used to give you, if you think they care for money or anything else more than for goodness, and if they think highly of themselves when they are of no value. Reprove them, as I reproved you, for failing to care for the things they should, and for thinking highly of themselves when they are worthless. If you will do that, then I shall have received my own just deserts from you, as will my sons.

But enough. It is now time to leave—for me to die, and for you to live—though which of us has the better destiny is unclear to everyone, save only to God.

NOTES

1. It is striking that the *Defence of Socrates* begins, as it ends, with a disavowal of knowledge.

2. Socrates' reputation for skill in argument enabled Aristophanes to caricature him as an instructor in logical trickery. Cf. *Clouds* (112–15).

3. The reference is to Aristophanes.

4. Speeches in Athenian lawcourts were timed.

5. This describes Socrates' first appearance in the *Clouds* (223–5), where he is swung around in a basket in the air, and says he is walking on air and thinking about the sun.

6. Professional educators who offered instruction in many subjects.

7. A mina equalled 100 silver drachmas. At the end of the fifth century a drachma was roughly equivalent to one day's pay for a man employed in public works. Evenus' fees were therefore not as "modest" as Socrates pretends.

8. The god Apollo, though nowhere named in the *Defence,* is the deity whose servant Socrates claim to be. In what follows, however, when he speaks of "the god," it is not always clear whether he means Apollo, or a personal God distinct from any deity of traditional Greek religion.

9. Politicians of the democratic party had fled from Athens during the regime of the Thirty Tyrants. They returned under an amnesty in 403 B.C. when the Thirty were overthrown.

10. Literally, "by the dog," a favourite Socratic oath, which may have originated as a euphemism.

11. Socrates alludes to the labours of Heracles, twelve tasks of prodigious difficulty imposed upon a hero of legendary strength and courage.

12. The dithyramb was an emotionally powerful lyric poem, performed by a chorus of singers and dancers.

13. The Athenian Council was a body of 500, with fifty members from each of the ten tribes, elected annually by lot from citizens over the age of 30. In conjunction with the magistrates it carried on state business, and prepared an agenda for the Assembly.

14. Socrates' denial that he corrupts the young intentionally relies upon the principle that human beings never intentionally follow a course of action which they know or believe to be harmful to themselves. Since, in Socrates' view, all wrongdoing is harmful to the agent, it follows that all wrongdoing is unintentional, and curable by the removal of ignorance. This doctrine, one of the so-called Socratic Paradoxes, is often summarized in the slogan "Virtue Is Knowledge." It is elaborated in the *Meno*.

15. The sun and moon, even though not the objects of an official cult at Athens, were widely believed to be divine.

16. According to one tradition, Anaxagoras had been prosecuted for heresies regarding the composition of the sun and moon.

17. The "riddle" which Socrates attributes to Meletus consists in the self-contradictory statement "Socrates acknowledges gods and does not acknowledge gods." Greek riddles often take the form of paradoxes generated by apparent self-contradiction.

18. Spirits were sometimes begotten by gods through union with nymphs or mortals.

19. Site of the legendary war between the Greeks and Trojans, which is the context of Homer's *Iliad*.

20. Achilles, heroic Greek warrior in the Trojan War. As the offspring of a goddess mother by a mortal father, he is referred to as a "demigod."

21. Potidaea, in Thrace, was the scene of a campaign in 432 B.C.

22. Socrates here confirms that his well-known mysterious "sign" had been used to substantiate the charge of "introducing new spiritual realities."

23. Fifty representatives from each of the ten tribes who made up the Council took turns during the year to provide an executive for the entire body.

24. In 406 B.C., after a sea-battle off the Ionian coast at Arginusae, several Athenian commanders were charged for their failure to rescue the ship-wrecked survivors and recover the dead. A motion to try them collectively was endorsed by the Council and referred to the Assembly. Although a collective trial was unconstitutional, the motion was passed by the Assembly after a stormy debate, and six surviving commanders were convicted and executed.

25. A building also called the "sun-shade" from its shape. It was commandeered as a seat of government by the Thirty.

26. An island separated by a narrow channel from the coast of Africa.

27. Socrates is probably alluding, especially, to two of his former associates who had become notorious enemies of the Athenian democracy, Alcibiades and Critias. The former was a brilliant but wayward politician, who had turned against Athens and helped her enemies. The latter was an unscrupulous oligarch, who had become a leading member of the Thirty Tyrants.

28. Socrates here, in effect, contrasts himself with the sophists, in that he did not set himself up as a professional teacher.

29. For example, the Delphic oracle, whose answer had led Socrates to undertake his mission. Dreams had long been believed to be a source of divine communication with human beings, and are often so treated by Plato.

30. At the time of the trial Socrates had two little boys, Sophroniscus and Menexenus, and an older son, Lamprocles.

31. This is one of many disparaging remarks in Plato about women. Open displays of emotion, especially grief, are regarded as distinctively female, an indulgence of the "female side" of our nature.

32. The verdict was "Guilty." Socrates here begins his second speech, proposing an alternative to the death penalty demanded by the prosecution.

33. With a jury of 500, this implies that the vote was 280–220, since at the time of Socrates' trial an evenly split vote (250–250) would have secured his acquittal.

34. The court had to decide between the penalty demanded by the prosecution and a counter-penalty proposed by the defence, with no option of substituting a different one.

35. The Prytaneum was the building on the north-east slope of the Acropolis, in which hospitality was given to honoured guests of the state, and to Olympic victors and other sports-heroes.

36. This was the law at Sparta, because of the irrevocability of capital punishment.

37. This seems to have been a normal amount for a fine, and was a considerable sum.

38. The jury has now voted for the death penalty, and Socrates begins his final speech.

39. This monarch embodied the popular ideal of happiness.

40. It is not clear whether Socrates envisages them merely as judging disputes among the dead, or as passing judgment upon the earthly life of those who enter Hades.

41. Agamemnon, chief of the Greek forces in the Trojan War.

INDEX OF NAMES

Adimantus: older brother of Plato.

Aeacus: one of the three judges in Hades. He also appears as a judge and lawgiver of the island Aegina, and an arbiter of disputes among the gods.

Aeantodorus: brother of APOLLODORUS, but otherwise unknown.

Aeschines: devotee of Socrates, who wrote speeches for the lawcourts, taught oratory, and was admired as an author of Socratic dialogues. A few fragments of his writings are extant.

Ajax: Greek hero of the Trojan War, mentioned as a victim of an "unjust verdict." This refers to the award of Achilles' armour to ODYSSEUS in a contest with Ajax. The latter's resulting madness and suicide are the subject of *Ajax,* one of the extant tragedies by Sophocles.

Anaxagoras: Presocratic philosopher, originally from Clazomenae in Ionia. Important fragments of his work are extant. He spent many years in Athens and was prominent in Athenian intellectual life.

Antiphon: from Cephisia, father of EPIGENES and supporter of Socrates at his trial, but not otherwise known.

Anytus: leading Athenian democratic politician and accuser of Socrates, and the main instigator of the prosecution.

Apollodorus: ardent devotee of Socrates, notorious for his emotional volatility.

Ariston: Athenian of distinguished lineage, and father of Plato.

Aristophanes: *c.* 450–385. The most famous playwright of Athenian Old Comedy. Eleven of his plays and many fragments are extant.

Callias: wealthy Athenian patron of sophistic culture.

Cebes: citizen of Thebes in Boeotia, who had studied there with the Pythagorean philosopher Philolaus. A disciple of Socrates.

Chaerephon: long-time faithful follower of Socrates. Expelled from Athens in 404 during the regime of the Thirty Tyrants, he returned when the democracy was restored in the following year. The comic poets nicknamed him "the bat" from his squeaky voice.

Crito: Socrates' contemporary, fellow demesman, and one of his closest friends.

Critobulus: son of CRITO and member of the Socratic circle, who was present at Socrates' trial and death.

Demodocus: father of THEAGES.

Epigenes: an associate of Socrates. He was present at Socrates' death.

Evenus: a professional teacher of human excellence, or "sophist."

Gorgias: *c.* 480–376, from Leontini in Sicily; commonly but perhaps wrongly classified as a "sophist." He cultivated an artificial but influential prose style, and gave lessons in rhetoric, or effective public speaking.

Hades: the underworld inhabited by the dead. The name belongs, properly, to the mythical king of that realm, who was the brother of ZEUS and Poseidon.

Hector: son of Priam, and leading Trojan hero in the war between Greece and Troy. In HOMER's *Iliad* he kills PATROCLUS, squire of Achilles, who in turn avenges his friend's death by slaying Hector.

Hesiod: one of the earliest extant Greek poets. His *Theogony* contains an account of the origin of the traditional gods. His *Works and Days* is a didactic poem giving moral and practical precepts about rural life.

Hippias: itinerant teacher or "sophist," probably a close contemporary of Socrates, who claimed expertise in many subjects.

Hipponicus: member of wealthy Athenian family, and father of CALLIAS.

Homer: greatest epic poet of Greece, and composer of the *Iliad* and the *Odyssey*. The *Iliad* contains episodes from the legendary Trojan War, while the *Odyssey* recounts the travels and adventures of the hero ODYSSEUS during his journey home after the war.

Leon: resident of Salamis, unjustly arrested and murdered by the Thirty Tyrants in 404.

Lycon: Athenian politician and co-accuser of Socrates with MELETUS and ANYTUS.

Lysanias: of Sphettus, father of AESCHINES, but otherwise unknown.

Meletus: youthful co-accuser of Socrates with ANYTUS and LYCON. He drew up the indictment against Socrates, but was evidently a mere tool of Anytus.

Minos: legendary king of Crete, and traditional judge in the underworld.

Musaeus: mythical bard or singer, closely connected with ORPHEUS.

Nicostratus: supporter of Socrates, present at his trial, but otherwise unknown.

Odysseus: legendary hero in HOMER's *Iliad*, and central figure in the *Odyssey,* which recounts his wanderings after the Trojan War.

Orpheus: legendary bard and founder of the archaic mystical or religious movement known as "Orphism."

Palamedes: Greek hero of the Trojan War, credited with invention of the alphabet.

Paralius: supporter of Socrates who was present at his trial, but is not otherwise known.

Patroclus: squire and close friend of Achilles in HOMER's *Iliad*, slain by HECTOR and avenged by Achilles.

Prodicus: itinerant teacher from Ceos, and one of the sophists.

Rhadamanthys: with AEACUS and MINOS one of the three traditional judges in the underworld.

Simmias: citizen of Thebes and follower of Socrates, who was prepared to finance his escape.

Sisyphus: mythical wrongdoer, famous for his endless punishment in the underworld. His task was to push a boulder up to the top of a hill, from which it always rolled down again.

Telamon: legendary king of Salamis and father of AJAX.

Theages: disciple of Socrates, whose brother PARALIUS was present at the trial, though Theages himself was already dead.

Theodotus: associate of Socrates who died before his trial, but is not otherwise known.

Theozotides: father of NICOSTRATUS and THEODOTUS. Though deceased by the time of Socrates' trial, he is known to have introduced two important democratic measures after the fall of the Thirty Tyrants. Plato may therefore have mentioned him to counter suspicion that Socrates had antidemocratic leanings.

Thetis: sea-nymph or goddess, given in marriage to the mortal Peleus. Achilles was her only child.

Triptolemus: mythical agricultural hero from Eleusis, and a central figure in its mystery cults.

Study Questions

1. According to Socrates, why did the Delphic oracle declare that no one was wiser than Socrates?
2. According to Socrates, what mistake is involved in the fear of death?
3. Why is Socrates unwilling to give up the study of philosophy?
4. According to Socrates, what is far harder to avoid than death?

Part II

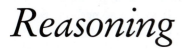

Reasoning

The Scope of Logic

WESLEY C. SALMON

To assert a belief is simple; defending it is far more difficult. Yet if a belief is not defended adequately, why accept it?

Saying something is true does not make it true. Suppose Smith says that both Charles Darwin, who developed the theory of evolution, and Abraham Lincoln were born on February 12, 1809. Jones denies this claim. If saying something is true proves it true, then what Smith says is true and what Jones says is also true—which is impossible, because one of them denies exactly what the other affirms. Their statements are contradictory, and asserting both of them amounts to saying nothing at all. (Incidentally, Smith is correct.)

To reason effectively, we need to avoid contradiction and accept beliefs that are adequately defended. But what are the appropriate standards by which we can determine if our beliefs are consistent with each other and well-confirmed by the available evidence? Logic is the subject that offers answers to these questions, and the scope of logic is explained in the following essay by Wesley C. Salmon, (1925–2001), who was Professor of Philosophy at the University of Pittsburgh.

The remainder of my remarks should be read after Salmon's article. Therefore please proceed now to the selection, and return to this point after finishing it.

In his last paragraph Salmon refers to deductive correctness as "validity." If you have followed his account to that point, you will realize that a valid argument may have false premises and a false conclusion, false premises and a true conclusion, or true premises and a true conclusion. What is not possible is for a valid argument to have true premises and a false conclusion, for a valid argument is one in which if the premises are true, then so is the conclusion.

For purposes of review, consider the following arguments:

1. The capital of Massachusetts is Springfield.
   No banks are located in the capital of Massachusetts.
   Therefore Springfield has no banks.

2. The capital of Massachusetts is Springfield.
   Springfield is the home of the Boston Red Sox.
   Therefore the capital of Massachusetts is the home of the Boston Red Sox.

3. The capital of Massachusetts is Boston.
   Boston is the home of the Boston Red Sox.
   Therefore the capital of Massachusetts is the home of the Boston Red Sox.

Example (1) illustrates a valid argument with false premises and a false conclusion. Example (2) illustrates a valid argument with false premises and a true conclusion. Example (3) illustrates a valid argument with true premises and a true conclusion.

A valid argument with true premises is referred to by philosophers as a "sound" argument. Because a sound argument has true premises and its conclusion follows from its premises, the conclusion of a sound argument is sure to be true. No wonder philosophers prize sound arguments.

In one of his celebrated adventures, Sherlock Holmes comes into possession of an old felt hat. Although Holmes is not acquainted with the owner of the hat, he tells Dr. Watson many things about the man—among them, that he is highly intellectual. This assertion, as it stands, is unsupported. Holmes may have evidence for his statement, but so far he has not given it.

Dr. Watson, as usual, fails to see any basis for Holmes's statement, so he asks for substantiation. "For answer Holmes clapped the hat upon his head. It came right over the forehead and settled upon the bridge of his nose. 'It is a question of cubic capacity,' said he; 'a man with so large a brain must have something in it.'"[1] Now, the statement that the owner of the hat is highly intellectual is no longer an unsupported assertion. Holmes has given the evidence, so his statement is supported. It is the conclusion of an argument. . . .

An argument consists of one statement which is the conclusion and one or more statements of supporting evidence. The statements of evidence are called "premises." There is no set number of premises which every argument must have, but there must be at least one.

When Watson requested a justification for the statement about the owner of the hat, Holmes gave an indication of an argument. Although he did not spell out his argument in complete detail, he did say enough to show what it would be. We can reconstruct it as follows:

a] 1. This is a large hat.
2. Someone is the owner of this hat.
3. The owners of large hats are people with large heads.
4. People with large heads have large brains.
5. People with large brains are highly intellectual.
6. The owner of this hat is highly intellectual.

This is an argument; it consists of six statements. The first five statements are the premises; the sixth statement is the conclusion.

The premises of an argument are supposed to present evidence for the conclusion. Presenting evidence in premises involves two aspects. First, the premises are statements of fact. Second, these facts are offered as *evidence for* the conclusion. . . .

If an argument is offered as a justification of its conclusion, two questions arise. First, are the premises true? Second, are the premises properly related to the conclusion? If either question has a negative answer, the justification is unsatisfactory. It is absolutely essential, however, to avoid confusing these two questions. In logic we are concerned with the second question only. When an argument is subjected to logical analysis, the question of relevance is at issue. *Logic deals with the relation between premises and conclusion, not with the truth of the premises.*

One of our basic purposes is to provide methods of distinguishing between logically correct and incorrect arguments. *The logical correctness or incorrectness of an argument depends solely upon the relation between premises and conclusion.* In a logically correct argument, the premises have the following relation to the conclusion: *If the premises were true, this fact would constitute good grounds for accepting the conclusion as true.* If the facts alleged by the premises of a logically correct argument are, indeed, facts, then they do constitute good evidence for the conclusion. That is what we shall mean by saying that the premises of a logically correct argument *support* the conclusion. The premises of an argument support the conclusion if the truth of the premises would constitute good reason for asserting that the conclusion is true. When we say that the premises of an argument support the conclusion, we are *not* saying that the premises are true; we are saying that there would be good evidence for the conclusion *if* the premises were true.

The premises of a logically incorrect argument may *seem* to support the conclusion, but actually they do not. Logically incorrect arguments are called "fallacious." Even if the premises of a logically incorrect argument were true, this would not constitute good grounds for accepting the conclusion. The premises of a logically incorrect argument do not have the proper relevance to the conclusion.

Since the logical correctness or incorrectness of an argument depends solely upon the relation between premises and conclusion, *logical correctness or incorrectness is completely independent of the truth of the premises.* In particular, it is wrong to call an argument "fallacious" just because it has one or more false premises. Consider the argument concerning the hat in example *a*. You may already have recognized that there is something wrong with the argument from the size of the hat to the intellectuality of the owner; you might have been inclined to reject it on grounds of faulty logic. It would have been a mistake to do so. The argument is logically correct—it is not fallacious—but it does have at least one false premise. As a matter

of fact, not everyone who has a large brain is highly intellectual. However, you should be able to see that the conclusion of this argument would have to be true if all of the premises were true. It is not the business of logic to find out whether people with large brains are intellectual; this matter can be decided only by scientific investigation. Logic *can* determine whether these premises support their conclusion.

As we have just seen, a logically correct argument may have one or more false premises. A logically incorrect or fallacious argument may have true premises; indeed, it may have a true conclusion as well.

b]   *Premises:*   All mammals are mortal.
                  All dogs are mortal.
      Conclusion: All dogs are mammals.

This argument is obviously fallacious. The fact that the premises and the conclusion are all true statements does not mean that the premises support the conclusion. They do not. . . . It happens that the conclusion, "All dogs are mammals," is true, but there is nothing in the premises which provides any basis for it.

Since the logical correctness or incorrectness of an argument depends solely upon the relation between the premises and the conclusion and is completely independent of the truth of the premises, we can analyze arguments without knowing whether the premises are true—indeed, we can do so even when they are known to be false. This is a desirable feature of the situation. It is often useful to know what conclusions can be drawn from false or doubtful premises. For example, intelligent deliberation involves the consideration of the consequences of various alternatives. We may construct arguments with various premises in order to see what the consequences are. In so doing, we do not pretend that the premises are true; rather, we can examine the arguments without even raising the question of the truth of the premises. Up to this point we have proceeded as if the only function of arguments is to provide justifications for conclusions. We see now that this is only one among several uses for arguments. In general, arguments serve to show the conclusions that can be drawn from given premises, whether these premises are known to be true, known to be false, or are merely doubtful.

For purposes of logical analysis it is convenient to present arguments in standard form. We shall adopt the practice of writing the premises first and identifying the conclusion by a triplet of dots.

c]   Everyone who served on the jury was a registered voter.
Jones served on the jury.
∴Jones was a registered voter.

This argument is logically correct. Outside of logic books, we should not expect to find arguments expressed in this neat form. We must learn to recognize arguments when they occur in ordinary prose, for they are not usually set off in the middle of the page and labeled. Furthermore, we have to identify the premises and the conclusion, for they are not usually explicitly labeled. It is not necessary for the premises to precede the conclusion. Sometimes the conclusion comes last, sometimes first, and sometimes in the middle of the argument. For stylistic reasons arguments may be given in a variety of ways; for example, any of the following variations of *c* would be quite proper:

d]   Everyone who served on the jury was a registered voter and Jones served on the jury; *therefore,* Jones was a registered voter.
e]   Jones was a registered voter *because* Jones served on the jury, and everyone who served on the jury was a registered voter.
f]   *Since* everyone who served on the jury was a registered voter, Jones *must have been* a registered voter, *for* Jones served on the jury.

The fact that an argument is being given is usually conveyed by certain words or phrases which indicate that a statement is functioning as a premise or as a conclusion. Terms like "therefore," "hence," "consequently," "so," and "it follows that" indicate that what comes immediately after

is a conclusion. The premises from which it follows should be stated nearby. Also, certain verb forms which suggest necessity, such as "must have been," indicate that the statement in which they occur is a conclusion. They indicate that this statement follows necessarily (i.e., deductively) from stated premises. Other terms indicate that a statement is a premise: "since," "for," and "because" are examples. The statement which follows such a word is a premise. The conclusions based upon this premise should be found nearby. Terms which indicate parts of arguments should be used if, and only if, arguments are being presented. If no argument occurs, it is misleading to use these terms. For instance, if a statement is prefaced by the word "therefore," the reader has every right to expect that it follows from something which has already been said. When arguments are given, it is important to indicate that fact, and to indicate exactly which statements are intended as premises and which as conclusions. It is up to the reader to be sure he understands which statements are premises and which are conclusions before he proceeds to subject arguments to analysis.

There is another respect in which arguments encountered in most contexts fail to have the standard logical form. When we subject arguments to logical analysis, all of the premises must be given explicitly. Many arguments, however, involve premises which are so obvious that it would be sheer pedantry to state them in ordinary speech and writing. We have already seen an example of an argument with missing premises. Holmes's argument about the hat was incomplete; we attempted to complete it in example *a*. Outside a logic book, example *c* might appear in either of the following forms, depending on which premise is considered more obvious:

g]   Jones must have been a registered voter, for he served on the jury.
h]   Jones was a registered voter, because everyone who served on the jury was a registered voter.

In neither case would there be any difficulty in finding the missing premise.

It would be unreasonable to insist that arguments always be presented in complete form without missing premises. Nevertheless, the missing premise can be a great pitfall. Although a missing premise is often a statement too obvious to bother making, sometimes a missing premise can represent a crucial hidden assumption. When we attempt to complete the arguments we encounter, we bring to light the assumptions which would be required to make them logically correct. This step is often the most illuminating aspect of logical analysis. It sometimes turns out that the required premises are extremely dubious or obviously false.

Logical analysis of discourse involves three preliminary steps which we have discussed.

1. Arguments must be recognized; in particular, unsupported statements must be distinguished from conclusions of arguments.
2. When an argument has been found, the premises and conclusions must be identified.
3. If the argument is incomplete, the missing premises must be supplied.

When an argument has been set out in complete and explicit form, logical standards can be applied to determine whether it is logically correct or fallacious. . . .

What we have said so far applies to all types of arguments. The time has come to distinguish two major types: *deductive* and *inductive*. There are logically correct and incorrect forms of each. Here are correct examples.

a]   *Deductive:*   Every mammal has a heart.
                          All horses are mammals.
                          ∴ Every horse has a heart.
b]   *Inductive:*   Every horse that has ever been
                          observed has had a heart.
                          ∴ Every horse has a heart.

There are certain fundamental characteristics which distinguish between correct deductive and correct inductive arguments. We will mention two primary ones.

DEDUCTIVE	INDUCTIVE
I. If all of the premises are true, the conclusion *must be true*.	I. If all of the premises are true, the conclusion is probably true but not necessarily true.
II. All of the information or factual content in the conclusion was already contained, at least implicitly, in the premises.	II. The conclusion contains information not present, even implicitly, in the premises.

It is not difficult to see that the two examples satisfy these conditions.

Characteristic I. The only way in which the conclusion of a could be false—that is, the only possible circumstance under which it could fail to be true that every horse has a heart—is that either not all horses are mammals or not all mammals have hearts. In other words, for the conclusion of a to be false, one or both of the premises must be false. If both premises are true, the conclusion must be true. On the other hand, in b, it is quite possible for the premise to be true and the conclusion false. This would happen if at some future time, a horse is observed which does not have a heart. The fact that no horse without a heart has yet been observed is some evidence that none ever will be. In this argument, the premise does not necessitate the conclusion, but it does lend some weight to it.

Characteristic II. When the conclusion of a says that all horses have hearts, it says something which has already been said, in effect, by the premises. The first premise says that all mammals have hearts, and that includes all horses according to the second premise. In this argument, as in all other correct deductive arguments, the conclusion states explicitly or reformulates information already given in the premises. It is for this reason that deductive arguments also have characteristic I. The conclusion must be true if the premises are true, because the conclusion says nothing which was not already stated by the premises. On the other hand, the premise of our inductive argument *b* refers only to horses that have been observed up to the present, while the conclusion refers to horses that have not yet been observed. Thus, the conclusion makes a statement which goes beyond the information given in the premise. It is because the conclusion says something not given in the premise that the conclusion might be false even though the premise is true. The additional content of the conclusion might be false, rendering the conclusion as a whole false. Deductive and inductive arguments fulfill different functions. The deductive argument is designed to make explicit the content of the premises; the inductive argument is designed to extend the range of our knowledge.

We may summarize by saying that the inductive argument expands the content of premises by sacrificing necessity, whereas the deductive argument achieves necessity by sacrificing any expansion of content.

It follows immediately from these characteristics that deductive correctness (known as *validity* . . .) is an all or nothing affair. An argument either qualifies fully as a correct deduction or it fails completely; there are no degrees of deductive validity. The premises either completely necessitate the conclusion or they fail entirely to do so. Correct inductive arguments, in contrast, admit of degrees of strength, depending upon the amount of support the premises furnish for the conclusion. There are degrees of probability which the premises of an inductive argument can supply to a conclusion, but the logical necessity which relates premises to conclusion in a deductive argument is never a matter of degree.

NOTE

1. A. Conan Doyle, "The Adventure of the Blue Carbuncle," *Adventures of Sherlock Holmes* (New York and London: Harper & Row, n.d.), p. 157. Direct quotation and use of literary material from this story by permission of the Estate of Sir Arthur Conan Doyle.

Study Questions

1. How does a deductive argument differ from an inductive one?
2. Give an example of a valid argument with two false premises, one true premise, and a true conclusion.
3. If all the premises of a valid argument are false, is the conclusion sure to be false?
4. If all the premises of a valid argument are true, is the conclusion sure to be true?

Improving Your Thinking

STEPHEN F. BARKER

Effective reasoning calls for avoiding fallacious arguments and clarifying ambiguous terms. Our next selection, written by Stephen F. Barker, Professor Emeritus of Philosophy at Johns Hopkins University, addresses both of these issues.

You can strengthen your own thinking by being alert to some commonly used words that are so notoriously vague that their appearance in any argument signals trouble. Here are some examples: subjective, natural, relative, pragmatic, diverse. Next time you hear someone use one of these terms, ask what it means. Everyone will benefit from the clarification.

1. FALLACIES

If we want to become more skillful at playing chess, or football, or any other game, it is a good idea to study not only the shrewd moves that experts make, but also the poor moves that less experienced players make—we can learn from their mistakes. Similarly, as we try to improve our ability to reason logically, we should not confine our attention to specimens of good reasoning; we should also consider plenty of tempting examples of bad reasoning. By becoming more aware of how these bad arguments are bad, we strengthen our ability to distinguish between good and bad reasoning.

In ordinary talk the term "fallacy" is often loosely applied to any sort of mistaken belief or untrue sentence. "It's a fallacy to believe that handling a toad causes warts," people say. Here the thing being called a fallacy is just a belief, not a piece of reasoning. But in logic the term "fallacy" is restricted to mistakes in reasoning: a *fallacy* is a logical mistake in reasoning, especially one that it is tempting to make. There is a logical fallacy only when there are premises and a conclusion which is erroneously thought to be proved by them.

Many types of fallacies have been given special names, especially those types that are rather tempting and likely to deceive people. . . .

An argument is called a *petitio principii* (or begging of the question) if the argument fails to prove anything because it somehow takes for granted what it is supposed to prove. Suppose a man says "Jones is insane, you know," and we reply "Really? Are you sure?" and he responds, "Certainly, I can prove it. Jones is demented; therefore he is insane." This is a valid argument in the sense that if the premise is true, the conclusion must be true too; but the argument is unsatisfactory, for it does not really prove anything. The premise is merely another statement of the conclusion, so that practically anyone who doubts the truth of the conclusion ought to be equally doubtful about the truth of the premise, and the argument is useless for the purpose of convincing us of the truth of the conclusion. Thus the argument takes for granted just what it is supposed to prove; it begs the question.

Consider a longer chain of reasoning:

"We must not drink liquor."
"Why do you say that?"
"Drinking is against the will of Allah."
"How do you know?"
"The Koran says so."
"But how do you know that the Koran is right?"
"Everything said in the Koran is right."
"How do you know that?"
"Why, it's all divinely inspired."
"But how do you know that?"
"Why, the Koran itself declares that it is divinely inspired."
"But why believe that?"
"You've got to believe the Koran, because everything in the Koran is right."

This chain of reasoning is a more extended case of begging the question; the speaker is reasoning in a large circle, taking for granted one of the things that is supposed to be proved.

One specific form of *petitio principii,* or begging of the question, has a special name of its own: the fallacy of *complex question.* This is the fallacy of framing a question so as to take for granted something controversial that ought to be proved.

Suppose Mr. White is trying to prove that Mr. Green has a bad character, and White asks Green the famous question "Have you stopped beating your wife yet?" If Green answers "Yes" to this question, White will argue that Green is admitting to having been a wife-beater; if he answers "No," then White will argue that Green is admitting to still being a wife-beater. The questioner has framed his question in such a way as to take for granted that Green has a wife whom he has been beating. The fallacy is that this is a controversial proposition that is at least as doubtful as is the conclusion (that Green has a bad character) supposedly being established. It is not proper in this debate to take for granted this controversial proposition; it needs to be proved if White is to make use of it at all. . . .

One important type of fallacy . . . is the *ad hominem* fallacy. An argument is *ad hominem* (Latin: "to the man") if it is directed at an opponent in a controversy rather than being directly relevant to proving the conclusion under discussion. Such arguments are often, but not always, fallacious. For example, suppose someone argues: "Of course Karl Marx must have been mistaken in maintaining that capitalism is an evil form of economic and social organization. Why, he was a miserable failure of a man who couldn't even earn enough money to support his family." This is an *ad hominem* argument, for it attacks Marx the man instead of offering direct reasons why his views are incorrect. . . .

Another quite different fallacy of irrelevance is the appeal to unsuitable authority. . . . We

commit this fallacy when we appeal to some admired or famous person as if that person were an authority on the matter being discussed—but when we have no good reason for thinking that the person is a genuine authority on it. Of course it is not always fallacious to appeal to authorities, but we are not entitled to appeal to persons as authorities unless there are good reasons for believing them to be authorities, and we should not trust an authority outside his or her special proven field of competence. A famous guitarist may be an expert on one type of music, but this does not make her an authority on philosophy of life. A movie star may be an authority on how to look attractive to the opposite sex, but is not likely to be an authority on which pain reliever is most healthful or which toothpaste tastes best. . . .

We conclude with . . . the fallacy of *black-and-white* thinking. A wife may say to her husband "So you think the soup is too cold, do you? Well, I suppose you would like to have had it scalding hot then, instead." The second remark is presented as if it followed logically from the first, and yet there is no logical connection whatever. But people find it very easy to fall into this sort of thinking in extremes, especially in the heat of controversy.

2. DEFINITIONS

When we encounter words that cause confusion because their meanings are ambiguous, it is often helpful to define them. . . .

Definitions that are useful in preventing ambiguity may be subdivided into two types. Some of them serve the purpose of describing the meaning that a word already has in language. We might call these *analytical* definitions. In giving this kind of definition of a word, the speaker does not aim to change its meaning; he aims only to characterize the meaning it already has. Dictionary definitions are of this type. When a definition has this purpose, we can properly ask whether the definition is correct or incorrect.

In order to be correct in its description of the meaning of a word, an analytical definition must not be *too broad;* that is, it must not embrace things that do not really belong. (To define "pneumonia" as "disease of the lungs" would be too broad, for there are many lung diseases besides pneumonia.) Also, in order to be correct in its description of the meaning of a word, an analytical definition must not be *too narrow;* that is, it must not exclude things that really belong. (To define "psychosis" as "schizophrenia" would be too narrow, for there are other kinds of psychoses. . . .)

Finally, a definition cannot serve much useful purpose if it is circular. . . . For example, to define "straight line" as "the line along which a ray of light travels when it goes straight" is circular and uninformative. . . .

A second type of definition useful in preventing ambiguity is the *stipulative* definition, whose purpose is to declare how a speaker intends that a certain word, phrase, or symbol shall be understood ("Let '*S*' mean 'Samoans'"; "Let 'heavy truck' mean 'truck that can carry a load of 5 tons or more'"; etc.). Perhaps the expression being defined is one that previously had no meaning, or perhaps it had a different or a vaguer meaning. At any rate, the point of the stipulative definition is that the expression now is deliberately endowed with a particular meaning. Obviously, a stipulative definition cannot be of much use if it is unclear or circular. However, we do not have to worry about whether it is too broad or too narrow, for that sort of correctness cannot pertain to stipulative definitions. A stipulative definition is arbitrary, in that it expresses only the speaker's intention to use the word in the stipulated manner, and the speaker is, after all, entitled to use it in any desired way, so long as it does not cause confusion.

In order to avoid causing confusion, however, a stipulative definition should not assign to a word that already has an established meaning some new meaning that is likely to be confused with it. Consider the following dialogue:

SMITH: General Green is insane, you know. He ought to be dismissed.

JONES: He is? I agree that we should not have insane persons serving in the Army. But how do you know he's insane?

SMITH: It's obvious. He says he believes in extrasensory perception, and according to my definition—surely I'm entitled to use words as I please—anyone who does that is insane.

Here the stipulative definition is used to promote ambiguity rather than to prevent it. In the ordinary sense of the term "insane," Jones agrees with Smith that insane persons ought not to be generals. But Smith offers no evidence that General Green is insane in this sense. All that Smith shows is that the general is "insane" in a special, idiosyncratic sense of the word. From that, nothing follows about whether he ought to be dismissed. Smith is causing confusion by failing to keep distinct these two very different senses of the word; this happens because he fails to recognize the difference here between a stipulative and an analytical definition. . . .

The two kinds of definitions mentioned so far both aim to inform us about verbal usage. . . . It would be a mistake, however, to suppose that everything called a definition belongs to one of these two kinds. In fact, the profoundest and most valuable definitions usually do not fit tidily into either kind. When Newton defined force as the product of mass times acceleration, when Einstein defined simultaneity of distant events in terms of the transmission of light rays . . . [w]hat these definitions did was to propose new verbal usages growing out of the previously established usages. It was felt that these new usages perfected tendencies of thought implicit in the old usages and offered more insight into the subject matter being treated.

We might give the name *revelatory* definitions to definitions like these, which do not fit into either of the two categories of stipulative and analytical. Revelatory definitions constitute a third category. Further examples of revelatory definitions can be found in other, diverse fields. For example, when a nineteenth-century writer defined architecture as frozen music, he was not trying to describe how the word "architecture" is used in our language. (He took it for granted that his readers would know what kinds of constructions are considered architecture.) Nor was he proposing some arbitrary new usage. We should not censure his definition on the ground that it is unhelpful for the purpose of preventing ambiguity; that is not the purpose of this kind of definition. This definition is a metaphor, and it suggests a new way of looking at architecture, comparing the structural organization of the parts of a building with the structural organization of the parts of a musical composition. In trying to decide whether the definition is a good one or not, we must reflect about the extent and validity of this comparison between music and buildings; the definition is a good one if and only if the comparison is revealing. . . .

How frequently are definitions needed? People sometimes think that one always should define one's terms at the beginning of any discussion. But this idea becomes absurd if carried too far. Suppose that we as speakers did undertake to define all our terms in noncircular ways. However far we proceeded, we would always still have . . . undefined terms; therefore this task is an impossible one to complete. Moreover, we do have a fairly adequate understanding of the meanings of many words that we have never bothered to define and also of many words that we would not know how to define satisfactorily even if we tried. Thus, it would be foolish to try indiscriminately to define all or even most of our terms before proceeding with our thinking. What we should do at the beginning of a discussion is seek definitions of those particular words which are especially likely to make trouble in the discussion because they are harmfully ambiguous, obscure, or vague.

This is especially true with regard to discussions in which confusion is caused by failure to notice the different meanings of a term. A *verbal dispute* is a dispute arising solely from the fact that some word is being used with different meanings; this kind of dispute can be settled merely by giving the definitions that clarify the situation (though this is not to say that such disputes always are *easy* to settle).

The American philosopher William James gives a classic example of such a verbal dispute. . . . Suppose there is a squirrel on the trunk of a tree, and a man walks around the tree. The squirrel moves around the tree trunk so as to stay out of sight, always facing the man but keeping the tree between them. Has the man gone around the squirrel or not? Some of James's friends disputed hotly for a long time about this question. Here is a purely verbal dispute; it can be settled by pointing out that in one sense the man has gone "around" the squirrel, for he has moved from the north to the west and then to the south and east of the squirrel's location, but in another sense the man has not gone "around" the squirrel, for the squirrel has always been facing him. Once we have pointed out these two different senses of the word, we have done all that can reasonably be done; there is nothing more worth discussing (though this does not ensure that discussion will cease). With a verbal dispute like this, giving definitions is the way to resolve the dispute. But it would be utterly wrong to assume that all disputes are verbal in this way. There are many serious problems for the settling of which definitions are not needed, and there are many other problems where if definitions help, they mark only the beginning of the thinking needed to resolve the issue.

Study Questions

1. Give an example of an argument that begs the question.
2. Give your own example of an *ad hominem* argument.
3. Explain the danger involved in offering a stipulative definition that uses an ordinary word in an idiosyncratic manner.
4. Give your own example of a purely verbal dispute.

Scientific Inquiry

CARL G. HEMPEL

The scientific method of explanation involves formulating a hypothesis and testing it, then accepting, rejecting, or modifying it in light of the experimental results. But how do we test a hypothesis? That is the subject of the following selection by the celebrated philosopher of science Carl G. Hempel (1905–1997), who was Professor of Philosophy at Princeton University.

As you read about hypothesis testing, you may wonder how hypotheses are developed. What is their source? No mechanical procedures are available; the answer lies in creative imagination. While giving free rein to ingenuity, however, scientific method requires that our intuitions be accepted only if they pass the rigors of careful testing.

1. A CASE HISTORY AS AN EXAMPLE

As a simple illustration of some important aspects of scientific inquiry let us consider Semmelweis' work on childbed fever. Ignaz Semmelweis, a physician of Hungarian birth, did this work during the years from 1844 to 1848 at the Vienna General Hospital. As a member of the medical staff of the First Maternity Division in the hospital, Semmelweis was distressed to find that a large proportion of the women who were delivered of their babies in that division contracted a serious and often fatal illness known as puerperal fever or childbed fever. In 1844, as many as 260 out of 3,157 mothers in the First Division, or 8.2 per cent, died of the disease; for 1845, the death rate was 6.8 per cent, and for 1846, it was 11.4 per cent. These figures were all the more alarming because in the adjacent Second Maternity Division of the same hospital, which accommodated almost as many women as the First, the death toll from childbed fever was much lower: 2.3, 2.0, and 2.7 per cent for the same years. In a book that he wrote later on the causation and the prevention of childbed fever, Semmelweis describes his efforts to resolve the dreadful puzzle.[1]

He began by considering various explanations that were current at the time; some of these he rejected out of hand as incompatible with well-established facts; others he subjected to specific tests.

One widely accepted view attributed the ravages of puerperal fever to "epidemic influences," which were vaguely described as "atmospheric-cosmic-telluric changes" spreading over whole districts and causing childbed fever in women in confinement. But how, Semmelweis reasons, could such influences have plagued the First Division for years and yet spared the Second? And how could this view be reconciled with the fact that while the fever was raging in the hospital, hardly a case occurred in the city of Vienna or in its surroundings: a genuine epidemic, such as cholera, would not be so selective. Finally, Semmelweis notes that some of the women admitted to the First Division, living far from the hospital, had been overcome by labor on their way and had given birth in the street: yet despite these adverse conditions, the death rate from childbed fever among these cases of "street birth" was lower than the average for the First Division.

On another view, overcrowding was a cause of mortality in the First Division. But Semmelweis points out that in fact the crowding was heavier in the Second Division, partly as a result of the desperate efforts of patients to avoid assignment to the notorious First Division. He also rejects two similar conjectures that were current, by noting that there were no differences between the two Divisions in regard to diet or general care of the patients.

In 1846, a commission that had been appointed to investigate the matter attributed the prevalence of illness in the First Division to injuries resulting from rough examination by the medical students, all of whom received their obstetrical training in the First Division. Semmelweis notes in refutation of this view that (*a*) the injuries resulting naturally from the process of birth are much more extensive than those that might be caused by rough examination; (*b*) the

midwives who received their training in the Second Division examined their patients in much the same manner but without the same ill effects; (*c*) when, in response to the commission's report, the number of medical students was halved and their examinations of the women were reduced to a minimum, the mortality, after a brief decline, rose to higher levels than ever before.

Various psychological explanations were attempted. One of them noted that the First Division was so arranged that a priest bearing the last sacrament to a dying woman had to pass through five wards before reaching the sickroom beyond: the appearance of the priest, preceded by an attendant ringing a bell, was held to have a terrifying and debilitating effect upon the patients in the wards and thus to make them more likely victims of childbed fever. In the Second Division, this adverse factor was absent, since the priest had direct access to the sickroom. Semmelweis decided to test this conjecture. He persuaded the priest to come by a roundabout route and without ringing of the bell, in order to reach the sick chamber silently and unobserved. But the mortality in the First Division did not decrease.

A new idea was suggested to Semmelweis by the observation that in the First Division the women were delivered lying on their backs; in the Second Division, on their sides. Though he thought it unlikely, he decided "like a drowning man clutching at a straw," to test whether this difference in procedure was significant. He introduced the use of the lateral position in the First Division, but again, the mortality remained unaffected.

At last, early in 1847, an accident gave Semmelweis the decisive clue for his solution of the problem. A colleague of his, Kolletschka, received a puncture wound in the finger, from the scalpel of a student with whom he was performing an autopsy, and died after an agonizing illness during which he displayed the same symptoms that Semmelweis had observed in the victims of childbed fever. Although the role of microorganisms in such infections had not yet been recognized at the time, Semmelweis realized that "cadaveric matter" which the student's scalpel had introduced into Kolletschka's blood stream had caused his colleague's fatal illness. And the similarities between the course of Kolletschka's disease and that of the women in his clinic led Semmelweis to the conclusion that his patients had died of the same kind of blood poisoning: he, his colleagues, and the medical students had been the carriers of the infectious material, for he and his associates used to come to the wards directly from performing dissections in the autopsy room, and examine the women in labor after only superficially washing their hands, which often retained a characteristic foul odor.

Again, Semmelweis put his idea to a test. He reasoned that if he were right, then childbed fever could be prevented by chemically destroying the infectious material adhering to the hands. He therefore issued an order requiring all medical students to wash their hands in a solution of chlorinated lime before making an examination. The mortality from childbed fever promptly began to decrease, and for the year 1848 it fell to 1.27 per cent in the First Division, compared to 1.33 in the Second.

In further support of his idea, or of his hypothesis, as we will also say, Semmelweis notes that it accounts for the fact that the mortality in the Second Division consistently was so much lower: the patients there were attended by midwives, whose training did not include anatomical instruction by dissection of cadavers.

The hypothesis also explained the lower mortality among "street births": women who arrived with babies in arms were rarely examined after admission and thus had a better chance of escaping infection.

Similarly, the hypothesis accounted for the fact that the victims of childbed fever among the newborn babies were all among those whose mothers had contracted the disease during labor; for then the infection could be transmitted to the baby before birth, through the common bloodstream of mother and child, whereas this was impossible when the mother remained healthy.

Further clinical experiences soon led Semmelweis to broaden his hypothesis. On one occasion, for example, he and his associates, having carefully disinfected their hands, examined first a woman in labor who was suffering from a festering cervical cancer; then they proceeded to examine twelve other women in the same room, after only routine washing without renewed disinfection. Eleven of the twelve patients died of puerperal fever. Semmelweis concluded that childbed fever can be caused not only by cadaveric material, but also by "putrid matter derived from living organisms."

2. BASIC STEPS IN TESTING A HYPOTHESIS

We have seen how, in his search for the cause of childbed fever, Semmelweis examined various hypotheses that had been suggested as possible answers. . . . [L]et us examine how a hypothesis, once proposed, is tested.

Sometimes, the procedure is quite direct. Consider the conjectures that differences in crowding, or in diet, or in general care account for the difference in mortality between the two divisions. As Semmelweis points out, these conflict with readily observable facts. There are no such differences between the divisions; the hypotheses are therefore rejected as false.

But usually the test will be less simple and straightforward. Take the hypothesis attributing the high mortality in the First Division to the dread evoked by the appearance of the priest with his attendant. The intensity of that dread, and especially its effect upon childbed fever, are not as directly ascertainable as are differences in crowding or in diet, and Semmelweis uses an indirect method of testing. He asks himself: Are there any readily observable effects that should occur if the hypothesis were true? And he reasons: *If* the hypothesis were true, *then* an appropriate change in the priest's procedure should be followed by a decline in fatalities. He checks this implication by a simple experiment and finds it false, and he therefore rejects the hypothesis.

Similarly, to test his conjecture about the position of the women during delivery, he reasons: *If* this conjecture should be true, *then* adoption of the lateral position in the First Division will reduce the mortality. Again, the implication is shown false by his experiment, and the conjecture is discarded.

In the last two cases, the test is based on an argument to the effect that *if* the contemplated hypothesis, say *H,* is true, *then* certain observable events (e.g., decline in mortality) should occur under specified circumstances (e.g., if the priest refrains from walking through the wards, or if the women are delivered in lateral position); or briefly, if *H* is true, then so is *I,* where *I* is a statement describing the observable occurrences to be expected. For convenience, let us say that *I* is inferred from, or implied by, *H;* and let us call *I* a *test implication of the hypothesis H.* . . .

In our last two examples, experiments show the test implication to be false, and the hypothesis is accordingly rejected. The reasoning that leads to the rejection may be schematized as follows:

2*a*]   If *H* is true, then so is *I*.
            But (as the evidence shows) *I* is not true.
            H is not true.

Any argument of this form, called *modus tollens* in logic, is deductively valid; that is, if its premisses (the sentences above the horizontal line) are true, then its conclusion (the sentence below the horizontal line) is unfailingly true as well. Hence, if the premisses of (2*a*) are properly established, the hypothesis *H* that is being tested must indeed be rejected.

Next, let us consider the case where observation or experiment bears out the test implication *I.* From his hypothesis that childbed fever is blood poisoning produced by cadaveric matter, Semmelweis infers that suitable antiseptic

measures will reduce fatalities from the disease. This time, experiment shows the test implication to be true. But this favorable outcome does not conclusively prove the hypothesis true, for the underlying argument would have the form

2*b*]   If *H* is true, then so is *I*.
            (As the evidence shows) *I* is true.
            H is true.

And this mode of reasoning, which is referred to as the *fallacy of affirming the consequent,* is deductively invalid, that is, its conclusion may be false even if its premises are true. This is in fact illustrated by Semmelweis' own experience. The initial version of his account of childbed fever as a form of blood poisoning presented infection with cadaveric matter essentially as the one and only source of the disease; and he was right in reasoning that if this hypothesis should be true, then destruction of cadaveric particles by antiseptic washing should reduce the mortality. Furthermore, his experiment did show the test implication to be true. Hence, in this case, the premises of (2*b*) were both true. Yet, his hypothesis was false, for as he later discovered, putrid material from living organisms, too, could produce childbed fever.

Thus, the favorable outcome of a test, i.e., the fact that a test implication inferred from a hypothesis is found to be true, does not prove the hypothesis to be true. Even if many implications of a hypothesis have been borne out by careful tests, the hypothesis may still be false. The following argument still commits the fallacy of affirming the consequent:

2*c*]   If *H* is true, then so are $I_1, I_2, \ldots, I_n$.
            (As the evidence shows) $I_1, I_2, \ldots, I_n$ are
                all true.
            H is true.

This, too, can be illustrated by reference to Semmelweis' final hypothesis in its first version. As we noted earlier, his hypothesis also yields the test implications that among cases of street births admitted to the First Division, mortality from puerperal fever should be below the average for the

Division, and that infants of mothers who escape the illness do not contract childbed fever; and these implications, too, were borne out by the evidence—even though the first version of the final hypothesis was false.

But the observation that a favorable outcome of however many tests does not afford conclusive proof for a hypothesis should not lead us to think that if we have subjected a hypothesis to a number of tests and all of them have had a favorable outcome, we are no better off than if we had not tested the hypothesis at all. For each of our tests might conceivably have had an unfavorable outcome and might have led to the rejection of the hypothesis. A set of favorable results obtained by testing different test implications, $I_1, I_2, \ldots, I_n$, of a hypothesis, shows that as far as these particular implications are concerned, the hypothesis has been borne out; and while this result does not afford a complete proof of the hypothesis, it provides at least some support, some partial corroboration or confirmation for it.

NOTE

1. The story of Semmelweis' work and of the difficulties he encountered forms a fascinating page in the history of medicine. A detailed account, which includes translations and paraphrases of large portions of Semmelweis' writings, is given in W. J. Sinclair, *Semmelweis: His Life and His Doctrine* (Manchester, England: Manchester University Press, 1909). Brief quoted phrases in this chapter are taken from this work. The highlights of Semmelweis' career are recounted in the first chapter of P. de Kruif, *Men Against Death* (New York: Harcourt, Brace & World, Inc., 1932).

Study Questions

1. Give your own example of testing a hypothesis by use of scientific method.
2. Give your own example of an argument in the form of *modus tollens*.
3. If an implication inferred from a hypothesis is found to be true, is the hypothesis thereby proven to be true?
4. What is the value of a partial confirmation of a hypothesis?

Science and the Practices of Women

NANCY TUANA

Nancy Tuana is Professor of Philosophy at Pennsylvania State University. She considers how scientific inquiry can be affected by the gender of those conducting research.

Women's differences, both their differences from men and their differences from one another, can highlight overlooked or minimized aspects of the knowledge process in science. I will here limit my analysis to three of these, each of which is relevant to transformations of the traditional epistemological question "How do we know?" and the rejection of the ideal of value-neutrality in science:

1. replacing the traditional model of the knower as a detached, disinterested individual with the dynamic model of engaged, committed individuals in communities;

2. recognition of the epistemic value of affective processes;

3. examination of the role of embodiment in the knowledge process.

INDIVIDUALS IN COMMUNITIES

A careful study of the actual practice of science . . . necessitates a rejection of the model of the isolated knower and replaces it with a dynamic model of individuals in communities. An examination of the complexity of the communities relevant to the production of knowledge in science also reveals that the production of good science does not require disinterested, dispassionate scientists. . . . The ideal of a pure science, a science uninfluenced by values, and the scientist as a neutral recorder of facts are myths, ones that can be rejected without abandoning objectivity.

Changing the Subject of Evolution

The development of "woman, the gatherer" theories of human evolution has been the subject of much discussion in feminist science literature because this example is an excellent illustration of not only the inescapable fact of value within the construction of scientific theories, but also the potential epistemic significance of the various communities, including political communities, in which the knower participates.

Feminist discussions of the epistemological significance of being part of the feminist community have found the science of primatology to be particularly relevant due to the fact that its stories of human evolution arise out of origin myths, that is, accounts of the origins of the family, of the sexes and their roles, as well as of the divisions between human and nonhuman animals. In other words, accounts of human evolution wear the metaphysics of their authors "on their sleeves" and thus provide clear accounts of the ways participation in alternative communities can be epistemologically significant.

To understand the androcentrism of traditional "man, the hunter" accounts of evolution, we need only attend to the respective roles of women and men. "Man, the hunter" theories of human evolution attribute the evolution of *Homo sapiens* to those activities and behaviors engaged in and exhibited by male ancestors. Males, the explanation goes, having the important and dangerous task of hunting big animals to provide the central food source, invented not only tools but also a social organization, including the development of language, that enabled them to do so most successfully. Hunting behavior is posited as the rudimentary beginnings of social and political organization. "In a very real sense our intellect, interests, emotions, and basic social life—all are evolutionary products of the success of the hunting adaptation. . . . The biology, psychology, and customs that separate us from apes—all these we owe to the hunters of time past" (Washburn and Lancaster, 1976, pp. 293, 303).

Such accounts do not omit women, but place them firmly "at home." While men are out hunting, women are taking care of hearth and children, dependent upon the men for sustenance and protection. Note the assumptions embedded in this account. Only male activities are depicted as skilled or socially oriented. Women's actions are represented as biologically oriented and based on "nature." This definition of woman's functions as natural curtails any analysis of them, such as their relation to the physical and social environments or the role they might play in determining other social arrangements. Men are depicted as actively transforming their nature, while women are portrayed as constrained by it.

The alternative origin stories told by feminist primatologists transform women from a passive, sexual resource for males to active agents and creators. . . . One key to understanding the explosion of alternative images of women's nature lies in the woman's movement of the 1960s that contested the definitions of woman as the second sex, definitions that simultaneously relegated her role to the private realm of family while designating the public realm of culture and politics as that which makes one fully human.

Feminist attention to perceptions of women's roles and the linkage of woman and nature provided the basis for a rethinking of evolution for a number of scientists. The anthropologist Sally Linton Slocum, for example, in her 1970 essay "Woman the Gatherer: Male Bias in Anthropology" identified ways in which females were being obscured within evolutionary theories by the association of their actions with nature and began to question the assumption that women's actions were unimportant because they were derived from instinct and thus not relevant to the evolutionary process. Slocum's position was in turn developed by the paleoanthropological research of Adrienne Zihlman and Nancy Tanner. This shift of attention was the result not of any biological difference between women and men scientists, but because women scientists were more likely to be affected by and participate in the feminist community—a community that had been actively exposing the history and the impact of the androcentric bias of associating women with nature and men with culture, as well as working to revalue the socially defined work of women, including childcare and housework. This political awareness arising from the influences of the feminist community changed the focus of attention for researchers like Slocum, Tanner, and Zihlman and contributed to the construction of alternative questions.

But it would be inaccurate to see the accounts of these scientists as influenced only by their participation in communities that were redefining woman's nature. These women were also influenced by their membership in scientific communities and the then current theories of evolution. The point is that accounts by women primatologists, particularly feminist primatologists, while marked both by their gender and their politics as they attempt to carve a role for women out of the standard narrative of evolution, nevertheless evolve out of and are influenced by the accepted narratives and standards of evidence of their scientific communities.

Nor should alternative evolutionary accounts such as "woman, the gatherer" be seen simply as feminist "correctives," that is, as an ideological image imposed onto the data. I will argue that this alternative model of evolution arose in response to changes within the scientific community, provided more accurate accounts of the evidence, and was therefore the result of better science. But this is not incompatible with saying that the model emerged from the practice of feminist scientists who, because of the impact of their communities, attended differently to the data. To say that the practice of science is marked by gender and by politics is not the same as claiming that it arises out of wishful thinking or ideological concerns. A scientific theory can provide consistent methods for obtaining reliable knowledge, yet be influenced by certain values or interests. Objectivity and neutrality are not the same thing. . . .

Zihlman's creation of an alternative to the androcentric "man, the hunter" theory was made possible by the knowledge she gained from the communities of which she was a member, in this case both scientific and nonscientific. However, it is not a coincidence that the "woman, the gatherer" hypothesis was initiated by the work of Sally Linton Slocum, and developed by Nancy Tanner and Adrienne Zihlman. Being a feminist scientist can affect one's practice of science. In the words of Lynn Hankinson Nelson, "it makes a difference to one's observations, appraisals of theories, and one's own theorizing, if one *recognizes* androcentric and sexist assumptions, categories, or questions and if one questions the inevitability of male dominance and/or the universality of hierarchical dominance relationships. In short, it makes a difference if one is working from a feminist perspective" (Nelson, 1990, p. 224). But Zihlman's participation within particular scientific communities was also a crucial factor in the development of her research. The point is that a scientist is simultaneously a member of a number of different epistemic communities and subcommunities. The values and beliefs of these various communities often interact in complex ways over the course of the knowledge process. Fully understanding the development of knowledge then requires an appreciation of the interactive effects of all relevant communities and an understanding of the underlying presuppositions, metaphysical as well as aesthetic and moral values, of each community's system of beliefs.

ENGAGED KNOWERS

. . . Many feminist theorists of science contend that women's relative absence from the practice of science is not due simply to institutional barriers such as limited access to advanced science training, but is also an aspect of a model of the scientist that privileges traits that have historically been associated with masculinity (autonomous, detached, disinterested) and suppress those traditionally associated with femininity (dependent, connected, engaged). . . .

Such a model, for example, does not account for the epistemic role of the complex relationships between agents of knowledge as evidenced in examples like that of "woman, the gatherer" theories of human evolution. Equally problematic, this model overlooks the epistemic significance of subjective aspects of the relationship between scientists and the subject of inquiry,

such as the scientist's commitments, desires, and interests. It also ignores the fact and nature of a scientist's embodiment. In this section I examine the role of what has traditionally been labeled "the passions" in the knowledge process in science, reserving the question of the role of the body for the final section of the essay.

A Feeling for the Organism

Evelyn Fox Keller offers a portrait of the geneticist Barbara McClintock that provides a very different image of the scientist than that of the disinterested, detached observer. McClintock describes herself as having developed a close relationship with the objects of her investigation. "I start with the seedling [of maize], I don't want to leave it. I don't feel I really know the story if I don't watch the plant all the way along. So I know every plant in the field. I know them intimately, and I find it a great pleasure to know them" (Keller, 1983, p. 198). McClintock viewed the complexity of nature as being beyond full human comprehension. "Organisms can do all types of things; they do fantastic things. They do everything that we do, and they do it better, more efficiently, more marvelously. . . . Trying to make everything fit into set dogma won't work. . . . There's no such thing as a central dogma into which everything will fit." . . .

[O]nly by listening carefully can one "let the material tell you." "I feel that much of the work [in science] is done because one wants to impose an answer on it. They have the answer ready, and they [know what they] want the material to tell them. [Anything else it tells them] they don't really recognize as there, or they think it's a mistake and throw it out. . . . *If you'd only just let the material tell you*" (Keller, 1983, p. 179). . . .

Knowing Other People

. . . Influenced by examples like that of McClintock, many feminists are developing epistemologies that include the tenet that subjectivity is an important and indispensable component of the process of gaining knowledge. But successfully doing so requires offering alternative models of knowledge. Lorraine Code has offered such an alternative, the model of "knowing other people." While S-knows-that-p models of knowledge are based on what Code calls ordinary knowledge of medium-sized objects in the immediate environment—the red book, the open door—Code's model is based on the centrality of our relationships with others. "Developmentally, recognizing other people, learning what can be expected of them, is both one of the first and one of the most essential kinds of knowledge a child acquires" (Code, 1991, p. 37). Code presents this model as an *addition* to the S-knows-that-p epistemologies that perhaps work for simple objects in simple settings. She argues that the latter model is not sufficient for more complex instances in which knowledge requires constant learning, is open to interpretation at various levels, admits of degree, and is not primarily propositional. For such cases, a standard of knowledge modeled after our knowledge of other people would be more accurate.

Code, influenced by examples like that of McClintock, argues for a remapping of the epistemic terrain. A model that posits knowing other people as a paradigmatic kind of knowing challenges the desirability or even possibility of the disinterested and dislocated view from nowhere. Code's model of knowing other people is a dynamic, interactive model. It is a vision of a process of coming to know, "knowing other people in relationships requires constant learning: how to be with them, respond to them, and act toward them" (Code, 1993, p. 33). It is a model of knowledge that admits of degree, that is not fixed or complete, that is not primarily propositional, and is acquired interactively.

Code's model embraces the subjective components of the knowledge process illustrated in McClintock's method. McClintock's desire to develop an intimate relationship with the subject of her study, to take the time to listen, to get right down there, to develop a feeling for the organism, are all aspects of the knowing process accounted for by Code's model. "Rocks, cells,

and scientists are located in multiple relations to one another, all of which are open to analysis and critique. Singling out and privileging the asymmetrical observer-observed relation is but one possibility" (Code, 1991, p. 164). Code's alternative model, unlike S-knows-that-p models, embraces McClintock's metaphysical belief that nature, like other people, is far too complex to allow for complete and universal knowledge. For McClintock, our knowledge of nature will always be partial, always changing, always in process—just as is our knowledge of people. This is not a critique or belittlement of our knowledge capacities, but rather a recognition and appreciation of the extraordinary complexity and continual evolution of both nature and of people. Such recognition leads to a model of knowledge that embraces the importance of empathy and imagination as a resource for "letting the material tell you." It is a model that, while acknowledging the importance of categories and theories, does not privilege them over and above the importance of listening attentively and responsibly to the stories told to us—accounting for the differences rather than imposing a model upon the world.

Code's point and one that is shared by many feminist epistemologists is that the traditional image of the dispassionate scientist removed from her or his object of study has blinded us to the complexity of the possible relationships between subjects and objects. Code argues that McClintock gained her knowledge *because* of her engaged relationship with the object of her study. That is, McClintock's fascination with the maize is epistemically significant. She is drawn to it not just to predict the genetic patterns, but because she desires a full understanding of the organism in all its stages. When she refers to her study of maize, she does so with affection—"these were my friends."

Code posits nothing like an essential femininity that entails that all and only women will embrace an engaged style of knowledge production. She argues rather that McClintock's femaleness is one aspect of the complex conjunction of subjective factors at play in her practice of science. Code's goal and the goal of other feminists is to open epistemology and science education and practice to the importance of such subjective features and to argue that S-knows-that-p models of scientific knowledge are inadequate to the full complexity of knowing. Code's intention is to reclaim subjective components of the knowledge process, components often defined as "feminine" and suppressed from traditional accounts. The aim is not to create a "feminine" science, but "to make a space in scientific research for suppressed practices and values that, coincidentally or otherwise, are commonly associated with 'the feminine'" (Code, 1991, p. 152).

EMBODIED KNOWERS

The feminist rejection of the supposedly "generic" knower thus requires that attention be paid to the characteristics and situation of the knower as an important part of the knowledge process. As illustrated in my example of Zihlman's practice of science, the various communities of which one is a part, including one's political beliefs, can be epistemically significant to the knowledge process. As we see with McClintock, a knower's emotive capacities and her or his openness to their relevance to the knowing process, can also be epistemically significant. This is the content of Code's claim that a person's gender can be epistemically significant. In contemporary Western culture, one who is female is more likely than one who is male to be socialized in such a way as to make her more proficient in and accepting of the usefulness of emotions such as empathy and imagination. Just as a feminist is more likely to question the categorization of female activities as "natural" and male activities as "cultural," a woman in contemporary Western culture is more likely to be accepting of and skilled in the employment of emotions in the knowledge process.

But an additional aspect of the knowing subject that is epistemically significant is the fact of

and nature of their embodiment. The model of the generic knower has traditionally rejected the relevance of our bodily differences. Attention to the body calls attention to the specificities and partiality of human knowledge, as well as reminding us of the importance of acknowledging the body, and its variations, in the knowledge process. Once we admit the body into our theories of knowledge, we must also recognize its variations; we must, for example, examine the ways in which bodies are "sexed."

Vision

Traditional models of knowledge privilege vision over the other senses. The association of knowledge and vision provides a model of knowledge as disembodied. Vision, perceived as the most detached of the senses, is employed in such a way as to conceal the action of the body. The world appears to my gaze without any apparent movement or action on my part. The action of the body disappears into the background and with it as a model of knowledge, the philosopher places the world at a distance from the observer, thereby dematerializing knowledge. The perceived scene, as well as the perceiver, is to be physically unaffected by the gaze.

There have been many studies that have examined the ways in which this conception of vision has shaped traditional Western conceptions of knowledge. The construction of an image of reason based on metaphors of vision has led to the notion of a "mind's eye" and a conception of knowledge in which the world is separated from the observer who sees it and thereby gains knowledge of it, without in any way contaminating it or being affected by it.

But these disembodied images of vision are possible only by "forgetting" the fact of our embodiment. What we are capable of seeing and what we attend to are part of our location within the world. Let me begin by using a very different case study than those I've so far employed. Let us think about frogs and dogs.

There are many ways to remember the significance of the situatedness of vision and thereby inhibit the tendency to use visual metaphors to construct allegedly generic images of reason. One of these is to reflect upon the significance of the specificities of human vision. A frog's visual cortex is different from ours. Neural response is linked to small objects in rapid, erratic motion. Objects at rest elicit little neural response and large objects evoke a qualitatively different response than small ones. Although this makes sense for frogs, let us imagine, along with Katherine Hayles, that a frog is presented with Newton's law of motion:

> The first law, you recall, says that an object at rest remains so unless acted upon by a force. Encoded into the formulation is the assumption that the object stays the same; the new element is the force. This presupposition, so obvious from a human point of view, would be almost unthinkable from a frog's perspective, since for the frog moving objects are processed in an entirely different way than stationary ones. Newton's first law further states, as a corollary, that an object moving in a straight line continues to move so unless compelled to change by forces acting upon it. The proposition would certainly not follow as a corollary for the frog, for variation of motion rather than continuation counts in his perceptual scheme. Moreover, it ignores the *size* of the object, which from a frog's point of view is crucial to how information about movement is processed (Hayles, 1993, p. 28).

The point is that bodily differences in perceptual organs and neural patterns organize perception in highly specific, in this case species specific, ways. Far from being the neutral receptor or static mirroring of the visual metaphors informing traditional accounts of knowledge, observation is a dynamic process of organization in which our bodily being plays a central role.

The image of disembodied vision is similarly discounted by imagining a walk with one's dog. Haraway reminds us of the lessons that can be learned from such a walk. "I learned in part walking with my dog and wondering how the world looks without a fovea and very few retinal cells for colour vision, but with a huge neural processing and sensory area for smells . . . . [that] all eyes, including our own organic ones, are active perceptual systems, building in translations and specific *ways* of seeing, that is ways of life" (Haraway, 1991, p. 190).

Although the walk with your dog may remind you of human emphasis on color and shape over a canine attention to smell, it may also remind you, depending on your focus of attention, of the essential and intimate connection of vision with our kinaesthetic sense and our sense of touch. As you walk through a meadow you may meditate upon the way in which your two eyes integrate to produce a unified vision of your dog, and as you reach out to pet her be reminded of the ways in which vision is woven together with motility and touch. Such a walk can impress upon us the realization that the image of vision as disembodied is a circumscribed perspective, and that its emphasis has been the result of complex factors. That is, it is an example of a partial, situated knowledge.

When we consider the human specificities of vision, those mandated by our bodies as well as by the social contexts which shape our experiences of it, we are reminded that the privileging of an image of vision which views it as passive, detached, and disinterested is itself a partial and biased perspective. As any loving parent who looks into the eyes of her or his six month old child or any lover who gazes into the eyes of the person she or he loves know, vision can also be a way in which we actively connect and interact with other people. It can be a way in which we express feelings and negotiate our relationships. Such vision is active, engaged, and reciprocal. An emphasis on vision as passive, detached, and disinterested is a situated vision, one that arises out of particular social situations and values. We are reminded again that vision, as well as objectivity, is not about neutrality, but is embedded in particular and specific embodiments.

A recognition of the epistemic importance of our embodiment requires a conception of knowledge as embodied, in which the emphasis on vision as the primary source of knowledge is replaced by an appreciation of the multiplicity of senses involved in the process of knowledge and an understanding of the ways in which faculties such as empathy, intuition, and reason enter into and interact in this process. . . .

CONCLUSION

[T]his study, and others like it, serve as case studies of the very model of knowledge I am here professing. . . .

I and many other feminists came to positions like these *because* of our participation in feminist communities. This obviously was not the only epistemically significant community; we are also philosophers, historians, sociologists, and scientists. Nor does it mean that *only* feminists will hold such views. There are many theorists of science who do not participate in feminist communities who argue for versions of the above tenets. But a difference of feminist analyses is the persistent attention to gender as a variable of analysis. This is how our feminism is epistemologically significant.

REFERENCES

Code, Lorraine: 1991, *What Can She Know? Feminist Theory and the Construction of Knowledge.* Cornell University Press, Ithaca.

Code, Lorraine: 1993, 'Taking Subjectivity into Account,' in Linda Alcoff and Elizabeth Potter (eds.), *Feminist Epistemologies.* Routledge, New York, pp. 15–48.

Haraway, Donna: 1991, 'Situated Knowledges: The Science Question in Feminism and the Privilege of Partial Perspective,' in *Simians, Cyborgs, and Women: The Reinvention of Nature.* Routledge, New York.

Hayles, N. Katherine: 1993, 'Constrained Constructivism: Locating Scientific Inquiry in the Theater of Representation,' in George Levine (ed.), *Realism and Representation.* University of Wisconsin Press, Madison.

Keller, Evelyn Fox: 1983, *A Feeling for the Organism.* W. H. Freeman and Company, New York.

Nelson, Lynn Hankinson: 1990, *Who Knows: From Quine to a Feminist Empiricism.* Temple University Press, Philadelphia.

Washburn, Sherwood L. and C. S. Lancaster: 1976, 'Evolution of Hunting,' in R. B. Lee and I. DeVore (eds.), *Kalahari Hunter–Gatherers.* Harvard University Press, Cambridge.

Study Questions

1. According to Tuana, how does objectivity differ from neutrality?
2. Is a scientist's work always affected by the communities of which the scientist is a member?
3. Is gaining scientific knowledge akin to acquiring knowledge of other people?
4. Does Tuana's position on the importance of gender in the process of science also imply the importance of other factors such as a scientist's racial background, religious affiliation, or sexual orientation?

Part III

⊠

Knowledge

Meditations on First Philosophy

RENÉ DESCARTES

We now turn to a fundamental field of philosophy: The theory of knowledge, or, as philosophers often refer to it, "epistemology," from the Greek word *epistēmē*, meaning "knowledge." But what can we be certain that we know?

This question lies at the heart of one of the most influential of all philosophical works, the *Meditations on First Philosophy*, published in Latin in 1641, and authored by the Frenchman René Descartes (1596–1650), mathematician, scientist, and one of the most famous of all philosophers. The book's combination of personal narrative and rigorous argument is highly unusual.

Descartes is driven by his desire to place philosophy on an unshakable foundation. He searches for a starting point that can withstand all doubt. Because the evidence of our senses sometimes misleads us, it does not provide a secure basis for knowledge. Furthermore, we cannot be certain that we are awake and not dreaming. Nor can we be sure that we are not being systematically fooled by an evil genius who wishes to deceive us. Given such possibilities, can we be sure of any truth?

The *Meditations* is universally regarded as a philosophical classic, even by the many who do not accept all the steps in Descartes' argument. What continues to fascinate philosophers is the provocative manner in which Descartes formulated and pursued such crucial issues. To meditate along with him is as good a way as any to come to an understanding of philosophical inquiry.

What follows is the first of Descartes' six meditations. We shall return to the second meditation in the next section of the book.

FIRST MEDITATION

What Can Be Called into Doubt

Some years ago I was struck by the large number of falsehoods that I had accepted as true in my childhood, and by the highly doubtful nature of the whole edifice that I had subsequently based on them. I realized that it was necessary, once in the course of my life, to demolish everything completely and start again right from the foundations if I wanted to establish anything at all in the sciences that was stable and likely to last. But the task looked an enormous one, and I began to wait until I should reach a mature enough age to ensure that no subsequent time of life would be more suitable for tackling such inquiries. This led me to put the project off for so long that I would now be to blame if by pondering over it any further I wasted the time still left for carrying it out. So today I have expressly rid my mind of all worries and arranged for myself a clear stretch of free time. I am here quite alone, and at last I will devote myself sincerely and without reservation to the general demolition of my opinions.

But to accomplish this, it will not be necessary for me to show that all my opinions are false, which is something I could perhaps never manage. Reason now leads me to think that I should hold back my assent from opinions which are not completely certain and indubitable just as carefully as I do from those which are patently false. So, for the purpose of rejecting all my opinions, it will be enough if I find in each of them at least some reason for doubt. And to do this I will not need to run through them all individually, which would be an endless task. Once the foundations of a building are undermined, anything built on them collapses of its own accord; so I will go straight for the basic principles on which all my former beliefs rested.

Whatever I have up till now accepted as most true I have acquired either from the senses or through the senses. But from time to time I have found that the senses deceive, and it is prudent never to trust completely those who have deceived us even once.

Yet although the senses occasionally deceive us with respect to objects which are very small or in the distance, there are many other beliefs about which doubt is quite impossible, even though they are derived from the senses—for example, that I am here, sitting by the fire, wearing a winter dressing-gown, holding this piece of paper in my hands, and so on. Again, how could it be denied that these hands or this whole body are mine? Unless perhaps I were to liken myself to madmen, whose brains are so damaged by the persistent vapours of melancholia that they firmly maintain they are kings when they are paupers, or say they are dressed in purple when they are naked, or that their heads are made of earthenware, or that they are pumpkins, or made of glass. But such people are insane, and I would be thought equally mad if I took anything from them as a model for myself.

A brilliant piece of reasoning! As if I were not a man who sleeps at night, and regularly has all the same experiences while asleep as madmen do when awake—indeed sometimes even more improbable ones. How often, asleep at night, am I convinced of just such familiar events—that I am here in my dressing-gown, sitting by the fire—when in fact I am lying undressed in bed! Yet at the moment my eyes are certainly wide awake when I look at this piece of paper; I shake my head and it is not asleep; as I stretch out and feel my hand I do so deliberately, and I know what I am doing. All this would not happen with such distinctness to someone asleep. Indeed! As if I did not remember other occasions when I have been tricked by exactly similar thoughts while asleep! As I think about this more carefully, I see plainly that there are never any sure signs by means of which being awake can be distinguished from being asleep. The result is that I begin to feel dazed, and this very feeling only reinforces the notion that I may be asleep.

Suppose then that I am dreaming, and that these particulars—that my eyes are open, that I am moving my head and stretching out my hands—are not true. Perhaps, indeed, I do not even have such hands or such a body at all. Nonetheless, it must surely be admitted that the visions which come in sleep are like paintings, which must have been fashioned in the likeness of things that are real, and hence that at least these general kinds of things—eyes, head, hands, and the body as a whole—are things which are not imaginary but are real and exist. For even when painters try to create sirens and satyrs with the most extraordinary bodies, they cannot give them natures which are new in all respects; they simply jumble up the limbs of different animals. Or if perhaps they manage to think up something so new that nothing remotely similar has ever been seen before—something which is therefore completely fictitious and unreal—at least the colours used in the composition must be real. By similar reasoning, although these general kinds of things—eyes, head, hands and so on—could be imaginary, it must at least be admitted that certain other even simpler and more universal things are real. These are as it were the real colours from which we form all the images of things, whether true or false, that occur in our thought.

This class appears to include corporeal nature in general, and its extension; the shape of extended things; the quantity, or size and number of these things; the place in which they may exist, the time through which they may endure, and so on.

So a reasonable conclusion from this might be that physics, astronomy, medicine, and all other disciplines which depend on the study of composite things, are doubtful; while arithmetic, geometry, and other subjects of this kind, which deal only with the simplest and most general things, regardless of whether they really exist in nature or not, contain something certain and indubitable. For whether I am awake or asleep, two and three added together are five, and a square has no more than four sides. It seems impossible that such transparent truths should incur any suspicion of being false.

And yet firmly rooted in my mind is the long-standing opinion that there is an omnipotent God who made me the kind of creature that I am. How do I know that he has not brought it about that there is no earth, no sky, no extended thing, no shape, no size, no place, while at the same time ensuring that all these things appear to me to exist just as they do now? What is more, just as I consider that others sometimes go astray in cases where they think they have the most perfect knowledge, how do I know that God has not brought it about that I too go wrong every time I add two and three or count the sides of a square, or in some even simpler matter, if that is imaginable? But perhaps God would not have allowed me to be deceived in this way, since he is said to be supremely good. But if it were inconsistent with his goodness to have created me such that I am deceived all the time, it would seem equally foreign to his goodness to allow me to be deceived even occasionally; yet this last assertion cannot be made.

Perhaps there may be some who would prefer to deny the existence of so powerful a God rather than believe that everything else is uncertain. Let us not argue with them, but grant them that everything said about God is a fiction. According to their supposition, then, I have arrived at my present state by fate or chance or a continuous chain of events, or by some other means; yet since deception and error seem to be imperfections, the less powerful they make my original cause, the more likely it is that I am so imperfect as to be deceived all the time. I have no answer to these arguments, but am finally compelled to admit that there is not one of my former beliefs about which a doubt may not properly be raised; and this is not a flippant or ill-considered conclusion, but is based on powerful and well thought-out reasons. So in future I must withhold my assent from these former beliefs just as carefully as I would from obvious falsehoods, if I want to discover any certainty.

But it is not enough merely to have noticed this; I must make an effort to remember it. My habitual opinions keep coming back, and, despite my wishes, they capture my belief, which is as it were bound over to them as a result of long occupation and the law of custom. I shall never get out of the habit of confidently assenting to these opinions, so long as I suppose them to be what in fact they are, namely, highly probable opinions—opinions which, despite the fact that they are in a sense doubtful, as has just been shown, it is still much more reasonable to believe than to deny. In view of this, I think it will be a good plan to turn my will in completely the opposite direction and deceive myself, by pretending for a time that these former opinions are utterly false and imaginary. I shall do this until the weight of preconceived opinion is counter-balanced and the distorting influence of habit no longer prevents my judgement from perceiving things correctly. In the meantime, I know that no danger or error will result from my plan, and that I cannot possibly go too far in my distrustful attitude. This is because the task now in hand does not involve action but merely the acquisition of knowledge.

I will suppose therefore that not God, who is supremely good and the source of truth, but rather some malicious demon of the utmost power and cunning has employed all his energies in order to deceive me. I shall think that the sky, the air, the earth, colours, shapes, sounds, and all external things are merely the delusions of dreams which he has devised to ensnare my judgement. I shall consider myself as not having hands or eyes, or flesh, or blood or senses, but as falsely believing that I have all these things. I shall stubbornly and firmly persist in this meditation; and, even if it is not in my power to know any truth, I shall at least do what is in my power, that is, resolutely guard against assenting to any falsehoods, so that the deceiver, however powerful and cunning he may be, will be unable to impose on me in the slightest degree. But this is an arduous undertaking, and a kind of laziness brings me back to normal life. I am like a prisoner who is enjoying an imaginary freedom while asleep; as he begins to suspect that he is asleep, he dreads being woken up, and goes along with the pleasant illusion as long as he can. In the same way, I happily slide back into my old opinions and dread being shaken out of them, for fear that my peaceful sleep may be followed by hard labour when I wake, and that I shall have to toil not in the light, but amid the inextricable darkness of the problems I have now raised.

A Treatise Concerning the Principles of Human Knowledge

GEORGE BERKELEY

George Berkeley (1685–1753), born in Ireland, published his most important works during his twenties. At one time he lived in Rhode Island, then returned to his homeland to become bishop of Cloyne.

A few words about the history of modern philosophy will help place Berkeley's work in context. Philosophers like Descartes, who base knowledge on reason alone rather than sense experience, are known as *rationalists*. Those who base knowledge on sense experience rather than pure reason are known as *empiricists*, and the leading historical exponents of empiricism are the Englishman John Locke (1632–1704), George Berkeley, and David Hume.

Locke argues that we can be mistaken in our beliefs about the external world; they fall short of Descartes' standard of absolute certainty. Nevertheless, our understanding of physical objects is a paradigm of knowledge, thus demonstrating that Descartes was mistaken in the standard he set.

Locke claims that all our ideas can be traced to two sources: sensation (i.e., sense perception) and reflection (i.e., awareness of the operations of our mind). Our knowledge of the world has its source in sensation. For example, I know a solid, brown table is in front of me, and the basis for my knowledge is the evidence of my senses.

From *A Treatise Concerning the Principles of Human Knowledge* by George Berkeley (1710).

Locke draws a crucial distinction between an object's primary and secondary qualities. The primary qualities are those inseparable from an object, such as its solidity, size, or velocity. The secondary qualities are powers in an object to produce sensations in us, for example, color, taste, and odor. Thus the solid brown table I see in front of me is in itself solid but only perceived as brown. If I looked at it in a different light, it would still be solid but might look black or some other color.

Berkeley accepts Locke's view of secondary qualities as mind-dependent and extends Locke's position to primary qualities, arguing that they too are mind-dependent. For example, an object that appears solid to one perceiver may not appear solid to another (the basis for many magic tricks).

But if both the primary and secondary qualities are mind-dependent, what remains of the material object? Berkeley's startling answer is: nothing. Physical objects exist but only as ideas in the minds of perceivers, who are themselves immaterial spirits. Does a table go out of existence when not being perceived by us? No, for it is being perceived by the "governing Spirit" we call God. He sends us our sensations in an orderly manner, thus giving rise to a world of sensations exhibiting the laws of nature.

Berkeley, after all, was a clergyman. Therefore his epistemological and theological views are in harmony. Berkeley's idealism, his position that reality is fundamentally mental in nature, may not persuade many readers, but finding errors in his reasoning is no easy matter.

---

1. It is evident to anyone who takes a survey of the objects of human knowledge, that they are either ideas actually imprinted on the senses, or else such as are perceived by attending to the passions and operations of the mind, or lastly ideas formed by help of memory and imagination, either compounding, dividing, or barely representing those originally perceived in the aforesaid ways. By sight I have the ideas of light and colours with their several degrees and variations. By touch I perceive, for example, hard and soft, heat and cold, motion and resistance, and of all these more and less either as to quantity or degree. Smelling furnishes me with odours; the palate with tastes, and hearing conveys sounds to the mind in all their variety of tone and composition. And as several of these are observed to accompany each other, they come to be marked by one name, and so to be reputed as one thing. Thus, for example, a certain colour, taste, smell, figure and consistence having been observed to go together, are accounted one distinct thing, signified by the name *apple*. Other collections of ideas constitute a stone, a tree, a book, and the like sensible things; which, as they are pleasing or disagreeable, excite the passions of love, hatred, joy, grief, and so forth.

2. But besides all that endless variety of ideas or objects of knowledge, there is likewise something which knows or perceives them, and exercises divers operations, as willing, imagining, remembering about them. This perceiving, active being is what I call *mind, spirit, soul* or *myself*. By which words I do not denote any one of my ideas, but a thing entirely distinct from them, wherein they exist, or, which is the same thing, whereby they are perceived; for the existence of an idea consists in being perceived.

3. That neither our thoughts, nor passions, nor ideas formed by the imagination, exist without the mind, is what everybody will allow. And it seems no less evident that the various sensations or ideas imprinted on the sense, however blended or combined together (that is, whatever

objects they compose) cannot exist otherwise than in a mind perceiving them. I think an intuitive knowledge may be obtained of this, by anyone that shall attend to what is meant by the term *exist* when applied to sensible things. The table I write on, I say, exists, that is, I see and feel it; and if I were out of my study I should say it existed, meaning thereby that if I was in my study I might perceive it, or that some other spirit actually does perceive it. There was an odour, that is, it was smelled; there was a sound, that is to say, it was heard; a colour or figure, and it was perceived by sight or touch. This is all that I can understand by these and the like expressions. For as to what is said of the absolute existence of unthinking things without any relation to their being perceived, that seems perfectly unintelligible. Their *esse* is *percipi,* nor is it possible they should have any existence, out of the minds or thinking things which perceive them.

4. It is indeed an opinion strangely prevailing amongst men, that houses, mountains, rivers, and in a word all sensible objects have an existence natural or real, distinct from their being perceived by the understanding. But with how great an assurance and acquiescence soever this principle may be entertained in the world; yet whoever shall find in his heart to call it in question, may, if I mistake not, perceive it to involve a manifest contradiction. For what are the forementioned objects but the things we perceive by sense, and what do we perceive besides our own ideas or sensations; and is it not plainly repugnant that any one of these or any combination of them should exist unperceived?

5. If we thoroughly examine this tenet, it will, perhaps, be found at bottom to depend on the doctrine of *abstract ideas.* For can there be a nicer strain of abstraction than to distinguish the existence of sensible objects from their being perceived, so as to conceive them existing unperceived? Light and colours, heat and cold, extension and figures, in a word the things we see and feel, what are they but so many sensations, notions, ideas or impressions on the sense; and is it possible to separate, even in thought, any of

these from perception? For my part I might as easily divide a thing from itself. I may indeed divide in my thoughts or conceive apart from each other those things which, perhaps, I never perceived by sense so divided. Thus I imagine the trunk of a human body without, the limbs, or conceive the smell of a rose without thinking on the rose itself. So far I will not deny I can abstract, if that may properly be called *abstraction,* which extends only to the conceiving separately such objects, as it is possible may really exist or be actually perceived asunder. But my conceiving or imagining power does not extend beyond the possibility of real existence or perception. Hence as it is impossible for me to see or feel anything without an actual sensation of that thing, so is it impossible for me to conceive in my thoughts any sensible thing or object distinct from the sensation or perception of it.

6. Some truths there are so near and obvious to the mind, that a man need only open his eyes to see them. Such I take this important one to be, to wit, that all the choir of heaven and furniture of the earth, in a word all those bodies which compose the mighty frame of the world, have not any subsistence, without a mind, that their being is to be perceived or known; that consequently so long as they are not actually perceived by me, or do not exist in my mind or that of any other created spirit, they must either have no existence at all, or else subsist in the mind of some eternal spirit: it being perfectly unintelligible and involving all the absurdity of abstraction, to attribute to any single part of them an existence independent of a spirit. To be convinced of which, the reader need only reflect and try to separate in his own thoughts the being of a sensible thing from its being perceived.

7. From what has been said, it follows, there is not any other substance than *spirit,* or that which perceives. But for the fuller proof of this point, let it be considered, the sensible qualities are colour, figure, motion, smell, taste, and such like, that is, the ideas perceived by sense. Now for an idea to exist in an unperceiving thing, is a manifest contradiction; for to have an idea is all

one as to perceive; that therefore wherein colour, figure, and the like qualities exist, must perceive them; hence it is clear there can be no unthinking substance or *substratum* of those ideas.

8. But say you, though the ideas themselves do not exist without the mind, yet there may be things like them whereof they are copies or resemblances, which things exist without the mind, in an unthinking substance. I answer, an idea can be like nothing but an idea; a colour or figure can be like nothing but another colour or figure. If we look but ever so little into our thoughts, we shall find it impossible for us to conceive a likeness except only between our ideas. Again, I ask whether these supposed originals or external things, of which our ideas are the pictures or representations, be themselves perceivable or no? If they are, then they are ideas, and we have gained our point; but if you say they are not, I appeal to anyone whether it be sense, to assert a colour is like something which is invisible, hard or soft, like something which is intangible; and so of the rest.

9. Some there are who make a distinction betwixt *primary* and *secondary* qualities: by the former, they mean extension, figure, motion, rest, solidity or impenetrability and number: by the latter they denote all other sensible qualities, as colours, sounds, tastes, and so forth. The ideas we have of these they acknowledge not to be the resemblances of anything existing without the mind or unperceived; but they will have our ideas of the primary qualities to be patterns or images of things which exist without the mind, in an unthinking substance which they call *matter*. By matter therefore we are to understand an inert, senseless substance, in which extension, figure, and motion, do actually subsist. But it is evident from what we have already shewn, that extension, figure and motion are only ideas existing in the mind, and that an idea can be like nothing but another idea, and that consequently neither they nor their archetypes can exist in an unperceiving substance. Hence it is plain, that the very notion of what is called *matter* or *corporeal substance,* involves a contradiction in it.

10. They who assert that figure, motion, and the rest of the primary or original qualities do exist without the mind, in unthinking substances, do at the same time acknowledge that colours, sounds, heat, cold, and such like secondary qualities, do not, which they tell us are sensations existing in the mind alone, that depend on and are occasioned by the different size, texture and motion of the minute particles of matter. This they take for an undoubted truth, which they can demonstrate beyond all exception. Now if it be certain, that those original qualities are inseparably united with the other sensible qualities, and not, even in thought, capable of being abstracted from them, it plainly follows that they exist only in the mind. But I desire anyone to reflect and try, whether he can by any abstraction of thought, conceive the extension and motion of a body, without all other sensible qualities. For my own part, I see evidently that it is not in my power to frame an idea of a body extended and moved, but I must withal give it some colour or other sensible quality which is acknowledged to exist only in the mind. In short, extension, figure, and motion, abstracted from all other qualities, are inconceivable. Where therefore the other sensible qualities are, there must these be also, to wit, in the mind and nowhere else.

14. I shall farther add, that after the same manner, as modern philosophers prove certain sensible qualities to have no existence in matter, or without the mind, the same thing may be likewise proved of all other sensible qualities whatsoever. Thus, for instance, it is said that heat and cold are affections only of the mind, and not at all patterns of real beings, existing in the corporeal substances which excite them, for that the same body which appears cold to one hand, seems warm to another. Now why may we not as well argue that figure and extension are not patterns or resemblances of qualities existing in matter, because to the same eye at different stations, or eyes of a different texture at the same station, they appear various, and cannot therefore be the images of anything settled and

determinate without the mind? Again, it is proved that sweetness is not really in the sapid thing because the thing remaining unaltered the sweetness is changed into bitter, as in case of a fever or otherwise vitiated palate. Is it not as reasonable to say, that motion is not without the mind, since if the succession of ideas in the mind become swifter, the motion, it is acknowledged, shall appear slower without any alteration in any external object.

15. In short, let anyone consider those arguments, which are thought manifestly to prove that colours and tastes exist only in the mind, and he shall find they may with equal force, be brought to prove the same thing of extension, figure, and motion? Though it must be confessed this method of arguing doth not so much prove that there is no extension or colour in an outward object, as that we do not know by sense which is the true extension or colour of the object. But the arguments foregoing plainly shew it to be impossible that any colour or extension at all, or other sensible quality whatsoever, should exist in an unthinking subject without the mind, or in truth, that there should be any such thing as an outward object.

16. But let us examine a little the received opinion. It is said extension is a mode or accident of matter, and that matter is the *substratum* that supports it. Now I desire that you would explain what is meant by matter's *supporting* extension: say you, I have no idea of matter, and therefore cannot explain it. I answer, though you have no positive, yet if you have any meaning at all, you must at least have a relative idea of matter; though you know not what it is, yet you must be supposed to know what relation it bears to accidents, and what is meant by its supporting them. It is evident *support* cannot here be taken in its usual or literal sense, as when we say that pillars support a building: in what sense therefore must it be taken?

17. If we inquire into what the most accurate philosophers declare themselves to mean by *material substance;* we shall find them acknowledge, they have no other meaning annexed to those sounds, but the idea of being in general, together with the relative notion of its supporting accidents. The general idea of being appeareth to me the most abstract and incomprehensible of all other; and as for its supporting accidents, this, as we have just now observed, cannot be understood in the common sense of those words; it must therefore be taken in some other sense, but what that is they do not explain. So that when I consider the two parts or branches which make the signification of the words *material substance,* I am convinced there is no distinct meaning annexed to them. But why should we trouble ourselves any farther, in discussing this material *substratum* or support of figure and motion, and other sensible qualities? Does it not suppose they have an existence without the mind? And is not this a direct repugnancy, and altogether inconceivable?

18. But though it were possible that solid, figured, moveable substances may exist without the mind, corresponding to the ideas we have of bodies, yet how is it possible for us to know this? Either we must know it by sense, or by reason. As for our senses, by them we have the knowledge only of our sensations, ideas, or those things that are immediately perceived by sense, call them what you will: but they do not inform us that things exist without the mind, or unperceived, like to those which are perceived. This the materials themselves acknowledge. It remains therefore that if we have any knowledge at all of external things, it must be by reason, inferring their existence from what is immediately perceived by sense. But what reason can induce us to believe the existence of bodies without the mind, from what we perceive, since the very patrons of matter themselves do not pretend, there is any necessary connexion betwixt them and our ideas? I say it is granted on all hands (and what happens in dreams, phrensies, and the like, puts it beyond dispute) that it is possible we might be affected with all the ideas we have now, though no bodies existed without, resembling them. Hence it is evident the supposition of external bodies is not

necessary for the producing our ideas: since it is granted they are produced sometimes, and might possibly be produced always in the same order we see them in at present, without their concurrence.

19. But though we might possibly have all our sensations without them, yet perhaps it may be thought easier to conceive and explain the manner of their production, by supposing external bodies in their likeness rather than otherwise; and so it might be at least probable there are such things as bodies that excite their ideas in our minds. But neither can this be said; for though we give the materialists their external bodies, they by their own confession are never the nearer knowing how our ideas are produced; since they own themselves unable to comprehend in what manner body can act upon spirit, or how it is possible it should imprint any idea in the mind. Hence it is evident the production of ideas or sensations in our minds, can be no reason why we should suppose matter or corporeal substances, since that is acknowledged to remain equally inexplicable with, or without this supposition. If therefore it were possible for bodies to exist without the mind, yet to hold they do so, must needs be a very precarious opinion; since it is to suppose, without any reason at all, that God has created innumerable beings that are entirely useless, and serve to no manner of purpose.

22. I am afraid I have given cause to think me needlessly prolix in handling this subject. For to what purpose is it to dilate on that which may be demonstrated with the utmost evidence in a line or two, to anyone that is capable of the least reflexion? It is but looking into your own thoughts, and so trying whether you can conceive it possible for a sound, or figure, or motion, or colour, to exist without the mind, or unperceived. This easy trial may make you see, that what you contend for, is a downright contradiction. Insomuch that I am content to put the whole upon this issue; if you can but conceive it possible for one extended moveable substance, or in general, for any one idea or anything like an idea, to exist otherwise than in a mind

perceiving it, I shall readily give up the cause: and as for all that *compages* of external bodies which you contend for, I shall grant you its existence, though you cannot either give me any reason why you believe it exists, or assign any use to it when it is supposed to exist. I say, the bare possibility of your opinion's being true, shall pass for an argument that it is so.

23. But you say, surely there is nothing easier than to imagine trees, for instance, in a park, or books existing in a closet, and nobody by to perceive them. I answer, you may so, there is no difficulty in it: but what is all this, I beseech you, more then framing in your mind certain ideas which you call *books* and *trees,* and at the same time omitting to frame the idea of anyone that may perceive them? But do not you yourself perceive or think of them all the while? This therefore is nothing to the purpose: it only shows you have the power of imagining or forming ideas in your mind; but it doth not shew that you can conceive it possible, the objects of your thought may exist without the mind: to make out this, it is necessary that you conceive them existing unconceived or unthought of, which is a manifest repugnancy. When we do our utmost to conceive the existence of external bodies, we are all the while only contemplating our own ideas. But the mind taking no notice of itself, is deluded to think it can and doth conceive bodies existing unthought of or without the mind; though at the same time they are apprehended by or exist in itself. A little attention will discover to anyone the truth and evidence of what is here said, and make it unnecessary to insist on any other proofs against the existence of material substance.

25. All our ideas, sensations, or the thing which we perceive, by whatsoever names they may be distinguished, are visibly inactive, there is nothing of power or agency included in them. So that one idea or object of thought cannot produce, or make any alteration in another. To be satisfied of the truth of this, there is nothing else requisite but a bare observation of our ideas. For since they and every part of them exist only in the mind, it follows that there is nothing in

them but what is perceived. But whoever shall attend to his ideas, whether of sense or reflexion, will not perceive in them any power or activity; there is therefore no such thing contained in them. A little attention will discover to us that the very being of an idea implies passiveness and inertness in it, insomuch that it is impossible for an idea to do anything, or, strictly speaking, to be the cause of anything: neither can it be the resemblance or pattern of any active being, as is evident from *Sect*. 8. Whence it plainly follows that extension, figure and motion, cannot be the cause of our sensations. To say therefore, that these are the effects of powers resulting from the configuration, number, motion, and size of corpuscles, must certainly be false.

26. We perceive a continual succession of ideas, some are anew excited, others are changed or totally disappear. There is therefore some cause of these ideas whereon they depend, and which produces and changes them. That this cause cannot be any quality or idea or combination of ideas, is clear from the preceding section. It must therefore be a substance; but it has been shewn that there is no corporeal or material substance; it remains therefore that the cause of ideas is an incorporeal active substance or spirit.

27. A spirit is one simple, undivided, active being: as it perceives ideas, it is called the *understanding*, and as it produces or otherwise operates about them, it is called the *will*. Hence there can be no idea formed of a soul or spirit: for all ideas whatever, being passive and inert, *vide Sect*. 25, they cannot represent unto us, by way of image or likeness, that which acts. A little attention will make it plain to anyone, that to have an idea which shall be like that active principle of motion and change of ideas, is absolutely impossible. Such is the nature of *spirit* or that which acts, that it cannot be of itself perceived, but only by the effects which it produceth. If any man shall doubt of the truth of what is here delivered, let him but reflect and try if he can frame the idea of any power or active being; and whether he hath ideas of two principal powers, marked by the names *will* and *understanding*, distinct from each other

as well as from a third idea of substance or being in general, with a relative notion of its supporting or being the subject of the aforesaid powers, which is signified by the name *soul* or *spirit*. This is what some hold; but so far as I can see, the words *will, soul, spirit*, do not stand for different ideas, or in truth, for any idea at all, but for something which is very different from ideas, and which being an agent cannot be like unto, or represented by, any idea whatsoever. Though it must be owned at the same time, that we have some notion of soul, spirit, and the operations of the mind, such as willing, loving, hating, in as much as we know or understand the meaning of those words.

28. I find I can excite ideas in my mind at pleasure, and vary and shift the scene as oft as I think fit. It is no more than willing, and straightway this or that idea arises in my fancy: and by the same power it is obliterated, and makes way for another. This making and unmaking of ideas doth very properly denominate the mind active. Thus much is certain, and grounded on experience: but when we talk of unthinking agents, or of exciting ideas exclusive of volition, we only amuse ourselves with words.

29. But whatever power I may have over my own thoughts, I find the ideas actually perceived by sense have not a like dependence on my will. When in broad day-light I open my eyes, it is not in my power to choose whether I shall see or no, or to determine what particular objects shall present themselves to my view; and so likewise as to the hearing and other senses, the ideas imprinted on them are not creatures of my will. There is therefore some other will or spirit that produces them.

30. The ideas of sense are more strong, lively, and distinct than those of the imagination; they have likewise a steadiness, order, and coherence, and are not excited at random, as those which are the effects of human wills often are, but in a regular train or series, the admirable connexion whereof sufficiently testifies the wisdom and benevolence of its Author. Now the set rules or established methods, wherein the mind we depend

on excites in us the ideas of sense, are called the *Laws of Nature:* and these we learn by experience, which teaches us that such and such ideas are attended with such and such other ideas, in the ordinary course of things.

31. This gives us a sort of foresight, which enables us to regulate our actions for the benefit of the life. And without this we should be eternally at a loss: we could not know how to act anything that might procure us the least pleasure, or remove the least pain of sense. That food nourishes, sleep refreshes, and fire warms us; that to sow in the seed-time is the way to reap in the harvest, and, in general, that to obtain such or such ends, such or such means are conducive, all this we know, not by discovering any necessary connexion between our ideas, but only by the observation of the settled Laws of Nature, without which we should be all in uncertainty and confusion, and a grown man no more know how to manage himself in the affairs of life, than an infant just born.

32. And yet this consistent uniform working, which so evidently displays the goodness and wisdom of that governing spirit whose will constitutes the Laws of Nature, is so far from leading our thoughts to him, that it rather sends them a wandering after second causes. For when we perceive certain ideas of sense constantly followed by other ideas, and we know this is not of our doing, we forthwith attribute power and agency to the ideas themselves, and make one the cause of another, than which nothing can be more absurd and unintelligible. Thus, for example, having observed that when we perceive by sight a certain round luminous figure, we at the same time perceive by touch the idea of sensation called *heat,* we do from thence conclude the sun to be the cause of heat. And in like manner perceiving the motion and collision of bodies to be attended with sound, we are inclined to think the latter an effect of the former.

33. The ideas imprinted on the senses by the Author of Nature are called *real things:* and those excited in the imagination being less regular, vivid and constant, are more properly termed *ideas,* or *images of things,* which they copy and represent. But then our sensations, be they never so vivid and distinct, are nevertheless *ideas,* that is, they exist in the mind, or are perceived by it, as truly as the ideas of its own framing. The ideas of sense are allowed to have more reality in them, that is, to be more strong, orderly, and coherent than the creatures of the mind; but this is no argument that they exist without the mind. They are also less dependent on the spirit, or thinking substance which perceives them, in that they are excited by the will of another and more powerful spirit: yet still they are *ideas,* and certainly no *idea,* whether faint or strong, can exist otherwise than in a mind perceiving it.

Study Questions

1. Do you believe that Berkeley succeeds in his attack on Locke's distinction between primary and secondary qualities?
2. How does Berkeley reply to the claim that nothing is easier to imagine than trees in a park with nobody there to perceive them?
3. How does Berkeley distinguish real things and images of things?
4. How do you distinguish real things and images of things?

An Enquiry Concerning Human Understanding

DAVID HUME

The Scotsman David Hume (1711–1776), essayist, historian, and philosopher, developed one of the most influential of all philosophical systems. He presented it first in his monumental *Treatise of Human Nature,* published when he was twenty-eight years old. Later he reworked the material to make it more accessible, and the selection that follows is from *An Enquiry Concerning Human Understanding,* which appeared in 1748.

The fundamental principle of Hume's philosophy is that our knowledge of the world depends entirely on the evidence provided by our senses. While this premise may appear uncontroversial, as developed by Hume it has startling consequences.

To use an example he offers, suppose you see one billiard ball hit a second, and then the second ball moves. You would say the first made the second move. Hume points out, however, that all you see is one event followed by another; you do not actually see any connection between them. You assume the connection, but the force of Hume's argument is that your assumption violates the principle that our knowledge rests only on the evidence of our senses, for you did not sense any necessary connection between the two events, but presumed it anyway.

Hume extends this reasoning and argues that, so far as we know, the world consists of entirely separate events, some regularly following others but all unconnected. He concludes that our beliefs about the necessity of causation are instinctive, not rational.

OF THE ORIGIN OF IDEAS

Everyone will readily allow that there is a considerable difference between the perceptions of the mind, when a man feels the pain of excessive heat, or the pleasure of moderate warmth, and when he afterwards recalls to his memory this sensation, or anticipates it by his imagination. These faculties may mimic or copy the perceptions of the senses; but they never can entirely reach the force and vivacity of the original sentiment. The utmost we say of them, even when they operate with greatest vigor, is that they represent their object in so lively a manner, that we could *almost* say we feel or see it: But, except the mind be disordered by disease or madness, they never can arrive at such a pitch of vivacity, as to render these perceptions altogether undistinguishable. All the colors of poetry, however splendid, can never paint natural objects in such a manner as to make the description be taken for a real landscape. The most lively thought is still inferior to the dullest sensation.

We may observe a like distinction to run through all the other perceptions of the mind. A man in a fit of anger is actuated in a very different

---

From *An Enquiry Concerning Human Understanding* by David Hume (1748).

manner from one who only thinks of that emotion. If you tell me, that any person is in love, I easily understand your meaning, and form a just conception of his situation; but never can mistake that conception for the real disorders and agitations of the passion. When we reflect on our past sentiments and affections, our thought is a faithful mirror, and copies its objects truly; but the colors which it employs are faint and dull, in comparison of those in which our original perceptions were clothed. It requires no nice discernment or metaphysical head to mark the distinction between them.

Here therefore we may divide all the perceptions of the mind into two classes or species, which are distinguished by their different degrees of force and vivacity. The less forcible and lively are commonly denominated *thoughts* or *ideas.* The other species want a name in our language, and in most others; I suppose, because it was not requisite for any, but philosophical purposes, to rank them under a general term or appellation. Let us, therefore, use a little freedom, and call them *impressions;* employing that word in a sense somewhat different from the usual. By the term *impression,* then, I mean all our more lively perceptions, when we hear, or see, or feel, or love, or hate, or desire, or will. And impressions are distinguished from ideas, which are the less lively perceptions, of which we are conscious, when we reflect on any of those sensations or movements above mentioned.

Nothing, at first view, may seem more unbounded than the thought of man, which not only escapes all human power and authority, but is not even restrained within the limits of nature and reality. To form monsters, and join incongruous shapes and appearances, costs the imagination no more trouble than to conceive the most natural and familiar objects. And while the body is confined to one planet, along which it creeps with pain and difficulty; the thought can in an instant transport us into the most distant regions of the universe; or even beyond the universe, into the unbounded chaos, where nature is supposed to lie in total confusion.

What never was seen, or heard of, may yet be conceived; nor is anything beyond the power of thought, except what implies an absolute contradiction.

But though our thought seems to possess this unbounded liberty, we shall find, upon a nearer examination, that it is really confined within very narrow limits, and that all this creative power of the mind amounts to no more than the faculty of compounding, transposing, augmenting, or diminishing the materials afforded us by the senses and experience. When we think of a golden mountain, we only join two consistent ideas, *gold,* and *mountain,* with which we were formerly acquainted. A virtuous horse we can conceive; because, from our own feeling, we can conceive virtue; and this we may unite to the figure and shape of a horse, which is an animal familiar to us. In short, all the materials of thinking are derived either from our outward or inward sentiment: the mixture and composition of these belongs alone to the mind and will. Or, to express myself in philosophical language, all our ideas or more feeble perceptions are copies of our impressions or more lively ones.

To prove this, the two following arguments will, I hope, be sufficient. First, when we analyze our thoughts or ideas, however compounded or sublime, we always find that they resolve themselves into such simple ideas as were copied from a precedent feeling or sentiment. Even those ideas, which, at first view, seem the most wide of this origin, are found, upon a nearer scrutiny, to be derived from it. The idea of God, as meaning an infinitely intelligent, wise, and good Being, arises from reflecting on the operations of our own mind, and augmenting, without limit, those qualities of goodness and wisdom. We may prosecute this inquiry to what length we please; where we shall always find, that every idea which we examine is copied from a similar impression. Those who would assert that this position is not universally true nor without exception, have only one, and that an easy method of refuting it; by producing that idea, which, in their opinion, is not derived from this source. It will then be incumbent on us, if we would maintain our doctrine, to produce the impression, or lively perception, which corresponds to it.

Secondly. If it happen, from a defect of the organ, that a man is not susceptible of any species of sensation, we always find that he is as little susceptible of the correspondent ideas. A blind man can form no notion of colors; a deaf man of sounds. Restore either of them that sense in which he is deficient; by opening this new inlet for his sensations, you also open an inlet for the ideas; and he finds no difficulty in conceiving these objects. . . . When we entertain, therefore, any suspicion that a philosophical term is employed without any meaning or idea (as is but too frequent), we need but inquire, *from what impression is that supposed idea derived?* And if it be impossible to assign any, this will serve to confirm our suspicion. By bringing ideas into so clear a light we may reasonably hope to remove all dispute, which may arise, concerning their nature and reality. . . .

SCEPTICAL DOUBTS CONCERNING THE OPERATIONS OF THE UNDERSTANDING

Part I

All the objects of human reason or inquiry may naturally be divided into two kinds, to wit, *relations of ideas,* and *matters of fact.* Of the first kind are the sciences of geometry, algebra, and arithmetic; and in short, every affirmation which is either intuitively or demonstratively certain. *That the square of the hypotenuse is equal to the squares of the two sides,* is a proposition which expresses a relation between these figures. *That three times five is equal to the half of thirty,* expresses a relation between these numbers. Propositions of this kind are discoverable by the mere operation of thought, without dependence on what is anywhere existent in the universe.

Though there never was a circle or triangle in nature, the truths demonstrated by Euclid would for ever retain their certainty and evidence.

Matters of fact, which are the second objects of human reason, are not ascertained in the same manner; nor is our evidence of their truth, however great, of a like nature with the foregoing. The contrary of every matter of fact is still possible; because it can never imply a contradiction, and is conceived by the mind with the same facility and distinctness, as if ever so conformable to reality. *That the sun will not rise tomorrow* is no less intelligible a proposition, and implies no more contradiction than the affirmation, *that it will rise.* We should in vain, therefore, attempt to demonstrate its falsehood. Were it demonstratively false, it would imply a contradiction, and could never be distinctly conceived by the mind.

It may, therefore, be a subject worthy of curiosity, to inquire what is the nature of that evidence which assures us of any real existence and matter of fact, beyond the present testimony of our senses, or the records of our memory. This part of philosophy, it is observable, has been little cultivated, either by the ancients or moderns; and therefore our doubts and errors, in the prosecution of so important an inquiry, may be the more excusable; while we march through such difficult paths without any guide or direction. They may even prove useful, by exciting curiosity, and destroying that implicit faith and security, which is the bane of all reasoning and free inquiry. The discovery of defects in the common philosophy, if any such there be, will not, I presume, be a discouragement, but rather an incitement, as is usual, to attempt something more full and satisfactory than has yet been proposed to the public.

All reasonings concerning matter of fact seem to be founded on the relation of *cause and effect.* By means of that relation alone we can go beyond the evidence of our memory and senses. If you were to ask a man, why he believes any matter of fact, which is absent; for instance, that his friend is in the country, or in France;

he would give you a reason; and this reason would be some other fact; as a letter received from him, or the knowledge of his former resolutions and promises. A man finding a watch or any other machine in a desert island, would conclude that there had once been men in that island. All our reasonings concerning fact are of the same nature. And here it is constantly supposed that there is a connection between the present fact and that which is inferred from it. Were there nothing to bind them together, the inference would be entirely precarious. The hearing of an articulate voice and rational discourse in the dark assures us of the presence of some person: Why? because these are the effects of the human make and fabric, and closely connected with it. If we anatomize all the other reasonings of this nature, we shall find that they are founded on the relation of cause and effect, and that this relation is either near or remote, direct or collateral. Heat and light are collateral effects of fire, and the one effect may justly be inferred from the other.

If we would satisfy ourselves, therefore, concerning the nature of that evidence, which assures us of matters of fact, we must inquire how we arrive at the knowledge of cause and effect.

I shall venture to affirm, as a general proposition, which admits of no exception, that the knowledge of this relation is not, in any instance, attained by reasonings a priori; but arises entirely from experience, when we find that any particular objects are constantly conjoined with each other. Let an object be presented to a man of ever so strong natural reason and abilities; if that object be entirely new to him, he will not be able, by the most accurate examination of its sensible qualities, to discover any of its causes or effects. Adam, though his rational faculties be supposed, at the very first, entirely perfect, could not have inferred from the fluidity and transparency of water that it would suffocate him, or from the light and warmth of fire that it would consume him. No object ever discovers, by the qualities which appear to the senses, either the causes which produced it, or the effects which will arise from it; nor can our reason, unassisted by experience, ever draw any inference concerning real existence and matter of fact.

This proposition, *that causes and effects are discoverable, not by reason but by experience,* will readily be admitted with regard to such objects, as we remember to have once been altogether unknown to us; since we must be conscious of the utter inability, which we then lay under, of foretelling what would arise from them. Present two smooth pieces of marble to a man who has no tincture of natural philosophy; he will never discover that they will adhere together in such a manner as to require great force to separate them in a direct line, while they make so small a resistance to a lateral pressure. Such events, as bear little analogy to the common course of nature, are also readily confessed to be known only by experience; nor does any man imagine that the explosion of gunpowder, or the attraction of a loadstone, could ever be discovered by arguments a priori. In like manner, when an effect is supposed to depend upon an intricate machinery or secret structure of parts, we make no difficulty in attributing all our knowledge of it to experience. Who will assert that he can give the ultimate reason, why milk or bread is proper nourishment for a man, not for a lion or a tiger?

But the same truth may not appear, at first sight, to have the same evidence with regard to events, which have become familiar to us from our first appearance in the world, which bear a close analogy to the whole course of nature, and which are supposed to depend on the simple qualities of objects, without any secret structure of parts. We are apt to imagine that we could discover these effects by the mere operation of our reason, without experience. We fancy, that were we brought on a sudden into this world, we could at first have inferred that one billiard ball would communicate motion to another upon impulse; and that we needed not to have waited for the event, in order to pronounce with certainty concerning it. Such is the influence of custom, that, where it is strongest, it not only covers our natural ignorance, but even conceals itself, and seems not to take place, merely because it is found in the highest degree.

But to convince us that all the laws of nature, and all the operations of bodies without exception, are known only by experience, the following reflections may, perhaps, suffice. Were any object presented to us, and were we required to pronounce concerning the effect, which will result from it, without consulting past observation; after what manner, I beseech you, must the mind proceed in this operation? It must invent or imagine some event, which it ascribes to the object as its effect; and it is plain that this invention must be entirely arbitrary. The mind can never possibly find the effect in the supposed cause, by the most accurate scrutiny and examination. For the effect is totally different from the cause, and consequently can never be discovered in it. Motion in the second billiard ball is a quite distinct event from motion in the first: nor is there anything in the one to suggest the smallest hint of the other. A stone or piece of metal raised into the air, and left without any support, immediately falls: but to consider the matter a priori, is there anything we discover in this situation which can beget the idea of a downward, rather than an upward, or any other motion, in the stone or metal?

And as the first imagination or invention of a particular effect, in all natural operations, is arbitrary, where we consult not experience; so must we also esteem the supposed tie or connection between the cause and effect, which binds them together, and renders it impossible that any other effect could result from the operation of that cause. When I see, for instance, a billiard ball moving in a straight line towards another; even suppose motion in the second ball should by accident be suggested to me, as the result of their contact or impulse; may I not conceive, that a hundred different events might as well follow from that cause? May not both these balls remain at absolute rest? May not the first ball return in a straight line, or leap off from the second in any line or direction? All these suppositions are consistent and conceivable. Why then should we give the preference to one, which is no more consistent or conceivable than the rest? All our reasonings a priori, will never be able to show us any foundation for this preference.

In a word, then, every effect is a distinct event from its cause. It could not, therefore, be discovered in the cause, and the first invention or conception of it, a priori, must be entirely arbitrary. And even after it is suggested, the conjunction of it with the cause must appear equally arbitrary; since there are always many other effects, which, to reason, must seem fully as consistent and natural. In vain, therefore, should we pretend to determine any single event, or infer any cause or effect, without the assistance of observation and experience. . . .

Part II

But we have not yet attained any tolerable satisfaction with regard to the question first proposed. Each solution still gives rise to a new question as difficult as the foregoing, and leads us on to farther inquiries. When it is asked, *What is the nature of all our reasonings concerning matter of fact?* the proper answer seems to be, that they are founded on the relation of cause and effect. When again it is asked, *What is the foundation of all our reasonings and conclusions concerning that relation?* it may be replied in one word, *experience.* But if we still carry on our sifting humor, and ask, *What is the foundation of all conclusions from experience?* this implies a new question, which may be of more difficult solution and explication. Philosophers, that give themselves airs of superior wisdom and sufficiency, have a hard task when they encounter persons of inquisitive dispositions, who push them from every corner to which they retreat, and who are sure at last to bring them to some dangerous dilemma. The best expedient to prevent this confusion, is to be modest in our pretensions; and even to discover the difficulty ourselves before it is objected to us. By this means, we may make a kind of merit of our very ignorance.

I shall content myself, in this section, with an easy task, and shall pretend only to give a negative answer to the question here proposed. I say then, that, even after we have experience of the operations of cause and effect, our conclusions from that experience are *not* founded on reasoning, or any process of the understanding. This answer we must endeavor both to explain and to defend.

It must certainly be allowed, that nature has kept us at a great distance from all her secrets, and has afforded us only the knowledge of a few superficial qualities of objects; while she conceals from us those powers and principles on which the influence of those objects entirely depends. Our senses inform us of the color, weight, and consistence of bread; but neither sense nor reason can ever inform us of those qualities which fit it for the nourishment and support of a human body. Sight or feeling conveys an idea of the actual motion of bodies; but as to that wonderful force or power, which would carry on a moving body forever in a continued change of place, and which bodies never lose but by communicating it to others; of this we cannot form the most distant conception. But notwithstanding this ignorance of natural powers and principles, we always presume, when we see like sensible qualities, that they have like secret powers, and expect that effects, similar to those which we have experienced, will follow from them. If a body of like color and consistence with that bread, which we have formerly eat, be presented to us, we make no scruple of repeating the experiment, and foresee, with certainty, like nourishment and support. Now this is a process of the mind or thought, of which I would willingly know the foundation. It is allowed on all hands that there is no known connection between the sensible qualities and the secret powers; and consequently, that the mind is not led to form such a conclusion concerning their constant and regular conjunction, by anything which it knows of their nature. As to past *experience*, it can be allowed to give *direct* and *certain* information of those precise objects only, and

that precise period of time, which fell under its cognizance: but why this experience should be extended to future times, and to other objects, which, for aught we know, may be only in appearance similar; this is the main question on which I would insist. The bread, which I formerly eat, nourished me; that is, a body of such sensible qualities was, at that time, endued with such secret powers: but does it follow, that other bread must also nourish me at another time, and that like sensible qualities must always be attended with like secret powers? The consequence seems no wise necessary. At least, it must be acknowledged that there is here a consequence drawn by the mind; that there is a certain step taken; a process of thought, and an inference, which wants to be explained. These two propositions are far from being the same, *I have found that such an object has always been attended with such an effect,* and *I foresee, that other objects, which are, in appearance, similar, will be attended with similar effects.* I shall allow, if you please, that the one proposition may justly be inferred from the other; I know, in fact, that it always is inferred. But if you insist that the inference is made by a chain of reasoning, I desire you to produce that reasoning. . . .

To say it is experimental is begging the question. For all inferences from experience suppose, as their foundation, that the future will resemble the past, and that similar powers will be conjoined with similar sensible qualities. If there be any suspicion that the course of nature may change, and that the past may be no rule for the future, all experience becomes useless, and can give rise to no inference or conclusion. It is impossible, therefore, that any arguments from experience can prove this resemblance of the past to the future; since all these arguments are founded on the supposition of that resemblance. Let the course of things be allowed hitherto ever so regular; that alone, without some new argument or inference, proves not that, for the future, it will continue so. In vain do you pretend to have learned the nature of bodies from your past experience. Their secret nature, and consequently all their effects and influence, may change, without any change in their sensible qualities. This happens sometimes, and with regard to some objects: Why may it not happen always, and with regard to all objects? What logic, what process of argument secures you against this supposition? My practice, you say, refutes my doubts. But you mistake the purport of my question. As an agent, I am quite satisfied in the point; but as a philosopher, who has some share of curiosity, I will not say scepticism, I want to learn the foundation of this inference. No reading, no inquiry has yet been able to remove my difficulty, or give me satisfaction in a matter of such importance. Can I do better than propose the difficulty to the public, even though, perhaps, I have small hopes of obtaining a solution? We shall, at least, by this means, be sensible of our ignorance, if we do not augment our knowledge. . . .

SCEPTICAL SOLUTION OF THESE DOUBTS

. . . Suppose a person, though endowed with the strongest faculties of reason and reflection, to be brought on a sudden into this world; he would, indeed, immediately observe a continual succession of objects, and one event following another; but he would not be able to discover anything farther. He would not, at first, by any reasoning, be able to reach the idea of cause and effect; since the particular powers, by which all natural operations are performed, never appear to the senses; nor is it reasonable to conclude, merely because one event, in one instance, precedes another, that therefore the one is the cause, the other the effect. Their conjunction may be arbitrary and casual. There may be no reason to infer the existence of one from the appearance of the other. And in a word, such a person, without more experience, could never employ his conjecture or reasoning concerning any matter of fact, or be assured of anything beyond what was immediately present to his memory and senses.

Suppose, again, that he has acquired more experience, and has lived so long in the world as to have observed familiar objects or events to be constantly conjoined together; what is the consequence of this experience? He immediately infers the existence of one object from the appearance of the other. Yet he has not, by all his experience, acquired any idea or knowledge of the secret power by which the one object produces the other; nor is it, by any process of reasoning, he is engaged to draw this inference. But still he finds himself determined to draw it: And though he should be convinced that his understanding has no part in the operation, he would nevertheless continue in the same course of thinking. There is some other principle which determines him to form such a conclusion.

This principle is *custom* or *habit*. For wherever the repetition of any particular act or operation produces a propensity to renew the same act or operation, without being impelled by any reasoning or process of the understanding, we always say, that this propensity is the effect of *custom*. By employing that word, we pretend not to have given the ultimate reason of such a propensity. We only point out a principle of human nature, which is universally acknowledged, and which is well known by its effects. Perhaps we can push our inquiries no farther, or pretend to give the cause of this cause; but must rest contented with it as the ultimate principle, which we can assign, of all our conclusions from experience. . . .

Custom, then, is the great guide of human life. It is that principle alone which renders our experience useful to us, and makes us expect, for the future, a similar train of events with those which have appeared in the past. Without the influence of custom, we should be entirely ignorant of every matter of fact beyond what is immediately present to the memory and senses. We should never know how to adjust means to ends, or to employ our natural powers in the production of any effect. There would be an end at once of all action, as well as of the chief part of speculation. . . .

What, then, is the conclusion of the whole matter? A simple one; though, it must be confessed, pretty remote from the common theories of philosophy. All belief of matter of fact or real existence is derived merely from some object, present to the memory or senses, and a customary conjunction between that and some other object. Or in other words; having found, in many instances, that any two kinds of objects—flame and heat, snow and cold—have always been conjoined together; if flame or snow be presented anew to the senses, the mind is carried by custom to expect heat or cold, and to *believe* that such a quality does exist, and will discover itself upon a nearer approach. This belief is the necessary result of placing the mind in such circumstances. It is an operation of the soul, when we are so situated, as unavoidable as to feel the passion of love, when we receive benefits; or hatred, when we meet with injuries. All these operations are a species of natural instincts, which no reasoning or process of the thought and understanding is able either to produce or to prevent.

Study Questions

1. Explain Hume's distinction between "relations of ideas" and "matters of fact."
2. According to Hume, what is the foundation for all reasonings concerning matters of fact?
3. What does Hume mean by "custom"?
4. According to Hume, why is custom "the great guide of human life"?

What Is Knowledge?

A. J. AYER

A traditional definition of knowledge is that you know that something is the case if (1) you are sure of it, (2) what you are sure of is true, and (3) you have a right to be sure. In our next selection A. J. Ayer (1910–1989), who was Professor of Philosophy at the University of Oxford and one of the most eminent philosophers of the twentieth century, explains the reasoning behind these three conditions.

The first requirement [of knowing that something is the case] is that what is known should be true, but this is not sufficient; not even if we add to it the further condition that one must be completely sure of what one knows. For it is possible to be completely sure of something which is in fact true, but yet not to know it. The circumstances may be such that one is not entitled to be sure. For instance, a superstitious person who had inadvertently walked under a ladder might be convinced as a result that he was about to suffer some misfortune; and he might in fact be right. But it would not be correct to say that he knew that this was going to be so. He arrived at his belief by a process of reasoning which would not be generally reliable; so, although his prediction came true, it was not a case of knowledge. Again, if someone were fully persuaded of a mathematical proposition by a proof which could be shown to be invalid, he would not, without further evidence, be said to know the proposition, even though it was true. But while it is not hard to find examples of true and fully confident beliefs which in some ways fail to meet the standards required for knowledge, it is not at all easy to determine exactly what these standards are.

One way of trying to discover them would be to consider what would count as satisfactory answers to the question How do you know? Thus people may be credited with knowing truths of mathematics or logic if they are able to give a valid proof of them, or even if, without themselves being able to set out such a proof, they have obtained this information from someone who can. Claims to know empirical statements may be upheld by a reference to perception, or to memory, or to testimony, or to historical records, or to scientific laws. But such backing is not always strong enough for knowledge. Whether it is so or not depends upon the circumstances of the particular case. If I were asked how I knew that a physical object of a certain sort was in such and such a place, it would, in general, be a sufficient answer for me to say that I could see it; but if my eyesight were bad and the light were dim, this answer might not be sufficient. Even though I was right, it might still be said that I did not really know that the object was there. If I have a poor memory and the event which I claim to remember is remote, my memory of it may still not amount to knowledge, even though in this instance it does not fail me. If a witness is unreliable, his unsupported evidence may not enable us to know that what he says is true, even in a case where we completely trust him and he is not in fact

deceiving us. In a given instance it is possible to decide whether the backing is strong enough to justify a claim to knowledge. But to say in general how strong it has to be would require our drawing up a list of the conditions under which perception, or memory, or testimony, or other forms of evidence are reliable. And this would be a very complicated matter, if indeed it could be done at all.

Moreover, we cannot assume that, even in particular instances, an answer to the question How do you know? will always be forthcoming. There may very well be cases in which one knows that something is so without its being possible to say how one knows it. . . . Suppose that someone were consistently successful in predicting events of a certain kind, events, let us say, which are not ordinarily thought to be predictable, like the results of a lottery. If his run of successes were sufficiently impressive, we might very well come to say that he knew which number would win, even though he did not reach this conclusion by any rational method, or indeed by any method at all. We might say that he knew it by intuition, but this would be to assert no more than that he did know it but that we could not say how. In the same way, if someone were consistently successful in reading the minds of others without having any of the usual sort of evidence, we might say that he knew these things telepathically. But in default of any further explanation this would come down to saying merely that he did know them, but not by any ordinary means. Words like "intuition" and "telepathy" are brought in just to disguise the fact that no explanation has been found.

But if we allow this sort of knowledge to be even theoretically possible, what becomes of the distinction between knowledge and true belief? How does our man who knows what the results of the lottery will be differ from one who only makes a series of lucky guesses? The answer is that, so far as the man himself is concerned, there need not be any difference. His procedure and his state of mind, when he is said to know what will happen, may be exactly the same as when it is said that he is only guessing. The difference is that to say that he knows is to concede to him the right to be sure, while to say that he is only guessing is to withhold it. Whether we make this concession will depend upon the view which we take of his performance. Normally we do not say that people know things unless they have followed one of the accredited routes to knowledge. If someone reaches a true conclusion without appearing to have any adequate basis for it, we are likely to say that he does not really know it. But if he were repeatedly successful in a given domain, we might very well come to say that he knew the facts in question, even though we could not explain how he knew them. We should grant him the right to be sure, simply on the basis of his success. . . .

I conclude then that the necessary and sufficient conditions for knowing that something is the case are first that what one is said to know be true, secondly that one be sure of it, and thirdly that one should have the right to be sure.

Study Questions

1. Can you be sure of something, yet not know it?
2. Can you know something without being able to say how you know it?
3. How does knowledge differ from true belief?
4. Give an example of a situation in which you believe a claim to be true, it is true, and you have the right to be sure it is true.

Is Justified True Belief Knowledge?

EDMUND L. GETTIER

Ayer's definition of knowledge may appear unexceptionable, but a type of counter-example is offered in a much-discussed article by Edmund L. Gettier, Professor Emeritus of Philosophy at the University of Massachusetts at Amherst. Here for your consideration is a case he presents.

Ayer has stated the necessary and sufficient condition for [S knows that P] as follows:

(i) P is true,
(ii) S is sure that P is true, and
(iii) S has the right to be sure that P is true.

I shall argue that the conditions stated therein do not constitute a *sufficient* condition for the truth of the proposition that S knows that P. . . .

Suppose that Smith and Jones have applied for a certain job. And suppose that Smith has

---

From Edmund L. Gettier, *Analysis,* 23 (1963). Reprinted by permission of the author.

strong evidence for the following conjunctive proposition:

> (d) Jones is the man who will get the job, and Jones has ten coins in his pocket.

Smith's evidence for (d) might be that the president of the company assured him that Jones would in the end be selected, and that he, Smith, had counted the coins in Jones's pocket ten minutes ago. Proposition (d) entails:

> (e) The man who will get the job has ten coins in his pocket.

Let us suppose that Smith sees the entailment from (d) to (e), and accepts (e) on the grounds of (d), for which he has strong evidence. In this case, Smith is clearly justified in believing that (e) is true.

But imagine, further, that unknown to Smith, he himself, not Jones, will get the job. And, also, unknown to Smith, he himself has ten coins in his pocket. Proposition (e) is then true, though proposition (d), from which Smith inferred (e), is false. In our example, then, all of the following are true: (*i*) (e) is true, (*ii*) Smith believes that (e) is true, and (*iii*) Smith is justified in believing that (e) is true. But it is equally clear that Smith does not *know* that (e) is true; for (e) is true in virtue of the number of coins in Smith's pocket, while Smith does not know how many coins are in Smith's pocket, and bases his belief in (e) on a count of the coins in Jones's pocket, whom he falsely believes to be the man who will get the job.

Study Questions

1. What is the point of Gettier's example?
2. Is Smith justified in believing that the man who will get the job has ten coins in his pocket?
3. Does Smith know that Jones will get the job?
4. Can you develop your own example along the same lines as Gettier's case?

The Project of Feminist Epistemology

UMA NARAYAN

Uma Narayan is Professor of Philosophy at Vassar College. She considers how who we are may affect what we know. She argues that oppressed groups, whether women, racial minorities, or colonized peoples, may derive an epistemic advantage from understanding both their own situations and those of dominant groups.

A fundamental thesis of feminist epistemology is that our location in the world as women makes it possible for us to perceive and understand different aspects of both the world and human activities in ways that challenge the male bias of existing perspectives. Feminist epistemology is a particular manifestation of the general insight that the nature of women's experiences as individuals and as social beings, our contributions to work, culture, knowledge, and our history and political interests have been systematically ignored or misrepresented by mainstream discourses in different areas.

Women have been often excluded from prestigious areas of human activity (for example, politics or science) and this has often made these activities seem clearly "male." In areas where women were not excluded (for example, subsistence work), their contribution has been misrepresented as secondary and inferior to that of men. Feminist epistemology sees mainstream theories about various human enterprises, including mainstream theories about human knowledge, as one-dimensional and deeply flawed because of the exclusion and misrepresentation of women's contributions.

Feminist epistemology suggests that integrating women's contribution into the domain of science and knowledge will not constitute a mere adding of details; it will not merely widen the canvas but result in a shift of perspective enabling us to see a very different picture. The inclusion of women's perspective will not merely amount to women participating in greater numbers in the existing practice of science and knowledge, but it will change the very nature of these activities and their self-understanding. . . .

At the most general level, feminist epistemology resembles the efforts of many oppressed groups to reclaim for themselves the value of their own experience. The writing of novels that focused on working-class life in England or the lives of black people in the United States shares a motivation similar to that of feminist epistemology—to depict an experience different from the norm and to assert the value of this difference.

In a similar manner, feminist epistemology also resembles attempts by third-world writers and historians to document the wealth and complexity of local economic and social structures that existed prior to colonialism. These attempts are useful for their ability to restore to colonized peoples a sense of the richness of their own history and culture. These projects also mitigate the tendency of intellectuals in former colonies who are westernized through their education to think that anything western is necessarily better and more "progressive." In some cases, such studies help to preserve the knowledge of many local arts, crafts, lore, and techniques that were part of the former way of life before they are lost not only to practice but even to memory.

These enterprises are analogous to feminist epistemology's project of restoring to women a sense of the richness of their history, to mitigate our tendency to see the stereotypically "masculine" as better or more progressive, and to preserve for posterity the contents of "feminine" areas of knowledge and expertise—medical lore, knowledge associated with the practices of childbirth and child rearing, traditionally feminine crafts, and so on. Feminist epistemology, like these other enterprises, must attempt to balance the assertion of the value of a different culture or experience against the dangers of romanticizing it to the extent that the limitations and oppressions it confers on its subjects are ignored. . . .

I think that one of the most interesting insights of feminist epistemology is the view that oppressed groups, whether women, the poor, or racial minorities, may derive an "epistemic advantage" from having knowledge of the practices of both their own contexts and those of their oppressors. The practices of the dominant groups (for instance, men) govern a society; the dominated group (for instance, women) must acquire some fluency with these practices in order to survive in that society.

There is no similar pressure on members of the dominant group to acquire knowledge of the practices of the dominated groups. For instance, colonized people had to learn the language and culture of their colonizers. The colonizers seldom found it necessary to have more than a sketchy acquaintance with the language and culture of the "natives." Thus, the oppressed are seen as having an "epistemic advantage" because they can operate with two sets of practices and in two different contexts. This advantage is thought to lead to critical insights because each framework provides a critical perspective on the other.

I would like to balance this account with a few comments about the "dark side," the disadvantages, of being able to or of having to inhabit two mutually incompatible frameworks that provide differing perspectives on social reality. I suspect that nonwestern feminists, given the often complex and troublesome interrelationships between the contexts they must inhabit, are less likely to express unqualified enthusiasm about the benefits of straddling a multiplicity of contexts. Mere access to two different and incompatible contexts is not a guarantee that a critical stance on the part of an individual will result. There are many ways in which she may deal with the situation.

First, the person may be tempted to dichotomize her life and reserve the framework of a different context for each part. The middle class of nonwestern countries supplies numerous examples of people who are very westernized in public life but who return to a very traditional lifestyle in the realm of the family. Women may choose to live their public lives in a "male" mode, displaying characteristics of aggressiveness, competition, and so on, while continuing to play dependent and compliant roles in their private lives. The pressures of jumping between two different lifestyles may be mitigated by justifications of how each pattern of behavior is appropriate to its particular context and of how it enables them to "get the best of both worlds."

Second, the individual may try to reject the practices of her own context and try to be as much as possible like members of the dominant group. Westernized intellectuals in the nonwestern world often may almost lose knowledge of their own cultures and practices and be ashamed of the little that they do still know. Women may try both to acquire stereotypically male characteristics, like aggressiveness, and to expunge stereotypically female characteristics, like emotionality. Or the individual could try to reject entirely the framework of the dominant group and assert the virtues of her own despite the risks of being marginalized from the power structures of the society; consider, for example, women who seek a certain sort of security in traditionally defined roles.

The choice to inhabit two contexts critically is an alternative to these choices and, I would argue, a more useful one. But the presence of alternative contexts does not by itself guarantee that one of the other choices will not be made. Moreover, the decision to inhabit two contexts critically, although it may lead to an "epistemic advantage," is likely to exact a certain price. It may lead to a sense of totally lacking roots or any space where one is at home in a relaxed manner.

This sense of alienation may be minimized if the critical straddling of two contexts is part of an ongoing critical politics, due to the support of others and a deeper understanding of what is going on. When it is not so rooted, it may generate ambivalence, uncertainty, despair, and even madness, rather than more positive critical emotions and attitudes. However such a person determines her locus, there may be a sense of being an outsider in both contexts and a sense of clumsiness or lack of fluency in both sets of practices. Consider this simple linguistic example: most people who learn two different languages that are associated with two very different cultures seldom acquire both with equal fluency; they may find themselves devoid of vocabulary in one language for certain contexts of life or be unable to match real objects with terms they have acquired in their vocabulary. For instance, people from my sort of background would know words in Indian languages for some spices, fruits, and vegetables that they do not know in English. Similarly, they might be unable to discuss "technical" subjects like economics or biology in their own languages because they learned about these subjects and acquired their technical vocabularies only in English.

The relation between the two contexts the individual inhabits may not be simple or straightforward. The individual subject is seldom in a position to carry out a perfect "dialectical synthesis" that preserves all the advantages of both contexts and transcends all their problems. There may be a number of different "syntheses," each of which avoids a different subset of the problems and preserves a different subset of the benefits.

No solution may be perfect or even palatable to the agent confronted with a choice. For example, some Indian feminists may find some western modes of dress (say trousers) either more comfortable or more their "style" than some local modes of dress. However, they may find that wearing the local mode of dress is less socially troublesome, alienates them less from more traditional people they want to work with, and so on. Either choice is bound to leave them partly frustrated in their desires.

Feminist theory must be temperate in the use it makes of this doctrine of "double vision"—the claim that oppressed groups have an epistemic advantage and access to greater critical conceptual space. Certain types and contexts of oppression certainly may bear out the truth of this claim. Others certainly do not seem to do so; and even if they do provide space for critical insights, they may also rule out the possibility of actions subversive of the oppressive state of affairs.

Certain kinds of oppressive contexts, such as the contexts in which women of my grandmother's background lived, rendered their subjects entirely devoid of skills required to function as independent entities in the culture. Girls were married off barely past puberty, trained for nothing beyond household tasks and the rearing of children, and passed from economic dependency on their fathers to economic dependency on their husbands to economic dependency on their sons in old age. Their criticisms of their lot were articulated, if at all, in terms that precluded a desire for any radical change. They saw themselves sometimes as personally unfortunate, but they did not locate the causes of their misery in larger social arrangements.

I conclude by stressing that the important insight incorporated in the doctrine of "double vision" should not be reified into a metaphysics that serves as a substitute for concrete social analysis. Furthermore, the alternative to "buying" into an oppressive social system need not be a celebration of exclusion and the mechanisms of marginalization. The thesis that oppression may bestow an epistemic advantage should not tempt us in the direction of idealizing or romanticizing oppression and blind us to its real material and psychic deprivations.

Study Questions

1. Are any people, men or women, free of bias?
2. Do you acquire any specific items of knowledge as a result of being oppressed?
3. What does Narayan mean by "double vision"?
4. Would Narayan's analysis be equally applicable to those discriminated against based on age, religion, nationality, sexual orientation, bodily appearance, or other personal characteristics?

Buddhist Epistemology

CHRISTOPHER W. GOWANS

Buddhism, with over 300 million adherents, is one of the world's leading religions. The older of its two main branches, Theravada Buddhism, or "The Doctrine of the Elders," is today found primarily in Sri Lanka and throughout Southeast Asia; the other branch, Mahayana Buddhism, or "The Greater Vehicle," is widespread in Vietnam, Tibet, China, Korea, and Japan. Relatively few Buddhists remain in India, where the religion originated approximately 2,500 years ago.

Theravada Buddhism is atheistic, viewing the Buddha as a supreme teacher, and stressing individual effort to achieve understanding through intense concentration. In contrast, Mahayana Buddhism recognizes an ultimate reality, of which the Buddha is a manifestation, thus serving as a source of spiritual strength.

Buddhist meditation is supposed to yield knowledge, and in this selection Christopher W. Gowans, Professor of Philosophy at Fordham University, assesses the reliability of the results of that process. In later readings we shall examine the Buddhist concept of self as well as Buddhist ethics.

The person we know as the Buddha was born . . . near the present-day border of India and Nepal, sometime between the seventh and the fifth centuries B.C.E. He was called Siddhattha Gotama (Siddhārtha Gautama in Sanskrit). . . .

His father was determined that [Siddhattha] should become a ruler, and to ensure this outcome he protected [Siddhattha] from everything unpleasant in life. . . . Eventually, [Siddhattha] discovered what everyone comes to know—that . . . aging, illness, and death are facts of every human life. . . . He wondered: What is the meaning of human suffering? What is its cause? Can it be overcome? . . .

A central contention of the Buddha is that the most important avenue to acquiring . . . knowledge is not reason but meditation, and Buddhist meditation has no significant correlate in Western epistemological discussions. Meditation is not rooted in subjective feelings or desires, nor is its aim a non-cognitive, dream-like condition. On the contrary, meditation is said to provide us with a form of objective knowledge of reality, the knowledge that enables us to overcome suffering. But the knowledge meditation gives us is not based on a rational grasp of self-evident truths, it is not the result of logical inferences, and it is not grounded in the ordinary experience of the five senses. Buddhist understanding as a whole may draw on all these epistemological sources. But meditation itself is *sui generis* and cannot be reduced to or understood in terms of any of them.

The Buddha taught two kinds of meditation: serenity meditation (*samatha-bhāvanā*) and insight meditation (*vipassanā-bhāvanā*). For both, to be effective, a good deal of intellectual, emotional, and moral preparation is required. The aim of serenity meditation is to purify the mind of various obstacles so that it may attain the highest degree of concentration. The Buddha thought our minds were typically in so much turmoil that, in the absence of radical modification, they had no hope of truly understanding reality. Serenity meditation involves extensive training in focusing our attention wholly and exclusively on a single object so as to end this turmoil and gain the ability to concentrate.

This provides a foundation for insight meditation. Here, the purpose is to directly know reality as it truly is. Insight meditation is a matter of heightened and attentive awareness rather than intellectual or theoretical thought. It involves detailed and mindful observation of all aspects of one's person. . . . Insight meditation is a kind of experience, in a broad sense of the term, but experience that is quite different from, and beyond that ordinarily provided by, the five senses. The eventual outcome is . . . an immediate comprehension of the unconditioned realm beyond the ordinary world of sense experience, an understanding that cannot adequately be described in language, but that liberates us from attachment and enables us to live with compassion, joy, and tranquility.

The knowledge Buddhist meditation is supposed to provide purports to be objective in two senses of the word: it gives us knowledge of the way the universe really is, and this knowledge is something that anyone, with proper training, can acquire. . . . Whether meditation actually results in objective knowledge is another question, but that it does is a central contention of the Buddha's teaching. . . .

Let us assume that both the Buddha and many of his followers, during his lifetime and since, have sincerely reported to have gained enlightenment on the basis of meditation. . . . How should stream-observers[1] assess the epistemic worth of these reports?

It might be contended that, in order to answer this question, we first need to establish where the burden of proof lies. On the one hand, someone might say that the burden rests with Buddhists to prove to us stream-observers that meditation produces genuine knowledge. Against this, it may be said that stream-observers

are not now in a position to directly confirm or disconfirm the reports of Buddhist meditators. What we now know or think we know, Buddhists might say, is not an adequate criterion for judging the worth of Buddhist meditation because we are caught up in craving and attachment to things of the world. On the other hand, someone else might say that the burden rests with skeptics to establish that meditation does not produce knowledge. Buddhism has a long and established tradition, and we should assume that the claim that meditation gives knowledge is correct unless there are sufficient reasons to doubt this. Against this, skeptics may reply that all sorts of bizarre claims to knowledge may be difficult to refute, but it does not follow that we should accept these claims.

It is unlikely that we can resolve this debate about the burden of proof. Both the Buddhists and the skeptics have a point. All we can do is consider some specific questions that might be raised about Buddhist meditation and reflect on what may be said in response to them. It will then be up to each of us to determine whether or not, in the context of his overall teaching, the Buddha's meditation techniques have enough prima facie credibility to make them worth pursuing. . . .

We have an account of what the life of an *arahant*[2] is supposed to be like. Suppose it turned out that purported *arahants* did not generally live in this way. For example, suppose they lacked compassion or were rather attached to material goods. Since the knowledge they are said to have is supposed to bring it about that they do not live this way, this would be a reason to doubt that they have this knowledge. Of course, there can always be fraudulent cases. However, it may be said on behalf of the Buddha that *arahants*—and perhaps more generally persons who are especially accomplished in the teaching of the Buddha—do largely live the lives they are expected to live. If this were true, the objection would be answered. On the other hand, the fact that they live this way, though it might encourage our confidence, would not necessarily show that they have the knowledge claimed. There could be other explanations.

Similarly, if persons who report meditative knowledge were known to be unreliable in various ways (for example, by having a bad memory, being especially gullible, giving inconsistent reports, and so on), then this would be another ground for doubt. Once again, it may be said in support of the Buddha that this is not generally the case (not that no such person is unreliable, but that they are not typically so). If this were correct, we would have a response to the objection. Also, as before, reliability in these respects would not necessarily confirm meditative knowledge. In both this and the previous case, empirical research presumably could confirm or disconfirm the claims made on behalf of the Buddha.

Another source of doubt might be found in the apparent disanalogies between sense-experience and meditative experience. To a very great extent, sense-experience is a common possession of all human beings, but nothing close to this can be said of meditative experience. On account of this, reports based on sense-experience can be checked by numerous persons, but reports about . . . ultimate reality . . . cannot similarly be checked. In response, it may be said in defense of the Buddha that there are forms of knowledge based on sense-experience that are possessed by only a few persons—for instance, knowledge of coffee or wine based on its taste, or knowledge of the medical significance of an X-ray. These are cases of genuine knowledge based on sense-experience, but they require special abilities and training to acquire. Something similar might be said about Buddhist meditation. Moreover, it may be said that to a large extent reports based on Buddhist meditation can be checked by others, but only those who have undertaken the Eightfold Path.[3] Hence, there is a significant role for intersubjective verification of these reports. Finally, it may also be noted that there are some kinds of reports we accept as generally authoritative even though they cannot be verified by other persons—for example, introspective reports about whether a person has a headache. Perhaps intersubjective verification is not essential for knowledge.

Suspicion may also be raised by the claim that the knowledge meditators are said to acquire is so heavily influenced by their expectations, given their Buddhist beliefs, that it is not reliable. In effect, meditators experience in meditation what they expect to experience, not what is objectively there to be experienced. Of course, it is often the case that our expectations influence what we think we observe. But from this fact we ordinarily conclude not that all beliefs where this can happen are doubtful, but that particular ones are doubtful that we have reason to suspect are adversely influenced by expectations. By parity of reasoning, it may be said on the Buddha's behalf, this cannot be a basis for casting doubt on all reports based on meditation unless it can be shown that all or nearly all meditators are unduly influenced in this way. And it seems unlikely that this could be shown. Just as there are persons who are capable of an objective assessment of their own team's chances in the championship game, so there may be meditators who are capable of an objective assessment of what meditation reveals.

It might also be said that the beliefs of meditators can be explained in purely naturalistic terms on the basis of psychology or physiology. For example, it might be claimed that serenity meditation puts the brain in a highly unusual state, and that the supposed knowledge that meditators gain is nothing more than an effect of this state. One difficulty with this critique is that all beliefs have a naturalistic explanation. Whether a particular naturalistic explanation supplies a basis for skepticism about some class of beliefs depends on whether we have grounds for thinking the explanation undermines the reliability of the beliefs. For example, we might think that a particular kind of drug-induced state was unreliable if persons in that state made reports we could show on independent grounds to be false (say, if they always forgot their address). Conversely, we might believe that another kind of drug-induced state was especially reliable if persons in that state performed much better intellectually (say, if they could do more complex mathematical calculations). A Buddhist might respond that meditation may well alter the state of the brain. What must be shown, but cannot be, is that there are independent grounds for supposing the reports of Buddhist meditation are unreliable. In any case, it seems clear that the issue of reliability would have to be brought into this discussion.

Finally, it might be argued that reports based on Buddhist meditation are part of a larger class of reports based on religious experience in many different traditions (Hindu, Jewish, Christian, Muslim, and so on), and that the reports in this larger class often contradict one another. Therefore, there is reason to question all these reports, including the Buddhist ones. The Buddhist might respond that it is not evident why Buddhist meditation should be considered part of the larger class of religious experiences. Buddhist meditation is a highly specific set of techniques that are quite different from anything found in other religious traditions. Why should the fact that persons in those other traditions who rely on different approaches and give reports incompatible with Buddhism count against the authority of the reports based on Buddhist meditation? Since the reports from other traditions are not based on Buddhist techniques, there is no reason to expect that they would be consistent with the teachings of the Buddha.

In response, a modification of this objection may be given that does not depend on classifying Buddhist meditation as one form of religious experience. It contends that the conflicting experience-based reports of other religious traditions could be justified to the same extent as the reports based on Buddhist meditation. That is, analogous and equally plausible responses to the objections already given could be made on behalf of the reports in these different traditions, and since these reports cannot all be true, we have reason to question all of them, including the Buddhist ones. This is a more serious objection. However, in order to be established, it would have to be shown that equally plausible responses could be made in all the traditions, and this is a large agenda. There are several possibilities here. Perhaps a close look at reports that genuinely could be said to be equally plausible do not conflict to the extent supposed. Or perhaps the respects in which these religious traditions do conflict are not directly based on religious experiences. Or perhaps we do not know enough about these issues to adequately assess this objection. The defender of the Buddha would probably say that, insofar as there is real conflict, the reports based on Buddhist meditation are better justified. It would be difficult to prove this, but it may be just as difficult to refute it.

In short, there are a number of grounds for challenging the epistemic credentials of Buddhist meditation, but Buddhists are not without resources for answering these challenges. Stream-observers can determine for themselves whether these responses are adequate.

NOTES

1. [Those who are culturally part of the contemporary Western world and have no Buddhist upbringing—S.M.C.]

2. [Fully enlightened ones; the Buddhist's first followers.]

3. [Training that leads to enlightenment.]

Study Questions

1. Can knowledge be acquired in different ways?
2. Might meditation be a source of knowledge?
3. How can the outcome of meditative experience be tested?
4. Do conflicting claims made by different religions undermine the epistemic credentials of Buddhist meditation?

Part IV

⊠

Reality

A.   Mind and Body

Meditations on First Philosophy

RENÉ DESCARTES

Philosophers sometimes consider questions about the fundamental nature of the world. Does every event have a cause? Do human beings possess free will? What is a self? Such issues belong to the field of philosophy known as "metaphysics," a Greek term meaning "after physics," so called because when Aristotle's works were first catalogued more than two millennia ago, the treatise in which he discussed such matters was placed after his treatise on physics.

One of the central issues in metaphysics is commonly referred to by philosophers as "the mind-body problem." Are you identical with your body, your mind, or some combination of the two? If you are a combination, how are the mind and body connected so as to form one person?

An influential starting point for exploring these questions is the Second Meditation of Descartes. We left off at the point at which he had wondered whether we can be sure of any truth. He believes we can. The principle he proposes as certain is best known as formulated in another of his works as "I think, therefore, I am," in Latin, "Cogito, ergo sum." According to Descartes, the Cogito, as it is called by philosophers, is undeniable, for, in the act of attempting to deny one is thinking, one thinks and so renders the denial false.

Using the Cogito as the premise of his philosophical system, Descartes argues that because he is certain he is thinking but not certain of the existence of anything other than his own mind, he is to be identified with his mind. He claims further that by relying on the judgments of his mind rather than the evidence of his senses he can attain knowledge.

SECOND MEDITATION

The Nature of the Human Mind, and How It Is Better Known Than the Body

So serious are the doubts into which I have been thrown as a result of yesterday's mediation that I can neither put them out of my mind nor see any way of resolving them. It feels as if I have fallen unexpectedly into a deep whirlpool which tumbles me around so that I can neither stand on the bottom nor swim up to the top. Nevertheless I will make an effort and once more attempt the same path which I started on yesterday. Anything which admits of the slightest doubt I will set aside just as if I had found it to be wholly false;

and I will proceed in this way until I recognize something certain, or, if nothing else, until I at least recognize for certain that there is no certainty. Archimedes used to demand just one firm and immovable point in order to shift the entire earth; so I too can hope for great things if I manage to find just one thing, however slight, that is certain and unshakeable.

I will suppose then, that everything I see is spurious. I will believe that my memory tells me lies, and that none of the things that it reports ever happened. I have no senses. Body, shape, extension, movement, and place are chimeras. So what remains true? Perhaps just the one fact that nothing is certain.

Yet apart from everything I have just listed, how do I know that there is not something else which does not allow even the slightest occasion for doubt? Is there not a God, or whatever I may call him, who puts into me the thoughts I am now having? But why do I think this, since I myself may perhaps be the author of these thoughts? In that case am not I, at least, something? But I have just said that I have no senses and no body. This is the sticking point: what follows from this? Am I not so bound up with a body and with senses that I cannot exist without them? But I have convinced myself that there is absolutely nothing in the world, no sky, no earth, no minds, no bodies. Does it now follow that I too do not exist? No: if I convinced myself of something then I certainly existed. But there is a deceiver of supreme power and cunning who is deliberately and constantly deceiving me. In that case I too undoubtedly exist, if he is deceiving me; and let him deceive me as much as he can, he will never bring it about that I am nothing so long as I think that I am something. So after considering everything very thoroughly, I must finally conclude that this proposition, *I am, I exist,* is necessarily true whenever it is put forward by me or conceived in my mind.

But I do not yet have a sufficient understanding of what this "I" is, that now necessarily exists. So I must be on my guard against carelessly taking something else to be this "I," and so making a mistake in the very item of knowledge that I maintain is the most certain and evident of all. I will therefore go back and meditate on what I originally believed myself to be, before I embarked on this present train of thought. I will then subtract anything capable of being weakened, even minimally, by the arguments now introduced, so that what is left at the end may be exactly and only what is certain and unshakeable.

What then did I formerly think I was? A man. But what is a man? Shall I say "a rational animal"? No; for then I should have to inquire what an animal is, what rationality is, and in this way one question would lead me down the slope to other harder ones, and I do not now have the time to waste on subtleties of this kind. Instead I propose to concentrate on what came into my thoughts spontaneously and quite naturally whenever I used to consider what I was. Well, the first thought to come to mind was that I had a face, hands, arms, and the whole mechanical structure of limbs which can be seen in a corpse, and which I called the body. The next thought was that I was nourished, that I moved about, and that I engaged in sense-perception and thinking; and these actions I attributed to the soul. But as to the nature of this soul, either I did not think about this or else I imagined it to be something tenuous, like a wind or fire or ether, which permeated my more solid parts. As to the body, however, I had no doubts about it, but thought I knew its nature distinctly. If I had tried to describe the mental conception I had of it, I would have expressed it as follows: by a body I understand whatever has a determinable shape and a definable location and can occupy a space in such a way as to exclude any other body; it can be perceived by touch, sight, hearing, taste, or smell, and can be moved in various ways, not by itself but by whatever else comes into contact with it. For, according to my judgement, the power of self-movement, like the power of sensation or of thought, was quite foreign to the nature of a body; indeed, it was a source of wonder to me that certain bodies were found to contain faculties of this kind.

But what shall I now say that I am, when I am supposing that there is some supremely powerful and, if it is permissible to say so, malicious deceiver, who is deliberately trying to trick me in every way he can? Can I now assert that I possess even the most insignificant of all the attributes which I have just said belong to the nature of a body? I scrutinize them, think about them, go over them again, but nothing suggests itself; it is tiresome and pointless to go through the list once more. But what about the attributes I assigned to the soul? Nutrition or movement? Since now I do not have a body, these are mere fabrications. Sense-perception? This surely does not occur without a body, and besides, when asleep I have appeared to perceive through the senses many things which I afterwards realized I did not perceive through the senses at all. Thinking? At last I have discovered it—thought; this alone is inseparable from me. I am, I exist—that is certain. But for how long? For as long as I am thinking. For it could be that were I totally to cease from thinking, I should totally cease to exist. At present I am not admitting anything except what is necessarily true. I am, then, in the strict sense only a thing that thinks; that is, I am a mind, or intelligence, or intellect, or reason—words whose meaning I have been ignorant of until now. But for all that I am a thing which is real and which truly exists. But what kind of a thing? As I have just said—a thinking thing.

What else am I? I will use my imagination. I am not that structure of limbs which is called a human body. I am not even some thin vapour which permeates the limbs—a wind, fire, air, breath, or whatever I depict in my imagination; for these are things which I have supposed to be nothing. Let this supposition stand; for all that I am still something. And yet may it not perhaps be the case that these very things which I am supposing to be nothing, because they are unknown to me, are in reality identical with the "I" of which I am aware? I do not know, and for the moment I shall not argue the point, since

I can make judgements only about things which are known to me. I know that I exist; the question is, what is this "I" that I know? If the "I" is understood strictly as we have been taking it, then it is quite certain that knowledge of it does not depend on things of whose existence I am as yet unaware; so it cannot depend on any of the things which I invent in my imagination. And this very word "invent" shows me my mistake. It would indeed be a case of fictitious invention if I used my imagination to establish that I was something or other; for imagining is simply contemplating the shape or image of a corporeal thing. Yet now I know for certain both that I exist and at the same time that all such images and, in general, everything relating to the nature of body, could be mere dreams (and chimeras). Once this point has been grasped, to say "I will use my imagination to get to know more distinctly what I am" would seem to be as silly as saying "I am now awake, and see some truth; but since my vision is not yet clear enough, I will deliberately fall asleep so that my dreams may provide a truer and clearer representation." I thus realize that none of the things that the imagination enables me to grasp is at all relevant to this knowledge of myself which I possess, and that the mind must therefore be most carefully diverted from such things if it is to perceive its own nature as distinctly as possible.

But what then am I? A thing that thinks. What is that? A thing that doubts, understands, affirms, denies, is willing, is unwilling, and also imagines and has sensory perceptions.

This is a considerable list, if everything on it belongs to me. But does it? Is it not one and the same "I" who is now doubting almost everything, who nonetheless understands some things, who affirms that this one thing is true, denies everything else, desires to know more, is unwilling to be deceived, imagines many things even involuntarily, and is aware of many things which apparently come from the senses? Are not all these things just as true as the fact that I exist, even if I am asleep all the time, and even if he who created me is doing all he can to deceive me?

Which of all these activities is distinct from my thinking? Which of them can be said to be separate from myself? The fact that it is I who am doubting and understanding and willing is so evident that I see no way of making it any clearer. But it is also the case that the "I" who imagines is the same "I." For even if, as I have supposed, none of the objects of imagination are real, the power of imagination is something which really exists and is part of my thinking. Lastly, it is also the same "I" who has sensory perceptions, or is aware of bodily things as it were through the senses. For example, I am now seeing light, hearing a noise, feeling heat. But I am asleep, so all this is false. Yet I certainly *seem* to see, to hear, and to be warmed. This cannot be false; what is called "having a sensory perception" is strictly just this, and in this restricted sense of the term it is simply thinking.

From all this I am beginning to have a rather better understanding of what I am. But it still appears—and I cannot stop thinking this—that the corporeal things of which images are formed in my thought, and which the senses investigate, are known with much more distinctness than this puzzling "I" which cannot be pictured in the imagination. And yet it is surely surprising that I should have a more distinct grasp of things which I realize are doubtful, unknown, and foreign to me, than I have of that which is true and known—my own self. But I see what it is: my mind enjoys wandering off and will not yet submit to being restrained within the bounds of truth. Very well then; just this once let us give it a completely free rein, so that after a while, when it is time to tighten the reins, it may more readily submit to being curbed.

Let us consider the things which people commonly think they understand most distinctly of all; that is, the bodies which we touch and see. I do not mean bodies in general—for general perceptions are apt to be somewhat more confused—but one particular body. Let us take, for example, this piece of wax. It has just been taken from the honeycomb; it has not yet quite lost the taste of the honey; it retains some of the scent of the flowers from which it was gathered; its colour, shape, and size are plain to see; it is hard, cold and can be handled without difficulty; if you rap it with your knuckle, it makes a sound. In short, it has everything which appears necessary to enable a body to be known as distinctly as possible. But even as I speak, I put the wax by the fire, and look: the residual taste is eliminated, the smell goes away, the colour changes, the shape is lost, the size increases; it becomes liquid and hot; you can hardly touch it, and if you strike it, it no longer makes a sound. But does the same wax remain? It must be admitted that it does; no one denies it, no one thinks otherwise. So what was it in the wax that I understood with such distinctness? Evidently none of the features which I arrived at by means of the senses; for whatever came under taste, smell, sight, touch, or hearing has now altered—yet the wax remains.

Perhaps the answer lies in the thought which now comes to my mind; namely, the wax was not after all the sweetness of the honey, or the fragrance of the flowers, or the whiteness, or the shape, or the sound, but was rather a body which presented itself to me in these various forms a little while ago, but which now exhibits different ones. But what exactly is it that I am now imagining? Let us concentrate, take away everything which does not belong to the wax, and see what is left: merely something extended, flexible, and changeable. But what is meant here by "flexible" and "changeable"? Is it what I picture in my imagination: that this piece of wax is capable of changing from a round shape to a square shape, or from a square shape to a triangular shape? Not at all; for I can grasp that the wax is capable of countless changes of this kind, yet I am unable to run through this immeasurable number of changes in my imagination, from which it follows that it is not the faculty of imagination that gives me my grasp of the wax as flexible and changeable. And what is meant by "extended"? Is the extension of the wax also unknown? For it increases if the wax melts, increases again if it boils, and is greater still if the heat is increased. I would not be making a correct judgement about the nature of wax unless I believed it capable of being extended in many more different ways than I will ever encompass in my imagination. I must therefore admit that the nature of this piece of wax is in no way revealed by my imagination, but is perceived by the mind alone. (I am speaking of this particular piece of wax; the point is even clearer with regard to wax in general.) But what is this wax which is perceived by the mind alone? It is of course the same wax which I see, which I touch, which I picture in my imagination, in short the same wax which I thought it to be from the start. And yet, and here is the point, the perception I have of it is a case not of vision or touch or imagination—nor has it ever been, despite previous appearances—but of purely mental scrutiny; and this can be imperfect and confused, as it was before, or clear and distinct as it is now, depending on how carefully I concentrate on what the wax consists in.

But as I reach this conclusion I am amazed at how (weak and) prone to error my mind is. For although I am thinking about these matters within myself, silently and without speaking, nonetheless the actual words bring me up short, and I am almost tricked by ordinary ways of talking. We say that we see the wax itself, if it is there before us, not that we judge it to be there from its colour or shape; and this might lead me to conclude without more ado that knowledge of the wax comes from what the eye sees, and not from the scrutiny of the mind alone. But then if I look out of the window and see men crossing the square, as I just happen to have done, I normally say that I see the men themselves, just as I say that I see the wax. Yet do I see any more than hats and coats which could conceal automatons? I *judge* that they are men. And so something which I thought I was seeing with my eyes is in fact grasped solely by the faculty of judgement which is in my mind.

However, one who wants to achieve knowledge above the ordinary level should feel ashamed at having taken ordinary ways of talking as a basis for doubt. So let us proceed, and consider on which occasion my perception of the nature of the wax was more perfect and evident. Was it when I first looked at it, and believed I knew it by my external senses, or at least by what they call the "common" sense—that is, the power of imagination? Or is my knowledge more perfect now, after a more careful investigation of the nature of the wax and of the means by which it is known? Any doubt on this issue would clearly be foolish; for what distinctness was there in my earlier perception? Was there anything in it which an animal could not possess? But when I distinguish the wax from its outward forms—take the clothes off, as it were, and consider it naked—then although my judgement may still contain errors, at least my perception now requires a human mind.

But what am I to say about this mind, or about myself? (So far, remember, I am not admitting that there is anything else in me except a mind.) What, I ask, is this "I" which seems to perceive the wax so distinctly? Surely my awareness of my own self is not merely much truer and more certain than my awareness of the wax, but also much more distinct and evident. For if I judge that the wax exists from the fact that I see it, clearly this same fact entails much more evidently that I myself also exist. It is possible that what I see is not really the wax; it is possible that I do not even have eyes with which to see anything. But when I see, or think I see (I am not here distinguishing the two), it is simply not possible that I who am now thinking am not something. By the same token, if I judge that the wax exists from the fact that I touch it, the same result follows, namely, that I exist. If I judge that it exists from the fact that I imagine it, or for any other reason, exactly the same thing follows. And the result that I have grasped in the case of the wax may be applied to everything else located outside me.

Moreover, if my perception of the wax seemed more distinct after it was established not just by sight or touch but by many other considerations, it must be admitted that I now know myself even more distinctly. This is because every consideration whatsoever which contributes to my perception of the wax, or of any other body, cannot but establish even more effectively the nature of my own mind. But besides this, there is so much else in the mind itself which can serve to make my knowledge of it more distinct, that it scarcely seems worth going through the contributions made by considering bodily things.

I see that without any effort I have now finally got back to where I wanted. I now know that even bodies are not strictly perceived by the senses or the faculty of imagination but by the intellect alone, and that this perception derives not from their being touched or seen but from their being understood; and in view of this I know plainly that I can achieve an easier and more evident perception of my own mind than of anything else. But since the habit of holding on to old opinions cannot be set aside so quickly, I should like to stop here and meditate for some time on this new knowledge I have gained, so as to fix it more deeply in my memory.

Study Questions

1. According to Descartes, which proposition is necessarily true?
2. By what argument does Descartes reach the conclusion that he is a mind?
3. What implications does Descartes draw from the example of the piece of wax?
4. Do you agree with Descartes that you can achieve an easier understanding of your own mind than of anything else?

The Ghost in the Machine

GILBERT RYLE

An influential writer on the mind-body problem is Gilbert Ryle (1900–1976), who was Professor of Philosophy at the University of Oxford. He argues that we should not suppose that the mind is something inside the body, a "ghost in the machine." Such a misconception he calls a "category mistake," the sort of error that would be committed by one who, having been shown a college's classrooms, offices, playing fields, and libraries, would then ask, "But where is the university?" The university, of course, is not a separate building that one can see, and Ryle believes that the mind is not a separate entity that one can sense.

From *The Concept of Mind,* by Gilbert Ryle, Hutchinson and Co., 1949. Reprinted by permission of Taylor & Francis Books UK and the Principal, Fellows and Scholars of Hertford College at Oxford University.

THE OFFICIAL DOCTRINE

There is a doctrine about the nature and place of minds which is so prevalent among theorists and even among laymen that it deserves to be described as the official theory. Most philosophers, psychologists and religious teachers subscribe, with minor reservations, to its main articles and, although they admit certain theoretical difficulties in it, they tend to assume that these can be overcome without serious modifications being made to the architecture of the theory. It will be argued here that the central principles of the doctrine are unsound and conflict with the whole body of what we know about minds when we are not speculating about them.

The official doctrine, which hails chiefly from Descartes, is something like this. With the doubtful exceptions of idiots and infants in arms every human being has both a body and a mind. Some would prefer to say that every human being is both a body and a mind. His body and his mind are ordinarily harnessed together, but after the death of the body his mind may continue to exist and function.

Human bodies are in space and are subject to the mechanical laws which govern all other bodies in space. Bodily processes and states can be inspected by external observers. So a man's bodily life is as much a public affair as are the lives of animals and reptiles and even as the careers of trees, crystals and planets.

But minds are not in space, nor are their operations subject to mechanical laws. The workings of one mind are not witnessable by other observers; its career is private. Only I can take direct cognisance of the states and processes of my own mind. A person therefore lives through two collateral histories, one consisting of what happens in and to his body, the other consisting of what happens in and to his mind. The first is public, the second private. The events in the first history are events in the physical world, those in the second are events in the mental world.

It has been disputed whether a person does or can directly monitor all or only some of the episodes of his own private history; but, according to the official doctrine, of at least some of these episodes he has direct and unchallengeable cognisance. In consciousness, self-consciousness and introspection he is directly and authentically apprised of the present states and operations of his mind. He may have great or small uncertainties about concurrent and adjacent episodes in the physical world, but he can have none about at least part of what is momentarily occupying his mind.

It is customary to express this bifurcation of his two lives and of his two worlds by saying that the things and events which belong to the physical world, including his own body, are external, while the workings of his own mind are internal. This antithesis of outer and inner is of course meant to be construed as a metaphor, since minds, not being in space, could not be described as being spatially inside anything else, or as having things going on spatially inside themselves. But relapses from this good intention are common and theorists are found speculating how stimuli, the physical sources of which are yards or miles outside a person's skin, can generate mental responses inside his skull, or how decisions framed inside his cranium can set going movements of his extremities.

Even when "inner" and "outer" are construed as metaphors, the problem how a person's mind and body influence one another is notoriously charged with theoretical difficulties. What the mind wills, the legs, arms and the tongue execute; what affects the ear and the eye has something to do with what the mind perceives; grimaces and smiles betray the mind's moods; and bodily castigations lead, it is hoped, to moral improvement. But the actual transactions between the episodes of the private history and those of the public history remain mysterious, since by definition they can belong to neither series. They could not be reported among the happenings described in a person's autobiography of his inner life, but nor could they be reported among those described in someone else's biography of that person's overt career. They can be inspected neither by introspection nor by laboratory experiment. They are theoretical shuttlecocks which are forever being bandied from the physiologist back to the psychologist and from the psychologist back to the physiologist.

Underlying this partly metaphorical representation of the bifurcation of a person's two lives there is a seemingly more profound and philosophical assumption. It is assumed that there are two different kinds of existence or status. What exists or happens may have the status of physical existence, or it may have the status of mental existence. Somewhat as the faces of coins are either heads or tails, or somewhat as living creatures are either male or female, so, it is supposed, some existing is physical existing, other existing is mental existing. It is a necessary feature of what has physical existence that it is in space and time; it is a necessary feature of what has mental existence that it is in time but not in space. What has physical existence is composed of matter, or else is a function of matter; what has mental existence consists of consciousness, or else is a function of consciousness.

There is thus a polar opposition between mind and matter, an opposition which is often brought out as follows. Material objects are situated in a common field, known as "space," and what happens to one body in one part of space is mechanically connected with what happens to other bodies in other parts of space. But mental happenings occur in insulated fields, known as "minds," and there is, apart maybe from telepathy, no direct causal connection between what happens in one mind and what happens in another. Only through the medium of the public physical world can the mind of one person make a difference to the mind of another. The mind is its own place and in his inner life each of us lives the life of a ghostly Robinson Crusoe. People can see, hear and jolt one another's bodies, but they are irremediably blind and deaf to the workings of one another's minds and inoperative upon them. . . .

THE ABSURDITY OF THE OFFICIAL DOCTRINE

Such in outline is the official theory. I shall often speak of it, with deliberate abusiveness, as "the dogma of the Ghost in the Machine." I hope to prove that it is entirely false, and false not in detail but in principle. It is not merely an assemblage of particular mistakes. It is one big mistake and a mistake of a special kind. It is, namely, a category mistake. It represents the facts of mental life as if they belonged to one logical type or category (or range of types or categories), when they actually belong to another. The dogma is therefore a philosopher's myth. . . .

I must first indicate what is meant by the phrase "category mistake." This I do in a series of illustrations.

A foreigner visiting Oxford or Cambridge for the first time is shown a number of colleges, libraries, playing fields, museums, scientific departments and administrative offices. He then asks, "But where is the University? I have seen where the members of the Colleges live, where the Registrar works, where the scientists experiment and the rest. But I have not yet seen the University in which reside and work the members of your University." It has then to be explained to him that the University is not another collateral institution, some ulterior counterpart to the colleges, laboratories and offices which he has seen. The University is just the way in which all that he has already seen is organized. When they are seen and when their coordination is understood, the University has been seen. His mistake lay in his innocent assumption that it was correct to speak of Christ Church, the Bodleian Library, the Ashmolean Museum *and* the University, to speak, that is, as if "the University" stood for an extra member of the class of which these other units are members. He was mistakenly allocating the University to the same category as that to which the other institutions belong.

The same mistake would be made by a child witnessing the march-past of a division, who, having had pointed out to him such and such battalions, batteries, squadrons, etc., asked when the division was going to appear. He would be supposing that a division was a counterpart to the units already seen, partly similar to them and partly unlike them. He would be shown his mistake by being told that in watching the battalions, batteries, and squadrons marching past he had been watching the division marching past. The march-past was not a parade of battalions, batteries, squadrons *and* a division; it was a parade of the battalions, batteries and squadrons *of* a division.

One more illustration. A foreigner watching his first game of cricket learns what are the functions of the bowlers, the batsmen, the fielders, the umpires and the scorers. He then says, "But there is no one left on the field to contribute the famous element of team spirit. I see who does the bowling, the batting and the wicket-keeping; but I do not see whose role it is to exercise *esprit de corps*." Once more, it would have to be explained that he was looking for the wrong type of thing. Team spirit is not another cricketing-operation supplementary to all of the other special tasks. It is, roughly, the keenness with which each of the special tasks is performed, and performing a task keenly is not performing two tasks. Certainly exhibiting team spirit is not the same thing as bowling or catching, but nor is it a third thing such that we can say that the bowler first bowls *and* then exhibits team spirit or that a fielder is at a given moment *either* catching *or* displaying *esprit de corps*.

These illustrations of category mistakes have a common feature which must be noticed. The mistakes were made by people who did not know how to wield the concepts *University, division* and *team spirit*. Their puzzles arose from inability to use certain items in the English vocabulary.

The theoretically interesting category mistakes are those made by people who are perfectly competent to apply concepts, at least in the situations with which they are familiar, but are still liable in their abstract thinking to allocate those concepts to logical types to which they do not belong. An instance of a mistake of this sort would be the following story. A student of politics has learned the main differences between the British, the French and the American Constitutions, and has learned also the differences and connections between the Cabinet, Parliament, the various Ministries, the Judicature and the Church of England. But he still becomes embarrassed when asked questions about the connections between the Church of England, the Home Office and the British Constitution. For while the Church and the Home Office are institutions, the British Constitution is not another institution in the same sense of that noun. So inter-institutional relations which can be asserted or denied to hold between the Church and the Home Office cannot be asserted or denied to hold between either of them and the British Constitution. "The British Constitution" is not a term of the same logical type as "the Home Office" and "the Church of England." In a partially similar way, John Doe may be a relative, a friend, an enemy or a stranger to Richard Roe; but he cannot be any of these things to the Average Taxpayer. He knows how to talk sense in certain sorts of discussions about the Average Taxpayer, but he is baffled to say why he could not come across him in the street as he can come across Richard Roe.

It is pertinent to our main subject to notice that, so long as the student of politics continues to think of the British Constitution as a counterpart to the other institutions, he will tend to describe it as a mysteriously occult institution; and so long as John Doe continues to think of the Average Taxpayer as a fellow citizen, he will tend to think of him as an elusive insubstantial man, a ghost who is everywhere yet nowhere.

My destructive purpose is to show that a family of radical category mistakes is the source of the double-life theory. The representation of a person as a ghost mysteriously ensconced in a machine derives from this argument.

Study Questions

1. What does Ryle mean by "the dogma of the Ghost in the Machine"?
2. What does Ryle mean by a "category mistake"?
3. According to Ryle, how does the dogma of the Ghost in the Machine involve a category mistake?
4. Present your own example of a category mistake.

The Mind-Body Problem

PAUL M. CHURCHLAND

Paul M. Churchland is Professor Emeritus of Philosophy at the University of California, San Diego. He explores different forms of dualism, concluding that none is persuasive.

The dualistic approach to mind encompasses several quite different theories, but they are all agreed that the essential nature of conscious intelligence resides in something *nonphysical,* in something forever beyond the scope of sciences like physics, neurophysiology, and computer science. Dualism is not the most widely held view in the current philosophical and scientific community but is to the public the most common theory of mind, is deeply entrenched in most of the world's religions, and has been the dominant theory of mind for most of Western history. Let us therefore consider dualism carefully.

SUBSTANCE DUALISM

The distinguishing claim of this view is that each mind is a distinct nonphysical thing, an individual "package" of nonphysical substance, a thing whose identity is independent of any physical body to which it may be temporarily "attached." Mental states and activities derive their special character, on this view, from their being states and activities of this unique, nonphysical substance.

This leaves us wanting to ask for more in the way of a *positive* characterization of the proposed mind-stuff. It is a frequent complaint with the substance dualist's approach that his characterization of it is so far almost entirely negative. This need not be a fatal flaw, however, since we no doubt have much to learn about the underlying nature of mind, and perhaps the deficit here can eventually be made good. On this score, the philosopher René Descartes (1596–1650) has done as much as anyone to provide a positive

From Paul M. Churchland, *Matter and Consciousness,* third edition, MIT Press, 2013. Reprinted by permission of the publisher.

account of the nature of the proposed mind-stuff, and his views are worthy of examination.

Descartes theorized that reality divides into two basic kinds of substance. The first is ordinary matter, and the essential feature of this kind of substance is that it is extended in space: any instance of it has length, breadth, height, and occupies a determinate position in space. Descartes did not attempt to play down the importance of this type of matter. On the contrary, he was one of the most imaginative physicists of his time, and he was an enthusiastic advocate of what was then called "the mechanical philosophy." But there was one isolated corner of reality he thought could not be accounted for in terms of the mechanics of matter: the conscious reason of Man. This was his motive for proposing a second and radically different kind of substance, a substance that has no spatial extension or spatial position whatever, a substance whose essential feature is the activity of *thinking*. This view is known as *Cartesian dualism*.

As Descartes saw it, the real *you* is not your material body, but rather a non-spatial thinking substance, an individual unit of mind-stuff quite distinct from your material body. This nonphysical mind is in systematic causal interaction with your body. The physical state of your body's sense organs, for example, causes visual/auditory/tactile experiences in your mind. And the desires and decisions of your nonphysical mind cause your body to behave in purposeful ways. Its causal connections to your mind are what make your body yours, and not someone else's.

The main reasons offered in support of this view were straightforward enough. First, Descartes thought that he could determine, by direct introspection alone, that he was essentially a thinking substance and nothing else. And second, he could not imagine how a purely physical system could ever use *language* in a relevant way, or engage in mathematical *reasoning*, as any normal human can. Whether these are good reasons, we shall discuss presently. Let us first notice a difficulty that even Descartes regarded as a problem.

If "mind-stuff" is so utterly different from "matter-stuff" in its nature—different to the point that it has no mass whatever, no shape whatever, and no position anywhere in space—then how is it possible for my mind to have any causal influence on my body at all? As Descartes himself was aware (he was one of the first to formulate the law of the conservation of momentum), ordinary matter in space behaves according to rigid laws, and one cannot get bodily movement (= momentum) from nothing. How is this utterly insubstantial "thinking substance" to have any influence on ponderous matter? How can two such different things be in any sort of causal contact? Descartes proposed a very subtle material substance—"animal spirits"—to convey the mind's influence to the body in general. But this does not provide us with a solution, since it leaves us with the same problem with which we started: how something ponderous and spatial (even 'animal spirits') can interact with something entirely nonspatial.

In any case, the basic principle of division used by Descartes is no longer as plausible as it was in his day. It is now neither useful nor accurate to characterize ordinary matter as that-which-has-extension-in-space. Electrons, for example, are bits of matter, but our best current theories describe the electron as a point-particle with no extension whatever (it even lacks a determinate spatial position). And according to Einstein's theory of gravity, an entire star can achieve this same status, if it undergoes a complete gravitational collapse. If there truly is a division between mind and body, it appears that Descartes did not put his finger on the dividing line.

Such difficulties with Cartesian dualism provide a motive for considering a less radical form of substance dualism, and that is what we find in a view I shall call *popular dualism*. This is the theory that a person is literally a "ghost in a machine," where the machine is the human body, and the ghost is a spiritual substance, quite unlike physical matter in its internal constitution, but fully possessed of spatial properties even so. In particular, minds are commonly held to be *inside* the bodies they control; inside the head, on most views, in intimate contact with the brain.

This view need not have the difficulties of Descartes'. The mind is right there in contact with the brain, and their interaction can perhaps be understood in terms of their exchanging energy of a form that our science has not yet recognized or understood. Ordinary matter, you may recall, is just a form or manifestation of energy. (You may think of a grain of sand as a great deal of energy condensed or frozen into a small package, according to Einstein's relation, $E = mc^2$.) Perhaps mind-stuff is a well-behaved form or manifestation of energy also, but a different form of it. It is thus *possible* that a dualism of this alternative sort be consistent with familiar laws concerning the conservation of momentum and energy. This is fortunate for dualism, since those particular laws are very well established indeed.

This view will appeal to many for the further reason that it at least holds out the possibility (though it certainly does not guarantee) that the mind might survive the death of the body. It does not guarantee the mind's survival because it remains possible that the peculiar form of energy here supposed to constitute a mind can be produced and sustained only in conjunction with the highly intricate form of matter we call the brain, and must disintegrate when the brain disintegrates. So the prospects for surviving death are quite unclear even on the assumption that popular dualism is true. But even if survival were a clear consequence of the theory, there is a pitfall to be avoided here. Its promise of survival might be a reason for *wishing* dualism to be true, but it does not constitute a reason for *believing* that it *is* true. For that, we would need independent empirical evidence that minds do indeed survive the permanent death of the body. Regrettably, and despite the exploitative blatherings of the supermarket tabloids (TOP DOCS PROVE LIFE AFTER DEATH!!!), we possess no such evidence.

As we shall see later in this section, when we turn to evaluation, positive evidence for the existence of this novel, nonmaterial, thinking *substance* is in general on the slim side. This has moved many dualists to articulate still less extreme forms of dualism, in hopes of narrowing further the gap between theory and available evidence.

PROPERTY DUALISM

The basic idea of the theories under this heading is that while there is no *substance* to be dealt with here beyond the physical brain, the brain has a special set of *properties* possessed by no other kind of physical object. It is these special properties that are nonphysical: hence the term *property dualism*. The properties in question are the ones you would expect: the property of having a pain, of having a sensation of red, of thinking that *P*, of desiring that *Q*, and so forth. These are the properties that are characteristic of conscious intelligence. They are held to be nonphysical in the sense that they cannot ever be reduced to or explained solely in terms of the concepts of the familiar physical sciences. They will require a wholly new and autonomous science—the "science of mental phenomena"—if they are ever to be adequately understood.

From here, important differences among the positions emerge. Let us begin with what is perhaps the oldest version of property dualism: *epiphenomenalism*. This term is rather a mouthful, but its meaning is simple. The Greek prefix "epi-" means "above," and the position at issue holds that mental phenomena are not a part of the physical phenomena in the brain that ultimately determine our actions and behavior, but rather ride "above the fray." Mental phenomena are thus *epi*phenomena. They are held to just appear or emerge when the growing brain passes a certain level of complexity.

But there is more. The epiphenomenalist holds that while mental phenomena are caused to occur by the various activities of the brain, *they do not have any causal effects in turn*. They are entirely impotent with respect to causal effects on the physical world. They are *mere* epiphenomena. (To fix our ideas, a vague metaphor may be helpful here. Think of our conscious mental states as little sparkles of shimmering light that occur on the wrinkled surface of the brain, sparkles which are caused to occur by physical activity in the brain, but which have no causal effects on the brain in return.) This means that the universal conviction that one's actions are determined by one's desires, decisions, and volitions is false! One's actions are exhaustively determined by physical events in the brain, which events *also* cause the epiphenomena we call desires, decisions, and volitions. There is therefore a constant conjunction between volitions and actions. But according to the epiphenomenalist, it is mere illusion that the former cause the latter.

What could motivate such a strange view? In fact, it is not too difficult to understand why someone might take it seriously. Put yourself in the shoes of a neuroscientist who is concerned to trace the origins of behavior back up the motor nerves to the active cells in the motor cortex of the cerebrum, and to trace in turn their activity into inputs from other parts of the brain, and from the various sensory nerves. She finds a thoroughly physical system of awesome structure and delicacy, and much intricate activity, all of it unambiguously chemical or electrical in nature, and she finds no hint at all of any nonphysical inputs of the kind that substance dualism proposes. What is she to think? From the standpoint of her researches, human behavior is exhaustively a function of the activity of the physical brain. And this opinion is further supported by her confidence that the brain has the behavior-controlling features it does exactly because those features have been ruthlessly selected for during the brain's long evolutionary history. In sum, the seat of human behavior appears entirely physical in its constitution, in its origins, and in its internal activities.

On the other hand, our neuroscientist has the testimony of her own introspection to account for as well. She can hardly deny that she has experiences, beliefs, and desires, nor that they are connected in some way with her behavior. One bargain that can be struck here is to admit the *reality* of mental properties, as nonphysical properties, but demote them to the status of impotent epiphenomena that have nothing to do with the scientific explanation of human and animal behavior. This is the position the epiphenomenalist takes, and the reader can now perceive the rationale behind it. It is a bargain struck between the desire to respect a rigorously scientific approach to the explanation of behavior, and the desire to respect the testimony of introspection.

The epiphenomenalist's "demotion" of mental properties—to causally impotent byproducts of brain activity—has seemed too extreme for most property dualists, and a theory closer to the convictions of common sense has enjoyed somewhat greater popularity. This view, which we may call *interactionist property dualism*, differs from the previous view in only one essential respect: the interactionist asserts that mental properties do indeed have causal effects on the brain, and thereby, on behavior. The mental properties of the brain are an integrated part of the general causal fray, in systematic interaction with the brain's physical properties. One's actions, therefore, are held to be caused by one's desires and volitions after all.

As before, mental properties are here said to be *emergent* properties, properties that do not appear at all until ordinary physical matter has managed to organize itself, through the evolutionary process, into a system of sufficient complexity. Examples of properties that are emergent in this sense would be the property of being *solid*, the property of being *colored*, and the property of being *alive*. All of these require matter to be suitably organized before they can be displayed. With this much, any materialist will agree. But any property dualist makes the further claim that mental states and properties are *irreducible,* in the sense that they are not just organizational features of physical matter, as are the examples cited. They are said to be novel properties beyond prediction or explanation by physical science.

This last condition—the irreducibility of mental properties—is an important one, since this is what makes the position a dualist position. But it sits poorly with the joint claim that mental properties emerge from nothing more than the organizational achievements of physical matter. If that is how mental properties are produced, then one would expect a physical account of them to be possible. The simultaneous claim of evolutionary emergence *and* physical irreducibility is prima facie puzzling.

A property dualist is not absolutely bound to insist on both claims. He could let go the thesis of evolutionary emergence, and claim that mental properties are *fundamental* properties of reality, properties that have been here from the universe's inception, properties on a par with length, mass, electric charge, and other fundamental properties. There is even an historical precedent for a position of this kind. At the turn of this century it was still widely believed that electromagnetic phenomena (such as electric charge and magnetic attraction) were just an unusually subtle manifestation of purely *mechanical* phenomena. Some scientists thought that a reduction of electromagnetics to mechanics was more or less in the bag. They thought that radio waves, for example, would turn out to be just travelling oscillations in a very subtle but jelly-like aether that fills space everywhere. But the aether turned out not to exist. So electromagnetic properties turned out to be fundamental properties in their own right, and we were forced to add electric charge to the existing list of fundamental properties (mass, length, and duration).

Perhaps mental properties enjoy a status like that of electromagnetic properties: irreducible, but not emergent. Such a view may be called *elemental-property dualism,* and it has the advantage of clarity over the previous view.

Unfortunately, the parallel with electromagnetic phenomena has one very obvious failure. Unlike electromagnetic properties, which are displayed at all levels of reality from the subatomic level on up, mental properties are displayed only in large physical systems that have evolved a very complex internal organization. The case for the evolutionary emergence of mental properties through the organization of matter is extremely strong. They do not appear to be basic or elemental at all. This returns us, therefore, to the issue of their irreducibility. Why should we accept this most basic of the dualist's claims? Why be a dualist?

ARGUMENTS FOR DUALISM

Here we shall examine some of the main considerations commonly offered in support of dualism. Criticism will be postponed for a moment so that we may appreciate the collective force of these supporting considerations.

A major source of dualistic convictions is the religious belief many of us bring to these issues. Each of the major religions is in its way a theory about the cause or purpose of the universe, and Man's place within it, and many of them are committed to the notion of an immortal soul—that is, to some form of substance dualism. Supposing that one is consistent, to consider disbelieving dualism is to consider disbelieving one's religious heritage, and some of us find that difficult to do. Call this the *argument from religion.*

A more universal consideration is the *argument from introspection.* The fact is, when you center your attention on the contents of your consciousness, you do not clearly apprehend a neural network pulsing with electrochemical activity: you apprehend a flux of thoughts, sensations, desires, and emotions. It seems that mental states and properties, as revealed in introspection, could hardly be more different from physical states and properties if they tried. The verdict of introspection, therefore, seems strongly on the side of some form of dualism—on the side of property dualism, at a minimum.

A cluster of important considerations can be collected under the *argument from irreducibility*. Here one points to a variety of mental phenomena where it seems clear that no purely physical explanation could possibly account for what is going on. Descartes has already cited our ability to use language in a way that is relevant to our changing circumstances, and he was impressed also with our faculty of Reason, particularly as it is displayed in our capacity for mathematical reasoning. These abilities, he thought, must surely be beyond the capacity of any physical system. More recently, the introspectible qualities of our sensations (sensory "qualia"), and the meaningful content of our thoughts and beliefs, have also been cited as phenomena that will forever resist reduction to the physical. Consider, for example, seeing the color or smelling the fragrance of a rose. A physicist or chemist might know everything about the molecular structure of the rose, and of the human brain, argues the dualist, but that knowledge would not enable him to predict or anticipate the quality of these inexpressible experiences.

Finally, parapsychological phenomena are occasionally cited in favor of dualism. Telepathy (mind reading), precognition (seeing the future), telekinesis (thought control of material objects), and clairvoyance (knowledge of distant objects) are all awkward to explain within the normal confines of psychology and physics. If these phenomena are real, they might well be reflecting the superphysical nature that the dualist ascribes to the mind. Trivially they are *mental* phenomena, and if they are also forever beyond physical explanation, then at least some mental phenomena must be irreducibly nonphysical.

Collectively, these considerations may seem compelling. But there are serious criticisms of each, and we must examine them as well. Consider first the argument from religion. There is certainly nothing wrong in principle with appealing to a more general theory that bears on the case at issue, which is what the appeal to religion amounts to. But the appeal can only be as good as the scientific credentials of the religion(s) being appealed to, and here the appeals tend to fall down rather badly. In general, attempts to decide scientific questions by appeal to religious orthodoxy have a very sorry history. That the stars are other suns, that the earth is not the center of the universe, that diseases are caused by microorganisms, that the earth is billions of years old, that life is a physicochemical phenomenon; all of these crucial insights were strongly and sometimes viciously resisted, because the dominant religion of the time happened to think otherwise. Giordano Bruno was burned at the stake for urging the first view; Galileo was forced by threat of torture in the Vatican's basement to recant the second view; the firm belief that disease was a punishment visited by the Devil allowed public health practices that brought chronic plagues to most of the cities of Europe; and the age of the earth and the evolution of life were forced to fight an uphill battle against religious prejudice even in an age of supposed enlightenment.

History aside, the almost universal opinion that one's own religious convictions are the reasoned outcome of a dispassionate evaluation of all of the major alternatives is almost demonstrably false for humanity in general. If that really were the genesis of most people's convictions, then one would expect the major faiths to be distributed more or less randomly or evenly over the globe. But in fact they show a very strong tendency to cluster: Christianity is centered in Europe and the Americas, Islam in Africa and the Middle East, Hinduism in India, and Buddhism in the Orient. Which illustrates what we all suspected anyway: that *social forces* are the primary determinants of religious belief for people in general. To decide scientific questions by appeal to religious orthodoxy would therefore be to put social forces in place of empirical evidence. For all of these reasons, professional scientists and philosophers concerned with the nature of mind generally do their best to keep religious appeals out of the discussion entirely.

The argument from introspection is a much more interesting argument, since it tries to appeal to the direct experience of everyman. But the argument is deeply suspect, in that it assumes that our faculty of inner observation or introspection reveals things as they really are in their innermost nature. This assumption is suspect because we already know that our other forms of observation—sight, hearing, touch, and so on—do no such thing. The red surface of an apple does not *look* like a matrix of molecules reflecting photons at certain critical wavelengths, but that is what it is. The sound of a flute does not *sound* like a sinusoidal compression wave train in the atmosphere, but that is what it is. The warmth of the summer air does not *feel* like the mean kinetic energy of millions of tiny molecules, but that is what it is. If one's pains and hopes and beliefs do not *introspectively* seem like electrochemical states in a neural network, that may be only because our faculty of introspection, like our other senses, is not sufficiently penetrating to reveal such hidden details. Which is just what one would expect anyway. The argument from introspection is therefore entirely without force, unless we can somehow argue that the faculty of introspection is quite different from all other forms of observation.

The argument from irreducibility presents a more serious challenge, but here also its force is less than first impression suggests. Consider first our capacity for mathematical reasoning which so impressed Descartes. The last ten years have made available, to anyone with fifty dollars to spend, electronic calculators whose capacity for mathematical reasoning—the calculational part, at least—far surpasses that of any normal human. The fact is, in the centuries since Descartes' writings, philosophers, logicians, mathematicians, and computer scientists have managed to isolate the general principles of mathematical reasoning, and electronics engineers have created machines that compute in accord with

those principles. The result is a hand-held object that would have astonished Descartes. This outcome is impressive not just because machines have proved capable of some of the capacities boasted by human reason, but because some of those achievements invade areas of human reason that past dualistic philosophers have held up as forever closed to mere physical devices.

Although debate on the matter remains open, Descartes' argument from language use is equally dubious. The notion of a *computer language* is by now a commonplace: consider BASIC, PASCAL, FORTRAN, APL, LISP, and so on. Granted, these artificial "languages" are much simpler in structure and content than human natural language, but the differences may be differences only of degree, and not of kind. As well, the theoretical work of Noam Chomsky and the generative grammar approach to linguistics have done a great deal to explain the human capacity for language use in terms that invite simulation by computers. I do not mean to suggest that truly conversational computers are just around the corner. We have a great deal yet to learn, and fundamental problems yet to solve (mostly having to do with our capacity for inductive or theoretical reasoning). But recent progress here does nothing to support the claim that language use must be forever impossible for a purely physical system. On the contrary, such a claim now appears rather arbitrary and dogmatic.

The next issue is also a live problem: How can we possibly hope to explain or to predict the intrinsic qualities of our sensations, or the meaningful content of our beliefs and desires, in purely physical terms? This is a major challenge to the materialist. But as we shall see in later sections, active research programs are already under way on both problems, and positive suggestions are being explored. It is in fact not impossible to imagine how such explanations might go, though the materialist cannot yet pretend to have solved either problem. Until he does, the dualist will retain a bargaining chip here, but that is about all. What the dualists need in order to establish their case is the conclusion that a physical reduction is outright impossible, and that is a conclusion they have failed to establish. Rhetorical questions, like the one that opens this paragraph, do not constitute arguments. And it is equally difficult, note, to imagine how the relevant phenomena could be explained or predicted solely in terms of the substance dualist's nonphysical mind-stuff. The explanatory problem here is a major challenge to everybody, not just to the materialist. On this issue then, we have a rough standoff.

The final argument in support of dualism urged the existence of parapsychological phenomena such as telepathy and telekinesis, the point being that such mental phenomena are (a) real, and (b) beyond purely physical explanation. This argument is really another instance of the argument from irreducibility discussed above, and as before, it is not entirely clear that such phenomena, even if real, must forever escape a purely physical explanation. The materialist can already suggest a possible mechanism for telepathy, for example. On his view, thinking is an electrical activity within the brain. But according to electromagnetic theory, such changing motions of electric charges must produce electromagnetic waves radiating at the speed of light in all directions, waves that will contain information about the electrical activity that produced them. Such waves can subsequently have effects on the electrical activity of other brains, that is, on their thinking. Call this the "radio transmitter/receiver" theory of telepathy.

I do not for a moment suggest that this theory is true; the electromagnetic waves emitted by the brain are fantastically weak (billions of times weaker than the ever present background electromagnetic flux produced by commercial radio stations), and they are almost certain to be hopelessly jumbled together as well. This is one reason why, in the absence of systematic, compelling, and repeatable evidence for the existence of telepathy, one must doubt its possibility. But it is significant that the materialist has the theoretical resources to suggest a

detailed possible explanation of telepathy, if it were real, which is more than any dualist has so far done. It is not at all clear, then, that the materialist *must* be at an explanatory disadvantage in these matters. Quite the reverse.

Put the preceding aside, if you wish, for the main difficulty with the argument from parapsychological phenomena is much, much simpler. Despite the endless pronouncements and anecdotes in the popular press, and despite a steady trickle of serious research on such things, there is no significant or trustworthy evidence that such phenomena even exist. The wide gap between popular conviction on this matter, and the actual evidence, is something that itself calls for research. For there is not a single parapsychological effect that can be repeatedly or reliably produced in any laboratory suitably equipped to perform and control the experiment. Not one. Honest researchers have been repeatedly hoodwinked by "psychic" charlatans with skills derived from the magician's trade, and the history of the subject is largely a history of gullibility, selection of evidence, poor experimental controls, and outright fraud by the occasional researcher as well. If someone really does discover a repeatable parapsychological effect, then we shall have to reevaluate the situation, but as things stand, there is nothing here to support a dualist theory of mind.

Upon critical examination, the arguments in support of dualism lose much of their force. But we are not yet done: there are arguments against dualism, and these also require examination.

ARGUMENTS AGAINST DUALISM

The first argument against dualism urged by the materialists appeals to the greater *simplicity* of their view. It is a principle of rational methodology that, if all else is equal, the simpler of two competing hypotheses should be preferred. This principle is sometimes called "Ockham's Razor"—after William of Ockham, the medieval philosopher who first enunciated it—and it can also be expressed as follows: "Do not multiply entities beyond what is strictly necessary to explain the phenomena." The materialist postulates only one kind of substance (physical matter), and one class of properties (physical properties), whereas the dualist postulates two kinds of matter and/or two classes of properties. And to no explanatory advantage, charges the materialist.

This is not yet a decisive point against dualism, since neither dualism nor materialism can yet explain all of the phenomena to be explained. But the objection does have some force, especially since there is no doubt at all that physical matter exists, while spiritual matter remains a tenuous hypothesis.

If this latter hypothesis brought us some definite explanatory advantage obtainable in no other way, then we would happily violate the demand for simplicity, and we would be right to do so. But it does not, claims the materialist. In fact, the advantage is just the other way around, he argues, and this brings us to the second objection to dualism: the relative *explanatory impotence* of dualism as compared to materialism.

Consider, very briefly, the explanatory resources already available to the neurosciences. We know that the brain exists and what it is made of. We know much of its microstructure: how the neurons are organized into systems and how distinct systems are connected to one another, to the motor nerves going out to the muscles, and to the sensory nerves coming in from the sense organs. We know much of their microchemistry: how the nerve cells fire tiny electrochemical pulses along their various fibers, and how they make other cells fire also, or cease firing. We know some of how such activity processes sensory information, selecting salient or subtle bits to be sent on to higher systems. And we know some of how such activity initiates and coordinates bodily behavior. Thanks mainly to neurology (the branch of medicine concerned with brain pathology), we know a great deal about the correlations between damage to various parts of the human brain, and various behavioral and cognitive deficits from which the victims suffer. There are a great many isolated deficits—some gross, some subtle—that are familiar to neurologists (inability to speak, or to read, or to understand speech, or to recognize faces, or to add/subtract, or to move a certain limb, or to put information into long-term memory, and so on), and their appearance is closely tied to the occurrence of damage to very specific parts of the brain.

Nor are we limited to cataloguing traumas. The growth and development of the brain's microstructure is also something that neuroscience has explored, and such development appears to be the basis of various kinds of learning by the organism. Learning, that is, involves lasting chemical and physical changes in the brain. In sum, the neuroscientist can tell us a great deal about the brain, about its constitution and the physical laws that govern it; he can already explain much of our behavior in terms of the physical, chemical, and electrical properties of the brain; and he has the theoretical resources available to explain a good deal more as our explorations continue.

Compare now what the neuroscientist can tell us about the brain, and what he can do with that knowledge, with what the dualist can tell us about spiritual substance, and what he can do with those assumptions. Can the dualist tell us anything about the internal constitution of mind-stuff? Of the nonmaterial elements that make it up? Of the laws that govern their behavior? Of the mind's structural connections with the body? Of the manner of its operations? Can he explain human capacities and pathologies in terms of its structures and its defects? The fact is, the dualist can do none of these things, because no detailed theory of mind-stuff has ever been formulated. Compared to the rich resources and explanatory successes of current materialism, dualism is less a theory of mind than it is an empty space waiting for a genuine theory of mind to be put in it.

Thus argues the materialist. But again, this is not a completely decisive point against dualism. The dualist can admit that the brain plays a major role in the administration of both perception and behavior—on his view the brain is the *mediator* between the mind and the body—but he may attempt to argue that the materialist's current successes and future explanatory prospects concern only the mediative functions of the brain, not the *central* capacities of the nonphysical mind, capacities such as reason, emotion, and consciousness itself. On these latter topics, he may argue, both dualism *and* materialism currently draw a blank.

But this reply is not a very good one. So far as the capacity for reasoning is concerned, machines already exist that execute in minutes sophisticated deductive and mathematical calculations that would take a human a lifetime to execute. And so far as the other two mental capacities are concerned, studies of such things as depression, motivation, attention, and sleep have revealed many interesting and puzzling facts about the neurochemical and neurodynamical basis of both emotion and consciousness. The *central* capacities, no less than the peripheral, have been addressed with profit by various materialist research programs.

In any case, the (substance) dualist's attempt to draw a sharp distinction between the unique "mental" capacities proper to the nonmaterial mind, and the merely mediative capacities of the brain, prompts an argument that comes close to being an outright refutation of (substance) dualism. If there really is a distinct entity in which reasoning, emotion, and consciousness take place, and if that entity is dependent on the brain for nothing more than sensory experiences as input and volitional executions as output, *then one would expect reason, emotion, and consciousness to be relatively invulnerable to direct control or pathology by manipulation or damage to the brain.* But in fact the exact opposite is true. Alcohol, narcotics, or senile degeneration of nerve tissue will impair, cripple, or even destroy one's capacity for rational thought. Psychiatry knows of hundreds of emotion-controlling chemicals (lithium, chlorpromazine, amphetamine, cocaine, and so on) that do their work when vectored into the brain. And the vulnerability of consciousness to the anesthetics, to caffeine, and to something as simple as a sharp blow to the head, shows its very close dependence on neural activity in the brain. All of this makes perfect sense if reason, emotion, and consciousness are activities of the brain itself. But it makes very little sense if they are activities of something else entirely.

We may call this the argument from the *neural dependence* of all known mental phenomena. Property dualism, note, is not threatened by this argument, since, like materialism, property dualism reckons the brain as the seat of all mental activity. We shall conclude this section, however, with an argument that cuts against both varieties of dualism: the argument from *evolutionary history.*

What is the origin of a complex and sophisticated species such as ours? What, for that matter, is the origin of the dolphin, the mouse, or the housefly? Thanks to the fossil record, comparative anatomy, and the biochemistry of proteins and nucleic acids, there is no longer any significant doubt on this matter. Each existing species is a surviving type from a number of variations on an earlier type of organism; each earlier type is in turn a surviving type from a number of variations on a still earlier type of organism; and so on down the branches of the evolutionary tree until, some three billion years ago, we find a trunk of just one or a handful of very simple organisms. These organisms, like their more complex offspring, are just self-repairing, self-replicating, energy-driven molecular structures. (That evolutionary trunk has its own roots in an earlier era of purely chemical evolution, in which the molecular elements of life were themselves pieced together.) The mechanism of development that has structured this tree has two main elements: (1) the occasional blind variation in types of reproducing creature, and (2) the selective survival of some of these types due to the relative reproductive advantage enjoyed by individuals of those types. Over periods of geological time, such a process can produce an enormous variety of organisms, some of them very complex indeed.

For purposes of our discussion, the important point about the standard evolutionary story is that the human species and all of its features are the wholly physical outcome of a purely physical process. Like all but the simplest of organisms, we have a nervous system. And for the same reason: a nervous system permits the discriminative guidance of behavior. But a nervous system is just an active matrix of cells, and a cell is just an active matrix of molecules. We are

notable only in that our nervous system is more complex and powerful than those of our fellow creatures. Our inner nature differs from that of simpler creatures in degree, but not in kind.

If this is the correct account of our origins, then there seems neither need, nor room, to fit any nonphysical substances or properties into our theoretical account of ourselves. We are creatures of matter. And we should learn to live with that fact.

Arguments like these have moved most (but not all) of the professional community to embrace some form of materialism. This has not produced much unanimity, however, since the differences between the several materialist positions are even wider than the differences that divide dualism.

Study Questions

1. Explain the difference between substance dualism and property dualism.
2. Present two arguments in favor of dualism.
3. Present two arguments against dualism.
4. According to Churchland, what is the connection between evolution and dualism?

What Is It Like to Be a Bat?

THOMAS NAGEL

If materialism is correct and a person is identical with a body, can we explain the phenomenon we all experience of being conscious? How can my body be conscious? Is my consciousness like yours? Is ours like that of animals? This last question is explored by Thomas Nagel, Professor of Philosophy at New York University, who wonders what it would be like to be a bat and goes on to explain how the question bears directly on the mind-body problem.

From Thomas Nagel, "What Is It Like to Be a Bat?" in *The Philosophical Review*, Volume LXXXIII, no. 4, pp. 435–450.

Conscious experience is a widespread phenomenon. It occurs at many levels of animal life, though we cannot be sure of its presence in the simpler organisms, and it is very difficult to say in general what provides evidence of it. (Some extremists have been prepared to deny it even of mammals other than man.) No doubt it occurs in countless forms totally unimaginable to us, on other planets in other solar systems throughout the universe. But no matter how the form may vary, the fact that an organism has conscious experiences *at all* means, basically, that there is something it is like to *be* that organism. . . .

We may call this the subjective character of experience. . . . It is useless to base the defense of materialism on any analysis of mental phenomena that fails to deal explicitly with their subjective character. . . . [T]o make evident the importance of subjective features, it will help to explore the matter in relation to an example. . . .

I assume we all believe that bats have experience. After all, they are mammals, and there is no more doubt that they have experience than that mice or pigeons or whales have experience. I have chosen bats instead of wasps or flounders because if one travels too far down the phylogenetic tree, people gradually shed their faith that there is experience there at all. Bats, although more closely related to us than those other species, nevertheless present a range of activity and a sensory apparatus so different from ours that the problem I want to pose is exceptionally vivid (though it certainly could be raised with other species). Even without the benefit of philosophical reflection, anyone who has spent some time in an enclosed space with an excited bat knows what it is to encounter a fundamentally *alien* form of life.

I have said that the essence of the belief that bats have experience is that there is something that it is like to be a bat. Now we know that most bats (the microchiroptera, to be precise) perceive the external world primarily by sonar, or echolocation, detecting the reflections, from objects within range, of their own rapid, subtly modulated, high-frequency shrieks. Their brains are designed to correlate the outgoing impulses with the subsequent echoes, and the information thus acquired enables bats to make precise discrimination of distance, size, shape, motion, and texture comparable to those we make by vision. But bat sonar, though clearly a form of perception, is not similar in its operation to any sense that we possess, and there is no reason to suppose that it is subjectively like anything we can experience or imagine. This appears to create difficulties for the notion of what it is like to be a bat. We must consider whether any method will permit us to extrapolate to the inner life of the bat from our own case,[1] and if not, what alternative methods there may be for understanding the notion.

Our own experience provides the basic material for our imagination, whose range is therefore limited. It will not help to try to imagine that one has webbing on one's arms, which enables one to fly around at dusk and dawn catching insects in one's mouth; that one has very poor vision, and perceives the surrounding world by a system of reflected high-frequency sound signals; and that one spends the day hanging upside down by one's feet in an attic. Insofar as I can imagine this (which is not very far), it tells me only what it would be like for *me* to behave as a bat behaves. But that is not the question. I want know what it is like for a *bat* to be a bat. Yet if I try to imagine this, I am restricted to the resources of my own mind, and those resources are inadequate to the task. I cannot perform it either by imagining additions to my present experience, or by imagining segments gradually subtracted from it, or by imagining some combination of additions, subtractions, and modifications.

To the extent that I could look and behave like a wasp or a bat without changing my fundamental structure, my experiences would not be anything like the experiences of those animals. On the other hand, it is doubtful that any meaning can be attached to the supposition that I should possess the internal neurophysiological constitution of a bat. Even if I could by gradual degrees be transformed into a bat, nothing in my present constitution enables me to imagine what the experiences of such a future stage of myself thus metamorphosed would be like. The best evidence would come from the experiences of bats, if we only knew what they were like.

So if extrapolation from our own case is involved in the idea of what it is like to be a bat, the extrapolation must be incompletable. We cannot form more than a schematic conception of what it *is* like. For example, we may ascribe general *types* of experience on the basis of the animal's structure and behavior. Thus we describe bat sonar as a form of three-dimensional forward perception; we believe that bats feel some versions of pain, fear, hunger, and lust, and that they have other, more familiar types of perception besides sonar. But we believe that these experiences also have in each case a specific subjective character, which it is beyond our ability to conceive. And if there is conscious life elsewhere in the universe, it is likely that some of it will not be describable even in the most general experiential terms available to us.[2] (The problem is not confined to exotic cases, however, for it exists between one person and another. The subjective character of the experience of a person deaf and blind from birth is not accessible to me, for example, nor presumably is mine to him. This does not prevent us each from believing that the other's experience has such a subjective character.)

If anyone is inclined to deny that we can believe in the existence of facts like this whose exact nature we cannot possibly conceive, he should reflect that in contemplating the bats we are in much the same position that intelligent bats or Martians[3] would occupy if they tried to form a conception of what it was like to be us. The structure of their own minds might make it impossible for them to succeed, but we know they would be wrong to conclude that there is not anything precise that it is like to be us: that only certain general types of mental state could be ascribed to us (perhaps perception and appetite would be concepts common to us both;

perhaps not). We know they would be wrong to draw such a skeptical conclusion because we know what it is like to be us. And we know that while it includes an enormous amount of variation and complexity, and while we do not possess the vocabulary to describe it adequately, its subjective character is highly specific, and in some respects describable in terms that can be understood only by creatures like us. The fact that we cannot expect ever to accommodate in our language a detailed description of Martian or bat phenomenology should not lead us to dismiss as meaningless the claim that bats and Martians have experiences fully comparable in richness of detail to our own. It would be fine if someone were to develop concepts and a theory that enabled us to think about those things, but such an understanding may be permanently denied to us by the limits of our nature. . . .

My realism about the subjective domain in all its forms implies a belief in the existence of facts beyond the reach of human concepts. Certainly it is possible for a human being to believe that there are facts which humans never *will* possess the requisite concepts to represent or comprehend. Indeed, it would be foolish to doubt this, given the finiteness of humanity's expectations. . . . But one might also believe that there are facts which *could* not ever be represented or comprehended by human beings, even if the species lasted forever—simply because our structure does not permit us to operate with concepts of the requisite type. . . . Reflection on what it is like to be a bat seems to lead us, therefore, to the conclusion that there are facts that do not consist in the truth of propositions expressible in a human language. . . .

This bears directly on the mind-body problem. For if the facts of experience—facts about what it is like *for* the experiencing organism— are accessible only from one point of view, then it is a mystery how the true character of experiences could be revealed in the physical operation of that organism. The latter is a domain of objective facts par excellence—the kind that can be observed and understood from many points of view and by individuals with differing perceptual systems. There are no comparable imaginative obstacles to the acquisition of knowledge about bat neurophysiology by human scientists, and intelligent bats or Martians might learn more about the human brain than we ever will. . . .

In the case of experience, on the other hand, the connexion with a particular point of view seems much closer. It is difficult to understand what could be meant by the *objective* character of an experience, apart from the particular point of view from which its subject apprehends it. After all, what would be left of what it was like to be a bat if one removed the viewpoint of the bat?

NOTES

1. By "our own case," I do not mean just "my own case," but rather the mentalistic ideas that we apply unproblematically to ourselves and other human beings.

2. Therefore the analogical form of the English expression "what it is *like*" is misleading. It does not mean "what (in our experience) it *resembles*," but rather "how it is for the subject himself."

3. Any intelligent extraterrestrial beings totally different from us.

Study Questions

1. What does Nagel mean by "the subjective character of experience"?
2. Do you agree that bats have experiences?
3. Does Nagel believe in the existence of facts beyond the reach of any concept?
4. According to Nagel, how does reflection on what it is like to be a bat relate to the mind-body problem?

Do Computers Think?

JOHN SEARLE

John Searle, Professor of Philosophy at the University of California, Berkeley, asks us to consider a man with no knowledge of Chinese who is placed in a room containing a basket of Chinese symbols and a rule book telling him which Chinese symbols to match with others solely on the basis of their shape. Using the rule book he is able to answer in Chinese questions posed in Chinese. His successful manipulation of the Chinese symbols, however, does not give him an understanding of Chinese. So too, according to Searle, a computer's following its program does not give it thought.

From John Searle, "Is the Brain's Mind a Computer Program?" *Scientific American*, 1990. Reprinted by permission of the journal.

Can a machine think? Can a machine have conscious thoughts in exactly the same sense that you and I have? If by "machine" one means a physical system capable of performing certain functions (and what else can one mean?), then humans are machines of a special biological kind, and humans can think, and so of course machines can think. And, for all we know, it might be possible to produce a thinking machine out of different materials altogether—say, out of silicon chips or vacuum tubes. Maybe it will turn out to be impossible, but we certainly do not know that yet.

In recent decades, however, the question of whether a machine can think has been given a different interpretation entirely. The question that has been posed in its place is, Could a machine think just by virtue of implementing a computer program? Is the program by itself constitutive of thinking? This is a completely different question because it is not about the physical, causal properties of actual or possible physical systems but rather about the abstract, computational properties of formal computer programs that can be implemented in any sort of substance at all, provided only that the substance is able to carry the program.

A fair number of researchers in artificial intelligence (AI) believe the answer to the second question is yes; that is, they believe that by designing the right programs with the right inputs and outputs, they are literally creating minds. They believe furthermore that they have a scientific test for determining success or failure: the Turing test devised by Alan M. Turing, the founding father of artificial intelligence. The Turing test, as currently understood, is simply this: if a computer can perform in such a way that an expert cannot distinguish its performance from that of a human who has a certain cognitive ability—say, the ability to do addition or to understand Chinese—then the computer also has that ability. So the goal is to design programs that will simulate human cognition in such a way as to pass the Turing test. What is more, such a program would not merely be a model of the mind; it would literally be a mind, in the same sense that a human mind is a mind.

By no means does every worker in artificial intelligence accept so extreme a view. A more cautious approach is to think of computer models as being useful in studying the mind in the same way that they are useful in studying the weather, economics or molecular biology. To distinguish these two approaches, I call the first strong AI and the second weak AI. It is important to see just how bold an approach strong AI is. Strong AI claims that thinking is merely the manipulation of formal symbols, and that is exactly what the computer does: manipulate formal symbols. This view is often summarized by saying, "The mind is to the brain as the program is to the hardware."

Strong AI is unusual among theories of the mind in at least two respects: it can be stated clearly, and it admits of a simple and decisive refutation. The refutation is one that any person can try for himself or herself. Here is how it goes. Consider a language you don't understand. In my case, I do not understand Chinese. To me Chinese writing looks like so many meaningless squiggles. Now suppose I am placed in a room containing baskets full of Chinese symbols. Suppose also that I am given a rule book in English for matching Chinese symbols with other Chinese symbols. The rules identify the symbols entirely by their shapes and do not require that I understand any of them. The rules might say such things as, "Take a squiggle-squiggle sign from basket number one and put it next to a squoggle-squoggle sign from basket number two."

Imagine that people outside the room who understand Chinese hand in small bunches of symbols and that in response I manipulate the symbols according to the rule book and hand back more small bunches of symbols. Now, the rule book is the "computer program." The people who wrote it are "programmers," and

I am the "computer." The baskets full of symbols are the "data base," the small bunches that are handed in to me are "questions" and the bunches I then hand out are "answers."

Now suppose that the rule book is written in such a way that my "answers" to the "questions" are indistinguishable from those of a native Chinese speaker. For example, the people outside might hand me some symbols that unknown to me mean, "What's your favorite color?" and I might after going through the rules give back symbols that, also unknown to me, mean, "My favorite is blue, but I also like green a lot." I satisfy the Turing test for understanding Chinese. All the same, I am totally ignorant of Chinese. And there is no way I could come to understand Chinese in the system as described, since there is no way that I can learn the meanings of any of the symbols. Like a computer, I manipulate symbols, but I attach no meaning to the symbols.

The point of the thought experiment is this: if I do not understand Chinese solely on the basis of running a computer program for understanding Chinese, then neither does any other digital computer solely on that basis. Digital computers merely manipulate formal symbols according to rules in the program.

What goes for Chinese goes for other forms of cognition as well. Just manipulating the symbols is not by itself enough to guarantee cognition, perception, understanding, thinking and so forth. And since computers, qua computers, are symbol-manipulating devices, merely running the computer program is not enough to guarantee cognition.

This simple argument is decisive against the claims of strong AI.

Study Questions

1. Does Searle believe a machine can think?
2. Explain the experiment that uses Chinese symbols.
3. What does Searle believe that the experiment proves?
4. What do you believe that the experiment proves?

The Body Problem

BARBARA MONTERO

Barbara Montero is Professor of Philosophy at the College of Staten Island and The Graduate Center of The City University of New York. She points out that the question whether the mind is physical presumes an understanding of what counts as physical, a point on which agreement is lacking.

From Steven M. Cahn and Maureen Eckert, eds., *Philosophical Horizons*, second edition, Wadsworth, 2012. Reprinted by permission of the publisher.

Is the mind physical? Are mental properties, such as the property of *being in pain* or *thinking about the higher orders of infinity,* actually physical properties? Many philosophers think that they are. For no matter how strange and remarkable consciousness and cognition may be, many hold that they are, nevertheless, entirely physical. While some take this view as a starting point in their discussions about the mind, others, well aware that there are dissenters among the ranks, argue for it strenuously. One wonders, however, just what is being assumed, argued for, or denied. In other words, one wonders: Just what does it mean to be physical? This is the question I call, "the body problem."

As I see it, there is little use in arguing about whether the mind is physical, or whether mental properties are physical properties unless we have at least some understanding of what it means to be physical. In other words, in order to solve the mind-body problem, we must solve the body problem. It strikes me as odd that while bookstores and journals are overflowing with debates about whether consciousness is physical, hardly anyone is concerned with "What counts as physical?" Moreover, it would not be much of an exaggeration to say today, as John Earman did more than twenty years ago, that "attempts to answer this question that have appeared in the philosophical literature are for the most part notable only for their glaring inadequacies."[1] If we want to discuss whether the mind is physical, we should say something about what it means to be physical.

Some may argue that such clarification is unnecessary. They may point out that while we cannot provide necessary and sufficient conditions for *tablehood,* we nonetheless understand the concept, because we can readily identify things that are clearly tables and things that are clearly not. They claim the same is true of our notion of the physical. But the situations are not analogous. While we can identify central cases of being physical—what could be clearer examples of physical than rocks and trees (except, perhaps, quarks and leptons)?—an extra wrinkle

is that rocks and trees (as well as quarks and leptons) are clear cases only assuming that idealism is false. In any case, something needs to be said about how to determine what we can place in the category along with rocks and trees. In certain ways, beliefs and desires *are* like rocks and trees, while quarks and leptons are not. For example, talk of beliefs and desires plays a role in our ordinary folk understanding of the world, while talk of quarks and leptons does not. Beliefs and desires also are part of the same macro-level causal network as rocks and trees, while quarks and leptons are not. But few physicalists think that from our central examples of physical objects we should infer that quarks and leptons are nonphysical.

Perhaps these problems could be overlooked if we had clear intuitions regarding the nonphysical. But do we? The stock example of a nonphysical entity is some kind of ghost. For example, Jaegwon Kim defines "ontological physicalism" as the view that "there are no nonphysical residues (e.g. Cartesian souls, entelechies, and the like)."[2] And Jeffrey Poland states that the physicalist's bottom line is really: "There are no ghosts!"[3] But why is a ghost nonphysical? Is it that they can pass through walls without disturbing them? Neutrinos, I am told, can pass right through the earth without disturbing it, yet neutrinos are classified as physical. Is it that they have no mass? Photons have no mass yet are considered physical. Perhaps it is that they supposedly do not take up space. But if taking up no space shows that something is nonphysical, point particles (if they exist) would have to be classified as nonphysical. Yet physicalists, I take it, would not accept this view. So to say that the physical means "no spooky stuff" does not help matters.

Perhaps physicalism at least excludes the possibility of a ghost in a machine, that is, the view that there is some type of mental substance completely different in kind from physical substance. But what does this view amount to, since most physicalists are happy to admit that there is more than one kind of elementary particle?

Perhaps the idea is that whether only one basic particle exists, say, strings, or it turns out that in addition to strings there are also Ferris wheels, physicalism holds that everything nonbasic is composed of the same kind, or kinds of basic particles. But this view cannot be right. For example, some evidence indicates that what physicists call "dark matter" is composed entirely of axions, hypothetical new elementary particles.[4] Yet dark matter is no threat to physicalism. So the simple notion of *stuff of a different kind* does not provide us with a notion of nonphysical. But what, then, does?

Philosophers commonly answer this question by deferring to the physicists. The physical is said to be whatever the physicist, or more precisely, the particle physicist, tells us exists (what we might now think of as quarks and leptons, as well as the exchange particles, gluons, gravitons, etc.). And the nonphysical is whatever remains, if there is anything. On this view, physicalists—that is, those who hold that everything is physical—claim that physics provides us with an exhaustive and exclusive line to all reality. Here is a straightforward answer to the body problem, but one that is too simple, since most philosophers believe that things like rocks, tables, and chairs are just as physical as quarks, leptons, and gluons.

Granted, whether to say that the physical is only what the physicists take as fundamental is partially a terminological issue. But while the question whether to reserve the name "physical" for just the fundamental constituents of reality or to use it more broadly *is* terminological, the question of how many layers of reality to countenance is not. Because most physicalists allow for not only the smallest stuff, but also for atoms, molecules, rocks and galaxies, the leave-it-to-the-physicists approach is usually amended to the view that the physical world is the world of the fundamental particles, forces, laws and such *as well as* whatever depends on this physical stuff. As such, we can allow for the possibility that rocks may be physical.

My concern, however, is not with the dependence relation *per se* but with what everything is being related to: the lower level dependence base or what is often referred to as "the microphysical." One thinks of microphysical phenomena as described by the most recent microphysics. But if the physical is defined in terms of current microphysics, and a new particle is discovered next week, the particle will not be physical—a consequence most philosophers want to avoid. But if not current microphysics, what else could the microphysical be?

Carl Hempel posed a dilemma for those attempting to define the physical in reference to microphysics.[5] On the one hand, we cannot define the physical in terms of current microphysics since today's microphysics is probably neither entirely true (some of our theories may look as wrong-headed to future generations as phlogiston theory looks to us now) nor complete (more remains to be explained). On the other hand, if we take microphysics to be some future unspecified theory, the claim that the mind is physical is vague, since we currently have no idea of that theory. Faced with this dilemma, what is a physicalist to do?

Some try to take the middle road, explaining the "microphysical" by referring to "something like current microphysics—but just improved."[6] But in what respect is this future microphysics like current microphysics? And in what respect will it be improved? Since these questions are usually not addressed (save, of course, for the implication that it is similar enough to be intelligible yet different enough to be true) it seems that Hempel's dilemma recurs for these compromise views. For the theory in question will be false if it is significantly similar to current physics, and if not, we are left with no clear notion of the physical.

Taking the first horn of Hempel's dilemma, that is, defining the physical in terms of current microphysics, does not provide us with a comfortable solution to the body problem. For it is rather awkward to hold a theory that one knows is false.[7] But does taking the second horn fare any better? David Armstrong thinks so. He explicitly tells us that when he says "physical properties" he is not talking about the properties specified by current physics, but rather "whatever set of properties the physicist in the end will appeal to."[8] Similarly, Frank Jackson holds that the physical facts encompass "everything in a completed physics, chemistry, and neurophysiology, and all there is to know about the causal and relational facts consequent upon all this."[9] As Barry Loewer puts it, "what many have on their minds when they speak of fundamental physical properties is that they are the properties expressed by simple predicates of the true comprehensive fundamental physical theory."[10] So for Armstrong and others the physical is to be defined over a completed physics, a physics in the end. But what is this final physics? The answer, as Hempel has pointed out, is unknown.

Basing one's notion of the physical on an unfathomable theory seems to be a serious enough problem to discourage defining the physical over a final theory. But most philosophers ignore this problem and charge ahead to the more juicy questions, such as whether knowledge of all the physical facts, (whatever they may be) enables us to know what it is like to see colors. So consider that another consequence of using the notion of a completed physics to explain the physical is that, at least under one interpretation, it trivially excludes the possibility that the mind is not physical. For on one understanding of it, a completed physics amounts to a physics that explains *everything*. So if mentality is a feature of the world, a completed physics, on this definition, will explain it too. While there is nothing wrong with trivial truth *per se,* this is not the solution to the mind-body problem most philosophers would accept. For neither physicalists nor their foes think that we already know by definition that the mind is physical.

Chomsky has identified a related problem for those who define the physical in terms of a final physics. His point is that since we cannot predict the course of physics, we cannot be sure that a final physics will not include mental properties, qua mental, as fundamental properties.[11] Yet if final physics takes the mental realm to be

fundamental, the difference dissolves between physicalists who claim that mental properties will be accounted for in final physics and dualists who claim that mental properties are fundamental.

A solution to the body problem is not forthcoming. Perhaps, we should focus on questions other than the question "Is the mind physical?" So let me conclude with a suggestion. Physicalism is, at least partly, motivated by the belief that the mental is ultimately non-mental, that is, that mental properties are not fundamental properties, whereas dualism holds, precisely, that they are. So a crucial question is whether the mental is ultimately nonmental. Of course, the notion of the non-mental is also open-ended. And, for this reason, it may be just as difficult to see what sort of considerations are relevant in determining what counts as non-mental as it is to see what sort of considerations are relevant in determining what counts as physical. However, we do have a grasp of one side of the divide—that is, the mental. So, rather than worrying about whether the mind is physical, we should be concerned with whether it is non-mental. And this question has little to do with what current physics, future physics, or a final physics says about the world.

NOTES

1. John Earman, "What is Physicalism?" *Journal of Philosophy* 72 (1975), p. 566.

2. Jaegwon Kim, "Supervenience, Emergence, Realization in Philosophy of Mind," in M. Carrier and P. Machamer (eds.), *Mindscapes: Philosophy, Science, and the Mind,* Pittsburgh, University of Pittsburgh Press, 1997.

3. Jeffery Poland, *Physicalism: The Philosophical Foundations,* Oxford: Oxford University Press, 1994, p. 15. He emphasizes this point again later: "ghosts, gods, and the paranormal are genuine threats to physicalism" (p. 228). That is, according to Poland, if ghosts were to exist, physicalism would be false.

4. See Leslie Rosenberg, "The Search for Dark Matter Axions," *Particle World* 4 (1995), pp. 3–10.

5. See Carl Hempel, "Comments on Goodman's Ways of Worldmaking," *Synthese* 45 (1980), pp. 193–9. Also see Hempel, "Reduction: Ontological and Linguistic Facets," in S. Morgenbesser, P. Suppes and M. Whit (eds.), *Philosophy, Science and Method: Essays in Honor of Ernest Nagel,* New York: St. Martin's Press, 1969. I am using different terminology from Hempel, and my emphasis is on the question of whether the mind is physical rather than the question of physicalism in general, but the point is essentially the same.

6. See for example, David Lewis, "New Work for a Theory of Universals," *Australasian Journal of Philosophy* 61 (1983), pp. 343–77 and Robert Kirk, *Raw Feeling: A Philosophical Account of the Essence of Consciousness,* New York: Oxford University Press, 1994.

7. For further discussion of this point see Barbara Montero, "The Body Problem," *Nous* 33 (1999), pp. 183–200.

8. David Armstrong, "The Causal Theory of Mind," in D. Rosenthal (ed.) *The Nature of Mind,* New York: Oxford University Press, 1991, p. 186. Of course, not all properties the physicist appeals to are relevant: when a physicist is explaining a proposed budget in a grant application or explaining to her supervisor why she was late to work, she may be appealing to very different properties than when she is applying her mathematical skills in computing a wave function. But perhaps this distinction is intuitive enough.

9. Frank Jackson, "What Mary Didn't Know," in D. Rosenthal (ed.), *The Nature of Mind,* New York: Oxford University Press, 1991, p. 291.

10. Barry Loewer, "Humean Supervenience," *Philosophical Topics* 24 (1996), p. 103.

11. See Noam Chomsky, "Language and Nature," *Mind* 104 (1995), pp. 1–61 and *Language and Thought,* Rhode Island: Moyer Bell, 1993.

Study Questions

1. According to Montero, what is "the body problem"?
2. How does the body problem differ from the mind-body problem?
3. Does Montero agree that a ghost is nonphysical?
4. According to Montero, do we have a clearer grasp of the mental than the physical?

B.   The Self

Hinduism and the Self

JOEL KUPPERMAN

Over 4,000 years old and composed of numerous sects, Hinduism is the religion of the vast majority of the people of India. Hindus seek liberation from suffering by achieving union with the divine.

Hinduism supports a caste system, according to which all people are born into one of four social groups: from lower to higher, they are servants and unskilled laborers, merchants and farmers, rulers and warriors, and spiritual and intellectual leaders, the *Brahmins*. Each has its characteristic rules and customs.

In this article Joel Kupperman, Professor Emeritus of Philosophy at the University of Connecticut, explains the central doctrine of Hindu metaphysics, the claim that *atman*, the true Self, is identical with Brahman, the single divine reality. Later we shall explore the Hindu doctrines of karma and rebirth.

The Upanishads, written in India mainly in the ninth to sixth centuries B.C.E. . . . were—and remain—the core texts of Hinduism, which continues to be by far the dominant religion of India to have adherents in some other countries of South Asia as well.

The Upanishads also are philosophy. Indeed, they are widely viewed as the foundational texts of some major traditions of Indian philosophy, as well as central to the Hindu religion. Further, they are exceptionally subtle and interesting as philosophy. . . .

[T]he metaphysics of the Upanishads . . . centers on a single, deceptively simple claim: *Atman is Brahman*.

Atman (pronounced "aht-man") and Brahman are central to classical Hindu philosophy. Are they central to experience? Perhaps this is not true, at least explicitly, for most of us. But the ancient Indian argument is that it should become true. The right kind of experience is claimed to provide evidence for the identification of *atman* with Brahman.

Let us begin with Brahman. . . . [T]he ancient religion of India worshipped many gods and goddesses. Three gods were paramount: Brahma the creator, Vishnu the preserved, and Shiva the destroyer. . . .

One needs to be mindful of the difference between Brahma, who is merely one god, and Brahman, who is everything. . . . The gods and goddesses all are—if they are properly understood—aspects or personae of the single divine reality, Brahman. This is subtly accommodating to popular religion. The gods and goddesses can continue to be worshipped, but those in the know will be mindful that they are all aspects of Brahman.

Thus far I have been presenting the outlines of a worldview without giving the reasons for it. The reasons for identifying all gods and goddesses with Brahman will emerge when we look at the sources of the idea of *atman*. The link is that gods and goddesses, like human beings, have desires, aversions, and characteristic forms of behavior. In short they have personalities. The central argument underlying the metaphysics of the Upanishads is that personality has only a superficial kind of reality.

The best way of appreciating this view is to examine a persistent feature of human experience, sense of self. Most of us have a feeling, which is familiar but hard to analyze, that there is a "me" close to the surface of our normal experience. When we wake up in unfamiliar surroundings we may not know where we are, but there is the familiar "me." Usually we know who we are by name, but even in cases of amnesia there will be the "me" (although now it is more mysterious).

This "me" gives us a strong sense of ways in which actions and experience in a life—our life—are unified. It enables us to have immediate knowledge, not based on evidence, of connections. Sydney Shoemaker has given the example of knowing that it was I who broke the window yesterday. He points out that it would be over-simple to regard this knowledge as simply based on memory. Memory tells me that *someone* broke the window, but the claim that it was I requires the additional step of judging that I am identical with that person. Normally we do not need to look at videotape, or to consult eyewitnesses, in order to make this judgment.

What most people, quite possibly in every culture, firmly believe is that each of us has a "me" that persists through a life (and perhaps beyond) and that (in some sense) remains the same "me" throughout. This is intuitive and pre-philosophical. The obvious questions are "How do we know this?" and "What does this really mean?"

"How do we know this?" may be one of those questions that does not have a good answer. One thought is that we introspectively can take stock. We could look inside ourselves, that is, for something that looks like a "me," tracking it then as a stable element in our experience. The eighteenth-century Scottish philosopher David Hume tried this experiment and came up empty. This led him, in book 1 of his *Treatise of Human Nature*, to deny that any of us has a self, at least in the sense of a stable, unchanging element of our minds. More than two thousand years earlier, Buddha, reacting against a philosophical tradition that provided the base for what became known as Hinduism, tried the same experiment with the same result.

We need not conclude that the notion of a persistent and stable "me" is nonsense or is wrong. Perhaps the experiment of looking inward for a real self was miscast? Critics of Hume have sometimes asked, "If Hume looked for his self and failed to find it, what was doing the looking?" The difficulty of introspective search would seem to be that it is naturally "dualistic": that is, there is a separation between something looking and something looked for. But maybe a self, if there is one, includes both elements. Perhaps, then, a form of experience that is nondual, if such be possible, would be more successful?

Another alternative is that the self, rather than being an element of experience, is something posited in relation to all possible experience. This was the view of the eighteenth-century philosopher Immanuel Kant. He held that the self (at least the self connected with experience) is a unifying feature of the structure of experience and not something that could be an item within the structure.

The Upanishads offer an answer different from this, one that does appeal to a special kind of experience. Unlike Hume's introspection, this special kind of experience is not available to everyone. It requires extensive preparation and hard work. Its features are more easily explained if we first become clear about what the Upanishads mean by *atman*, and also how they are sure that it can be found if one searches for it in the proper way.

We have seen that there is a widespread assumption that each of us has a stable, persistent self. Can such a self change? Intuitively it might seem that the answer is "Yes." You are the same person you were a few years ago, even though undoubtedly you have changed in some respects. Reflective examination, though, undermines this intuitive confidence. We could imagine someone who is more like you were a few years ago than you now are. What then? The usual response is that, all the same, you (now) are you (then). Given continuous surveillance, we could have tracked you during the intervening period; and this continuity strengthens our sense of identity, even if the changes in you were in fact very great.

This line of thought would leave us with an identity that looks tempered by matters of degree. The ancient Greek philosopher Heraclitus is famous for the cryptic utterance "You can't step in the same river twice." What he presumably meant is that the river is constantly changing (different water flows through, there can be tiny variations in the positions of the river banks, etc.) so that, strictly speaking, today's river is not (entirely) the same as yesterday's river. In much the same spirit he might have argued that you can't be the same person today that you were yesterday. But a possible response is that we have conventions of language that enable rivers and persons to keep their names, and to count as the same by being pretty much the same.

These conventions usually work pretty well. But there are imaginable cases in which they start to break down. Some of these involve great change. If the river became very like what we would normally call a lake, that would put our sense of being confronted with the "same" river under considerable pressure. We could imagine cases in which someone's brain were entirely taken over by a terrible virus that had its own personality (and perhaps even its own name), in which there would be great hesitation in judging that what we were confronting is the same person we had known.

There also are imaginable cases in which what we might normally judge to be the same has close competitors that also might seem the same, thus introducing doubt. The Oxford philosopher Derek Parfit, in his *Reasons and Persons,* has given a nice example of this. He imagines your traveling to Mars by Teletransporter. This process involves going to a room on Earth and pressing a green button. You lose consciousness; all your cells are destroyed on Earth, and at the same time you are reassembled on Mars. After you have made several trips this way, there is one in which there is a malfunctioning of the apparatus. You regain consciousness on Earth but now there is also a you on Mars. This duplication might seem to create problems, but an attendant assures you that the you still on Earth will within a short time suffer cardiac arrest. (So, not to worry!?)

This hypothetical case raises questions of whether either or both of the you's in this story can be considered identical to the old you. Also, do the previous instances of Teletransportation count as cases in which a you on Mars was identical to the you that had been on Earth? Or were these cases in which death on Earth was combined with duplication on Mars (i.e., a new person on Mars who was, as it were, a xerox copy of the old you on Earth)?

Parfit throughout his book devises a variety of ingenious cases in which—despite our conventions of what counts as the same person—we have trouble in deciding what to say. We might have assumed that questions of "Is it me?" in general have an objective "Yes" or "No" answer. But Parfit's examples are not like this.

The best example of a problem case that might occur soon is this. Imagine a future transplant operation in which half of your brain is put in one body, and the other half is put in another body. Are both of these people you? If the answer is "Yes," are both of them the same person?

All of this exploration does not exactly prove that you cannot both hold that you have a persistent "me," and at the same time accept that this "me" continually changes. But it does place the combination under argumentative pressure. There may be cases in which there is not a straightforward right answer, especially if there is a competing candidate to count as "you," or if the changes are very great.

Despite this, our intuitive sense of having a persistent "me" is hardly the sense of having one that is largely the same as yesterday's me, or pretty much the same as last year's. Rather we tend to assume that the "me" that persists through a lifetime has an identity that, as the eighteenth-century philosopher Bishop Butler put it, is "strict and philosophical" rather than "loose and popular." You are you, period—not 90 percent you, not 99 percent you—but simply you.

Most contemporary philosophers who work on problems of the self have come to think (largely on the basis of arguments like those just referred to) that this is indefensible. You have a self, in their view, only in a conventional sense governed by our criteria for what counts as the "same" person. There are interesting and positive things to be said about how such a "self" is developed. Hume, the pioneer in Western philosophy of this line of thought, explores it at length in book 2 of his *Treatise of Human Nature.*

There is an alternative response, though. One might simply deny that the persistent "me" changes. Personality, the thoughts and feelings we have, and our physical appearance all change. But perhaps there is something underlying all of these things, some core of our being, that does not change?

The late-twentieth-century philosopher Roderick Chisholm, in his *Person and Object,* suggested such a view: that each of us has an inner self-nature, a "haecceity," which is available to introspective experience. This suggestion (which Chisholm later appeared to drop) had the appeal of having it both ways, preserving individuality (everyone's haecceity is different from everyone else's) while insisting on changelessness. However, there was the difficulty that our experiences of individuality are all bound up with things, including our thoughts and styles of behavior, that do change.

There is one alternative remaining, if we want to do justice to our intuitive sense of an unchanging "me" throughout life. This is to look for a core of self that has no elements of individual natures that grow and change. This would be a core that underlies (and is separate from) personality, thought patterns, bodily nature, and so forth.

This is *atman*. In the view of the Upanishads, this is what, at the deepest level, you are.

What I am suggesting is that the Upanishads' view of *atman* makes good philosophical sense if it is seen as the conclusion of the following (largely implicit) argument.

Each of us has a persistent "me."
This "me" (as it intuitively seems) must be unchanging.
But personality, thought patterns, and so on, do change.
Therefore the persistent "me" cannot include such elements.

The further conclusion is that your persistent "me," lacking all elements of individuality, is the same as anyone else's persistent "me." Once individuality is subtracted, what is there to distinguish you (qualitatively) from anyone else? The Upanishads indeed assume something broader: that the inner nature of all things, and not merely of all conscious beings, will be the same. This yields an image of the universe as a field of inner realities that are all at bottom the same. The inner realities of gods and goddesses, once their individualities are discounted, are included in this. The name for this field of inner realities is Brahman. *Atman*, then, is Brahman in somewhat the way in which a drop of water is the ocean of which it is a part. Whether the identity of *atman* and Brahman should be viewed straightforwardly as a matter of the same thing in two different guises, or as an identity between part and whole, becomes a debatable subject in Hindu philosophy. . . .

The philosophical implications of the claimed identity of *atman* and Brahman are complicated. They include a philosophical monism—the entire universe is one thing. . . . But they include also an account of what we are that is more complex and qualified than one might at first think.

There is the sense, of course, in which (if the Upanishads are right) you never change: Brahman is always Brahman. But, on the other hand, there are obvious respects in which you *do* change, especially as you come to think of yourself as Brahman.

There also is the problem of the layers of individual personality that surround the *atman*. According to the Upanishads, they are not the real you or any part of the real you. . . .

Are [they] then an illusion? They certainly are not a *delusion*: that is, they are not like introspective hallucinations that have no footing in the world as it really is. An illusion, as opposed to a delusion, is something that distorts a reality that is there (but in a different form from the one that you take it to have). In this sense, the Upanishads do hold that individual personality is an illusion.

Nevertheless, it is an illusion that has an experiential life of its own. One of the striking things about the progress to enlightenment, though, is that the experiential life of individual personality is more ample and noticeable at the beginning than it is toward the end. Ancient Hindu texts convey a sense that to be enlightened or nearly enlightened is to be highly impersonal in affect, manner, and self-presentation. It is as if the layers of individual personality, once seen through, also begin to fade away. When you have seen one enlightened person, you have seen them all.

It sometimes seems as if the Upanishads want to say two divergent things at the same time. One is that there is a sense in which to become enlightened, fully engrossed in the mode of thought that goes along with the claim that *atman* is Brahman, is to become Brahman. Certainly the person on the way to enlightenment becomes more Brahman-ish, losing personality characteristics that might look as if they distinguish a person from the rest of the universe. But the Upanishads clearly insist that such a person (like all of us) always was Brahman. Everything is Brahman.

Along this line there are clear statements that individual personality characteristics are parts of the reality that Brahman spins out of itself, creating the universe out of itself like a spider spinning a web. If our atman is Brahman, then these personality characteristics also are Brahman. Are they equally Brahman? A recurrent metaphor is that each of us is like a drop of water in the ocean that is Brahman. Perhaps the individual personality characteristics could be compared to froth surrounding the drops of water?

The puzzle here should be related to a set of puzzling characteristics of the general Hindu thought system in which the Upanishads play a central role. On one hand, both the ideal presented by the Upanishads and the reality it claims is fundamental are highly impersonal. We all are one. On the other hand, the social reality that Hinduism (before fairly recently) endorsed hardly treats all humans as one, and indeed takes caste distinctions very seriously.

It might be held that all religions as actually practiced, and perhaps all great systems of thought in general, have internal contradictions. The pulls and counterpulls can be part of the fascination and the tension of the system of thought. The Upanishads, though, may be a special case. They are unusually philosophically self-conscious texts. There is a consistent tendency also to describe the universe both as Brahman and at the same time in more specific terms keyed to individual realities. This consistency makes me think that there is actually *not* an internal contradiction. If there were, it would have been too obvious to everyone concerned.

Here is an analogy that may be helpful. The scientist and philosopher Sir Arthur Eddington, in the introduction to his *The Nature of the Physical World*, remarks that the table in front of him is in a way two tables. One is the solid and dense table of common sense. The other is the largely empty table of nuclear physics, with elementary particles moving about. This allows the formulation of true statements that on the surface appear incompatible with one another. It is true (in the framework of common sense) that the table is solid and dense. It also is true (in the framework of nuclear physics) that it is largely empty space.

Some people, of course, would want to insist that there is only one system of truth. One option might be to reject nuclear physics utterly, or alternatively to regard it as a kind of mythic structure whose true meanings are to be found only in ordinary experience. Alternatively one might flatly reject the commonsense picture of the world as pre-scientific or as "folk science."

Both of these simplifications have real difficulties. Rejecting nuclear physics of course would be stupid. It is far from clear, though, that we can do justice to its meanings, and to the quality of the evidence to which it appeals, if we regard it as merely a mythic superstructure that can be "cashed" in ordinary experience. Conversely, by ordinary criteria the table in front of Eddington (as distinguished from one that was in fact hollow) presumably *was* solid and dense.

A basic philosophical point is that one cannot separate sharply what is meant by calling a statement "true" from acceptable criteria for judging that it is true. There are acceptable criteria within the framework of nuclear physics for judging that the table was largely empty space.

There also were acceptable criteria for judging that it was solid and dense.

So it looks highly plausible to hold that there genuinely can be two different sets of statements that provide a picture of something real (e.g., a table), that both can count as true even if the pictures they provide are very different. We can accept this without necessarily holding that the two sets of statements are on a par. We can consistently claim that, say, the statements of nuclear physics present a deeper truth than those of common sense.

In much this spirit, we can take the Upanishads to be presenting two different frameworks within which what is real can be understood and described. What is thought of as the deeper truth is provided by the framework that is informed by "*atman* is Brahman." In this framework there is only one reality, Brahman. Everything is Brahman, and nothing ever changes.

Let us call this framework Ultimate Reality. There is also a framework of Superficial Reality, which represents the view of anyone whose thinking has not been entirely engrossed by the idea that *atman* is Brahman. In this framework there are countless individuals, including humans, animals, plants, pieces of furniture, gods and goddesses. Each of these things has its own characteristics. There is change, including processes of creation, preservation, destruction, life and death, spiritual fulfillment, spiritual sloth, and outright sin.

It is important to the Upanishads that there are truths within the framework of Superficial Reality. The phrase "superficial reality" may sound belittling, but anyone who writes a book, for which it is expected there will be readers, is (from the point of view of the authors of the Upanishads) operating within a framework of superficial reality. People who are fully enlightened do not write books. It is highly doubtful that they even know who (as individuals) they are or that there are differences between them and other people.

Study Questions

1. Explain the concept of *atman*.
2. Explain the concept of Brahman.
3. What is meant by the claim that *atman* is Brahman?
4. Can the claim that *atman* is Brahman be proven or disproven?

The Buddhist Concept of Self

THOMAS P. KASULIS

The Buddhist outlook on the self diverges in crucial ways from the Hindu perspective. The similarities and differences between the two are discussed in our next selection. Its author is Thomas P. Kasulis, Professor in the Departments of Comparative Studies and of East Asian Languages and Literatures at The Ohio State University.

Buddhism did not begin twenty-five centuries ago as a philosophical system. Yet, insofar as its founder Gautama Siddartha made claims about the nature of self and reality, the seeds of philosophical reflection, analysis, and argument were already planted. The Buddha himself may not have been a philosopher in the strictest sense of the term: the earliest texts give us less of a philosophical system than a set of practical sermons, intriguing metaphors, and provocative parables. At around the time of the Buddha, however, a tradition of Indian thought that can be loosely identified as "Hindu" was already well underway, as can be seen in sections of some later Vedas and especially the early Upaniṣads. As the Hindu philosophers sharpened their own skills and became more systematic in their rationales, the Buddha's followers found themselves in philosophical competition with not only a set of indigenous beliefs, but increasingly also with sophisticated analyses supporting those beliefs.

The issue of personhood and its nature turned out to be a key point of contention. No idea in Hinduism was more central and had more philosophical luster than *ātman*, which could mean simply "self" but in Hindu thought typically added the connotations of "true self" or "soul." In fact, some early Hindu texts identified the true self with the oneness of reality, *brahman*. Buddhism, on the other hand, explicitly took the position of denying the reality of such a self. The Buddha himself made *anātman*, the negation of *ātman*, an emblem of his break from the Hindu tradition around him. . . .

In developing an understanding of Buddhist philosophical views in relation to personhood, it is useful to bear in mind two general principles behind Buddhist thought. First, Buddhist philosophy arises out of Buddhist praxis. Of course, one could claim that there is always a connection between theory and praxis on some level, but there are important distinctions in how the two may interrelate. For example, sometimes a theory of reality precedes the development of a certain praxis that is then used as a means of verification within the theory. In the case of controlled laboratory experimentation, for instance, the scientist's practical procedures developed out of a theory that events follow a specific kind of reproducible pattern ("causes") that can be observed and measured by strictly empirical means. It is not always true, however, that theory precedes praxis in this way. For example, the praxis of learning and using language preceded the subsequent development of linguistic theory about language acquisition. In such cases, the praxis (of acquiring and using speech) was not acquired to confirm or disconfirm a theory, but rather the theory of reality (including the linguistics and cognitive science of how the mind and body work) was a metapractical reflection on the praxis in order to explain how and why the praxis works. In an analogous fashion, as we shall see, Buddhist philosophies about the self tend to arise out of metapractical reflection rather than prior theoretical systematization.

This point about the priority of praxis has clear philosophical implications. For example, Buddhism generally shies away from speculative metaphysics and argumentation about cosmic realities. It is typically less interested in analyzing reality to increase our understanding of it and more interested in probing and eliminating our resistance to accepting realities that, at least on some level, we already recognize. For example, what we ordinarily experience is impermanent and not eternal. Buddhism's inclination is to examine our flight from accepting that apparent fact and our quest to try to access some other reality transcendent to our ordinary sensory experience. To put this in terms more familiar to the contemporary West, Buddhism is more interested in the psychological than in the metaphysical aspects of philosophical reflection.

Of course, no philosophical position can be totally devoid of all assumptions about reality. Any philosophical position ultimately makes some initial assumptions within which it then develops its case. There is one premise that Buddhism does take as an unprovable starting point—namely, that there is a real presence besides the workings of the mind, and that the presence does not disguise itself to our ordinary ways of knowing. Again, using a Western terminology that offers only a rough fit, we can say that Buddhism is foundationally *realist* rather than, say, idealist or even constructivist.

In discussing phenomenal appearance, it is important to add one further point about the general Indian context. In Buddhism, as in most other Indian philosophical systems, the "ordinary sensory experience" to which we have referred are products of six, not five, senses. Besides the five outwardly directed senses usually recognized in the West, Buddhism includes also the sense of inner awareness or introspection. From the Buddhist standpoint, that I feel hungry or embarrassed, for example, are as "empirical" and "objective" as that I see the color red or hear a thud. Introspection is not considered a different order of knowing from extrospection. The acceptance of the reality and objective accessibility of psychological states is important to Buddhist praxis as the foundation for its understanding of self.

According to tradition, the Buddha developed his distinctive forms of praxis in response to a pervasive sense of anguish, anxiety, or unsatisfactoriness (*duḥkha*). Through a series of meditations that allowed him to cease making conceptual constructions, he introspectively focused on the stream of immediately available psychophysical events. He concluded that what we directly experience is what actually is and that anguish arises from our refusal to accept what exists for what it is. Ordinarily, he claimed, we project onto the immediately accessible phenomena a desire for things to be otherwise: to be "mine" rather than simply "to be"; to be enduring instead of transient; to be substantial—to be independently existing entities—instead of interdependent processes. Through the meditative praxis, the Buddha was purportedly able to disengage those projections. In so doing, he was able to gain the insight that allowed him not to form the fixations or attachments that lead to our ordinary sense of ego, substantiality, permanence, and self-dependency. In other

words, the fruits of the praxis carried over into his ordinary life by liberating him from the tendency to structure his experiences around those categories. Freed of their effects, he was said to be able to accept things for what they are. The anguish disappeared.

The story of the Buddha's awakening ("*buddha*" means "awakened one") is peppered with various accounts of his achieving supernormal or paranormal powers (the ability to remember previous lifetimes, for example). It is significant, however, that none of those powers were considered necessary for underpinning his account of reality and of the self. To duplicate the Buddha's insight, one need not add something to what one ordinarily experiences. On the contrary, the Buddhist praxis is aimed at disengaging the conditioned responses that lead one to think things are other than they are. The praxis is a therapy that eliminates delusional, anxiety-provoking behaviors or constructions of reality. In this context philosophical analysis, with its propensity to build systems around fixed categories, could be a liability rather than a positive tool. The early Buddhist texts relate the Buddha's own hesitation to enter into analyses not conducive to breaking the patterns leading to delusion. For better or worse, however, Buddhism developed in India at a time when Hindu philosophical reflection, speculation, and analysis were beginning to blossom. The Buddhists found themselves being asked philosophical questions that could not be avoided. To understand Indian Buddhist philosophy, especially its analysis of the self as *anātman*, we need to appreciate that larger intellectual context of the time.

In the Buddha's era there was already an Indian trend toward distrusting the ordinary senses. It is significant, therefore, that Buddhist praxis worked against that tendency. The Hindu texts often referred to *māyā*, the idea that reality takes on an illusory mask that must be understood if its true nature is to be fathomed. According to this common Hindu view, reality does not appear to us the way it essentially is.

What we see as multiplicity, evanescence, and distinctions may be, in fact, only the superficial appearance of a deeper, transcendent reality of oneness and changelessness (*brahman*). Therefore, with the proper knowledge, we may still see the illusion, but also see through it to the reality beyond. This allows a detached (sometimes even playful) engagement with the world analogous to how we might find ourselves caught up in the illusion of a magic show or cinema. While enjoying the show, we also *know* that the distinctions with which we are engaged are illusions.

Buddhism disagrees fundamentally with the Hindu viewpoint. In Buddhism, the issue to be addressed is not illusion, but delusion. According to Buddhism, we experience the unreal not because the real presents a false appearance, but because we project our own desires onto what is presented. In that projection we delude ourselves. The goal of Buddhism, therefore, is not to see through the appearances, but instead to accept them without the distortion of egocentric projections. The phenomenal world is not illusion (*māyā*), but "suchness" or "thusness" (*tathatā*). This difference had a fundamental impact on the *ātman/anātman* debate between Hindu and Buddhist philosophies of self.

The general position developed in many Hindu Upaniṣads was that behind the sensory functions, there must be a faculty or agency possessing the function. If there is seeing or hearing, for example, there must be that which sees or hears. Yet whatever the seer or hearer is, it itself must be unseen or unheard, or there would be an infinite regress: we could endlessly ask, if the seer is itself seen, then what sees that seer? Therefore, argued this group of Hindu philosophers, there must be something that is the subject, but never the object, of human sensory experience (including introspection). It is the unseen, unheard, untasted, untouched, unsmelled, and unintrospected self behind a person's various experiences. It itself is unchanging and inaccessible to ordinary sensory knowing, yet it defines what one is: it is the *ātman*, the "true self."

The gist of this Hindu argument already existed in the early Upaniṣads current at the time of the Buddha and the details were further developed by subsequent philosophical analysis in the ensuing few centuries. It is important to point out, however, that the acceptance of *ātman* was not just the result of abstract reasoning. There was an experiential or practical component to the belief as well.

For understanding the Hindu position, the central point is what we mean by "direct experiential knowledge." If we limit such knowledge to what is accessible to the six senses, then *ātman's* very definition excludes its verification. We need not limit "direct experiential knowledge" in that way, however. Yogic disciplines for controlling the mind and body were already highly developed in ancient India, and adepts were said to be capable of achieving a state of complete quiet in which sensory experience (including inner awareness) disappeared altogether. This "experience" (if that Western term can be stretched to apply to such an event) was said to have no subject–object distinction and to be simply a state of oneness. The "I" would be doing nothing other than being "I"—a state of pure *ātman* awareness without discrimination or distinctions.

One might question the possibility of such an event. For example, what continuity would there be between the trance state and the return to normal consciousness? With no distinctions, what or who would emerge from such a state and how would that be connected to the person who existed before the trance event? To such questions, a common reply was to refer to the everyday event of dreamless sleep. It lacks content, the subject–object distinction, and even inner awareness. Yet, when we awake every morning, we remember who we are and have been. To the proponents of the *ātman* theory this was further evidence that personal identity resides in a level of reality not accessible to ordinary sensory experience and which is beyond distinctions. This justified, in their view, the identification of the true self (*ātman*) with monistic reality (*brahman*).

At least in general form, it is that type of theory of *ātman* that the Buddha rejected in his position of *anātman*. Even in its earliest texts, Buddhism rejected both parts of the Hindu theory of *ātman*—namely, (1) the logical argument that action requires an independently existing agent (for there to be seeing, there must be a seer that is not itself seen); and (2) the metapractical argument that the possibility of having events of sensory cessation implies there is a "true self" behind the experience. Let us consider Buddhism's critique of each of these issues.

As we have seen in our discussion of Buddhist praxis, the Buddha maintained that what we experience through the senses (and, therefore, what really is) is a nexus of interconnected processes, not unchanging things (such as *ātman*). Buddhism insists that a process does not require an agent that has or undergoes the change. Ordinary language can be misleading. We say "the river flows in its channel," but this does not mean that the river is something other than the continuing process of water's flowing in the channel. Similarly, nature does not "cause" or "undergo" the change of seasons; the changing of the seasons is one of the processes that constitutes "nature." The analogy to an idea of self is clear: "I" am not what "has" or "undergoes" the processes of psychophysical change. Rather, those processes themselves constitute what is called "I."

According to traditional Buddhist thought, there are five interrelated processes constituting the self: the physical bodily form, sensations or feelings, sense perceptions, habitual mental formations or volitional tendencies, and consciousness. The self is, therefore, the name for the continuities and interactions among those five processes and not something in addition to them. An implication of this theory is that the self is an activity, not a thing, and that its nature is to be the locus where the five processes intersect. Not only is there no "soul" or "true self" behind that locus of events, but there is also no tendency to identify the "real self" with consciousness alone. For Buddhism, there are no sharp lines demarcating the boundaries of the self. In everyday circumstances it may often be convenient to think of a person's existence as strictly bounded, but that is no different from thinking of the boundaries of a river as clearly defined. If we try to be too precise, however, the sharp distinctions disappear. As the river is interdependent with its riverbank—splashing up against its sides, eroding chunks to settle into its own riverbed—so too is the self conditioned by surrounding factors separated from the self by fuzzy boundaries.

With this process image of the self, the various schools of Buddhist philosophy addressed in slightly different ways the issue of continuity. Common to all of them was the idea that the self is an ongoing interaction with other processes. Persons have an identity not because they contain some unchanging core, but precisely because they do change. The self is a pattern of the linked changes, each changing condition leading to reconfigurations that help set the conditions for the next phase. The continuity of the self is in the continuity of those patterned, conditioned changes.

This Buddhist critique undercuts the Hindu argument for *ātman* as the "true self" or the "unseen seer." If seeing, for example, is a psychophysical process, there does not have to be some self or seer behind the process. The interrelated psychophysical processes themselves are what we call "I." A Buddhist philosopher can be as sophisticated in the analysis of these constituent processes as a scientist might be in analyzing a river in terms of the geology of the riverbed and the water's erosion patterns, the rainfall cycles, the seepage of minerals or artificial toxins into the water, the biosystem of river life, and so forth. Yet, just as the scientist does not find, nor feel any need to look for, the "river" as something other than those processes, so too does the Buddhist rest content with a characterization of the self as the name for a set of interrelated psychophysical processes.

With this logical critique behind us, let us turn to Buddhism's metapractical ground for rejecting the Hindu assertion of *ātman*: the reflection on the nature and meaning of the trance state of sensory cessation. Significantly, the Buddha did not deny the possibility of such an experience. In fact, a famous account of his death reports that while giving his last sermon to his assembled disciples, he interrupted his talk because of stomach pain to enter a trance. Re-energized, he then continued his lecture. The disagreement with Hinduism, then, is not whether such a state of sensory-cessation is possible, but the metapractical issue of the meaning of that state. For at least some Hindus, that state suggests what the true self may be. For Buddhists, on the other hand, it means only that under the right conditions the flow of sensory experience can be temporarily frozen. There is for them no reason to jump to the conclusion that such a frozen state is more fundamental or truer than other states. For the Buddhist, it is noteworthy that such trance states and dreamless sleep are temporary events. Those purported experiences of eternity are themselves transient and temporary. Even in dreamless sleep or trance states, there is a continuity of some processes defining the self— the physical processes of the body, for example.

In summation, by rejecting the contemporaneous notion of *ātman*, the early Indian Buddhist philosophers were not denying the existence of the self, but only insisting that there were logical, empirical, and metapractical reasons for denying the self as a substantial, permanent, transcendent entity. The Buddhists certainly maintain that the self exists, but only as a name, like "river" or "nature," for a set of interrelated processes.

Study Questions

1. How does illusion differ from delusion?
2. What is Buddhism's critique of the Hindu theory of *atman*?
3. According to Buddhism, what is the self?
4. According to Buddhism, what is the sixth sense?

C. Identity

A Case of Identity

BRIAN SMART

A perplexing metaphysical issue is personal identity. What makes you the same person today that you were yesterday? The question is much more difficult to answer than may at first appear.

From Brian Smart, "How to Reidentify the Ship of Theseus," *Analysis*, 32:5, 1972. Reprinted by permission of the author.

But rather than beginning our discussion with the identities of persons, let us start simply with the identities of objects. Imagine that you leave your car in a parking lot and return some hours later to discover that your vehicle has been hit by a huge truck and smashed to smithereens. A towing service arrives and takes the remaining pieces of your car to a repair garage, where you are assured that your car will be completely fixed. When you come to the garage two weeks later you are shown a car in perfect condition and told that it's your old car, now repaired. But is this car the same one you had left in the parking lot, or is it a new car? And how would you know? Suppose the original automobile was a gift that you valued highly. Do you still have that gift? Or has it been lost and replaced?

The following selection is by Brian Smart, who was Professor of Philosophy at the University of Keele. His example concerns a ship rather than a car, and he shows how a metaphysical issue about identity can lie at the heart of a legal dispute about ownership. See whether you believe the judges in the case ruled correctly.

A ship, X, is composed of a thousand old, but perfectly seaworthy, planks. It is brought into dock A where at hour 1 one of X's planks is removed to dock B and is replaced by a new plank. At hour 2 the same process is repeated so that by hour 1000 we have a ship Y in dock A composed of a thousand new planks and (since X's old planks have been reassembled as a ship) a ship Z in dock B composed of a thousand old planks. The problem is: with which ship—Y or Z—, if either, is X identical?

Let us give this problem a fictitious, but practical, setting.

Two shipowners, Morion and Bombos, are involved in a legal dispute. Morion had ordered a new ship from the Proteus brothers, shipbuilders and shiprepairers. Bombos had sent his ship, X, along to the same firm for a complete renewal of all its parts. (It should be explained that such a renewal would involve only half the labour costs of building a new ship from scratch.) Now the scheming Proteus brothers had persuaded Morion that what he wanted was a ship with well-seasoned timber and told him that his "new" ship was under construction in dock B. They saw their way to an enormous profit. For, while they would require a thousand new planks for renovating the ship that belonged to the shrewder and potentially more troublesome

Bombos, they would clearly not need a second batch of new planks for building Morion's ship: they would use Bombos's old ones.

However the brothers' plans misfired all too literally. Just after Morion and Bombos had paid their bills, but before they had taken possession of Y and Z, there was a fire in dock B and Z was reduced to ashes. Under the law of Oudamou, where all these events occurred, the brothers were responsible for Z until Morion had taken possession. Unfortunately, they had not had Z insured. The insurance would have had to be for a "new" ship but under Oudamou law the newness of a ship was decided by the newness of its component parts.

Seeing their vast profits about to disappear the Proteus brothers, in heavy disguise, left Oudamou abandoning Y in dock A.

Morion was quickly persuaded by his lawyer to claim ownership of Y as he had paid for a new ship and Y was new under Oudamou law. Bombos's lawyer naturally put in a claim on his client's behalf for possession of Y on the ground that Y was identical with X.

When the case was heard . . . Bombos's lawyer argued . . . as follows. Over a period of time objects like the human body can undergo a change of identity in all their parts. All that is required is that the overall *form* of the object is retained and that it occupies a continuous space-time path. The ship in dock A satisfies this condition, and so X, his client's ship, is identical with Y. X is not identical with Z precisely because the form of Z cannot be linked to the form of X by a continuous space-time path.

Morion's lawyer attacked this argument. . . . He urged that the spatio-temporal continuity of form was neither a necessary nor a sufficient condition of identity. It was not a necessary condition since a watch could be dismantled and the same parts reassembled to form the same watch. X had in fact been gradually dismantled in dock A and reassembled in dock B. The necessary and sufficient condition to be met was the identity of the parts of X with the parts of Z. This condition had been met by Z. Hence it was Bombos's ship that had been destroyed and his client's ship which remained. . . .

The judges agreed that objects could be dismantled and reassembled elsewhere, still retaining their identity. . . . They contended that the requirement was that the object's *parts* had been reassembled. . . . They claimed that Z did not contain X's parts at all. If the case had been one in which only the original planks were involved there would be no difficulty over identifying Z's parts with X's parts. But the case was not as simple as that.

Their reasoning was this. When a plank had been removed from X and replaced by a new plank, it was the new plank that was now a part of X. The old plank *had been* a part of X but was no longer. Rather it was a part of Z which gradually came into being from hour 1 onwards. When completed Z was not composed of any of X's parts but rather of what had been X's parts. "Being a part of X" was merely a temporary role in the career of the old planks which were now parts of Z. Using this line of argument it was clear that X had simply changed the identity of its parts and that now its parts were identical with the parts of Y. Hence X was identical with Y. X was not identical with Z for they had no parts in common.

Thus they found in favour of Bombos.

Study Questions

1. Explain in your own words the case of Morion versus Bombos.
2. What are the strongest arguments Morion can offer?
3. What are the strongest arguments Bombos can offer?
4. Is any decision in the case arbitrary?

The Problem of Personal Identity

JOHN PERRY

So much for the identity of objects. Now what about the identity of persons? The issue is explained here by John Perry, Professor Emeritus of Philosophy at Stanford University.

From John Perry, ed., *Personal Identity,* Berkeley, University of California Press, 1975. Reprinted by permission of the publisher.

Imagine the following. Elected to the Senate from your home state, you have become a key member of the Committee on Health, Education, and Welfare. This committee meets tomorrow to vote on a bill to fund a feasibility study of a new method for manufacturing shoes, which is alleged to produce a high quality, inexpensive shoe that never wears out. Your support of the bill is essential; it has faced the bitter and unflagging opposition of the American Cobblers Association (ACA), led by their high pressure lobbyist Peter Pressher, and a number of committee members intend to vote against it.

The morning of the committee vote you wake up, open your eyes, and glance at the clock on the shelf beyond the bed. Something seems strange. The bump in the covers you take to be your feet seems strangely distant. As you get out of bed you hit your head on a shelf that used to be a good three or four inches above it. You notice you are wearing a leather apron, which you are certain you didn't wear to bed. Puzzled, you go to the mirror. Staring out you see not your familiar cleanshaven face and squatty body, but the strapping frame and bearded countenance of Peter Pressher.

You don't know what to think. Are you dreaming? Is this some kind of a trick? But you perform various tests to eliminate these possibilities. No doubt can remain: the body you have looks just like the body Peter Pressher normally has; it seems to be that very body.

Hearing laughter, you turn toward your living room. There on the sofa sits a person who looks exactly like you. That is exactly like you used to look, down to the inevitable magenta hollyhock (your state's flower) in the lapel. Before you can speak, he says,

"Surprised, Senator? I've made sacrifices for the Cobblers before. Getting this squatty body must take the prize. But I'll vote to kill that bill this afternoon, and it will be worth it . . ."

He speaks with your own deep and resonant voice, but the syntax and the fanatic overtones are unmistakably those of . . .

"Peter Pressher! . . ."

"Right, Senator, it's me. But as far as the rest of the world will ever know, it's really you. We snuck into your apartment last night and my brother Bimo, the brain surgeon, carefully removed your brain and put it in my body—or should I say your body. And vice-versa. It's a new operation he's pioneering; he calls it a 'body-transplant.'"

"You'll never get away with it . . ."

"Forget it. You have two choices. You can go around telling people that you're you, in which case I will sue you and my family, thinking they are your family, will sign papers to have you put away. Or you can start acting like me—become Peter Pressher—we think you'd make a good lobbyist. Almost as good a lobbyist as I'll make a senator!"

An incredible story? Let's hope so. Impossible? In one sense, yes. Physicians cannot now perform body-transplants with human beings. But in another sense the case is perfectly possible. The day when such operations can be performed may not be so far away. Such an operation is possible in the sense of being conceivable. The story was not self-contradictory or incoherent. As a piece of science fiction, it's pretty mild stuff. . . .

Why are such cases puzzling, and why is the puzzlement of philosophical interest? Because they seem to disprove the view that a person is just a live human body. If we can have the same person on two different occasions when we don't have the same live human body, then it seems that a person cannot be identified with his body, and personal identity cannot be identified with bodily identity. This is puzzling simply because the assumption that the two go together plays a large role in our daily lives. We make it when we identify others on the basis of appearance, or observed movements, or fingerprints. What is the justification for this assumption? The abandonment of the simple theory that personal identity is just bodily identity carries with it the need to formulate an alternative account of personal identity. On such attempts this anthology focuses.

But perhaps we are moving too fast. Are we so sure that the puzzle cases prove what they are alleged to? Perhaps the events imagined have been wrongly described, and the right description would go something like this:

You are a senator from your home state. One morning you wake up on the sofa, seeming to remember being Peter Pressher, a lobbyist for the ACA. A man emerges from a bedroom, who seems to remember being you. But subsequent tests—fingerprints, testimony of close friends, comparison of medical records, etc.—establishes, to your delight and his dismay, that you are a duly elected senator with delusions (which you keep quiet about) of having been a lobbyist, while he is a lobbyist with delusions of having been a senator. His situation is rather ironic. He willingly participated in a scheme where his brain (and so various of his psychological characteristics) were exchanged for your brain (and so various of your psychological characteristics). He seems to have thought that would somehow constitute a "body transfer," and he would wind up in the Senate. (He was taught this by a philosophy professor in college, whom he is suing.) What actually happened, of course, is that two people underwent radical changes in character and personality, and acquired delusive memories, as a result of brain surgery.

How shall we decide between these two descriptions? In a sense, they do not disagree about what happened—which sounds emanated from which bodies, and so forth. So neither can be proven incorrect by reference to the occurrence of these events. But in another sense they are blatantly contradictory, and one must be wrong.

Study Questions

1. In Perry's story, are you Peter Pressher?
2. How do you decide the matter?
3. Could you be mistaken about who you are?
4. Is any decision in the matter arbitrary?

D.   Free Will

Free Will

THOMAS NAGEL

We turn next to one of the most-discussed philosophical questions: do human beings ever act freely? It might seem obvious that they do. Consider an ordinary human action, for instance, raising your hand at a meeting to attract the speaker's attention.

If you are attending a lecture and the time comes for questions from the audience, you believe it is within your power to raise your hand and within your power not to raise it. The choice is yours.

Equally obvious, however, is that whenever an event occurs, a causal explanation can account for the occurrence of the event. If you feel a pain in your arm, then something is causing that pain. If nothing were causing it, you wouldn't be in pain. This same line of reasoning applies whether the event to be explained is a loud noise, a change in the weather, or an individual's action. If the event were uncaused, it wouldn't have occurred.

But if all actions are part of a causal chain extending back beyond your birth, how is it possible that any of your actions is free?

Our first reading is by Thomas Nagel, whose work we read previously. He explains the problem and concludes by suggesting that perhaps the feeling of free will is an illusion.

Suppose you're going through a cafeteria line and when you come to the desserts, you hesitate between a peach and a big wedge of chocolate cake with creamy icing. The cake looks good, but you know it's fattening. Still, you take it and eat it with pleasure. The next day you look in the mirror or get on the scale and think, "I wish I hadn't eaten that chocolate cake. I could have had a peach instead."

"I could have had a peach instead." What does that mean, and is it true?

Peaches were available when you went through the cafeteria line: you had the *opportunity* to take a peach instead. But that isn't all you mean. You mean you could have *taken* the peach instead of the cake. You could have *done* something different from what you actually did. Before you made up your mind, it was open whether you would take fruit or cake, and it was only your choice that decided which it would be.

Is that it? When you say, "I could have had a peach instead," do you mean that it depended only on your choice? You chose chocolate cake, so that's what you had, but *if* you had chosen the peach, you would have had that.

This still doesn't seem to be enough. You don't mean only that *if* you had chosen the peach, you would have had it. When you say, "I could have had a peach instead," you also mean that you *could have chosen* it—no "ifs" about it. But what does that mean?

It can't be explained by pointing out other occasions when you *have* chosen fruit. And it can't be explained by saying that if you had thought about it harder, or if a friend had been with you who eats like a bird, you *would* have chosen it. What you are saying is that you could have chosen a peach instead of chocolate cake *just then, as things actually were.* You think you could have chosen a peach even if everything else had been exactly the same as it was up to the point when you in fact chose chocolate cake. The only difference would have been that instead of thinking, "Oh well," and reaching for the cake, you would have thought, "Better not," and reached for the peach.

This is an idea of "can" or "could have" which we apply only to people (and maybe some animals). When we say, "The car could have climbed to the top of the hill," we mean the car had enough power to reach the top of the hill *if* someone drove it there. We don't mean that on an occasion when it was parked at the bottom of the hill, the car could have just taken off and climbed to the top, instead of continuing to sit there. Something else would have had to happen differently first, like a person getting in and starting the motor. But when it comes to people, we seem to think that they can do various things they don't actually do, *just like that,* without anything else happening differently first. What does this mean?

Part of what it means may be this: Nothing up to the point at which you choose determines irrevocably what your choice will be. It remains an *open possibility* that you will choose a peach until the moment when you actually choose chocolate cake. It isn't determined in advance.

Some things that happen *are* determined in advance. For instance, it seems to be determined in advance that the sun will rise tomorrow at a certain hour. It is not an open possibility that tomorrow the sun won't rise and night will just continue. That is not possible because it could happen only if the earth stopped rotating, or the sun stopped existing, and there is nothing going on in our galaxy which might make either of those things happen. The earth will continue rotating unless it is stopped, and tomorrow morning its rotation will bring us back around to face inward in the solar system, toward the sun, instead of outward, away from it. If there is no possibility that the earth will stop or that the sun won't be there, there is no possibility that the sun won't rise tomorrow.

When you say you could have had a peach instead of chocolate cake, part of what you mean may be that it wasn't determined in advance what you would do, as it *is* determined in advance that the sun will rise tomorrow. There were no processes or forces at work before you made your choice that made it inevitable that you would choose chocolate cake.

That may not be all you mean, but it seems to be at least part of what you mean. For if it was really determined in advance that you would choose cake, how could it also be true that you could have chosen fruit? It would be true that nothing would have prevented you from having a peach if you had chosen it instead of cake. But these *ifs* are not the same as saying you could have chosen a peach, period. You couldn't have chosen it unless the possibility remained open until you closed it off by choosing cake.

Some people have thought that it is never possible for us to do anything different from what we actually do, in this absolute sense. They acknowledge that what we do depends on our choices, decisions, and wants, and that we make different choices in different circumstances: we're not like the earth rotating on its axis with monotonous regularity. But the claim is that, in each case, the circumstances that exist before we act determine our actions and make them inevitable. The sum total of a person's experiences, desires and knowledge, his hereditary constitution, the social circumstances and the nature of the choice facing him, together with other factors that we may not know about, all combine to make a particular action in the circumstances inevitable.

This view is called determinism. The idea is not that we can know all the laws of the universe and use them to *predict* what will happen. First of all, we can't know all the complex circumstances that affect a human choice. Secondly, even when we do learn something about the circumstances, and try to make a prediction, that is itself a *change* in the circumstances, which may change the predicted result. But predictability isn't the point. The hypothesis is that there *are* laws of nature, like those that govern the movement of the planets, which govern everything that happens in the world—and that in accordance with those laws, the circumstances before an action determine that it will happen, and rule out any other possibility.

If that is true, then even while you were making up your mind about dessert, it was already determined by the many factors working on you and in you that you would choose cake. You *couldn't* have chosen the peach, even though you thought you could: the process of decision is just the working out of the determined result inside your mind.

If determinism is true for everything that happens, it was already determined before you were born that you would choose cake. Your choice was determined by the situation immediately before, and *that* situation was determined by the situation before *it,* and so on as far back as you want to go.

Even if determinism isn't true for everything that happens—even if some things just happen without being determined by causes that were there in advance—it would still be very significant if everything *we did* were determined before we did it. However free you might feel when choosing between fruit and cake, or between two candidates in an election, you would really be able to make only one choice in those circumstances—though if the circumstances or your desires had been different, you would have chosen differently.

If you believed that about yourself and other people, it would probably change the way you felt about things. For instance, could you blame yourself for giving in to temptation and having the cake? Would it make sense to say, "I really should have had a peach instead," if you *couldn't* have chosen a peach instead? It certainly wouldn't make sense to say it if there *was* no fruit. So how can it make sense if there *was* fruit, but you couldn't have chosen it because it was determined in advance that you would choose cake?

This seems to have serious consequences. Besides not being able sensibly to blame yourself for having had cake, you probably wouldn't be able sensibly to blame anyone at all for doing something bad, or praise them for doing something good. If it was determined in advance that they would do it, it was inevitable: they couldn't have done anything else, given the circumstances as they were. So how can we hold them responsible?

You may be very mad at someone who comes to a party at your house and steals all your Glenn Gould records, but suppose you believed that his action was determined in advance by his nature and the situation. Suppose you believed that everything he did, including the earlier actions that had contributed to the formation of his character, was determined in advance by earlier circumstances. Could you still hold him responsible for such low-grade behavior? Or would

it be more reasonable to regard him as a kind of natural disaster—as if your records had been eaten by termites?

People disagree about this. Some think that if determinism is true, no one can reasonably be praised or blamed for anything, any more than the rain can be praised or blamed for falling. Others think that it still makes sense to praise good actions and condemn bad ones, even if they were inevitable. After all, the fact that someone was determined in advance to behave badly doesn't mean that he *didn't* behave badly. If he steals your records, that shows inconsiderateness and dishonesty, whether it was determined or not. Furthermore, if we don't blame him, or perhaps even punish him, he'll probably do it again.

On the other hand, if we think that what he did was determined in advance, this seems more like punishing a dog for chewing on the rug. It doesn't mean we hold him responsible for what he did: we're just trying to influence his behavior in the future. I myself don't think it makes sense to blame someone for doing what it was impossible for him not to do. (Though of course determinism implies that it was determined in advance that I would think this.)

These are the problems we must face if determinism is true. But perhaps it isn't true. Many scientists now believe that it isn't true for the basic particles of matter—that in a given situation, there's more than one thing that an electron may do. Perhaps if determinism isn't true for human actions, either, this leaves room for free will and responsibility. What if human actions, or at least some of them, are not determined in advance? What if, up to the moment when you choose, it's an open possibility that you will choose either chocolate cake or a peach? Then, so far as what has happened before is concerned, you *could* choose either one. Even if you actually choose cake, you could have chosen a peach.

But is even this enough for free will? Is this all you mean when you say, "I could have chosen fruit instead?"—that the choice wasn't determined in advance? No, you believe something more. You believe that *you* determined what you would do, by *doing* it. It wasn't determined in advance, but it didn't *just happen,* either. *You did it*, and you could have done the opposite. But what does that mean?

This is a funny question: we all know what it means to *do* something. But the problem is, if the act wasn't determined in advance, by your desires, beliefs, and personality, among other things, it seems to be something that just happened, without any explanation. And in that case, how was it *your doing*?

One possible reply would be that there is no answer to that question. Free action is just a basic feature of the world, and it can't be analyzed. There's a difference between something just happening without a cause and an action just being *done* without a cause. It's a difference we all understand, even if we can't explain it.

Some people would leave it at that. But others find it suspicious that we must appeal to this unexplained idea to explain the sense in which you could have chosen fruit instead of cake. Up to now it has seemed that determinism is the big threat to responsibility. But now it seems that even if our choices are not determined in advance, it is still hard to understand in what way we *can* do what we don't do. Either of two choices may be possible in advance, but unless I determine which of them occurs, it is no more my responsibility than if it was determined by causes beyond my control. And how can *I* determine it if *nothing* determines it?

This raises the alarming possibility that we're not responsible for our actions whether determinism is true *or* whether it's false. If determinism is true, antecedent circumstances are responsible. If determinism is false, nothing is responsible. That would really be a dead end.

There is another possible view, completely opposite to most of what we've been saying. Some people think responsibility for our actions *requires* that our actions be determined, rather than requiring that they not be. The claim is that for an action to be something

you have done, it has to be produced by certain kinds of causes in you. For instance, when you chose the chocolate cake, that was something you did, rather than something that just happened, because you wanted chocolate cake more than you wanted a peach. Because your appetite for cake was stronger at the time than your desire to avoid gaining weight, it resulted in your choosing the cake. In other cases of action, the psychological explanation will be more complex, but there will always be one—otherwise the action wouldn't be yours. This explanation seems to mean that what you did was determined in advance after all. If it wasn't determined by anything, it was just an unexplained event, something that happened out of the blue rather than something that you did.

According to this position, causal determination by itself does not threaten freedom—only a certain *kind* of cause does that. If you grabbed the cake because someone else pushed you into it, then it wouldn't be a free choice. But free action doesn't require that there be no determining cause at all: it means that the cause has to be of a familiar psychological type.

I myself can't accept this solution. If I thought that everything I did was determined by my circumstances and my psychological condition, I would feel trapped. And if I thought the same about everybody else, I would feel that they were like a lot of puppets. It wouldn't make sense to hold them responsible for their actions any more than you hold a dog or a cat or even an elevator responsible.

On the other hand, I'm not sure I understand how responsibility for our choices makes sense if they are *not* determined. It's not clear what it means to say I determine the choice, if nothing about me determines it. So perhaps the feeling that you could have chosen a peach instead of a piece of cake is a philosophical illusion, and couldn't be right whatever was the case.

Study Questions

1. What is determinism?
2. If you chose one apple rather than another seemingly as good, was your choice determined?
3. Would you, like Nagel, believe yourself trapped if everything you did was determined by your circumstances and psychological conditions?
4. Why does Nagel doubt that we are responsible for our choices if they are not determined?

Free Will and Determinism

W. T. STACE

In the previous essay Nagel defended the view that free will and determinism are incompatible, that one or the other is false. Many philosophers, however, believe the two theses are compatible and that both are true.

These philosophers are sympathetic to the sort of argument presented in our next selection by W. T. Stace (1886–1967), an Englishman who became Professor of Philosophy at Princeton University. He maintains that once we define "free will" properly, any apparent incompatibility with determinism disappears.

[T]hose learned professors of philosophy or psychology who deny the existence of free will do so only in their professional moments and in their studies and lecture rooms. For when it comes to doing anything practical, even of the most trivial kind, they invariably behave as if they and others were free. They inquire from you at dinner whether you will choose this dish or that dish. They will ask a child why he told a lie, and will punish him for not having chosen the way of truthfulness. All of which is inconsistent with a disbelief in free will. This should cause us to suspect that the problem is not a real one; and this, I believe, is the case. The dispute is merely verbal, and is due to nothing but a confusion about the meanings of words. . . .

Throughout the modern period, until quite recently, it was assumed, both by the philosophers who denied free will and by those who defended it, that *determinism is inconsistent with free will*. If a man's actions were wholly determined by chains of causes stretching back into the remote past, so that they could be predicted beforehand by a mind which knew all the causes, it was assumed that they could not in that case be free. This implies that a certain definition of actions done from free will was assumed, namely that they are actions *not* wholly determined by causes or predictable beforehand. Let us shorten this by saying that free will was defined as meaning indeterminism. This is the incorrect definition which has led to the denial of free will. As

Specified excerpts from *Religion and the Modern Mind* by W. T. Stace. Copyright © 1952 by W. T. Stace. Copyright renewed. Reprinted by permission of HarperCollins Publishers, Inc.

soon as we see what the true definition is we shall find that the question whether the world is deterministic, as Newtonian science implied, or in a measure indeterministic, as current physics teaches, is wholly irrelevant to the problem. . . .

At a recent murder trial in Trenton some of the accused had signed confessions, but afterwards asserted that they had done so under police duress. The following exchange might have occurred:

JUDGE: Did you sign this confession of your own free will?

PRISONER: No. I signed it because the police beat me up.

Now suppose that a philosopher had been a member of the jury. We could imagine this conversation taking place in the jury room.

FOREMAN OF THE JURY: The prisoner says he signed the confession because he was beaten, and not of his own free will.

PHILOSOPHER: This is quite irrelevant to the case. There is no such thing as free will.

FOREMAN: Do you mean to say that it makes no difference whether he signed because his conscience made him want to tell the truth or because he was beaten?

PHILOSOPHER: None at all. Whether he was caused to sign by a beating or by some desire of his own—the desire to tell the truth, for example—in either case his signing was causally determined, and therefore in neither case did he act of his own free will. Since there is no such thing as free will, the question whether he signed of his own free will ought not to be discussed by us.

The foreman and the rest of the jury would rightly conclude that the philosopher must be making some mistake. What sort of a mistake could it be? There is only one possible answer. The philosopher must be using the phrase "free will" in some peculiar way of his own which is not the way in which men usually use it. . . .

What, then, is the difference between acts which are freely done and those which are not? . . . The free acts are all caused by desires, or motives, or by some sort of internal psychological states of the agent's mind. The unfree acts, on the other hand, are all caused by physical forces or physical conditions, outside the agent. . . . We may therefore frame the following rough definitions. *Acts freely done are those whose immediate causes are psychological states in the agent. Acts not freely done are those whose immediate causes are states of affairs external to the agent.*

It is plain that if we define free will in this way, then free will certainly exists, and the philosopher's denial of its existence is seen to be what it is—nonsense. For it is obvious that all those actions of men which we should ordinarily attribute to the exercise of their free will, or of which we should say that they freely chose to do them, are in fact actions which have been caused by their own desires, wishes, thoughts, emotions, impulses, or other psychological states.

In applying our definition we shall find that it usually works well, but that there are some puzzling cases which it does not seem exactly to fit. These puzzles can always be solved by paying careful attention to the ways in which words are used, and remembering that they are not always used consistently. I have space for only one example. Suppose that a thug threatens to shoot you unless you give him your wallet, and suppose that you do so. Do you, in giving him your wallet, do so of your own free will or not? If we apply our definition, we find that you acted freely, since the immediate cause of the action was not an actual outside force but the fear of death, which is a psychological cause. Most people, however, would say that you did not act of your own free will but under compulsion. Does this show that our definition is wrong? I do not think so. . . . In the case under discussion, though no actual force was used, the gun at your forehead so nearly approximated to actual force that we tend to say the case was one of compulsion. It is a borderline case.

Here is what may seem like another kind of puzzle. According to our view an action may be free though it could have been predicted beforehand with certainty. But suppose you told a lie, and it was certain beforehand that you would tell it. How could one then say, "You could have told the truth"? The answer is that it is perfectly true that you could have told the truth *if* you had wanted to. In fact you would have done so, for in that case the causes producing your action, namely your desires, would have been different, and would therefore have produced different effects. It is a delusion that predictability and free will are incompatible. This agrees with common sense. For if, knowing your character, I predict that you will act honorably, no one would say when you do act honorably, that this shows you did not do so of your own free will.

Study Questions

1. If you deny the existence of free will, is your position undermined by the observation that you act as if people had free will?
2. How does Stace argue in behalf of the compatibility of free will and determinism?
3. What does Stace believe is the difference between acts that are freely done and those that are not?
4. If someone can predict with certainty what you will do, might your action nevertheless be free?

Freedom or Determinism?

STEVEN M. CAHN

In the next essay I offer an overview of the problem of free will and argue against Stace's view that freedom is compatible with determinism. The discussion begins with an account of one of the twentieth century's most famous criminal trials. How did it involve a philosophical issue? Let us see.

In 1924 the American people were horrified by a senseless crime of extraordinary brutality. The defendants were eighteen-year-old Nathan Leopold and seventeen-year-old Richard Loeb, the sons of Chicago millionaires, and brilliant students who had led seemingly idyllic lives. Leopold was the youngest graduate in the history of the University of Chicago, and Loeb the youngest graduate in the history of the University of Michigan. Suddenly they were accused of the kidnapping and vicious murder of fourteen-year-old Bobby Franks, a cousin of Loeb's. Before the trial even began, Leopold and Loeb both confessed, and from across the country came an outcry for their execution.

The lawyer who agreed to defend them was Clarence Darrow, the outstanding defense attorney of his time. Because Leopold and Loeb

From *Puzzles & Perplexities: Collected Essays*, 2d edition by Steven M. Cahn. Copyright © 2007 by the author and reprinted with his permission.

had already admitted their crime, Darrow's only chance was to explain their behavior in such a way that his clients could escape the death penalty. He was forced to argue that Leopold and Loeb were not morally responsible for what they had done, that they were not to be blamed for their actions. But how could he possibly maintain that position?

Darrow's defense was a landmark in the history of criminal law. He argued that the actions of his clients were a direct and necessary result of hereditary and environmental forces beyond their control.[1] Leopold suffered from a glandular disease that left him depressed and moody. Originally shy with girls, he had been sent to an all-girls school as a cure but had sustained deep psychic scars from which he never recovered. In addition, his parents instilled in him the belief that his wealth absolved him of any responsibility toward others. Pathologically inferior because of his diminutive size, and pathologically superior because of his wealth, he became an acute schizophrenic.

Loeb suffered from a nervous disorder that caused fainting spells. During his unhappy childhood, he had often thought of committing suicide. He was under the control of a domineering governess and was forced to lie and cheat to deceive her. His wealth led him to believe that he was superior to all those around him, and he developed a fascination for crime, an activity in which he could demonstrate his superiority. By the time he reached college he was severely psychotic.

In his final plea Darrow recounted these facts. His central theme was that Leopold and Loeb were in the grip of powers beyond their control, that they themselves were victims.

> I do not know what it was that made these boys do this mad act, but I do know there is a reason for it. I know they did not beget themselves. I know that any one of an infinite number of causes reaching back to the beginning might be working out in these boys' minds, whom you are asked to hang in malice and in hatred and in injustice, because someone in the past

has sinned against them . . . What had this boy to do with it? He was not his own father; he was not his own mother; he was not his own grandparents. All of this was handed to him. He did not surround himself with governesses and wealth. He did not make himself. And yet he is to be compelled to pay.[2]

Darrow's plea was successful, for Leopold and Loeb escaped execution and were sentenced to life imprisonment. Although they had committed crimes and were legally responsible for their actions, the judge believed they were not morally responsible, for they had not acted freely.

If the line of argument that Darrow utilized in the Leopold-Loeb case is sound, then not only were Leopold and Loeb not to blame for what they had done, but no person is ever to blame for any actions. As Darrow himself put it, "We are all helpless."[3] But is Darrow's argument sound? Does the conclusion follow from the premises, and are the premises true?

We can formalize his argument as follows:

Premise 1: No action is free if it must occur.
Premise 2: In the case of every event that occurs, antecedent conditions, known or unknown, ensure the event's occurrence.
Conclusion: Therefore, no action is free.

Premise (1) assumes that an action is free only if it is within the agent's power to perform it and within the agent's power not to perform it. In other words, whether a free action will occur is up to the agent. If circumstances require the agent to perform a certain action or require the agent not to perform that action, then the action is not free.

Premise (2) is the thesis known as *determinism*. Put graphically, it is the claim that if at any time a being knew the position of every particle in the universe and all the forces acting on each particle, then that being could predict with certainty every future event. Determinism does not presume such a being exists; the being is only imagined in order to illustrate what the world would be like if determinism were true.

Darrow's conclusion, which is supposed to follow from premises (1) and (2), is that no person has free will. Note that to have free will does not imply being free with regard to all actions, for only the mythical Superman is free to leap tall buildings at a single bound. But so long as at least some of an agent's actions are free, the agent is said to have free will. What Darrow's argument purports to prove is that not a single human action that has ever been performed has been performed freely.

Does the conclusion of Darrow's argument follow from the premises? If premise (2) is true, then every event that occurs must occur, for its occurrence is ensured by antecedent conditions. Because every action is an event, it follows from premise (2) that every action that occurs must occur. But according to premise (1), no action is free if it must occur. Thus, if premises (1) and (2) are true, it follows that no action is free—the conclusion of Darrow's argument.

Even granting that Darrow's reasoning is unassailable, we need not accept the conclusion of his argument unless we grant the truth of his premises. Should we do so?

Hard determinism is the view that both premises of Darrow's argument are correct. In other words, a hard determinist believes that determinism is true and that, as a consequence, no person has free will.[4] Determinists note that whenever an event occurs, we all assume that a causal explanation can account for the occurrence of the event. Suppose, for example, you feel a pain in your arm and are prompted to visit a physician. After examining you, the doctor announces that the pain has no cause, either physical or psychological. In other words, you are supposed to be suffering from an uncaused pain. On hearing this diagnosis, you would surely switch doctors. After all, no one may be able to discover the cause of your pain, but surely something is causing it. If nothing were causing it, you wouldn't be in pain. This same line of reasoning applies whether the event to be explained is a loud noise, a change in the weather, or an individual's action. If the event were uncaused, it wouldn't have occurred.

We may agree, however, that the principle of determinism holds in the vast majority of cases, yet doubt its applicability in the realm of human action. While causal explanations may be found for rocks falling and birds flying, people are far more complex than rocks or birds.

The determinist responds to this objection by asking us to consider any specific action: for instance, your decision to read this book. You may suppose your decision was uncaused, but did you not wish to acquire information about philosophy? The determinist argues that your desire for such information, together with your belief that the information is found in this book, caused you to read. Just as physical forces cause rocks and birds to do things, so human actions are caused by desires and beliefs.

If you doubt this claim, the determinist can call attention to our success in predicting people's behavior. For example, a store owner who reduces prices can depend on increasing visits by shoppers; an athlete who wins a major championship can rely on greater attention from the press. Furthermore, when we read novels or see plays, we expect to understand why the characters act as they do, and an author who fails to provide such explanations is charged with poor writing. The similarity of people's reactions to the human condition also accounts for the popularity of the incisive psychological insights of a writer such as La Rochefoucauld, the French aphorist. We read one of his maxims, for instance, "When our integrity declines, our taste does also,"[5] and nod our heads with approval, but are we not agreeing to a plausible generalization about the workings of the human psyche?

Granted, people's behavior cannot be predicted with certainty, but the hard determinist reminds us that each individual is influenced by a unique combination of hereditary and environmental factors. Just as each rock is slightly different from every other rock, and each bird is somewhat different from every other bird, so human beings differ from each other. Yet just as rocks and birds are part of an unbroken chain of causes and effects, so human beings, too, are part of that chain. Just as a rock falls because it breaks off from a cliff, so people act because of their desires and beliefs. And just as a rock has no control over the wind that causes it to break off, so people have no control over the desires and beliefs that cause them to act. In short, we are said to have no more control over our desires and beliefs than Leopold and Loeb had over theirs. If you can control your desire for food and your friend cannot, the explanation is that your will is of a sort that can control your desire and your friend's will is of a sort that cannot. That your will is of one sort and your friend's will of another is not within the control of either of you. As one hard determinist has written, "If we can overcome the effects of early environment, the ability to do so is itself a product of the early environment. We did not give ourselves this ability; and if we lack it we cannot be blamed for not having it."[6]

At this point in the argument an antideterminist is apt to call attention to recent developments in physics that have been interpreted by some thinkers as a refutation of determinism. They claim that work in quantum mechanics demonstrates that certain subatomic events are uncaused and inherently unpredictable. Yet some physicists and philosophers of science argue that determinism has not been refuted, because the experimental results can be understood in causal terms.[7] The outcome of this dispute, however, seems irrelevant to the issue of human freedom, because the events we are discussing are not subatomic, and indeterminism on that level is compatible with the universal causation of events on the much larger level of human action.

Here, then, is a summary of hard determinism: According to this view, determinism is true and no person has free will. Every event that occurs is caused to occur, for otherwise why

would it occur? Your present actions are events caused by your previous desires and beliefs, which themselves are accounted for by hereditary and environmental factors. These are part of a causal chain extending back far before your birth, and each link of the chain determines the succeeding link. Because you obviously have no control over events that occurred before your birth, and because these earlier events determined the later ones, it follows that you have no control over your present actions. In short, you do not have free will.

The hard determinist's argument may appear plausible, yet few of us are inclined to accept its shocking conclusion. We opt, therefore, to deny one of its two premises. *Soft determinism* is the view that the conclusion is false because premise (1) is false. In other words, a soft determinist believes both that determinism is true and that human beings have free will. The implication of the position is that an action may be free even if it is part of a causal chain extending back to events outside the agent's control. While this view may at first appear implausible, it has been defended throughout the centuries by many eminent philosophers, including David Hume and John Stuart Mill.

An approach employed explicitly or implicitly by many soft determinists has come to be known as "the paradigm-case argument." Consider it first in another setting, where its use is a classic of philosophical argumentation.

In studying physics, we learn that ordinary objects like tables and chairs are composed of sparsely scattered, minute particles. This fact may lead us to suppose that such objects are not solid. As Sir Arthur Eddington, the noted physicist, put it, a "plank has no solidity of substance. To step on it is like stepping on a swarm of flies."[8]

Eddington's view that a plank is not solid was forcefully attacked by the British philosopher L. Susan Stebbing. She pointed out that the word "solid" derives its meaning from examples such as planks.

For "solid" just is the word we use to describe a certain respect in which a plank of wood resembles a block of marble, a piece of paper, and a cricket ball, and in which each of these differs from a sponge, from the interior of a soap-bubble, and from the holes in a net. . . . The point is that the common usage of language enables us to attribute a meaning to the phrase "a solid plank"; but there is no common usage of language that provides a meaning for the word "solid" that would make sense to say that the plank on which I stand is not solid.[9]

In other words, a plank is a paradigm case of solidity. Anyone who claims that a plank is not solid does not know how the word "solid" is used in the English language. Note that Stebbing is not criticizing Eddington's scientific views but only the manner in which he interpreted them.

The paradigm-case argument is useful to soft determinists, for in the face of the hard determinist's claim that no human action is free, soft determinists respond by pointing to a paradigm case of a free action, for instance, a person walking down the street. They stipulate that the individual is not under the influence of drugs, is not attached to ropes, is not sleepwalking, and so on; in other words, they refer to a normal, everyday instance of a person walking down the street. Soft determinists claim that the behavior described is a paradigm case of a free action, clearly distinguishable from instances in which a person is, in fact, under the influence of drugs, attached to ropes, or sleepwalking. These latter cases are not examples of free actions, or are at best problematic examples, while the case the soft determinists cite is clear and seemingly indisputable. Indeed, according to soft determinists, anyone who claims the act of walking down the street is not free does not know how the word "free" is used in English. Thus people certainly have free will, for we can cite obvious cases in which they act freely.

How do soft determinists define a "free action"? According to them, actions are free if the persons who perform them wish to do so and could, if they wished, not perform them. If your arm is forcibly raised, you did not act freely, for you did not wish to raise your arm. If you were locked in a room, you would also not be free, even if you wished to be there, for if you wished to leave, you couldn't.

Soft determinists emphasize that once we define "freedom" correctly, any apparent incompatibility between freedom and determinism disappears. Consider some particular action I perform that is free in the sense explicated by soft determinists. Even if the action is one link in a causal chain extending far back beyond my birth, nevertheless I am free with regard to that action, for I wish to perform it, and if I did not wish to, I would not do so. This description of the situation is consistent with supposing that my wish is a result of hereditary and environmental factors over which I have no control. The presence of such factors is, according to the soft determinists, irrelevant to the question of whether my action is free. I may be walking down a particular street because of my desire to buy a coat and my belief that I am heading toward a clothing store, and this desire and belief may themselves be caused by any number of other factors. But because I desire to walk down the street and could walk down some other street if I so desired, it follows that I am freely walking down the street. By this line of reasoning soft determinists affirm both free will and determinism, finding no incompatibility between them.

Soft determinism is an inviting doctrine, for it allows us to maintain a belief in free will without having to relinquish the belief that every event has a cause. Soft determinism, however, is open to objections that have led some philosophers to abandon the position.

The fundamental problem for soft determinists is that their definition of "freedom" does not seem in accordance with the ordinary way in which we use the term. Note that soft determinists and hard determinists offer two different definitions of "freedom." According to the hard determinist, an action is free if it is within my power to perform it and also within my power not to perform it. According to the soft determinist, an action is free if it is such that if I wish to perform it I can, and if I wish not to perform it I also can. To highlight the difference between these definitions, consider the case of a man who has been hypnotized and rolls up the leg of his pants as if to cross a stream. Is his action free? According to the hard determinist, the man's action is not free, for it is not within his power to refrain from rolling up the leg of his pants. According to the soft determinist's definition of "freedom," the action would be considered free, for the agent desires to perform it, and if he didn't desire to, he wouldn't. But a man under hypnosis is not free. Therefore, the soft determinist's definition of "freedom" seems unsatisfactory.

Perhaps this objection to soft determinism is unfair, because the desires of the hypnotized man are not his own but are controlled by the hypnotist. The force of the objection to soft determinism, however, is that the soft determinist overlooks whether a person's wishes or desires are themselves within that individual's control. The hard determinist emphasizes that my action is free only if it is up to me whether to perform it. But in order for an action to be up to me, I need to have control over my own wishes or desires. If I do not, my desires might be controlled by a hypnotist, a brainwasher, my family, hereditary factors, and so on, and thus I would not be free. Soft determinists do not appear to take such possibilities seriously, because, according to them, I would be free even if my desires were not within my control, so long as I was acting according to my desires and could act differently if my desires were different. But could my desires have been different? That is the crucial question. If my desires could not have been different, then I could not have acted in any way other than I did, which is the description of a person who is not free.

By failing to consider the ways in which a person's desires can be controlled by external forces beyond the individual's control, soft determinists offer a definition of "freedom" that I find not in accord with our normal use of the term. They may, of course, define terms as they wish, but we are interested in the concept of freedom relevant to questions of moral responsibility. Any concept of freedom implying that hypnotized or brainwashed individuals are morally responsible for their actions is not the concept in question.

What of the soft determinist's claim that a person's walking down the street is a paradigm case of a free action? Although I agree that the paradigm-case argument can sometimes be used effectively, the soft determinist's appeal to it does not seem convincing. To see why, imagine that we traveled to a land in which the inhabitants believed that every woman born on February 29 was a witch, and that every witch had the power to cause droughts. If we refused to believe that any woman was a witch, the philosophically sophisticated inhabitants might try to convince us by appealing to the paradigm-case argument, claiming that anyone born on February 29 is a paradigm case of a witch.

What would we say in response? How does this appeal to a paradigm case differ from Susan Stebbing's appeal to a plank as a paradigm case of solidity? No one doubts that a plank can hold significant weight and is, in that sense, solid. But until women born on February 29 demonstrate supernatural powers and are in that sense witches, the linguistic claim alone has no force.

Are soft determinists appealing to an indisputable instance when they claim that a person's walking down the street is a paradigm case of a free action? Not at all, for as we saw in the trial of Leopold and Loeb, such apparently free actions may not turn out to be judged as free. By appealing to a disputable example as a paradigm case, soft determinists assume what they are supposed to be proving. They are supposed to demonstrate that actions such as walking down the street are examples of free actions. Merely asserting that such actions are free is to overlook the hard determinist's argument that such actions are not free. No questionable instance can be used as a paradigm case, and walking down the street is, as Darrow demonstrated, a questionable example of a free action. Thus soft determinism appears to have a serious weakness.

Remember that the hard determinist argues that because premises (1) and (2) of Darrow's argument are true, so is the conclusion. Soft determinists argue that premise (1) is false. If they are mistaken, then the only way to avoid hard determinism is to reject premise (2). That position is known as *libertarianism*.

The libertarian agrees with the hard determinist that if an action must occur, it is not free. For the libertarian as well as for the hard determinist, I am free with regard to a particular action only if it is within my power to perform the action and within my power not to perform it. But do persons ever act freely? The hard determinist believes that people are never free, because in the case of every action, antecedent conditions, known or unknown, ensure the action's occurrence. Libertarians refuse to accept this conclusion, but find it impossible to reject premise (1) of Darrow's argument. Therefore their only recourse is to reject premise (2). As Sherlock Holmes noted, "When you have eliminated the impossible, whatever remains, however improbable, must be the truth."[10] The libertarian thus denies that every event has a cause.

But why is the libertarian so convinced that people sometimes act freely? Consider an ordinary human action—for instance, raising your hand at a meeting to attract the speaker's attention. If you are attending a lecture and the time comes for questions from the audience, you believe it is within your power to raise your hand and also within your power not to raise it. The choice is yours. Nothing forces you to ask a question, and nothing prevents you from asking one. What could be more obvious? If this description of the situation is accurate, then hard determinism is incorrect, for

you are free with regard to the act of raising your hand.

The heart of the libertarian's position is that innumerable examples of this sort are conclusive evidence for free will. Indeed, we normally accept them as such. We assume on most occasions that we are free with regard to our actions, and, moreover, we assume that other persons are free with regard to theirs. If a friend agrees to meet us at six o'clock for dinner and arrives an hour late claiming to have lost track of time, we blame her for her tardiness, because we assume she had it within her power to act otherwise. All she had to do was glance at her watch, and assuming no special circumstances were involved, it was within her power to do so. She was simply negligent and deserves to be blamed, for she could have acted conscientiously. But to believe she could have acted in a way other than she did is to believe she was free.

How do hard determinists respond to such examples? They argue that such situations need to be examined in greater detail. In the case of our friend who arrives an hour late for dinner, we assume she is to blame for her actions, but the hard determinist points out that some motive impelled her to be late. Perhaps she was more interested in finishing her work at the office than in arriving on time for dinner. But why was she more interested in finishing her work than in arriving on time? Perhaps her parents had instilled in her the importance of work but not promptness. Hard determinists stress that whatever the explanation for her lateness, the motive causing it was stronger than the motive impelling her to arrive on time. She acted as she did because her strongest motive prevailed. Which motive was the strongest, however, was not within her control, and thus she was not free.

The hard determinist's reply may seem persuasive. How can I deny that I am invariably caused to act by my strongest motive? Analysis reveals, however, that the thesis is tautological, immune from refutation, and so devoid of empirical content. No matter what example of a human action is presented, a defender of the thesis could argue that the person's action resulted from the strongest motive. If I take a swim, taking a swim must have been my strongest motive. If I decide to forgo the swim and read a book instead, then reading a book must have been my strongest motive. How do we know that my motive to read a book was stronger than my motive to take a swim? Because I read a book and did not take a swim. If this line of argument appears powerful, the illusion will last only so long as we do not ask how we are to identify a person's strongest motive. The only possible answer appears to be that the strongest motive is the motive that prevails, the motive that causes the person to act. If the strongest motive is the motive causing the person to act, what force is there in the claim that the motive causing a person to act is causing the person to act? No insight into the complexities of human action is obtained by trumpeting such an empty redundancy.

Thus the hard determinist does not so easily succeed in overturning the examples of free actions offered by the libertarian. However, both hard and soft determinists have another argument to offer against the libertarian's position. If the libertarian is correct that free actions are uncaused, why do they occur? Are they inexplicable occurrences? If so, to act freely would be to act in a random, chaotic, unintelligible fashion. Yet holding people morally blameworthy for inexplicable actions is unreasonable. If you are driving a car and, to your surprise, find yourself turning the wheel to the right, we can hardly blame you if an accident occurs, for what happened was beyond your control.

So determinists argue that libertarians are caught in a dilemma. If we are caused to do whatever we do, libertarians assert we are not morally responsible for our actions. Yet if our actions are uncaused and inexplicable, libertarians again must deny our moral responsibility.

How then can libertarians claim we ever act responsibly?

To understand the libertarian response, consider the simple act of a man picking up a telephone. Suppose we want to understand what he is doing and are told he is calling his stockbroker. The man has decided to buy some stock and wishes his broker to place the appropriate order. With this explanation, we now know why this man has picked up the telephone. Although we may be interested in learning more about the man or his choice of stocks, we have a complete explanation of his action, which turns out not to be random, chaotic, or unintelligible. We may not know what, if anything, is causing the man to act, but we do know the reason for the man's action. The libertarian thus replies to the determinist's dilemma by arguing that an action can be uncaused yet understandable, explicable in terms of the agent's intentions or purposes.

Now contrast the libertarian's description of a particular action with a determinist's. Let the action be your moving your arm to adjust your television set. A determinist claims you were caused to move your arm by your desire to adjust the set and your belief that you could make this adjustment by turning the dials. A libertarian claims you moved your arm in order to adjust the set.

Note that the libertarian explains human actions fundamentally differently from the way in which we explain the movements of rocks or rivers. If we speak of a rock's purpose in falling off a cliff or a river's purpose in flowing south, we do so only metaphorically, for we believe that rocks and rivers have no purposes of their own but are caused to do what they do. Strictly speaking, a rock does not fall in order to hit the ground, and a river does not flow in order to reach the south. But libertarians are speaking not metaphorically but literally when they say that people act in order to achieve their purposes. After all, not even the most complex machine can act as a person does. A machine can break down and fail to operate, but only a human being can protest and stop work on purpose.

Is the libertarian's view correct? I doubt anyone is justified in answering that question with certainty, but if the libertarian is right, human beings are often morally responsible for their actions. They deserve praise when acting admirably and blame when acting reprehensibly. Darrow may have been correct in arguing that Leopold and Loeb were not free agents, but if the libertarian is right, the burden of proof lay with Darrow, for he had to demonstrate that these boys were in that respect unlike the rest of us.

What if the libertarian is not correct? What if all human actions are caused by antecedent conditions, known or unknown, that ensure their occurrence? Moral responsibility would vanish, but even so people could be held legally responsible for their actions. Just as we need to be safeguarded against mad dogs, so we need protection from dangerous people. Thus even if no person were morally responsible, we would still have a legal system, courts, criminals, and prisons. Remember that Darrow's eloquence did not free his clients; indeed, he did not ask that they be freed. Although he did not blame them for their actions, he did not want those actions repeated. To Darrow, Leopold and Loeb were sick men who needed the same care as sick persons with a contagious disease. After all, in a world without freedom, events need not be viewed as agreeable; they should, however, be understood as necessary.

Notes

1. The following information is found in Irving Stone, *Clarence Darrow for the Defense* (Garden City, NY: Doubleday, Doran, 1941), pp. 384–91.

2. *Attorney for the Damned*, ed. Arthur Weinberg (New York: Simon and Schuster, 1957), pp. 37, 65.

3. Ibid., p. 37.

4. The expressions "hard determinism" and "soft determinism" were coined by William James in his essay "The Dilemma of Determinism," reprinted in *Essays on Faith and Morals* (Cleveland: World, 1962).

5. *The Maxims of La Rochefoucauld*, trans. Louis Kronenberger (New York: Random House, 1959), #379.

6. John Hospers, "What Means This Freedom," *Determinism and Freedom in the Age of Modern Science*, ed. Sidney Hook (New York: Collier, 1961), p. 138.

7. For a detailed discussion of the philosophical implications of quantum mechanics, see Ernest Nagel, *The Structure of Science* (New York: Harcourt Brace Jovanovich, 1961), ch. 10.

8. A. S. Eddington, *The Nature of the Physical World* (New York: Macmillan, 1928), p. 342.

9. L. Susan Stebbing, *Philosophy and the Physicists* (New York: Dover, 1958), pp. 51–52.

10. Sir Arthur Conan Doyle, "The Sign of Four," in *The Complete Sherlock Holmes* (Garden City, NY: Doubleday, n.d.), p. 111.

Study Questions

1. Is a hard determinist more committed to determinism than a soft determinist?
2. What reply does Cahn offer to the sort of argument presented by Stace in the preceding selection?
3. Are reasons a type of cause?
4. Can a machine make a mistake on purpose?

The Principle of Alternative Possibilities

HARRY FRANKFURT

Our previous selections on free will have taken for granted that if people cannot act otherwise than as they do, then they do not act freely. But is this assumption correct? Harry Frankfurt, who is Professor Emeritus of Philosophy at Princeton University, argues that the assumption is mistaken, and he offers an intriguing example to defend his position.

A dominant role in nearly all recent inquiries into the free-will problem has been played by a principle which I shall call "the principle of alternate possibilities." This principle states that a person is morally responsible for what he has done only if he could have done otherwise.... Practically no one ... seems inclined to deny or even to question that the principle of alternate possibilities ... is true....

But the principle of alternate possibilities is false. A person may well be morally responsible for what he has done even though he could not have done otherwise. The principle's plausibility is an illusion, which can be made to vanish by bringing the relevant moral phenomena into sharper focus....

Suppose someone—Black, let us say—wants Jones to perform a certain action. Black is prepared to go to considerable lengths to get his way, but he prefers to avoid showing his hand unnecessarily. So he waits until Jones is about to make up his mind what to do, and he does nothing unless it is clear to him (Black is an excellent judge of such things) that Jones is going to decide to do something *other* than what he wants him to do. If it does become clear that Jones is going to decide to do something else, Black takes effective steps to ensure that Jones decides to do, and that he does do, what he wants him to do. Whatever Jones's initial preferences and inclinations, then, Black will have his way.

What steps will Black take, if he believes he must take steps, in order to ensure that Jones decides and acts as he wishes? Anyone with a theory concerning what "could have done otherwise" means may answer this question for himself by describing whatever measures he would regard as sufficient to guarantee that, in the relevant sense, Jones cannot do otherwise. Let Black pronounce a terrible threat, and in this way both force Jones to perform the desired action and prevent him from performing a forbidden one. Let Black give Jones a potion, or put him under hypnosis, and in some such way as these generate in Jones an irresistible inner compulsion to perform the act Black wants performed and to avoid others. Or let Black manipulate the minute processes of Jones's brain and nervous system in some more direct way, so that causal forces running in and out of his synapses and along the poor man's nerves determine that he chooses to act and that he does act in the one way and not in any other. Given any conditions under which it will be maintained that Jones cannot do otherwise, in other words,

From Harry Frankfurt, "Alternative Possibilities and Moral Responsibility," *The Journal of Philosophy*, LXVI, 23 (1969). Reprinted by permission of the journal and the author.

let Black bring it about that those conditions prevail. The structure of the example is flexible enough, I think, to find a way around any charge of irrelevance by accommodating the doctrine on which the charge is based.

Now suppose that Black never has to show his hand because Jones, for reasons of his own, decides to perform and does perform the very action Black wants him to perform. In that case, it seems clear, Jones will bear precisely the same moral responsibility for what he does as he would have borne if Black had not been ready to take steps to ensure that he do it. It would be quite unreasonable to excuse Jones for his action, or to withhold the praise to which it would normally entitle him, on the basis of the fact that he could not have done otherwise. This fact played no role at all in leading him to act as he did. He would have acted the same even if it had not been a fact. Indeed, everything happened just as it would have happened without Black's presence in the situation and without his readiness to intrude into it.

In this example there are sufficient conditions for Jones's performing the action in question. What action he performs is not up to him. Of course it is in a way up to him whether he acts on his own or as a result of Black's intervention. That depends upon what action he himself is inclined to perform. But whether he finally acts on his own or as a result of Black's intervention, he performs the same action. He has no alternative but to do what Black wants him to do. If he does it on his own, however, his moral responsibility for doing it is not affected by the fact that Black was lurking in the background with sinister intent, since this intent never comes into play. . . .

This, then, is why the principle of alternate possibilities is mistaken. It asserts that a person bears no moral responsibility—that is, he is to be excused—for having performed an action if there were circumstances that made it impossible for him to avoid performing it. But there may be circumstances that make it impossible for a person to avoid performing some action without those circumstances in any way bringing it about that he performs that action. It would surely be no good for the person to refer to circumstances of this sort in an effort to absolve himself of moral responsibility for performing the action in question. For those circumstances, by hypothesis, actually had nothing to do with his having done what he did. He would have done precisely the same thing, and he would have been led or made in precisely the same way to do it, even if they had not prevailed. . . .

Study Questions

1. What is "the principle of alternate possibilities"?
2. Explain in your own words the case of Black and Jones.
3. Does this case disprove the principle of alternate possibilities?
4. Is Frankfurt's view consistent with soft determinism?

Part V

⬚

Religion

A.   Religious Beliefs

The Ontological Argument

ANSELM AND GAUNILO

One metaphysical issue that interests us all is whether God exists. A theist believes God does exist. An atheist believes God does not exist. An agnostic believes the available evidence is insufficient to decide the matter. Which of these positions is the most reasonable?

The first step in answering this question is to determine what is meant by the term "God." Let us adopt a view common to many religious believers that "God" refers to an all-good, all-powerful, eternal Creator of the world. The question then is whether a being of that description exists.

Throughout the history of philosophy, various arguments have been offered to prove God's existence. Only one, however, the ontological argument, is *a priori,* making no appeal to empirical evidence and relying solely on an analysis of the concept of God.

Its classic formulation was provided by Saint Anselm (1033–1109), who was born in a village that is now part of Italy, was educated in a Benedictine monastery, and became Archbishop of Canterbury. He understood God to be the Being greater than which none can be conceived. Anselm reasoned that if God did not exist, then a greater being could be conceived, namely, a being that exists. In that case, the Being greater than which none can be conceived would not be the Being greater than which none can be conceived, which is a contradiction. So the Being greater than which none can be conceived must exist, that is, God must exist. Indeed, Anselm goes on to claim that God cannot even be thought not to exist, because a being that *cannot* be thought not to exist is greater than one that *can* be thought not to exist.

The first known response to Anselm's argument was offered by his contemporary Gaunilo, a monk of Marmoutier, France, about whom little is known. Gaunilo maintained that Anselm's line of reasoning could be used to prove the existence of an island greater than which none can be conceived, an absurd conclusion. In reply, Anselm maintained that the argument did not apply to an island because, unlike God, an island has a beginning and end and so can be thought not to exist.

The ontological argument has continued to intrigue thinkers throughout the centuries. While its intricacy may not win many converts to theism, the argument retains the power to fascinate philosophers.

From Brian Davies and G. R. Evans, eds., *Anselm of Canterbury: The Major Works.* Reprinted by permission of Oxford University Press. The words enclosed in brackets have been interpolated by the translator, M. J. Charlesworth, to make the meaning clearer.

PROSLOGION

2

Well then, Lord, You who give understanding to faith, grant me that I may understand, as much as You see fit, that You exist as we believe You to exist, and that You are what we believe You to be. Now we believe that You are something than which nothing greater can be thought. Or can it be that a thing of such a nature does not exist, since "the Fool has said in his heart, there is no God" [Ps. 13:1; 52:1]? But surely, when this same Fool hears what I am speaking about, namely, "something-than-which-nothing-greater-can-be-thought," he understands what he hears, and what he understands is in his mind, even if he does not understand that it actually exists. For it is one thing for an object to exist in the mind, and another thing to understand that an object actually exists. Thus, when a painter plans beforehand what he is going to execute, he has [the picture] in his mind, but he does not yet think that it actually exists because he has not yet executed it. However, when he has actually painted it, then he both has it in his mind and understands that it exists because he has now made it. Even the Fool, then, is forced to agree that something-than-which-nothing-greater-can-be-thought exists in the mind, since he understands this when he hears it, and whatever is understood is in the mind. And surely that-than-which-a-greater-cannot-be-thought cannot exist in the mind alone. For if it exists solely in the mind, it can be thought to exist in reality also, which is greater. If then that-than-which-a-greater-cannot-be-thought exists in the mind alone, this same that-than-which-a-greater-*cannot*-be-thought is that-than-which-a-greater-*can*-be-thought. But this is obviously impossible. Therefore there is absolutely no doubt that something-than-which-a-greater-cannot-be-thought exists both in the mind and in reality.

3

And certainly this being so truly exists that it cannot be even thought not to exist. For something can be thought to exist that cannot be thought not to exist, and this is greater than that which can be thought not to exist. Hence, if that-than-which-a-greater-cannot-be-thought can be thought not to exist, then that-than-which-a-greater-cannot-be-thought is not the same as that-than-which-a-greater-cannot-be-thought, which is absurd. Something-than-which-a-greater-cannot-be-thought exists so truly then, that it cannot be even thought not to exist.

And You, Lord our God, are this being. You exist so truly, Lord my God, that You cannot even be thought not to exist. And this is as it should be, for if some intelligence could think of something better than You, the creature would be above its Creator and would judge its Creator—and that is completely absurd. In fact, everything else there is, except You alone, can be thought of as not existing. You alone, then, of all things most truly exist and therefore of all things possess existence to the highest degree; for anything else does not exist as truly, and so possesses existence to a lesser degree. Why then did 'the Fool say in his heart, there is no God' [Ps. 13:1; 52:1] when it is so evident to any rational mind that You of all things exist to the highest degree? Why indeed, unless because he was stupid and a fool?

4

How indeed has he "said in his heart" what he could not think; or how could he not think what he "said in his heart," since to "say in one's heart" and to "think" are the same? But if he really (indeed, since he really) both thought because he "said in his heart" and did not "say in his heart" because he could not think, there is not only one sense in which something is "said in one's heart" or thought. For in one sense a thing is thought when the word signifying it is thought; in another sense when the very object which the thing is is understood. In the first sense, then, God can be thought not to exist, but not at all in the second sense. No one, indeed, understanding what God is can think that God does not exist, even though he may say these words in his heart either without any [objective] signification or with some peculiar signification. For God is that-than-which-nothing-greater-can-be-thought. Whoever really understands this understands clearly that this same being so exists that not even in thought can it not exist. Thus whoever understands that God exists in such a way cannot think of Him as not existing.

I give thanks, good Lord, I give thanks to You, since what I believed before through Your free gift I now so understand through Your illumination, that if I did not want to *believe* that You existed, I should nevertheless be unable not to *understand* it.

ON BEHALF OF THE FOOL

Gaunilo

1

To one doubting whether there is, or denying that there is, something of such a nature than which nothing greater can be thought, it is said here that its existence is proved, first because the very one who denies or doubts it already has it in his mind, since when he hears it spoken of he understands what is said; and further, because what he understands is necessarily such that it exists not only in the mind but also in reality. And this is proved by the fact that it is greater to exist both in the mind and in reality than in the mind alone. For if this same being exists in the mind alone, anything that existed also in reality would be greater than this being, and thus that which is greater than everything would be less than some thing and would not be greater than everything, which is obviously contradictory. Therefore, it is necessarily the case that that which is greater than everything, being already proved to exist in the mind, should exist not only in the mind but also in reality, since otherwise it would not be greater than everything.

2

But he [the Fool] can perhaps reply that this thing is said already to exist in the mind only in the sense that I understand what is said. For could I not say that all kinds of unreal things, not existing in themselves in any way at all, are equally in the mind since if anyone speaks about them I understand whatever he says? . . .

6

For example: they say that there is in the ocean somewhere an island which, because of the difficulty (or rather the impossibility) of finding that which does not exist, some have called the "Lost Island." And the story goes that it is blessed with all manner of priceless riches and delights in abundance, much more even than the Happy Isles, and, having no owner or inhabitant, it is superior everywhere in abundance of riches to all those other lands that men inhabit. Now, if anyone tell me that it is like this, I shall easily understand what is said, since nothing is difficult about it. But if he should then go on to say, as though it were a logical consequence of this: You cannot any more doubt that this island that is more excellent than all other lands truly exists somewhere in reality than you can doubt that it is in your mind; and since it is more excellent to exist not only in the mind alone but also in reality, therefore it must needs be that it exists. For if it did not exist, any other land existing in reality would be more excellent than it, and so this island, already conceived by you to be more excellent than others, will not be more excellent. If, I say, someone wishes thus to persuade me that this island really exists beyond all doubt, I should either think that he was joking, or I should find it hard to decide which of us I ought to judge the bigger fool—I, if I agreed with him, or he, if he thought that he had proved the existence of this island with any certainty, unless he had first convinced me that its very excellence exists in my mind precisely as a thing existing truly and indubitably and not just as something unreal or doubtfully real.

REPLY TO GAUNILO

You claim, however, that this is as though someone asserted that it cannot be doubted that a certain island in the ocean (which is more fertile than all other lands and which, because of the difficulty or even the impossibility of discovering what does not exist, is called the "Lost Island") truly exists in reality since anyone easily understands it when it is described in words. Now, I truly promise that if anyone should discover for me something existing either in reality or in the mind alone—except "that-than-which-a-greater-cannot-be-thought"—to which the logic of my argument would apply, then I shall find that Lost Island and give it, never more to be lost, to that person. It has already been clearly seen, however, that "that-than-which-a-greater-cannot-be-thought" cannot be thought not to exist, because it exists as a matter of such certain truth. Otherwise it would not exist at all. In short, if anyone says that he thinks that this being does not exist, I reply that, when he thinks of this, either he thinks of something than which a greater cannot be thought, or he does not think of it. If he does not think of it, then he does not think that what he does not think of does not exist. If, however, he does think of it, then indeed he thinks of something which cannot be even thought not to exist. For if it could be thought not to exist, it could be thought to have a beginning and an end—but this cannot be. Thus, he who thinks of it thinks of something that cannot be thought not to exist; indeed, he who thinks of this does not think of it as not existing, otherwise he would think what cannot be thought. Therefore "that-than-which-a-greater-cannot-be-thought" cannot be thought not to exist.

Study Questions

1. Why is the ontological argument considered an *a priori* argument?
2. What are the premises Anselm uses to prove the existence of God?
3. What is Gaunilo's criticism of Anselm's argument?
4. Do you find Gaunilo's criticism persuasive?

The Five Ways

THOMAS AQUINAS

St. Thomas Aquinas (1225–1274), born near Naples, was the most influential philosopher of the medieval period. He joined the Dominican order and taught at the University of Paris. In his vast writings, composed in Latin, he sought to demonstrate that all Christian doctrines were consistent with reason, even if some transcended reason and were believed on faith, for example, that the world did not always exist but was created at a particular time.

Aquinas' greatest work was the *Summa Theologiae*, and its most famous passage, reprinted here, is the five ways to prove the existence of God. These arguments are *a posteriori*, relying on empirical evidence. They are typically grouped as "cosmological arguments," because they depend on observing features of the world and deducing from them that God exists.

In the fourth way Aquinas cites "*Metaph.* ii." The reference is to the second book of the *Metaphysics* of Aristotle, and serves as a reminder of Aquinas' high regard for that influential Greek thinker.

The existence of God can be proved in five ways.

The first and more manifest way is the argument from motion. It is certain, and evident to our senses, that in the world some things are in motion. Now whatever is moved is moved by another, for nothing can be moved except it is in potentiality to that towards which it is moved; whereas a thing moves inasmuch as it is in act. For motion is nothing else than the reduction of something from potentiality to actuality. But nothing can be reduced from potentiality to actuality, except by something in a state of actuality. Thus that which is actually hot, as fire, makes wood, which is potentially hot, to be actually hot, and thereby moves and changes it. Now it is not possible that the same thing should be at once in actuality and potentiality in the same respect, but only in different respects. For what is actually hot cannot simultaneously be potentially hot; but it is simultaneously potentially cold. It is therefore impossible that in the same respect and in the same way a thing should be both mover and moved, i.e., that it should move itself. Therefore, whatever is moved must be moved by another. If that by which it is moved be itself moved, then this also must needs be moved by another, and that by another again. But this cannot go on to infinity, because then there would be no first mover, and, consequently, no other mover, seeing that subsequent movers move only inasmuch as they are moved by the first mover; as the staff moves only because it is moved by the hand. Therefore it is necessary to arrive at a first mover, moved by no other; and this everyone understands to be God.

The second way is from the nature of efficient cause. In the world of sensible things we find there is an order of efficient causes. There is no case known (neither is it, indeed, possible) in which a thing is found to be the efficient cause of itself; for so it would be prior to itself, which is impossible. Now in efficient causes it is not possible to go on to infinity, because in all efficient causes following in order, the first is the cause of the intermediate cause, and the intermediate is the cause of the ultimate cause, whether the intermediate cause be several, or one only. Now to take away the cause is to take away the effect. Therefore, if there be no first cause among efficient causes, there will be no ultimate, nor any intermediate, cause. But if in efficient causes it is possible to go on to infinity, there will be no first efficient cause, neither will there be an ultimate effect, nor any intermediate efficient causes; all of which is plainly false. Therefore it is necessary to admit a first efficient cause, to which everyone gives the name of God.

The third way is taken from possibility and necessity, and runs thus. We find in nature things that are possible to be and not to be, since they are found to be generated, and to be corrupted, and consequently, it is possible for them to be and not to be. But it is impossible for these always to exist, for that which can not-be at some time is not. Therefore, if everything can not-be, then at one time there was nothing in existence. Now if this were true, even now there would be nothing in existence, because that which does not exist begins to exist only through something already existing. Therefore, if at one time nothing was in

existence, it would have been impossible for anything to have begun to exist; and thus even now
nothing would be in existence—which is absurd.
Therefore, not all beings are merely possible, but
there must exist something the existence of which
is necessary. But every necessary thing either has
its necessity caused by another, or not. Now it is
impossible to go on to infinity in necessary things
which have their necessity caused by another, as
has been already proved in regard to efficient
causes. Therefore we cannot but admit the existence of some being having of itself its own necessity, and not receiving it from another, but rather
causing in others their necessity. This all men
speak of as God.

The fourth way is taken from the gradation to
be found in things. Among beings there are
some more and some less good, true, noble, and
the like. But *more* and *less* are predicated of different things according as they resemble in their
different ways something which is the maximum, as a thing is said to be hotter according as
it more nearly resembles that which is hottest; so
that there is something which is truest,
something best, something noblest, and, consequently, something which is most being, for
those things that are greatest in truth are greatest in being, as it is written in *Metaph.* ii. Now
the maximum in any genus is the cause of all in
that genus, as fire, which is the maximum of
heat, is the cause of all hot things, as is said in
the same book. Therefore there must also be
something which is to all beings the cause of
their being, goodness, and every other perfection: and this we call God.

The fifth way is taken from the governance of
the world. We see that things which lack knowledge, such as natural bodies, act for an end, and
this is evident from their acting always, or nearly
always, in the same way, so as to obtain the best
result. Hence it is plain that they achieve their
end, not fortuitously, but designedly. Now whatever lacks knowledge cannot move towards an
end, unless it be directed by some being endowed
with knowledge and intelligence; as the arrow is
directed by the archer. Therefore some intelligent
being exists by whom all natural things are directed to their end; and this being we call God.

Study Questions

1. Do Aquinas' five ways all reach the same conclusion?
2. If whatever is moved must be moved by another, how is an unmoved mover possible?
3. Do the terms "more" and "less" always presuppose a maximum?
4. Does a river flowing toward the sea act for an end?

The Kalam Cosmological Argument

WILLIAM L. ROWE

In the next selection William L. Rowe, who is Professor Emeritus of Philosophy at
Purdue University, assesses a version of the cosmological argument that has its origin
in medieval Arabic philosophy but has recently been the subject of much discussion.

The argument has been dubbed "the Kalam argument," a term derived from an Arabic word referring to the interpretation of Islamic doctrine. The argument rests on the claim that the world necessarily had a beginning, and because time began with the beginning of the world, we can conclude that the cause of the world must be a timeless being, who is God.

A version of the Cosmological Argument that has its origin in Arabic philosophy is also receiving attention in contemporary philosophy of religion. . . . [A]ccording to the Kalam argument it is *impossible* for an *actual infinite* to exist. If the Kalam argument is correct on this point, then, since an actual series of events stretching endlessly into the past would be an actual infinite, it is impossible that such a series should exist. This does not mean that there could not be a series that is *potentially infinite,* a series that at any moment it is considered is finite, but that can be successively added to ad infinitum. For such a series would never be *actually* infinite. But why is an *actual infinite* series of past events leading up to the present claimed to be impossible? Consider such an unending series of events into the past. Suppose each of these events takes a certain amount of time, however small, to occur. No matter how little time it takes each event to occur, the claim is that since there is no *first event* in the series of past events, one could never reach the point where we now are, the present.

If we grant the impossibility of an actual infinite, we can be confident that our universe *had a beginning.* For if our universe never had a beginning, then the series of events of which its past temporal existence consists would constitute an actual infinite. But our confidence that our universe had a beginning need not rely on this philosophical argument; for according to the best estimates of current science our universe did have a beginning. It came into existence about 14.5 billion years ago, with the planet Earth coming into existence about 4.5 billion years ago, and living things on earth coming into existence about 3.5 billion years ago.

We can now state the first step in the Kalam Cosmological Argument as follows:

1. If our universe never had a beginning, an actual infinite series of past events has occurred.
2. An actual infinite series of events in time is impossible. Therefore,
3. Our universe had a beginning.

The second step of the Kalam argument raises the question of whether the beginning of our universe had a cause. It is important to note that according to current science the beginning of our universe also marks that beginning of time. So, there simply is no temporal moment *before* the beginning of our universe, no prior moment at which something or someone might act so as to cause our universe to begin. This means that if our universe were to have a cause, the cause (whatever it may be) could not have caused our universe by existing at some temporal moment *before* our universe existed and then acting so as to bring about the existence of our universe. How then could our universe have been caused to exist? A prominent advocate of the Kalam Cosmological Argument, William Lane Craig, has noted that a number of philosophers have countenanced *simultaneous causation.* He cites an example provided by Immanuel Kant: a heavy ball's resting on a cushion being the cause of a depression in that cushion. Craig concludes:

There seems to be no conceptual difficulty in saying that the cause of the origin of the universe acted simultaneously (or coincidentally) with the origination of the universe. We should therefore say that the cause of the origin of the universe is causally prior to the Big Bang, though not temporally prior to the Big Bang.

The idea, then, is that time begins with the beginning of the universe. The cause of the universe, whatever it may be, is itself not temporal, since its existence is required in order for the universe (and time) to come into existence. What properties must some timeless entity possess in order for it to nontemporally cause a temporal universe to exist, assuming that reason requires us to suppose that there must be a cause of the Big Bang? Craig reasons that such an entity would have the properties constituting the God of traditional theism: perfect goodness, omniscience, and omnipotence. The question that remains is whether a being must have these three properties in order for it to be the nontemporal cause of the temporal universe. Presumably, a being with these properties would be able to cause the existence of the temporal universe. But in inferring from what appears to us to have been caused (our universe) to the nature of the being that caused it, we cannot simply assume the being to have properties that aren't in any way required for it to be successful in being the cause of our universe. A being with sufficient power and knowledge to cause a temporal universe need not possess knowledge of absolutely everything that is knowable (omniscience). Nor need it possess perfect goodness. Moreover, if we look at the quality of a part of the product that has been produced, the one planet in the universe with which we are acquainted, we will be hard pressed to think that the cause of our universe would have to be a morally perfect being. It is rather difficult to argue that a being with sufficient power and knowledge, although lacking perfect goodness, would be unable to cause the existence of our universe. This objection, however, does not show that the Kalam Cosmological Argument can play no significant role in support of traditional theism. For the Cosmological argument, in either its traditional form as presented by Clarke or as represented in the Kalam version, is only one of several important arguments for the existence of the theistic God. If the Kalam argument supports the existence of a creator of the universe, some other argument may support the conclusion that a creator would possess moral perfection. And just as one branch may be insufficient to support a heavy object, but several tied together will be sufficient, so too the several arguments taken together may be sufficient to support the existence of a being that is omniscient, omnipotent, perfectly good, and the creator of the world.

Study Questions

1. Restate in your own words the Kalam cosmological argument.
2. How does the Kalam cosmological argument differ from the five arguments of Thomas Aquinas?
3. Assuming the existence of a creator of the universe, need that being be omniscient, omnipotent, or perfectly good?
4. Is a metaphysical claim about the beginning of the universe relevant to our present lives?

Does God Exist?

ERNEST NAGEL

Ernest Nagel (1901–1985) was Professor of Philosophy at Columbia University. In the next selection he considers the arguments for the existence of God and finds them unpersuasive. Then he considers an argument against the existence of God, the "problem of evil." The world contains many ills. But should we suffer them if our world was created by an all-good, all-powerful being? An all-good being would do everything possible to abolish evils. An all-powerful being would be able to abolish evils. So if an all-good, all-powerful being existed, evils would not. But evils do exist. Hence an all-good, all-powerful being does not. Nagel finds this argument persuasive and, therefore, is an atheist.

1

I want now to discuss three classical arguments for the existence of God, arguments which have constituted at least a partial basis for theistic commitments. As long as theism is defended simply as a dogma, asserted as a matter of direct revelation or as the deliverance of authority, belief in the dogma is impregnable to rational argument. In fact, however, reasons are frequently advanced in support of the theistic creed, and these reasons have been the subject of acute philosophical critiques.

One of the oldest intellectual defenses of theism is the cosmological argument, also known as the argument from a first cause. Briefly put, the argument runs as follows. Every event must have a cause. Hence an event A must have as cause some event B, which in turn must have a cause C, and so on. But if there is no end to this backward progression of causes, the progression will be infinite; and in the opinion of those who use this argument, an infinite series of actual events is unintelligible and absurd. Hence there must be a first cause, and this first cause is God, the initiator of all change in the universe.

The argument is an ancient one, and . . . it has impressed many generations of exceptionally keen minds. The argument is nonetheless a weak reed on which to rest the theistic thesis. Let us waive any question concerning the validity of the principle that every event has a cause, for though the question is important, its discussion would lead us far afield. However, if the principle is assumed, it is surely incongruous to postulate a first cause as a way of escaping from the coils of an infinite series. For if everything must have a cause, why does not God require one for His own existence? The standard answer is that He does not need any, because He is self-caused. But if God can be self-caused, why cannot the world itself be self-caused? Why do we require a God transcending the world to bring the world into existence and to initiate changes in it? On the other hand, the supposed inconceivability and absurdity of an infinite series of regressive causes will be admitted by no one who has competent familiarity with the modern mathematical analysis of infinity. The cosmological argument does not stand up under scrutiny.

The second "proof" of God's existence is usually called the ontological argument. It too has a long history going back to early Christian days, though it acquired great prominence only in medieval times. The argument can be stated in several ways, one of which is the following. Since God is conceived to be omnipotent, he is a perfect being. A perfect being is defined as one whose essence or nature lacks no attributes (or properties) whatsoever, one whose nature is complete in every respect. But it is evident that we have an idea of a perfect being, for we have just defined the idea; and since this is so, the argument continues, God who is the perfect being must exist. Why must he? Because his existence follows from his defined nature. For if God lacked the attribute of existence, he would be lacking at least one attribute, and would therefore not be perfect. To sum up, since we have an idea of God as a perfect being, God must exist.

There are several ways of approaching this argument, but I shall consider only one. The argument was exploded by the eighteenth century philosopher Immanuel Kant. The substance of Kant's criticism is that it is just a confusion to say that existence is an attribute, and that though the *word* "existence" may occur as the grammatical predicate in a sentence, no attribute is being predicated of a thing when we say that the thing exists or has existence. Thus, to use Kant's example, when we think of $100 we are thinking of the nature of this sum of money; but the nature of $100 remains the same whether we have $100 in our pockets or not. Accordingly, we are confounding grammar with logic if we suppose that some characteristic is being attributed to the nature of $100 when we say that a hundred dollar bill exists in someone's pocket.

To make the point clearer, consider another example. When we say that a lion has a tawny color, we are predicating a certain attribute of the animal, and similarly when we say that the lion is fierce or is hungry. But when we say the lion exists, all that we are saying is that something is (or has the nature of) a lion; we are not specifying an attribute which belongs to the nature of anything that is a lion. In short, the word "existence" does not signify any attribute, and in consequence no attribute that belongs to the nature of anything. Accordingly, it does not follow from the assumption that we have an idea of a perfect being that such a being exists. For the idea of a perfect being does not involve the attribute of existence as a constituent of that idea, since there is no such attribute. The ontological argument thus has a serious leak, and it can hold no water.

2

The two arguments discussed thus far are purely dialectical, and attempt to establish God's existence without any appeal to empirical data. The next argument, called the argument from design, is different in character, for it is based on what purports to be empirical evidence. I wish to examine two forms of this argument.

One variant of it calls attention to the remarkable way in which different things and processes in the world are integrated with each other, and concludes that this mutual "fitness" of things can be explained only by the assumption of a divine architect who planned the world and everything in it. For example, living organisms can maintain themselves in a variety of environments, and do so in virtue of their delicate mechanisms which adapt the organisms to all sorts of environmental changes. There is thus an intricate pattern of means and ends throughout the animate world. But the existence of this pattern is unintelligible, so the argument runs, except on the hypothesis that the pattern has been deliberately instituted by a Supreme Designer. If we find a watch in some deserted spot, we do not think it came into existence by chance, and we do not hesitate to conclude that an intelligent creature designed and made it. But the world and all its contents exhibit mechanisms and mutual adjustments that are far more complicated and subtle than are those of a watch. Must we not therefore conclude that these things too have a Creator?

The conclusion of this argument is based on an inference from analogy: the watch and the world are alike in possessing a congruence of parts and an adjustment of means to ends; the watch has a watch-maker; hence the world has a world-maker. But is the analogy a good one? Let us once more waive some important issues, in particular the issue whether the universe is the unified system such as the watch admittedly is. And let us concentrate on the question what is the ground for our assurance that watches do not come into existence except through the operations of intelligent manufacturers. The answer is plain. We have never run across a watch which has not been deliberately made by someone. But the situation is nothing like this in the case of the innumerable animate and inanimate systems with which we are familiar. Even in the case of living organisms, though they are generated by their parent organisms, the parents do not "make" their progeny in the same sense in which watch-makers make watches. And once this point is clear, the inference from the existence of living organisms to the existence of a supreme designer no longer appears credible.

Moreover, the argument loses all its force if the facts which the hypothesis of a divine designer is supposed to explain can be understood on the basis of a better supported assumption. And indeed, such an alternative explanation is one of the achievements of Darwinian biology. For Darwin showed that one can account for the variety of biological species, as well as for their adaptations to their environments, without invoking a divine creator and acts of special creation. The Darwinian theory explains the diversity of biological species in terms of chance variations in the structure of organisms, and of a mechanism of selection which retains those variant forms that possess some advantages for survival. The evidence for these assumptions is considerable; and developments subsequent to Darwin have only strengthened the case for a thoroughly naturalistic explanation of the facts of biological adaptation. In any event, this version of the argument from design has nothing to recommend it.

A second form of this argument has been recently revived in the speculations of some modern physicists. No one who is familiar with the facts can fail to be impressed by the success with which the use of mathematical methods has enabled us to obtain intellectual mastery of many parts of nature. But some thinkers have therefore concluded that since the book of nature is ostensibly written in mathematical language, nature must be the creation of a divine mathematician. However, the argument is most dubious. For it rests, among other things, on the assumption that mathematical tools can be successfully used only if the events of nature exhibit some *special* kind of order, and on the further assumption that if the structure of things were different from what they are, mathematical language would be inadequate for describing such structure. But it can be shown that no matter what the world were like—even if it impressed us as being utterly chaotic—it would still possess some order, and would in principle be amenable to a mathematical description. In point of fact, it makes no sense to say that there is absolutely *no* pattern in any conceivable subject matter. To be sure, there are differences in complexities of structure, and if the patterns of events were sufficiently complex, we might not be able to unravel them. But however that may be, the success of mathematical physics in giving us some understanding of the world around us does not yield the conclusion that only a mathematician could have devised the patterns of order we have discovered in nature.

3

The inconclusiveness of the three classical arguments for the existence of God was already made evident by Kant, in a manner substantially not different from the above discussion. There are, however, other types of arguments for theism that have been influential in the history of thought, two of which I wish to consider, even if only briefly.

Indeed, though Kant destroyed the classical intellectual foundations for theism, he himself invented a fresh argument for it. Kant's attempted proof is not intended to be a purely theoretical demonstration, and is based on the supposed facts of our moral nature. It has exerted an enormous influence on subsequent theological speculation. In barest outline, the argument is as follows. According to Kant, we are subject not only to physical laws like the rest of nature, but also to moral ones. These moral laws are categorical imperatives, which we must heed not because of their utilitarian consequences, but simply because as autonomous moral agents it is our duty to accept them as binding. However, Kant was keenly aware that though virtue may be its reward, the virtuous man (that is, the man who acts out of a sense of duty and in conformity with the moral law) does not always receive his just desserts in this world; nor did he shut his eyes to the fact that evil men frequently enjoy the best things this world has to offer. In short, virtue does not always reap happiness. Nevertheless, the highest human good is the realization of happiness commensurate with one's virtue; and Kant believed that it is a practical postulate of the moral life to promote this good. But what can guarantee that the highest good is realizable? Such a guarantee can be found only in God, who must therefore exist if the highest good is not to be a fatuous ideal. The existence of an omnipotent, omniscient, and omnibenevolent God is thus postulated as a necessary condition for the possibility of a moral life.

Despite the prestige this argument has acquired, it is difficult to grant it any force. It is easy enough to postulate God's existence. But as Bertrand Russell observed in another connection, postulation has all the advantages of theft over honest toil. No postulation carries with it any assurance that what is postulated is actually the case. And though we may postulate God's existence as a means to guaranteeing the possibility of realizing happiness together with virtue, the postulation establishes neither the actual realizability of this ideal nor the fact of his existence. Moreover, the argument is not made more cogent when we recognize that it is based squarely on the highly dubious conception that considerations of utility and human happiness must not enter into the determination of what is morally

obligatory. Having built his moral theory on a radical separation of means from ends, Kant was driven to the desperate postulation of God's existence in order to relate them again. The argument is thus at best a tour de force, contrived to remedy a fatal flaw in Kant's initial moral assumptions. It carries no conviction to anyone who does not commit Kant's initial blunder.

One further type of argument, pervasive in much Protestant theological literature, deserves brief mention. Arguments of this type take their point of departure from the psychology of religious and mystical experience. Those who have undergone such experiences often report that during the experience they feel themselves to be in the presence of the divine and holy, that they lose their sense of self-identity and become merged with some fundamental reality, or that they enjoy a feeling of total dependence upon some ultimate power. The overwhelming sense of transcending one's finitude which characterizes such vivid periods of life, and of coalescing with some ultimate source of all existence, is then taken to be compelling evidence for the existence of a supreme being. In a variant form of this argument, other theologians have identified God as the object which satisfies the commonly experienced need for integrating one's scattered and conflicting impulses into a coherent unity, or as the subject which is of ultimate concern to us. In short, a proof of God's existence is found in the occurrence of certain distinctive experiences.

It would be flying in the face of well-attested facts were one to deny that such experiences frequently occur. But do these facts constitute evidence for the conclusion based on them? Does the fact, for example, that an individual experiences a profound sense of direct contact with an alleged transcendent ground of all reality constitute competent evidence for the claim that there is such a ground and that it is the immediate cause of the experience? If well-established canons for evaluating evidence are accepted, the answer is surely negative. No one will dispute that many men do have vivid experiences in which such things as ghosts or pink elephants appear before them; but only the hopelessly credulous will without further ado count such experiences as establishing the existence of ghosts and pink elephants. To establish the existence of such things, evidence is required that is obtained under controlled conditions and that can be confirmed by independent inquirers. Again, though a man's report that he is suffering pain may be taken at face value, one cannot take at face value the claim, were he to make it, that it is the food he ate which is the cause (or a contributory cause) of his felt pain—not even if the man were to report a vivid feeling of abdominal disturbance. And similarly, an overwhelming feeling of being in the presence of the Divine is evidence enough for admitting the genuineness of such feeling; it is no evidence for the claim that a supreme being with a substantial existence independent of the experience is the cause of the experience.

4

Thus far the discussion has been concerned with noting inadequacies in various arguments widely used to support theism. However, much atheistic criticism is also directed toward exposing incoherencies in the very thesis of theism. I want therefore to consider this aspect of the atheistic critique, though I will restrict myself to the central difficulty in the theistic position which arises from the simultaneous attribution of omnipotence, omniscience, and omnibenevolence to the Deity. The difficulty is that of reconciling these attributes with the occurrence of evil in the world. Accordingly, the question to which I now turn is whether, despite the existence of evil, it is possible to construct a theodicy which will justify the ways of an infinitely powerful and just God to man.

Two main types of solutions have been proposed for this problem. One way that is frequently used is to maintain that what is commonly called evil is only an illusion, or at worst only the "privation" or absence of good. Accordingly, evil is not "really real," it is only the "negative" side of God's beneficence, it is only the product of our limited

intelligence which fails to plumb the true character of God's creative bounty. A sufficient comment on this proposed solution is that facts are not altered or abolished by rebaptizing them. Evil may indeed be only an appearance and not genuine. But this does not eliminate from the realm of appearance the tragedies, the sufferings, and the iniquities which men so frequently endure. And it raises once more, though on another level, the problem of reconciling the fact that there is evil in the realm of appearance with God's alleged omnibenevolence. In any event, it is small comfort to anyone suffering a cruel misfortune for which he is in no way responsible, to be told that what he is undergoing is only the absence of good. It is a gratuitous insult to mankind, a symptom of insensitivity and indifference to human suffering, to be assured that all the miseries and agonies men experience are only illusory.

Another gambit often played in attempting to justify the ways of God to man is to argue that the things called evil are evil only because they are viewed in isolation; they are not evil when viewed in proper perspective and in relation to the rest of creation. Thus, if one attends to but a single instrument in an orchestra, the sounds issuing from it may indeed be harsh and discordant. But if one is placed at a proper distance from the whole orchestra, the sounds of that single instrument will mingle with the sounds issuing from the other players to produce a marvellous bit of symphonic music. Analogously, experiences we call painful undoubtedly occur and are real enough. But the pain is judged to be an evil only because it is experienced in a limited perspective—the pain is there for the sake of a more inclusive good, whose reality eludes us because our intelligences are too weak to apprehend things in their entirety.

It is an appropriate retort to this argument that of course we judge things to be evil in a human perspective, but that since we are not God this is the only proper perspective in which to judge them. It may indeed be the case that what is evil for us is not evil for some other part of creation. However, we are not this other part of creation, and it is irrelevant to argue that were we something other than what we are, our evaluations of what is good and bad would be different. Moreover, the worthlessness of the argument becomes even more evident if we remind ourselves that it is unsupported speculation to suppose that whatever is evil in a finite perspective is good from the purported perspective of the totality of things. For the argument can be turned around: what we judge to be a good is a good only because it is viewed in isolation; when it is viewed in proper perspective, and in relation to the entire scheme of things, it is an evil. This is in fact a standard form of the argument for a universal pessimism. Is it any worse than the similar argument for a universal optimism? The very raising of this question is a *reductio ad absurdum* of the proposed solution to the ancient problem of evil.

I do not believe it is possible to reconcile the alleged omnipotence and omnibenevolence of God with the unvarnished facts of human existence. In point of fact, many theologians have concurred in this conclusion; for in order to escape from the difficulty which the traditional attributes of God present, they have assumed that God is not all powerful, and that there are limits as to what He can do in his efforts to establish a righteous order in the universe. But whether such a modified theology is better off is doubtful; and in any event, the question still remains whether the facts of human life support the claim that an omnibenevolent Deity, though limited in power, is revealed in the ordering of human history. It is pertinent to note in this connection that though there have been many historians who have made the effort, no historian has yet succeeded in showing to the satisfaction of his professional colleagues that the hypothesis of a Divine Providence is capable of explaining anything which cannot be explained just as well without this hypothesis.

Study Questions

1. What connection does Nagel find between Darwinian biology and the design argument?
2. What is Nagel's assessment of the evidence for God's existence drawn from mystical experience?
3. How does Nagel respond to the claim that evil is only an illusion?
4. If the existence of God is compatible with the worst evils imaginable, what comfort is provided by believing in God?

Why God Allows Evil

RICHARD SWINBURNE

Richard Swinburne, who taught at the University of Oxford, is a leading proponent of theism and other tenets of Christianity. In our next selection he offers a theodicy, a defense of God's goodness and omnipotence in the face of the existence of evil.

The world . . . contains much evil. An omnipotent God could have prevented this evil, and surely a perfectly good and omnipotent God would have done so. So why is there this evil? Is not its existence strong evidence against the existence of God? It would be unless we can construct what is known as a theodicy, an explanation of why God would allow such evil to occur. I believe that that can be done, and I shall outline a theodicy. . . . I emphasize that . . . in writing that God would do this or that, I am not taking for granted the existence of God, but merely claiming that, if there is a God, it is to be expected that he would do certain things, including allowing the occurrence of certain evils; and so, I am claiming, their occurrence is not evidence against his existence.

It is inevitable that any attempt by myself or anyone else to construct a theodicy will sound callous, indeed totally insensitive to human suffering. Many theists, as well as atheists, have felt that any attempt to construct a theodicy evinces an immoral approach to suffering. I can only ask the reader to believe that I am not totally insensitive to human suffering, and that I do mind about the agony of poisoning, child abuse, bereavement, solitary imprisonment, and marital infidelity as much as anyone else. True, I would not in most cases recommend that a pastor give this chapter to victims of sudden distress at their worst moment to read for consolation. But this is not because its arguments are unsound; it is simply that most people in deep distress need comfort, not argument. Yet there is a problem about why God allows evil, and, if the theist does not have (in a cool moment) a satisfactory answer to it, then his belief in God is less than rational, and there is no reason why the atheist should share it. To appreciate the argument of this chapter, each of us needs to stand back a bit from the particular situation of his or her own life and that of close relatives and friends (which can so easily seem the only important thing in the world), and ask very generally what good things would a generous and everlasting God give to human beings in the course of a short earthly life. Of course thrills of pleasure and periods of contentment are good things, and—other things being equal—God would certainly seek to provide plenty of those. But a generous God will seek to give deeper good things than these. He will seek to give us great responsibility for ourselves, each other, and the world, and thus a share in his own creative activity of determining what sort of world it is to be. And he will seek to make our lives valuable, of great use to ourselves and each other. The problem is that God cannot give us these goods in full measure without allowing much evil on the way. . . .

[T]here are plenty of evils, positive bad states, which God could if he chose remove. I divide these into moral evils and natural evils. I understand by "natural evil" all evil which is not deliberately produced by human beings and which is not allowed by human beings to occur as a result of their negligence. Natural evil includes both physical suffering and mental suffering, of animals as well as humans; all the trial of suffering which disease, natural disasters, and accidents unpredictable by humans bring in their train. "Moral evil" I understand as including all evil caused deliberately by humans doing what they ought not to do (or allowed to occur by humans negligently failing to do what they ought to do) *and* also the evil constituted by such deliberate actions or negligent failure. It includes the sensory pain of the blow inflicted by the bad parent on his child, the mental pain of the parent depriving the child of love, the starvation allowed to occur in Africa because of negligence by members of foreign governments who could have prevented it, and also the evil of the parent or politician deliberately bringing about the pain or not trying to prevent the starvation.

MORAL EVIL

The central core of any theodicy must, I believe, be the "free-will defence," which deals—to start with—with moral evil, but can be extended to deal with much natural evil as well. The free-will defence claims that it is a great good that humans have a certain sort of free will which I shall call free and responsible choice, but that, if they do, then necessarily there will be the natural possibility of moral evil. (By the "natural possibility" I mean that it will not be determined in advance whether or not the evil will occur.) A God who gives humans such free will necessarily brings about the possibility, and puts outside his own control whether or not that evil occurs. It is not logically possible—that is, it would be self-contradictory to suppose—that God could give us such free will and yet ensure that we always use it in the right way.

Free and responsible choice is not just free will in the narrow sense of being able to choose between alternative actions, without our choice being causally necessitated by some prior cause. . . . [H]umans could have that kind of free will merely in virtue of being able to choose freely between two equally good and unimportant alternatives. Free and responsible choice is rather free will (of the kind discussed) to make significant choices between good and evil, which make a big difference to the agent, to others, and to the world.

Given that we have free will, we certainly have free and responsible choice. Let us remind ourselves of the difference that humans can make to themselves, others, and the world. Humans have opportunities to give themselves and others pleasurable sensations, and to pursue worthwhile activities—to play tennis or the piano, to acquire knowledge of history and science and philosophy, and to help others to do so, and thereby to build deep personal relations founded upon such sensations and activities. And humans are so made that they can form their characters. Aristotle famously remarked: "we become just by doing just acts, prudent by doing prudent acts, brave by doing brave acts." That is, by doing a just act when it is difficult—when it goes against our natural inclinations (which is what I understand by desires)—we make it easier to do a just act next time. We

can gradually change our desires, so that—for example—doing just acts becomes natural. Thereby we can free ourselves from the power of the less good desires to which we are subject. And, by choosing to acquire knowledge and to use it to build machines of various sorts, humans can extend the range of the differences they can make to the world—they can build universities to last for centuries, or save energy for the next generation; and by cooperative effort over many decades they can eliminate poverty. The possibilities for free and responsible choice are enormous.

It is good that the free choices of humans should include *genuine* responsibility for other humans, and that involves the opportunity to benefit *or* harm them. God has the power to benefit or to harm humans. If other agents are to be given a share in his creative work, it is good that they have that power too (although perhaps to a lesser degree). A world in which agents can benefit each other but not do each other harm is one where they have only very limited responsibility for each other. If my responsibility for you is limited to whether or not to give you a camcorder, but I cannot cause you pain, stunt your growth, or limit your education, then I do not have a great deal of responsibility for you. A God who gave agents only such limited responsibilities for their fellows would not have given much. God would have reserved for himself the all-important choice of the kind of world it was to be, while simply allowing humans the minor choice of filling in the details. He would be like a father asking his elder son to look after the younger son, and adding that he would be watching the elder son's every move and would intervene the moment the elder son did a thing wrong. The elder son might justly retort that, while he would be happy to share his father's work, he could really do so only if he were left to make his own judgements as to what to do within a significant range of the options available to the father. A good God, like a good father, will delegate responsibility. In order to allow creatures a share in creation, he will allow them the choice of hurting and maiming, of frustrating the divine plan. Our world is one where creatures have just such deep responsibility for each other. I cannot only benefit my children, but harm them. One way in which I can harm them is that I can inflict physical pain on them. But there are much more damaging things which I can do to them. Above all I can stop them growing into creatures with significant knowledge, power, and freedom; I can determine whether they come to have the kind of free and responsible choice which I have. The possibility of humans bringing about significant evil is a logical consequence of their having this free and responsible choice. Not even God could give us this choice without the possibility of resulting evil.

Now . . . an action would not be intentional unless it was done for a reason—that is, seen as in some way a good thing (either in itself or because of its consequences). And, if reasons alone influence actions, that regarded by the subject as most important will determine what is done; an agent under the influence of reason alone will inevitably do the action which he regards as overall the best. If an agent does not do the action which he regards as overall the best, he must have allowed factors other than reason to exert an influence on him. In other words, he must have allowed desires for what he regards as good only in a certain respect, but not overall, to influence his conduct. So, in order to have a choice between good and evil, agents need already a certain depravity, in the sense of a system of desires for what they correctly believe to be evil. I need to *want* to overeat, get more than my fair share of money or power, indulge my sexual appetites even by deceiving my spouse or partner, want to see you hurt, if I am to have choice between good and evil. This depravity is itself an evil which is a necessary condition of a greater good. It makes possible a choice made seriously and deliberately, because made in the face of a genuine alternative. I stress that, according to the free-will defence, it is the natural possibility of moral evil which is the necessary

condition of the great good, not the actual evil itself. Whether that occurs is (through God's choice) outside God's control and up to us.

Note further and crucially that, if I suffer in consequence of your freely chosen bad action, that is not by any means pure loss for me. In a certain respect it is a good for *me*. My suffering would be pure loss for me if the only good thing in life was sensory pleasure, and the only bad thing sensory pain; and it is because the modern world tends to think in those terms that the problem of evil seems so acute. If these were the only good and bad things, the occurrence of suffering would indeed be a conclusive objection to the existence of God. But we have already noted the great good of freely choosing and influencing our future, that of our fellows, and that of the world. And now note another great good—the good of our life serving a purpose, of being of use to ourselves and others. Recall the words of Christ, "it is more blessed to give than to receive" (as quoted by St. Paul (Acts 20: 35)). We tend to think, when the beggar appears on our doorstep and we feel obliged to give and do give, that that was lucky for him but not for us who happened to be at home. That is not what Christ's words say. They say that *we* are the lucky ones, not just because we have a lot, out of which we can give a little, but because we are privileged to contribute to the beggar's happiness—and that privilege is worth a lot more than money. And, just as it is a great good freely to choose to do good, so it is also a good to be used by someone else for a worthy purpose (so long, that is, that he or she has the right, the authority, to use us in this way). Being allowed to suffer to make possible a great good is a privilege, even if the privilege is forced upon you. Those who are allowed to die for their country and thereby save their country from foreign oppression are privileged. Cultures less obsessed than our own by the evil of purely physical pain have always recognized that. And they have recognized that it is still a blessing, even if the one who died had been conscripted to fight.

And even twentieth-century man can begin to see that—sometimes—when he seeks to help prisoners, not by giving them more comfortable quarters, but by letting them help the handicapped; or when he pities rather than envies the "poor little rich girl" who has everything and does nothing for anyone else. And one phenomenon prevalent in end-of-century Britain draws this especially to our attention—the evil of unemployment. Because of our system of Social Security, the unemployed on the whole have enough money to live without too much discomfort; certainly they are a lot better off than are many employed in Africa or Asia or Victorian Britain. What is evil about unemployment is not so much any resulting poverty but the uselessness of the unemployed. They often report feeling unvalued by society, of no use, "on the scrap heap." They rightly think it would be a good for them to contribute; but they cannot. Many of them would welcome a system where they were obliged to do useful work in preference to one where society has no use for them.

It follows from that fact that being of use is a benefit for him who is of use, and that those who suffer at the hands of others, and thereby make possible the good of those others who have free and responsible choice, are themselves benefited in this respect. I am fortunate if the natural possibility of my suffering if you choose to hurt me is the vehicle which makes your choice really matter. My vulnerability, my openness to suffering (which necessarily involves my actually suffering if you make the wrong choice), means that you are not just like a pilot in a simulator, where it does not matter if mistakes are made. That our choices matter tremendously, that we can make great differences to things for good or ill, is one of the greatest gifts a creator can give us. And if my suffering is the means by which he can give you that choice, I too am in this respect fortunate. Though of course suffering is in itself a bad thing, my good fortune is that the suffering is not random, pointless suffering. It is suffering which is a consequence of my vulnerability which makes me of such use.

Someone may object that the only good thing is not *being* of use (dying for one's country or being vulnerable to suffering at your hands), but *believing* that one is of use—believing that one is dying for one's country and that this is of use; the "feel-good" experience. But that cannot be correct. Having comforting beliefs is only a good thing if they are true beliefs. It is not a good thing to believe that things are going well when they are not, or that your life is of use when it is not. Getting pleasure out of a comforting falsehood is a cheat. But if I get pleasure out of a true belief, it must be that I regard the state of things which I believe to hold to be a good thing. If I get pleasure out of the true belief that my daughter is doing well at school, it must be that I regard it as a good thing that my daughter does well at school (whether or not I believe that she is doing well). If I did not think the latter, I would not get any pleasure out of believing that she is doing well. Likewise, the belief that I am vulnerable to suffering at your hands, and that that is a good thing, can only be a good thing if being vulnerable to suffering at your hands is itself a good thing (independently of whether I believe it or not). Certainly, when my life is of use and that is a good for me, it is even better if I believe it and get comfort therefrom; but it can only be even better if it is already a good for me whether I believe it or not.

But though suffering may in these ways serve good purposes, does God have the right to allow me to suffer for your benefit, without asking my permission? For surely, an objector will say, no one has the right to allow one person A to suffer for the benefit of another one B without A's consent. We judge that doctors who use patients as involuntary objects of experimentation in medical experiments which they hope will produce results which can be used to benefit others are doing something wrong. After all, if my arguments about the utility of suffering are sound, ought we not all to be causing suffering to others in order that those others may have the opportunity to react in the right way?

There are, however, crucial differences between God and the doctors. The first is that God as the author of our being has certain rights, a certain authority over us, which we do not have over our fellow humans. He is the cause of our existence at each moment of our existence and sustains the laws of nature which give us everything we are and have. To allow someone to suffer for his own good or that of others, one has to stand in some kind of parental relationship towards him. I do not have the right to let some stranger suffer for the sake of some good, when I could easily prevent this, but I do have *some* right of this kind in respect of my own children. I may let the younger son suffer *somewhat* for his own good or that of his brother. I have this right because in small part I am responsible for the younger son's existence, his beginning and continuance. If I have begotten him, nourished, and educated him, I have some limited rights over him in return; to a *very limited* extent I can use him for some worthy purpose. If this is correct, then a God who is so much more the author of our being than are our parents has so much more right in this respect. Doctors do have over us even the rights of parents.

But secondly and all-importantly, the doctors *could* have asked the patients for permission; and the patients, being free agents of some power and knowledge, could have made an informed choice of whether or not to allow themselves to be used. By contrast, God's choice is not about how to use already existing agents, but about the sort of agents to make and the sort of world into which to put them. In God's situation there are no agents to be asked. I am arguing that it is good that one agent A should have deep responsibility for another B (who in turn could have deep responsibility for another C). It is not logically possible for God to have asked B if he wanted things thus, for, if A is to be responsible for B's growth in freedom, knowledge, and power, there will not be a B with enough freedom and knowledge to make any choice, before God has to choose whether or not to give

A responsibility for him. One cannot ask a baby into which sort of world he or she wishes to be born. The creator has to make the choice independently of his creatures. He will seek on balance to benefit them—all of them. And, in giving them the gift of life—whatever suffering goes with it—that is a substantial benefit. But when one suffers at the hands of another, often perhaps it is not enough of a benefit to outweigh the suffering. Here is the point to recall that it is an additional benefit to the sufferer that his suffering is the means whereby the one who hurt him had the opportunity to make a significant choice between good and evil which otherwise he would not have had.

Although for these reasons, as I have been urging, God has the right to allow humans to cause each other to suffer, there must be a limit to the amount of suffering which he has the right to allow a human being to suffer for the sake of a great good. A parent may allow an elder child to have the power to do some harm to a younger child for the sake of the responsibility given to the elder child; but there are limits. And there are limits even to the moral right of God, our creator and sustainer, to use free sentient beings as pawns in a greater game. Yet, if these limits were too narrow, God would be unable to give humans much real responsibility; he would be able to allow them only to play a toy game. Still, limits there must be to God's rights to allow humans to hurt each other; and limits there are in the world to the extent to which they can hurt each other, provided above all by the short finite life enjoyed by humans and other creatures—one human can hurt another for no more than eighty years or so. And there are a number of other safety-devices in-built into our physiology and psychology, limiting the amount of pain we can suffer. But the primary safety limit is that provided by the shortness of our finite life. Unending, unchosen suffering would indeed to my mind provide a very strong argument against the existence of God. But that is not the human situation.

So then God, without asking humans, has to choose for them between the kinds of world in which they can live—basically either a world in which there is very little opportunity for humans to benefit or harm each other, or a world in which there is considerable opportunity. How shall he choose? There are clearly reasons for both choices. But it seems to me (just, on balance) that his choosing to create the world in which we have considerable opportunity to benefit or harm each other is to bring about a good at least as great as the evil which he thereby allows to occur. *Of course* the suffering he allows is a bad thing; and, other things being equal, to be avoided. But having the natural possibility of causing suffering makes possible a greater good. God, in creating humans who (of logical necessity) cannot choose for themselves the kind of world into which they are to come, plausibly exhibits his goodness in making for them the heroic choice that they come into a risky world where they may have to suffer for the good of others.

NATURAL EVIL

Natural evil is not to be accounted for along the same lines as moral evil. Its main role rather, I suggest, is to make it possible for humans to have the kind of choice which the free-will defence extols, and to make available to humans specially worthwhile kinds of choice.

There are two ways in which natural evil operates to give humans those choices. First, the operation of natural laws producing evils gives humans knowledge (if they choose to seek it) of how to bring about such evils themselves. Observing you catch some disease by the operation of natural processes gives me the power either to use those processes to give that disease to other people, or through negligence to allow others to catch it, or to take measures to prevent others from catching the disease. Study of the mechanisms of nature producing various evils (and goods) opens up for humans a wide range of

choice. This is the way in which in fact we learn how to bring about (good and) evil. But could not God give us the requisite knowledge (of how to bring about good or evil) which we need in order to have free and responsible choice by a less costly means? Could he not just whisper in our ears from time to time what are the different consequences of different actions of ours? Yes. But anyone who believed that an action of his would have some effect because he believed that God had told him so would see all his actions as done under the all-watchful eye of God. He would not merely believe strongly that there was a God, but would know it with real certainty. That knowledge would greatly inhibit his freedom of choice, would make it very difficult for him to choose to do evil. This is because we all have a natural inclination to wish to be thought well of by everyone, and above all by an all-good God; that we have such an inclination is a very good feature of humans, without which we would be less than human. Also, if we were directly informed of the consequences of our actions, we would be deprived of the choice whether to seek to discover what the consequences were through experiment and hard co-operative work. Knowledge would be available on tap. Natural processes alone give humans knowledge of the effects of their actions without inhibiting their freedom, and if evil is to be a possibility for them they must know how to allow it to occur.

The other way in which natural evil operates to give humans their freedom is that it makes possible certain kinds of action towards it between which agents can choose. It increases the range of significant choice. A particular natural evil, such as physical pain, gives to the sufferer a choice—whether to endure it with patience, or to bemoan his lot. His friend can choose whether to show compassion towards the sufferer, or to be callous. The pain makes possible these choices, which would not otherwise exist. There is no guarantee that our actions in response to the pain will be good ones, but the pain gives us the opportunity to perform good actions. The good or bad actions which we perform in the face of natural evil themselves provide opportunities for further choice—of good or evil stances towards the former actions. If I am patient with my suffering, you can choose whether to encourage or laugh at my patience; if I bemoan my lot, you can teach me by word and example what a good thing patience is. If you are sympathetic, I have then the opportunity to show gratitude for the sympathy; or to be so self-involved that I ignore it. If you are callous, I can choose whether to ignore this or to resent it for life. And so on. I do not think that there can be much doubt that natural evil, such as physical pain, makes available these sorts of choice. The actions which natural evil makes possible are ones which allow us to perform at our best and interact with our fellows at the deepest level.

It may, however, be suggested that adequate opportunity for these great good actions would be provided by the occurrence of moral evil without any need for suffering to be caused by natural processes. You can show courage when threatened by a gunman, as well as when threatened by cancer; and show sympathy to those likely to be killed by gunmen as well as to those likely to die of cancer. But just imagine all the suffering of mind and body caused by disease, earthquake, and accident unpreventable by humans removed at a stroke from our society. No sickness, no bereavement in consequence of the untimely death of the young. Many of us would then have such an easy life that we simply would not have much opportunity to show courage or, indeed, manifest much in the way of great goodness at all. We need those insidious processes of decay and dissolution which money and strength cannot ward off for long to give us the opportunities, so easy otherwise to avoid, to become heroes.

God has the right to allow natural evils to occur (for the same reason as he has the right to allow moral evils to occur)—up to a limit. It would, of course, be crazy for God to multiply evils more and more in order to give endless opportunity for heroism, but to have *some*

significant opportunity for real heroism and consequent character formation is a benefit for the person to whom it is given. Natural evils give to us the knowledge to make a range of choices between good and evil, and the opportunity to perform actions of especially valuable kinds.

There is, however, no reason to suppose that animals have free will. So what about their suffering? Animals had been suffering for a long time before humans appeared on this planet— just how long depends on which animals are conscious beings. The first thing to take into account here is that, while the higher animals, at any rate the vertebrates, suffer, it is most unlikely that they suffer nearly as much as humans do. Given that suffering depends directly on brain events (in turn caused by events in other parts of the body), then, since the lower animals do not suffer at all and humans suffer a lot, animals of intermediate complexity (it is reasonable to suppose) suffer only a moderate amount. So, while one does need a theodicy to account for why God allows animals to suffer, one does not need as powerful a theodicy as one does in respect of humans. One only needs reasons adequate to account for God allowing an amount of suffering much less than that of humans. That said, there is, I believe, available for animals parts of the theodicy which I have outlined above for humans.

The good of animals, like that of humans, does not consist solely in thrills of pleasure. For animals, too, there are more worthwhile things, and in particular intentional actions, and among them serious significant intentional actions. The life of animals involves many serious significant intentional actions. Animals look for a mate, despite being tired and failing to find one. They take great trouble to build nests and feed their young, to decoy predators and explore. But all this inevitably involves pain (going on despite being tired) and danger. An animal cannot intentionally avoid forest fires, or take trouble to rescue its offspring from forest fires, unless there exists a serious danger of getting caught in a forest fire. The action of rescuing despite danger simply cannot be done unless the danger exists—and the danger will not exist unless there is a significant natural probability of being caught in the fire. Animals do not choose freely to do such actions, but the actions are nevertheless worthwhile. It is great that animals feed their young, not just themselves; that animals explore when they know it to be dangerous; that animals save each other from predators, and so on. These are the things that give the lives of animals their value. But they do often involve some suffering to some creature.

To return to the central case of humans—the reader will agree with me to the extent to which he or she values responsibility, free choice, and being of use very much more than thrills of pleasure or absence of pain. There is no other way to get the evils of this world into the right perspective, except to reflect at length on innumerable very detailed thought experiments (in addition to actual experiences of life) in which we postulate very different sorts of worlds from our own, and then ask ourselves whether the perfect goodness of God would require him to create one of these (or no world at all) rather than our own. But I conclude with a very small thought experiment, which may help to begin this process. Suppose that you exist in another world before your birth in this one, and are given a choice as to the sort of life you are to have in this one. You are told that you are to have only a short life, maybe of only a few minutes, although it will be an adult life in the sense that you will have the richness of sensation and belief characteristic of adults. You have a choice as to the sort of life you will have. You can have either a few minutes of very considerable pleasure, of the kind produced by some drug such as heroin, which you will experience by yourself and which will have no effects at all in the world (for example, no one else will know about it); or you can have a few minutes of considerable pain, such as the pain of childbirth, which will have (unknown to you at the time of pain) considerable good effects on others over a few years. You are told that, if you do not make the second

choice, those others will never exist—and so you are under no moral obligation to make the second choice. But you seek to make the choice which will make *your* own life the best life for *you* to have led. How will you choose? The choice is, I hope, obvious. You should choose the second alternative.

For someone who remains unconvinced by my claims about the relative strengths of the good and evils involved—holding that, great though the goods are, they do not justify the evils which they involve—there is a fall-back position. My arguments may have convinced you of the greatness of the goods involved sufficiently for you to allow that a perfectly good God would be justified in bringing about the evils for the sake of the good which they make possible, if and only if God also provided compensation in the form of happiness after death to the victims whose sufferings make possible the goods. . . . While believing that God does provide at any rate for many humans such life after death, I have expounded a theodicy without relying on this assumption. But I can understand someone thinking that the assumption is needed, especially when we are considering the worst evils. (This compensatory afterlife need not necessarily be the everlasting life of Heaven.)

It remains the case, however, that evil is evil, and there is a substantial price to pay for the goods of our world which it makes possible. God would not be less than perfectly good if he created instead a world without pain and suffering, and so without the particular goods which those evils make possible. Christian, Islamic, and much Jewish tradition claims that God has created worlds of both kinds—our world, and the Heaven of the blessed. The latter is a marvellous world with a vast range of possible deep goods, but it lacks a few goods which our world contains, including the good of being able to reject the good. A generous God might well choose to give some of us the choice of rejecting the good in a world like ours before giving to those who embrace it a wonderful world in which the former possibility no longer exists.

1. Explain Swinburne's distinction between moral evil and natural evil.
2. According to Swinburne, what amount of human suffering, if any, would be unjustifiable?
3. If a drought contributes to greater goods, why should we hope it ends?
4. If evil enhances our world, would evil also enhance heaven?

Karma and Rebirth

RAYNOR JOHNSON

If we understand the problem of evil as the challenge of explaining how an all-good, all-powerful God can create a world containing evil, then that issue presents no difficulty for anyone who does not affirm the existence of such a deity. But the problem of evil can be reformulated as the challenge of explaining how a good world can contain evil. In other words, if the world has a moral structure, why do bad things happen to good people, and good things happen to bad people?

The major religions of South Asia, including Jainism, Hinduism, and Buddhism, explain the existence of evil by invoking two related doctrines: karma and rebirth. Karma is the English form of the Sanskrit word "karman," meaning "action." The term refers to impersonal causal laws that describe how the world works, ensuring that an individual's good acts lead to pleasant results, while bad acts lead to unpleasant results. Admittedly, such consequences may not occur in the course of a single life. They take effect, however, when we are reborn. If our actions have been morally good, our next life will occur in more favorable circumstances; if our actions have been morally bad, our next life will occur in less favorable circumstances.

In our next selection Raynor Johnson (1901–1987), an English physicist who developed an interest in psychical research, presents a case for karma and rebirth.

We start from indisputable ground. Here we are on earth, going through a set of experiences in physical form along with millions of others. We were born into these conditions, into a particular nation and a particular family, without, so far as we are aware, having had any opportunity of choice in these matters. Let us look particularly at the tragic side of life, because this presents the thoughtful person with doubts and problems far more than does the attractive and happy side of life. We see children born into the world under the greatest variety of conditions. Some have sound, healthy bodies with good brains, keen, alert and capable, when fully

From *The Imprisoned Splendor*. Copyright © 1953 by Hodder and Stoughton.

matured, of sustaining great thoughts. Others are handicapped from the beginning with unhealthy bodies, blindness, deafness, disease and defective intelligence. For some the environment is one of security and affection, encouragement, culture and aesthetic interest; for others it is depravity, squalor and ugliness, and one of indifference or gross cruelty by the parents. For some, opportunity stands knocking at the door waiting to welcome and assist; for others it passes by, or knocks too late. Are these things just chance, or are they "planned by God"? If neither of these alternatives is acceptable, what explanation have we to offer which carries with it the reasonable assurance that we live in a just world? If God is just, and good and all-loving, the person who supposes each soul born into the world to be a new creation of God is faced with a real dilemma. There is no doubt that the conditions into which some souls are born preclude their proper development in this life. In some cases the physical body is a wretched tenement. . . . In other cases the environment of fear, cruelty and brutality is calculated to crush and brutalise before the child's personality can possibly resist it. Is it conceivable that God is capable of doing something which any ordinary decent person would do all in his power to prevent or mitigate? The Christian, at least, should remember the words of Jesus, "If ye then, being evil, know how to give good gifts unto your children, *how much more* shall your Father which is in heaven give good things to them that ask Him?" The commonplace orthodox answer to this dilemma is quite frankly an evasion. It runs something like this. "Certainly there is inequality, but in the light of a future state there is justice too. Life, we must remember, is a handicap race. To whom much was given, from him much will be required. Shakespeares and Newtons must make good use of their talents. The . . . suffering and crushed must do their best, realising that God is just and merciful, that He only expects achievement commensurate with their talents, and that in the end all will have been found to

be worth while." However true these affirmations may be, they do not face the problem, which is concerned not with compensations in a future state, but with an explanation of the present state. There is an obvious way out of the difficulty—namely, to abandon the idea that each soul born into this world is in some mysterious way a fresh creation of God. If we do so we need not assume that chance or accident is an alternative "explanation" of the gross inequalities at birth. We can take our stand on the Law of Cause and Effect, and say that all these grossly unequal conditions of birth and childhood are the results of prior causes. Since these causes are not by any means apparent in the present lives, this involves as a logical necessity the pre-existence of souls. It is then possible to affirm that we are the product of our past, that present circumstances arise as the result of self-generated forces in states of prior existence.

It is curious that in the West we have come to accept the Law of Cause and Effect without question in the scientific domain, but seem reluctant to recognise its sway on other levels of significance. Yet every great religion teaches this as part of its ethical code. "Whatsoever a man sows that shall he also reap." In [Asian] philosophy this is the great Law of Karma. Whatsoever a man sows, whether in the field of action or thought, sometime and somewhere the fruits of it will be reaped by him. As a boomerang thrown by a skilled person will move rapidly away to a great distance on a circular path, but finally returns to the hand of the thrower, so there is an inexorable law of justice which runs through the world on all these levels. There is no question of rewards and punishments at all: it is simply a question of inevitable consequence, and applies equally to good things and evil things. . . .

Such a viewpoint is logical, and avoids the incredible supposition that God places one newly created soul in a position of advantage and another in a position of extreme disadvantage, and in effect tells them both to make the best of it. If we suppose that a man is born [disabled] because of his activity in previous lives it may seem brutal, but let us be clear that it is not the explanation which is brutal, but the facts. Heredity, of course, is operative: no one denies this. It must, however, be seen as an effect as well as a cause. Looking behind the heredity, we infer, on this view, that the Law of Karma operates so as to direct or draw a person to be born to certain parents under certain conditions.

The pre-existence of the human soul is also supported by the widely different degrees of spiritual achievement we find around us. There is a vast gulf between the spiritual quality of the best person we know and the worst, between the saint or sage on the one hand and a degenerate wretch on the other. It is so great a gulf that many consider it cannot be accounted for in terms of failure or achievement in one life-span of seventy years. It seems to me to represent a gulf quite as enormous as that which on the physical evolutionary level separates primitive and advanced forms of life. It suggests the probability that the two spiritual states are the culmination of very varying moral and spiritual struggle through a long past. . . .

The commonplace matter of family differences is one which must frequently create speculation. Physical differences and likenesses are doubtless covered by genetical laws, but differences of a profound kind in mental, moral and artistic characteristics sometimes occur, and remain quite inexplicable on biological grounds. This would not be unreasonable if we assume that each soul has a long past behind it, and was drawn to incarnate according to karmic laws in a family whose parents could provide him with the physical vehicle and environment most suited to his further development. It has been remarked that Johann Sebastian Bach was born into a family with a long musical tradition, but we need not infer from this that his genius could be accounted for by his heredity. Rather the view would be that his musical genius needed a special quality of physical vehicle and a certain environment for its satisfactory expression and further progress, and his soul chose,

or was directed towards, parents capable of providing that opportunity. The soul determines the heredity, not the heredity the soul. . . .

If the case for pre-existence is considered a strong one, then the idea of re-incarnation presents no logical difficulties, whatever be the emotional reaction to it. What the soul has done once by the process of incarnation in a physical body, it can presumably do again. . . . We should of course bear in mind that what is meant by the phrase "have lived before" is not that the physical form Raynor Johnson has lived on earth previously, but rather that Raynor Johnson is only a particular and temporary expression of an underlying immortal soul which has adopted previous and quite possibly different appearances. . . .

There [are] a number of questions which inevitably arise in the mind of anyone who seriously considers this subject.

Why do persons not remember their past lives? It is, I think, a reasonable reply to say that when we know how memory works we may hope to have an answer. The memory of events in our present life gets more and more sparse and uncertain as we go back to early years. Few people can recall much of the third year of their life, and almost certainly nothing of the second year of life. This datum of observation suggests that we ought not *normally* to expect to recover memories of pre-existent life, and their absence should not be taken as evidence against pre-existence. It may be remarked that under hypnosis extremely early memories have been recovered from the deeper mind, which must clearly store them somehow. All that we may deduce from this is that if the memories of pre-existent lives are in fact recoverable, we should only expect it to be possible in unusual circumstances or with a special technique. . . .

There are some persons who feel antipathetic to the conception of Karma on the ground that it leads to fatalism. By fatalism we understand a philosophy of life which assumes that all that we experience arises from a destiny or powers outside ourselves which we can in no way influence or control. It makes human life the sport of destiny, and necessarily leads to resigned indifference or cynicism. Such a philosophy is not a legitimate deduction from the idea of Karma, which says, rather, that there is no fate or destiny which we have not made and do not make for ourselves. We are today the product of our long past, and we shall be tomorrow what we make of ourselves today.

Study Questions

1. How could a theist explain what Johnson describes as "grossly unequal conditions of birth and childhood"?
2. How does Johnson explain those conditions?
3. Does the idea of reincarnation present any logical difficulties?
4. How does Johnson reconcile the doctrine of reincarnation with people not remembering their past lives?

Karma, Rebirth, and the Problem of Evil

WHITLEY R. P. KAUFMAN

In our next selection Whitley R. P. Kaufman, Professor of Philosophy at the University of Massachusetts Lowell, argues that the doctrines of karma and rebirth do not provide a satisfactory explanation of how a moral world can contain evil.

According to the seed that's sown
So is the fruit ye reap therefrom.
Doer of good will gather good,
Doer of evil, evil reaps.
Sown is the seed, and thou shalt taste
The fruit thereof.

Samyutta Nikaya[1]

The doctrine of karma and rebirth represents perhaps the most striking difference between Western (Judeo-Christian and Islamic) religious thought and the great Indian religious traditions (Hindu, Buddhist, Jain). To be sure, Western theology also makes use of a retributive explanation of evil in which an individual's suffering is accounted for by his previous wrongdoing. But given the obviously imperfect correlation between sin and suffering in an individual's lifetime, Western religions have resorted to other explanations of suffering (including, notoriously, that of Original Sin). However, Indian thought

From "Karma, Rebirth, and the Problem of Evil," *Philosophy East & West* 59:1, 2005. Reprinted by permission of the University of Hawaii Press.

boldly combines this retributionism with the idea of multiple human incarnations, so that all suffering in this life can be explained by each individual's prior wrongdoing, whether in this or in a prior life, and all wrongdoing in the present life will be punished in either this or a future life. In this way, Indian thought is able to endorse a complete and consistent retributive explanation of evil: all suffering can be explained by the wrongdoing of the sufferer himself. As Ananda Coomaraswamy declares, in answer to the question "Who did sin, this man or his parents, that he was born blind?": "The Indian theory replies without hesitation, *this man*."[2]

It is frequently claimed that the doctrine of karma and rebirth provides Indian religion with a more emotionally and intellectually satisfying account of evil and suffering than do typical Western solutions to the problem of evil. Thus, for Max Weber, karma

> stands out by virtue of its consistency as well as by its extraordinary metaphysical achievement: It unites virtuoso-like self-redemption by man's own effort with universal accessibility of salvation, the strictest rejection of the world with organic social ethics, and contemplation as the paramount path to salvation with an inner-worldly vocational ethic.[3]

Arthur Herman, in his classic *The Problem of Evil and Indian Thought*, similarly asserts the superiority of karma to all Western theodicies: "Unlike the Western theories, . . . the doctrine of rebirth is capable of meeting the major objections against which those Western attempts all failed" (Herman 1976, p. 287).[4] Michael Stoeber also claims that the Indian idea of rebirth is "more plausible" than traditional Christian ideas such as purgatory (Stoeber 1992, p. 167). And the karma doctrine appears to be increasing in popularity in the West as well, perhaps because of these perceived advantages.

However, despite these and similar enthusiastic endorsements, karma as a theodicy has still received comparatively little critical analysis in comparison with the scrutiny to which dominant

Western ideas such as Original Sin or free will have been subjected. . . . In this essay . . . I will limit my discussion to the specific question of whether a karma-and-rebirth theory, even if true, could solve the problem of evil. That is, can it provide a satisfactory explanation of the (apparent) unfairness, injustice, and innocent suffering in the world? I will argue here that the doctrine, in whatever form it is proposed, suffers from serious limitations that render it unlikely to provide a satisfactory solution to the problem of evil. . . .

KARMA AS SYSTEMATIC THEODICY: FIVE MORAL OBJECTIONS

The advantages of the karma theory are obvious and I will not dwell on them here. It is repeatedly pointed out, for example, that it can explain the suffering of innocent children, or congenital illnesses, with which Western thought has great difficulty. It is further argued that it is a more profoundly just doctrine, in that the fact of multiple existences gives the possibility of multiple possibilities for salvation—indeed, that in the end there can be universal salvation. This is again in contrast to the Western tradition, in which there is only one bite at the apple; those who fail in this life are doomed to eternal perdition. However, the doctrine as a whole is subject to a number of serious objections. Here I will present five distinct objections to the rebirth doctrine, all of which raise serious obstacles to the claim that rebirth can provide a convincing solution to the Problem of Evil. I do not claim this to be an exhaustive list, nor do I claim that everyone will agree with each of them. However, I think that they are serious enough as to require at the very least a fuller and more detailed defense of karma as theodicy than has so far been given.

The Memory Problem

An oft-raised objection to the claim of prior existences is the utter lack of any memory traces of previous lives. Both Paul Edwards and Bruce

Reichenbach point out the oddity that all of us have had long, complex past lives, yet none of us have any recollection of them at all. More often, this objection is raised to cast doubt on whether we did in fact have any past lives at all. But my concern here is the *moral* issue raised by this deficiency: justice demands that one who is being made to suffer for a past crime be made aware of his crime and understand why he is being punished for it. Thus, even Christmas Humphreys in his vigorous defense of karma concedes the "injustice of our suffering for the deeds of someone about whom we remember nothing" (Humphreys 1983, p. 84). A conscientious parent explains to his child just why he is being punished; our legal system treats criminal defendants in just the same way. Would not a compassionate deity or a just system make sure the guilty party knows what he has done wrong? It is true that one's belief that all crime is eventually punished might serve a disciplinary function even where one is not aware just what one is being punished for at the time. However, the fact that the sufferer can never know just what crime he is being punished for at a given time, that the system of meting out punishments is so random and unpredictable, constitutes a violation of a basic principle of justice.

Moreover, the memory problem renders the karmic process essentially useless as a means of moral education. Yet, strikingly, it is regularly claimed by adherents that one of the great virtues of karma and rebirth is precisely that "the doctrine presupposes the possibility of moral growth" and that rewards and punishments "constitute a discipline of natural consequences to educate man morally."[5] For example, suppose I am diagnosed with cancer: this must be a punishment for something I have done wrong—but I have no idea what I did to deserve this, or whether it occurred yesterday, last week, or infinitely many past lives ago. For that matter, I might be committing a sin right now—only I will not know it is a sin, because the punishment might occur next week, next year, or in the next life. Radakrishnan

suggests that retaining memory could be a hindrance to our moral development, since it would bring in memories of lower existences in the past (see Minor 1986, p. 32). But even if this is occasionally true, it is hardly plausible to say it is better *never* or even rarely to remember past deeds or lives; acknowledging past mistakes is in general an important (even essential) educating force in our lives. Yet none of us does remember such past events, nor is there definitive evidence that anyone has *ever* recalled a past life.

The memory problem is particularly serious for the karmic doctrine, since most wrongs will be punished in a later life, and most suffering is the result of wrongdoing in prior existences. (Recall that the theory is forced into this position in order to explain the obvious fact that most misdeeds do *not* get automatically punished in this world, and most suffering is not obviously correlated with wickedness.) How, then, can it be said that the doctrine promotes moral education? It is not an answer to say that our knowledge of moral duties can come from elsewhere, from religious scripture, for example. For the point is that the mechanism of karma itself is poorly designed for the purposes of moral education or progress, given the apparently random and arbitrary pattern of rewards and punishments. If moral education were truly the goal of karma and rebirth, then either punishment would be immediately consequent on sin, or at least one would have some way of knowing what one was being punished (or rewarded) for.

In fact, the difficulty is not merely one of moral education. It has been pointed out that the total lack of memory renders the theory more of a *revenge* theory than a retributive one—and hence morally unacceptable.[6] That is, it suggests that justice is satisfied merely because satisfaction has been taken on the perpetrator of the crime, ignoring completely a central moral element of punishment: that the offender where possible be made aware of his crime, that he acknowledge what he has done wrong and repent for it, that he attempt to atone for his crime, and so forth.

As such the rebirth theory fails to respect the moral agency of the sinner in that it is apparently indifferent to whether or not he understands that what he has done is wrong. As Reichenbach rightly points out, the lack of memory prevents one from undergoing the moral process involved in repentance for one's crimes and even attempted rectification for them (p. 95). Further, as Francis Clooney recognizes, the lack of memory of prior lives undermines the pastoral effectiveness of karma as providing comfort to the sufferer: "little comfort is given to the suffering person who is usually thought not to remember anything of the culprit's past deeds" (p. 535). A vague assurance that one must have done unremembered terrible deeds in the past is hardly satisfactory.

The Proportionality Problem

The rebirth solution to the Problem of Evil purports to explain every ill and benefit of this life by prior good or bad conduct. To be a morally adequate solution it must presuppose as well (although this is rarely stated explicitly) a proportionality principle—that the severity of suffering be appropriately proportioned to the severity of the wrong. But herein lies a problem: given the kinds and degrees of suffering we see in this life, it is hard to see what sort of sins the sufferers could have committed to deserve such horrible punishment. Think of those who slowly starve to death along with their family in a famine; those with severe depression or other mental illness; those who are tortured to death; young children who are rendered crippled for life in a car accident; those who die of incurable brain cancer; those burned to death in a house fire. It is difficult to believe that every bit of this kind of suffering was genuinely earned. One may grant that we as finite humans are not always in a position to judge what is just or unjust from God's perspective; nevertheless, the point of the rebirth theory is precisely to make suffering comprehensible to us as a form of justice. Indeed,

belief in karma might make us tend to enact even more brutal and cruel penalties (e.g., torturing to death) if we try to model human justice on this conception of what apparently counts as divine justice.

The evidence from our own practices is that in fact we do not consider such punishments morally justified. For example, capital punishment is considered excessive and inappropriate as punishment even for a crime as serious as rape. Yet according to the karma theory every one of us without exception is condemned to "capital punishment," that is, inevitable physical death, even apart from the various other sufferings we have to endure. An eye-for-an-eye version of the rebirth theory holds that if one is raped in this life it is because one must have been a rapist in a past life, and what could be fairer than that whatever harm one caused to others will be caused to you later? But it is hard to believe that we are all subject to death because we have all been murderers in a past life. Moreover, this answer simply will not work for most diseases (one cannot "cause" another to have Parkinson's or brain cancer). (It also leads to an infinite regress problem, on which see below). It is certainly hard to stomach the notion that the inmates of Auschwitz and Buchenwald did something so evil in the past that they merely got what was coming to them—but the rebirth theory is committed to just this position.

Nor does the idea of the "pool of karmic residues" solve this problem: it is equally hard to believe that even an enormous accumulation of past bad acts could justify the horrible suffering of this world, or indeed that fairness would allow all one's lesser wrongs to accumulate and generate a single, horrible punishment rather than smaller punishments over a longer period. Indeed, it raises the question of fairness of the mechanism: why would some people be punished separately for each individual wrong, while others are punished only all at once and horribly (further undermining the possibility of moral education, one might note)?

The Infinite Regress Problem

In order to explain an individual's circumstances in the present life, karma refers to the events of his prior life. But in order to explain the circumstances of that prior life, we need to invoke the events of his previous life—and so on, ad infinitum. The problem is quite general: how did the karmic process begin? What was the first wrong? Who was the original sufferer? This familiar objection points out that rebirth provides no solution at all, but simply pushes the problem back.[7] And the response typically given by defenders of rebirth is quite inadequate: they claim that the process is simply beginningless (*anādi*), that the karmic process extends back infinitely in time.[8] But this is no answer at all; indeed, it violates a basic canon of rationality, that the "explanation" not be equally as problematic as the problem being explained. Thus, explains Wendy O'Flaherty: "Karma 'solves' the problem of the origin of evil by saying that there *is* no origin. . . . But this ignores rather than solves the problem" (p. 17).

Roy Perrett has responded to this criticism by arguing that the doctrine of karma satisfactorily explains each individual instance of suffering, and it is unreasonable to demand that it give an "ultimate explanation" of the origin of suffering. After all, he says, "explanation has to come to an end somewhere" (Perrett 1985, p. 7). However, the fallacy in this argument can be illustrated by analogy. Consider the "theory" that the world is supported on the back of an elephant, which in turn rests on the back of a tortoise. Now if this is to be an explanatory account of what supports the world, it only begs the question: what supports the tortoise? A famous (probably apocryphal) exchange between Bertrand Russell and an anonymous woman goes as follows:

WOMAN: The world rests on the back of a giant turtle.
RUSSELL: What does the turtle rest on?
WOMAN: Another turtle.
RUSSELL: What does *it* rest on?
WOMAN: Another turtle.
RUSSELL: What does *it* rest on?

The discussion goes on this way for quite some time, until the woman becomes exasperated and blurts out: "Don't you see, Professor Russell, it's turtles *all the way down*!" It will hardly do for the woman to claim that, as her solution explains how the world is supported in each individual instance, she need not worry about the infinite regress. This solution is the equivalent of borrowing money in order to pay off a debt: a solution that merely postpones the problem is no solution at all.

It is also noteworthy that the denial of a beginning to the process sidesteps the question of divine responsibility for the beginning of evil in the world. If there is a creator, then why is he not responsible for the misdeeds of his creations? There is no easy answer to this question, but neither can it be avoided altogether. Christianity has long been criticized for its doctrine of the Fall of Man and Original Sin for these same reasons. I do not claim here that the Christian solution succeeds, but only that the Indian solution does not evade these difficulties, either.

The Problem of Explaining Death

If rebirth is to account for all human suffering, it must, of course, explain the paradigmatic case of innocent suffering: death itself. But the problem here is that in the typical rebirth theory death seems not to be presented as punishment for wrong, but rather is *presupposed* as the mechanism by which karma operates. That is, it is through rebirth that one is rewarded or punished for one's past wrongs (by being born in high or low station, healthy or sickly, etc.). But there can be no rebirth unless there is death. So even if one is moving up in the scale of karma to a very high birth for one's great virtue, one must still undergo death. This would appear to undermine the moral justification for (arguably) the greatest of evils, death itself. For in most versions of the theory death is not even taken as something that needs explaining, but is rather assumed as simply the causal process by which karma operates. Indeed, one might well ask why *everyone* is mortal; why are there not at least some who have been virtuous enough to live indefinitely? Did we all commit such terrible wrongs right away that we have always been subject to death? Typically, though, death and rebirth are not themselves morally justified but simply taken as the neutral mechanism of karma (see, e.g., Humphreys, p. 22).

There are several ways one might try to get around this problem. Max Weber suggests that the finiteness of good deeds in our life accounts for the finiteness of our life span.[9] But this entails a quite different karmic system, one in which one is punished not for positive misdeeds, but for the lack of infinitely many good deeds. It also seems to suggest that we are morally required to be infinitely good to avoid death—a rather implausible moral demand on us and one that undermines the moral justification of karma to be a fair system of rewards and punishments (one might ask why we are not rewarded with infinitely long life for not committing "infinite evil"). Moreover, there is a troublesome hint of circularity in Weber's solution: it seems odd to say that the finiteness of our life span derives from the finiteness of our goodness; to do infinitely much good one apparently needs an infinitely long life.

Another possible solution is simply to deny that death is indeed an evil, since it is the means by which one reaches greater rewards in life. But this is hardly satisfying, for there is no reason at all that death needs to be the mechanism by which one attains one's rewards: why not simply reward the person with health, wealth, and long life, without having to undergo rebirth in the first place? Karma certainly does not need death and rebirth: as soon as one accumulates sufficient merit, one could be instantly transformed into a higher state of existence. Further, this solution simply resorts to denial of the commonsense fact that death usually involves a terrible and often physically painful disruption of one's existence, including the separation from all one's loved ones and from all that one holds dear.

A different strategy might be to say that the ultimate reward is indeed escape from death, the release from the cycle of *samsāra* or rebirth, as many Indians believe. The trouble with this solution is, to put it colloquially, that it throws out the baby with the bathwater. The problem of evil arises not because life itself is an unmitigated evil, but because it contains such a strange mixture of good and evil. Karma implies that all of the good in life—health, wealth, happiness—is due to our good deeds. Why, then, is not perfect goodness rewarded with a perfectly good earthly life (one without death, pain, sickness, poverty, etc.)? If the idea that the ultimate goal is escape from life itself, it simply goes too far.[10] The idea of Nirvāna in Indian thought is often identified with release from not only the evil in life, but from all aspects of life, the good and the bad.[11] But to say that life itself (not just the bad aspects of it) is the problem cannot be a solution to the problem of evil, but rather an admission of failure to solve it. For why is life bad, full of suffering and misery, rather than good? It is also an implausible claim, since experience shows that life can be very good indeed, so why is it not good all the time?

The Free Will Problem

The karma solution is often presented as the ideal solution that respects free moral agency: one determines one's own future by one's present deeds. In fact, as is often pointed out, karma is paradoxically both a fatalist and a freewill theory. For Keyes, karma "manages to affirm and deny human responsibility at the same time" (p. 175); Walli tries to account for this peculiarity by interpreting karma in two stages: in the early stages of existence it is fatalistic, but later it becomes a "moral force" (Walli 1977, p. 328). It is often noted that, despite the promise of control over one's destiny, in practice the doctrine of karma can often result instead in an attitude of fatalistic pessimism in the believer.

Thus, Berger argues that by legitimating the conditions of all social classes, karma "constitutes the most thoroughly conservative religious system devised in history" (p. 65).

Karma is also praised as a freewill theory on the grounds that it gives the individual multiple (infinitely many?) chances to reach salvation in future lives. However, it is not clear whether the multiple-life theory in fact constitutes an advantage over Christian doctrine. Since in Christianity the individual has but one life in which to earn salvation, this entails a high degree of moral importance to one's life (especially given that death could come at any time). In contrast, for karma there is no such urgency, for all mistakes and misdeeds can be rectified in the fullness of future lives. The significance of a particular lifetime, let alone a particular action, is radically diminished if the "life of the individual is only an ephemeral link in a causal chain that extends infinitely into both past and future" (Berger, p. 65). Again, this could encourage fatalism, a sense that one's choice here and now does not matter much in the greater scheme of things.

But a deeper problem is whether the doctrine of karma can in fact be squared at all with the existence of free moral agency. The difficulty can be illustrated with the following example. Consider the potential terrorist, who is deciding whether to draw attention to his political cause by detonating a bomb in a civilian area. How are we to reconcile the automatic functioning of karma with the man's choice? The karma solution must face a dilemma here. There is either of the following possibilities:

(1) Karma functions in a determinate and mechanical fashion. Then, whomever the terrorist kills will not be innocent but deserving of their fate. From the terrorist's perspective, if he is the agent of karma his action is no more blameworthy than that of the executioner who delivers the lethal injection. Indeed, no matter what evils he does in the world, he can always justify them to himself by saying he is merely an agent for karma, carrying out the necessary punishments for these

"wicked" people. Alternatively, it may be that his potential victims do not deserve to die this way, in which case the man must be determined not to kill them. In either case, freedom of the will (supposedly a virtue of the karma theory) is absent.

(2) The other possibility might be countenanced as a way to preserve freedom of the will. Perhaps it really is up to the terrorist to choose whether to kill his victims. Indeed, let us say that he has the potential to create genuine evil: to kill innocent, undeserving civilians. But now the problem is that a central, indeed crucial, tenet of the karma theory has been abandoned: that *all suffering* is deserved and is justified by one's prior wrongful acts. For now we have admitted the genuine possibility of gratuitous evil, innocent suffering—just what the theory was designed to deny. One could, of course, suggest that such gratuitous suffering will eventually be fully compensated for in a future life. But this, as Arthur Herman recognizes, would be a theory very different from that of karma. It would be a doctrine that asserts that all suffering will be *compensated* for (eventually) rather than holding that all suffering is *justified* (i.e., by one's misdeeds). Herman rightly rejects this alternative version of the theory as a recompense, not a karma, theory (p. 213).[12]

This dilemma also undermines the idea of karma as a predictive, causal law (a status often asserted for it). Further, either horn of the dilemma undermines the moral-education function of karma as well (see Herman, p. 215). In (1) one cannot learn because one apparently cannot do wrong. In (2) if one suffers, one can never know if it is because one has done wrong or because of the gratuitous harm caused by the wrongdoing of others. Similarly, if one enjoys success one can never know if it is because of one's merits or because it is payback for the gratuitous evil one suffered earlier.

Reichenbach (p. 94) suggests a way in which some defenders of the doctrine of karma have tried to evade this difficulty and preserve the reality of free will: by asserting that karma explains only evil that is not caused by wrongful human choices (i.e., karma is a theory of "moral evil" rather than of "natural evil"). But this strategy is troublesome. First, there are innumerable cases where the categories of moral-versus-natural evil seem to break down: harm caused or contributed to by human negligence (negligent driving of a car, failing to make buildings earthquake proof); harm that was not directly caused but that was anticipated and could have been prevented (starvation in Africa); harm caused in cases of insanity or diminished mental capacity; harm caused while in a state of intoxication (drunk driving); and so forth. In such cases it is doubtful that we could draw a clear distinction between moral and natural evil, but the strategy fails if one cannot draw such a line. Moreover, the great comforting and consoling function of the karma doctrine is gone: one cannot be sure whether or not one's suffering is retribution for past wrong, and one cannot even know which of one's sufferings are punishments for one's prior wrongs and which are not. Even more importantly, this strategy represents not so much a solution to the difficulty as a whole-hearted concession to the radical limitations of the theory, an admission that enormous amounts of suffering cannot be explained or justified in terms of just punishment for past wrongs. One can no longer be sure whether the circumstances one is born into (e.g., poverty) are the result of one's previous sins or of someone else's wrongdoing. This revised explanation of moral evil presumes that suffering can be random, inexplicable, meaningless, freely chosen without regard to the victim's deserts, while the explanation of natural evil presumes that all suffering is explicable and justified. One might wonder whether the explanations of moral and natural evil are now so much at such cross-purposes that the rebirth theory as a whole loses its coherence.

Thus, the dilemma seems to show that karma is simply not consistent with the genuine possibility of free moral choice. The basic problem here is the deep tension (even incompatibility) between the causal determinism implicit in the karma doctrine and the ideal of free moral responsibility, which makes one fully responsible for one's actions. Most commentators never successfully reconcile the two, if indeed they can be reconciled. An example is Hiriyanna, who insists that "everything that happens in the moral realm is preordained;" but that this is fully consistent with human freedom, by which he means "being determined by oneself" (pp. 46–7 and n. 23). It is not clear how one can escape this contradiction. The more one insists on human freedom, the less are events in the world subject to karmic determination.

The difficulty is even worse for the interpretation of karma that extends the idea of causal determinism to one's character or disposition in future lives. Thus, someone who does evil will inherit in the next life not only lowly circumstances but also a wicked, malevolent disposition; those who have a good disposition owe it to their good deeds in previous lives. Now even one's character and moral choice are influenced, even determined by, one's past lives; this threatens to do away with free moral choice altogether. And once one has a wicked disposition, it is a puzzle how one can escape spiraling down into further wrongdoing, or at best being permanently stuck at a given moral level, if karma has already determined one's moral character. (The problem is exaggerated even further if one accepts the view that particularly bad people become animals; how could one ever escape one's animal state, since animals do not appear to be capable of moral choice at all?)

There is in the end a fatalistic dilemma for the theory. Either the karma theory is a complete and closed causal account of evil and suffering or it is not. That is, either the present state of affairs is fully explained causally by reference to prior events (including human actions) or it is not. If it is fully explained, then there can be no progress or indeed no change at all in the world. Past evil will generate present evil, and present evil will in turn cause equivalent future evil. There is no escape from the process. Alternatively, if there is the possibility of change, then karma must no longer be a complete causal account. That is, it fails as a systematic theory and therefore cannot in fact solve the problem of evil, since there must be evil in the world for which it cannot account.

KARMA AND THE VERIFIABILITY PROBLEM

There is one final matter that I think has significant moral relevance in this debate: the charge that the rebirth (or preexistence) doctrine is objectionable because it is *unveritiable* (or unfalsifiable).[13] Whatever happens is consistent with the theory; no fact could apparently falsify it. Whatever the terrorist does is (as Humphreys insists) simply the determination of karma. Further, one has no capacity effectively to predict the future by this theory. Even if one has done wrong (assuming that there are precise guidelines for what counts as wrongdoing, a difficult assumption in a world of moral dilemmas), one has no way of knowing just what the punishment will be, or when it will occur, in this life or the next. A remarkable example of the willing endorsement of the advantages of unfalsifiability is made by Arthur Herman in defending karma:

> Thus no matter how terrible and awe-inspiring the suffering may be, the rebirth theorist can simply attribute the suffering to previous misdeeds done in previous lives, and the puzzle is over. Extraordinary evil is solved with no harm done to the majesty and holiness of deity.[14]

Another defender of karma and transmigration also unwittingly demonstrates the problem with such theories. He claims that the evidence for transmigration is provided by the law of karma itself (i.e., the law of moral cause and effect), since without the transmigration of souls, karma would be an inadequate solution to the Problem of Evil.[15] Such a justification is transparently circular: it presupposes that the karma solution is true in order to defend it.

Now, one might fairly doubt whether, in general, religious claims can meaningfully be held to

the same standards of empirical verification as scientific claims. Nonetheless, the virtue of testability and falsifiability is that it provides a check against all of the familiar human biases: dogmatism, ethnocentrism, and so on. This is a particular problem for the karma theory, since the very unfalsifiability of the doctrine can be used to rationalize the status quo or justify oppression or unfairness on the grounds that their suffering is punishment for their prior wrongs (for they would simply have to pay their debt later). It is widely acknowledged that the repressive caste system in India lasted so long in large part because the doctrine of karma encouraged Indians to accept social oppression as the mechanical workings of karma. Hiriyanna remarkably presents it as an *advantage* of the karma theory that in India sufferers cannot blame God or their neighbors for their troubles, but only themselves (even if their neighbors are indeed unjustly oppressing them).[16] Human fallibility being what it is, the idea that all suffering is due to a previous wrongful action provides a great temptation to rationalize the status quo with reference to unverifiable claims about one's past wrongs. This is surely too great a price to pay for whatever pastoral comfort such fatalistic reassurance provides.

CONCLUSION

I conclude that the doctrine of karma and rebirth, taken as a systematic rational account of human suffering by which all individual suffering is explained as a result of that individual's wrongdoing, is unsuccessful as a theodicy.

NOTES

1. Cited in Keyes, p. 262.
2. Coomaraswamy 1964, p. 108. The reference, of course, is to John 9:2, in which Jesus rejects the retributive explanation of a man's blindness.
3. Weber 1947, p. 359.
4. In the second edition, Herman backs off this claim, and says that he now thinks that the tradiional problem of evil is "insolvable" (p. viii).

5. Hiriyanna, p. 49; see also Stoeber, p. 178.

6. See, for example, Nayak, quoted in Stoeber, p. 178.

7. See, for example, Watts 1964, p. 38; Hick 1976, pp. 309, 314; Hick 1990, p. 139; and O'Flaherty, p. 17.

8. See Herman, p. 263, and Hiriyanna, pp. 47, 198....

9. Weber 1964, p. 145.

10. See Hick 1976, pp. 321, 437.

11. Hiriyanna, p. 69.

12. See also Reichenbach, p. 17.

13. A problem raised both by Paul Edwards (1996) and Bruce Reichenbach (1990).

14. Herman, p. 287.

15. Hiriyanna, p. 47.

16. Ibid., p. 48 (although he does not specifically mention caste). See Humphreys, p. 55 (the condition of cripples and dwarfs can be justified by their sins).

REFERENCES

Berger, Peter, 1967. *The Sacred Canopy*. Garden City, NY: Doubleday.

Clooney, Francis. 1989. "Evil, Divine Omnipotence, and Human Freedom: Vedanta's Theology of Karma." *Journal of Religion* 69: 530–48.

Coomaraswamy, Ananda. 1964. *Buddha and the Gospel of Buddhism*. New York: Harper and Row.

Edwards, Paul. 1996. *Reincarnation: A Critical Examination*. New York: Prometheus Books.

Herman, Arthur. 1976. *The Problem of Evil in Indian Thought*. Delhi: Motilal Banarsidass.

Hick, John. 1976. *Death and Eternal Life*. New York: Harper and Row.

———. 1990. *Philosophy of Religion*. Englewood Cliffs, NJ: Prentice-Hall.

Hiriyanna, M. 1995. *The Essentials of Indian Philosophy*. Delhi: Motilal Banarsidass.

Humphreys, Christmas. 1983. *Karma and Rebirth*. London: Curzon Press.

Keyes, Charles. 1983. "Merit-Transference in the Kammic Theory of Popular Theravada Buddhism." In *Karma*, edited by Charles Keyes and Valentine Daniel. Berkeley: University of California Press.

Minor, Robert. 1986. "In Defense of Karma and Rebirth: Evolutionary Karma." In Ronald Neufeldt, ed., *Karma and Rebirth*. Albany: State University of New York Press.

O'Flaherty, Wendy Doniger. 1976. *The Origins of Evil in Hindu Mythology*. Berkeley: University of California Press.

Perrett, Roy. 1985. "Karma and the Problem of Suffering." *Sophia* 24: 4–10.

Reichenbach, Bruce. 1990. *The Law of Karma*. Honolulu: University of Hawai'i Press.

Stoeber, Michael. 1992. *Evil and the Mystics' God*. Toronto: University of Toronto Press.

Walli, Koshelya. 1977. *Theory of Karman in Indian Thought*. Bharata Mahisha.

Watts, Alan. 1964. *Beyond Theology*. New York: Vintage Books.

Weber, Max. 1947. *Essays in Sociology*. Translated by H. H. Certh and C. Wright Mills. London: K. Paul, Trench, Trubner.

———. 1964. *The Sociology of Religion*. Translated by Ephraim Fischoff. Boston: Beacon Press. (Original publication date in German: 1922).

Study Questions

1. To which philosophical problems are the doctrines of karma and rebirth supposed to provide an answer?

2. According to Kaufman, what is the infinite regress problem with karma?

3. Is the doctrine of karma consistent with free will?

4. Is reincarnation more plausible than the doctrine of resurrection?

The Wager

BLAISE PASCAL

If philosophical arguments are inadequate to prove the existence of God, might other reasons suffice to justify theism? Blaise Pascal (1623–1662), the French mathematician, physicist, and philosopher, offered an argument that belief in God is useful even if not supported by the available evidence.

According to Pascal's celebrated "wager," if we believe in God, and God exists, then we attain heavenly bliss; if we believe in God, and God doesn't exist, little is lost. On the other hand, if we don't believe in God, and God does exist, then we are doomed to the torments of damnation; if we don't believe in God, and God doesn't exist, little is gained. So belief is the safest strategy.

If there is a God, he is infinitely beyond our comprehension, since, having neither parts nor limits, he bears no relation to ourselves. We are therefore incapable of knowing either what he is, or if he is. That being so, who will dare to undertake a resolution of this question? It cannot be us, who bear no relationship to him.

Who will then blame the Christians for being unable to provide a rational basis for their belief, they who profess a religion for which they cannot provide a rational basis? They declare that it is a folly (1 Cor. 1: 18) in laying it before the world: and then you complain that they do not prove it! If they did prove it, they would not be keeping their word. It is by the lack of proof that they do not lack sense. "Yes, but although that excuses those who offer their religion as it is, and that takes away the blame from them of producing it without a rational basis, it does not excuse those who accept it."

Let us therefore examine this point, and say: God is, or is not. But towards which side will we lean? Reason cannot decide anything. There is an infinite chaos separating us. At the far end of this infinite distance a game is being played and the coin will come down heads or tails. How will you wager? Reason cannot make you choose one way or the other, reason cannot make you defend either of the two choices.

So do not accuse those who have made a choice of being wrong, for you know nothing about it! "No, but I will blame them not for having made this choice, but for having made any choice. For, though the one who chooses heads and the other one are equally wrong, they are both wrong. The right thing is not to wager at all."

Yes, but you have to wager. It is not up to you, you are already committed. Which then will you choose? Let us see. Since you have to choose, let us see which interests you the least. You have two things to lose: the truth and the good, and two things to stake: your reason and will, your knowledge and beatitude; and your nature has two things to avoid: error and wretchedness. Your reason is not hurt more by choosing one rather than the other, since you do have to make the choice. That is one point disposed of. But

From Blaise Pascal, *Pensées,* trans. Honor Levi. Reprinted by permission of Oxford University Press.

your beatitude? Let us weigh up the gain and the loss by calling heads that God exists. Let us assess the two cases: if you win, you win everything; if you lose, you lose nothing. Wager that he exists then, without hesitating! "This is wonderful. Yes, I must wager. But perhaps I am betting too much." Let us see. Since there is an equal chance of gain and loss, if you won only two lives instead of one, you could still put on a bet. But if there were three lives to win, you would have to play (since you must necessarily play), and you would be unwise, once forced to play, not to chance your life to win three in a game where there is an equal chance of losing and winning. But there is an eternity of life and happiness. And that being so, even though there were an infinite number of chances of which only one were in your favour, you would still be right to wager one in order to win two, and you would be acting wrongly, since you are obliged to play, by refusing to stake one life against three in a game where out of an infinite number of chances there is one in your favour, if there were an infinitely happy infinity of life to be won. But here there is an infinitely happy infinity of life to be won, one chance of winning against a finite number of chances of losing, and what you are staking is finite. That removes all choice: wherever there is infinity and where there is no infinity of chances of losing against one of winning, there is no scope for wavering, you have to chance everything. And thus, as you are forced to gamble, you have to have discarded reason if you cling on to your life, rather than risk it for the infinite prize which is just as likely to happen as the loss of nothingness.

For it is no good saying that it is uncertain if you will win, that it is certain you are taking a risk, and that the infinite distance between the *certainty* of what you are risking and the *uncertainty* of whether you win makes the finite good of what you are certainly risking equal to the uncertainty of the infinite. It does not work like that. Every gambler takes a certain risk for an uncertain gain; nevertheless he certainly risks the finite uncertainty in order to win a finite

gain, without sinning against reason. There is no infinite distance between this certainty of what is being risked and the uncertainty of what might be gained: that is untrue. There is, indeed, an infinite distance between the certainty of winning and the certainty of losing. But the uncertainty of winning is proportional to the certainty of the risk, according to the chances of winning or losing. And hence, if there are as many chances on one side as on the other, the odds are even, and then the certainty of what you risk is equal to the uncertainty of winning. It is very far from being infinitely distant from it. So our argument is infinitely strong, when the finite is at stake in a game where there are equal chances of winning and losing, and the infinite is to be won.

That is conclusive, and, if human beings are capable of understanding any truth at all, this is the one.

"I confess it, I admit it, but even so . . . Is there no way of seeing underneath the cards?" "Yes, Scripture and the rest, etc." "Yes, but my hands are tied and I cannot speak a word. I am being forced to wager and I am not free, they will not let me go. And I am made in such a way that I cannot believe. So what do you want me to do?" "That is true. But at least realize that your inability to believe, since reason urges you to do so and yet you cannot, arises from your passions. So concentrate not on convincing yourself by increasing the number of proofs of God but on diminishing your passions. You want to find faith and you do not know the way? You want to cure yourself of unbelief and you ask for the remedies? Learn from those who have been bound like you, and who now wager all they have. They are people who know the road you want to follow and have been cured of the affliction of which you want to be cured. Follow the way by which they began: by behaving just as if they believed, taking holy water, having masses said, etc. That will make you believe quite naturally, and according to your animal reactions." "But that is what I am afraid of." "Why? What do you have to lose?"

Pascal's Wager: An Assessment

LINDA TRINKAUS ZAGZEBSKI

In the next selection Linda Trinkhaus Zagzebski, who is Professor of Philosophy at the University of Oklahoma, considers three objections to Pascal's wager. She finds that they point to problems in the wager but may not require that Pascal's line of reasoning be abandoned.

Pascal's wager has a number of well-known objections, some of them coming from theists and some from non-theists. Let us consider three of them.

1. *The many gods objection.* Pascal assumes the wager is over belief in the Christian God. It is a God who promises eternal life for belief in him. But this means that the wager is between the existence of a God of a certain kind and no God. That is not a forced wager because there are other possibilities. To put the point another way, there are many wagers: Christian God or no Christian God, Muslim God or no Muslim God, Hindu God or no Hindu God, etc. And this is a problem because for some of these you could make the same kind of wager, yet you really can only bet on one, assuming that betting on one commits you to betting against the others. But which one should you bet on?

One answer to this objection is that Pascal is thinking of live options, something you could really believe. Presumably he thinks that the God of only one religion would be a possibility for you. Pascal's era was not one in which there were churches, temples, mosques, and synagogues within easy driving distance of the average person making the wager. So it means that Pascal's wager is not intended for everybody. It is for people who: (1) think both Christianity and atheism are intellectually unproven but also unrefuted, so from a rational viewpoint both are live options; (2) have a roughly Christian view of God as a being who rewards his worshipers with heaven; and (3) are in the emotional position of struggle, trying to choose. Presumably that would apply to many people, and many other people would be in the analogous position of betting on the God of a different religion. Clearly, though, the situation is much more complex for a person for whom more than one religion that promises an infinite payoff is a live option.

2. *The wager presupposes a low view of God and religious faith.* A second objection is that God does not want believers who believe on the basis of a wager motivated by self-interest. This is not what religious faith is all about. This objection is often expressed by religious people who find the wager repugnant. The reply to this objection is that Pascal is formulating an appeal to a certain kind of person, one who is perched precariously between belief and unbelief. Given that he thought of the wager as the precursor to real faith, not faith itself, the person who makes the wager would sincerely try to believe in God. She would not remain indefinitely in the state of the gambler who is motivated only by potential gain. There is no guarantee that she will eventually acquire real faith, but she won't unless she tries, just as the entrepreneur has no guarantee of success in business, but he knows for sure that he won't succeed if he doesn't make the attempt. If the theistic bettor succeeds, her original motive will eventually be replaced by the attitude of religious faith. . . .

3. *We can't believe by making a choice.* There are many things you can't just decide to believe. Suppose somebody tries to bribe you into believing there will be an earthquake in Antarctica on April 19, 2020. Could you do it? You can't just believe because it is in your interest to do so. No matter how much money you are offered, it is probably impossible to make yourself believe certain things if the evidence does not support it. If the choice is not forced, your reason tells you to withhold judgment. And it is hard to see how you could muster the motive to believe, given that earthquakes in Antarctica probably do not connect to anything you already care about at all.

But there are several disanalogies between the Antarctica example and Pascal's wager. As we have seen, Pascal does not think you can start believing in an instant. Second, Pascal thinks the choice is forced, and it is about something you already care about. If you take the time to cultivate the belief by acting as if you believe, you may eventually end up really believing. Here is an analogy given by James Cargile[1] defending Pascal's view that you could get yourself to believe in God given (a) the right motivation, (b) no firm belief to begin with, and (c) a bit of time. Suppose a billionaire jazz lover declares that in two years he will toss a coin. If it comes up heads he will give a million dollars to every devoted jazz fan. If it comes up tails he won't do anything. Every Sunday for the next two years a one-hour jazz concert is scheduled. If you attend these concerts religiously, listen to jazz at every other opportunity, and avoid listening to any other kind of music, it is quite likely that you will become a lover of jazz. Of course, it's not likely to work if you hated jazz from the beginning, but if you start out neutral, there is a good chance it will work. In any case, Pascal is addressing someone who is neutral about the existence of God.

But here is another analogy that is more problematic. It highlights both the issue of whether you can make yourself feel something, and whether it is morally reprehensible to do so even if you can. Suppose a wealthy man falls in love with a poor woman and wants to marry her, but she feels nothing for him, neither positive nor negative. If she can get herself to love him, she will get a lot of money. One problem is that she has to try to love the man, and while the chances that she will succeed vary with the case, there is rarely a very high probability that it will. But that is not an unsurmountable problem, since even a low probability of success may be enough to make the effort to love him worthwhile. The real problem is that the motive is suspect. No one objects when a woman tries to love a man in order to have a happy relationship with someone she does not want to hurt, but the situation is problematic when she is motivated by the prospect of a reward external to the relationship itself. Nonetheless, human motives are complex, and we often consider it acceptable, even commendable, when people consider the external rewards of a marriage to some extent. Parents routinely advise their children to pick a mate with a good income, and nobody considers that deplorable. But it would be a foolhardy parent who would advise her child to choose a mate with the best income and *then* try to love the person. Is Pascal's wager analogous to the foolhardy parent? If so, can it be altered to avoid the problematic features of the marriage analogy?

NOTE

1. James Cargile, "Pascal's Wager," in Steven M. Cahn and David Shatz, eds., *Contemporary Philosophy of Religion.* Oxford University Press, 1982, pp. 229–236.

Study Questions

1. What is "the many gods objection" to Pascal's wager?
2. What is Zagzebski's response to the many gods objection?
3. Can you decide to believe a claim knowing the evidence is against it?
4. Might acting as certain religious adherents act lead you to believe what they believe?

A Discussion of Heaven

XUNZI

Xunzi (pronounced shun-see), or Master Xun, was a Confucian scholar of the third century B.C.E. His philosophical system rested on the view that human nature is selfish but open to improvement through study and moral education. He considered any belief in supernaturalism to be pointless, because whatever Heaven may be, it is not concerned with human action, has no mind or will, and provides no rewards or punishments. Rites are not appeals to otherworldly forces but human inventions that ornament social life and serve as expressions of emotion.

Heaven's ways are constant. It does not prevail because of a sage like Yao; it does not cease to prevail because of a tyrant like Jie. Respond to it with good government, and good fortune will result; respond to it with disorder, and misfortune will result. If you encourage agriculture and are frugal in expenditures, then Heaven cannot make you poor. If you provide the people with the goods they need and demand their labor only at the proper time, then Heaven cannot afflict you with illness. If you practice the Way and are not of two minds, then Heaven cannot bring you misfortune. Flood or drought cannot make your people starve, extremes of heat or cold cannot make them

From *Xunzi: Basic Writings,* trans. Burton Watson, Columbia University Press, 2003. Reprinted by permission of the publisher.

fall ill, and strange and uncanny occurrences cannot cause them harm. But if you neglect agriculture and spend lavishly, then Heaven cannot make you rich. If you are careless in your provisions and slow to act, then Heaven cannot make you whole. If you turn your back upon the Way and act rashly, then Heaven cannot give you good fortune. Your people will starve even when there are no floods or droughts; they will fall ill even before heat or cold come to oppress them; they will suffer harm even when no strange or uncanny happenings occur. The seasons will visit you as they do a well-ordered age, but you will suffer misfortunes that a well-ordered age does not know. Yet you must not curse Heaven, for it is merely the natural result of your own actions. Therefore, he who can distinguish between the activities of Heaven and those of mankind is worthy to be called the highest type of man.

To bring to completion without acting, to obtain without seeking—this is the work of Heaven. Thus, although the sage has deep understanding, he does not attempt to exercise it upon the work of Heaven; though he has great talent, he does not attempt to apply it to the work of Heaven; though he has keen perception, he does not attempt to use it on the work of Heaven. Hence it is said that he does not compete with Heaven's work. Heaven has its seasons; earth has its riches; man has his government. Hence man may form a triad with the other two. But if he sets aside that which allows him to form a triad with the other two and longs for what they have, then he is deluded. The ranks of stars move in progression, the sun and moon shine in turn, the four seasons succeed each other in good order, the yin and yang[1] go through their great transformations, and the wind and rain pass over the whole land. All things obtain what is congenial to them and come to life, receive what is nourishing to them and grow to completion. One does not see the process taking place, but sees only the results. Thus it is called godlike. All men understand that the process has reached completion, but none understands the formless forces that bring it about. Hence it is

called the accomplishment of Heaven. Only the sage does not seek to understand Heaven. . . .

Are order and disorder due to the heavens? I reply, the sun and moon, the stars and constellations revolved in the same way in the time of Yu as in the time of Jie. Yu achieved order; Jie brought disorder. Hence order and disorder are not due to the heavens.

Are they then a matter of the seasons? I reply, the crops sprout and grow in spring and summer, and are harvested and stored away in autumn and winter. It was the same under both Yu and Jie. Yu achieved order; Jie brought disorder. Hence; order and disorder are not a matter of the seasons.

Are they due to the land? I reply, he who acquires land may live; he who loses it will die. It was the same in the time of Yu as in the time of Jie. Yu achieved order; Jie brought disorder. Hence order and disorder are not due to the land. . . .

Heaven does not suspend the winter because men dislike cold; earth does not cease being wide because men dislike great distances; the gentleman does not stop acting because petty men carp and clamor. Heaven has its constant way; earth has its constant dimensions; the gentleman has his constant demeanor. The gentleman follows what is constant; the petty man reckons up his achievements. This is what the *Odes* means when it says:

> *If you have no faults of conduct,*
> *Why be distressed at what others say?*

The king of Chu has a retinue of a thousand chariots, but not because he is wise. The gentleman must eat boiled greens and drink water, but not because he is stupid. These are accidents of circumstance. To be refined in purpose, rich in virtuous action, and clear in understanding; to live in the present and remember the past—these are things which are within your own power. Therefore the gentleman cherishes what is within his power and does not long for what is within the power of Heaven alone. The petty man, however, puts aside what is within his power and longs for what is within the power of Heaven. Because the gentleman cherishes what is within his power and does not long for what is within Heaven's power, he goes forward day by day. Because the petty man sets aside what is within his power and longs for what is within Heaven's power, he goes backward day by day. The same cause impels the gentleman forward day by day, and the petty man backward. What separates the two originates in this one point alone.

When stars fall or trees make strange sounds, all the people in the country are terrified and go about asking, "Why has this happened?" For no special reason, I reply. It is simply that, with the changes of Heaven and earth and the mutations of the yin and yang, such things once in a while occur. You may wonder at them, but you must not fear them. The sun and moon are subject to eclipses, wind and rain do not always come at the proper season, and strange stars occasionally appear. There has never been an age that was without such occurrences. If the ruler is enlightened and his government just, then there is no harm done even if they all occur at the same time. But if the ruler is benighted and his government ill-run, then it will be no benefit to him even if they never occur at all. Stars that fall, trees that give out strange sounds—such things occur once in a while with the changes of Heaven and earth and the mutations of the yin and yang. You may wonder at them, but do not fear them.

Among all such strange occurrences, the ones really to be feared are human portents. When the plowing is poorly done and the crops suffer, when the weeding is badly done and the harvest fails; when the government is evil and loses the support of the people; when the fields are neglected and the crops badly tended; when grain must be imported from abroad and sold at a high price, and the people are starving and die by the roadside—these are what I mean by human portents. When government commands are unenlightened, public works are undertaken at the wrong season, and agriculture is not properly attended to, these too are human portents. . . .

[W]hen ritual principles are not obeyed, family affairs and outside affairs are not properly separated, and men and women mingle wantonly, so that fathers and sons begin to doubt each other, superior and inferior become estranged, and bands of invaders enter the state—these too are human portents. Portents such as these are born from disorder, and if all three types occur at once, there will be no safety for the state. The reasons for their occurrence may be found very close at hand; the suffering they cause is great indeed. You should not only wonder at them, but fear them as well. . . .

You pray for rain and it rains. Why? For no particular reason, I say. It is just as though you had not prayed for rain and it rained anyway. The sun and moon undergo an eclipse and you try to save them; a drought occurs and you pray for rain; you consult the arts of divination before making a decision on some important matter. But it is not as though you could hope to accomplish anything by such ceremonies. They are done merely for ornament. Hence the gentleman regards them as ornaments, but the common people regard them as supernatural. He who considers them ornaments is fortunate; he who considers them supernatural is unfortunate.

NOTE

1. [The polar extremes that are the fundamental categories of the Chinese worldview.—S.M.C.]

Study Questions

1. According to Xunzi, why does only the sage not seek to understand Heaven?
2. What argument does Xunzi offer to prove that order and disorder are not due to the heavens?
3. According to Xunzi, which strange occurrences should be feared?
4. According to Xunzi, if you pray for rain, and then rain comes, what lesson should be drawn?

B.   Religious Diversity

The Challenge of Religious Diversity

PHILIP L. QUINN AND KEVIN MEEKER

Religious beliefs vary greatly from one religious tradition to another. Christianity, for instance, places heavy emphasis on an afterlife, whereas the central concern of Judaism is life in this world, not the next. What is the philosophical significance of the diversity of religions? Does the existence of many undermine the reasonableness of commitment to one? The problem is presented in the following piece by Philip L. Quinn (1940–2004), who was Professor of Philosophy at the University of Notre Dame, and Kevin Meeker, Professor of Philosophy at the University of South Alabama.

In subsequent readings we shall consider some religions that may be unfamiliar to you. Their different perspectives on the human condition raise philosophical issues about religious pluralism that will be explored in later articles.

Imagine that you were raised in a small, mostly evangelical Christian farming community in South Dakota. As far back as you can remember, you have believed in a personal God. While growing up, you were taught various Christian doctrines in Sunday School. Almost all the adults you knew accepted these doctrines, and so you took most of them for granted. You tried your best to live a good Christian life.

But now you are at the university. You elect to take a course in religious studies on Hinduism. In it you learn that advaita Hindus do not believe in a personal God; instead, for them, ultimate reality is the nonpersonal Brahman. As it happens, a classmate who also resides on your dormitory floor is a practicing advaita Hindu. The material from the class and discussions with this classmate inspire you to study the issue of what reasons there are for being a Christian.

You discover that arguments for the existence of a personal God come in many varieties: ontological, cosmological, teleological, and so on. But you also learn that scholars disagree on whether such arguments are any good. By the same token, you find out that there are arguments for the existence of Brahman and learn that they too are disputed. You read about Christians who report experiences of God. Indeed, when you reflect on the matter, you recall a couple of experiences of your own that could well be taken to be experiences of God guiding you. But you also read reports by advaita Hindus about their experiential contact with Brahman. You read reports about how the Christian system of belief and practice has helped many people become good and holy, but you also find out that there are reports of a lot of good and holy people among the advaita

Hindus. You quickly realize that it is unlikely that you will discover undisputed arguments or reasons that will establish the superiority of your own evangelical Christianity to advaita Hinduism or vice versa. And, of course, you recognize that you probably would have reached similar conclusions if you had been investigating Buddhism or Islam or Judaism or Taoism instead of advaita Hinduism.

So what should you do? Should you stick with the Christian system of belief and practice in which you were raised? Should you try to switch to one of its competitors? Or should you become a skeptic about all the religious systems of belief and take a stand outside all the religious practices? Once you have become genuinely puzzled by questions like these, you have felt the challenge of religious diversity. Of course, you need not doubt your own religion to feel the force of this challenge; simply wondering what justifies you in remaining in a tradition as opposed to switching to some other perspective poses similar questions. Or you might wonder how rationally to convince someone from another tradition that yours is true. In all such situations, the challenge of religious diversity looms large.

Needless to say, the awareness of religious diversity is not new. But many scholars argue that this awareness has recently acquired new significance. . . . Among the factors involved in this change is the better acquaintance people have with religions other than their own. After all, modern technologies of travel and communication facilitate contacts between adherents of different religions. Along the same lines, modern scholarship has produced fine translations of texts from a variety of religious traditions, and cultural anthropologists have provided fascinating thick descriptions of the practices of such traditions. Moreover, those who live in religiously pluralistic democracies have ample opportunities to develop first-hand familiarity with religions other than their own without leaving home. Finally, twenty-four hour a day news broadcasts have confronted us with graphic illustrations of what can transpire when diverging religions clash in such places as Belfast, Beirut, and Bosnia. Brief reflection on these factors should make it easy to see why the issue of religious diversity has become increasingly significant. . . .

It is also worth noting that the issue of religious diversity in general has not been on the radar screen of *academic* philosophy in the twentieth century as much as one might expect. For philosophy of religion in the middle part of the century was almost exclusively preoccupied with abstract questions about the meaningfulness of religious language. Now that the range of topics discussed has widened considerably, the issue of religious diversity is again receiving critical attention. And this is a healthy sign. For religious diversity is a practical problem for many people. As we noted earlier, modern technology and demographics have made the problem more acute and pressing. Unlike many very abstract philosophical problems, then, this one has the potential to engage nonphilosophers in a down-to-earth issue, and the philosophical discussion of it promises to aid nonphilosophers in further reflecting about what is at stake.

Study Questions

1. What is religious diversity?
2. Is religious diversity a strength or a weakness of religion?
3. Is religious diversity a reason for not accepting any particular religion?
4. Might belonging to a religion be important even if choosing any particular religion is not?

The Jain Path

JEFFERY D LONG

Jainism is an ancient nontheistic Indian religion still practiced today. Jains believe in the principle of karma, the idea of reincarnation, and the ultimate goal of Nirvāna, or unending bliss.

The Jain tradition stresses nonviolence against any living being. Its adherents are vegetarians and do not serve as butchers or soldiers. Its monks and nuns wear a gauze mask over the mouth to prevent the unintentional inhalation of an insect. They also sweep the ground in front of them as they walk, so as not to crush anything alive. The ascetic goal of neglecting every personal interest can in rare cases lead monks or nuns to starve themselves to death, thus ridding the soul of all passions and bringing an appropriate close to an ethical life.

Although accounting for less than 0.5 percent of India's population, Jains have had a significant impact on the country's religious, social, political, and economic life. Our next selection, written by Jeffery D Long, Professor of Religious Studies at Elizabethtown College in Pennsylvania, assesses this influential religious tradition.

Jainism is an ancient tradition of nonviolence and, according to many of its contemporary adherents, deep ecological wisdom. Originating in India and having many affinities with Hinduism and Buddhism, it is a tradition that is relatively unknown in the West.

Like Hindus and Buddhists, Jains affirm the reality of a universal moral principle of cause and effect called *karma*. Derived from a Sanskrit word meaning 'act', karma governs all action. It can be likened to Newton's Third Law of Motion: for every action there is an equal and opposite reaction. But traditional Indic worldviews do not make the sharp distinction, so typical of modern Western thought, between the realms of fact and value. Karma thus manifests not only in the form of physical laws, such as gravity, but also as a moral law governing action. If one engages in actions that are violent, or motivated by hatred, selfishness, or egotism,

the universe will respond in kind, producing suffering in the one who has caused suffering to others. Similarly, if one engages in actions that are benevolent, pure, and kind, the universe will respond benevolently, and one will have pleasant experiences. There are Western expressions that convey a similar sensibility to that of the idea of karma: You reap what you sow. What goes around comes around.

Like Hindus and Buddhists, Jains deduce from the principle of karma the idea of rebirth, or reincarnation. All religions must address the issue of why bad things happen to good people and good things happen to bad people. Why, if there is universal justice—which is essentially what karma amounts to—does the world in which we live appear to be as unjust as it does? Indic religions explain this phenomenon in terms of past and future lives. Today's joy or suffering may be the fruit of karma from a previous life. And the actions one takes today will inevitably bear fruit, if not in this life, then in a future one.

Like Hindus and Buddhists, Jains see the ultimate good as escape from the cycle of rebirth—*mokṣa,* or liberation from karmic bondage, or *nirvāṇa,* as it is also called in all of these traditions, a state of absorption in unending bliss. But, as for most Hindus and Buddhists, this final goal is widely conceived as remote and difficult to attain, the more immediate goal of religious activity being merit-making: the acquisition of 'good karma'.

Like Buddhists, and unlike most Hindus, Jains do not affirm the idea of a God, at least as this idea is understood in the Abrahamic religions—a creator and moral arbiter of the universe. Karmic 'reward' and 'punishment' is a wholly impersonal process, and we are each responsible for our own joy and suffering. There is no divine judge. It is up to us to follow the path that leads to ultimate freedom, or not. . . .

For those Westerners who have heard of Jainism, it may bring to mind images of ascetics—of monks and nuns—wearing what appear to be surgical face-masks in order to protect insects and microorganisms from being inhaled, and sweeping the ground in front of them with a broom or whisk to protect tiny creatures from being stepped on—a practice of nonviolence so radical as to defy easy comprehension.

But though this picture is not an inaccurate one, it is one-sided. The commitment of the Jains to a radically ascetic practice of nonviolence should not be minimized; but it should also not be exaggerated. A tiny percentage of Jains are actually monks or nuns who practice the kind of nonviolent asceticism most Western representations of Jainism bring to mind—a life of constant mindfulness of what one could call one's environmental impact. Though such asceticism evokes great admiration and reverence from the typical, lay practitioner of Jainism, it is not uncommon to hear lay Jains admit, quite frankly, that such asceticism is beyond their own, current ability to practice. One also hears

the hope expressed that the layperson may someday, perhaps later in life or in a future rebirth, feel the call of renunciation and take up the life of the Jain ascetic. The point is that although, as Jains, laypersons understand and admire what Jain ascetics do, they regard such ascetic practice much as many non-Jains do: as extraordinary and extremely difficult. . . .

Today, there are approximately 4.2 million Jains in the world. Although there are Jain communities in the UK, North America, and elsewhere—such as . . . [a] community in central Pennsylvania—the vast majority of Jains continue to live in India, where they have existed for over two and a half millennia as a small but highly influential minority. . . .

A common stereotype of the Jains, in both India and the West, is that they constitute a highly affluent merchant community. In fact, although many Jains do practice business professions—and many have been quite successful in these pursuits—there are also Jains who practice other professions, such as farming, and whose level of material wealth is relatively modest.

And then there are of course the Jain *sādhus* and *sādhvīs,* or monks and nuns, who have practically no material possessions to speak of, and who live a life of deliberate simplicity and nonviolence. Indeed, the strict commitment to *ahiṃsā,* or nonviolence, which the Jain monks and nuns embody, is the source of another stereotype of the Jains as a whole: that all Jains wear a face-mask to avoid accidentally ingesting insects, or that they carefully sweep the ground free of insects to avoid treading upon them as they walk. Only monks and nuns practice nonviolence to such a strict degree. . . .

According to a Jain understanding, however, it is very difficult to avoid doing any harm whatsoever to living beings. The universe is filled with microscopic organisms. . . . The most basic of these are called *nigodas.* For human beings, the very act of being alive involves the destruction of such tiny life forms. Eating, digesting food, breathing, sitting, and moving about: all involve the destruction of *nigodas* on a massive scale.

Such activities are generally not carried out with the intention of doing harm. One could argue that the requisite intent to do harm—and so the passion with which this intent is normally associated—is absent from such activities, and that they must therefore be without karmic consequence. But this is not a traditional Jain understanding. Once one is aware of the existence of tiny life forms in the air one breathes, in the water one drinks, and on the surfaces on which one travels and rests one's body, one becomes responsible for the harm that one does. Also, unlike Buddhism, which sees motive as the chief determinant of the morality of an act—of whether it involves a good or a bad karmic result—Jainism teaches that the actual consequences of action are always a major factor.

Jain monks and nuns therefore spend a good deal of their time in the effort to have a minimal negative impact upon their environment. Jain asceticism consists primarily of curbing activities that might lead to the accidental destruction of life, and to cultivating mindfulness of the life forms with which one shares the physical universe. A well-known symbol of this ascetic ideal is the *muhpatti,* a cloth that some Jain monks and nuns wear over their mouths to avoid accidentally inhaling or ingesting small organisms.

Central though the ascetic ideal of *ahiṃsā* is to the Jain community and its view of itself, it would be an exaggeration to suggest that all, or even most, Jains are constantly preoccupied with avoiding harm to microorganisms. There is a frank recognition in the Jain community, as in Buddhism, that most people are not yet at the spiritual level where they would wish to renounce life as a layperson and the activities that go with day-to-day existence. . . .

For the layperson, of course, avoidance of the destruction of life on a microscopic level may be simply impossible. One needs to eat, to drink, and to prepare food both for oneself and for one's children, as well as for wandering Jain ascetics (though ascetics are forbidden from taking food prepared explicitly for them). Where do Jains draw the line? For the layperson, it is a matter of intention. One knows that one's daily actions involve the destruction of life on a microscopic scale. But one does not willfully or deliberately take the life of any being. Even for laypersons, this is not simply a matter of behavior, but of cultivating an attitude of harmlessness toward all living things.

In practical terms, this means Jains overwhelmingly—if they are practicing and not merely nominal Jains—are vegetarian. Jains are not traditionally, as is sometimes thought, vegans, though in recent years a growing number of Jains have become vegan. A vegan does not consume any animal products at all. Jains in India do drink milk and use milk products, since cows are not harmed in the process. But they do not eat eggs.

Jains are also forbidden to engage in activities for their livelihood which involve the direct taking of life. One will not typically find a Jain butcher or Jain executioner, for example. Indeed, the injunction to avoid direct taking of life is the reason so many Jains go into business professions. Trading in goods made by others is less likely to force one into situations where one must directly take life oneself. . . .

The most controversial of Jain ascetic practices—though, it must be emphasized, a quite rare one—is the practice of self-starvation—known as *sallekhanā* or *santhārā*—occasionally undertaken by Jain monks and nuns, and the rare layperson . . .

This practice—as Jains emphasize quite strongly—is *not* a form of suicide. It is not undertaken out of passion or because of despair or anger. It can only be undertaken with the permission of one's spiritual preceptor, or *guru.* The guru's duty is to ensure that one's motives in undertaking this fast to the death are pure—that one is doing it out of a genuine sense of detachment from the body and out of compassion for all of the living beings that one will save by not continuing to eat, breathe, and consume resources. Such a holy death is seen as having great capacity to advance the soul on its path to liberation, and to be possible only for beings who have perfected their compassion and their wisdom to such a degree that they would rather die than cause pain or death for even the tiniest of creatures.

Study Questions

1. How does Jainism differ from most Western religions?
2. Is belief in God essential to religion?
3. What is the focus of Jain devotion?
4. Need asceticism be religious?

The Confucian Way

HERBERT FINGARETTE

Confucius (c. 551–c. 479 B.C.E.), whose original name was K'ung Ch'ui, or Master K'ung, was a Chinese sage who urged the adoption of an ethical system that stressed benevolence and personal integrity, thereby seeking to preserve peace and stable government. His sayings are found in the *Analects*, a work probably arranged by his disciples. For more than two millennia his thought has permeated the Chinese religious outlook.

While his ideas about God and the afterlife remain unclear, he stressed the importance of virtuous action in this life and close attention to *li*, a Chinese term referring to ceremony performed with care and conviction. This key concept is explored in our next selection, which was written by Herbert Fingarette, Professor Emeritus of Philosophy at the University of California, Santa Barbara. He stresses that for Confucius the proper object of attention is action in this world, not speculation about a transcendent realm.

Confucius saw, and tried to call to our attention, that the truly, distinctively human powers have, characteristically, a magical quality. His task, therefore, required, in effect, that he reveal what is already so familiar and universal as to be unnoticed. What is necessary in such cases is that one come upon this "obvious" dimension of our existence in a new way, in the right way. Where can one find such a new path to this familiar area, one which provides a new and revealing perspective? Confucius found the path: we go by way of the notion of *li*.

From *Confucius: The Secular as Sacred*, Waveland Press, 1998. Reprinted by permission of HarperCollins Publishers, Inc.

One has to labor long and hard to learn *li.* The word in its root meaning is close to "holy ritual," "sacred ceremony." Characteristic of Confucius's teaching is the use of the language and imagery of *li* as a medium within which to talk about the entire body of the *mores,* or more precisely, of the authentic tradition and reasonable conventions of society. Confucius taught that the ability to act according to *li* and the will to submit to *li* are essential to that perfect and peculiarly human virtue or power which can be man's. Confucius thus does two things here: he calls our attention to the entire body of tradition and convention, and he calls upon us to see all this by means of a metaphor, through the imagery of sacred ceremony, holy rite.

The (spiritually) noble man is one who has labored at the alchemy of fusing social forms (*li*) and raw personal existence in such a way that they transmuted into a way of being which realizes *te,* the distinctively human virtue or power.

Te is realized in concrete acts of human intercourse, the acts being of a pattern. These patterns have certain general features, features common to all such patterns of *li:* they are all expressive of "man-to-man-ness," of reciprocal loyalty and respect. But the patterns are also specific: they differentiate and they define in detail the ritual performance-repertoires which constitute civilized, i.e., truly human patterns of mourning, marrying and fighting, of being a prince, a father, a son and so on. However, men are by no means conceived as being mere standardized units mechanically carrying out prescribed routines in the service of some cosmic or social law. Nor are they self-sufficient, individual souls who happen to consent to a social contract. Men become truly human as their raw impulse is shaped by *li.* And *li* is the fulfillment of human impulse, the civilized expression of it—not a formalistic dehumanization. *Li* is the specifically humanizing form of the dynamic relation of man-to-man.

The novel and creative insight of Confucius was to see this aspect of human existence, its form as learned tradition and convention, in terms of a particular revelatory image: *li,* i.e, "holy rite," "sacred ceremony," in the usual meaning of the term prior to Confucius.

In well-learned ceremony, each person does what he is supposed to do according to a pattern. My gestures are coordinated harmoniously with yours—though neither of us has to force, push, demand, compel or otherwise "make" this happen. Our gestures are in turn smoothly followed by those of the other participants, all effortlessly. If all are "self-disciplined, ever turning to *li,*" then all that is needed—quite literally—is an initial ritual gesture in the proper ceremonial context; from there onward everything "happens." What action did Shun (the Sage-ruler) take? "He merely placed himself gravely and reverently with his face due south; that was all." Let us consider in at least a little detail the distinctive features of action emphasized by this revelatory image of Holy Rite.

It is important that we do not think of this effortlessness as "mechanical" or "automatic." If it is so, then, as Confucius repeatedly indicates, the ceremony is dead, sterile, empty: there is no *spirit* in it. The truly ceremonial "takes place"; there is a kind of spontaneity. It happens "of itself." There is life in it because the individuals involved do it with seriousness and sincerity. For ceremony to be authentic one must "participate in the sacrifice"; otherwise it is as if one "did not sacrifice at all." To put it another way, there are two contrasting kinds of failure in carrying out *li:* the ceremony may be awkwardly performed for lack of learning and skill; or the ceremony may have a surface slickness but yet be dull, mechanical for lack of serious purpose and commitment. Beautiful and effective ceremony requires the personal "presence" to be fused with learned ceremonial skill. This ideal fusion is true *li* as sacred rite.

Confucius characteristically and sharply contrasts the ruler who uses *li* with the ruler who seeks to attain his ends by means of commands, threats, regulations, punishments and force. The force of coercion is manifest and tangible, whereas the vast (and sacred) forces at work in *li* are invisible and intangible. *Li* works through spontaneous coordination rooted in reverent dignity. The perfection in Holy Rite is esthetic as well as spiritual.

Having considered holy ceremony in itself, we are now prepared to turn to more everyday aspects of life. This is in effect what Confucius invites us to do; it is the foundation for his perspective on man.

I see you on the street; I smile, walk toward you, put out my hand to shake yours. And behold—without any command, stratagem, force, special tricks or tools, without any effort on my part to make you do so, you spontaneously turn toward me, return my smile, raise your hand toward mine. We shake hands—not by my pulling your hand up and down or your pulling mine but by spontaneous and perfect cooperative action. Normally we do not notice the subtlety and amazing complexity of this coordinated "ritual" act. This subtlety and complexity become very evident, however, if one has had to learn the ceremony only from a book of instructions, or if one is a foreigner from a non-handshaking culture.

Nor normally do we notice that the "ritual" has "life" in it, that we are "present" to each other, at least to some minimal extent. As Confucius said, there are always the general and fundamental requirements of reciprocal good faith and respect. This mutual respect is not the same as a conscious feeling of mutual respect; when I am *aware* of a respect for you, I am much more likely to be piously fatuous or perhaps self-consciously embarrassed; and no doubt our little "ceremony" will reveal this in certain awkwardnesses. (I put out my hand too soon and am left with it hanging in midair.) No, the authenticity of the mutual respect does not require that I consciously feel respect or focus my attention on my respect for you; it is fully expressed in the correct "live" and spontaneous performance of the *act*. Just as an aerial acrobat must, at least for the purpose at hand, possess (but not think about his) complete trust in his partner if the trick is to come off, so we who shake hands,

though the stakes are less, must have (but not think about) respect and trust. Otherwise we find ourselves fumbling awkwardly or performing in a lifeless fashion, which easily conveys its meaninglessness to the other.

Clearly it is not necessary that our reciprocal respect and good faith go very far in order for us to accomplish a reasonably successful handshake and greeting. Yet even here, the sensitive person can often plumb the depths of another's attitude from a handshake. This depth of human relationship expressible in a "ceremonial" gesture is in good part possible because of the remarkable specificity of the ceremony. For example, if I am your former teacher, you will spontaneously be rather obvious in walking toward me rather than waiting for me to walk toward you. You will allow a certain subtle reserve in your handshake, even though it will be warm. You will not slap me on the back, though conceivably I might grasp you by the shoulder with my free hand. There are indescribably many subtleties in the distinctions, nuances and minute but meaningful variations in gesture. If we do try to describe these subtle variations and their rules, we immediately sound like Book 10 of the *Analects*, whose ceremonial recipes initially seem to the modern American reader to be the quintessence of quaint and extreme traditionalism. It is in just such ways that social activity is coordinated in civilized society, without effort or planning, but simply by spontaneously initiating the appropriate ritual gesture in an appropriate setting. This power of *li*, Confucius says, depends upon prior learning. It is not inborn.

The effortless power of *li* can also be used to accomplish physical ends, though we usually do not think of it this way. Let us suppose I wish to bring a book from my office to my classroom. If I have no magic powers, I must literally take steps—walk to my office, push the door open, lift the book with my own muscles, physically carry it back. But there is also magic—the proper ritual expression of my wish which will accomplish my wish with no such effort on my part. I turn politely, i.e., ceremonially, to one of my students in class and merely express in an appropriate and polite (ritual) formula my wish that he bring me the book. This proper ceremonial expression of my wish is all; I do not need to force him, threaten him, trick him. I do not need to do anything more myself. In almost no time the book is in my hands, as I wished! This is a uniquely human way of getting things done.

The examples of handshaking and of making a request are humble; the moral is profound. These complex but familiar gestures are characteristic of human relationships at their most human: we are least like anything else in the world when we do not treat each other as physical objects, as animals or even as subhuman creatures to be driven, threatened, forced, maneuvered. Looking at these "ceremonies" through the image of *li*, we realize that explicitly sacred rite can be seen as an emphatic, intensified and sharply elaborated extension of everyday *civilized* intercourse.

The notion that we can use speech only to talk *about* action or indirectly to *evoke* action has dominated modern Western thought. Yet contemporary "linguistic" analysis in philosophy has revealed increasingly how much the ritual word is itself the critical act rather than a report of, or stimulus to, action. . . . Professor J. L. Austin was one of those who brought the reality and pervasiveness of this phenomenon to a focus in his analyses of what he called the "performative utterance."[1] These are the innumerable statements we make which function somewhat like the "operative" clause in a legal instrument. They are statements, but they are not statements *about* some act or inviting some action; instead they are the very execution of the act itself.

"I give and bequeath my watch to my brother," duly said or written is not a report of what I have already done but is the very act of bequeathal itself. In a marriage ceremony, the "I do" is not a report of an inner mental act of acceptance; it is itself the act which seals my part of the bargain. "I promise . . ." is not a report of what I have done a moment before inside my head, nor is it indeed a report of anything at all; the uttering of the words is itself the act of promising. It is by words, and by the ceremony of which the words form a part, that I bind myself in a way which, for a man "ever turning to *li*," is more powerful, more inescapable than strategies or force. Confucius truly tells us that the man who uses the power of *li* can influence those above him—but not the man who has only physical force at his command.

There is no power of *li* if there is no learned and accepted convention, or if we utter the words and invoke the power of the convention in an inappropriate setting, or if the ceremony is not fully carried out, or if the persons carrying out the ceremonial roles are not those properly authorized ("authorization"—again a ceremony). In short, the peculiarly moral yet binding power of ceremonial gesture and word cannot be abstracted from or used in isolation from ceremony. It is not a distinct power we happen to use in ceremony; it is the power *of* ceremony. I cannot effectively go through the ceremony of bequeathing my servant to someone if, in our society, there is no accepted convention of slavery; I cannot bet two dollars if no one completes the bet by accepting; I cannot legally plead "Guilty" to a crime while eating dinner at home. Thus the power of *li* cannot be used except as the *li* is fully respected. . . .

For present purposes it is enough to note how many are the obvious performative formulas in our own language and ceremony,[2] and also to note that there may be less obvious but no less important performative formulas, for example, those formulas in which one expresses one's own wish or preference or choice. "I choose this one" excludes the objection, made after one receives it, that one was not speaking truly. For to say it in the proper circumstances is not to report something already done but is to take the "operative" step in making the choice.

The upshot of this approach to language and its "ceremonial" context was, in the reasoning of Professor Austin, paradoxical. He came to feel forced toward the conclusion that ultimately *all* utterances are in some essential way performative. This remains an open question, but it suffices for us to recall that it is now a commonplace of contemporary analytical philosophy (as it was a basic thesis of pragmatist philosophies) that we use words to *do* things, profoundly important and amazingly varied things.

Indeed, the central lesson of these new philosophical insights is not so much a lesson about language as it is about ceremony. What we have come to see, in our own way, is how vast is the area of human existence in which the substance of that existence *is* the ceremony. Promises, commitments, excuses, pleas, compliments, pacts—these and so much more are ceremonies or they are nothing. It is thus in the medium of ceremony that the peculiarly human part of our life is lived. The ceremonial act is the primary, irreducible event; language cannot be understood in isolation from the conventional practice in which it is rooted; conventional practice cannot be understood in isolation from the language that defines and is part of it. No purely physical motion is a promise; no word alone, independent of ceremonial context, circumstances and roles can be a promise. Word and motion are only abstractions from the concrete ceremonial act.

From this standpoint, it is easy to see that not only motor skills must be learned but also correct use of language. For correct use of language is *constitutive* of effective action as gesture is. Correct language is not merely a useful adjunct; it is of the essence of executing the ceremony. . . .

Of course we must be leery of reading our own contemporary philosophical doctrines into an ancient teaching. Yet I think that the text of the *Analects,* in letter and spirit, supports and enriches our own quite recently emerging vision of man as a ceremonial being.

In general, what Confucius brings out in connection with the workings of ceremony is not only its distinctively human character, its linguistic and magical character, but also its moral and religious character. Here, finally, we must recall and place at the focus of our analysis the fact that for Confucius it is the imagery of

Holy Ceremony that unifies and infuses all these dimensions of human existence. . . .

Rite brings out forcefully not only the harmony and beauty of social forms, the inherent and ultimate dignity of human intercourse; it brings out also the moral perfection implicit in achieving one's ends by dealing with others as beings of equal dignity, as free coparticipants in *li.* Furthermore, to act by ceremony is to be completely open to the other; for ceremony is public, shared, transparent; to act otherwise is to be secret, obscure and devious, or merely tyrannically coercive. It is in this beautiful and dignified, shared and open participation with others who are ultimately like oneself that man realizes himself. Thus perfect community of men—the Confucian analogue to Christian brotherhood—becomes an inextricable part, the chief aspect, of Divine worship—again an analogy with the central Law taught by Jesus.

Confucius wanted to teach us, as a corollary, that sacred ceremony in its narrower, root meaning is not a totally mysterious appeasement of spirits external to human and earthly life. Spirit is no longer an external being influenced by the ceremony; it is that that is expressed and comes most alive *in* the ceremony. Instead of being diversion of attention from the human realm to another transcendent realm, the overtly holy ceremony is to be seen as the central symbol, both expressive of and participating in the holy as a dimension of all truly human existence.

NOTES

1. J. L. Austin, "Performative Utterances," in *Philosophical Papers* (London: Oxford University Press, 1961), pp. 220–239; *How to Do Things with Words* (London: Oxford University Press, 1962); "Performatif-Constatif," in *La Philosophic Analytique,* Cahiers de Royaumont, Phil. No. V (Editions de Mincit, Paris, 1962), 271–305.

I have offered a systematic analysis of the concept of the performative, which I believe concords with and amplifies the points I am here making in connection with Confucius, though my analysis of performativeness was intended to be entirely general. See Herbert Fingarette, "Performatives," *American Philosophical Quarterly*, Vol. 4 (1967).

2. Though the list could go on interminably, I mention here just a few more terms which commonly enter into formulas having an obvious performative function: "I christen you," "I appoint you," "I pick this (or him)," "I congratulate you," "I welcome you," "I authorize you," "I challenge you," "I order you," "I request you."

Study Questions

1. What does a Confucian mean by "*li*"?
2. In what circumstances does an individual display *li*?
3. What role in religion is played by ceremony?
4. Why do certain ceremonies arouse strong emotions?

The Tao

RAY BILLINGTON

Along with Confucianism and Zen Buddhism, Taoism stands as one of the three major religious traditions in China. Its central focus is not God but "the Tao," the first principle of the universe, which is unknowable. But if words fail us, how can we follow the central precept of Taoism, to live in harmony with the Tao?

In our next selection Ray Billington (1930–2012) offers a brief exposition of the Taoist outlook. He was a Methodist minister who turned against Christianity, became an exponent of Eastern philosophy, and headed the Philosophy Department at the University of West Bristol, England.

What . . . does 'Tao' mean? To be able to give a direct answer to this seemingly straightforward question would, paradoxically, be to fall into error, since, as the opening verse of the most famous of all Taoist classics states unambiguously,

The tao that can be told is not the eternal Tao;
The name that can be named is not the eternal Name.

This couplet is from the *Tao Te Ching*, the 'classic of the way and its power'. According to Chinese tradition, it was written by Lao Tzu, a famous teacher and mystic of the sixth century BCE, just before he removed himself from civilisation in order to become a recluse. It is now generally agreed by sinologists that the work is the product of many hands (Lao Tzu means 'great master', which is more a title than a name); that it was compiled over some centuries; and was finalised in its present form around the second century BCE.

According to the *Tao Te Ching*, the Tao is *the first principle of the universe, the all-embracing*

From *Religion Without God*, Routledge, 2002. Reprinted by permission of Taylor & Francis.

reality from which everything else arises. Although the Tao remains eternally unknowable, its power (Te) can enter into every human being, so that the test of one's commitment to Taoism is viewed as the extent to which one's life is in harmony with the Tao. (The Chinese hieroglyphic for 'philosophy' depicts a hand and a mouth, symbolising a condition where words are consistent with deeds.) . . . Taoism does not proceed to make any case for God, or gods, as divine powers operating under the Tao's auspices, so to speak. Section 42 of the *Tao Te Ching* puts the matter rather differently:

> The Tao gives birth to One.
> One gives birth to Two.
> Two gives birth to Three.
> Three gives birth to all things.

The 'One' to which the Tao gives birth . . . is Ch'i, or primordial breath (wind, spirit, energy, like the Hebrew word *Ruach* as used in Genesis 1: 2: 'The spirit of God moved upon the face of the waters'). It is the life-force that pervades and vitalises all things, the cosmic energy which brought the universe into being and continues to sustain it. . . .

For Taoists even the Ch'i remains remote. It can be experienced, but only with time and dedication. If the Te, the power of the Tao in each individual life, is to be evinced, a force is needed which can be experienced more immediately. It is here that Taoists turn to the 'Two' to which the Ch'i gives birth. These are the twin forces of yin and yang, the polar opposites by which the universe functions, such as negative and positive, cold and heat, darkness and light, intuition and rationality, femininity and masculinity, earth and heaven. Neither of these can be without the other, and neither has any meaning without the other. We know the meaning of 'hot' only in relation to 'cold', of 'wet' to 'dry', of 'tall' to 'short', of 'dark' to 'light', of 'life' to 'death'. (We know that we are alive only because we know that we were once, and shall again be, dead. If we were eternal,

there would be no word either for 'eternal' or for 'living'.) . . .

[N]either yin nor yang is ever motionless; each is continuously moving into the other, which means that one must learn to recognise when to apply yin, and when yang, energies. This again means allowing the intuition to exert itself: to know when to speak out and when to remain quiet; when to be gentle and when to be violent; when to be active and when to stand and stare. Both the workaholic and the playboy are, according to the yin-yang doctrine, living distorted and incomplete lives because only half of their natures is being allowed expression. Neither the ant nor the grasshopper in Aesop's fable would receive Taoism's stamp of approval.

The 'Three' to which the Two give birth are heaven, earth and humanity. [I]t is when there is harmony between these three—the yang of heaven, the yin of earth, and the human occupants of the arena which between them they bring into being—that the Te can be identified in people's lives. The final stage is the creation of 'all things' which we encounter and experience, for which 'the Three' are responsible.

The important consideration with Taoism, however, . . . is not to speculate on the meaning of the idea of the Tao, but to find out how to respond to its power (Te) in one's own life. The aim . . . is to be natural, and the *Tao Te Ching* gives many hints about how this state may be achieved. One way is to practise *wu-wei*. This is often translated as living a life of 'non-action', but a more accurate translation would be not to take any *inappropriate* action. The most famous exponent of Taoism who was unquestionably a historical figure was the teacher of the third century BCE, Chuang-Tzu (Master Chuang). He argued that many of the things we do and the words we speak are simply a waste of time and breath, since the situation we are discussing or trying to affect cannot be changed by our efforts: all we're actually doing, he said, was 'flaying the air'. Or worse: our frenetic efforts may actually lead to the loss of what was wholesome and acceptable in itself. We destroy a lily by gilding it; a snake is no longer a snake if we paint legs on it; we shall not help young wheat to grow by tugging at it. We must practise patience . . . acting only at the right time and with the minimum amount of effort. In fact, if we learn how to wait, we shall frequently find that no action is necessary in any case. The *Tao Te Ching* states:

> Do you have the patience to wait
> till your mud settles and the water is clear?
> Can you remain unmoving
> till the right action arises by itself?

* * *

Wu-wei means striking only when the iron is hot, sowing one's seed—whether in deed or word—and leaving it time to burgeon. Where disagreement with another person occurs, its approach is to present one's viewpoint unambiguously, then leave it time to germinate—if there is any worth in the idea—in the mind of the other, rather than to overcome the other with decibels or, worse, to force him to accept a viewpoint or an activity against either his will or his personal assessment of the situation. Wu-wei is the way of the diplomat, not the dictator; of the philosopher, not the proselytiser.

Another concept in Taoism with which wu-wei is linked is *fu*, meaning 'returning'. This could be interpreted as aligning oneself with the yin and yang by understanding that seasons, whether in nature or in a nation's culture and values, arrive and pass, only to return again and pass away again, so that the wise person will accommodate his living to the eternal process of change. More basically Taoism is the concept of fu as returning, or, at any rate, remaining loyal, to one's roots:

> If you let yourself be blown to and fro, you lose touch with your root.
> If you let restlessness move you, you lose touch with who you are.

* * *

[A]nother Taoist virtue . . . is *p'u* literally an unhewn block, and is an image used to denote simplicity, even innocence: not arising from ignorance, but from a backcloth of full awareness of the human condition: childlikeness without being childish. . . . To live according to p'u is to speak as one feels, to behave according to the person one is, or has become; in other words, to act naturally. The *Tao Te Ching* states:

> Man follows the earth.
> Earth follows the universe.
> The universe follows the Tao.
> The Tao follows only itself.

That final phrase has also been translated as 'suchness', the spontaneous and intuitive state of *tzu-yan*, meaning 'being such of itself, 'being natural'. In human beings, it includes everything which is free of human intention or external influences: that which is in harmony with itself. It may therefore be linked with wu-wei with its call for action only when it is appropriate—that is, when it is the natural action for those particular circumstances. When a person achieves this condition (which is not easy), he or she can be described as being at one with the Tao. It will not be achieved by academic research, or the study of sacred texts, or through a correct observance of ritual: . . . Taoism relegates all these activities to a low ranking on the scale of spiritual aids. It will be gained by living one's life in accordance with the natural forces of the universe, expressed both in nature itself and in human nature.

Study Questions

1. Can we knowingly act in accord with an unknowable principle?
2. What does Taoism mean by "*wu-wei*"?
3. What does Billington mean by "childlikeness without being childish"?
4. Does Taoism, like Confucianism, stress correct observance of ritual?

Twelve Zen Stories

Buddhism was introduced in China in the first century. After hundreds of years, Buddhist and Taoist ideas blended to yield Zen Buddhism, which more than a millennium later spread to Japan.

Zen places comparatively little emphasis on ritual, morality, or book learning. Rather, Zen finds enlightenment in spontaneous experience and challenges adherents with koans, puzzles that seek to force respondents to abandon reason. Such a query is this famous one: "Can you show me the sound of one hand clapping?"

Our next selection contains a dozen Zen stories that illustrate how paradox can provide a path to understanding, even when intellect appears to fail. The ultimate lesson is supposed to be the elimination of all dualities, including any separation between consciousness and the object of meditation.

A CUP OF TEA

Nan-in, a Japanese master during the Meiji era (1868–1912), received a university professor who came to inquire about Zen.

Nan-in served tea. He poured his visitor's cup full, and then kept on pouring.

The professor watched the overflow until he no longer could restrain himself. "It is overfull. No more will go in!"

"Like this cup," Nan-in said, "you are full of your own opinions and speculations. How can I show you Zen unless you first empty your cup?"

IS THAT SO?

The Zen master Hakuin was praised by his neighbors as one living a pure life.

A beautiful Japanese girl whose parents owned a food store lived near him. Suddenly, without any warning, her parents discovered she was with child.

This made her parents angry. She would not confess who the man was, but after much harassment at last named Hakuin.

In great anger the parents went to the master. "Is that so?" was all he would say.

After the child was born it was brought to Hakuin. By this time he had lost his reputation, which did not trouble him, but he took very good care of the child. He obtained milk from his neighbors and everything else the little one needed.

A year later the girl-mother could stand it no longer. She told her parents the truth—that the real father of the child was a young man who worked in the fishmarket.

The mother and father of the girl at once went to Hakuin to ask his forgiveness, to apologize at length, and to get the child back again.

Hakuin was willing. In yielding the child, all he said was: "Is that so?"

THE MOON CANNOT BE STOLEN

Ryokan, a Zen master, lived the simplest kind of life in a little hut at the foot of a mountain. One evening a thief visited the hut only to discover there was nothing in it to steal.

From *Zen Flesh/Zen Bones,* compiled by Paul Reps and Nyogen Senzaki, Tuttle Publishing, 1957.

Ryokan returned and caught him. "You may have come a long way to visit me," he told the prowler, "and you should not return empty-handed. Please take my clothes as a gift."

The thief was bewildered. He took the clothes and slunk away.

Ryokan sat naked, watching the moon. "Poor fellow," he mused, "I wish I could give him this beautiful moon."

HAPPY CHINAMAN

Anyone walking about Chinatowns in America will observe statues of a stout fellow carrying a linen sack. Chinese merchants call him Happy Chinaman or Laughing Buddha.

This Hotei [sage] lived in the T'ang dynasty. He had no desire to call himself a Zen master or to gather many disciples about him. Instead he walked the streets with a big sack into which he would put gifts of candy, fruit, or doughnuts. These he would give to children who gathered around him in play. He established a kindergarten of the streets.

Whenever he met a Zen devotee he would extend his hand and say: "Give me one penny." And if anyone asked him to return to a temple to teach others, again he would reply: "Give me one penny."

Once as he was about his play-work another Zen master happened along and inquired: "What is the significance of Zen?"

Hotei immediately plopped his sack down on the ground in silent answer.

"Then," asked the other, "what is the actualization of Zen?"

At once the Happy Chinaman swung the sack over his shoulder and continued on his way.

MUDDY ROAD

Tanzan and Ekido were once traveling together down a muddy road. A heavy rain was still falling.

Coming around a bend, they met a lovely girl in a silk kimono and sash, unable to cross the intersection.

"Come on, girl," said Tanzan at once. Lifting her in his arms, he carried her over the mud.

Ekido did not speak again until that night when they reached a lodging temple. Then he no longer could restrain himself. "We monks don't go near females," he told Tanzan, "especially not young and lovely ones. It is dangerous. Why did you do that?"

"I left the girl there," said Tanzan. "Are you still carrying her?"

THE SOUND OF ONE HAND

The master of Kennin temple was Mokurai, Silent Thunder. He had a little protégé named Toyo who was only twelve years old. Toyo saw the older disciples visit the master's room each morning and evening to receive instruction in sanzen or personal guidance in which they were given koans to stop mind-wandering.

Toyo wished to do sanzen also.

"Wait a while," said Mokurai. "You are too young."

But the child insisted, so the teacher finally consented.

In the evening little Toyo went at the proper time to the threshold of Mokurai's sanzen room. He struck the gong to announce his presence, bowed respectfully three times outside the door, and went to sit before the master in respectful silence.

"You can hear the sound of two hands when they clap together," said Mokurai. "Now show me the sound of one hand."

Toyo bowed and went to his room to consider this problem. From his window he could hear the music of the geishas. "Ah, I have it!" he proclaimed.

The next evening, when his teacher asked him to illustrate the sound of one hand, Toyo began to play the music of the geishas.

"No, no," said Mokurai. "That will never do. That is not the sound of one hand. You've not got it at all."

Thinking that such music might interrupt, Toyo moved his abode to a quiet place. He meditated again. "What can the sound of one hand be?" He happened to hear some water dripping. "I have it," imagined Toyo.

When he next appeared before his teacher, Toyo imitated dripping water.

"What is that?" asked Mokurai. "That is the sound of dripping water, but not the sound of one hand. Try again."

In vain Toyo meditated to hear the sound of one hand. He heard the sighing of the wind. But the sound was rejected.

He heard the cry of an owl. This also was refused.

The sound of one hand was not the locusts.

For more than ten times Toyo visited Mokurai with different sounds. All were wrong. For almost a year he pondered what the sound of one hand might be.

At last little Toyo entered true meditation and transcended all sounds. "I could collect no more," he explained later, "so I reached the soundless sound."

Toyo had realized the sound of one hand.

EVERY-MINUTE ZEN

Zen students are with their masters at least ten years before they presume to teach others. Nan-in was visited by Tenno, who, having passed his apprenticeship, had become a teacher. The day happened to be rainy, so Tenno wore wooden clogs and carried an umbrella. After greeting him Nanin remarked: "I suppose you left your wooden clogs in the vestibule. I want to know if your umbrella is on the right or left side of the clogs."

Tenno, confused, had no instant answer. He realized that he was unable to carry his Zen every minute. He became Nan-in's pupil, and he studied six more years to accomplish his every-minute Zen.

IN THE HANDS OF DESTINY

A great Japanese warrior named Nobunaga decided to attack the enemy although he had only one-tenth the number of men the opposition commanded. He knew that he would win, but his soldiers were in doubt.

On the way he stopped at a Shinto shrine and told his men: "After I visit the shrine I will toss a coin. If heads comes, we will win; if tails, we will lose. Destiny holds us in her hand."

Nobunaga entered the shrine and offered a silent prayer. He came forth and tossed a coin. Heads appeared. His soldiers were so eager to fight that they won their battle easily.

"No one can change the hand of destiny," his attendant told him after the battle.

"Indeed not," said Nobunaga, showing a coin which had been doubled, with heads facing either way.

THE SUBJUGATION OF A GHOST

A young wife fell sick and was about to die. "I love you so much," she told her husband, "I do not want to leave you. Do not go from me to any other woman. If you do, I will return as a ghost and cause you endless trouble."

Soon the wife passed away. The husband respected her last wish for the first three months, but then he met another woman and fell in love with her. They became engaged to be married.

Immediately after the engagement a ghost appeared every night to the man, blaming him for not keeping his promise. The ghost was clever too. She told him exactly what had transpired between himself and his new sweetheart. Whenever he gave his fiancée a present, the ghost would describe it in detail. She would even repeat conversations, and it so annoyed the man that he could not sleep. Someone advised him to take his problem to a Zen master who lived close to the village. At length, in despair, the poor man went to him for help.

"Your former wife became a ghost and knows everything you do," commented the master. "Whatever you do or say, whatever you give your beloved, she knows. She must be a very wise ghost. Really you should admire such a ghost. The next time she appears, bargain with her. Tell her that she knows so much you can hide nothing from her, and that if she will answer you one question, you promise to break your engagement and remain single."

"What is the question I must ask her?" inquired the man.

The master replied: "Take a large handful of soy beans and ask her exactly how many beans you hold in your hand. If she cannot tell you, you will know she is only a figment of your imagination and will trouble you no longer."

The next night, when the ghost appeared the man flattered her and told her that she knew everything.

"Indeed," replied the ghost, "and I know you went to see that Zen master today."

"And since you know so much," demanded the man, "tell me how many beans I hold in this hand!"

There was no longer any ghost to answer the question.

ONE NOTE OF ZEN

After Kakua visited the emperor he disappeared and no one knew what became of him. He was the first Japanese to study Zen in China, but since he showed nothing of it, save one note, he is not remembered for having brought Zen into his country.

Kakua visited China and accepted the true teaching. He did not travel while he was there. Meditating constantly, he lived on a remote part of a mountain. Whenever people found him and asked him to preach he would say a few words and then move to another part of the mountain where he could be found less easily.

The emperor heard about Kakua when he returned to Japan and asked him to preach Zen for his edification and that of his subjects.

Kakua stood before the emperor in silence. He then produced a flute from the folds of his robe, and blew one short note. Bowing politely, he disappeared.

REAL PROSPERITY

A rich man asked Sengai to write something for the continued prosperity of his family so that it might be treasured from generation to generation.

Sengai obtained a large sheet of paper and wrote: "Father dies, son dies, grandson dies."

The rich man became angry. "I asked you to write something for the happiness of my family! Why do you make such a joke as this?"

"No joke is intended," explained Sengai. "If before you yourself die your son should die, this would grieve you greatly. If your grandson should pass away before your son, both of you would be broken-hearted. If your family, generation after generation, passes away in the order I have named, it will be the natural course of life. I call this real prosperity."

A LETTER TO A DYING MAN

Bassui wrote the following letter to one of his disciples who was about to die:

"The essence of your mind is not born, so it will never die. It is not an existence, which is perishable. It is not an emptiness, which is a mere void. It has neither color nor form. It enjoys no pleasures and suffers no pains.

"I know you are very ill. Like a good Zen student, you are facing that sickness squarely. You may not know exactly who is suffering, but question yourself: What is the essence of this mind? Think only of this. You will need no more. Covet nothing. Your end which is endless is as a snowflake dissolving in the pure air."

Study Questions

1. Do you have to empty your cup of opinions in order to learn?
2. What do you take to be the lesson of "Muddy Road"?
3. What is meant by the action of blowing one short note on a flute?
4. What significance do you find in "A Letter to a Dying Man"?

God Is Red: A Native View of Religion

VINE DELORIA, JR.

Vine Deloria, Jr. (1933–2005), was Professor of Political Science and later of Law at the University of Arizona and was active in a variety of Native American organizations. In the next selection he describes the religious outlook of Native Americans that stresses the sacredness of lands.

A belief in the sacredness of lands in the non-Indian context may become the preferred belief of an individual or group of people based on their experiences or on an intensive study of preselected evidence. But this belief becomes the subject of intense criticism and does not, except under unusual circumstances, become an operative principle in the life and behavior of the non-Indian group. The same belief, when seen in the Indian context, is an integral part of the experiences of the people—past, present, and future. The idea does not become a bone of contention among the people for even if someone does not have the experience or belief in the sacredness of lands, he or she accords tradition the respect that it deserves. Indians who have never visited certain sacred sites nevertheless know of these places from the community knowledge, and they intuit this knowing to be an essential part of their being. . . .

If we were to subject the topic of the sacredness of lands to a Western rational analysis, fully recognizing that such an analysis is merely for our convenience in discussion and does not represent the nature of reality, we would probably find four major categories of description. Some of these categories are overlapping because some groups might not agree with the description of certain sites in the categories in which other Indians would place them. Nevertheless, it is the principle of respect for the sacred that is important.

The first and most familiar kind of sacred lands are places to which we attribute sanctity because the location is a site where, within our own history, something of great importance has taken place. Unfortunately, many of these places are related to instances of human violence. Gettysburg National Cemetery is a good example of this kind of sacred land. Abraham Lincoln properly noted that we cannot hallow the Gettysburg

From *God Is Red: A Native View of Religion*, 30th Anniversary Edition, Fulcrum Publishing, 2003. Reprinted by permission of the publisher.

battlefield because others, the men who fought there, had already consecrated it by giving "that last full measure of devotion." We generally hold these places sacred because people did there what we might one day be required to do—give our lives in a cause we hold dear. Wounded Knee, South Dakota, has become such a place for many Indians where a band of Sioux Indians were massacred. On the whole, however, the idea of regarding a battlefield as sacred was entirely foreign to most tribes because they did not see war as a holy enterprise. The Lincoln Memorial in Washington, D.C., might be an example of a nonmartial location, and . . . it is important to recognize that we should have some sense of reverence in these places.

Every society needs these kinds of sacred places because they help to instill a sense of social cohesion in the people and remind them of the passage of generations that have brought them to the present. A society that cannot remember and honor its past is in peril of losing its soul. Indians, because of our considerably longer tenure on this continent, have many more sacred places than do non-Indians. Many different ceremonies can be and have been held at these locations; there is both an exclusivity and an inclusiveness, depending upon the occasion and the ceremony. In this classification the site is all important, but it is sanctified each time ceremonies are held and prayers offered.

A second category of sacred lands has a deeper, more profound sense of the sacred. It can be illustrated in Old Testament stories that have become the foundation of three world religions. After the death of Moses, Joshua led the Hebrews across the River Jordan into the Holy Land. On approaching the river with the Ark of the Covenant, the waters of the Jordan "rose up" or parted and the people, led by the Ark, crossed over on "dry ground," which is to say they crossed without difficulty. After crossing, Joshua selected one man from each of the Twelve Tribes and told him to find a large stone. The twelve stones were then placed together in a monument to mark the spot where the people

had camped after having crossed the river successfully. When asked about this strange behavior, Joshua then replied, "That this may be a sign among you, that when your children ask their fathers in time to come, saying 'What mean ye by these stones?' Then you shall answer them: That the waters of Jordan were cut off before the Ark of the Covenant of the Lord, when it passed over Jordan."[1]

In comparing this site with Gettysburg, we must understand a fundamental difference. Gettysburg is made sacred by the actions of men. It can be described as exquisitely dear to us, but it is not a location where we have perceived that something specifically other than ourselves is present, something mysteriously religious in the proper meaning of those words has happened or been made manifest. In the crossing of the River Jordan, the sacred or higher powers have appeared in the lives of human beings. Indians would say something holy has appeared in an otherwise secular situation. No matter how we might attempt to explain this event in later historical, political, or economic terms, the essence of the event is that the sacred has become a part of our experience.

Some of the sites that traditional religious leaders visit are of this nature. Buffalo Gap at the southeastern edge of the Black Hills of South Dakota marks the location where the buffalo emerged each spring to begin the ceremonial year of the Plains Indians, and it has this aspect of sacred/secular status. It may indeed be the starting point of the Great Race that determined the primacy between two-legged and four-legged creatures at the beginning of the world. Several mountains in New Mexico and Arizona mark places where the Pueblo, Hopi, and Navajo peoples completed their migrations, were told to settle, or where they first established their spiritual relationships with bear, deer, eagle, and other peoples who participate in the ceremonials.

Every identifiable region has sacred places peculiar to its geography and as we extend the circle geographically from any point in

North America, we begin to include an ever-increasing number of sacred sites. Beginning in the American Southwest we must include the Apache, Ute, Comanche, Kiowa, and other tribes as we move away from the Pueblo and Navajo lands. These lands would be sacred to some tribes but secular to the Pueblo, Hopi, and Navajo. The difference would be in the manner of revelation and what the people experienced. There is immense particularity in the sacred and it is not a blanket category to be applied indiscriminately. Even east of the Mississippi, though many places have been nearly obliterated, people retain knowledge of these sacred sites. Their sacredness does not depend on human occupancy but on the stories that describe the revelation that enabled human beings to experience the holiness there.

In the religious world of most tribes, birds, animals, and plants compose the "other peoples" of creation. Depending on the ceremony, various of these "peoples" participate in human activities. If Jews and Christians see the action of a deity at sacred places in the Holy Land and in churches and synagogues, traditional Indian people experience spiritual activity as the whole of creation becomes active participants in ceremonial life. Because the relationship with the "other peoples" is so fundamental to the human community, most traditional practitioners are reluctant to articulate the specific elements of either the ceremony or the locations. Because some rituals involve the continued prosperity of the "other peoples," discussing the nature of the ceremony would violate the integrity of these relationships. Thus, traditional people explain that these ceremonies are being held for "all our relatives" but are reluctant to offer any further explanations. . . .

It is not likely that non-Indians have had many of these kinds of religious experiences, particularly because most churches and synagogues have special rituals that are designed to cleanse the buildings so that their services can be held there untainted by the natural world. Non-Indians have simply not been on this continent very long; their families have rarely settled in one place for any period of time so that no profound relationship with the environment has been possible. Additionally, non-Indians have engaged in the senseless killing of wildlife and utter destruction of plant life. It is unlikely that they would have understood efforts by other forms of life to communicate with humans. Although, some non-Indian families who have lived continuously in isolated rural areas tell stories about birds and animals similar to the traditions of many tribes indicating that lands and the "other peoples" do seek intimacy with our species.

The third kind of sacred lands are places of overwhelming holiness where the Higher Powers, on their own initiative, have revealed Themselves to human beings. Again, we can illustrate this in the Old Testament narrative. Prior to his journey to Egypt, Moses spent his time herding his father-in-law's sheep on or near Mount Horeb. One day he took the flock to the far side of the mountain and to his amazement saw a bush burning with fire but not being consumed by it. Approaching this spot with the usual curiosity of a person accustomed to the outdoor life, Moses was startled when the Lord spoke to him from the bush, warning, "Draw not hither; put off thy shoes from thy feet, for the place where on thou standest is holy ground."[2]

This tradition tells us that there are places of unquestionable, inherent sacredness on this earth, sites that are holy in and of themselves. Human societies come and go on this earth and any prolonged occupation of a geographical region will produce shrines and sacred sites discerned by the occupying people, but there will always be a few sites at which the highest spirits dwell. The stories that explain the sacred nature of these locations will frequently provide startling parallels to the account about the burning bush. One need only look at the shrines of present-day Europe. Long before Catholic or Protestant churches were built in certain places, other religions had established shrines and temples of that spot. These holy places are locations where people have always gone to communicate and commune with higher spiritual powers.

This phenomenon is worldwide and all religions find that these places regenerate people and fill them with spiritual powers. In the Western Hemisphere these places, with few exceptions, are known only by American Indians. . . . People have been commanded to perform ceremonies at these holy places so that the earth and all its forms of life might survive and prosper. Evidence of this moral responsibility that sacred places command has come through the testimony of traditional people when they have tried to explain to non-Indians at various times in this century— in court, in conferences, and in conversations— that they must perform certain ceremonies at specific times and places in order that the sun may continue to shine, the earth prosper, and the stars remain in the heavens. Tragically, this attitude is interpreted by non-Indians as indicative of the traditional leader's personal code or philosophy and is not seen as a simple admission of a moral duty.

Skeptical non-Indians, and representatives of other religions seeking to discredit tribal religions, have sometimes deliberately violated some of these holy places with no ill effects. They have then come to believe that they have demonstrated the false nature of Indian beliefs. These violations reveal a strange non-Indian belief in a form of mechanical magic that is touchingly adolescent, a belief that an impious act would, or could trigger an immediate response from the higher spiritual powers. Surely these impious acts suggest a deity who jealously guards his or her prerogatives and wreaks immediate vengeance for minor transgressions— much as some Protestant sects have envisioned God and much as an ancient astronaut wanting to control lesser beings might act.

It would be impossible for the thoughtless or impious acts of one species to have an immediate drastic effect on the earth. The cumulative effect of continuous secularity, however, poses a different kind of danger. Long-standing prophecies tell us of the impious people who would come here, defy the creator, and cause the massive destruction of the planet. Many traditional people believe that we are now quite near that time. The cumulative evidence of global warming, acid rain, the disappearance of amphibians, overpopulation, and other products of civilized life certainly testify to the possibility of these prophecies being correct.

Of all the traditional ceremonies extant and actively practiced at the time of contact with non-Indians, ceremonies derived from or related to these holy places have the highest retention rate because of their extraordinary planetary importance. Ironically, traditional people have been forced to hold these ceremonies under various forms of subterfuge and have been abused and imprisoned for doing them. Yet the ceremonies have very little to do with individual or tribal prosperity. Their underlying theme is one of gratitude expressed by human beings on behalf of all forms of life. They act to complete and renew the entire and complete cycle of life, ultimately including the whole cosmos present in its specific realizations, so that in the last analysis one might describe ceremonials as the cosmos becoming thankfully aware of itself.

Having used Old Testament examples to show the objective presence of the holy places, we can draw additional conclusions about the nature of these holy places from the story of the Exodus. Moses did not demand that the particular location of the burning bush become a place of worship for his people, although there was every reason to suppose that he could have done so. Lacking information, we must conclude that the holiness of this place precluded its use as a shrine. If Moses had been told to perform annual ceremonies at that location during specific days or times of the year, world history would have been entirely different.

Each holy site contains its own revelation. This knowledge is not the ultimate in the sense that Near Eastern religions like to claim the universality of their ideas. Traditional religious leaders tell us that in many of the ceremonies new messages are communicated to them. The ceremonies enable humans to have continuing relationships with higher spiritual powers so that each bit of information is specific to the time, place, and circumstances of the people. No revelation can be regarded as universal because times and conditions change.

The second and third kinds of sacred lands result from two distinctly different forms of sacred revelations where the sacred is actively involved in secular human activities and where the sacred takes the initiative to chart out a new historical course for humans. Because there are higher spiritual powers who can communicate with people, there has to be a fourth category of sacred lands. People must always be ready to experience new revelations at new locations. If this possibility did not exist, all deities and spirits would be dead. Consequently, we always look forward to the revelation of new sacred places and ceremonies. . . .

We live in time and space and receive most of our signals about proper behavior from each other and the environment around us. Under these circumstances, the individual and the group must both have some kind of sanctity if we are to have a social order at all. By recognizing the various aspects of the sacredness of lands as we have described, we place ourselves in a realistic context in which the individual and the group can cultivate and enhance the sacred experience. Recognizing the sacredness of lands on which previous generations have lived and died is the foundation of all other sentiment. Instead of denying this dimension of our emotional lives, we should be setting aside additional places that have transcendent meaning. Sacred sites that higher spiritual powers have chosen for manifestation enable us to focus our concerns on the specific form of our lives. These places remind us of our unique relationship with the spiritual forces that govern the universe and call us to fulfill our religious vocations. These kinds of religious experiences have shown us something of the nature of the universe by an affirmative manifestation of themselves and this knowledge illuminates everything else that we know. . . .

Sacred places are the foundation of all other beliefs and practices because they represent the presence of the sacred in our lives. They properly inform us that we are not larger than nature and that we have responsibilities to the rest of the natural world that transcend our own personal desires and wishes. This lesson must be learned by each generation; unfortunately the technology of industrial society always leads us in the other direction. Yet it is certain that as we permanently foul our planetary nest, we shall have to learn a most bitter lesson. There probably is not sufficient time for the non-Indian population to understand the meaning of sacred lands and incorporate the idea into their lives and practices. We can but hope that some protection can be afforded these sacred places before the world becomes wholly secular and is destroyed.

Notes

1. Joshua 4:6–7.
2. Exodus 3:5.

Study Questions

1. What is the meaning of "sacredness"?
2. In what different ways can land be sacred?
3. How is a new sacred place revealed?
4. How might a disagreement about the sacredness of a place be rationally resolved?

Religious Pluralism and Salvation

JOHN H. HICK

John H. Hick (1922–2012) was Professor of the Philosophy of Religion at Claremont Graduate University and Professor Emeritus of Theology at the University of Birmingham. He believes that despite the differences among religions, in at least one crucial respect all are fundamentally similar. Each can be viewed as offering a path to salvation, a way of shifting believers from self-centeredness to concentration on a divine reality. In light of this consideration, Hick urges all religious adherents to reject the view that their own religions are superior to all others.

In particular, Hick maintains that Christians should recognize the "arbitrary and contrived notion" that the salvation of all persons depends on their believing in the Trinity and resurrection. Whether such a doctrinal transformation would undermine or enhance Christianity is a crucial question.

I

The fact that there is a plurality of religious traditions, each with its own distinctive beliefs, spiritual practices, ethical outlook, art forms, and cultural ethos, creates an obvious problem for those of us who see them, not simply as human phenomena, but as responses to the Divine. For each presents itself, implicitly or explicitly, as in some important sense absolute and unsurpassable and as rightly claiming a total allegiance. The problem of the relationship between these different streams of religious life has often been posed in terms of their divergent belief-systems. For whilst there are various overlaps between their teachings there are also radical differences: is the divine reality (let us refer to it as the Real) personal or non-personal; if personal, is it unitary or triune; is the universe created, or emanated, or itself eternal; do we live only once on this earth or are we repeatedly reborn? and so on and so on. When the problem of understanding religious plurality is approached through these rival truth-claims it appears particularly intractable.

I want to suggest, however, that it may more profitably be approached from a different direction, in terms of the claims of the various traditions to provide, or to be effective contexts of, salvation. "Salvation" is primarily a Christian term, though I shall use it here to include its functional analogues in the other major world traditions. In this broader sense we can say that both Christianity and these other faiths are paths of salvation. For whereas preaxial religion was (and is) centrally concerned to keep life going on an even keel, the post-axial traditions, originating or rooted in the "axial age" of the first millennium B.C.E.—principally Hinduism, Judaism, Buddhism, Christianity, Islam—are centrally concerned with a radical transformation of the human situation.

It is of course possible, in an alternative approach, to define salvation in such a way that it becomes a necessary truth that only one

From "Religious Pluralism and Salvation," *Faith and Philosophy* 5 (1998). Reprinted by permission of the journal.

particular tradition can provide it. If, for example, from within Christianity we define salvation as being forgiven by God because of Jesus' atoning death, and so becoming part of God's redeemed community, the church, then salvation is by definition Christian salvation. If on the other hand, from within Mahayana Buddhism, we define it as the attainment of *satori* or awakening, and so becoming an ego-free manifestation of the eternal Dharmakaya, then salvation is by definition Buddhist liberation. And so on. But if we stand back from these different conceptions to compare them, we can, I think, very naturally and properly see them as different forms of the more fundamental conception of a radical change from a profoundly unsatisfactory state to one that is limitlessly better because rightly related to the Real. Each tradition conceptualizes in its own way the wrongness of ordinary human existence—as a state of fallenness from paradisal virtue and happiness, or as a condition of moral weakness and alienation from God, or as the fragmentation of the infinite One into false individualities, or as a self-centeredness which pervasively poisons our involvement in the world process, making it to us an experience of anxious, unhappy unfulfillment. But each at the same time proclaims a limitlessly better possibility, again conceptualized in different ways—as the joy of conforming one's life to God's law; as giving oneself to God in Christ, so that "it is no longer I who live, but Christ who lives in me" (Galatians 2:20), leading to eternal life in God's presence; as a complete surrender (*islam*) to God, and hence peace with God, leading to the bliss of paradise; as transcending the ego and realizing oneness with the limitless being-consciousness-bliss (*satchitananda*) of Brahman; as overcoming the ego point of view and entering into the serene selflessness of nirvana. I suggest that these different conceptions of salvation are specifications of what, in a generic formula, is the transformation of human existence from self-centeredness to a new orientation, centered in the divine Reality. And in each case the good news that is proclaimed is that this limitlessly better possibility is

actually available and can be entered upon, or begin to be entered upon, here and now. Each tradition sets forth the way to attain this great good: faithfulness to the Torah, discipleship to Jesus, obedient living out of the Qur'anic way of life, the Eightfold Path of the Buddhist dharma, or the three great Hindu *margas* of mystical insight, activity in the world, and self-giving devotion to God.

II

The great world religions, then, are ways of salvation. Each claims to constitute an effective context within which the transformation of human existence can and does take place from self-centeredness to Reality-centeredness. How are we to judge such claims? We cannot directly observe the inner spiritual quality of a human relationship to the Real; but we can observe how that relationship, as one's deepest and most pervasive orientation, affects the moral and spiritual quality of a human personality and of a man's or woman's relationship to others. It would seem, then, that we can only assess these salvation-projects insofar as we are able to observe their fruits in human life. The inquiry has to be, in a broad sense, empirical. For the issue is one of fact, even though hard to define and difficult to measure fact, rather than being settleable by a priori stipulation.

The word "spiritual" which occurs above is notoriously vague; but I am using it to refer to a quality or, better, an orientation which we can discern in those individuals whom we call saints—a Christian term which I use here to cover such analogues as arahat, bodhisattva, jivanmukti, mahatma. In these cases the human self is variously described as becoming part of the life of God, being "to the Eternal Goodness what his own hand is to a man"; or being permeated from within by the infinite reality of Brahman; or becoming one with the eternal Buddha nature. There is a change in their deepest orientation from centeredness in the ego to a new centering in the Real as manifested in their own tradition. One is conscious in the presence of such a person that he or she is, to a startling extent, open to the transcendent, so as to be largely free from self-centered concerns and anxieties and empowered to live as an instrument of God/Truth/Reality.

It is to be noted that there are two main patterns of such a transformation. There are saints who withdraw from the world into prayer or meditation and saints who seek to change the world—in the medieval period a contemplative Julian of Norwich and a political Joan of Arc, or in our own century a mystical Sri Aurobindo and a political Mahatma Gandhi. In our present age of sociological consciousness, when we are aware that our inherited political and economic structures can be analyzed and purposefully changed, saintliness is more likely than in earlier times to take social and political forms. But, of whichever type, the saints are not a different species from the rest of us; they are simply much more advanced in the salvific transformation.

The ethical aspect of this salvific transformation consists in observable modes of behavior. But how do we identify the kind of behavior which, to the degree that it characterizes a life, reflects a corresponding degree of reorientation to the divine Reality? Should we use Christian ethical criteria, or Buddhist, or Muslim . . . ? The answer, I suggest, is that at the level of their most basic moral insights the great traditions use a common criterion. For they agree in giving a central and normative role to the unselfish regard for others that we call love or compassion. This is commonly expressed in the principle of valuing others as we value ourselves, and treating them accordingly. Thus in the ancient Hindu *Mahabharata* we read that "One should never do to another that which one would regard as injurious to oneself. This, in brief, is the rule of Righteousness" (*Anushana parva,* 113:7). Again, "He who . . . benefits persons of all orders, who is always devoted to the good of all beings, who does not feel aversion to anybody . . . succeeds in ascending to Heaven"

(*Anushana parva,* 145:24). In the Buddhist *Sutta Nipata* we read, "As a mother cares for her son, all her days, so towards all living things a man's mind should be all-embracing" (149). In the Jain scriptures we are told that one should go about "treating all creatures in the world as he himself would be treated" (*Kitanga Sutra,* I.ii.33). Confucius, expounding humaneness (*jen*), said, "Do not do to others what you would not like yourself" (*Analects,* xxi, 2). In a Taoist scripture we read that the good man will "regard [others'] gains as if they were his own, and their losses in the same way" (*Thai Shang,* 3). The Zoroastrian scriptures declare, "That nature only is good when it shall not do unto another whatever is not good for its own self" (*Dadistan-i-dinik,* 94:5). We are all familiar with Jesus' teaching, "As ye would that men should do to you, do ye also to them likewise" (Luke 6:31). In the Jewish Talmud we read "What is hateful to yourself do not do to your fellow man. That is the whole of the Torah" (*Babylonian Talmud,* Shabbath 31a). And in the Hadith of Islam we read Muhammad's words, "No man is a true believer unless he desires for his brother that which he desires for himself" (*Ibn Madja,* Intro. 9). Clearly, if everyone acted on this basic principle, taught by all the major faiths, there would be no injustice, no avoidable suffering, and the human family would everywhere live in peace.

When we turn from this general principle of love/compassion to the actual behavior of people within the different traditions, wondering to what extent they live in this way, we realize how little research has been done on so important a question. We do not have, much more to go on than general impressions, supplemented by travellers' tales and anecdotal reports. We observe among our neighbors within our own community a great deal of practical loving-kindness; and we are told, for example, that a remarkable degree of self-giving love is to be found among the Hindu fishing families in the mud huts along the Madras shore; and we hear various other similar accounts from other lands. We read biographies, social histories, and novels of Muslim village life in Africa, Buddhist life in Thailand, Hindu life in India, Jewish life in New York, as well as Christian life around the world, both in the past and today, and we get the impression that the personal virtues (as well as vices) are basically much the same within these very different religion-cultural settings and that in all of them unselfish concern for others occurs and is highly valued. And, needless to say, as well as love and compassion we also see all-too-abundantly, and apparently spread more or less equally in every society, cruelty, greed, hatred, selfishness, and malice.

All this constitutes a haphazard and impressionistic body of data. Indeed I want to stress, not how easy it is, but on the contrary how difficult it is, to make responsible judgments in this area. For not only do we lack full information, but the fragmentary information that we have has to be interpreted in the light of the varying natural conditions of human life in different periods of history and in different economic and political circumstances. And I suggest that all that we can presently arrive at is the cautious and negative conclusion that we have no good reason to believe that any one of the great religious traditions has proved itself to be more productive of love/compassion than another.

The same is true when we turn to the large-scale social outworkings of the different salvation-projects. Here the units are not individual human lives, spanning a period of decades, but religious cultures spanning many centuries. For we can no more judge a civilization than a human life by confining our attention to a single temporal cross-section. Each of the great streams of religious life has had its times of flourishing and its times of deterioration. Each has produced its own distinctive kinds of good and its own distinctive kinds of evil. But to assess either the goods or the evils cross-culturally is difficult to say the least. How do we weigh, for example, the lack of economic progress, and consequent widespread poverty, in traditional Hindu and Buddhist cultures against the endemic violence and racism of Christian civilization, culminating

in the twentieth century Holocaust? How do we weigh what the west regards as the hollowness of arranged marriages against what the east regards as the hollowness of a marriage system that leads to such a high proportion of divorces and broken families? From within each culture one can see clearly enough the defects of the others. But an objective ethical comparison of such vast and complex totalities is at present an unattainable ideal. And the result is that we are not in a position to claim an over-all moral superiority for any one of the great living religious traditions.

Let us now see where we have arrived. I have suggested that if we identify the central claim of each of the great religious traditions as the claim to provide, or to be an effective context of, salvation; and if we see salvation as an actual change in human beings from self-centeredness to a new orientation centered in the ultimate divine Reality; and if this new orientation has both a more elusive "spiritual" character and a more readily observable moral aspect—then we arrive at the modest and largely negative conclusion that, so far as we can tell, no one of the great world religions is salvifically superior to the rest.

III

If this is so, what are we to make of the often contradictory doctrines of the different traditions? In order to make progress at this point, we must distinguish various kinds and levels of doctrinal conflict.

There are, first, conceptions of the ultimate as Jahweh, or the Holy Trinity, or Allah, or Shiva, or Vishnu, or as Brahman, or the Dharmakaya, the Tao, and so on.

If salvation is taking place, and taking place to about the same extent, within the religious systems presided over by these various deities and absolutes, this suggests that they are different manifestations to humanity of a yet more ultimate ground of all salvific transformation. Let us then consider the possibility that an infinite transcendent divine reality is being differently conceived, and therefore differently experienced, and therefore differently responded to from within our different religio-cultural ways of being human. This hypothesis makes sense of the fact that the salvific transformation seems to have been occurring in all the great traditions. Such a conception is, further, readily open to philosophical support. For we are familiar today with the ways in which human experience is partly formed by the conceptual and linguistic frameworks within which it occurs. The basically Kantian insight that the mind is active in perception, and that we are always aware of our environment as it appears to a consciousness operating with our particular conceptual resources and habits, has been amply confirmed by work in cognitive psychology and the sociology of knowledge and can now be extended with some confidence to the analysis of religious awareness. If, then, we proceed inductively from the phenomenon of religious experience around the world, adopting a religious as distinguished from a naturalistic interpretation of it, we are likely to find ourselves making two moves. The first is to postulate an ultimate transcendent divine reality (which I have been referring to as the Real) which, being beyond the scope of our human concepts, cannot be directly experienced by us as it is in itself but only as it appears through our various human thought-forms. And the second is to identify the thought-and-experienced deities and absolutes as different manifestations of the Real within different historical forms of human consciousness. In Kantian terms, the divine noumenon, the Real *an sich,* is experienced through different human receptivities as a range of divine phenomena, in the formation of which religious concepts have played an essential part.

These different "receptivities" consist of conceptual schemas within which various personal, communal, and historical factors have produced yet further variations. The most basic concepts in terms of which the Real is humanly thought-and-experienced are those of (personal) deity and of the (non-personal) absolute. But the Real is not actually experienced either as deity in general or as the absolute in general. Each basic concept becomes (in Kantian terminology) schematized in more concrete form. It is at this point that individual and cultural factors enter the process. The religious tradition of which we are a part, with its history and ethos and its great exemplars, its scriptures feeding our thoughts and emotions, and perhaps above all its devotional or meditative practices, constitutes an uniquely shaped and coloured "lens" through which we are concretely aware of the Real specifically as the personal Adonai, or as the Heavenly Father, or as Allah, or Vishnu, or Shiva . . . or again as the non-personal Brahman, or Dharmakaya, or the Void or the Ground. . . . Thus, one who uses the forms of Christian prayer and sacrament is thereby led to experience the Real as the divine Thou, whereas one who practices advaitic yoga or Buddhist zazen is thereby brought to experience the Real as the infinite being-consciousness-bliss of Brahman, or as the limitless emptiness of *sunyata* which is at the same time the infinite fullness of immediate reality as "wondrous being."

Three explanatory comments at this point before turning to the next level of doctrinal disagreement. First, to suppose that the experienced deities and absolutes which are the intentional objects of worship or content of religious meditation, are appearances or manifestations of the Real, rather than each being itself the Real *an sich,* is not to suppose that they are illusions—any more than the varying ways in which a mountain may appear to a plurality of differently placed observers are illusory. That the same reality may be variously experienced and described is true even of physical objects. But in the case of the infinite, transcendent divine reality there may well be much greater scope for the use of varying human conceptual schemas producing varying modes of phenomenal experience. Whereas the concepts in terms of which we are aware of mountains and rivers and houses are largely (though by no means entirely) standard throughout the human race, the religious concepts in terms of which we become aware of the Real have developed in widely different ways within the different cultures of the earth.

As a second comment, to say that the Real is beyond the range of our human concepts is not intended to mean that it is beyond the scope of purely formal, logically generated concepts—such as the concept of being beyond the range of (other than purely formal) concepts. We would not be able to refer at all to that which cannot be conceptualized in any way, not even by the concept of being unconceptualizable! But the other than purely formal concepts by which our experience is structured must be presumed not to apply to its noumenal ground. The characteristics mapped in thought and language are those that are constitutive of human experience. We have no warrant to apply them to the noumenal ground of the phenomenal, i.e., experienced, realm. We should therefore not think of the Real *an sich* as singular or plural, substance or process, personal or non-personal, good or bad, purposive or non-purposive. This has long been a basic theme of religious thought. For example, within Christianity, Gregory of Nyssa declared that:

> The simplicity of the True Faith assumes God to be that which He is, namely, incapable of being grasped by any term, or any idea, or any other device of our apprehension, remaining beyond the reach not only of the human but of the angelic and all supramundane intelligence, unthinkable, unutterable, above all expression in words, having but one name that can represent His proper nature, the single name being "Above Every Name" (*Against Eunomius*, I, 42).

Augustine, continuing this tradition, said that "God transcends even the mind" (*True Religion*, 36:67), and Aquinas that "by its immensity, the divine substance surpasses every form that our intellect reaches" (*Contra Gentiles*, I, 14, 3). In Islam the Qur'an affirms that God is "beyond what they describe" (6:101). The Upanishads declare of Brahman, "There the eye goes not, speech goes not, nor the mind" (*Kena Up.*, 1, 3), and Shankara wrote that Brahman is that "before which words recoil, and to which no understanding has ever attained" (Otto, *Mysticism East and West*, E. T. 1932, p. 28).

But, third, we might well ask, why postulate an ineffable and unobservable divine-reality-in-itself? If we can say virtually nothing about it, why affirm its existence? The answer is that the reality or non-reality of the postulated noumenal ground of the experienced religious phenomena constitutes the difference between a religious and a naturalistic interpretation of religion. If there is no such transcendent ground, the various forms of religious experience have to be categorized as purely human projections. If on the other hand there is such a transcendent ground, then these phenomena may be joint products of the universal presence of the Real and of the varying sets of concepts and images that have crystallized within the religious traditions of the earth. To affirm the transcendent is thus to affirm that religious experience is not solely a construction of the human imagination but is a response—though always culturally conditioned—to the Real.

Those doctrinal conflicts, then, that embody different conceptions of the ultimate arise, according to the hypothesis I am presenting, from the variations between different sets of human conceptual schema and spiritual practice. And it seems that each of these varying ways of thinking-and-experiencing the Real has been able to mediate its transforming presence to human life. For the different major concepts of the ultimate do not seem—so far as we can tell—to result in one religious totality being soteriologically more effective than another.

IV

The second level of doctrinal difference consists of metaphysical beliefs which cohere with although they are not exclusively linked to a particular conception of the ultimate. These are beliefs about the relation of the material universe to the Real: creation ex nihilo, emanation, an eternal universe, an unknown form of dependency . . .? And about human destiny: reincarnation or a single life, eternal identity or transcendence of the self . . .? Again, there are questions about the existence of heavens and hells and purgatories and angels and devils and many other subsidiary states and entities. Out of this mass of disputed religious issues let me pick two major examples: is the universe created ex nihilo, and do human beings reincarnate?

I suggest that we would do well to apply to such questions a principle that was taught by the Buddha two and a half millennia ago. He listed a series of "undetermined questions" (*avyakata*)—whether the universe is eternal, whether it is spatially infinite, whether (putting it in modern terms) mind and brain are identical, and what the state is of a completed project of human existence (a Tathagata) after bodily death. He refused to answer these questions, saying that we do not need to have knowledge of these things in order to attain liberation or awakening (nirvana); and indeed that to regard such information as soteriologically essential would only divert us from the single-minded quest for liberation. I think that we can at this point profitably learn from the Buddha, even extending his conception of the undetermined questions further than he did—for together with almost everyone else in his own culture he regarded one of our examples, reincarnation, as a matter of assured knowledge. Let us, then, accept that we do not *know* whether, e.g., the universe was created ex nihilo, nor whether human beings are reincarnated; and, further, that it is not necessary for salvation to hold a correct opinion on either matter.

I am not suggesting that such issues are unimportant. On their own level they are extremely important, being both of great interest to us and also having widely ramifying implications within our belief systems and hence for our lives. The thought of being created out of nothing can nourish a salutary sense of absolute dependence.

(But other conceptions can also nurture that sense.) The idea of reincarnation can offer the hope of future spiritual progress; though, combined with the principle of karma, it can also serve to validate the present inequalities of human circumstances. (But other eschatologies also have their problems, both theoretical and practical). Thus these—and other—disputed issues do have a genuine importance. Further, it is possible that some of them may one day be settled by empirical evidence. It might become established, for example, that the "big bang" of some fifteen billion years ago was an absolute beginning, thus ruling out the possibility that the universe is eternal. And again, it might become established, by an accumulation of evidence, that reincarnation does indeed occur in either some or all cases. On the other hand it is possible that we shall never achieve agreed knowledge in these areas. Certainly, at the present time, whilst we have theories, preferences, hunches, inherited convictions, we cannot honestly claim to have secure knowledge. And the same is true, I suggest, of the entire range of metaphysical issues about which the religions dispute. They are of intense interest, properly the subject of continuing research and discussion, but are not matters concerning which absolute dogmas are appropriate. Still less is it appropriate to maintain that salvation depends upon accepting some one particular opinion or dogma. We have seen that the transformation of human existence from self-centeredness to Reality-centeredness seems to be taking place within each of the great traditions despite their very different answers to these debated questions. It follows that a correct opinion concerning them is not required for salvation.

V

The third level of doctrinal disagreement concerns historical questions. Each of the great traditions includes a larger or smaller body of historical beliefs. In the case of Judaism these include at least the main features of the history described in the Hebrew scriptures; in the case of Christianity, these plus the main features of the life, death, and resurrection of Jesus as described in the New Testament; in the case of Islam, the main features of the history described in the Qur'an; in the case of Vaishnavite Hinduism, the historicity of Krishna; in the case of Buddhism, the historicity of Guatama and his enlightenment at Bodh Gaya; and so on. But although each tradition thus has its own records of the past, there are rather few instances of direct disagreement between these. For the strands of history that are cherished in these different historical memories do not generally overlap; and where they do overlap they do not generally involve significant differences. The overlaps are mainly within the thread of ancient Near Eastern history that is common to the Jewish, Christian, and Muslim scriptures; and within this I can only locate two points of direct disagreement—the Torah's statement that Abraham nearly sacrificed his son Isaac at Mount Moriah (Genesis 22) versus the Muslim interpretation of the Qur'anic version (in Sura 37) that it was his other son Ishmael; and the New Testament witness that Jesus died on the cross versus the Qur'anic teaching that "they did not slay him, neither crucified him, only a likeness of that was shown them" (Sura 4:156). (This latter however would seem to be a conflict between an historical report, in the New Testament, and a theological inference—that God would not allow so great a prophet to be killed—in the Qur'an.)

All that one can say in general about such disagreements, whether between two traditions or between any one of them and the secular historians, is that they could only properly be settled by the weight of historical evidence. However, the events in question are usually so remote in time, and the evidence so slight or so uncertain, that the question cannot be definitively settled. We have to be content with different communal memories, enriched as they are by the mythic halo that surrounds all long-lived human memories of events of transcendent significance. Once again, then, I suggest that differences of historical judgment, although having their own

proper importance, do not prevent the different traditions from being effective, and so far as we can tell equally effective, contexts of salvation. It is evidently not necessary for salvation to have correct historical information. (It is likewise not necessary for salvation, we may add, to have correct scientific information.)

VI

Putting all this together, the picture that I am suggesting can be outlined as follows: our human religious experience, variously shaped as it is by our sets of religious concepts, is a cognitive response to the universal presence of the ultimate divine Reality that, in itself, exceeds human conceptuality. This Reality is however manifested to us in ways formed by a variety of human concepts, as the range of divine personae and metaphysical impersonae witnessed to in the history of religions. Each major tradition, built around its own distinctive way of thinking-and-experiencing the Real, has developed its own answers to the perennial questions of our origin and destiny, constituting more or less comprehensive and coherent cosmologies and eschatologies. These are human creations which have, by their association with living streams of religious experience, become invested with a sacred authority. However they cannot all be wholly true; quite possibly none is wholly true; perhaps all are partly true. But since the salvific process has been going on through the centuries despite this unknown distribution of truth and falsity in our cosmologies and eschatologies, it follows that it is not necessary for salvation to adopt any one of them. We would therefore do well to learn to tolerate unresolved, and at present unresolvable, differences concerning these ultimate mysteries.

One element, however, to be found in the belief-systems of most of the traditions raises a special problem, namely that which asserts the sole salvific efficacy of that tradition. I shall discuss this problem in terms of Christianity because it is particularly acute for those of us who are Christians. We are all familiar with such New Testament texts as "There is salvation in no one else [than Jesus Christ], for there is no other name under heaven given among men by which we must be saved" (Acts 4:12), and with the Catholic dogma *Extra ecclesiam nulla salus* (No salvation outside the church) and its Protestant equivalent—never formulated as an official dogma but nevertheless implicit within the eighteenth and nineteenth century Protestant missionary expansion—no salvation outside Christianity. Such a dogma differs from other elements of Christian belief in that it is not only a statement about the potential relationship of Christians to God but at the same time about the actual relationship of non-Christians to God. It says that the latter, in virtue of being non-Christians, lack salvation. Clearly such a dogma is incompatible with the insight that the salvific transformation of human existence is going on, and so far as we can tell going on to a more or less equal extent, within all the great traditions. Insofar, then, as we accept that salvation is not confined to Christianity we must reject the old exclusivist dogma.

This has in fact now been done by most thinking Christians, though exceptions remain, mostly within the extreme Protestant fundamentalist constituencies. The *Extra ecclesiam* dogma, although not explicitly repealed, has been outflanked by the work of such influential Catholic theologians as Karl Rahner, whose new approach was in effect endorsed by Vatican II. Rahner expressed his more inclusivist outlook by suggesting that devout people of other faiths are "anonymous Christians," within the invisible church even without knowing it, and thus within the sphere of salvation. The Pope [John Paul II] in his Encyclical *Redemptor Hominis* (1979), expressed this thought even more comprehensively by saying that "every man without exception has been redeemed by Christ" and "with every man without any exception whatever Christ is in a way united, even when man is unaware of it" (para. 14). And a number of Protestant theologians have advocated a comparable position.

The feature that particularly commends this kind of inclusivism to many Christians today is that it recognizes the spiritual values of other religions, and the occurrence of salvation within them, and yet at the same time preserves their conviction of the ultimate superiority of their own religion over all others. For it maintains that salvation, wherever it occurs, is Christian salvation; and Christians are accordingly those who alone know and preach the source of salvation, namely in the atoning death of Christ.

This again, like the old exclusivism, is a statement not only about the ground of salvation for Christians but also for Jews, Muslims, Hindus, Buddhists, and everyone else. But we have seen that it has to be acknowledged that the immediate ground of their transformation is the particular spiritual path along which they move. It is by living in accordance with the Torah or with the Qur'anic revelation that Jews and Muslims find a transforming peace with God; it is by one or other of their great *margas* that Hindus attain to *moksha*; it is by the Eightfold Path that Theravada Buddhists come to *nirvana*; it is by *zazen* that Zen Buddhists attain to *satori*; and so on. The Christian inclusivist is, then, by implication, declaring that these various spiritual paths are efficacious, and constitute authentic contexts of salvation, because Jesus died on the cross; and, by further implication, that if he had not died on the cross they would not be efficacious.

This is a novel and somewhat astonishing doctrine. How are we to make sense of the idea that the salvific power of the dharma taught five hundred years earlier by the Buddha is a consequence of the death of Jesus in approximately 30 C.E.? Such an apparently bizarre conception should only be affirmed for some very good reason. It was certainly not taught by Jesus or his apostles. It has emerged only in the thought of twentieth century Christians who have come to recognize that Jews are being salvifically transformed through the spirituality of Judaism, Muslims through that of Islam, Hindus and

Buddhists through the paths mapped out by their respective traditions, and so on, but who nevertheless wish to retain their inherited sense of the unique superiority of Christianity. The only outlet left for this sense, when one has acknowledged the salvific efficacy of the various great spiritual ways, is the arbitrary and contrived notion of their metaphysical dependency upon the death of Christ. But the theologian who undertakes to spell out this invisible causality is not to be envied. The problem is not one of logical possibility—it only requires logical agility to cope with that—but one of religious or spiritual plausibility. It would be a better use of theological time and energy, in my opinion, to develop forms of trinitarian, christological, and soteriological doctrine which are compatible with our awareness of the independent salvific authenticity of the other great world faiths. Such forms are already available in principle in conceptions of the Trinity, not as ontologically three but as three ways in which the one God is humanly thought and experienced; conceptions of Christ as a man so fully open to and inspired by God as to be, in the ancient Hebrew metaphor, a "son of God"; and conceptions of salvation as an actual human transformation which has been powerfully elicited and shaped, among his disciples, by the influence of Jesus.

There may indeed well be a variety of ways in which Christian thought can develop in response to our acute late twentieth century awareness of the other world religions, as there were of responding to the nineteenth century awareness of the evolution of the forms of life and the historical character of the holy scriptures. And likewise there will no doubt be a variety of ways in which each of the other great traditions can rethink its inherited assumption of its own unique superiority. But it is not for us to tell people of other traditions how to do their own business. Rather, we should attend to our own.

Study Questions

1. What does Hick mean by "salvation"?
2. How does Hick explain the often contradictory doctrines of different traditions?
3. Can an individual be committed to a religion while agreeing that no religion is wholly true?
4. What attitude should a religious adherent take toward believers in other religions?

The Problem of Religious Diversity

LINDA TRINKAUS ZAGZEBSKI

In our next selection Linda Trinkaus Zagzebski, whose work we read previously, considers different responses to the issue of religious diversity. She explores the situation in which one trusts one's own beliefs yet admires those with conflicting beliefs.

EXCLUSIVISM AND INCLUSIVISM

The most common position on religious diversity among Christians until approximately the middle of the twentieth century was exclusivism: There is only one true religion—mine—and nobody who practices any other religion can be saved. This view is *exclusivist* in two senses. First, it is exclusivist about truth, since it maintains that the doctrines of only one religion are true. Of course, this view needs to be qualified because the teachings of every religion evolve over time even if the central teachings remain the same, so even from a perspective internal to a given religion, various prohibitions can change, such as eating meat on Friday among Catholics, and the teaching of a religion about other religions can also change, just to take some obvious examples. So exclusivism about truth needs to be clarified by reference to central doctrines, and the way to do that can be fairly complicated. How would we determine the set of central Christian doctrines? Does it include only the content of one of the creeds of the early Church? If so, which one? Does it include all the Hebrew and Christian Scriptures? Does it include documents of Church councils? Does it include the writings of prominent theologians? The answer to the last question is undoubtedly no, but the question is not silly and it shows the complexity of the position. Of course, exclusivism about truth does not commit a person to denying that other religions teach many truths. It is only when the teachings of other religions conflict with the teachings of one's own that exclusivism is relevant. Notice finally that exclusivism is the position that only one religion teaches the truth in its central doctrines, but exclusivists always add that that religion is their own. I've never heard of anyone who maintained that only one religion teaches the truth, but it is somebody else's religion that does so.

The position above is exclusivist in a second sense as well. It is exclusivist about salvation. Salvation or something comparable can be attained only in the way a certain religion says it can be attained. For religions that require belief, an individual has to believe in the doctrines of a particular religion in order to be saved. In the Christian form of salvation exclusivism, this means that only Christians can go to heaven. There are also forms of salvation in other religions and views that are exclusivist about the form of salvation they teach. For example, Buddhists teach that nirvana can only be reached by following certain practices. Exclusivism about salvation is obviously quite severe, and it is the first form of exclusivism to be rejected by many Christians.

Exclusivism about truth, and perhaps also about salvation, has sometimes been defended by an account that explains why the believers in a particular religion are epistemically privileged. Alvin Plantinga defends exclusivism about truth in Christianity by arguing that it is part of Christian doctrine that the Holy Spirit has given the gift of Faith in God to some people and not others. And surely Plantinga is right that, if there is a God, God could give a special gift to some people. If so, it would follow that the reason for diversity among religions is that some people are epistemically privileged in their religious beliefs and some are not. . . .

There is a third kind of exclusivism, exclusivism about rationality. This kind of exclusivism is much stronger than exclusivism about truth. The exclusivist about rationality maintains that the teachings of only one religion are rational. It is irrational to believe the teachings of any other religion in so far as they conflict with the teachings of the one that is rational. In my experience, religious people who have thought about religious diversity and who try to be as fair-minded as possible typically deny this form of exclusivism even when they accept exclusivism about truth. So they combine exclusivism about truth with inclusivism about rationality. They say, "Our beliefs are true and the beliefs of other religions are false in so far as they are incompatible with ours, but the beliefs of many other religions are still rational. The people who practice those religions are justified in believing what they believe, given their circumstances. If we had been born in their circumstances and had their experiences, we would probably believe what they believe."

It is hard to fault this position since it seems to go as far as possible in the direction of being understanding and non-judgmental, while not compromising one's commitment to one's own beliefs. But there is a problem in combining exclusivism about truth with inclusivism about rationality. One of the main reasons we want to have rational beliefs is that we think there is a close connection between rationality and truth. What makes it a good thing for humans to be rational is that it puts us in as good a position to get truth as we can get. There is a close correspondence between rationality and truth. But suppose there are nine religions, each of which has a different and incompatible teaching on the origin of the universe. At most one of these theories can be true. But are they all rational? Presumably we would want to say yes, assuming that there are no significant differences in intelligence, sensitivity to religious experience, and intellectual and moral virtue among the adherents of the different religions. But if we say that all nine of these beliefs about the origin of the universe are rational, then clearly rationality in this case does not make it likely that a person gets the truth—less than one chance in nine, and so we cannot maintain that what makes rationality a good thing is that it makes it likely that we are going to get the truth. It appears, then, that combining exclusivism about truth with inclusivism about rationality forces us to conclude either that rationality is not really such a good thing, or if it is a good thing, its goodness cannot come from its close connection to truth. I call this the problem of the gap.

Notice also that it does not help to opt for none of the nine, but to adopt some scientific theory on the origin of the universe that conflicts with all nine. . . . Even if such a theory satisfies the same conditions for rationality satisfied by the nine religions, its rationality does not put it in a better position to be true as long as there are many competitors, each of which is rational.

Of course, we should not exaggerate the extent of the problem of the gap. There *are* classes of belief for which we think there is a close connection between rationality and truth, but those beliefs do not help solve the problem of religious diversity because they are beliefs in which we can realistically expect agreement. And there are probably some religious beliefs in this category. For example, the belief that compassion is good is an almost universal belief, . . . And if we move to a sufficiently high level of generality, we can find agreement about some of the most fundamental religious beliefs—e.g., there is something wrong with the human condition, and when we are in contact with ultimate reality there is the possibility for both profound moral improvement and a higher level of consciousness. But belief at the level necessary for agreement is very thin, and unless we are content to ignore all but such thin beliefs, the fact that particular religious beliefs conflict with the beliefs of others remains a problem.

So religious diversity poses a problem for both religious believers and non-believers. No matter what we believe, we face a problem in our understanding of rationality. If we retain our beliefs because we judge that they are rational, and also judge that the conflicting beliefs of the atheist and of other religions are rational, we cannot maintain that the rationality of each such belief makes it likely to be true. It appears that we have no reason to think that one rational belief is preferable to a conflicting rational belief on the grounds that it is rational. The most we can say is that the rationality of a belief makes it preferable to an irrational alternative. Rationality may be more truth-conducive than irrationality, but one rational belief may not be preferable to another with respect to truth-conduciveness. On the other hand, if we give up our beliefs on the grounds that their rationality is not closely connected to getting the truth, we are forced to say that both atheists and believers in all of the world's major religions should give up their beliefs. That seems to force us into agnosticism, but if we take that option, we are forced to admit that we have given up any chance of getting the truth about a very important matter, an issue that directly impacts the desirability of our lives.

As far as I know, the problem of the gap has never been fully resolved. But in the next two sections I will propose two ways to resolve or avoid it.

THE PLURALISM OF JOHN HICK

An influential perspective on religious diversity is the theory of John Hick, who for some time has promoted a position about the comparative value of the major world religions he calls pluralism. Hick maintains that all the major religions are salvific in that they all offer a path to radically transform human persons from self-centeredness to reality-centeredness, a life centered in ultimate reality. Each religion has something analogous to Christian saints, who are the models for this transformation. The fruit of transformation is a life of love and compassion, and Hick proposes that, since we have evidence that all the great religions are productive of a life of love and compassion, we should conclude that they all offer genuine paths to salvation. Hick thinks that the metaphysical conclusion we ought to draw from this is that the salvific ground in ultimate reality is the same in all religions. Hick then uses Immanuel Kant's distinction between the noumenal and phenomenal worlds to explain how so many religions can all be in touch with the same ultimate reality.

Kant argued that it makes no sense to think that we can know the noumenal world, or the world as it is "in itself," independent of our capacity to experience it. What we can know is the world of possible experience, the phenomenal world. That world is necessarily connected to the ways in which it presents itself to our experience, through intuitions of space and time, and through the concepts that permit us to make judgments about it, such as the concepts of cause and of substance. Similarly, Hick argues that we cannot experience God/ultimate reality as he/it is in itself directly any more than we can experience the world of things-in-themselves according to Kant. All we can do is to experience ultimate reality through the experiential and conceptual forms that each culture has developed. Each religion is a different phenomenal manifestation of the one ultimate reality. And like Kant, Hick maintains that phenomenal reality is as real as it's going to get for us; it is not an illusion. It is the only way we humans can experience the world. So the Hindu world, the Christian world, the Muslim world, and the Buddhist world are distinct phenomenal worlds that are related to the world of reality-in-itself in the same way the world of ordinary human experience is related to the world of things-in-themselves.

There is an important difference between Hick and Kant. What Kant means by the phenomenal world is the world as it has to be in order to be experienced by human beings, and so there is only one such world. It is the world of trees, animals, chairs, and all the other objects of our experience that have spatial and temporal relations to each other and are potentially affected by our actions. But Hick cannot make the parallel claim about religious phenomenal worlds, since he maintains that there are as many of them as there are religious traditions. But he *can* say that ultimate reality cannot be experienced except through cultural forms, so each religion is a different lens through which ultimate reality is experienced. We are not equipped with a particular religious lens by nature the way we are equipped with Kant's conceptual categories, but we have to have one lens or another. The Muslim world, the Hindu world, the Buddhist world, and the Christian world are all phenomenally real worlds on a par with the reality of trees, houses, and animals in Kantian metaphysics.

Notice that Hick's pluralism solves the problem of the gap. All the great world religions are true in the sense that they all put human beings in contact with religious phenomenal reality. Of course, if you insist that a belief is not true unless it puts a person in contact with noumenal reality, the world of things-in-themselves, then all the world religions are false. But according to Hick, there is no more reason to complain about the lack of contact with noumenal reality in the religious realm than there is to complain about the lack of contact with things-in-themselves in Kant's metaphysics. The problem of the gap is solved, then, because all the great world religions are both rational and true in the sense just explained.

Hick does not think that every doctrine of every religion can be explained in this way, however. There are two types of religious teachings that do not fit the Kantian model. The doctrine of creation *ex nihilo* and the doctrine of reincarnation are examples of what Hick calls transhistorical truth claims. If one religion teaches that the supreme being created the entire material world out of nothing and another religion teaches that the material world is eternal, they cannot both be right and their differences cannot be explained by reference to different religious phenomenal worlds. If one religion teaches that after death you are reincarnated, and another religion teaches that your body will some day be resurrected and rejoined with your soul, and a third religion teaches that you will be annihilated as an individual person but assimilated into something else, one of these religions may be right and the others wrong, or maybe one is more right than another, but something is going to happen to you after death. It cannot be all three.

Some religions also make historical claims that cannot be explained on the Kantian model. Either Jesus raised Lazarus from the dead or he didn't. Either there was an empty tomb on Easter morning or there wasn't. Hick says that the grounds for these beliefs ought to be the same as the grounds for any historical belief if they are taken literally. Some of these beliefs are false and disputes about them cannot be resolved by reference to the pluralism of phenomenal worlds. But even if they are not literally true, they may be true as myths. A true myth evokes the response of transforming a person into one who is reality-centered, whereas a false myth does not. Hick thinks that the Incarnation is an example of a true myth.

Hick's position on religious diversity has many defenders and many detractors. I want to mention just three problems with it. First, if Hick truly means that each phenomenal world is a real one, then . . . he is a polytheist. Perhaps the charge of polytheism is not quite fair because Hick is a phenomenal polytheist and a noumenal mono-something (not "theist" because he is not willing to call the ultimate reality "God"). But on the noumenal level Hick is committed to the most negative of negative theologies: We cannot say that the ultimate reality is personal or impersonal, one or many, temporal or timeless, God or being itself. So Hick's position appears to be a combination of polytheism and negative theology. Neither of these positions may be very appealing, although . . . there is a strong strain of negative theology among the mystics who say that we cannot hope to know what God is really like, only what he is not.

A second problem involves the kind of belief that is justified if one accepts Hick's pluralism. Pluralism seems to threaten religious commitment. Christians who become convinced that Christianity is no more true than Hinduism are bound to interpret that as weakening the connection they thought obtained between Christian doctrine and the truth, and the same point applies to the convictions of Hindus, Muslims, Buddhists, and others. To wholeheartedly embrace a particular religion is to think of that religion as giving one a superior understanding of the nature of the universe and one's relationship to that universe than one would have had without it. This is particularly important for those who think that the universe had a personal creator who providentially guides the temporal world, hears prayers, and responds to them. To be told that the idea that I have a relationship with a personal God is no more true than the idea that there is an impersonal force of unknown qualities which may or may not relate to me at all is to be told that my faith is groundless, or at least, such a reaction is eminently understandable.

Third, Hick's separation of salvific beliefs that are phenomenal manifestations of ultimate reality from historical beliefs and transhistorical beliefs about the origin of the universe and the afterlife is not compatible with the central teachings of some religions. In Christianity, for example, beliefs about ultimate reality include historical beliefs about the Incarnation, the Redemption, and the Resurrection. These historical beliefs cannot be separated from the theological beliefs that on Hick's account are about phenomenal reality. Hick's pluralism, then, extends only to a limited subset of the beliefs of major religions and, as Hick is aware, some religions would not accept the way in which he distinguishes those beliefs that are religiously important from those that are not.

SELF-TRUST AND RELIGIOUS BELIEF

The problem of the gap between rationality and truth arises from a perspective external to the self. We look at our beliefs the same way we look at the beliefs of others and we think that from that perspective nobody has a privileged epistemic position. That follows if we assume that the external viewpoint is committed to intellectual egalitarianism. If one religion is rational, so are they all, barring special reason to think some of them are untrustworthy. But then there are no grounds for choice among them.

But how do we know what we would see from an external perspective? Maybe we would see that one religion does have a privileged connection to truth. When we say that from an external perspective all religions are roughly equal in rationality and one is no more likely to be true than another, aren't we really just admitting that we cannot figure out how to adopt the external perspective on religion? We *do* have some idea how this perspective works in physics and mathematics. We also have an idea how it works in the law and in ethics—it is the principle of impartiality. But what principle would the external observer of religion use to adjudicate among the different viewpoints on religion? Since we don't know, we assume there isn't one.

This problem is not limited to beliefs about religion. The vast majority of our important beliefs about morality and politics also suffer from this problem, as well as a host of beliefs about matters of personal interest—e.g., whether one movie is better than another, whether my alma mater is one of the most distinguished universities in the country, whether my spouse is looking good today, and so on. If we insist on adopting the external viewpoint on all our beliefs, we jeopardize many of the beliefs most important to us, including those we use in governing our lives.

We might think the problem does not arise when the belief is about an unimportant matter, but that is not the case. Suppose that I recall reading somewhere that coffee is very high in anti-oxidants and I encounter another person who believes that coffee has no such benefit. Suppose also that there is no reason to think one of us is an expert in this area and no reason to think one of us did a more careful reading of the news reports and any relevant follow-ups. If I evaluate my beliefs from an external viewpoint, I will withhold belief in whether coffee is high in anti-oxidants, and I might be willing to do that because it is not likely to have a significant impact on my life. But is it obvious that I should automatically trust another as much as myself? If I do, even though many of the beliefs I would have to give up are unimportant, the *quantity* of beliefs I would have to give up is very important. The conclusion is that if we evaluate our own beliefs the same way we evaluate the beliefs of other people, we are bound to end up with skepticism about all but a very few beliefs— not enough to base a worthwhile life upon.

Many philosophers these days are attempting to put the challenge of skepticism aside and get on with the business of living a life, which includes accepting with confidence the beliefs needed to live a life with energy and purpose. Doing that requires a substantial degree of trust in oneself and the forces that have shaped one into the person one is. . . . [A]ny normal, non-skeptical life will have to include a significant degree of self-trust in our intellectual faculties, procedures, and opinions. The reason is that any defense of our most fundamental faculties, procedures, and opinions will make use of those same faculties and opinions. For example, we test a memory by perception, we test one perception by another perception, we test much of what we believe by consulting other people, so we use beliefs about them to test other beliefs, and so on. We cannot get outside of the circle of our faculties and opinions to test the reliability of the faculties and opinions taken as a whole; we have to trust them.

An important element of self-trust is trust in our emotions. Emotion dispositions can be reliable or unreliable, and particular emotions may fit or not fit their objects. But we cannot tell whether our emotion dispositions are reliable without using those same dispositions in conjunction with our other faculties. How can we tell whether our disposition to pity is reliably directed at the pitiful, whether our disposition to disgust is reliably directed towards the disgusting, whether we reliably fear the fearsome, or admire the admirable without appealing to further emotions? We trust what we think we see when we take a hard look in good environmental conditions, and if others agree, we take that as confirmation. Similarly, we trust what we feel upon reflection when we feel admiration or pity or revulsion and we take the agreement of others as confirmation. We trust the emotion we have as an adult more than an emotion we had in the same circumstances as a child, just as we trust a belief we have as an adult more than our childish belief. So the grounds for trusting our emotions are similar to the grounds for trusting our perceptions and beliefs.

Furthermore, trust in the beliefs that lead to action requires emotional self-trust. My belief that I ought to escape a situation is often grounded in fear. The belief that I ought to help another person is typically grounded in compassion for her. The belief that I may not treat people in certain ways is grounded in respect for them. If I trust the belief, I must trust the emotion. So epistemic self-trust requires emotional self-trust. Both emotional and epistemic self-trust are compatible with revising what we trust, but it takes self-trust to trust that the process of revision is trustworthy.

One of the emotions I need to trust is admiration. Admiration is a basic emotion, one that does not have other emotions as parts, and I do not think we can explain what a basic emotion feels like. But I assume that all normal people have experienced the emotion of admiration, and so they know what it is in the same way they know what fear or love or anger is. I would describe the admirable as something like the imitably attractive. We feel a positive emotion towards the person we admire that would lead to imitating the person given the right practical conditions. To trust the emotion of admiration means to have confidence that it is appropriate to feel the kind of attraction and desire to imitate that is intrinsic to admiration. We trust our emotion of admiration for the same reason we trust our other emotions: we have no choice.

Trusting my emotion of admiration may lead me to trusting some of the beliefs of another person more than my own. That can happen when I notice that another person has the traits I admire in myself to a greater degree than I have myself, or she may form her belief in a more admirable way in the particular case than I have myself. Another possibility is that she is very much like my present self, only she has more experience, so she is related to me now the way I am related to my younger self. In such cases I can easily trust another person more than myself, either because I admire the other person more than myself and I trust my admiration, or because the other person has other elements

I trust in myself in a greater degree than I have myself, e.g., she has more experience. For the same reason, I will trust some people more than other people. I do that because of the way I trust myself. It follows that intellectual egalitarianism should be rejected.

Now let us return to conflict in beliefs. Suppose that I trust my emotion of admiration in some case more than I trust a given belief I have. And suppose that the person I admire has a belief that conflicts with mine, and there is no other person I admire just as much whose belief agrees with mine. Self-trust would lead me to trust the admired person's belief more than my own. If I am able to imitate the admired person by adopting her belief without changing anything else about myself that I trust even more than I trust the person I admire, then self-trust should lead me to change my belief. That is because admiration includes imitation, given the right circumstances.

But let's consider a harder case. Suppose a person I admire and therefore trust has a belief that conflicts with one of the beliefs I have that I trust. I am then faced with a conflict within self-trust. It is because of self-trust that I trust my belief, and it is because of self-trust that I trust the emotion of admiration that grounds my trust in the other person. But even if I trust my admiration more than the belief, it still does not follow that I should change it. Admiration is an emotion that leads me to imitate the admirable person in suitable circumstances, but often the circumstances are not suitable. I can easily admire Olympic gold medal winners without having the slightest inclination to imitate them, and I can admire the belief system of a Hindu without the inclination to adopt that system for myself. The reason why I would not is the same in both cases: I can't do it. It is not compatible with the self that I am. But the more interesting question is whether I should try. Some religious beliefs are not central to our sense of self, but many of them are. Whether I should change an important religious belief is not simply determined by how much I trust the belief itself, but

how much I trust the other aspects of myself that I would have to change if I changed the belief. Given the social construction of belief, trusting a belief commits me to trusting both the individual persons from whom I learned the belief, and the traditions and historical institutions upon which I depend to interpret the belief. Religious beliefs are usually connected to a network of other beliefs, emotions, experiences, institutional loyalties, and connections with many other admirable people, all of which I trust. So I can admire a Hindu for being a great Hindu and an Olympic swimmer for being a great swimmer without any inclination to imitate them. And I think that an intellectually conscientious person will often respond that way.

In the typical case, then, a person's trust in those aspects of himself that he would have to change if he converted to another religion will be greater than his trust in the way an admirable person of another religion believes in her religion. But sometimes trust in the latter can be greater, and so conversion can be compatible with intellectual conscientiousness. I think this is an important consequence of our analysis of self-trust. We should be suspicious of any account of conscientious belief that has the consequence that radical conversion is never a conscientious thing to do, and we also should be suspicious of any account of conscientious belief that requires us to give up the beliefs we have that conflict with the beliefs of others on the grounds that conscientiousness demands an external perspective on the self.

In a situation in which a choice whether to convert is made, some element of self-trust becomes the bottom line—that to which we refer in adjudicating between those elements of ourselves that pull us one way and those that pull in another direction. . . .

If I trust my admiration of others with beliefs that conflict with mine more than I trust the aspects of myself from which I gain my beliefs and the traditions that support them, then it is right for me to doubt my beliefs, and perhaps change them. But there is no standpoint outside of self-trust from which I can determine which is more trustworthy—myself or others—so it can easily happen that I have full confidence in my beliefs, emotions, and their sources in family, tradition, and the historical circumstances that shape me.

Admiration may not require me to change my beliefs, but it adds something important to the dialogue between people with conflicting religious beliefs that did not exist in the premodern era. What it adds is the feeling that I *would* imitate them if I had grown up with a different social construction of the self. That prevents me from taking the line "We're right, so they're wrong, and that's the end of that." Of course, we think we're right, but there's more to be said. Tolerance comes not from thinking that everybody is right, but trusting that we *are* right in the admiration we have for many people who have very different beliefs, and that logically requires us to think of them as like the self I could have been if I had been raised in a different way.

Study Questions

1. What does Zagzebski mean by "exclusivism"?
2. According to Zagzebski, why does Hick's pluralism threaten religious commitment?
3. Can we admire the beliefs of those with whom we disagree?
4. Might admiration for someone who practices a particular religion lead you to join that religion?

Interreligious Harmony

DALAI LAMA

The Dalai Lama, himself a practicing Buddhist, is the spiritual and temporal leader of the Tibetan people. He urges appreciation for the value of religious traditions other than one's own.

Perhaps the most significant obstruction to interreligious harmony is lack of appreciation of the value of others' faith traditions. Until comparatively recently, communication between different cultures, even different communities, was slow or nonexistent. For this reason, sympathy for other faith traditions was not necessarily very important—except of course where members of different religions lived side by side. But this attitude is no longer viable. In today's increasingly complex and interdependent world, we are compelled to acknowledge the existence

From *Ethics for the New Millennium*, Riverhead Books, 1999. Reprinted by permission.

of other cultures, different ethnic groups, and, of course, other religious faiths. Whether we like it or not, most of us now experience this diversity on a daily basis.

I believe that the best way to overcome ignorance and bring about understanding is through dialogue with members of other faith traditions. This I see occurring in a number of different ways. Discussions among scholars in which the convergence and perhaps more importantly the divergence between different faith traditions are explored and appreciated are very valuable. On another level, it is helpful when there are encounters between ordinary but practicing followers of different religions in which each shares their experiences. This is perhaps the most effective way of appreciating others' teachings. In my own case, for example, my meetings with the late Thomas Merton, a Catholic monk of the Cistercian order, were deeply inspiring. They helped me develop a profound admiration for the teachings of Christianity. I also feel that occasional meetings between religious leaders joining together to pray for a common cause are extremely useful. The gathering at Assisi in Italy in 1986, when representatives of the world's major religions gathered to pray for peace, was, I believe, tremendously beneficial to many religious believers insofar as it symbolized the solidarity and a commitment to peace of all those taking part.

Finally, I feel that the practice of members of different faith traditions going on joint pilgrimages together can be very helpful. It was in this spirit that in 1993 I went to Lourdes, and then to Jerusalem—a site holy to three of the world's great religions. I have also paid visits to various Hindu, Islamic, Jain, and Sikh shrines both in India and abroad. More recently, following a seminar devoted to discussing and practicing meditation in the Christian and Buddhist traditions, I joined an historic pilgrimage of practitioners of both traditions in a program of prayers, meditation, and dialogue under the Bodhi tree at Bodh Gaya in India. This is one of Buddhism's most important shrines.

When exchanges like these occur, followers of one tradition will find that, just as in the case of their own, the teachings of others' faiths are a source both of spiritual inspiration and of ethical guidance to their followers. It will also become clear that irrespective of doctrinal and other differences, all the major world religions are concerned with helping individuals to become good human beings. All emphasize love and compassion, patience, tolerance, forgiveness, humility, and so on, and all are capable of helping individuals to develop these. Moreover, the example given by the founders of each major religion clearly demonstrates a concern for helping others find happiness through developing these qualities. So far as their own lives were concerned, each conducted themselves with great simplicity. Ethical discipline and love for all others was the hallmark of their lives. They did not live luxuriously like emperors and kings. Instead, they voluntarily accepted suffering—without consideration of the hardships involved—in order to benefit humanity as a whole. In their teachings, all placed special emphasis on developing love and compassion and renouncing selfish desires. And each of them called on us to transform our hearts and minds. Indeed, whether we have faith or not, all are worthy of our profound admiration.

At the same time as engaging in dialogue with followers of other religions, we must, of course, implement in our daily life the teachings of our own religion. Once we have experienced the benefit of love and compassion, and of ethical discipline, we will easily recognize the value of others' teachings. But for this, it is essential to realize that religious practice entails a lot more than merely saying, "I believe" or, as in Buddhism, "I take refuge." There is also more to it than just visiting temples, or shrines, or churches. And taking religious teachings is of little benefit if they do not enter the heart but remain at the level of intellect alone. Simply relying on faith without understanding and without implementation is of limited value. I often tell Tibetans that carrying a *mala* (something like a rosary) does not make a person a genuine religious practitioner. The efforts we make sincerely to transform ourselves spiritually are what make us genuine religious practitioners.

We come to see the overriding importance of genuine practice when we recognize that, along with ignorance, individuals' unhealthy relationships with their beliefs is the other major factor in religious disharmony. Far from applying the teachings of their religion in our personal lives, we have a tendency to use them to reinforce our self-centered attitudes. We relate to our religion as something we own or as a label that separates us from others. Surely this is misguided? Instead of using the nectar of religion to purify the poisonous elements of our hearts and minds, there is a danger when we think like this of using these negative elements to poison the nectar of religion.

Yet we must acknowledge that this reflects another problem, one which is implicit in all religions. I refer to the claims each has of being the one "true" religion. How are we to resolve this difficulty? It is true that from the point of view of the individual practitioner, it is essential to have a single-pointed commitment to one's own faith. It is also true that this depends on the deep conviction that one's own path is the sole mediator of truth. But at the same time, we have to find some means of reconciling this belief with the reality of a multiplicity of similar claims. In practical terms, this involves individual practitioners finding a way at least to accept the validity of the teachings of other religions while maintaining a wholehearted commitment to their own. As far as the validity of the metaphysical truth claims of a given religion is concerned, that is of course the internal business of that particular tradition.

In my own case, I am convinced that Buddhism provides me with the most effective framework within which to situate my efforts to develop spiritually through cultivating love and compassion. At the same time, I must acknowledge that while Buddhism represents the best path for me—that is, it suits my character, my

temperament, my inclinations, and my cultural background—the same will be true of Christianity for Christians. For them, Christianity is the best way. On the basis of my conviction, I cannot, therefore, say that Buddhism is best for everyone.

I often think of religion in terms of medicine for the human spirit. Independent of its usage and suitability to a particular individual in a particular condition, we really cannot judge a medicine's efficacy. We are not justified in saying this medicine is very good because of such and such ingredients. If you take the patient and the medicine's effect on that person out of the equation, it hardly makes sense. What is relevant is to say that in the case of this particular patient with his or her particular illness, this medicine is the most effective. Similarly with different religious traditions, we can say that this one is most effective for this particular individual. But it is unhelpful to try to argue on the basis of philosophy or metaphysics that one religion is better than another. The important thing is surely its effectiveness in individual cases.

My way to resolve the seeming contradiction between each religion's claim to "one truth and one religion" and the reality of the multiplicity of faiths is thus to understand that in the case of a single individual, there can indeed be only one truth, one religion. However, from the perspective of human society at large, we must accept the concept of "many truths, many religions." To continue with our medical analogy, in the case of one particular patient, the suitable medicine is in fact the only medicine. But clearly that does not mean that there may not be other medicines suitable to other patients.

To my way of thinking, the diversity that exists among the various religious traditions is enormously enriching. There is thus no need to try to find ways of saying that ultimately all religions are the same. They are similar in that they all emphasize the indispensability of love and compassion in the context of ethical discipline. But to say this is not to say that they are all essentially one. The contradictory understanding of creation and beginninglessness articulated by Buddhism, Christianity, and Hinduism, for example, means that in the end we have to part company when it comes to metaphysical claims, in spite of the many practical similarities that undoubtedly exist. These contradictions may not be very important in the beginning stages of religious practice. But as we advance along the path of one tradition or another, we are compelled at some point to acknowledge fundamental differences. For example, the concept of rebirth in Buddhism and various other ancient Indian traditions may turn out to be incompatible with the Christian idea of salvation. This need not be a cause for dismay, however. Even within Buddhism itself, in the realm of metaphysics there are diametrically opposing views. At the very least, such diversity means that we have different frameworks within which to locate ethical discipline and the development of spiritual values. That is why I do not advocate a "super" or a new "world" religion. It would mean that we would lose the unique characteristics of the different faith traditions.

Some people, it is true, hold that the Buddhist concept of *shunyata,* or emptiness, is ultimately the same as certain approaches to understanding the concept of God. Nevertheless, there remain difficulties with this. The first is that while of course we can interpret these concepts, to what extent can we be faithful to the original teachings if we do so? There are compelling similarities between the Mahayana Buddhist concept of *dharmakaya, sambogakaya,* and *nirmanakaya*[1] and the Christian trinity of God as Father, Son, and Holy Spirit. But to say, on the basis of this, that Buddhism and Christianity are ultimately the same is to go a bit far, I think! As an old Tibetan saying goes, we must beware of trying to put a yak's head on a sheep's body—or vice versa.

What is required instead is that we develop a genuine sense of religious pluralism in spite of the different claims of different faith traditions. This is especially true if we are serious in our respect for human rights as a universal principle.

In this regard, I find the concept of a world parliament of religions very appealing. To begin with, the word "parliament" conveys a sense of democracy, while the plural "religions" underlines the importance of the principle of a multiplicity of faith traditions. The truly pluralist perspective on religion which the idea of such a parliament suggests could, I believe be, of great help. It would avoid the extremes of religious bigotry on the one hand, and the urge toward unnecessary syncretism on the other.

Connected with this issue of interreligious harmony, I should perhaps say something about religious conversion. This is a question which must be taken extremely seriously. It is essential to realize that the mere fact of conversion alone will not make an individual a better person—that is to say, a more disciplined, a more compassionate, a more warm-hearted person. Much more helpful, therefore, is for the individual to concentrate on transforming themselves spiritually through the practice of restraint, virtue, and compassion. To the extent that the insights or practices of other religions are useful or relevant to our own faith, it is valuable to learn from others. In some cases, it may even be helpful to adopt certain of them. Yet when this is done wisely, we can remain firmly committed to our own faith. This way is best because it carries with it no danger of confusion, especially with respect to the different ways of life that tend to go with different faith traditions.

Given the diversity to be found among individual human beings, it is of course bound to be the case that out of many millions of practitioners of a particular religion, a handful will find that another religion's approach to ethics and spiritual development is more satisfactory. For some, the concept of rebirth and karma will seem highly effective in inspiring the aspiration to develop love and compassion within the context of responsibility. For others, the concept of a transcendent, loving creator will come to seem more so. In such circumstances, it is crucial for those individuals to question themselves again and again. They must ask, "Am I attracted to this other religion for the right reasons? Is it merely the cultural and ritual aspects that are appealing? Or is it the essential teachings? Do I suppose that if I convert to this new religion it will be less demanding than my present one?" I say this because it has often struck me that when people do convert to a religion outside their own heritage, quite often they adopt certain superficial aspects of the culture to which their new faith belongs. But their practice may not go very much deeper than that.

In the case of a person who decides after a process of long and mature reflection to adopt a different religion, it is very important that they remember the positive contribution to humanity of each religious tradition. The danger is that the individual may, in seeking to justify their decision to others, criticize their previous faith. It is essential to avoid this. Just because that tradition is no long effective in the case of one individual does not mean it is no longer of benefit to humanity. On the contrary, we can be certain that it has been an inspiration to millions of people in the past, that it inspires millions today, and that it will inspire millions in the path of love and compassion in the future.

The important point to keep in mind is that ultimately the whole purpose of religion is to facilitate love and compassion, patience, tolerance, humility, forgiveness, and so on. If we neglect these, changing our religion will be of no help. In the same way, even if we are fervent believers in our own faith, it will avail us nothing if we neglect to implement these qualities in our daily lives. Such a believer is no better off than a patient with some fatal illness who merely reads a medical treatise but fails to undertake the treatment prescribed.

Moreover, if we who are practitioners of religion are not compassionate and disciplined, how can we expect it of others? If we can establish genuine harmony derived from mutual respect and understanding, religion has enormous potential to speak with authority on such vital moral questions as peace and disarmament, social and political justice, the natural environment, and many other matters affecting all humanity. But until we put our own spiritual teachings into practice, we will never be taken seriously. And this means, among other things, setting a good example through developing good relations with other faith traditions.

NOTE

1. [According to Mahayana Buddhism, the Buddha manifests himself in these three modes.—S.M.C.]

Study Questions

1. If you possess a wholehearted commitment to one religion, in what sense can you simultaneously accept the truth of another religion?
2. Is religion akin to medicine for the human spirit?
3. What does the Dalai Lama mean by "a world parliament of religions"?
4. Do all religions agree on their fundamental purpose?

Part VI

Moral Theory

God and Morality

STEVEN M. CAHN

We turn now to that major field of philosophy known as "ethics," a term derived from the Greek word *ethos*, meaning "character." The subject, which may also be known as "moral philosophy," focuses on the nature of a moral judgment, the principles that ought to guide a good life, or the resolution of such a thorny practical issue as abortion.

Some claim that belief in God provides the key to solving moral issues. This view is one with which many philosophers, including myself, disagree, and in the following selection I seek to explain why a theological conception of morality does not suffice as a basis for moral reasoning.

According to many religions, although not all, the world was created by God, an all-powerful, all-knowing, all-good being. Although God's existence has been doubted, let us for the moment assume its truth. What implications of this supposition would be relevant to our lives?

Some people would feel more secure in the knowledge that the world had been planned by an all-good being. Others would feel insecure, realizing the extent to which their existence depended on a decision of this being. In any case, most people, out of either fear or respect, would wish to act in accord with God's will.

Belief in God by itself, however, provides no hint whatsoever which actions God wishes us to perform or what we ought to do to please or obey God. We may affirm that God is all-good, yet have no way of knowing the highest moral standards. All we may presume is that, whatever these standards, God always acts in accordance with them. We might expect God to have implanted the correct moral standards in our minds, but this supposition is doubtful in view

of the conflicts among people's intuitions. Furthermore, even if consensus prevailed, it might be only a means by which God tests us to see whether we have the courage to dissent from popular opinion.

Some would argue that if God exists, then murder is immoral, because it destroys what God with infinite wisdom created. This argument, however, fails on several grounds. First, God also created germs, viruses, and disease-carrying rats. Because God created these things, ought they not be eliminated? Second, if God arranged for us to live, God also arranged for us to die. By killing, are we assisting the work of God? Third, God provided us with the mental and physical potential to commit murder. Does God wish us to fulfill this potential?

Thus God's existence alone does not imply any particular moral precepts. We may hope our actions are in accord with God's standards, but no test is available to check whether what we do is best in God's eyes. Some seemingly good people suffer great ills, whereas some seemingly evil people achieve happiness. Perhaps in a future life these outcomes will be reversed, but we have no way of ascertaining who, if anyone, is ultimately punished and who ultimately rewarded.

Over the course of history, those who believed in God's existence typically were eager to learn God's will and tended to rely on those individuals who claimed to possess such insight. Diviners, seers, and priests were given positions of great influence. Competition among them was severe, however, for no one could be sure which oracle to believe.

In any case prophets died, and their supposedly revelatory powers disappeared with them. For practical purposes what was needed was a permanent record of God's will. This requirement was met by the writing of holy books in which God's will was revealed to all.

But even though many such books were supposed to embody the will of God, they conflicted with one another. Which was to be accepted? Belief in the existence of God by itself yields no answer.

Let us suppose, however, that an individual becomes persuaded that a reliable guide to God's will is contained in the Ten Commandments. This person, therefore, believes it wrong to commit adultery, steal, or murder.

But why is it wrong? Is it wrong because God says it is wrong, or does God say it is wrong because it *is* wrong?

This crucial issue was raised more than two thousand years ago in Plato's remarkable dialogue, the *Euthyphro*. Plato's teacher, Socrates, who in most of Plato's works is given the leading role, asks the overconfident Euthyphro whether actions are right because God says they are right, or whether God says actions are right because they are right.

In other words, Socrates was inquiring whether actions are right because of God's fiat or whether God is subject to moral standards. If actions are right because of God's command, then anything God commands would be right. Had God commanded adultery, stealing, and

murder, then adultery, stealing, and murder would be right—surely an unsettling and to many an unacceptable conclusion.

Granted, some may be willing to adopt this discomforting view, but then they face another difficulty. If the good is whatever God commands, to say that God's commands are good amounts to saying that God's commands are God's commands, a mere tautology or repetition of words. In that case, the possibility of meaningfully praising the goodness of God would be lost.

The lesson here is that might does not make right, even if the might is the infinite might of God. To act morally is not to act out of fear of punishment; it is not to act as one is commanded to act. Rather, it is to act as one ought to act, and how one ought to act is not dependent on anyone's power, even if the power be divine.

Thus actions are not right because God commands them; on the contrary, God commands them because they are right. What is right is independent of what God commands, for in order to be right what God commands must conform to an independent standard.

We could act intentionally in accord with this independent standard without believing in the existence of God; therefore morality does not rest on that belief. Consequently, those who do not believe in God can be highly moral (as well as immoral) people, and those who do believe in the existence of God can be highly immoral (as well as moral) people. This conclusion should come as no surprise to anyone who has contrasted the benevolent life of the inspiring teacher, the Buddha, an atheist, with the malevolent life of the monk Torquemada, who devised and enforced the boundless cruelties of the Spanish Inquisition.

In short, believing in the existence of God does not by itself imply any specific moral principles, and knowing God's will does not provide any justification for morality. Thus regardless of our religious commitments, the moral dimension of our lives remains to be explored.

Study Questions

1. If God exists, is murder immoral?
2. Is murder wrong because God prohibits it, or does God prohibit murder because it is wrong?
3. Can those who do not believe in God be highly moral people?
4. Can people who practice different religions agree about how to resolve a moral disagreement?

Moral Isolationism

MARY MIDGLEY

Some would claim that the search for universal answers to moral questions is futile because morality differs from one culture to another. This view, sometimes referred to as "culture relativism," maintains that while we can seek understanding of a particular culture's moral system, we have no basis for judging it. Morality is just a matter of custom, as suggested by the origin of the term "morality," which comes from the Latin word *moralis*, relating to "custom."

In the next selection Mary Midgley, who was Senior Lecturer in Philosophy at Newcastle University in England, argues that moral reasoning requires the possibility of judging the practices of other cultures.

All of us are, more or less, in trouble today about trying to understand cultures strange to us. We hear constantly of alien customs. We see changes in our lifetime which would have astonished our parents. I want to discuss here one very short way of dealing with this difficulty, a drastic way which many people now theoretically favour. It consists in simply denying that we can ever understand any culture except our own well enough to make judgements about it. Those who recommend this hold that the world is sharply divided into separate societies, sealed units, each with its own system of thought. They feel that the respect and tolerance due from one system to another forbids us ever to take up a critical position to any other culture. Moral judgement, they suggest, is a kind of coinage valid only in its country of origin.

I shall call this position "moral isolationism". I shall suggest that it is certainly not forced upon us, and indeed that it makes no sense at all. People usually take it up because they think it is a respectful attitude to other cultures. In fact, however, it is not respectful. Nobody can

From Mary Midgley, *Heart and Mind: The Varieties of Moral Experience*, Routledge, 2003. Reprinted by permission of Taylor & Francis.

respect what is entirely unintelligible to them. To respect someone, we have to know enough about him to make a *favourable* judgement, however general and tentative. And we do understand people in other cultures to this extent. Otherwise a great mass of our most valuable thinking would be paralysed.

To show this, I shall take a remote example, because we shall probably find it easier to think calmly about it than we should with a contemporary one, such as female circumcision in Africa or the Chinese Cultural Revolution. The principles involved will still be the same. My example is this. There is, it seems, a verb in classical Japanese which means "to try out one's new sword on a chance wayfarer". (The word is *tsuji-giri*, literally "crossroads-cut".) A samurai sword had to be tried out because, if it was to work properly, it had to slice through someone at a single blow, from the shoulder to the opposite flank. Otherwise, the warrior bungled his stroke. This could injure his honour, offend his ancestors, and even let down his emperor. So tests were needed, and wayfarers had to be expended. Any wayfarer would do—provided, of course, that he was not another Samurai. Scientists will recognize a familiar problem about the rights of experimental subjects.

Now when we hear of a custom like this, we may well reflect that we simply do not understand it; and therefore are not qualified to criticize it at all, because we are not members of that culture. But we are not members of any other culture either, except our own. So we extend the principle to cover all extraneous cultures, and we seem therefore to be moral isolationists. But this is, as we shall see, an impossible position. Let us ask what it would involve.

We must ask first: Does the isolating barrier work both ways? Are people in other cultures equally unable to criticize *us*? This question struck me sharply when I read a remark in *The Guardian* by an anthropologist about a South American Indian who had been taken into a Brazilian town for an operation, which saved his life. When he came back to his village, he

made several highly critical remarks about the white Brazilians' way of life. They may very well have been justified. But the interesting point was that the anthropologist called these remarks "a damning indictment of Western civilization". Now the Indian had been in that town about two weeks. Was he in a position to deliver a damning indictment? Would we ourselves be qualified to deliver such an indictment on the Samurai, provided we could spend two weeks in ancient Japan? What do we really think about this?

My own impression is that we believe that outsiders can, in principle, deliver perfectly good indictments—only, it usually takes more than two weeks to make them damning. Understanding has degrees. It is not a slapdash yes-or-no matter. Intelligent outsiders can progress in it, and in some ways will be at an advantage over the locals. But if this is so, it must clearly apply to ourselves as much as anybody else.

Our next question is this: Does the isolating barrier between cultures block praise as well as blame? If I want to say that the Samurai culture has many virtues, or to praise the South American Indians, am I prevented from doing *that* by my outside status? Now, we certainly do need to praise other societies in this way. But it is hardly possible that we could praise them effectively if we could not, in principle, criticize them. Our praise would be worthless if it rested on no definite grounds, if it did not flow from some understanding. Certainly we may need to praise things which we do not *fully* understand. We say "there's something very good here, but I can't quite make out what it is yet". This happens when we want to learn from strangers. And we can learn from strangers. But to do this we have to distinguish between those strangers who are worth learning from and those who are not. Can we then judge which is which?

This brings us to our third question: What is involved in judging? Now plainly there is no question here of sitting on a bench in a red robe and sentencing people. Judging simply means forming an opinion, and expressing it if it is called for. Is there anything wrong about this? Naturally, we ought to avoid forming—and expressing—*crude* opinions, like that of a simple-minded missionary, who might dismiss the whole Samurai culture as entirely bad, because non-Christian. But this is a different objection. The trouble with crude opinions is that they are crude, whoever forms them, not that they are formed by the wrong people. Anthropologists, after all, are outsiders quite as much as missionaries. Moral isolationism forbids us to form *any* opinions on these matters. Its ground for doing so is that we don't understand them. But there is much that we don't understand in our own culture too. This brings us to our last question: If we can't judge other cultures, can we really judge our own? Our efforts to do so will be much damaged if we are really deprived of our opinions about other societies, because these provide the range of comparison, the spectrum of alternatives against which we set what we want to understand. We would have to stop using the mirror which anthropology so helpfully holds up to us.

In short, moral isolationism would lay down a general ban on moral reasoning. Essentially, this is the programme of immoralism, and it carries a distressing logical difficulty. Immoralists like Nietzsche are actually just a rather specialized sect of moralists. They can no more afford to put moralizing out of business than smugglers can afford to abolish customs regulations. The power of moral judgement is, in fact, not a luxury, not a perverse indulgence of the self-righteous. It is a necessity. When we judge something to be bad or good, better or worse than something else, we are taking it as an example to aim at or avoid. Without opinions of this sort, we would have no framework of comparison for our own policy, no chance of profiting by other people's insights or mistakes. In this vacuum, we could form no judgements on our own actions.

Now it would be odd if Homo sapiens had really got himself into a position as bad as this — a position where his main evolutionary asset, his brain, was so little use to him. None of us is going to accept this sceptical diagnosis. We cannot do so, because our involvement in moral isolationism does not flow from apathy, but from a rather acute concern about human hypocrisy and other forms of wickedness. But we polarize that concern around a few selected moral truths. We are rightly angry with those who despise, oppress or steam-roll other cultures. We think that doing these things is actually *wrong*. But this is itself a moral judgement. We could not condemn oppression and insolence if we thought that all our condemnation were just a trivial local quirk of our own culture. We could still less do it if we tried to stop judging altogether.

Real moral scepticism, in fact, could lead only to inaction, to our losing all interest in moral questions, most of all in those which concern other societies. When we discuss these things, it becomes instantly clear how far we are from doing this. Suppose, for instance, that I criticize the bisecting Samurai, that I say his behaviour is brutal. What will usually happen next is that someone will protest, will say that I have no right to make criticisms like that of another culture. But it is most unlikely that he will use this move to end the discussion of the subject. Instead, he will justify the Samurai. He will try to fill in the background, to make me understand the custom, by explaining the exalted ideals of discipline and devotion which produced it. He will probably talk of the lower value which the ancient Japanese placed on individual life generally. He may well suggest that this is a healthier attitude than our own obsession with security. He may add, too, that the wayfarers did not seriously mind being bisected, that in principle they accepted the whole arrangement.

Now an objector who talks like this is implying that it *is* possible to understand alien customs. That is just what he is trying to make me do. And he implies, too, that if I do succeed in understanding them, I shall do something better than giving up judging them. He expects me to change my present judgement to a truer one—namely, one that is favourable. And the standards I must use to do this cannot just be Samurai standards. They have to be ones current in my own culture. Ideals like discipline and devotion will not move anybody unless he himself accepts them. As it happens, neither discipline nor devotion is very popular in the West at present. Anyone who appeals to them may well have to do some more arguing to make *them* acceptable, before he can use them to explain the Samurai. But if he does succeed here, he will have persuaded us, not just that there was something to be said for them in ancient Japan, but that there would be here as well.

Isolating barriers simply cannot arise here. If we accept something as a serious moral truth about one culture, we can't refuse to apply it—in however different an outward form—to other cultures as well, wherever circumstances admit it. If we refuse to do this, we just are not taking the other culture seriously. This becomes clear if we look at the last argument used by my objector—that of justification by consent of the victim. It is suggested that sudden bisection is quite in order, *provided* that it takes place between consenting adults. I cannot now discuss how conclusive this justification is. What I am pointing out is simply that it can only work if we believe that *consent* can make such a transaction respectable—and this is a thoroughly modern and Western idea. It would probably never occur to a Samurai; if it did, it would surprise him very much. It is *our* standard. In applying it, too, we are likely to make another typically Western demand. We shall ask for good factual evidence that the wayfarers actually do have this rather surprising taste—that they are really willing to be bisected. In applying Western standards in this way, we are not being confused or irrelevant. We are asking the questions which arise *from where we stand,* questions which we can see the sense of. We do this because asking questions which you can't see the sense of is humbug. Certainly we can extend our questioning by

imaginative effort. We can come to understand other societies better. By doing so, we may make their questions our own, or we may see that they are really forms of the questions which we are asking already. This is not impossible. It is just very hard work. The obstacles which often prevent it are simply those of ordinary ignorance, laziness and prejudice.

If there were really an isolating barrier, of course, our own culture could never have been formed. It is no sealed box, but a fertile jungle of different influences—Greek, Jewish, Roman, Norse, Celtic and so forth, into which further influences are still pouring—American, Indian, Japanese, Jamaican, you name it. The moral isolationist's picture of separate unmixable cultures is quite unreal. People who talk about British history usually stress the value of this fertilizing mix, no doubt rightly. But this is not just an odd fact about Britain. Except for the very smallest and most remote, all cultures are formed out of many streams. All have the problem of digesting and assimilating things which, at the start, they do not understand. All have the choice of learning something from this challenge, or, alternatively, of refusing to learn, and fighting it mindlessly instead.

This universal predicament has been obscured by the fact that anthropologists used to concentrate largely on very small and remote cultures, which did not seem to have this problem. These tiny societies, which had often forgotten their own history, made neat, self-contained subjects for study. No doubt it was valuable to emphasize their remoteness, their extreme strangeness, their independence of our cultural tradition. This emphasis was, I think, the root of moral isolationism. But, as the tribal studies themselves showed, even there the anthropologists were able to interpret what they saw and make judgements—often favourable—about the tribesmen. And the tribesmen, too, were quite equal to making judgements about the anthropologists—and about the tourists and Coca-Cola salesmen who followed them. Both sets of judgements, no doubt, were somewhat hasty, both have been refined in the light of further experience. A similar transaction between us and the Samurai might take even longer. But that is no reason at all for deeming it impossible. Morally as well as physically, there is only one world, and we all have to live in it.

Study Questions

1. What does Midgley mean by "moral isolationism"?
2. Are those who oppose judging other cultures equally opposed to other cultures judging ours?
3. Do those who live in a culture necessarily understand it better than those who don't live in that culture?
4. If criticisms of other cultures are always inappropriate, can praise of other cultures ever be appropriate?

Egoism and Moral Skepticism

JAMES RACHELS

Morality involves taking into account interests apart from our own. Do we ever do so? According to psychological egoism, we don't, because all human behavior is motivated only by self-interest. According to ethical egoism, even if we could act in the interest of others, we ought not do so but should be concerned only with ourselves. In the next selection James Rachels (1941–2003), who was Professor of Philosophy at the University of Alabama at Birmingham, considers both psychological and ethical egoism, concluding that neither is acceptable.

1. Our ordinary thinking about morality is full of assumptions that we almost never question. We assume, for example, that we have an obligation to consider the welfare of other people when we decide what actions to perform or what rules to obey; we think that we must refrain from acting in ways harmful to others, and that we must respect their rights and interests as well as our own. We also assume that people are in fact capable of being motivated by such considerations, that is, that people are not wholly selfish and that they do sometimes act in the interests of others.

Both of these assumptions have come under attack by moral sceptics, as long ago as by Glaucon in Book II of Plato's *Republic*. Glaucon recalls the legend of Gyges, a shepherd who was said to have found a magic ring in a fissure

From Steven M. Cahn, *A New Introduction to Philosophy*. Copyright © 1971. Reprinted by permission of Steven M. Cahn.

opened by an earthquake. The ring would make its wearer invisible and thus would enable him to go anywhere and do anything undetected. Gyges used the power of the ring to gain entry to the Royal Palace, where he seduced the Queen, murdered the King, and subsequently seized the throne. Now Glaucon asks us to imagine that there are two such rings, one given to a man of virtue and one given to a rogue. The rogue, of course, will use his ring unscrupulously and do anything necessary to increase his own wealth and power. He will recognize no moral constraints on his conduct, and, since the cloak of invisibility will protect him from discovery, he can do anything he pleases without fear of reprisal. So, there will be no end to the mischief he will do. But how will the so-called virtuous man behave? Glaucon suggests that he will behave no better than the rogue: "No one, it is commonly believed, would have such iron strength of mind as to stand fast in doing right or keep his hands off other men's goods, when he could go to the market-place and fearlessly help himself to anything he wanted, enter houses and sleep with any woman he chose, set prisoners free and kill men at his pleasure, and in a word go about among men with the powers of a god. He would behave no better than the other; both would take the same course."[1] Moreover, why shouldn't he? Once he is freed from the fear of reprisal, why shouldn't a man simply do what he pleases, or what he thinks is best for himself? What reason is there for him to continue being "moral" when it is clearly not to his own advantage to do so?

These sceptical views suggested by Glaucon have come to be known as *psychological egoism* and *ethical egoism,* respectively. Psychological egoism is the view that all men are selfish in everything that they do, that is, that the only motive from which anyone ever acts is self-interest. On this view, even when men are acting in ways apparently calculated to benefit others, they are actually motivated by the belief that acting in this way is to their own advantage, and if they did not believe this, they would not be

doing that action. Ethical egoism is, by contrast, a normative view about how men *ought* to act. It is the view that, regardless of how men do in fact behave, they have no obligation to do anything except what is in their own interests. According to ethical egoists, a person is always justified in doing whatever is in his own interests, regardless of the effect on others.

Clearly, if either of these views is correct, then "the moral institution of life" (to use Butler's well-turned phrase) is very different than what we normally think. The majority of mankind is grossly deceived about what is, or ought to be, the case, where morals are concerned.

2. Psychological egoism seems to fly in the face of the facts. We are tempted to say, "Of course people act unselfishly all the time. For example, Smith gives up a trip to the country, which he would have enjoyed very much, in order to stay behind and help a friend with his studies, which is a miserable way to pass the time. This is a perfectly clear case of unselfish behavior, and if the psychological egoist thinks that such cases do not occur, then he is just mistaken." Given such obvious instances of "unselfish behavior," what reply can the egoist make? There are two general arguments by which he might try to show that all actions, including those such as the one just outlined, are in fact motivated by self-interest. Let us examine these in turn:

a. The first argument goes as follows: If we describe one person's action as selfish, and another person's action as unselfish, we are overlooking the crucial fact that in both cases, assuming that the action is done voluntarily, *the agent is merely doing what he most wants to do.* If Smith stays behind to help his friend, that only shows that he wanted to help his friend more than he wanted to go to the country. And why should he be praised for his "unselfishness" when he is only doing what he most wants to do? So, since Smith is only doing what he wants to do, he cannot be said to be acting unselfishly.

This argument is so bad that it would not deserve to be taken seriously except for the fact that so many otherwise intelligent people have been taken in by it. First, the argument rests on the premise that people never voluntarily do anything except what they want to do. But this is patently false; there are at least two classes of actions that are exceptions to this generalization. One is the set of actions which we may not want to do, but which we do anyway as a means to an end which we want to achieve, for example, going to the dentist in order to stop a toothache, or going to work every day in order to be able to draw our pay at the end of the month. These cases may be regarded as consistent with the spirit of the egoist argument, however, since the ends mentioned are wanted by the agent. But the other set of actions are those which we do, not because we want to, nor even because there is an end which we want to achieve, but because we feel ourselves *under an obligation* to do them. For example, someone may do something because he has promised to do it, and thus feels obligated, even though he does not want to do it. It is sometimes suggested that in such cases we do the action because, after all, we want to keep our promises; so, even here, we are doing what we want. However, this dodge will not work: if I have promised to do something, and if I do not want to do it, then it is simply false to say that I want to keep my promise. In such cases we feel a conflict precisely because we do *not* want to do what we feel obligated to do. It is reasonable to think that Smith's action falls roughly into this second category: he might stay behind, not because he wants to, but because he feels that this friend needs help.

But suppose we were to concede, for the sake of the argument, that all voluntary action is motivated by the agent's wants, or at least that Smith is so motivated. Even if this were granted, it would not follow that Smith is acting selfishly or from self-interest. For if Smith wants to do something that will help his friend, even when it means forgoing his own enjoyments, that is precisely what makes him *un*selfish. What else

could unselfishness be, if not wanting to help others? Another way to put the same point is to say that it is the *object* of a want that determines whether it is selfish or not. The mere fact that I am acting on *my* wants does not mean that I am acting selfishly; that depends on *what it is* that I want. If I want only my own good, and care nothing for others, then I am selfish; but if I also want other people to be well-off and happy, and if I act on *that* desire, then my action is not selfish. So much for this argument.

b. The second argument for psychological egoism is this: Since so-called unselfish actions always produce a sense of self-satisfaction in the agent,[2] and since this sense of satisfaction is a pleasant state of consciousness, it follows that the point of the action is really to achieve a pleasant state of consciousness, rather than to bring about any good for others. Therefore, the action is "unselfish" only at a superficial level of analysis. Smith will feel much better with himself for having stayed to help his friend—if he had gone to the country, he would have felt terrible about it—and that is the real point of the action. According to a well-known story, this argument was once expressed by Abraham Lincoln:

> Mr. Lincoln once remarked to a fellow-passenger on an old-time mud-coach that all men were prompted by selfishness in doing good. His fellow-passenger was antagonizing this position when they were passing over a corduroy bridge that spanned a slough. As they crossed this bridge they espied an old razor-backed sow on the bank making a terrible noise because her pigs had got into the slough and were in danger of drowning. As the old coach began to climb the hill, Mr. Lincoln called out, "Driver, can't you stop just a moment?" Then Mr. Lincoln jumped out, ran back, and lifted the little pigs out of the mud and water and placed them on the bank. When he returned, his companion remarked: "Now, Abe, where does selfishness come in on this little episode?" "Why, bless your soul, Ed, that was the very essence of selfishness. I should have had no peace of mind all day had I gone

on and left that suffering old sow worrying over those pigs. I did it to get peace of mind, don't you see?"³

This argument suffers from defects similar to the previous one. Why should we think that merely because someone derives satisfaction from helping others this makes him selfish? Isn't the unselfish man precisely the one who *does* derive satisfaction from helping others, while the selfish man does not? If Lincoln "got peace of mind" from rescuing the piglets, does this show him to be selfish, or, on the contrary, doesn't it show him to be compassionate and good-hearted? (If a man were truly selfish, why should it bother his conscience that *others* suffer—much less pigs?) Similarly, it is nothing more than shabby sophistry to say, because Smith takes satisfaction in helping his friend, that he is behaving selfishly. If we say this rapidly, while thinking about something else, perhaps it will sound all right; but if we speak slowly, and pay attention to what we are saying, it sounds plain silly.

Moreover, suppose we ask *why* Smith derives satisfaction from helping his friend. The answer will be, it is because Smith cares for him and wants him to succeed. If Smith did not have these concerns, then he would take no pleasure in assisting him; and these concerns, as we have already seen, are the marks of unselfishness, not selfishness. To put the point more generally: if we have a positive attitude toward the attainment of some goal, then we may derive satisfaction from attaining that goal. But the *object* of our attitude is *the attainment of that goal*; and we must want to attain the goal *before* we can find any satisfaction in it. We do not, in other words, desire some sort of "pleasurable consciousness" and then try to figure out how to achieve it; rather, we desire all sorts of different things—money, a new fishing boat, to be a better chess player, to get a promotion in our work, etc.—and because we desire these things, we derive satisfaction from attaining them. And so, if someone desires the welfare and happiness of another person, he will derive satisfaction

from that; but this does not mean that this satisfaction is the object of his desire, or that he is in any way selfish on account of it.

It is a measure of the weakness of psychological egoism that these insupportable arguments are the ones most often advanced in its favor. Why, then, should anyone ever have thought it a true view? Perhaps because of a desire for theoretical simplicity: In thinking about human conduct, it would be nice if there were some simple formula that would unite the diverse phenomena of human behavior under a single explanatory principle, just as simple formulae in physics bring together a great many apparently different phenomena. And since it is obvious that self-regard is an overwhelmingly important factor in motivation, it is only natural to wonder whether all motivation might not be explained in these terms. But the answer is clearly No; while a great many human actions are motivated entirely or in part by self-interest, only by a deliberate distortion of the facts can we say that all conduct is so motivated. This will be clear, I think, if we correct three confusions which are commonplace. The exposure of these confusions will remove the last traces of plausibility from the psychological egoist thesis.

The first is the confusion of selfishness with self-interest. The two are clearly not the same. If I see a physician when I am feeling poorly, I am acting in my own interest but no one would think of calling me "selfish" on account of it. Similarly, brushing my teeth, working hard at my job, and obeying the law are all in my self-interest but none of these are examples of selfish conduct. This is because selfish behavior is behavior that ignores the interests of others, in circumstances in which their interests ought not to be ignored. This concept has a definite evaluative flavor; to call someone "selfish" is not just to describe his action but to condemn it. Thus, you would not call me selfish for eating a normal meal in normal circumstances (although it may surely be in my self-interest); but you would call me selfish for hoarding food while others about are starving.

The second confusion is the assumption that every action is done *either* from self-interest or from other-regarding motives. Thus, the egoist concludes that if there is no such thing as genuine altruism then all actions must be done from self-interest. But this is certainly a false dichotomy. The man who continues to smoke cigarettes, even after learning about the connection between smoking and cancer, is surely not acting from self-interest, not even by his own standards—self-interest would dictate that he quit smoking at once—and he is not acting altruistically either. He *is*, no doubt, smoking for the pleasure of it, but all that this shows is that undisciplined pleasure-seeking and acting from self-interest are very different. This is what led Butler to remark that "the thing to be lamented is, not that men have so great regard to their own good or interest in the present world, for they have not enough."[4]

The last two paragraphs show (*a*) that it is false that all actions are selfish, and (*b*) that it is false that all actions are done out of self-interest. And it should be noted that these two points can be made, and were, without any appeal to putative examples of altruism.

The third confusion is the common but false assumption that a concern for one's own welfare is incompatible with any genuine concern for the welfare of others. Thus, since it is obvious that everyone (or very nearly everyone) does desire his own well-being, it might be thought that no one can really be concerned with others. But again, this is false. There is no inconsistency in desiring that everyone, including oneself *and* others, be well-off and happy. To be sure, it may happen on occasion that our own interests conflict with the interests of others, and in these cases we will have to make hard choices. But even in these cases we might sometimes opt for the interests of others, especially when the others involved are our family or friends. But more importantly, not all cases are like this: sometimes we are able to promote the welfare of others when our own interests are not involved at all. In these cases not even the strongest self-regard need prevent us from acting considerately toward others.

Once these confusions are cleared away, it seems to me obvious enough that there is no reason whatever to accept psychological egoism. On the contrary, if we simply observe people's behavior with an open mind, we may find that a great deal of it is motivated by self-regard, but by no means all of it; and that there is no reason to deny that "the moral institution of life" can include a place for the virtue of beneficence.[5]

3. The ethical egoist would say at this point, "Of course it is possible for people to act altruistically, and perhaps many people do act that way—but there is no reason why they *should* do so. A person is under no obligation to do anything except what is in his own interests."[6] This is really quite a radical doctrine. Suppose I have an urge to set fire to some public building (say, a department store) just for the fascination of watching the spectacular blaze: according to this view, the fact that several people might be burned to death provides no reason whatever why I should not do it. After all, this only concerns *their* welfare, not my own, and according to the ethical egoist the only person I need think of is myself.

Some might deny that ethical egoism has any such monstrous consequences. They would point out that it is really to my own advantage not to set the fire—for, if I do that I may be caught and put into prison (unlike Gyges, I have no magic ring for protection). Moreover, even if I could avoid being caught it is still to my advantage to respect the rights and interests of others, for it is to my advantage to live in a society in which people's rights and interests are respected. Only in such a society can I live a happy and secure life; so, in acting kindly toward others, I would merely be doing my part to create and maintain the sort of society which it is to my advantage to have.[7] Therefore, it is said, the egoist would not be such a bad man; he would be as kindly and considerate as anyone else, because he would see that it is to his own advantage to be kindly and considerate.

This is a seductive line of thought, but it seems to me mistaken. Certainly it is to everyone's advantage (including the egoist's) to preserve a stable society where people's interests are generally protected. But there is no reason for the egoist to think that merely because *he* will not honor the rules of the social game, decent society will collapse. For the vast majority of people are not egoists, and there is no reason to think that they will be converted by his example—especially if he is discreet and does not unduly flaunt his style of life. What this line of reasoning shows is not that the egoist himself must act benevolently, but that he must encourage *others* to do so. He must take care to conceal from public view his own self-centered method of decision making, and urge others to act on precepts very different from those on which he is willing to act.

The rational egoist, then, cannot advocate that egoism be universally adopted by everyone. For he wants a world in which his own interests are maximized; and if other people adopted the egoistic policy of pursuing their own interests to the exclusion of his interests, as he pursues his interests to the exclusion of theirs, then such a world would be impossible. So he himself will be an egoist, but he will want others to be altruists.

This brings us to what is perhaps the most popular "refutation" of ethical egoism current among philosophical writers—the argument that ethical egoism is at bottom inconsistent because it cannot be universalized.[8] The argument goes like this:

To say that any action or policy of action is *right* (or that it *ought* to be adopted) entails that it is right for *anyone* in the same sort of circumstances. I cannot, for example, say that it is right for me to lie to you, and yet object when you lie to me (provided, of course, that the circumstances are the same). I cannot hold that it is all right for me to drink your beer and then complain when you drink mine. This is just the requirement that we be consistent in our evaluations; it is a requirement of logic. Now it is said that ethical egoism cannot meet this requirement because, as we have already seen, the egoist would not want others to act in the same way that he acts. Moreover, suppose he *did*

advocate the universal adoption of egoistic policies: he would be saying to Peter, "You ought to pursue your own interests even if it means destroying Paul"; and he would be saying to Paul, "You ought to pursue your own interests even if it means destroying Peter." The attitudes expressed in these two recommendations seem clearly inconsistent—he is urging the advancement of Peter's interests at one moment, and countenancing their defeat at the next. Therefore, the argument goes, there is no way to maintain the doctrine of ethical egoism as a consistent view about how we ought to act. We will fall into inconsistency whenever we try.

What are we to make of this argument? Are we to conclude that ethical egoism has been refuted? Such a conclusion, I think, would be unwarranted; for I think that we can show, contrary to this argument, how ethical egoism can be maintained consistently. We need only to interpret the egoist's position in a sympathetic way: we should say that he has in mind a certain kind of world which he would prefer over all others; it would be a world in which his own interests were maximized, regardless of the effects on the other people. The egoist's primary policy of action, then, would be to act in such a way as to bring about, as nearly as possible, this sort of world. Regardless of however morally reprehensible we might find it, there is nothing *inconsistent* in someone's adopting this as his ideal and acting in a way calculated to bring it about. And if someone did adopt this as his ideal, then he would not advocate universal egoism; as we have already seen, he would want other people to be altruists. So, if he advocates any principles of conduct for the general public, they will be altruistic principles. This could not be inconsistent; on the contrary, it would be perfectly consistent with his goal of creating a world in which his own interests are maximized. To be sure, he would have to be deceitful; in order to secure the good will of others, and a favorable hearing for his exhortations to altruism, he would have to pretend that he was himself prepared to accept altruistic principles. But again, that would be all right; from the egoist's point of view, this would merely be a matter of adopting the necessary means to the achievement of his goal—and while we might not approve of this, there is nothing inconsistent about it. Again, it might be said, "He advocates one thing, but does another. Surely *that's* inconsistent." But it is not; for what he advocates and what he does are both calculated as means to an end (the *same* end, we might note); and as such, he is doing what is rationally required in each case. Therefore, contrary to the previous argument, there is nothing inconsistent in the ethical egoist's view. He cannot be refuted by the claim that he contradicts himself.

Is there, then, no way to refute the ethical egoist? If by "refute" we mean show that he has made some *logical* error, the answer is that there is not. However, there is something more that can be said. The egoist challenge to our ordinary moral convictions amounts to a demand for an explanation of why we should adopt certain policies of action, namely, policies in which the good of others is given importance. We can give an answer to this demand, albeit an indirect one. The reason one ought not to do actions that would hurt other people is other people would be hurt. The reason one ought to do actions that would benefit other people is other people would be benefited. This may at first seem like a piece of philosophical sleight-of-hand, but it is not. The point is that the welfare of human beings is something that most of us value *for its own sake,* and not merely for the sake of something else. Therefore, when *further* reasons are demanded for valuing the welfare of human beings, we cannot point to anything further to satisfy this demand. It is not that we have no reason for pursuing these policies, but that our reason *is* that these policies are for the good of human beings.

So if we are asked, "Why shouldn't I set fire to this department store?" one answer would be, "Because if you do, people may be burned to death." This is a complete, sufficient reason which does not require qualification or supplementation of any sort. If someone seriously wants to know why this action shouldn't be done, that's the reason. If we are pressed further and asked the sceptical question, "But why shouldn't I do actions that will harm others?" we may not know what to say—but this is because the questioner has included in his question the very answer we would like to give: "Why shouldn't you do actions that will harm others? Because, doing those actions would harm others."

The egoist, no doubt, will not be happy with this. He will protest that *we* may accept this as a reason, but *he* does not. And here the argument stops: there are limits to what can be accomplished by argument, and if the egoist really doesn't care about other people—if he honestly doesn't care whether they are helped or hurt by his actions—then we have reached those limits. If we want to persuade him to act decently toward his fellow humans, we will have to make our appeal to such other attitudes as he does possess, by threats, bribes, or other cajolery. That is all that we can do.

Though some may find this situation distressing (we would like to be able to show that the egoist is just *wrong*), it holds no embarrassment for common morality. What we have come up against is simply a fundamental requirement of rational action, namely, that the existence of reasons for action always depends on the prior existence of certain attitudes in the agent. For example, the fact that a certain course of action would make the agent a lot of money is a reason for doing it only if the agent wants to make money; the fact that practicing at chess makes one a better player is a reason for practicing only if one wants to be a better player; and so on. Similarly, the fact that a certain action would help the agent is a reason for doing the action only if the agent cares about his own welfare, and the fact that an action would help others is a reason for doing it only if the agent cares about others. In this respect ethical egoism and what we might call ethical altruism are in exactly the same fix: both require that the agent *care* about himself, or about other people, before they can get started.

So a nonegoist will accept "It would harm another person" as a reason not to do an action simply because he cares about what happens to that other person. When the egoist says that he does *not* accept that as a reason, he is saying something quite extraordinary. He is saying that he has no affection for friends or family, that he never feels pity or compassion, that he is the sort of person who can look on scenes of human misery with complete indifference, so long as he is not the one suffering. Genuine egoists, people who really don't care at all about anyone other than themselves, are rare. It is important to keep this in mind when thinking about ethical egoism; it is easy to forget just how fundamental to human psychological makeup the feeling of sympathy is. Indeed, a man without any sympathy at all would scarcely be recognizable as a man; and that is what makes ethical egoism such a disturbing doctrine in the first place.

4. There are, of course, many different ways in which the sceptic might challenge the assumptions underlying our moral practice. In this essay I have discussed only two of them, the two put forward by Glaucon in the passage that I cited from Plato's *Republic*. It is important that the assumptions underlying our moral practice should not be confused with particular judgments made within that practice. To defend one is not to defend the other. We may assume—quite properly, if my analysis has been correct—that the virtue of beneficence does, and indeed should, occupy an important place in "the moral institution of life"; and yet we may make constant and miserable errors when it comes to judging when and in what ways this virtue is to be exercised. Even worse, we may often be able to make accurate moral judgments, and know what we ought to do, but not do it. For these ills, philosophy alone is not the cure.

Notes

1. *The Republic of Plato,* translated by F. M. Cornford (Oxford, 1941), p. 45.

2. Or, as it is sometimes said, "It gives him a clear conscience," or "He couldn't sleep at night if he had done otherwise," or "He would have been ashamed of himself for not doing it," and so on.

3. Frank C. Sharp, *Ethics* (New York, 1928), pp. 74–75. Quoted from the Springfield (IL) *Monitor* in the *Outlook,* vol. 56, p. 1059.

4. *The Works of Joseph Butler,* edited by W. E. Gladstone (Oxford, 1896), vol. II, p. 26. It should be noted that most of the points I am making against psychological egoism were first made by Joseph Butler. Butler made all the important points; all that is left for us is to remember them.

5. The capacity for altruistic behavior is not unique to human beings. Some interesting experiments with rhesus monkeys have shown that these animals will refrain from operating a device for securing food if this causes other animals to suffer pain. See Jules H. Masserman, Stanley Wechkin, and William Terris, "'Altruistic' Behavior in Rhesus Monkeys," *American Journal of Psychiatry,* vol. 121 (1964), pp. 584–85.

6. I take this to be the view of Ayn Rand, insofar as I understand her confused doctrine.

7. Cf. Thomas Hobbes, *Leviathan* (London, 1651), chap. 17.

8. See, for example, Brian Medlin, "Ultimate Principles and Ethical Egoism," *Australasian Journal of Philosophy,* vol. 35 (1957), pp. 111–18; and D. H. Monro, *Empiricism and Ethics* (Cambridge, 1967), chap. 16.

Study Questions

1. Explain the distinction between psychological egoism and ethical egoism.
2. In the story about Abraham Lincoln, was his action motivated by selfishness?
3. Is a concern for one's own welfare incompatible with a concern for the welfare of others?
4. Is it self-defeating for an ethical egoist to urge everyone to act egoistically?

The Categorical Imperative

IMMANUEL KANT

We turn next to some of the most important moral theories, competing explanations of why certain actions are right and others are wrong.

One of the most influential of all ethical systems is that developed by the German philosopher Immanuel Kant (1724–1804), a dominant figure in the history of modern philosophy. Because his views are not easy to grasp, I shall offer a brief overview of them.

Kant argues that the moral worth of an action is to be judged not by its consequences but by the nature of the maxim or principle that motivated the action. Thus right actions are not necessarily those with favorable consequences but those performed in accordance with correct maxims. But which maxims are correct? According to Kant, the only correct ones are those that can serve as universal laws because they are applicable without exception to every person at any time. In other words, you should act only on a maxim that can be universalized without contradiction.

To see what Kant has in mind, consider a specific example he uses to illustrate his view. Suppose you need to borrow money, but it will be lent to you only if you promise to pay it back. You realize, however, that you will not be able to honor the debt. Is it permissible for you to promise to repay the money, knowing you will not keep the promise? Kant argues that doing so is not permissible because if it were a universal law that promises could be made with no intention of keeping them, then the practice of promising would be destroyed.

Kant refers to his supreme moral principle as the "categorical imperative"—categorical because it does not depend on anyone's particular desires, and an imperative because it is a command of reason. Kant also claims that the categorical imperative can be reformulated as follows: So act that you treat humanity, whether in your own person or in any other person, always at the same time as an end, never merely as a means. Using this version, Kant argues that a deceitful promise is immoral because a person making such a promise is using another person only as a means, not treating that individual as an end, a rational being worthy of respect.

It is impossible to imagine anything at all in the world, or even beyond it, that can be called good without qualification—except a *good will*. Intelligence, wit, judgement, and the other mental talents, whatever we may call them, or courage, decisiveness, and perseverance, are, as qualities of *temperament*, certainly good and desirable in many respects; but they can also be extremely bad and harmful when the will which makes use of these *gifts of nature* and whose

From Immanuel Kant, *Groundwork for the Metaphysics of Morals*, translated by Arnulf Zweig. Copyright © 2002. Reprinted by permission of Oxford University Press.

specific quality we refer to as *character*, is not good. It is exactly the same with *gifts of fortune*. Power, wealth, honour, even health and that total well-being and contentment with one's condition which we call "happiness," can make a person bold but consequently often reckless as well, unless a good will is present to correct their influence on the mind, thus adjusting the whole principle of one's action to render it conformable to universal ends. It goes without saying that the sight of a creature enjoying uninterrupted prosperity, but never feeling the slightest pull of a pure and good will, cannot excite approval in a rational and impartial spectator. Consequently, a good will seems to constitute the indispensable condition even of our worthiness to be happy.

Some qualities, even though they are helpful to this good will and can make its task very much easier, nevertheless have no intrinsic unconditional worth. Rather, they presuppose a good will which puts limits on the esteem in which they are rightly held and forbids us to regard them as absolutely good. Moderation in emotions and passions, self-control, and sober reflection are not only good in many respects: they may even seem to constitute part of the inner worth of a person. Yet they are far from being properly described as good without qualification (however unconditionally they were prized by the ancients). For without the principles of a good will those qualities may become exceedingly bad; the passionless composure of a villain makes him not merely more dangerous but also directly more detestable in our eyes than we would have taken him to be without it.

A good will is not good because of its effects or accomplishments, and not because of its adequacy to achieve any proposed end: it is good only by virtue of its willing—that is, it is good in itself. Considered in itself it is to be treasured as incomparably higher than anything it could ever bring about merely in order to satisfy some inclination or, if you like, the sum total of all inclinations. Even if it were to happen that, because of some particularly unfortunate face or

the miserly bequest of a step-motherly nature, this will were completely powerless to carry out its aims; if with even its utmost effort it still accomplished nothing, so that only good will itself remained (not, of course, as a mere wish, but as the summoning of every means in our power), even then it would still, like a jewel, glisten in its own right, as something that has its full worth in itself. . . .

We must thus develop the concept of a will estimable in itself and good apart from any further aim. This concept is already present in the natural, healthy mind, which requires not so much instruction as merely clarification. It is this concept that always holds the highest place in estimating the total worth of our actions and it constitutes the condition of all the rest. Let us then take up the concept of *duty*, which includes that of a good will, the latter however being here under certain subjective limitations and obstacles. These, so far from hiding a good will or disguising it, rather bring it out by contrast and make it shine forth more brightly. . . .

It is a duty to help others where one can, and besides this many souls are so compassionately disposed that, without any further motive of vanity or self-interest, they find an inner pleasure in spreading joy around them, taking delight in the contentment of others, so far as they have brought it about. Yet I maintain that, however dutiful and kind an action of this sort may be, it still has no genuinely moral worth. It is on a level with other inclinations—for example, the inclination to pursue honour, which if fortunate enough to aim at something generally useful and consistent with duty, something consequently honourable, deserves praise and encouragement but not esteem. For its maxim lacks the moral merit of such actions done not out of inclination but out of *duty*. Suppose then that the mind of this humanitarian were overclouded by sorrows of his own which extinguished all compassion for the fate of others, but that he still had the power to assist others in distress; suppose though that their adversity no longer stirred him, because he is preoccupied with his own; and now imagine that, though no longer moved by any inclination, he nevertheless tears himself out of this deadly apathy and does the action without any inclination, solely out of duty. Then for the first time his action has its genuine moral worth. Furthermore, if nature had put little sympathy into this or that person's heart; if he, though an honest man, were cold in temperament and in-different to the sufferings of others—perhaps because he has the special gifts of patience and fortitude in his own sufferings and he assumes or even demands the same of others; if such a man (who would in truth not be the worst product of nature) were not exactly fashioned by nature to be a humanitarian, would he not still find in himself a source from which he might give him-self a worth far higher than that of a good-natured temperament? Assuredly he would. It is precisely in this that the worth of character begins to show—a moral worth, and incompara-bly the highest—namely, that he does good, not out of inclination, but out of duty. . . .

The moral worth of an action done out of duty has its moral worth, not *in the objective* to be reached by that action, but in the maxim in accordance with which the action is decided upon; it depends, therefore, not on actualizing the object of the action, but solely on the *prin-ciple of volition* in accordance with which the action was done, without any regard for objects of the faculty of desire. It is clear from our previ-ous discussion that the objectives we may have in acting, and also our actions' effects consid-ered as ends and as what motivates our volition, can give to actions no unconditional or moral worth. Where then can this worth be found if not in the willing of the action's hoped for effect? It can be found nowhere but *in the prin-ciple of the will*, irrespective of the ends that can be brought about by such action. . . .

Duty is the necessity of an act done out of re-spect for the law. While I can certainly have an *inclination* for an object that results from my proposed action, I can never *respect* it, precisely because it is nothing but an effect of a will and not its activity. Similarly I cannot respect any

inclination whatsoever, whether it be my own inclination or that of another. At most I can ap-prove of that towards which I feel an inclination, and occasionally I can like the object of some-body else's inclination myself—that is, see it as conducive to my own advantage. But the only thing that could be an object of respect (and thus a commandment) for me is something that is conjoined with my will purely as a ground and never as a consequence, something that does not serve my inclination but overpowers it or at least excludes it entirely from my decision-making—consequently, nothing but the law itself. Now if an action done out of duty is sup-posed to exclude totally the influence of inclina-tion, and, along with inclination, every object of volition, then nothing remains that could de-termine the will except objectively *the law* and subjectively *pure respect* for this practical law. What is left therefore is the maxim, to obey this sort of law even when doing so is prejudicial to all my inclinations.

Thus the moral worth of an action depends neither on the result expected from that action nor on any principle of action that has to borrow its motive from this expected result. For all these results (such as one's own pleasurable condition or even the promotion of the happiness of others) could have been brought about by other causes as well. It would not require the will of a rational being to produce them, but it is only in such a will that the highest and unconditional good can be found. That pre-eminent good which we call "moral" consists therefore in nothing but *the idea of the law* in itself, which certainly *is present only in a rational being*—so far as that idea, and not an expected result, is the determining ground of the will. And this pre-eminent good is already present in the person who acts in accor-dance with this idea; we need not await the result of the action in order to find it. . . .

Everything in nature works in accordance with laws. Only a rational being has the power to act in accordance with the idea of laws—that is, in accordance with principles—and thus has a will. . . .

The idea of an objective principle, in so far as it constrains a will, is called a commandment (of reason), and the formulation of this commandment is called an Imperative. . . .

All imperatives command either hypothetically or categorically. Hypothetical imperatives declare a possible action to be practically necessary as a means to the attainment of something else that one wants (or that one may want). A categorical imperative would be one that represented an action as itself objectively necessary, without regard to any further end.

Since every practical law presents a possible action as good and therefore as necessary for a subject whose actions are determined by reason, all imperatives are therefore formulae for determining an action which is necessary according to the principle of a will in some way good. If the action would be good only as a means to something else, the imperative is hypothetical; if the action is thought of as good in itself and therefore as necessary for a will which of itself conforms to reason as its principle, then the imperative is categorical. . . .

There is, however, *one* end that we may presuppose as actual in all rational beings (so far as they are dependent beings to whom imperatives apply); and thus there is one aim which they not only *might* have, but which we can assume with certainty that they all *do* have by a necessity of nature and that aim is *perfect happiness*. The hypothetical imperative which affirms the practical necessity of an action as a means to the promotion of perfect happiness is an assertoric imperative. We must not characterize it as necessary merely for some uncertain, merely possible purpose, but as necessary for a purpose that we can presuppose a priori and with certainty to be present in everyone because it belongs to the essence of human beings. Now we can call skill in the choice of the means to one's own greatest well-being "prudence" in the narrowest sense of the word. So the imperative concerning the choice of means to one's own happiness—that is, the precept of prudence—still remains hypothetical; the action is commanded not absolutely but only as a means to a further end.

Finally, there is one imperative which commands a certain line of conduct directly, without assuming or being conditional on any further goal to be reached by that conduct. This imperative is categorical. It is concerned not with the material of the action and its anticipated result, but with its form and with the principle from which the action itself results. And what is essentially good in the action consists in the [agent's] disposition, whatever the result may be. This imperative may be called the imperative of morality. . . .

The question now arises "How are all these imperatives possible?" This question does not ask how an action commanded by the imperative can be performed, but merely how we can understand the constraining of the will, which imperatives express in setting us a task. How an imperative of skill is possible requires no special discussion. Whoever wills the end also wills (so far as reason has decisive influence on his actions) the means which are indispensably necessary and in his power. . . .

By contrast, "How is the imperative of morality possible?" is beyond all doubt the one question in need of solution. For the moral imperative is in no way hypothetical, and consequently the objective necessity, which it affirms, cannot be supported by any presupposition, as was the case with hypothetical imperatives. But we must never forget that it is impossible to settle by any example, i.e., empirically, whether there is any imperative of this kind at all; we should rather worry that all imperatives that seem to be categorical may yet be hypothetical in some hidden way. For example, when it is said, "You must abstain from making deceitful promises," one assumes that the necessity for this abstention is not mere advice so as to avoid some further evil—as though the meaning of what was said was, You ought not to make a deceitful promise lest, when it comes to light, you destroy your credit. On the contrary, an action of this kind would have to be considered as bad in itself, and the imperative of the prohibition would be therefore categorical. Even so, no example can show with certainty that the will would be determined here solely by the law without any further motivation, although it may appear to be so; for it is always possible that fear of disgrace, perhaps also hidden dread of other risks, may unconsciously influence the will. Who can prove by experience the non-existence of a cause? For experience shows only that we do not perceive it. In such a case, however, the so-called moral imperative, which as such appears to be categorical and unconditional, would in fact be only a pragmatic prescription calling attention to our own advantage and merely instructing us to take this into account. . . .

If I think of a *hypothetical* imperative as such, I do not know beforehand what it will contain—not until I am given its condition. But if I think of a *categorical imperative,* I know right away what it contains. For since this imperative contains, besides the law, only the necessity that the maxim conform to this law, while the law, as we have seen, contains no condition limiting it, there is nothing left over to which the maxim of action should conform except the universality of a law as such; and it is only this conformity that the imperative asserts to be necessary.

There is therefore only one categorical imperative and it is this: "Act only on that maxim by which you can at the same time will that it should become a universal law." . . .

We shall now enumerate some duties. . . .

1. A man feels sick of life as the result of a mounting series of misfortunes that has reduced him to hopelessness, but he still possesses enough of his reason to ask himself whether it would not be contrary to his duty to himself to take his own life. Now he tests whether the maxim of his action could really become a universal law of nature. His maxim, however, is: "I make it my principle out of self-love to shorten my life if its continuance threatens more evil than it promises advantage." The only further question is whether this principle of self-love can become a universal law of nature. But one sees at once that a nature whose law was that the very same feeling meant to promote life should

actually destroy life would contradict itself, and hence would not endure as nature. The maxim therefore could not possibly be a general law of nature and thus it wholly contradicts the supreme principle of all duty.

2. Another finds himself driven by need to borrow money. He knows very well that he will not be able to pay it back, but he sees too that nobody will lend him anything unless he firmly promises to pay it back within a fixed time. He wants to make such a promise, but he still has enough conscience to ask himself, "Isn't it impermissible and contrary to duty to get out of one's difficulties this way?" Suppose, however, that he did decide to do it. The maxim of his action would run thus: "When I believe myself short of money, I will borrow money and promise to pay it back, even though I know that this will never be done." Now this principle of self-love or personal advantage is perhaps quite compatible with my own entire future welfare; only there remains the question "Is it right?" I therefore transform the unfair demand of self-love into a universal law and frame my question thus: "How would things stand if my maxim became a universal law?" I then see immediately that this maxim can never qualify as a self-consistent universal law of nature, but must necessarily contradict itself. For the universality of a law that permits anyone who believes himself to be in need to make any promise he pleases with the intention of not keeping it would make promising, and the very purpose one has in promising, itself impossible. For no one would believe he was being promised anything, but would laugh at any such utterance as hollow pretense.

3. A third finds in himself a talent that, with a certain amount of cultivation, could make him a useful man for all sorts of purposes. But he sees himself in comfortable circumstances, and he prefers to give himself up to pleasure rather than to bother about increasing and improving his fortunate natural aptitudes. Yet he asks himself further "Does my maxim of neglecting my natural gifts, besides agreeing with my taste for

amusement, agree also with what is called duty?" He then sees that a nature could indeed endure under such a universal law, even if (like the South Sea Islanders) every man should let his talents rust and should be bent on devoting his life solely to idleness, amusement, procreation—in a word, to enjoyment. Only he cannot possibly *will* that this should become a universal law of nature or should be implanted in us as such a law by a natural instinct. For as a rational being he necessarily wills that all his powers should be developed, since they are after all useful to him and given to him for all sorts of possible purposes.

4. A fourth man, who is himself flourishing but sees others who have to struggle with great hardships (and whom he could easily help) thinks to himself: "What do I care? Let every one be as happy as Heaven intends or as he can make himself; I won't deprive him of anything; I won't even envy him; but I don't feel like contributing anything to his well-being or to helping him in his distress!" Now admittedly if such an attitude were a universal law of nature, the human race could survive perfectly well and doubtless even better than when everybody chatters about sympathy and good will, and even makes an effort, now and then, to practise them, but, when one can get away with it, swindles, traffics in human rights, or violates them in other ways. But although it is possible that a universal law of nature in accord with this maxim could exist, it is impossible to *will* that such a principle should hold everywhere as a law of nature. For a will that intended this would be in conflict with itself, since many situations might arise in which the man needs love and sympathy from others, and in which, by such a law of nature generated by his own will, he would rob himself of all hope of the help he wants.

These are some of the many actual duties—or at least of what we take to be actual—whose derivation from the single principle cited above is perspicuous. We must be able to will that a maxim of our action should become a universal law— this is the authoritative model for moral judging of action generally. Some actions are so

constituted that we cannot even *conceive* without contradiction that their maxim be a universal law of nature, let alone that we could *will* that it *ought* to become one. In the case of other actions, we do not find this inner impossibility, but it is still impossible to *will* that their maxim should be raised to the universality of a law of nature, because such a will would contradict itself. . . .

If we now look at ourselves whenever we transgress a duty, we find that we in fact do not intend that our maxim should become a universal law. For this is impossible for us. What we really intend is rather that its opposite should remain a law generally; we only take the liberty of making an *exception* to it, for ourselves or (of course just this once) to satisfy our inclination. Consequently if we weighed it all up from one and the same perspective—that of reason—we should find a contradiction in our own will, the contradiction that a certain principle should be objectively necessary as a universal law and yet subjectively should not hold universally but should admit of exceptions. . . .

Suppose, however, there were something *whose existence in itself* had an absolute worth, something that, as an end *in itself,* could be a ground of definite laws. Then in it and in it alone, would the ground of a possible categorical imperative, that is, of a practical law, reside.

Now, I say, a human being, and in general every rational being, *does exist* as an end in himself, *not merely as a means* to be used by this or that will as it pleases. In all his actions, whether they are directed to himself or to other rational beings, a human being must always be viewed *at the same time as an end.* . . . Beings whose existence depends not on our will but on nature still have only a relative value as means and are therefore called *things,* if they lack reason. Rational beings, on the other hand, are called *persons* because, their nature already marks them out as ends in themselves—that is, as something which ought not to be used *merely* as a means—and consequently imposes restrictions on all choice making (and is an object of respect). Persons, therefore, are not merely subjective ends whose existence as an effect of our actions has a value *for us*. They are *objective ends*—that is, things whose existence is in itself an end, and indeed an end such that no other end can be substituted for it, no end to which they should serve *merely* as a means. For if this were not so, there would be nothing at all having *absolute value* anywhere. But if all value were conditional, and thus contingent, then no supreme principle could be found for reason at all.

If then there is to be a supreme practical principle and a categorical imperative for the human will, it must be such that it forms an objective principle of the will from the idea of something which is necessarily an end for everyone because *it is an end in itself,* a principle that can therefore serve as a universal practical law. The ground of this principle is: *Rational nature exists as an end in itself.* This is the way in which a human being necessarily conceives his own existence, and it is therefore a *subjective* principle of human actions. But it is also the way in which every other rational being conceives his existence, on the same rational ground which holds also for me; hence it is at the same time an *objective* principle from which, since it is a supreme practical ground, it must be possible to derive all laws of the will. The practical imperative will therefore be the following: *Act in such a way that you treat humanity, whether in your own person or in any other person, always at the same time as an end, never merely as a means.* We will now see whether this can be carried out in practice.

Let us keep to our previous examples.

First, . . . the man who contemplates suicide will ask himself whether his action could be compatible with the Idea of humanity as *an end in itself.* If he damages himself in order to escape from a painful situation, he is making use of a person *merely as a means* to maintain a tolerable state of affairs till the end of his life. But a human being is not a thing—not something to be used *merely* as a means: he must always in all his actions be regarded as an end in himself. Hence I cannot dispose of a human being in my own person, by maiming, corrupting, or killing him. (I must here forego a more precise definition of this principle that would forestall any misunderstanding—for example, as to having limbs amputated to save myself or exposing my life to danger in order to preserve it, and so on—this discussion belongs to ethics proper.)

Secondly, . . . the man who has in mind making a false promise to others will see at once that he is intending to make use of another person *merely as a means* to an end which that person does not share. For the person whom I seek to use for my own purposes by such a promise cannot possibly agree with my way of treating him, and so cannot himself share the end of the action. This incompatibility with the principle of duty to others can be seen more distinctly when we bring in examples of attacks on the freedom and property of others. For then it is manifest that a violator of the rights of human beings intends to use the person of others merely as a means without taking into consideration that, as rational beings, they must always at the same time be valued as ends—that is, treated only as beings who must themselves be able to share in the end of the very same action.

Thirdly, . . . it is not enough that an action not conflict with humanity in our own person as an end in itself: it must also *harmonize with this end*. Now there are in humanity capacities for greater perfection that form part of nature's purpose for humanity in our own person. To neglect these can perhaps be compatible with the *survival* of humanity as an end in itself, but not with the *promotion* of that end.

Fourthly, . . . the natural end that all human beings seek is their own perfect happiness. Now the human race might indeed exist if everybody contributed nothing to the happiness of others but at the same time refrained from deliberately impairing it. This harmonizing with humanity *as an end in itself* would, however, be merely negative and not positive, unless everyone also endeavours, as far as he can, to further the ends of others. For the ends of any person who is an end in himself must, if this idea is to have its full effect in me, be also, as far as possible, *my* ends.

Study Questions

1. According to Kant, what is the only thing in the world that is good without limitation?
2. What does Kant mean by acting from duty?
3. How does Kant differentiate between a hypothetical and a categorical imperative?
4. By what argument does Kant seek to prove that the first formulation of the categorical imperative demonstrates the immorality of your making a promise you don't intend to keep?

Utilitarianism

JOHN STUART MILL

John Stuart Mill (1806–1873) was the leading English philosopher of the nineteenth century. Whereas Kant's ethical system concentrates exclusively on the reason for an action and does not take account of its results, Mill's system focuses only on consequences. Mill defends utilitarianism, the view that the supreme principle of morality is to act so as to produce as much happiness as possible, each person counting equally. By "happiness" Mill means pleasure and the absence of pain. He grants, however, that some pleasures are more worthwhile than others. "It is . . . better to be Socrates dissatisfied than a fool satisfied." His evidence for this claim is that anyone who knew the lives of both would choose the former rather than the latter.

Utilitarianism provides a means of dealing with the quandary of conflicting obligations. For instance, suppose you promised to meet someone for lunch but on the way encounter a child in need of immediate aid. What should you do? Utilitarianism solves the problem by telling you to give priority to helping the child because that course of action will produce more happiness. Shouldn't we keep our promises? Mill says that usually we should because the practice of keeping one's promises produces important social benefits. An exception should be made, however, on those occasions when more happiness will be produced by not keeping a promise.

CHAPTER II

WHAT UTILITARIANISM IS

. . . The creed which accepts as the foundation of morals "utility" or the "greatest happiness principle" holds that actions are right in proportion as they tend to promote happiness; wrong as they tend to produce the reverse of happiness. By happiness is intended pleasure and the absence of pain; by unhappiness, pain and the privation of pleasure. To give a clear view of the moral standard set up by the theory, much more requires to be said; in particular, what things it includes in

From John Stuart Mill, *Utilitarianism*, (1863).

the ideas of pain and pleasure, and to what extent this is left an open question. But these supplementary explanations do not affect the theory of life on which this theory of morality is grounded—namely, that pleasure and freedom from pain are the only things desirable as ends; and that all desirable things (which are as numerous in the utilitarian as in any other scheme) are desirable either for pleasure inherent in themselves or as means to the promotion of pleasure and the prevention of pain. . . .

It is quite compatible with the principle of utility to recognize the fact that some kinds of pleasure are more desirable and more valuable than others. It would be absurd that, while in estimating all other things quality is considered as well as quantity, the estimation of pleasure should be supposed to depend on quantity alone.

If I am asked what I mean by difference of quality in pleasures, or what makes one pleasure more valuable than another, merely as a pleasure, except its being greater in amount, there is but one possible answer. Of two pleasures, if there be one to which all or almost all who have experience of both give a decided preference, irrespective of any feeling of moral obligation to prefer it, that is the more desirable pleasure. If one of the two is, by those who are competently acquainted with both, placed so far above the other that they prefer it, even though knowing it to be attended with a greater amount of discontent, and would not resign it for any quantity of the other pleasure which their nature is capable of, we are justified in ascribing to the preferred enjoyment a superiority in quality so far outweighing quantity as to render it, in comparison, of small account.

Now it is an unquestionable fact that those who are equally acquainted with and equally capable of appreciating and enjoying both do give a most marked preference to the manner of existence which employs their higher faculties. Few human creatures would consent to be changed into any of the lower animals for a promise of the fullest allowance of a beast's pleasures; no

intelligent human being would consent to be a fool, no instructed person would be an ignoramus, no person of feeling and conscience would be selfish and base, even though they should be persuaded that the fool, the dunce, or the rascal is better satisfied with his lot than they are with theirs. They would not resign what they possess more than he for the most complete satisfaction of all the desires which they have in common with him. If they ever fancy they would, it is only in cases of unhappiness so extreme that to escape from it they would exchange their lot for almost any other, however undesirable in their own eyes. A being of higher faculties requires more to make him happy, is capable probably of more acute suffering, and certainly accessible to it at more points, than one of an inferior type; but in spite of these liabilities, he can never really wish to sink into what he feels to be a lower grade of existence. . . .

It is better to be a human being dissatisfied than a pig satisfied; better to be Socrates dissatisfied than a fool satisfied. And if the fool, or the pig, are of a different opinion, it is because they only know their own side of the question. The other party to the comparison knows both sides. . . .

From this verdict of the only competent judges, I apprehend there can be no appeal. On a question which is the best worth having of two pleasures, or which of two modes of existence is the most grateful to the feelings, apart from its moral attributes and from its consequences, the judgment of those who are qualified by knowledge of both, or, if they differ, that of the majority among them, must be admitted as final. And there needs be the less hesitation to accept this judgment respecting the quality of pleasures, since there is no other tribunal to be referred to even on the question of quantity. What means are there of determining which is the acutest of two pains, or the intensest of two pleasurable sensations, except the general suffrage of those who are familiar with both? . . .

I have dwelt on this point as being a necessary part of a perfectly just conception of utility or happiness considered as the directive rule of human conduct. But it is by no means an indispensable condition to the acceptance of the utilitarian standard; for that standard is not the agent's own greatest happiness, but the greatest amount of happiness altogether; and if it may possibly be doubted whether a noble character is always the happier for its nobleness, there can be no doubt that it makes other people happier, and that the world in general is immensely a gainer by it. Utilitarianism, therefore, could only attain its end by the general cultivation of nobleness of character, even if each individual were only benefited by the nobleness of others, and his own, so far as happiness is concerned, were a sheer deduction from the benefit. But the bare enunciation of such an absurdity as this last renders refutation superfluous.

According to the greatest happiness principle, as above explained, the ultimate end, with reference to and for the sake of which all other things are desirable—whether we are considering our own good or that of other people—is an existence exempt as far as possible from pain, and as rich as possible in enjoyments, both in point of quantity and quality; the test of quality and the rule for measuring it against quantity being the preference felt by those who, in their opportunities of experience, to which must be added their habits of self-consciousness and self-observation, are best furnished with the means of comparison. This, being according to the utilitarian opinion the end of human action, is necessarily also the standard of morality, which may accordingly be defined "the rules and precepts for human conduct," by the observance of which an existence such as has been described might be, to the greatest extent possible, secured to all mankind; and not to them only, but, so far as the nature of things admits, to the whole sentient creation. . . .

I must again repeat what the assailants of utilitarianism seldom have the justice to acknowledge, that the happiness which forms the utilitarian standard of what is right in conduct is not the agent's own happiness but that of all concerned. As between his own happiness and that of others, utilitarianism requires him to be as strictly impartial as a disinterested and benevolent spectator. In the golden rule of Jesus of Nazareth, we read the complete spirit of the ethics of utility. "To do as you would be done by," and "to love your neighbor as yourself," constitute the ideal perfection of utilitarian morality. As the means of making the nearest approach to this ideal, utility would enjoin, first, that laws and social arrangements should place the happiness or (as, speaking practically, it may be called) the interest of every individual as nearly as possible in harmony with the interest of the whole; and, secondly, that education and opinion, which have so vast a power over human character, should so use that power as to establish in the mind of every individual an indissoluble association between his own happiness and the good of the whole, especially between his own happiness and the practice of such modes of conduct, negative and positive, as regard for the universal happiness prescribes; so that not only he may be unable to conceive the possibility of happiness to himself, consistently with conduct opposed to the general good, but also that a direct impulse to promote the general good may be in every individual one of the habitual motives of action, and the sentiments connected therewith may fill a large and prominent place in every human being's sentient existence. If the impugners of the utilitarian morality represented it to their own minds in this its true character, I know not what recommendation possessed by any other morality they could possibly affirm to be wanting to it; what more beautiful or more exalted developments of human nature any other ethical system can be supposed to foster, or what springs of action, not accessible to the utilitarian, such systems rely on for giving effect to their mandates.

The objectors to utilitarianism cannot always be charged with representing it in a discreditable light. On the contrary, those among them who entertain anything like a just idea of its disinterested character sometimes find fault with its standard as being too high for humanity. They say it is exacting too much to require that people shall always act from the inducement of promoting the general interests of society. But this is to mistake the very meaning of a standard of morals and confound the rule of action with the motive of it. It is the business of ethics to tell us what are our duties, or by what test we may know them; but no system of ethics requires that the sole motive of all we do shall be a feeling of duty; on the contrary, ninety-nine hundredths of all our actions are done from other motives, and rightly so done if the rule of duty does not condemn them. It is the more unjust to utilitarianism that this particular misapprehension should be made a ground of objection to it, inasmuch as utilitarian moralists have gone beyond almost all others in affirming that the motive has nothing to do with the morality of the action, though much with the worth of the agent. He who saves a fellow creature from drowning does what is morally right, whether his motive be duty or the hope of being paid for his trouble; he who betrays the friend that trusts him is guilty of a crime, even if his object be to serve another friend to whom he is under greater obligations. But to speak only of actions done from the motive of duty, and in direct obedience to principle: it is a misapprehension of the utilitarian mode of thought to conceive it as implying that people should fix their minds upon so wide a generality as the world, or society at large. The great majority of good actions are intended not for the benefit of the world, but for that of individuals, of which the good of the world is made up; and the thoughts of the most virtuous man need not on these occasions travel beyond the particular persons concerned, except so far as is necessary to assure himself that in benefiting them he is not violating the rights, that is, the legitimate and authorized expectations, of anyone else. The multiplication of happiness is, according to the utilitarian ethics, the object of virtue: the occasions on which any person (except one in a thousand) has it in his power to do this on an extended scale—in other words, to be a public benefactor—are but exceptional; and on these occasions alone is he called on to consider public utility; in every other case, private utility, the interest or happiness of some few persons, is all he has to attend to. Those alone the influence of whose actions extends to society in general need concern themselves habitually about so large an object. In the case of abstinences indeed—of things which people forbear to do from moral considerations, though the consequences in the particular case might be beneficial—it would be unworthy of an intelligent agent not to be consciously aware that the action is of a class which, if practiced generally, would be generally injurious, and that this is the ground of the obligation to abstain from it. The amount of regard for the public interest implied in this recognition is no greater than is demanded by every system of morals, for they all enjoin to abstain from whatever is manifestly pernicious to society. . . .

Again, utility is often summarily stigmatized as an immoral doctrine by giving it the name of "expediency," and taking advantage of the popular use of that term to contrast it with principle. But the expedient, in the sense in which it is opposed to the right, generally means that which is expedient for the particular interest of the agent himself; as when a minister sacrifices the interests of his country to keep himself in place. When it means anything better than this, it means that which is expedient for some immediate object, some temporary purpose, but which violates a rule whose observance is expedient in a much higher degree. The expedient, in this sense, instead of being the same thing with the useful, is a branch of the hurtful. Thus it would often be expedient, for the purpose of getting over some momentary embarrassment, or attaining some object immediately useful to ourselves or others, to tell a lie. But inasmuch as the cultivation in ourselves of a sensitive feeling on the subject of veracity is one of the most useful, and the enfeeblement of that feeling one of the most hurtful, things to which our conduct can be instrumental; and inasmuch as any, even unintentional, deviation from truth does that much toward weakening the trustworthiness of human assertion, which is not only the principal support of all present social well-being, but the insufficiency of which does more than any one thing that can be named to keep back civilization, virtue, everything on which human happiness on the largest scale depends—we feel that the violation, for a present advantage, of a rule of such transcendent expediency is not expedient, and that he who, for the sake of convenience to himself or to some other individual, does what depends on him to deprive mankind of the good, and inflict upon them the evil, involved in the greater or less reliance which they can place in each other's word, acts the part of one of their worst enemies. Yet that even this rule, sacred as it is, admits of possible exceptions is acknowledged by all moralists; the chief of which is when the withholding of some fact (as of information from a malefactor, or of bad news from a person dangerously ill) would save an individual (especially an individual other than oneself) from great and unmerited evil, and when the withholding can only be effected by denial. But in order that the exception may not extend itself beyond the need, and may have the least possible effect in weakening reliance on veracity, it ought to be recognized and, if possible, its limits defined; and, if the principle of utility is good for anything, it must be good for weighing these conflicting utilities against one another and marking out the region within which one or the other preponderates.

CHAPTER IV

OF WHAT SORT OF PROOF THE PRINCIPLE OF UTILITY IS SUSCEPTIBLE

. . . Questions about ends are, in other words, questions about what things are desirable. The utilitarian doctrine is that happiness is desirable, and the only thing desirable, as an end; all other things being only desirable as means to that end. What ought to be required of this doctrine, what conditions is it requisite that the doctrine should fulfill—to make good its claim to be believed?

The only proof capable of being given that an object is visible is that people actually see it. The only proof that a sound is audible is that people hear it; and so of the other sources of our experience. In like manner, I apprehend, the sole evidence it is possible to produce that anything is desirable is that people do actually desire it. If the end which the utilitarian doctrine proposes to itself were not, in theory and in practice, acknowledged to be an end, nothing could ever convince any person that it was so. No reason can be given why the general happiness is desirable, except that each person, so far as he believes it to be attainable, desires his own happiness. This, however, being a fact, we have not only all the proof which the case admits of, but all which it is possible to require, that happiness is a good, that each person's happiness is a good to that person, and the general happiness, therefore, a good to the aggregate of all persons. Happiness has made out its title as *one* of the ends of conduct and, consequently, one of the criteria of morality.

But it has not, by this alone, proved itself to be the sole criterion. To do that, it would seem, by the same rule, necessary to show, not only that people desire happiness, but that they never desire anything else. Now it is palpable that they do desire things which, in common language, are decidedly distinguished from happiness. They desire, for example, virtue and the absence of vice no less really than pleasure and the absence of pain. The desire of virtue is not as universal, but it is as authentic a fact as the desire of happiness. And hence the opponents of the utilitarian standard deem that they have a right to infer that there are other ends of human action besides happiness, and that happiness is not the standard of approbation and disapprobation.

But does the utilitarian doctrine deny that people desire virtue, or maintain that virtue is not a thing to be desired? The very reverse. It maintains not only that virtue is to be desired, but that it is to be desired disinterestedly, for itself. Whatever may be the opinion of utilitarian moralists as to the original conditions by which virtue is made virtue, however they may believe (as they do) that actions and dispositions are only virtuous because they promote another end than virtue, yet this being granted, and it having been decided, from considerations of this description, what *is* virtuous, they not only place virtue at the very head of the things which are good as means to the ultimate end, but they also recognize as a psychological fact the possibility of its being, to the individual, a good in itself, without looking to any end beyond it; and hold that the mind is not in a right state, not in a state conformable to utility, not in the state most conducive to the general happiness, unless it does love virtue in this manner—as a thing desirable in itself, even although, in the individual instance, it should not produce those other desirable consequences which it tends to produce, and on account of which it is held to be virtue. This opinion is not, in the smallest degree, a departure from the happiness principle. The ingredients of happiness are very various, and each of them is desirable in itself, and not merely when considered as swelling an aggregate. The principle of utility does not mean that any given pleasure, as music, for instance, or any given exemption from pain, as for example health, is to be looked upon as means to a collective something termed happiness, and to be desired on that account. They are desired and desirable in and for themselves; besides being means, they are a part of the end. Virtue, according to the utilitarian doctrine is not naturally and originally part of the end, but it is capable of becoming so; and in those who live it disinterestedly it has become so, and is desired and cherished, not as a means to happiness, but as a part of their happiness.

To illustrate this further, we may remember that virtue is not the only thing originally a means, and which if it were not a means to anything else would be and remain indifferent, but which by association with what it is a means to comes to be desired for itself, and that too with the utmost intensity. What, for example, shall we say of the love of money? There is nothing originally more desirable about money than about any heap of glittering pebbles. Its worth is solely that of the things which it will buy; the desires for other things than itself, which it is a means of gratifying. Yet the love of money is not only one of the strongest moving forces of human life, but money is, in many cases, desired in and for itself; the desire to possess it is often stronger than the desire to use it, and goes on increasing when all the desires which point to ends beyond it, to be compassed by it, are falling off. It may, then, be said truly that money is desired not for the sake of an end, but as part of the end. From being a means to happiness, it has come to be itself a principal ingredient of the individual's conception of happiness. The same may be said of the majority of the great objects of human life: power, for example, or fame, except that to each of these there is a certain amount of immediate pleasure annexed, which has at least the semblance of being naturally inherent in them—a thing which cannot be said of money. Still, however, the strongest natural attraction, both of power and of fame, is the immense aid they give to the attainment of our other wishes; and it is the strong association thus generated between them and all our objects of desire which gives to the direct desire of them the intensity it often assumes, so as in some characters to surpass in strength all other desires. In these cases the means have become a part of the end, and a more important part of it than any of the things which they are means to. What was once desired as an instrument for the attainment of happiness has come to be desired for its own sake. In being desired for its own sake it is, however, desired as *part* of happiness. The person is made, or thinks he would be made, happy by its mere possession; and is made unhappy by failure to obtain it. The desire of it is not a different thing from the desire of happiness any more than the love of music or the desire of health. They are included in happiness. They are some of the elements of which the desire of happiness is made up. Happiness is not an abstract idea but a concrete whole; and these are some of its parts. And the utilitarian standard sanctions and approves their being so. Life would be a poor thing, very ill provided with sources of happiness, if there were not this provision of nature by which things originally indifferent, but conducive to, or otherwise associated with, the satisfaction of our primitive desires, become in themselves sources of pleasure more valuable than the primitive pleasures, both in permanency, in the space of human existence that they are capable of covering, and even in intensity.

Virtue, according to the utilitarian conception, is a good of this description. There was no original desire of it, or motive to it, save its conduciveness to pleasure, and especially to protection from pain. But through the association thus formed it may be felt a good in itself, and desired as such with as great intensity as any other good; and with this difference between it and the love of money, of power, or of fame—that all of these may, and often do, render the individual noxious to the other members of the society to which he belongs, whereas there is nothing which makes him so much a blessing to them as the cultivation of the disinterested love of virtue. And consequently, the utilitarian standard, while it tolerates and approves those other acquired desires, up to the point beyond which they would be more injurious to the general happiness than promotive of it, enjoins and requires the cultivation of the love of virtue up to the greatest strength possible, as being above all things important to the general happiness.

It results from the preceding considerations that there is in reality nothing desired except happiness. Whatever is desired otherwise than as a means to some end beyond itself, and ultimately to happiness, is desired as itself a part of happiness, and is not desired for itself until it has become so. Those who desire virtue for its own sake desire it either because the consciousness of it is a pleasure, or because the consciousness of being without it is a pain, or for both reasons united, as in truth the pleasure and pain seldom exist separately, but almost always together—the same person feeling pleasure in the degree of virtue attained, and pain in not having attained more. If one of these gave him no pleasure, and the other no pain, he would not love or desire virtue, or would desire it only for the other benefits which it might produce to himself or to persons whom he cared for.

We have now, then, an answer to the question, of what sort of proof the principle of utility is susceptible.

Study Questions

1. According to Mill, is the agent's own happiness the standard of right conduct?
2. Are some types of pleasure more worthwhile than others?
3. Why does Mill believe lying is wrong?
4. Does Mill believe the principle of utilitarianism can be proven?

The Nature of Virtue

ARISTOTLE

Aristotle had an enormous impact on the development of Western thought. He grounds morality in human nature, viewing the good as the fulfillment of the human potential to live well. To live well is to live in accordance with virtue. But how does one acquire virtue? Aristotle's answer is that we acquire it by habit; one becomes good by doing good. Repeated acts of justice and self-control result in a just, self-controlled person who not only performs just and self-controlled actions but does so from a fixed character. The virtuous act is a mean between two extremes, which are vices; for example, courage is the mean between rashness and cowardice.

Every art and every inquiry, and similarly every action and pursuit, is thought to aim at some good; and for this reason the good has rightly been declared to be that at which all things aim. . . .

If, then, there is some end of the things we do, which we desire for its own sake (everything else being desired for the sake of this), . . . clearly this must be . . . the chief good. . . .

Now such a thing happiness, above all else, is held to be; for this we choose always for itself and never for the sake of something else. . . .

Presumably, however, to say that happiness is the chief good seems a platitude, and a clearer account of what it is is still desired. This might perhaps be given, if we could first ascertain the function of man. For just as for a flute player, a sculptor, or any artist, and, in general, for all things that have a function or activity, the good and the "well" is thought to reside in the function, so would it seem to be for man, if he has a function. Have the carpenter, then, and the tanner certain functions or activities, and has man none? Is he born without a function? Or as eye, hand, foot, and in general each of the parts

evidently has a function, may one lay it down that man similarly has a function apart from all these? What then can this be? Life seems to belong even to plants, but we are seeking what is peculiar to man. Let us exclude, therefore, the life of nutrition and growth. Next there would be a life of perception, but *it* also seems to be shared even by the horse, the ox, and every animal. There remains, then, an active life of the element that has a rational principle. . . . Now if the function of man is an activity of soul which follows or implies a rational principle, and if . . . any action is well performed when it is performed in accordance with the appropriate excellence . . . human good turns out to be activity of soul exhibiting excellence. . . .

But we must add "in a complete life." For one swallow does not make a summer, nor does one day; and so too one day, or a short time, does not make a man blessed and happy. . . .

Virtue, then, being of two kinds, intellectual and moral, intellectual virtue in the main owes both its birth and its growth to teaching (for which reason it requires experience and time), while moral virtue comes about as a result of habit. . . . From this it is also plain that none of the moral virtues arises in us by nature; for nothing that exists by nature can form a habit contrary to its nature. For instance, the stone which by nature moves downwards cannot be habituated to move upwards, not even if one tries to train it by throwing it up ten thousand times; nor can fire be habituated to move downwards, nor can anything else that by nature behaves in one way be trained to behave in another. Neither by nature, then, nor contrary to nature do the virtues arise in us; rather we are adapted by nature to receive them, and are made perfect by habit.

Again, of all the things that come to us by nature we first acquire the potentiality and later exhibit the activity (this is plain in the case of the senses; for it was not by often seeing or often hearing that we got these senses, but on the contrary we had them before we used them, and did not come to have them by using them); but the virtues we get by first exercising them, as also happens in the case of the arts as well. For the things we have to learn before we can do them, we learn by doing them, e.g., men become builders by building and lyre players by playing the lyre; so too we become just by doing just acts, temperate by doing temperate acts, brave by doing brave acts. . . .

It makes no small difference, then, whether we form habits of one kind or of another from our very youth; it makes a very great difference, or rather *all* the difference.

Since, then, the present inquiry does not aim at theoretical knowledge like the others (for we are inquiring not in order to know what virtue is, but in order to become good, since otherwise our inquiry would have been of no use), we must examine the nature of actions, namely, how we ought to do them; for these determine also the nature of the states of character that are produced, as we have said. . . .

First, then, let us consider this, that it is the nature of such things to be destroyed by defect and excess, as we see in the case of strength and of health (for to gain light on things imperceptible

we must use the evidence of sensible things); exercise either excessive or defective destroys the strength, and similarly drink or food which is above or below a certain amount destroys the health, while that which is proportionate both produces and increases and preserves it. So too is it, then, in the case of temperance and courage and the other virtues. For the man who flies from and fears everything and does not stand his ground against anything becomes a coward, and the man who fears nothing at all but goes to meet every danger becomes rash; and similarly the man who indulges in every pleasure and abstains from none becomes self-indulgent, while the man who shuns every pleasure, as boors do, becomes in a way insensible; temperance and courage, then, are destroyed by excess and defect, and preserved by the mean.

But not only are the sources and causes of their origination and growth the same as those of their destruction, but also the sphere of their actualization will be the same; for this is also true of the things which are more evident to sense, e.g., of strength; it is produced by taking much food and undergoing much exertion, and it is the strong man that will be most able to do these things. So too is it with the virtues; by abstaining from pleasures we become temperate, and it is when we have become so that we are most able to abstain from them; and similarly too in the case of courage; for by being habituated to despise things that are fearful and to stand our ground against them we become brave, and it is when we have become so that we shall be most able to stand our ground against them. . . .

The question might be asked what we mean by saying that we must become just by doing just acts, and temperate by doing temperate acts; for if men do just and temperate acts, they are already just and temperate, exactly as if they do what is in accordance with the laws of grammar and of music, they are grammarians and musicians.

Or is this not true even of the arts? It is possible to do something that is in accordance with the laws of grammar, either by chance or under the guidance of another. A man will be a grammarian, then, only when he has both said something grammatical and said it grammatically; and this means doing it in accordance with the grammatical knowledge in himself.

Again, the case of the arts and that of the virtues are not similar; for the products of the arts have their goodness in themselves, so that it is enough that they should have a certain character, but if the acts that are in accordance with the virtues have themselves a certain character it does not follow that they are done justly or temperately. The agent also must be in a certain condition when he does them; in the first place he must have knowledge, secondly he must choose the acts, and choose them for their own sakes, and thirdly his action must proceed from a firm and unchangeable character. These are not reckoned in as conditions of the possession of the arts, except the bare knowledge, but as a condition of the possession of the virtues knowledge has little or no weight, while the other conditions count not for a little but for everything, i.e., the very conditions which result from often doing just and temperate acts.

Actions, then, are called just and temperate when they are such as the just or the temperate man would do; but it is not the man who does these that is just and temperate, but the man who also does them *as* just and temperate men do them. It is well said, then, that it is by doing just acts that the just man is produced, and by doing temperate acts the temperate man; without doing these no one would have even a prospect of becoming good.

But most people do not do these, but take refuge in theory and think they are being philosophers and will become good in this way, behaving somewhat like patients who listen attentively to their doctors, but do none of the things they are ordered to do. As the latter will not be made well in body by such a course of treatment, the former will not be made well in soul by such a course of philosophy. . . .

[E]very virtue or excellence both brings into good condition the thing of which it is the excellence and makes the work of that thing be done well; e.g., the excellence of the eye makes both the eye and its work good; for it is by the excellence of the eye that we see well. Similarly the excellence of the horse makes a horse both good in itself and good at running and at carrying its rider and at awaiting the attack of the enemy. Therefore, if this is true in every case, the virtue of man also will be the state of character which makes a man good and which makes him do his own work well.

How this is to happen we have stated already, but it will be made plain also by the following consideration of the specific nature of virtue. In everything that is continuous and divisible it is possible to take more, less, or an equal amount, and that either in terms of the thing itself or relatively to us; and the equal is an intermediate between excess and defect. By the intermediate in the object I mean that which is equidistant from each of the extremes, which is one and the same for all men; by the intermediate relatively to us that which is neither too much nor too little—and this is not one, nor the same for all. For instance, if ten is many and two is few, six is the intermediate, taken in terms of the object; for it exceeds and is exceeded by an equal amount; this is intermediate according to arithmetical proportion. But the intermediate relatively to us is not to be taken so; if ten pounds are too much for a particular person to eat and two too little, it does not follow that the trainer will order six pounds; for this also is perhaps too much for the person who is to take it, or too little—too little for Milo, too much for the beginner in athletic exercises. The same is true of running and wrestling. Thus a master of any art avoids excess and defect, but seeks the intermediate and chooses this—the intermediate not in the object but relatively to us.

If it is thus, then, that every art does its work well—by looking to the intermediate and judging its works by this standard (so that we often say of good works of art that it is not possible either to take away or to add anything, implying that excess and defect destroy the goodness of works of art, while the mean preserves it; and good artists, as we say, look to this in their work), and if, further, virtue is more exact and better than any art, as nature also is, then virtue must have the quality of aiming at the intermediate. I mean moral virtue; for it is this that is concerned with passions and actions, and in these there is excess, defect, and the intermediate. For instance, both fear and confidence and appetite and anger and pity and in general pleasure and pain may be felt both too much and too little, and in both cases not well; but to feel them at the right times, with reference to the right objects, towards the right people, with the right motive, and in the right way, is what is both intermediate and best, and this is characteristic of virtue. Similarly with regard to actions also there is excess, defect, and the intermediate. Now virtue is concerned with passions and actions, in which excess is a form of failure, and so is defect, while the intermediate is praised and is a form of success; and being praised and being successful are both characteristics of virtue. Therefore virtue is a kind of mean, since, as we have seen, it aims at what is intermediate. . . .

But not every action nor every passion admits of a mean; for some have names that already imply badness, e.g., spite, shamelessness, envy, and in the case of actions adultery, theft, murder; for all of these and suchlike things imply by their names that they are themselves bad, and not the excesses or deficiencies of them. It is not possible, then, ever to be right with regard to them; one must always be wrong. Nor does goodness or badness with regard to such things depend on committing adultery with the right woman, at the right time, and in the right way, but simply to do any of them is to go wrong. . . .

The moral virtue is a mean, then, and in what sense it is so, and that it is a mean between two vices, the one involving excess, the other deficiency, and that it is such because its character is to aim at what is intermediate in passions and in actions, has been sufficiently stated. Hence also it is no easy task to be good. For in everything it is no easy task to find the middle, e.g., to find the middle of a circle is not for everyone but for him who knows; so, too, anyone can get angry—that is easy—or give or spend money; but to do this to the right person, to the right extent, at the right time, with the right motive, and in the right way, *that* is not for everyone, nor is it easy; wherefore goodness is both rare and laudable and noble. . . .

But we must consider the things towards which we ourselves also are easily carried away; for some of us tend to one thing, some to another; and this will be recognizable from the pleasure and the pain we feel. We must drag ourselves away to the contrary extreme; for we shall get into the intermediate state by drawing well away from error. . . .

So much, then, is plain, that the intermediate state is in all things to be praised, but that we must incline sometimes towards the excess, sometimes towards the deficiency; for so shall we most easily hit the mean and what is right.

Study Questions

1. According to Aristotle, what is the function of a human being?
2. How does moral virtue differ from intellectual virtue?
3. How is moral virtue acquired?
4. What is Aristotle's doctrine of the mean?

The Ethics of Care

VIRGINIA HELD

Aristotelian ethics focuses not on what rules should be followed but on what sort of person I should be. Modern forms of this approach are known as "virtue ethics," which in a later reading we shall see applied to the problem of abortion. Now, however, we consider a related approach that has come to be known as "the ethics of care." Here it is explained by Virginia Held, Professor Emerita of Philosophy at Hunter College and the Graduate Center of the City University of New York.

I

The ethics of care is only a few decades old. Some theorists do not like the term "care" to designate this approach to moral issues and have tried substituting "the ethic of love," or "relational ethics," but the discourse keeps returning to "care" as the so far more satisfactory of the terms considered, though dissatisfactions with it remain. The concept of care has the advantage of not losing sight of the work involved in caring for people and of not lending itself to the interpretation of morality as ideal but impractical to which advocates of the ethics of care often object. . . .

I think one can discern among various versions of the ethics of care a number of major features.

First, the central focus of the ethics of care is on the compelling moral salience of attending to and meeting the needs of the particular others for whom we take responsibility. Caring for one's child, for instance, may well and defensibly be at the forefront of a person's moral concerns. The ethics of care recognizes that human beings are dependent for many years of their lives, that the moral claims of those dependent on us for the care they need is pressing, and that there are highly important moral aspects in developing the relations of caring that enable human beings to live and progress. All persons need care for at least their early years. Prospects for human progress and flourishing hinge fundamentally on the care that those needing it receive, and the ethics of care stresses the moral force of the responsibility to respond to the needs of the dependent. Many persons will become ill and dependent for some periods of their later lives, including in frail old age, and some who are permanently disabled will need care the whole of their lives. Moralities built on the image of the independent, autonomous, rational individual largely overlook the reality of human dependence and the morality for which it calls. The ethics of care attends to this central concern of human life and delineates the moral values involved. . . .

Second, in the epistemological process of trying to understand what morality would recommend and what it would be morally best for us to do and to be, the ethics of care values emotion rather than rejects it. Not all emotion is valued, of course, but in contrast with the dominant rationalist approaches, such emotions as sympathy, empathy, sensitivity, and responsiveness are seen as the kind of moral emotions that need to be cultivated not only to help in the implementation of the dictates of reason but to better ascertain what morality recommends. Even anger may be a component of the moral indignation that should be felt when people are treated unjustly or inhumanely, and it may contribute to (rather than interfere with) an appropriate interpretation of the moral wrong. This is not to say that raw emotion can be a guide to morality; feelings need to be reflected on and educated. But from the care perspective, moral inquiries that rely entirely on reason and rationalistic deductions or calculations are seen as deficient.

The emotions that are typically considered and rejected in rationalistic moral theories are the egoistic feelings that undermine universal moral norms, the favoritism that interferes with impartiality, and the aggressive and vengeful impulses for which morality is to provide restraints. The ethics of care, in contrast, typically appreciates the emotions and relational capabilities that enable morally concerned persons in actual interpersonal contexts to understand what would be best. Since even the helpful emotions can often become misguided or worse—as when excessive empathy with others leads to a wrongful degree of self-denial or when benevolent concern crosses over into controlling domination—we need an *ethics* of care, not just care itself. The various aspects and expressions of care and caring relations need to be subjected to moral scrutiny and *evaluated*, not just observed and described.

Third, the ethics of care rejects the view of the dominant moral theories that the more abstract the reasoning about a moral problem the better because the more likely to avoid bias and arbitrariness, the more nearly to achieve impartiality. The ethics of care respects rather than removes itself from the claims of particular others with whom we share actual relationships. It calls into question the universalistic and abstract rules of the dominant theories. When the latter consider such actual relations as between a parent and child, if they say anything about them at all, they may see them as permitted and cultivating them a preference that a person may have. Or they may recognize a universal obligation for all parents to care for their children. But they do not permit actual relations ever to take priority over the requirements of impartiality. . . .

The ethics of care may seek to limit the applicability of universal rules to certain domains where they are more appropriate, like the domain of law, and resist their extension to other domains. Such rules may simply be inappropriate in, for instance, the contexts of family and friendship, yet relations in these domains should certainly be *evaluated*, not merely described, hence morality should not be limited to abstract rules. We should be able to give moral guidance concerning actual relations that are trusting, considerate, and caring and concerning those that are not.

Dominant moral theories tend to interpret moral problems as if they were conflicts between egoistic individual interests on the one hand, and universal moral principles on the other. The extremes of "selfish individual" and "humanity" are recognized, but what lies between these is often overlooked. The ethics of care, in contrast, focuses especially on the area between these extremes. Those who conscientiously care for others are not seeking primarily to further their own *individual* interests; their interests are intertwined with the persons they care for. Neither are they acting for the sake of *all others* or *humanity in general*; they seek instead to preserve or promote an actual human relation between themselves and *particular others*. Persons in caring relations are acting for self-and-other together. Their characteristic stance is neither egoistic nor altruistic; these are the options in a conflictual situation, but the well-being of a caring relation involves the cooperative well-being of those in the relation and the well-being of the relation itself. . . .

II

What *is* care? What do we mean by the term "care"? Can we define it in anything like a precise way? There is not yet anything close to agreement among those writing on care on what exactly we should take the meaning of this term to be, but there have been many suggestions, tacit and occasionally explicit.

For over two decades, the concept of care as it figures in the ethics of care has been assumed, explored, elaborated, and employed in the development of theory. But definitions have often been imprecise, or trying to arrive at them has simply been postponed (as in my own case), in the growing discourse. Perhaps this is entirely appropriate for new explorations, but the time may have come to seek greater clarity. Some of those writing on care have attempted to be precise, with mixed results, whereas others have proceeded with the tacit understanding that of course to a considerable extent we know what we are talking about when we speak of taking care of a child or providing care for the ill. But care has many forms, and as the ethics of care evolves, so should our understanding of what care is.

The last words I spoke to my older brother after a brief visit and with special feeling were: "take care." He had not been taking good care of himself, and I hoped he would do better; not many days later he died, of problems quite possibly unrelated to those to which I had been referring. "Take care" was not an expression he and I grew up with. I acquired it over the years in my life in New York City. It may be illuminating to begin thinking about the meaning of "care" with an examination of this expression.

We often say "take care" as routinely as "goodbye" or some abbreviation and with as little emotion. But even then it does convey some sense of connectedness. More often, when said with some feeling, it means something like "take care of yourself because I care about you." Sometimes we say it, especially to children or to

someone embarking on a trip or an endeavor, meaning "I care what happens to you, so please don't do anything dangerous or foolish." Or, if we know the danger is inevitable and inescapable, it may be more like a wish that the elements will let the person take care so the worst can be evaded. And sometimes we mean it as a plea: Be careful not to harm yourself or others because our connection will make us feel with and for you. We may be harmed ourselves or partly responsible, or if you do something you will regret we will share that regret.

One way or another, this expression (like many others) illustrates human relatedness and the daily reaffirmations of connection. It is the relatedness of human beings, built and rebuilt, that the ethics of care is being developed to try to understand, evaluate, and guide. The expression has more to do with the feelings and awareness of the persons expressing and the persons receiving such expressions than with the actual tasks and work of "taking care" of a person who is dependent on us, or in need of care, but such attitudes and shared awareness seem at least one important component of care.

A seemingly easy distinction to make is between care as the activity of taking care of someone and the mere "caring about" of how we feel about certain issues. Actually "caring for" a small child or a person who is ill is quite different from merely "caring for" something (or not) in the sense of liking it or not, as in "I don't care for that kind of music." But these distinctions may not be as clear as they appear, since when we take care of a child, for instance, we usually also care about him or her, and although we could take care of a child we do not like, the caring will usually be better care if we care for the child in both senses. If we really do care about world hunger, we will probably be doing something about it, such as at least giving money to alleviate it or to change the conditions that bring it about, and thus establishing some connection between ourselves and the hungry we say we care about. And if we really do care about global climate change and the harm it will bring to future generations, we imagine a connection between ourselves and those future people who will judge our irresponsibility, and we change our consumption practices or political activities to decrease the likely harm. . . .

My own view, then, is that care is both a practice and a value. As a practice, it shows us how to respond to needs and why we should. It builds trust and mutual concern and connectedness between persons. It is not a series of individual actions, but a practice that develops, along with its appropriate attitudes. It has attributes and standards that can be described, but more important that can be recommended and that should be continually improved as adequate care comes closer to being good care. Practices of care should express the caring relations that bring persons together, and they should do so in ways that are progressively more morally satisfactory. Caring practices should gradually transform children and others into human beings who are increasingly morally admirable. . . .

In addition to being a practice, care is also a value. Caring persons and caring attitudes should be valued, and we can organize many evaluations of how persons are interrelated around a constellation of moral considerations associated with care or its absence. For instance, we can ask of a relation whether it is trusting and mutually considerate or hostile and vindictive. We can ask if persons are attentive and responsive to each other's needs or indifferent and self-absorbed. Care is not the same as benevolence, in my view, since it is more the characterization of a social relation than the description of an individual disposition, and social relations are not reducible to individual states. Caring relations ought to be cultivated, between persons in their personal lives and between the members of caring societies. Such relations are often reciprocal over time if not at given times. The values of caring are especially exemplified in caring relations, rather than in persons as individuals.

Study Questions

1. According to Held, what is "the ethics of care"?
2. What does Held mean by her claim that care is both a practice and a value?
3. Does the ethics of care focus on acting for the sake of humanity?
4. Does analyzing a moral problem from the perspective of the ethics of care sometimes yield a different result than that obtained by using either a Kantian or utilitarian standard?

Beyond Good and Evil

FRIEDRICH NIETZSCHE

One of the most controversial figures in the history of moral philosophy is Friedrich Nietzsche (1844–1900), a German philosopher and classical scholar who claimed that traditional notions of good and evil embody a "slave morality" that needed to be

From Friedrich Nietzsche, *Beyond Good and Evil: Prelude to a Philosophy of the Future,* translated and edited by Marion Faber. Copyright © 1998. Reprinted by permission of Oxford University Press. The notes are the translator's.

transcended by a higher form of humanity that would lead toward the enhancement of life in a world without God. The following selection offers a sample of his unconventional views and aphoristic style of writing.

201

As long as the utility that dominates moral judgements is still only the utility of the herd, as long as we confine our gaze solely to the preservation of the community, seeking out immorality exactly and exclusively in whatever seems dangerous to communal stability, there can be no 'morality of neighbourly love'. Assuming that here, too, there are already small ongoing acts of consideration, sympathy, fairness, gentleness, reciprocal help; and that at this stage of society, too, all the instincts are already at work that will later be designated by honourable names as 'virtues' and finally fit the concept 'morality'; during this period they are still in no way part of the realm of moral value judgements—they are still *extra-moral*. In the heyday of Rome for example, an act of pity was neither good nor evil, neither moral nor immoral; and even such praise as it may have received could well be accompanied by a kind of irritated disdain as soon as it was compared to an action that served to further the whole, the *res publica*.[1] Ultimately, 'neighbourly love' is always something secondary, in part convention and a deliberate fiction in relation to *fear of one's neighbour*. Once the social structure appears to be more or less established and secured against external dangers, it is this fear of one's neighbour that once again creates new perspectives for moral value judgements. Certain strong and dangerous instincts, such as adventurousness, recklessness, vengefulness, slyness, rapacity, lust for power, were previously not only honoured (by names other than the ones above, of course) as beneficial to the community, but they also had to be cultivated and bred, because people continually had need of them in their common danger against common enemies. But now

(when there are no drainage channels for them) these same instincts are felt to be doubly dangerous and are gradually stigmatized and slandered as immoral. Now the opposite drives and tendencies gain moral respect; step by step, the herd instinct draws its consequences. The moral perspective now considers how harmful or harmless an opinion, an emotional state, a will, a talent is to the community, to equality: here again, fear is the mother of morality. When an individual's highest and strongest instincts break forth with a passion, driving him far above and beyond the average, beyond the lowlands of the herd conscience, the community's self-regard is destroyed as a result; its belief in itself, its backbone, so to speak, is shattered: and that is why people do well to stigmatize and slander just these instincts above all. Exalted, self-directed spirituality, a will to solitude, even great powers of reason are felt as a danger; everything that raises an individual above the herd and causes his neighbour to fear him is henceforth called *evil*; a proper, modest, conforming, equalizing mentality, what is *average* on the scale of desires gains a moral name and respect. Finally, when conditions are very peaceable, there is less and less opportunity or necessity for educating one's feelings to be stern and harsh; and then every kind of sternness, even in matters of justice, begins to trouble the conscience; a harsh, exalted nobility or individual responsibility is almost considered offensive and awakens distrust, whereas 'a lamb', or better yet, 'a sheep' gains in esteem. There can come a point of such sickly morbidity and pampered indulgence in the history of a society that in all due seriousness it even takes the side of the one who does it harm, the *criminal*. Punishing: society thinks there is something unfair about it—it certainly finds the idea of 'punishment' and the 'need to punish' painful and frightening. 'Isn't it enough just to render him *innocuous*? Why do we have to punish him too? Real punishment is awful!'—with this question the herd morality, the morality of timidity, draws its final conclusion. Assuming that we could entirely abolish the danger, the grounds for fear, then we would have abolished this morality as well: it would no longer be necessary, it *would deem itself* no longer necessary!

Anyone who examines the conscience of a present-day European will have to extract from his thousand moral crannies and hiding places the same imperative, the imperative of herdlike timidity: 'At some point, we want there to be *nothing more to be afraid of*!' At some point—the will and the way *to that point* is what everyone in Europe today calls 'progress'.

202

Let us immediately say once again what we have already said a hundred times, for nowadays ears are reluctant to hear such truths—*our* truths. We know perfectly well how offensive it sounds when someone counts man among the animals plain and simple, without metaphorical intent; but we will almost be accounted a *criminal* for always using expressions such as 'herd', 'herd instincts', and the like when speaking about people of 'modern ideas'. What's the use! We can't do otherwise, for this is just what our new insight is about. We discovered that Europe, and those countries dominated by a European influence, are now of one mind in all their key moral judgements: it is obvious that Europeans nowadays *know* that which Socrates thought he did not know, and what that famous old serpent once promised to teach—people 'know' what is good and evil. It must sound harsh and trouble the ears, then, if we insist over and over that it is the instinct of man the herd animal that thinks it knows, that glorifies itself and calls itself good whenever it allots praise or blame. This instinct has had a breakthrough, has come to

predominance, has prevailed over the other instincts and continues to do so as a symptom of the increasing process of physiological approximations and resemblances. *Morality in Europe today is herd animal morality*—and thus, as we understand things, it is only one kind of human morality next to which, before which, after which many others, and especially *higher* moralities, are or should be possible. But this morality defends itself with all its strength against such 'possibilities', against such 'should be's'. Stubbornly and relentlessly it says, 'I am Morality itself, and nothing else is!' Indeed, with the help of a religion that played along with and flattered the most sublime desires of the herd animal, we have reached the point of finding an ever more visible expression of this morality even in political and social structures: the *democratic* movement is Christianity's heir. But its tempo is still far too slow and sleepy for the overeager, for patients or addicts of this above-mentioned instinct, as we can tell from the increasingly frantic howl, the ever more widely bared teeth of the anarchist dogs who now roam the alleys of European culture. They appear to be in conflict with the peaceably industrious democrats or ideologues of revolution, and even more with the foolish philosophasts and brotherhood enthusiasts who call themselves socialists and want a 'free society'; but in reality they are united with those others in their fundamental and instinctive enmity towards every form of society other than *autonomous* herds (right up to the point of even rejecting the concepts 'master' and 'servant'—*ni dieu ni maître*[2] is a socialist motto); united in their tough resistance to every exceptional claim, every exceptional right and privilege (and thus ultimately to *all* rights, for no one needs 'rights' any longer when everyone is equal); united in their distrust of any justice that punishes (as if it were a rape of the weaker party, unjust towards the *necessary* consequence of all earlier society); but also just as united in their religion of pity, in their empathy, wherever there are feelings, lives, or suffering (reaching down to the animal or up to 'God'—the eccentric notion of 'pity for God' suits a democratic age); united one and all in their impatient cry for pity, in their mortal hatred of any suffering, in their almost feminine incapacity to remain a spectator to it, to *allow* suffering; united in the involuntary depression and decadence which seems to hold Europe captive to a threatening new Buddhism; united in their belief in a morality of *communal* pity, as if it were Morality itself, the summit, the *conquered* summit of humankind, the only hope for the future, comfort in the present, the great redemption from all past guilt—united together in their belief in community as a *redeemer,* and thus a belief in the herd, a belief in 'themselves' . . .

203

We who hold a different belief—we who consider the democratic movement not merely a decadent form of political organization, but a decadent (that is to say, diminished) form of the human being, one that mediocritizes him and debases his value: what can *we* set our hopes on?

On *new philosophers,* we have no other choice; on spirits that are strong and original enough to give impetus to opposing value judgements and to revalue, to reverse 'eternal values'; on forerunners, on men of the future, who in the present will forge the necessary link to force a thousand-year-old will onto *new* tracks. They will teach humans that their future is their *will,* that the future depends on their human will, and they will prepare the way for great risk-taking and joint experiments in discipline and breeding in order to put an end to that terrible reign of nonsense and coincidence that until now has been known as 'history' (the nonsense about the 'greatest number' is only its most recent form). To accomplish this, new kinds of philosophers and commanders will eventually be necessary, whose image will make all the secretive, frightful, benevolent spirits that have existed in the world look pale and dwarfish. The image of such leaders is what hovers before *our* eyes—may I say it aloud, you free spirits? The

circumstances that would have to be in part created, in part exploited to give rise to these leaders; the probable paths and tests by which a soul would grow so great and powerful that it would feel *compelled* to accomplish these projects; a revaluation of values, under whose new hammer and pressure the conscience would be transformed into steel, the heart into bronze, so that they could bear the weight of such responsibility; the indispensability of such leaders; on the other hand, the terrible danger that they might not arrive or might go astray and degenerate—those are really the things that concern and worry *us*—do you know that, you free spirits?—those are the distant oppressive thoughts and thunderstorms that pass across the sky of *our* life. There are few pains so raw as to have once observed, understood, sympathized while an extraordinary man strayed from his path or degenerated: but a person with the rare vision to see the general danger that 'man' himself *is degenerating,* who has recognized as we have the tremendous randomness that thus far has been at play in determining the future of mankind (a play that has been guided by no one's hand, not even by 'God's finger!'), who has guessed the fate that lies hidden in all the stupid innocence and blissful confidence of 'modern ideas', and even more in the entire Christian-European morality: this person suffers from an anxiety that cannot be compared to any other. With one single glance he grasps everything that *mankind could be bred to be* if all its energies and endeavours were gathered together and heightened; with all the knowledge of his conscience, he knows how mankind's greatest possibilities have as yet been untapped, and how many mysterious decisions and new paths the human type has already encountered—he knows better yet, from his most painful memory, what kind of wretched things have usually caused the finest example of an evolving being to shatter, break apart, sink down, become wretched. The *overall degeneration of man,* right down to what socialist fools and flatheads call their 'man of the future' (their ideal!); this degeneration and diminution of man into a perfect herd animal (or, as they call it, man in a 'free society'); this bestialization of man into a dwarf animal with equal rights and claims is *possible,* no doubt about that! Anyone who has thought this possibility through to its end knows no disgust but other people—and also, perhaps, a new *project*! . . .

259

To refrain from injuring, abusing, or exploiting one another; to equate another person's will with our own: in a certain crude sense this can develop into good manners between individuals, if the preconditions are in place (that is, if the individuals have truly similar strength and standards and if they are united within one single social body). But if we were to try to take this principle further and possibly even make it the *basic principle of society,* it would immediately be revealed for what it is: a will to *deny* life, a principle for dissolution and decline. We must think through the reasons for this and resist all sentimental frailty: life itself *in its essence* means appropriating, injuring, overpowering those who are foreign and weaker; oppression, harshness, forcing one's own forms on others, incorporation, and at the very least, at the very mildest, exploitation—but why should we keep using this kind of language, that has from time immemorial been infused with a slanderous intent? Even that social body whose individuals, as we have just assumed above, treat one another as equals (this happens in every healthy aristocracy) must itself, if the body is vital and not moribund, do to other bodies everything that the individuals within it refrain from doing to one another: it will have to be the will to power incarnate, it will want to grow, to reach out around itself, pull towards itself, gain the upper hand—not out of some morality or immorality, but because it is *alive,* and because life simply *is* the will to power. This, however, more than anything else, is what the common European consciousness resists learning; people everywhere are rhapsodizing,

even under the guise of science, about future social conditions that will have lost their 'exploitative character'—to my ear that sounds as if they were promising to invent a life form that would refrain from all organic functions. 'Exploitation' is not part of a decadent or imperfect, primitive society: it is part of the *fundamental nature* of living things, as its fundamental organic function; it is a consequence of the true will to power, which is simply the will to life.

Assuming that this is innovative as theory—as reality it is the *original fact* of all history: let us at least be this honest with ourselves!

260

While perusing the many subtler and cruder moral codes that have prevailed or still prevail on earth thus far, I found that certain traits regularly recurred in combination, linked to one another—until finally two basic types were revealed and a fundamental difference leapt out at me. There are *master moralities* and *slave moralities.* I would add at once that in all higher and more complex cultures, there are also apparent attempts to mediate between the two moralities, and even more often a confusion of the two and a mutual misunderstanding, indeed sometimes even their violent juxtaposition—even in the same person, within one single breast. Moral value distinctions have emerged either from among a masterful kind, pleasantly aware of how it differed from those whom it mastered, or else from among the mastered, those who were to varying degrees slaves or dependants. In the first case, when it is the masters who define the concept 'good', it is the proud, exalted states of soul that are thought to distinguish and define the hierarchy. The noble person keeps away from those beings who express the opposite of these elevated, proud inner states: he despises them. Let us note immediately that in this first kind of morality the opposition 'good' and 'bad' means about the same thing as 'noble' and 'despicable'—the opposition 'good' and *'evil'* has a different origin. The person who is cowardly or anxious or petty or concerned with narrow utility is despised; likewise the distrustful person with his constrained gaze, the self-disparager, the craven kind of person who endures maltreatment, the importunate flatterer, and above all the liar: all aristocrats hold the fundamental conviction that the common people are liars. 'We truthful ones'—that is what the ancient Greek nobility called themselves. It is obvious that moral value distinctions everywhere are first attributed to *people* and only later and in a derivative fashion applied to *actions:* for that reason moral historians commit a crass error by starting with questions such as: 'Why do we praise an empathetic action?' The noble type of person feels *himself* as determining value—he does not need approval, he judges that 'what is harmful to me is harmful per se', he knows that he is the one who causes things to be revered in the first place, he *creates values.* Everything that he knows of himself he reveres: this kind of moral code is self-glorifying. In the foreground is a feeling of fullness, of overflowing power, of happiness in great tension, an awareness of a wealth that would like to bestow and share—the noble person will also help the unfortunate, but not, or not entirely, out of pity, but rather from the urgency created by an excess of power. The noble person reveres the power in himself, and also his power over himself, his ability to speak and to be silent, to enjoy the practice of severity and harshness towards himself and to respect everything that is severe and harsh. 'Wotan placed a harsh heart within my breast,' goes a line in an old Scandinavian saga: that is how it is written from the heart of a proud Viking—and rightly so. For this kind of a person is proud *not* to be made for pity; and so the hero of the saga adds a warning: 'If your heart is not harsh when you are young, it will never become harsh.' The noble and brave people who think like this are the most removed from that other moral code which sees the sign of morality in pity or altruistic behaviour or *désintéressement,*[3] belief in ourselves, pride in ourselves, a fundamental hostility and irony towards 'selflessness'—these are as surely a part of a noble morality as caution and a slight disdain towards empathetic feelings and 'warm hearts'.

It is the powerful who *understand* how to revere, it is their art form, their realm of invention. Great reverence for old age and for origins (all law is based upon this twofold reverence), belief in ancestors and prejudice in their favour and to the disadvantage of the next generation—these are typical in the morality of the powerful; and if, conversely, people of 'modern ideas' believe in progress and 'the future' almost by instinct and show an increasing lack of respect for old age, that alone suffices to reveal the ignoble origin of these 'ideas'. Most of all, however, the master morality is foreign and embarrassing to current taste because of the severity of its fundamental principle: that we have duties only towards our peers, and that we may treat those of lower rank, anything foreign, as we think best or 'as our heart dictates' or in any event 'beyond good and evil'—pity and the like should be thought of in this context. The ability and duty to feel enduring gratitude or vengefulness (both only within a circle of equals), subtlety in the forms of retribution, a refined concept of friendship, a certain need for enemies (as drainage channels for the emotions of envy, combativeness, arrogance—in essence, in order to be a good *friend*): these are the typical signs of a noble morality, which, as we have suggested, is not the morality of 'modern ideas' and is therefore difficult to sympathize with these days, also difficult to dig out and uncover.

It is different with the second type of morality, *slave morality.* Assuming that the raped, the oppressed, the suffering, the shackled, the weary, the insecure engage in moralizing, what will their moral value judgements have in common? They will probably express a pessimistic suspicion about the whole human condition, and they might condemn the human being along with his condition. The slave's eye does not readily apprehend the virtues of the powerful: he is sceptical and distrustful, he is *keenly* distrustful of everything that the powerful revere as 'good'—he would like to convince himself that even their happiness is not genuine. Conversely, those qualities that serve to relieve the sufferers' existence are brought into relief and bathed in light: this is where pity, a kind, helpful hand, a warm heart, patience, diligence, humility, friendliness are revered—for in this context, these qualities are most useful and practically the only means of enduring an oppressive existence. Slave morality is essentially a morality of utility. It is upon this hearth that the famous opposition 'good' and '*evil*' originates—power and dangerousness, a certain fear-inducing, subtle strength that keeps contempt from surfacing, are translated by experience into evil. According to slave morality, then, the 'evil' person evokes fear; according to master morality, it is exactly the 'good' person who evokes fear and wants to evoke it, while the 'bad' person is felt to be despicable. The opposition comes to a head when, in terms of slave morality, a hint of condescension (it may be slight and well intentioned) clings even to those whom this morality designates as 'good', since within a slave mentality a good person must in any event be *harmless*: he is good-natured, easily deceived, perhaps a bit stupid, a *bonhomme*.[4] Wherever slave morality gains the upper hand, language shows a tendency to make a closer association of the words 'good' and 'stupid'.

A last fundamental difference: the longing for *freedom,* an instinct for the happiness and nuances of feeling free, is as necessarily a part of slave morals and morality as artistic, rapturous reverence and devotion invariably signal an aristocratic mentality and judgement.

From this we can immediately understand why *passionate* love (our European speciality) absolutely must have a noble origin: the Provençal poet-knights are acknowledged to have invented it, those splendid, inventive people of the '*gai saber*'[5] to whom Europe owes so much—virtually its very self.

261

Among the things that a noble person finds most difficult to understand is vanity: he will be tempted to deny its existence, even when a different kind of person thinks that he grasps it with both hands. He has trouble imagining beings who would try to elicit a good opinion about themselves that they themselves do not hold (and thus do not 'deserve', either) and who then themselves nevertheless *believe* this good opinion. To him, that seems in part so tasteless and irreverent towards one's self, and in part so grotesquely irrational that he would prefer to consider vanity an anomaly and in most of the cases when it is mentioned, doubt that it exists. He will say, for example: 'I may be wrong about my worth, but on the other hand require that others recognize the worth that I assign—but that is not vanity (rather it is arrogance, or more often what is called "humility", and also "modesty").' Or he will say: 'There are many reasons to be glad about other people's good opinion of me, perhaps because I revere and love them and am happy about every one of their joys, or else perhaps because their good opinion underscores and strengthens my belief in my own private good opinion, or perhaps because the good opinion of others, even in the cases where I do not share it, is nevertheless useful or promises to be useful to me—but none of that is vanity.' It takes compulsion, particularly with the help of history, for the noble person to realize that in every sort of dependent social class, from time immemorial, a common person *was* only what he was *thought to be*—completely unused to determining values himself, he also attributed to himself no other value than what his masters attributed to him (creating values is truly the *master's privilege*). We may understand it as the result of a tremendous atavism that even now, the ordinary person first *waits* for someone else to have an opinion about him, and then instinctively submits to it—and by no means merely to 'good' opinions, but also to bad or improper ones (just think, for example, how most pious women esteem or under-esteem themselves in accordance with what they have learned from their father confessors, or what pious Christians in general learn from their Church). Now, in fact, in conformity with the slow emergence of a democratic order of things (this in turn caused by mixing the blood of masters and slaves), the originally noble and rare impulse to ascribe one's own value to oneself and to 'think well' of oneself, is more and more encouraged and widespread: but always working against it is an older, broader, and more thoroughly entrenched tendency—and when it comes to 'vanity', this older tendency becomes master of the newer. The vain person takes pleasure in *every* good opinion that he hears about himself (quite irrespective of any prospect of its utility, and likewise irrespective of truth or falsehood), just as he suffers at any bad opinion: for he submits himself to both, he *feels* submissive to both, from that old submissive instinct that breaks out in him.

It is the 'slave' in the blood of the vain person, a remnant of the slave's craftiness (and how much of the 'slave' is still left, for example, in women today!) that tries to *seduce* him to good opinions of himself; and it is likewise the slave who straightway kneels down before these opinions, as if he himself were not the one who had called them forth.

So I repeat: vanity is an atavism.

262

A *species* comes into being, a type grows strong and fixed, by struggling for a long time with essentially similar *unfavourable* conditions. Conversely, as we know from the experiences of stockbreeders, a species that is given overabundant nourishment and extra protection and care generally shows an immediate and very pronounced tendency to variations in type, and is rich in marvels and monstrosities (and in monstrous vices, too). Now let us consider an aristocratic community, such as the ancient Greek *polis*, say, or Venice, as an organization whose voluntary or involuntary purpose is to *breed*: there are people coexisting in it, relying on one another, who want to further their species, chiefly because they *must* further it or run some sort of terrible risk of extermination. In such a case, good will, excess, and protection, those conditions that favour variation, are missing; the species needs to remain a species, something that by virtue of its very harshness, symmetry, and simplicity of form, can be furthered and in general endure throughout all its continual struggles with its neighbours or with oppressed peoples who threaten rebellion or revolt. From its most diverse experience the species learns which qualities have particularly contributed to its survival, to its continuing victory in defiance of all gods and peoples: these qualities it calls virtues, and these are the only virtues that it cultivates. It is done harshly, indeed it demands harshness; every aristocratic moral code is intolerant, be it in educating its children, in disposing of its women, in its marital customs, in the relations of its old and young, or in its punitive laws (which apply only to the deviant); even intolerance itself is counted as a virtue, going by the name of 'justice'. A type like this, with few but very strong characteristics, a species of severe, warlike, prudently taciturn, closed and uncommunicative people (and as such most subtly attuned to the charms and nuances of society) thus becomes established beyond generational change; as mentioned above, its continual struggle with the same *unfavourable* conditions causes the type to become fixed and harsh. Eventually, however, it arrives at a period of good fortune, the tremendous tension relaxes; perhaps there are no longer any enemies among its neighbours and its means for living, even for enjoying life, are plentiful. At one single stroke the coercing bond of the old discipline is torn apart: it is no longer felt to be essential, critical for existence—if such discipline wished to endure, it could do so only as a kind of *luxury*, as an archaic *taste*. Variation, whether as deviance (into something higher, finer, more rare) or as degeneration and monstrosity is suddenly on the scene in all its greatest fullness and splendour; the individual dares to be an individual and stand out. During these historical turning points, we see splendid, manifold, jungle-like upgrowths and upsurges coexisting and often inextricably tangled up with one another; competition for growth assumes a kind of *tropical* tempo and there is a tremendous perishing and causing-to-perish, owing to the wild egoisms that challenge one another with seeming explosiveness, struggling 'for sun and light', and no longer knowing how to derive any set of limits, any restraint, any forbearance from their earlier moral code. It was this very moral code, in fact, that stored up the energy to such a monstrous extent, that tensed the bow so ominously—and now that code is, or is becoming 'obsolete'. The dangerous and sinister point is reached where the greater, more differentiated, richer life *survives beyond* the old morality; the 'individual' is left standing, forced to be his own lawgiver, to create his own arts and wiles of self-preservation, self-advancement, self-redemption. Nothing left but new 'What for?'s and new 'How to?'s; no more common formulae; misunderstanding and mistrust in league with one another; decline, decay, and the greatest aspirations terribly entangled; the genius of the race spilling good and bad out of all the horns of plenty; an ominous simultaneity of spring and autumn, full of new delights and veils that are intrinsic to the new, still unplumbed, still unwearied decay. Danger is present once again, the mother of morality, the great danger, this time displaced into the individual, into the neighbour or friend, into the street, into our own children, into our own hearts, into everything that is most secretly our own of wishing and wanting: what will the moral philosophers who emerge during this period find to preach about? They will discover, these keen observers and idlers, that things are quickly going downhill, that everything around them is turning to decay and causing decay, that nothing lasts past tomorrow, with the exception of one single species of human being,

the incurably *mediocre*. The mediocre alone have the prospect of continuing, of having descendants—they are the people of the future, the only survivors. 'Be like them! Become mediocre!' will henceforth be the only moral code that still makes sense, that can still find an ear.

But it is hard to preach, this morality of the mediocre!—it can never admit to itself what it is and what it wants! It has to talk of proportion and dignity and duty and brotherly love—it will not find it easy to *hide its irony*!

263

There is an *instinct for rank* that more than anything else is itself the sign of *high* rank; there is a *joy* in the nuances of reverence that hints at a noble origin and habits. The subtlety, kindness, and greatness of a soul are dangerously tested when it encounters something that is of the first rank, but as yet unprotected by awe of authority against crude, intrusive poking; something unmarked, undiscovered, tentative, perhaps capriciously cloaked or disguised, going its way like a living touchstone. A person who has taken upon himself the task and habit of sounding out souls and who wishes to establish the ultimate value of a soul, its irrevocable, inherent hierarchical position, will make manifold use of one particular art above all others: he will test the soul for its *instinct for reverence*. *Différence engendre haine.*[6] when a holy vessel, a jewel from a locked shrine, or a book with the sign of a great destiny is borne past, the commonness of certain natures suddenly splatters forth like dirty water; and on the other hand, there can be an involuntary loss of words, a hesitation in the eye, a quieting of all gestures which conveys the fact that a soul *feels* the proximity of something most worthy of reverence. The way that Europeans have so far more or less continued to revere the *Bible* may be the best part of the discipline and refinement in manners that Europe owes to Christianity: books with this kind of depth and ultimate significance must be protected by a tyrannical external authority in order to win those thousands of years of *duration* that are required for their full exploration and comprehension. Much has been achieved when the great crowd (the shallow and diarrhoeal of every kind) has finally been trained to feel that it may not touch everything; that there are holy experiences in the presence of which it must remove its shoes and keep its dirty hands off—this is virtually its highest ascent to humanity. Conversely, the so-called educated people, believers in 'modern ideas', stir our revulsion most of all perhaps by their lack of shame, their easy impertinent eyes and hands that go touching everything, licking, groping; and it is possible that among the common people, the low people, among today's peasants especially, there is *relatively* more nobility in taste and sense of reverence than in the newspaper-reading intellectual *demi-monde*, the educated.

NOTES

1. Commonwealth.
2. Neither God nor master.
3. Disinterested.
4. Simple man.
5. Gay science.
6. Difference engenders hatred.

Study Questions

1. What does Nietzsche mean by "master morality"?
2. Can you think of a real or fictional person who adheres to master morality? Do you admire that individual?
3. What does Nietzsche mean by "slave morality"?
4. Can you think of a real or fictional person who adheres to slave morality? Do you admire that individual?

The Myth of Sisyphus

ALBERT CAMUS

Albert Camus (1913–1960), the French novelist, playwright, and philosopher, explored how an ethical system can be developed within a world that he saw as without God, transcendent power, or meaningfulness. He believed the fundamental intellectual challenge to be the struggle to overcome despair in an absurd universe.

AN ABSURD REASONING

Absurdity and Suicide

There is but one truly serious philosophical problem, and that is suicide. Judging whether life is or is not worth living amounts to answering the fundamental question of philosophy. All the rest—whether or not the world has three dimensions, whether the mind has nine or twelve categories—comes afterwards. These are games; one must first answer. And if it is true, as Nietzsche claims, that a philosopher, to deserve our respect, must preach by example, you can appreciate the importance of that reply, for it will precede the definitive act. These are facts the heart can feel; yet they call for careful study before they become clear to the intellect.

If I ask myself how to judge that this question is more urgent than that, I reply that one judges by the actions it entails. I have never seen anyone die for the ontological argument. Galileo, who held a scientific truth of great importance, abjured it with the greatest ease as soon as it endangered his life. In a certain sense, he did right.[1] That truth was not worth the stake. Whether the earth or the sun revolves around the other is a matter of profound indifference. To tell the truth, it is a futile question. On the other hand, I see many people die because they judge that life is not worth living. I see others paradoxically getting killed for the ideas or illusions that give them a reason for living (what is called a reason for living is also an excellent reason for dying). I therefore conclude that the meaning of life is the most urgent of questions. How to answer it? On all essential problems (I mean thereby those that run the risk of leading to death or those that intensify the passion of living) there are probably but two methods of thought: the method of La Palisse and the method of Don Quixote. Solely the balance between evidence and lyricism can allow us to achieve simultaneously emotion and lucidity. In a subject at once so humble and so heavy with emotion, the learned and classical dialectic must yield, one can see, to a more modest attitude of mind deriving at one and the same time from common sense and understanding.

Suicide has never been dealt with except as a social phenomenon. On the contrary, we are concerned here, at the outset, with the relationship between individual thought and suicide. An act like this is prepared within the silence of the heart, as is a great work of art. The man himself is ignorant of it. One evening he pulls the trigger or jumps. Of an apartment-building manager who had killed himself I was told that he had lost his daughter five years before, that he had changed greatly since, and that that experience had "undermined" him. A more exact word cannot be imagined. Beginning to think is beginning to be undermined. Society has but little connection with such beginnings. The worm is in man's heart. That is where it must be sought. One must follow and understand this fatal game that leads from lucidity in the face of existence to flight from light.

There are many causes for a suicide, and generally the most obvious ones were not the most powerful. Rarely is suicide committed (yet the hypothesis is not excluded) through reflection. What sets off the crisis is almost always unverifiable. Newspapers often speak of "personal sorrows" or of "incurable illness." These explanations are plausible. But one would have to know whether a friend of the desperate man had not that very day addressed him indifferently. He is the guilty one. For that is enough to precipitate all the rancors and all the boredom still in suspension.[2]

But if it is hard to fix the precise instant, the subtle step when the mind opted for death, it is easier to deduce from the act itself the consequences it implies. In a sense, and as in melodrama, killing yourself amounts to confessing. It is confessing that life is too much for you or that you do not understand it. Let's not go too far in such analogies, however, but rather return to everyday words. It is merely confessing that that "is not worth the trouble." Living, naturally, is never easy. You continue making the gestures commanded by existence for many reasons, the first of which is habit. Dying voluntarily implies that you have recognized, even instinctively, the ridiculous character of that habit, the absence of any profound reason for living, the insane character of that daily agitation, and the uselessness of suffering.

What, then, is that incalculable feeling that deprives the mind of the sleep necessary to life? A world that can be explained even with bad reasons is a familiar world. But, on the other hand, in a universe suddenly divested of illusions and lights, man feels an alien, a stranger. His exile is without remedy since he is deprived of the memory of a lost home or the hope of a promised land. This divorce between man and his life, the actor and his setting, is properly the feeling of absurdity. All healthy men having thought of their own suicide, it can be seen, without further explanation, that there is a direct connection between this feeling and the longing for death. . . .

Absurd Walls

. . . All great deeds and all great thoughts have a ridiculous beginning. Great works are often born on a street corner or in a restaurant's revolving door. So it is with absurdity. The absurd world more than others derives its nobility from that abject birth. In certain situations, replying "nothing" when asked what one is thinking about may be pretense in a man. Those who are loved are well aware of this. But if that reply is sincere, if it symbolizes that odd state of soul in which the void becomes eloquent, in which the chain of daily gestures is broken, in which the heart vainly seeks the link that will connect it again, then it is as it were the first sign of absurdity.

It happens that the stage sets collapse. Rising, streetcar, four hours in the office or the factory, meal, streetcar, four hours of work, meal, sleep, and Monday Tuesday Wednesday Thursday Friday and Saturday according to the same rhythm—this path is easily followed most of the time. But one day the "why" arises and everything begins in that weariness tinged with amazement. "Begins"—this is important. Weariness comes at the end of the acts of a mechanical life, but at the same time it inaugurates the impulse of consciousness. It awakens consciousness and provokes what follows. What follows is the gradual return into the chain or it is the definitive awakening. At the end of the awakening comes, in time, the consequence: suicide or recovery. In itself weariness has something sickening about it. Here, I must conclude that it is good. For everything begins with consciousness and nothing is worth anything except through it. There is nothing original about these remarks. But they are obvious; that is enough for a while, during a sketchy reconnaissance in the origins of the absurd. Mere "anxiety," as Heidegger says, is at the source of everything.

Likewise and during every day of an unillustrious life, time carries us. But a moment always comes when we have to carry it. We live on the future: "tomorrow," "later on," "when you have made your way," "you will understand when you are old enough." Such irrelevancies are wonderful, for, after all, it's a matter of dying. Yet a day comes when a man notices or says that he is thirty. Thus he asserts his youth. But simultaneously he situates himself in relation to time. He takes his place in it. He admits that he stands at a certain point on a curve that he acknowledges having to travel to its end. He belongs to time, and by the horror that seizes him, he recognizes his worst enemy. Tomorrow, he was longing for tomorrow, whereas everything in him ought to reject it. That revolt of the flesh is the absurd.[3]

A step lower and strangeness creeps in: perceiving that the world is "dense," sensing to what a degree a stone is foreign and irreducible to us, with what intensity nature or a landscape can negate us. At the heart of all beauty lies something inhuman, and these hills, the softness of the sky, the outline of these trees at this very minute lose the illusory meaning with which we had clothed them, henceforth more remote than a lost paradise. The primitive hostility of the world rises up to face us across millennia. For a second we cease to understand it because for centuries we have understood in it solely the images and designs that we had attributed to it beforehand, because henceforth we lack the power to make use of that artifice. The world evades us because it becomes itself again. That stage scenery masked by habit becomes again what it is. It withdraws at a distance from us. Just as there are days when under the familiar face of a woman, we see as a stranger her we had loved months or years ago, perhaps we shall come even to desire what suddenly leaves us so alone. But the time has not yet come. Just one thing: that denseness and that strangeness of the world is the absurd.

Men, too, secrete the inhuman. At certain moments of lucidity, the mechanical aspect of their gestures, their meaningless pantomime makes silly everything that surrounds them. A man is talking on the telephone behind a glass partition; you cannot hear him, but you see his incomprehensible dumb show: you wonder why he is alive. This discomfort in the face of man's own inhumanity, this incalculable tumble before the image of what we are, this "nausea," as a writer of today calls it, is also the absurd. Likewise the stranger who at certain seconds comes to meet us in a mirror, the familiar and yet alarming brother we encounter in our own photographs is also the absurd. . . .

Absurd Freedom

Now I can broach the notion of suicide. It has already been felt what solution might be given. At this point the problem is reversed. It was previously a question of finding out whether or not life had to have a meaning to be lived. It now becomes clear, on the contrary, that it will be lived all the better if it has no meaning. Living an experience, a particular fate, is accepting it fully. Now, no one will live this fate, knowing it to be absurd, unless he does everything to keep before him that absurd brought to light by consciousness. Negating one of the terms of the opposition on which he lives amounts to escaping it. To abolish conscious revolt is to elude the problem. The theme of permanent revolution is thus carried into individual experience. Living is keeping the absurd alive. Keeping it alive is, above all, contemplating it. Unlike Eurydice, the absurd dies only when we turn away from it. One of the only coherent philosophical positions is thus revolt. It is a constant confrontation between man and his own obscurity. It is an insistence upon an impossible transparency. It challenges the world anew every second. Just as danger provided man the unique opportunity of seizing awareness, so metaphysical revolt extends awareness to the whole of experience. It is that constant presence of man in his own eyes. It is not aspiration, for it is devoid of hope. That revolt is the certainty of a crushing fate, without the resignation that ought to accompany it.

This is where it is seen to what a degree absurd experience is remote from suicide. It may be thought that suicide follows revolt—but wrongly. For it does not represent the logical outcome of revolt. It is just the contrary by the consent it presupposes. Suicide, like the leap, is acceptance at its extreme. Everything is over and man returns to his essential history. His future, his unique and dreadful future—he sees and rushes toward it. In its way, suicide settles the absurd. It engulfs the absurd in the same death. But I know that in order to keep alive, the absurd cannot be settled. It escapes suicide to the extent that it is simultaneously awareness and rejection of death. It is, at the extreme limit of the condemned man's last thought, that shoelace that despite everything he sees a few yards away, on the very brink of his dizzying fall. The contrary of suicide, in fact, is the man condemned to death.

That revolt gives life its value. Spread out over the whole length of a life, it restores its majesty to that life. To a man devoid of blinders, there is no finer sight than that of the intelligence at grips with a reality that transcends it. The sight of human pride is unequaled. No disparagement is of any use. That discipline that the mind imposes on itself, that will conjured up out of nothing, that face-to-face struggle have something exceptional about them. To impoverish that reality whose inhumanity constitutes man's majesty is tantamount to impoverishing him himself. I understand then why the doctrines that explain everything to me also debilitate me at the same time. They relieve me of the weight of my own life, and yet I must carry it alone. At this juncture, I cannot conceive that a skeptical metaphysics can be joined to an ethics of renunciation.

Consciousness and revolt, these rejections are the contrary of renunciation. Everything that is indomitable and passionate in a human heart quickens them, on the contrary, with its own life. It is essential to die unreconciled and not of one's own free will. Suicide is a repudiation. The absurd man can only drain everything to the bitter end, and deplete himself. The absurd is his extreme tension, which he maintains constantly by solitary effort, for he knows that in that consciousness and in that day-to-day revolt he gives proof of his only truth, which is defiance. This is a first consequence.

If I remain in that prearranged position which consists in drawing all the conclusions (and nothing else) involved in a newly discovered notion, I am faced with a second paradox. In order to remain faithful to that method, I have nothing to do with the problem of metaphysical liberty. Knowing whether or not man is free doesn't interest me. I can experience only my own freedom. As to it, I can have no general notions, but merely a few clear insights. The problem of "freedom as such" has no meaning. For it is linked in quite a different way with the problem of God. Knowing whether or not man is free involves knowing whether he can have a master. The absurdity peculiar to this problem comes from the fact that the very notion that makes the problem of freedom possible also takes away all its meaning. For in the presence of God there is less a problem of freedom than a problem of evil. You know the alternative: either

we are not free and God the all-powerful is responsible for evil. Or we are free and responsible but God is not all-powerful. All the scholastic subtleties have neither added anything to nor subtracted anything from the acuteness of this paradox.

This is why I cannot get lost in the glorification or the mere definition of a notion which eludes me and loses its meaning as soon as it goes beyond the frame of reference of my individual experience. I cannot understand what kind of freedom would be given me by a higher being. I have lost the sense of hierarchy. The only conception of freedom I can have is that of the prisoner of the individual in the midst of the State. The only one I know is freedom of thought and action. Now if the absurd cancels all my chances of eternal freedom, it restores and magnifies, on the other hand, my freedom of action. That privation of hope and future means an increase in man's availability.

Before encountering the absurd, the everyday man lives with aims, a concern for the future or for justification (with regard to whom or what is not the question). He weighs his chances, he counts on "someday," his retirement or the labor of his sons. He still thinks that something in his life can be directed. In truth, he acts as if he were free, even if all the facts make a point of contradicting that liberty. But after the absurd, everything is upset. That idea that "I am," my way of acting as if everything has a meaning (even if, on occasion, I said that nothing has)— all that is given the lie in vertiginous fashion by the absurdity of a possible death. Thinking of the future, establishing aims for oneself, having preferences—all this presupposes a belief in freedom, even if one occasionally ascertains that one doesn't feel it. But at that moment I am well aware that that higher liberty, that freedom *to be*, which alone can serve as basis for a truth, does not exist. Death is there as the only reality. After death the chips are down. I am not even free, either, to perpetuate myself, but a slave, and, above all, a slave without hope of an eternal revolution, without recourse to contempt. And who without revolution and without contempt can remain a slave? What freedom can exist in the fullest sense without assurance of eternity?

But at the same time the absurd man realizes that hitherto he was bound to that postulate of freedom on the illusion of which he was living. In a certain sense, that hampered him. To the extent to which he imagined a purpose to his life, he adapted himself to the demands of a purpose to be achieved and became the slave of his liberty. Thus I could not act otherwise than as the father (or the engineer or the leader of a nation, or the post-office sub-clerk) that I am preparing to be. I think I can choose to be that rather than something else. I think so unconsciously, to be sure. But at the same time I strengthen my postulate with the beliefs of those around me, with the presumptions of my human environment (others are so sure of being free, and that cheerful mood is so contagious!). However far one may remain from any presumption, moral or social, one is partly influenced by them and even, for the best among them (there are good and bad presumptions), one adapts one's life to them. Thus the absurd man realizes that he was not really free. To speak clearly, to the extent to which I hope, to which I worry about a truth that might be individual to me, about a way of being or creating, to the extent to which I arrange my life and prove thereby that I accept its having a meaning, I create for myself barriers between which I confine my life. I do like so many bureaucrats of the mind and heart who only fill me with disgust and whose only vice, I now see clearly, is to take man's freedom seriously.

The absurd enlightens me on this point: there is no future. Henceforth this is the reason for my inner freedom. I shall use two comparisons here. Mystics, to begin with, find freedom in giving themselves. By losing themselves in their god, by accepting his rules, they become secretly free. In spontaneously accepted slavery they recover a deeper independence. But what does that freedom mean? It may be said, above all, that they *feel* free with regard to themselves,

and not so much free as liberated. Likewise, completely turned toward death (taken here as the most obvious absurdity), the absurd man feels released from everything outside that passionate attention crystallizing in him. He enjoys a freedom with regard to common rules. It can be seen at this point that the initial themes of existential philosophy keep their entire value. The return to consciousness, the escape from everyday sleep represent the first steps of absurd freedom. But it is existential *preaching* that is alluded to, and with it that spiritual leap which basically escapes consciousness. In the same way (this is my second comparison) the slaves of antiquity did not belong to themselves. But they knew that freedom which consists in not feeling responsible.[4] Death, too, has patrician hands which, while crushing, also liberate.

Losing oneself in that bottomless certainty, feeling henceforth sufficiently remote from one's own life to increase it and take a broad view of it—this involves the principle of a liberation. Such new independence has a definite time limit, like any freedom of action. It does not write a check on eternity. But it takes the place of the illusions of *freedom*, which all stopped with death. The divine availability of the condemned man before whom the prison doors open in a certain early dawn, that unbelievable disinterestedness with regard to everything except for the pure flame of life—it is clear that death and the absurd are here the principles of the only reasonable freedom: that which a human heart can experience and live. This is a second consequence. The absurd man thus catches sight of a burning and frigid, transparent and limited universe in which nothing is possible but everything is given, and beyond which all is collapse and nothingness. He can then decide to accept such a universe and draw from it his strength, his refusal to hope, and the unyielding evidence of a life without consolation. But what does life mean in such a universe? Nothing else for the moment but indifference to the future and a desire to use up everything that is given. Belief in the meaning of life always implies a scale of values, a choice, our preferences. Belief in the absurd, according to our definitions, teaches the contrary. But this is worth examining.

Knowing whether or not one can live *without appeal* is all that interests me. I do not want to get out of my depth. This aspect of life being given me, can I adapt myself to it? Now, faced with this particular concern, belief in the absurd is tantamount to substituting the quantity of experiences for the quality. If I convince myself that this life has no other aspect than that of the absurd, if I feel that its whole equilibrium depends on that perpetual opposition between my conscious revolt and the darkness in which it struggles, if I admit that my freedom has no meaning except in relation to its limited fate, then I must say that what counts is not the best living but the most living. It is not up to me to wonder if this is vulgar or revolting, elegant or deplorable. Once and for all, value judgments are discarded here in favor of factual judgments. I have merely to draw the conclusions from what I can see and to risk nothing that is hypothetical. Supposing that living in this way were not honorable, then true propriety would command me to be dishonorable.

The most living; in the broadest sense, that rule means nothing. It calls for definition. It seems to begin with the fact that the notion of quantity has not been sufficiently explored. For it can account for a large share of human experience. A man's rule of conduct and his scale of values have no meaning except through the quantity and variety of experiences he has been in a position to accumulate. Now, the conditions of modern life impose on the majority of men the same quantity of experiences and consequently the same profound experience. To be sure, there must also be taken into consideration the individual's spontaneous contribution, the "given" element in him. But I cannot judge of that, and let me repeat that my rule here is to get along with the immediate evidence. I see, then, that the individual character of a common code of ethics lies not so much in the ideal importance of its basic principles as in the norm of an experience that it is possible to measure. To stretch a point somewhat, the Greeks had the code of their leisure just as we have the code of our eight-hour day. But already many men among the most tragic cause us to foresee that a longer experience changes this table of values. They make us imagine that adventurer of the everyday who through mere quantity of experiences would break all records (I am purposely using this sports expression) and would thus win his own code of ethics.[5] Yet let's avoid romanticism and just ask ourselves what such an attitude may mean to a man with his mind made up to take up his bet and to observe strictly what he takes to be the rules of the game.

Breaking all the records is first and foremost being faced with the world as often as possible. How can that be done without contradictions and without playing on words? For on the one hand the absurd teaches that all experiences are unimportant, and on the other it urges toward the greatest quantity of experiences. How, then, can one fail to do as so many of those men I was speaking of earlier—choose the form of life that brings us the most possible of that human matter, thereby introducing a scale of values that on the other hand one claims to reject?

But again it is the absurd and its contradictory life that teaches us. For the mistake is thinking that that quantity of experiences depends on the circumstances of our life when it depends solely on us. Here we have to be oversimple. To two men living the same number of years, the world always provides the same sum of experiences. It is up to us to be conscious of them. Being aware of one's life, one's revolt, one's freedom, and to the maximum, is living, and to the maximum. Where lucidity dominates, the scale of values becomes useless. Let's be even more simple. Let us say that the sole obstacle, the sole deficiency to be made good, is constituted by premature death. Thus it is that no depth, no emotion, no passion, and no sacrifice could render equal in the eyes of the absurd man (even if he wished it so) a conscious life of forty years and a lucidity spread over sixty years.[6]

Madness and death are his irreparables. Man does not choose. The absurd and the extra life it involves *therefore do not depend on man's will,* but on its contrary, which is death.[7] Weighing words carefully, it is altogether a question of luck. One just has to be able to consent to this. There will never be any substitute for twenty years of life and experience.

By what is an odd inconsistency in such an alert race, the Greeks claimed that those who died young were beloved of the gods. And that is true only if you are willing to believe that entering the ridiculous world of the gods is forever losing the purest of joys, which is feeling, and feeling on this earth. The present and the succession of presents before a constantly conscious soul is the ideal of the absurd man. But the word "ideal" rings false in this connection. It is not even his vocation, but merely the third consequence of his reasoning. Having started from an anguished awareness of the inhuman, the meditation on the absurd returns at the end of its itinerary to the very heart of the passionate flames of human revolt.[8]

Thus I draw from the absurd three consequences, which are my revolt, my freedom, and my passion. By the mere activity of consciousness I transform into a rule of life what was an invitation to death—and I refuse suicide. I know, to be sure, the dull resonance that vibrates throughout these days. Yet I have but a word to say: that it is necessary. When Nietzsche writes: "It clearly seems that the chief thing in heaven and on earth is to *obey* at length and in a single direction: in the long run there results something for which it is worth the trouble of living on this earth as, for example, virtue, art, music, the dance, reason, the mind—something that transfigures, something delicate, mad, or divine," he elucidates the rule of a really distinguished code of ethics. But he also points the way of the absurd man. Obeying the flame is both the easiest and the hardest thing to do. However, it is good for man to judge himself occasionally. He is alone in being able to do so.

"Prayer," says Alain, "is when night descends over thought." "But the mind must meet the night," reply the mystics and the existentials. Yes, indeed, but not that night that is born under closed eyelids and through the mere will of man—dark, impenetrable night that the mind calls up in order to plunge into it. If it must encounter a night, let it be rather that of despair, which remains lucid—polar night, vigil of the mind, whence will arise perhaps that white and virginal brightness which outlines every object in the light of the intelligence. At that degree, equivalence encounters passionate understanding. Then it is no longer even a question of judging the existential leap. It resumes its place amid the age-old fresco of human attitudes. For the spectator, if he is conscious, that leap is still absurd. In so far as it thinks it solves the paradox, it reinstates it intact. On this score, it is stirring. On this score, everything resumes its place and the absurd world is reborn in all its splendor and diversity.

But it is bad to stop, hard to be satisfied with a single way of seeing, to go without contradiction, perhaps the most subtle of all spiritual forces. The preceding merely defines a way of thinking. But the point is to live.

THE MYTH OF SISYPHUS

The gods had condemned Sisyphus to ceaselessly rolling a rock to the top of a mountain, whence the stone would fall back of its own weight. They had thought with some reason that there is no more dreadful punishment than futile and hopeless labor.

If one believes Homer, Sisyphus was the wisest and most prudent of mortals. According to another tradition, however, he was disposed to practice the profession of highwayman. I see no contradiction in this. Opinions differ as to the reasons why he became the futile laborer of the underworld. To begin with, he is accused of a certain levity in regard to the gods. He stole their secrets. Ægina, the daughter of Æsopus, was carried off by Jupiter. The father was shocked by that disappearance and complained to Sisyphus. He, who knew of the abduction, offered to tell about it on condition that Æsopus would give water to the citadel of Corinth. To the celestial thunderbolts he preferred the benediction of water. He was punished for this in the underworld. Homer tells us also that Sisyphus had put Death in chains. Pluto could not endure the sight of his deserted, silent empire. He dispatched the god of war, who liberated Death from the hands of her conqueror.

It is said also that Sisyphus, being near to death, rashly wanted to test his wife's love. He ordered her to cast his unburied body into the middle of the public square. Sisyphus woke up in the underworld. And there, annoyed by an obedience so contrary to human love, he obtained from Pluto permission to return to earth in order to chastise his wife. But when he had seen again the face of this world, enjoyed water and sun, warm stones and the sea, he no longer wanted to go back to the infernal darkness. Recalls, signs of anger, warnings were of no avail. Many years more he lived facing the curve of the gulf, the sparkling sea, and the smiles of earth. A decree of the gods was necessary. Mercury came and seized the impudent man by the collar and, snatching him from his joys, led him forcibly back to the underworld, where his rock was ready for him.

You have already grasped that Sisyphus is the absurd hero. He *is*, as much through his passions as through his torture. His scorn of the gods, his hatred of death, and his passion for life won him that unspeakable penalty in which the whole being is exerted toward accomplishing nothing. This is the price that must be paid for the passions of this earth. Nothing is told us about Sisyphus in the underworld. Myths are made for the imagination to breathe life into them. As for this myth, one sees merely the whole effort of a body straining to raise the huge stone, to roll it and push it up a slope a hundred times over; one sees the face screwed up, the cheek tight against the stone, the shoulder bracing the clay-covered mass, the foot wedging it, the fresh start with arms outstretched, the wholly human security of two earth-clotted hands. At the very end of his long effort measured by skyless space and time without depth, the purpose is achieved. Then Sisyphus watches the stone rush down in a few moments toward that lower world whence he will have to push it up again toward the summit. He goes back down to the plain.

It is during that return, that pause, that Sisyphus interests me. A face that toils so close to stones is already stone itself! I see that man going back down with a heavy yet measured step toward the torment of which he will never know the end. That hour like a breathing-space which returns as surely as his suffering, that is the hour of consciousness. At each of those moments when he leaves the heights and gradually sinks toward the lairs of the gods, he is superior to his fate. He is stronger than his rock.

If this myth is tragic, that is because its hero is conscious. Where would his torture be, indeed, if at every step the hope of succeeding upheld him? The workman of today works every day in his life at the same tasks, and this fate is no less absurd. But it is tragic only at the rare moments when it becomes conscious. Sisyphus, proletarian of the gods, powerless and rebellious, knows the whole extent of his wretched condition: it is what he thinks of during his descent. The lucidity that was to constitute his torture at the same time crowns his victory. There is no fate that cannot be surmounted by scorn.

If the descent is thus sometimes performed in sorrow, it can also take place in joy. This word is not too much. Again I fancy Sisyphus returning toward his rock, and the sorrow was in the beginning. When the images of earth cling too tightly to memory, when the call of happiness becomes too insistent, it happens that melancholy rises in man's heart: this is the rock's victory, this is the rock itself. The boundless grief is too heavy to bear. These are our nights of Gethsemane. But crushing truths perish from being acknowledged. Thus, Œdipus at the outset obeys fate without knowing it. But from the moment he knows, his tragedy begins. Yet at the same moment, blind and desperate, he realizes that the only bond linking him to the world is the cool hand of a girl. Then a tremendous remark rings out: "Despite so many ordeals, my advanced age and the nobility of my soul make me conclude that all is well." Sophocles' Œdipus, like Dostoevsky's Kirilov, thus gives the recipe for the absurd victory. Ancient wisdom confirms modern heroism.

One does not discover the absurd without being tempted to write a manual of happiness. "What! by such narrow ways—?" There is but one world, however. Happiness and the absurd are two sons of the same earth. They are inseparable. It would be a mistake to say that happiness necessarily springs from the absurd discovery. It happens as well that the feeling of the absurd springs from happiness. "I conclude that all is well," says Œdipus, and that remark is sacred. It echoes in the wild and limited universe of man. It teaches that all is not, has not been, exhausted. It drives out of this world a god who had come into it with dissatisfaction and a preference for futile sufferings. It makes of fate a human matter, which must be settled among men.

All Sisyphus' silent joy is contained therein. His fate belongs to him. His rock is his thing. Likewise, the absurd man, when he contemplates his torment, silences all the idols. In the universe suddenly restored to its silence, the myriad wondering little voices of the earth rise up. Unconscious, secret calls, invitations from all the faces, they are the necessary reverse and price of victory. There is no sun without shadow, and it is essential to know the night. The absurd man says yes and his effort will henceforth be unceasing. If there is a personal fate, there is no higher destiny, or at least there is but one which he concludes is inevitable and despicable. For the rest, he knows himself to be the master of his days. At that subtle moment when man glances backward over his life, Sisyphus returning toward his rock, in that slight pivoting he contemplates that series of unrelated actions which becomes his fate, created by him,

combined under his memory's eye and soon sealed by his death. Thus, convinced of the wholly human origin of all that is human, a blind man eager to see who knows that the night has no end, he is still on the go. The rock is still rolling.

I leave Sisyphus at the foot of the mountain! One always finds one's burden again. But Sisyphus teaches the higher fidelity that negates the gods and raises rocks. He too concludes that all is well. This universe henceforth without a master seems to him neither sterile nor futile. Each atom of that stone, each mineral flake of that night-filled mountain, in itself forms a world. The struggle itself toward the heights is enough to fill a man's heart. One must imagine Sisyphus happy.

NOTES

1. From the point of view of the relative value of truth. On the other hand, from the point of view of virile behavior, this scholar's fragility may well make us smile.

2. Let us not miss this opportunity to point out the relative character of this essay. Suicide may indeed be related to much more honorable considerations—for example, the political suicides of protest, as they were called, during the Chinese revolution.

3. But not in the proper sense. This is not a definition, but rather an *enumeration* of the feelings that may admit of the absurd. Still, the enumeration finished, the absurd has nevertheless not been exhausted.

4. I am concerned here with a factual comparison, not with an apology of humility. The absurd man is the contrary of the reconciled man.

5. Quantity sometimes constitutes quality. If I can believe the latest restatements of scientific theory, all matter is constituted by centers of energy. Their greater or lesser quantity makes its specificity more or less remarkable. A billion ions and one ion differ not only in quantity but also in quality. It is easy to find an analogy in human experience.

6. Same reflection on a notion as different as the idea of eternal nothingness. It neither adds anything to nor subtracts anything from reality. In psychological experience of nothingness, it is by the consideration of what will happen in two thousand years that our own

nothingness truly takes on meaning. In one of its aspects, eternal nothingness is made up precisely of the sum of lives to come which will not be ours.

7. The will is only the agent here: it tends to maintain consciousness. It provides a discipline of life, and that is appreciable.

8. What matters is coherence. We start out here from acceptance of the world. But Oriental thought teaches that one can indulge in the same effort of logic by choosing *against* the world. That is just as legitimate and gives this essay its perspectives and its limits. But when the negation of the world is pursued just as rigorously, one often achieves (in certain Vedantic schools) similar results regarding, for instance, the indifference of works. In a book of great importance, *Le Choix*, Jean Grenier establishes in this way a veritable "philosophy of indifference."

Study Questions

1. According to Camus, what is the fundamental question of philosophy?
2. What does Camus mean by "the absurd"?
3. Why does Camus believe that life will be lived all the better if it has no meaning?
4. Why does Camus conclude that "one must imagine Sisyphus happy"?

Existentialism Is a Humanism

JEAN-PAUL SARTRE

Jean-Paul Sartre (1905-1980) was a French philosopher, novelist, and dramatist who defended existentialism, the theory affirming that human agents, through their own thoughts and activities, freely shape themselves. His ethical theory stressed authenticity, the willingness to take responsibility for our choices.

What is meant by the term *existentialism*?

Most people who use the word would be rather embarrassed if they had to explain it, since, now that the word is all the rage, even the work of a musician or painter is being called existentialist. A gossip columnist in *Clartés* signs himself *The Existentialist,* so that by this time the word has been so stretched and has taken on so broad a meaning, that it no longer means anything at all. It seems that for want of an advance-guard doctrine analogous to surrealism, the kind of people who are eager for scandal and flurry turn to this philosophy which in other respects does not at all serve their purposes in this sphere.

Actually, it is the least scandalous, the most austere of doctrines. It is intended strictly for specialists and philosophers. Yet it can be defined easily. What complicates matters is that there are two kinds of existentialist; first, those who are Christian, among whom I would include Jaspers and Gabriel Marcel, both Catholic; and on the other hand the atheistic existentialists, among whom I class Heidegger, and then the French existentialists and myself. What they have in common is that they think that existence precedes essence, or, if you prefer, that subjectivity must be the starting point.

Just what does that mean? Let us consider some object that is manufactured, for example, a book or a paper-cutter: here is an object which has been made by an artisan whose inspiration came from a concept. He referred to the concept of what a paper-cutter is and likewise to a known method of production, which is part of the concept, something which is, by and large, a routine. Thus, the paper-cutter is at once an object produced in a certain way and, on the other hand, one having a specific use; and one can not postulate a man who produces a paper-cutter but does not know what it is used for. Therefore, let us say that, for the paper-cutter, essence— that is, the ensemble of both the production routines and the properties which enable it to be both produced and defined—precedes existence. Thus, the presence of the paper-cutter or book in front of me is determined. Therefore, we have here a technical view of the world whereby it can be said that production precedes existence.

When we conceive God as the Creator, He is generally thought of as a superior sort of artisan. Whatever doctrine we may be considering, whether one like that of Descartes or that of Leibnitz, we always grant that will more or less follows understanding or, at the very least, accompanies it, and that when God creates He knows exactly what He is creating. Thus, the concept of man in the mind of God is comparable to the concept of paper-cutter in the mind of the manufacturer, and, following certain techniques and a conception, God produces man, just as the artisan, following a definition and a technique, makes a paper-cutter. Thus,

the individual man is the realization of a certain concept in the divine intelligence.

In the eighteenth century, the atheism of the *philosophes* discarded the idea of God, but not so much for the notion that essence precedes existence. To a certain extent, this idea is found everywhere; we find it in Diderot, in Voltaire, and even in Kant. Man has a human nature; this human nature, which is the concept of the human, is found in all men, which means that each man is a particular example of a universal concept, man. In Kant, the result of this universality is that the wild-man, the natural man, as well as the bourgeois, are circumscribed by the same definition and have the same basic qualities. Thus, here too the essence of man precedes the historical existence that we find in nature.

Atheistic existentialism, which I represent, is more coherent. It states that if God does not exist, there is at least one being in whom existence precedes essence, a being who exists before he can be defined by any concept, and that this being is man, or, as Heidegger says, human reality. What is meant here by saying that existence precedes essence? It means that, first of all, man exists, turns up, appears on the scene, and, only afterwards, defines himself. If man, as the existentialist conceives him, is indefinable, it is because at first he is nothing. Only afterward will he be something, and he himself will have made what he will be. Thus, there is no human nature, since there is no God to conceive it. Not only is man what he conceives himself to be, but he is also only what he wills himself to be after this thrust toward existence.

Man is nothing else but what he makes of himself. Such is the first principle of existentialism. It is also what is called subjectivity, the name we are labeled with when charges are brought against us. But what do we mean by this, if not that man has a greater dignity than a stone or table? For we mean that man first exists, that is, that man first of all is the being who hurls himself toward a future and who is conscious of imagining himself as being in the future. Man is at the start a plan which is aware of itself, rather than a patch of moss, a piece of garbage, or a cauliflower; nothing exists prior to this plan; there is nothing in heaven; man will be what he will have planned to be. Not what he will want to be. Because by the word "will" we generally mean a conscious decision, which is subsequent to what we have already made of ourselves. I may want to belong to a political party, write a book, get married; but all that is only a manifestation of an earlier, more spontaneous choice that is called "will." But if existence really does precede essence, man is responsible for what he is. Thus, existentialism's first move is to make every man aware of what he is and to make the full responsibility of his existence rest on him. And when we say that a man is responsible for himself, we do not only mean that he is responsible for his own individuality, but that he is responsible for all men.

The word subjectivism has two meanings, and our opponents play on the two. Subjectivism means, on the one hand, that an individual chooses and makes himself; and, on the other, that it is impossible for man to transcend human subjectivity. The second of these is the essential meaning of existentialism. When we say that man chooses his own self, we mean that every one of us does likewise; but we also mean by that that in making this choice he also chooses all men. In fact, in creating the man that we want to be, there is not a single one of our acts which does not at the same time create an image of man as we think he ought to be. To choose to be this or that is to affirm at the same time the value of what we choose, because we can never choose evil. We always choose the good, and nothing can be good for us without being good for all.

If, on the other hand, existence precedes essence, and if we grant that we exist and fashion our image at one and the same time, the image is valid for everybody and for our whole age. Thus, our responsibility is much greater than we might have supposed, because it involves all mankind. If I am a workingman and choose to join a Christian trade-union rather than be a communist, and if by being a member I want to show that the best thing for man is resignation, that the kingdom of man is not of this world, I am not only involving my own case—I want to be resigned for everyone. As a result, my action has involved all humanity. To take a more individual matter, if I want to marry, to have children; even if this marriage depends solely on my own circumstances or passion or wish, I am involving all humanity in monogamy and not merely myself. Therefore, I am responsible for myself and for everyone else. I am creating a certain image of man of my own choosing. In choosing myself, I choose man.

This helps us understand what the actual content is of such rather grandiloquent words as anguish, forlornness, despair. As you will see, it's all quite simple.

First, what is meant by anguish? The existentialists say at once that man is anguish. What that means is this: the man who involves himself and who realizes that he is not only the person he chooses to be, but also a lawmaker who is, at the same time, choosing all mankind as well as himself, can not help escape the feeling of his total and deep responsibility. Of course, there are many people who are not anxious; but we claim that they are hiding their anxiety, that they are fleeing from it. Certainly, many people believe that when they do something, they themselves are the only ones involved, and when someone says to them, "What if everyone acted that way?" they shrug their shoulders and answer, "Everyone doesn't act that way." But really, one should always ask himself, "What would happen if everybody looked at things that way?" There is no escaping this disturbing thought except by a kind of double-dealing. A man who lies and makes excuses for himself by saying "not everybody does that," is someone with an uneasy conscience, because the act of lying implies that a universal value is conferred upon the lie.

Anguish is evident even when it conceals itself. This is the anguish that Kierkegaard called the anguish of Abraham. You know the story:

an angel has ordered Abraham to sacrifice his son; if it really were an angel who has come and said, "You are Abraham, you shall sacrifice your son," everything would be all right. But everyone might first wonder, "Is it really an angel, and am I really Abraham? What proof do I have?"

There was a madwoman who had hallucinations; someone used to speak to her on the telephone and give her orders. Her doctor asked her, "Who is it who talks to you?" She answered, "He says it's God." What proof did she really have that it was God? If an angel comes to me, what proof is there that it's an angel? And if I hear voices, what proof is there that they come from heaven and not from hell, or from the subconscious, or a pathological condition? What proves that they are addressed to me? What proof is there that I have been appointed to impose my choice and my conception of man on humanity? I'll never find any proof or sign to convince me of that. If a voice addresses me, it is always for me to decide that this is the angel's voice; if I consider that such an act is a good one, it is I who will choose to say that it is good rather than bad.

Now, I'm not being singled out as an Abraham, and yet at every moment I'm obliged to perform exemplary acts. For every man, everything happens as if all mankind had its eyes fixed on him and were guiding itself by what he does. And every man ought to say to himself, "Am I really the kind of man who has the right to act in such a way that humanity might guide itself by my actions?" And if he does not say that to himself, he is masking his anguish.

There is no question here of the kind of anguish which would lead to quietism, to inaction. It is a matter of a simple sort of anguish that anybody who has had responsibilities is familiar with. For example, when a military officer takes the responsibility for an attack and sends a certain number of men to death, he chooses to do so, and in the main he alone makes the choice. Doubtless, orders come from above, but they are too broad; he interprets them, and on this interpretation depend the lives of ten or fourteen or twenty men. In making a decision he cannot help having a certain anguish. All leaders know this anguish. That doesn't keep them from acting; on the contrary, it is the very condition of their action. For it implies that they envisage a number of possibilities, and when they choose one, they realize that it has value only because it is chosen. We shall see that this kind of anguish, which is the kind that existentialism describes, is explained, in addition, by a direct responsibility to the other men whom it involves. It is not a curtain separating us from action, but is part of action itself.

When we speak of forlornness, a term Heidegger was fond of, we mean only that God does not exist and that we have to face all the consequences of this. The existentialist is strongly opposed to a certain kind of secular ethics which would like to abolish God with the least possible expense. About 1880, some French teachers tried to set up a secular ethics which went something like this: God is a useless and costly hypothesis; we are discarding it; but, meanwhile, in order for there to be an ethics, a society, a civilization, it is essential that certain values be taken seriously and that they be considered as having an *a priori* existence. It must be obligatory, *a priori*, to be honest, not to lie, not to beat your wife, to have children, etc., etc. So we're going to try a little device which will make it possible to show that values exist all the same, inscribed in a heaven of ideas, though otherwise God does not exist. In other words—and this, I believe, is the tendency of everything called reformism in France—nothing will be changed if God does not exist. We shall find ourselves with the same norms of honesty, progress, and humanism, and we shall have made of God an outdated hypothesis which will peacefully die off by itself.

The existentialist, on the contrary, thinks it very distressing that God does not exist, because all possibility of finding values in a heaven of ideas disappears along with Him; there can no longer be an *a priori* Good, since there is no infinite and perfect consciousness to think it. Nowhere is it written that the Good exists, that we must be honest, that we must not lie; because the fact is we are on a plane where there are only men. Dostoevsky said, "If God didn't exist, everything would be possible." That is the very starting point of existentialism. Indeed, everything is permissible if God does not exist, and as a result man is forlorn, because neither within him nor without does he find anything to cling to. He can't start making excuses for himself.

If existence really does precede essence, there is no explaining things away by reference to a fixed and given human nature. In other words, there is no determinism, man is free, man is freedom. On the other hand, if God does not exist, we find no values or commands to turn to which legitimize our conduct. So, in the bright realm of values, we have no excuse behind us, nor justification before us. We are alone, with no excuses.

That is the idea I shall try to convey when I say that man is condemned to be free. Condemned, because he did not create himself, yet, in other respects is free; because, once thrown into the world, he is responsible for everything he does. The existentialist does not believe in the power of passion. He will never agree that a sweeping passion is a ravaging torrent which fatally leads a man to certain acts and is therefore an excuse. He thinks that man is responsible for his passion.

The existentialist does not think that man is going to help himself by finding in the world some omen by which to orient himself. Because he thinks that man will interpret the omen to suit himself. Therefore, he thinks that man, with no support and no aid, is condemned every moment to invent man. Ponge, in a very fine article, has said, "Man is the future of man." That's exactly it. But if it is taken to mean that this future is recorded in heaven, that God sees it, then it is false, because it would really no longer be a future. If it is taken to mean that, whatever a man may be, there is a future to be forged, a virgin future before him, then this remark is sound. But then we are forlorn.

To give you an example which will enable you to understand forlornness better, I shall cite the case of one of my students who came to see me under the following circumstances: his father was on bad terms with his mother, and, moreover, was inclined to be a collaborationist; his older brother had been killed in the German offensive of 1940, and the young man, with somewhat immature but generous feelings, wanted to avenge him. His mother lived alone with him, very much upset by the half-treason of her husband and the death of her older son; the boy was her only consolation.

The boy was faced with the choice of leaving for England and joining the Free French Forces—that is, leaving his mother behind—or remaining with his mother and helping her to carry on. He was fully aware that the woman lived only for him and that his going-off—and perhaps his death—would plunge her into despair. He was also aware that every act that he did for his mother's sake was a sure thing, in the sense that it was helping her to carry on, whereas every effort he made toward going off and fighting was an uncertain move which might run aground and prove completely useless; for example, on his way to England he might, while passing through Spain, be detained indefinitely in a Spanish camp; he might reach England or Algiers and be stuck in an office at a desk job. As a result, he was faced with two very different kinds of action: one, concrete, immediate, but concerning only one individual; the other concerned an incomparably vaster group, a national collectivity, but for that very reason was dubious, and might be interrupted en route. And, at the same time, he was wavering between two kinds of ethics. On the one hand, an ethics of sympathy, of personal devotion; on the other hand, a broader ethics, but one whose efficacy was more dubious. He had to choose between the two.

Who could help him choose? Christian doctrine? No. Christian doctrine says, "Be charitable, love your neighbor, take the more rugged path, etc., etc." But which is the more rugged path? Whom should he love as a brother? The fighting man or his mother? Which does the greater good, the vague act of fighting in a group, or the concrete one of helping a particular human being to go on living? Who can decide *a priori*? Nobody. No book of ethics can tell him. The Kantian ethics says, "Never treat any person as a means, but as an end." Very well, if I stay with my mother, I'll treat her as an end and not as a means; but by virtue of this very fact, I'm running the risk of treating the people around me who are fighting, as means; and, conversely, if I go to join those who are fighting, I'll be treating them as an end, and, by doing that, I run the risk of treating my mother as a means.

If values are vague, and if they are always too broad for the concrete and specific case that we are considering, the only thing left for us is to trust our instincts. That's what this young man tried to do; and when I saw him, he said, "In the end, feeling is what counts. I ought to choose whichever pushes me in one direction. If I feel that I love my mother enough to sacrifice everything else for her—my desire for vengeance, for action, for adventure—then I'll stay with her. If, on the contrary, I feel that my love for my mother isn't enough, I'll leave."

But how is the value of a feeling determined? What gives his feeling for his mother value? Precisely the fact that he remained with her. I may say that I like so-and-so well enough to sacrifice a certain amount of money for him, but I may say so only if I've done it. I may say "I love my mother well enough to remain with her" if I have remained with her. The only way to determine the value of this affection is, precisely, to perform an act which confirms and defines it. But, since I require this affection to justify my act, I find myself caught in a vicious circle.

On the other hand, Gide has well said that a mock feeling and a true feeling are almost indistinguishable; to decide that I love my mother and will remain with her, or to remain with her by putting on an act, amount somewhat to the

same thing. In other words, the feeling is formed by the acts one performs; so, I can not refer to it in order to act upon it. Which means that I can neither seek within myself the true condition which will impel me to act, nor apply to a system of ethics for concepts which will permit me to act. You will say, "At least, he did go to a teacher for advice." But if you seek advice from a priest, for example, you have chosen this priest; you already knew, more or less, just about what advice he was going to give you. In other words, choosing your adviser is involving yourself. The proof of this is that if you are a Christian, you will say, "Consult a priest." But some priests are collaborating, some are just marking time, some are resisting. Which to choose? If the young man chooses a priest who is resisting or collaborating, he has already decided on the kind of advice he's going to get. Therefore, in coming to see me he knew the answer I was going to give him, and I had only one answer to give: "You're free, choose, that is, invent." No general ethics can show you what is to be done; there are no omens in the world. The Catholics will reply, "But there are." Granted—but, in any case, I myself choose the meaning they have.

When I was a prisoner, I knew a rather remarkable young man who was a Jesuit. He had entered the Jesuit order in the following way: he had had a number of very bad breaks; in childhood, his father died, leaving him in poverty, and he was a scholarship student at a religious institution where he was constantly made to feel that he was being kept out of charity; then, he failed to get any of the honors and distinctions that children like; later on, at about eighteen, he bungled a love affair; finally at twenty-two, he failed in military training, a childish enough matter, but it was the last straw.

This young fellow might well have felt that he had botched everything. It was a sign of something, but of what? He might have taken refuge in bitterness or despair. But he very wisely looked upon all this as a sign that he was not made for secular triumphs, and that only the triumphs of religion, holiness, and faith were open to him. He saw the hand of God in all this, and so he entered the order. Who can help seeing that he alone decided what the sign meant?

Some other interpretation might have been drawn from this series of set-backs; for example, that he might have done better to turn carpenter or revolutionist. Therefore, he is fully responsible for the interpretation. Forlornness implies that we ourselves choose our being. Forlornness and anguish go together.

As for despair, the term has a very simple meaning. It means that we shall confine ourselves to reckoning only with what depends upon our will, or on the ensemble of probabilities which make our action possible. When we want something, we always have to reckon with probabilities. I may be counting on the arrival of a friend. The friend is coming by rail or street-car; this supposes that the train will arrive on schedule, or that the street-car will not jump the track. I am left in the realm of possibility; but possibilities are to be reckoned with only to the point where my action comports with the ensemble of these possibilities, and no further. The moment the possibilities I am considering are not rigorously involved by my action, I ought to disengage myself from them, because no God, no scheme, can adapt the world and its possibilities to my will. When Descartes said, "Conquer yourself rather than the world," he meant essentially the same thing.

The Marxists to whom I have spoken reply, "You can rely on the support of others in your action, which obviously has certain limits because you're not going to live forever. That means: rely on both what others are doing elsewhere to help you, in China, in Russia. and what they will do later on, after your death, to carry on the action and lead it to its fulfillment, which will be the revolution. You even *have* to rely upon that, otherwise you're immoral." I reply at once that I will always rely on fellow-fighters insofar as these comrades are involved with me in a common struggle, in the unity of a party or a group in which I can more or less make my weight felt; that is, one whose ranks I am in as a

fighter and whose movements I am aware of at every moment. In such a situation, relying on the unity and will of the party is exactly like counting on the fact that the train will arrive on time or that the car won't jump the track. But, given that man is free and that there is no human nature for me to depend on, I can not count on men whom I do not know by relying on human goodness or man's concern for the good of society. I don't know what will become of the Russian revolution; I may make an example of it to the extent that at the present time it is apparent that the proletariat plays a part in Russia that it plays in no other nation. But I can't swear that this will inevitably lead to a triumph of the proletariat. I've got to limit myself to what I see.

Given that men are free and that tomorrow they will freely decide what man will be, I can not be sure that, after my death, fellow-fighters will carry on my work to bring it to its maximum perfection. Tomorrow, after my death, some men may decide to set up Fascism, and the others may be cowardly and muddled enough to let them do it. Fascism will then be the human reality, so much the worse for us.

Actually, things will be as man will have decided they are to be. Does that mean that I should abandon myself to quietism? No. First, I should involve myself; then, act on the old saw, "Nothing ventured, nothing gained." Nor does it mean that I shouldn't belong to a party, but rather that I shall have no illusions and shall do what I can. For example, suppose I ask myself, "Will socialization, as such, ever come about?" I know nothing about it. All I know is that I'm going to do everything in my power to bring it about. Beyond that, I can't count on anything. Quietism is the attitude of people who say, "Let others do what I can't do." The doctrine I am presenting is the very opposite of quietism, since it declares, "There is no reality except in action." Moreover, it goes further, since it adds, "Man is nothing else than his plan; he exists only to the extent that he fulfills himself; he is therefore nothing else than the ensemble of his acts, nothing else than his life."

According to this, we can understand why our doctrine horrifies certain people. Because often the only way they can bear their wretchedness is to think, "Circumstances have been against me. What I've been and done doesn't show my true worth. To be sure, I've had no great love, no great friendship, but that's because I haven't met a man or woman who was worthy. The books I've written haven't been very good because I haven't had the proper leisure. I haven't had children to devote myself to because I didn't find a man with whom I could have spent my life. So there remains within me, unused and quite viable, a host of propensities, inclinations, possibilities, that one wouldn't guess from the mere series of things I've done."

Now, for the existentialist there is really no love other than one which manifests itself in a person's being in love. There is no genius other than one which is expressed in works of art; the genius of Proust is the sum of Proust's works; the genius of Racine is his series of tragedies. Outside of that, there is nothing. Why say that Racine could have written another tragedy, when he didn't write it? A man is involved in life, leaves his impress on it, and outside of that there is nothing. To be sure, this may seem a harsh thought to someone whose life hasn't been a success. But, on the other hand, it prompts people to understand that reality alone is what counts, that dreams, expectations, and hopes warrant no more than to define a man as a disappointed dream, as miscarried hopes, as vain expectations. In other words, to define him negatively and not positively. However, when we say, "You are nothing else than your life," that does not imply that the artist will be judged solely on the basis of his works of art; a thousand other things will contribute toward summing him up. What we mean is that a man is nothing else than a series of undertakings, that he is the sum, the organization, the ensemble of the relationships which make up these undertakings.

Study Questions

1. According to Sartre, what is the first principle of existentialism?
2. What does Sartre mean by "anguish"?
3. According to Sartre, why are we condemned to be free?
4. What lessons do you draw from the case of the boy faced with the choice of joining the Free French forces or staying with his mother?

The Buddha's Message

CHRISTOPHER W. GOWANS

The Buddha sought to enlighten people on the problem of suffering in life: its pervasiveness, cause, cure, and cessation. Wisdom is found in moral conduct and mental discipline. This teaching is explored in our next selection authored by Christopher W. Gowans, whose work we read previously.

A MORALLY ORDERED UNIVERSE

The Buddha's teaching was a radical challenge to the beliefs and practices of people in his social milieu—and to ours as well. This is not to deny that he was influenced by his environment. Human thought necessarily develops out of an historical context, and the thinking of the Buddha is no exception. Nonetheless, from the materials he found in his culture, he developed a unique and extraordinary message that deeply contested the intellectual, moral, and religious outlook of people then living in the Ganges river basin.

One important respect in which this was true concerned the fourfold division of persons into brahmins, rulers and warriors, farmers and traders, and servants. This rigid, hierarchical system of classification held that virtually everything important about a person—most significantly, a person's obligations and opportunities—was determined by birth. For example, the brahmins were supposed to have been born with a capacity for wisdom and virtue that no members of another class could achieve no matter what they did. The Buddha rejected this system. He declared that 'anyone from the four castes' could 'become emancipated through super-knowledge.' An important aspect of the Buddha's teaching is its *universalism*: it is put forth as an outlook that is true of, and has relevance for, all human beings—including us. The understanding, compassion, joy, and tranquillity that come with enlightenment are said to be available to anyone who undertakes the Eightfold Path. . . .

The Buddha believed every human being could achieve enlightenment because he thought human nature and the universe have certain objective features we can know. . . . . . It is true that the Buddha's teaching stresses the impermanence of things, but this goes hand-in-hand with an emphasis on the law-governed nature of the universe. Though the world is in constant change, it is very far from being in a state of chaos. Knowledge of the order of the universe is the key to enlightenment.

The world depicted by modern science is often said to be morally neutral or meaningless. By contrast, the universe portrayed by the Buddha is morally ordered. This need not mean the Buddha's teaching is incompatible with modern science, but it does mean the Buddha would regard the world of modern science as incomplete insofar as this world was taken to be morally neutral. . . .

SUFFERING AND ITS CAUSE

The Buddha's teaching is primarily practical rather than theoretical in its orientation. The aim is to show persons how to overcome suffering and attain *Nibbāna*.[1] The purpose is not to persuade them to accept certain doctrines as such. This practical approach is famously illustrated by a story the Buddha told Mālunkyāputta, a skeptically minded disciple, when he persisted in demanding answers to a series of philosophical questions the Buddha refused to answer. The Buddha described someone wounded by a poison arrow who would not allow a surgeon to treat him until he knew the name and class of the man who wounded him, his height and complexion, where he lived, and so on. The Buddha pointed out that the man would die before finding out the answers to all his questions, and that he did not need these answers in order for the surgeon to operate successfully to save his life. For the practical purpose of healing his wound, there was no reason to answer the questions. The point of the story is that the Buddha had not declared answers to Mālunkyāputta's questions because there was no practical need to do so. Answering these questions would have been 'unbeneficial' and would not have led 'to peace, to direct knowledge, to enlightenment, to *Nibbāna.*' The teaching of the Buddha does not consist of answers to any and all philosophical questions that might occur to us. Rather, it consists of answers that are needed for a practical purpose. The Buddha then gave the moral of the story: 'And what have I declared? "This is suffering" — I have declared. "This is the origin of suffering"—I have declared. "This is the cessation of suffering"—I have declared. "This is the way leading to the cessation of suffering"—I have declared.' The Buddha put forward these answers—the Four Noble Truths—because they were 'beneficial,' because they did lead 'to peace, to direct knowledge, to enlightenment, to *Nibbāna*'. The practical orientation of the Buddha's teaching does not mean it includes no theoretical doctrines, nor that it is unconcerned with the truth of these doctrines. It plainly contains such doctrines, and they are put forward as true and known to be true. Nonetheless, the Buddha would not have taught these doctrines unless they served the practical aim of overcoming human suffering. . . .

The Buddha's central teaching has the form of a medical diagnosis and plan of treatment: it describes a disease and its symptoms, identifies its cause, outlines what freedom from this disease would be like, and prescribes the course of treatment required to attain this healthy state. The story of the wounded man should be read in this light. We are to think of the Buddha as a physician who cures not strictly physical ailments, but broadly psychological ones, who shows 'wounded' human beings the way to the highest form of happiness. . . .

Here is the description of the disease and its symptoms:

> *First Noble Truth.* Now this, *bhikkhus,*[2] is the noble truth of suffering: birth is suffering, aging is suffering, illness is suffering, death is suffering; union with what is displeasing is suffering; separation from what is pleasing is suffering; not to get what one wants is suffering; in brief, the five aggregates subject to clinging are suffering.

The key term here and throughout is *dukkha*. It is ordinarily translated into English as 'suffering'. This is correct in part, but it is misleading. The description above features aging, sickness and death (the observation of which first led Siddhattha to seek enlightenment) and we naturally associate these with suffering. But for the other items listed—union with what is displeasing,

separation from what is pleasing, and not getting what one wants—'suffering' sometimes is the right term and sometimes seems too strong. The Buddha clearly has in mind a broad range of ways in which our lives may be unsatisfactory. For the time being, we may summarize the first Noble Truth as the claim that human lives regularly lack contentment, fulfillment, perfection, security, and the like.

Stream-observers[3] might regard this as a rather pessimistic diagnosis. They might be inclined to think that many (if not most) human lives are not so bad, that the positive aspects of life outweigh the negative ones. The Buddha would not have been surprised by this response and did not deny that many persons would question his analysis. His point may be illustrated by an analogy: if an alcoholic is told his life is in bad shape, he will probably point out, perhaps correctly, that he has lots of good times; nonetheless, he has a serious problem and could have a far better life without alcohol and the 'good times' it brings. Similarly, the Buddha thought, most of us can point to some positive features of life: he is not saying we are miserable all the time. However, there is something not fully satisfactory about the lives most of us live. We seek enduring happiness by trying to attach ourselves to things that are in constant change. This sometimes brings temporary and partial fulfillment, but the long-term result is frustration and anxiety. Because of the impermanence of the world, we do not achieve the real happiness we implicitly seek. The Buddha thought we could all sense the truth of this with a moderate amount of honest reflection on the realities of human life, but he also believed that full understanding of the first Truth was difficult to achieve and would require significant progress towards enlightenment.

The next Noble Truth is a claim about the cause of discontentment in human life. Here is how the Buddha explained it:

> *Second Noble Truth.* Now this, *bhikkhus,* is the noble truth of the origin of suffering: it is this craving which leads to renewed existence, accompanied by delight and lust, seeking delight

here and there; that is, craving for sensual pleasures, craving for existence, craving for
extermination.

There is much in this passage that is likely to
perplex us. For now, what is important is the
contention that suffering and other forms of
distress have a cause associated with various
kinds of desire—craving, clinging, attachment,
impulse, greed, lust, thirst, and so on are terms
frequently employed in this connection. The
Second Noble Truth states that the source of
our discontentment is found not simply in our
desires, but in the connection we forge between
desires and happiness. In its simplest form, it asserts that we are typically unhappy because we
do not get what we desire to have, or we do get
what we desire not to have. We do not get the
promotion we wanted, and we do get the disease we feared. Outcomes such as these are
common in human life. These outcomes, and
the anxieties their prospect produces, are causes
of our discontentment. . . .

NIBBĀNA

Many people would agree that suffering or unhappiness is rooted in desire, that it consists of
not getting what we want and getting what we
do not want. It may seem natural to infer from
this that happiness consists of the opposite, in
getting what we want and not getting what we
do not want. Happiness, in this view, is acquisition of all that we try to gain and security from
all that we seek to avoid.

The Buddha taught that this understanding
of happiness is a mistake. We can never achieve
true and complete happiness in these terms, and
there is another, far better form of happiness
that we can achieve. To revert to our earlier
analogy, someone who holds the first view is like
an alcoholic who reasons that, since he is unhappy when he is not drinking, he will be truly
happy only if he is always drinking. However,
what will really make him happy is to find a way
to stop the obsessive craving to drink, to stop

looking for happiness in drinking. The Buddha's striking assertion is a similar but broader
claim. Obtaining what we are hoping to gain
and safety from what we are trying to avoid will
not bring us real happiness. This can only be
achieved by a radical transformation of our desires and aversions—and especially of our attitudes towards them. We have arrived at the next
Truth:

> *Third Noble Truth.* Now this, *bhikkhus,* is the
> noble truth of the cessation of suffering: it is the
> remainderless fading away and cessation of that
> same craving, the giving up and relinquishing
> of it, freedom from it, nonreliance on it.

True happiness in life, the opposite of suffering, is brought about by reaching a state in
which, on my reading, we eliminate many of our
desires and stop clinging or attaching ourselves
to all of them. The Buddha referred to this state
with the term '*Nibbāna*'.

Why not seek happiness in the fulfillment of
our desires, in striving to get what we want and
to avoid what we do not want? The Buddha did
not deny that a measure of happiness may be
obtained from such striving, but he believed it
would always be unsatisfactory in some respects.
In part, the reason is that a life seeking such
happiness will always be precarious because of
the impermanent nature of the universe. What
would fulfill our typical desires—for status,
power, wealth, friends, and so on—is always
subject to change. Even if we were fortunate and
got all that we wanted (and can anyone truth-
fully say this?), old age, disease, and death would
always stand ready to take these things from us.
No matter what we have, we can never be secure
that we will continue to possess it, and so we
will never be truly happy. Another reason is that
fulfilling our desires does not always make us
happy. 'In this world there are only two tragedies,' said Oscar Wilde. 'One is not getting what
one wants, and the other is getting it' (*Lady
Windermere's Fan*: act 3).

For the Buddha, a better strategy than seeking
to fulfill desires would be to live a morally good

life: on account of *kamma*,[4] this would eventually produce greater happiness. However, the Buddha thought such happiness still would be temporary and imperfect, and he thought it would always be a struggle to live a truly good life as long as the belief that one is a self persisted. At best, this strategy might bring improvement, but ultimately it would only perpetuate the cycle of rebirth and its inherent suffering.

Considerations of this sort might be taken to show that these are inadequate roads to real happiness. But why suppose there is another form of happiness—*Nibbāna*—that is not only possible to achieve but better? The answer is the key to the Buddha's teaching and it involves the not-self doctrine. Sometimes it sounds as if *Nibbāna* involves the complete cessation of all desires (the word '*nibbāna*' literally means extinction or cessation), but this is not generally true of a person who has achieved enlightenment. This person does eliminate many desires, specifically all those that presuppose the belief that oneself has primary importance. This belief gives rise to an orientation to life in terms of what is mine and hence is more valuable, in contrast to what is not mine and hence is less valuable. The resulting thoughts and desires are the source of hatred, intolerance, anger, pride, greed, thirst for power and fame, and so on. These states bring unhappiness not only to others, but to those who possess them: a person full of hate does not have a happy life. On the other hand, full realization that I am not a distinct self would undermine the tendency to think myself has primary importance. The Buddha thought this would put an end to all desires associated with hatred and the like, and in fact would release my capacity for universal compassion. The result would be increased happiness for all concerned.

However, enlightenment does not mean the elimination of all desires—at least, not in a sustained way during this life (during meditative experiences of *Nibbāna*, and with the attainment of *Nibbāna* beyond death, desires are absent). For one thing, compassion clearly involves desire in some sense—namely, the desire

that others fare well. Moreover, no human life is possible that does not involve some elementary desires such as for food or sleep. Surely the Buddha did not mean to deny this (in fact, the extreme asceticism he rejected would seem to have been an endeavor to achieve freedom from any desires in this life). But the Buddha did think the realization that we are not selves would bring about a fundamental change in our attitude towards those desires that would remain. This realization would eliminate clinging or attachment to the satisfaction of these desires, and it would thereby cut through the bond we ordinarily forge between this satisfaction and happiness.

On my interpretation, there are at least two aspects of this difficult idea. First, in the absence of the belief that I am a self distinct from other selves, I would no longer think of some desires as mine, as things with which I deeply identify and so need to satisfy to achieve my well-being. As a result, there would no longer be an unhealthy drive or obsession to fulfill these desires. Second, in the absence of the belief that I am a self with identity, a substance persisting through time in some respects unchanged, I would no longer be preoccupied with regrets about the past unfulfillment of my desires and worries about the prospects for their future fulfillment. Liberated in these ways from attachment to desires as mine, from pinning my happiness on their satisfaction, there would be freedom to focus attention on the present moment at all times. The implicit message of the Buddha is that, in this state of awareness, no matter what happened, there would always be something of value, something good, in what was experienced. Not clinging to the fulfillment of our desires would release a capacity for joy at each moment in our lives.

For a person who has attained *Nibbāna*, life is a process of living selflessly in which, unencumbered by the false belief that we are selves, we are enabled to live compassionate and joyful lives. To this it may be added that our lives would also possess great peace and tranquility. They would be lives of perfect contentment and true happiness.

In addition to *Nibbāna* in this life, the Buddha described *Nibbāna* as a state beyond this life and the entire cycle of rebirth (henceforth, when it is important to distinguish these, I will refer to them respectively as *Nibbāna*-in-life and *Nibbāna*-after-death). Though he thought it could not be described adequately in our concepts, we may say by way of a preliminary that he believed *Nibbāna*-after-death is neither a state in which one exists as a self nor a state of absolute nothingness. It is a form of selfless existence in which there is realization of some union with *Nibbāna* understood as ultimate reality beyond change and conditioning. This is a state in which suffering, and all that causes suffering, is entirely absent. *Nibbāna* both in this life and beyond is a state of perfect well-being and tranquility, one that all conscious beings have reason to seek.

WISDOM, VIRTUE, AND CONCENTRATION

Even if we were convinced that *Nibbāna* would be the ultimate happiness, we might well wonder whether it would be possible for us to attain it. The Buddha's practical orientation made this a primary concern. He believed it is possible to achieve *Nibbāna*, but very difficult to do so. We have come to the final Truth:

> *Fourth Noble Truth.* Now this, *bhikkhus*, is the noble truth of the way leading to the cessation of suffering. It is this Noble Eightfold Path; that is right view, right intention, right speech, right action, right livelihood, right effort, right mindfulness, right concentration.

In the first discourse, addressed to the ascetic *samaṇas*,[5] the Buddha described the Eightfold Path as a 'middle way' that avoids two extremes: 'The pursuit of sensual happiness in sensual pleasures, which is low, vulgar, the way of worldlings, ignoble, unbeneficial; and the pursuit of self-mortification, which is painful, ignoble, unbeneficial.' Though the Buddha portrayed the Eightfold Path as a middle way between seeking sensual

happiness and undergoing self-mortification, it clearly involves a rigorous regime that is supposed to radically transform us. This path, the Buddha said, 'leads to peace, to direct knowledge, to enlightenment, to *Nibbāna*'.

The eight steps of the path are to be pursued not in sequence, but all together, with each step reinforcing the others (though the last two, right mindfulness and right concentration, are the culmination). The Buddha divided these steps into three parts: *wisdom* pertains primarily to intellectual development and conviction (right view and intention), *virtue* concerns moral or ethical training (right speech, action, and livelihood), and *concentration*—often rendered as 'meditation'—involves a set of mental disciplines (right effort, mindfulness, and concentration).

The first part, wisdom, instructs us to acquire a thorough comprehension of the Four Noble Truths and all that they involve. However, it does not require us to answer philosophical questions unrelated to attaining *Nibbāna*. In fact, this is discouraged, as we saw in the story of the man wounded by the arrow. Mālunkyāputta wanted the Buddha to tell him whether the world is eternal, whether it is finite, whether body and soul are one, and whether the *Tathāgata*[6] exists after death. The Buddha refused to answer these questions on the ground that attempts to do so would only hinder efforts to understand the Four Noble Truths.

Comprehension of the Four Noble Truths requires more than intellectual cultivation. We also need a fundamental commitment to understanding them, and our emotions and desires must be disciplined so that they do not distract us or lead us astray. Hence, the Buddha said we must renounce sensual desire, ill will, and cruelty. In this respect, he thought thinking and feeling, the mind and the heart, were closely connected.

The second part of the path concerns morality or ethics. Enlightenment requires moral as well as intellectual and emotional preparation. The Buddha spoke of morality at length, and he expected much more of members of the *Sangha*[7] than of lay followers. But there are basic precepts that apply to all persons. These fall into three categories. Right speech requires that we speak in ways that are truthful, friendly, useful, and productive of harmony. Right action dictates that we do not kill any living beings (human or animal), nor steal, nor have illegitimate sexual relations. Right livelihood says we should not earn our living by harming others (for example, by selling arms). Violation of these precepts, the Buddha thought, would only reinforce self-centered desires and would hinder attainment of *Nibbāna*.

The third part of the path—concentration, or meditation—is the least familiar to persons in the West, but the most significant for the Buddha. . . . Though the Buddha taught many forms of meditation, the general aim of these mental disciplines is twofold: first, to purify the mind of disturbances so as to bring about a peaceful, concentrated, attentive and mindful mental state; and second, to know reality as it actually is by observing that all things in our ordinary experience are impermanent, involve suffering, and are empty of any self. The ultimate aim is not to escape from the world nor to acquire special powers: it is to attain *Nibbāna*.

NOTES

1. [Sanskrit, *Nirvana*.—S.M.C.]
2. [Monks.]
3. [Those who are culturally part of the contemporary Western world and have no Buddhist upbringing.]
4. [Sanskrit, *Karma*.]
5. [Spiritual wanderers.]
6. [Truthfinder; Buddha's title for himself.]
7. [Fully enlightened ones; the Buddha's first followers.]

Study Questions

1. What are the Four Noble Truths?
2. How does Gowans distinguish "*Nibbāna*-in-life" and "*Nibbāna*-after-death"?
3. What is the Eightfold Path?
4. How does Buddhism link thought and action?

Confucian Morality

HENRY ROSEMONT, JR.

A Confucian stresses our obligations toward those with whom we stand in distinctive relationships. In particular, rituals are central to the moral life, for by performing them sincerely we cultivate our selves, show respect for others, and contribute to a better society. The Confucian outlook is explored in our next selection, authored by Henry Rosemont, Jr., Visiting Professor of Religious Studies at Brown University.

From *Living Well: Introductory Readings in Ethics*, ed. Steven Luper, Harcourt Brace, 2000. Reprinted by permission of the author.

Confucius (551–479 B.C.E.) may well be the most influential thinker in human history, if influence is determined by the sheer number of people who have lived their lives, and died, in accordance with that thinker's vision of how people ought to live, and die.

Long recognized and described as China's "First (or Premier) Teacher," his ideas have been the fertile soil in which the Chinese cultural tradition has been cultivated, although at the same time a number of the views and practices he championed were already evidenced in China centuries before his birth. Like many other epochal figures of the ancient world—Buddha, Socrates, Jesus—Confucius does not seem to have written anything that is clearly attributable to him; all that we know of his vision directly must be pieced together from the several accounts of his teachings, and his activities, found in the little work known as the *Analects*.

Beginning shortly after he died, a few of the disciples of Confucius began setting down what they remember the Master saying to them (very probably the present books 4–8). Some disciples of the disciples continued this process for the next 75 years or so, and an additional dozen little "books" were composed by we-know-not-whom during the following century, and it was to be still another century before a number of these little "books" were gathered together to make up the *Analects* as we have it today.

Thus it is not at all surprising that the text does not seem to form a coherent whole. Worse, if we take the writings of, say, Aristotle, or Spinoza, or Kant, as exemplary of philosophical texts, then the *Analects* does not seem to be properly philosophical, for it contains precious little metaphysics, puts forth no first principles, is not systematic, and the "sayings" which comprise it are not set down in a hypotheticodeductive mode of discourse.

On the other hand, if the New Testament—or the Hebrew scriptures, or the *Quran*—are taken as religious texts *par excellence,* then it would appear that the *Analects* isn't a religious text either, for it speaks not of God, nor of creation, salvation, or a transcendental realm of being; and no prophecies will be found in its pages.

However, if we are willing to construe philosophy and religion more broadly—i.e., as those domains that address the question "What kind of life should I live?"—then the *Analects* is both philosophical and religious, for it does indeed address this question; it does proffer models of what is right and what is good, models that are perhaps no less important and relevant today in the post-modern, post-industrial West than they were in pre-modern, pre-industrial China over two millennia ago. This is not at all to suggest that Confucius and his disciples were "just like us"; manifestly they were not. Hence, before coming to appreciate what they nevertheless may have to say to us today, we must first focus on how different they really were. . . .

. . . [W]e must first appreciate that for Confucius, we are fundamentally relational, not individual selves. The life of a hermit could not be a human life for him:

> *I cannot flock with the birds and beasts.*
> *If I am not to a person in the midst of others,*
> *what am I to be?*

In other words, Confucian selves are first and foremost sons and daughters; then siblings, friends, neighbors, students, teachers, lovers, spouses, and perhaps much else; but not autonomous individuals. In the contemporary West, these relationships are described in terms of roles, which we first consciously (i.e., rationally) choose, and thereafter "play"; just as actors and actresses play different roles on the theater stage, so do autonomous individuals play roles on the stage of life. These roles may be important for our lives, but are not of our essence.

Confucian selves, on the other hand, are the sum of the roles they *live*, not play, and when all the specific roles one lives have been specified, then that person has been fully accounted for as a unique person, with no remainder with which to construct a free, autonomous, individual self. Consider how Confucius would respond to the "identity crisis" so many undergraduate students undergo at some point during their college career. When Mary Smith asks "Who am I?" the Master will first respond straightforwardly "You are obviously the daughter of Mr. & Mrs. Smith, and the sister of Tom Smith; you are the friend of x, y, and z, the roommate of w, the student of professors a, b, c, and d," and so forth. To which Mary will undoubtedly reply "I don't mean *that*. I'm searching for the *real* me." To which Confucius could only respond sadly, shaking his head: "No wonder you call it a 'crisis,' for you have taken away everything that could possibly count as answers to your question."

This view of a fully relational rather than autonomous self has a number of immediate implications for moral philosophy. In Western thought the basis for moral analysis and evaluation is the *agent* and the *action*. "What did *you* do?" and "why did you do it?" are the central questions. But whereas the first question remains the same in a Confucian framework, the second becomes "with whom did you do it?" followed by a third, "When?" Put another way, Confucius focuses on interactions, not actions, and on specific, not general, interactors. Individual selves are agents who perform actions. Relational selves are always dynamically interacting in highly specific ways.

The roles we live are reciprocal and at the abstract level can be seen to hold between benefactors and beneficiaries. Thus we are, when young, beneficiaries of our parents, and when they age, become their benefactors; the converse holds with respect to our children. We are beneficiaries of our teachers, benefactors of our students, and are, at different times, benefactors and beneficiaries of and to our friends, spouses, neighbors, colleagues, lovers, and so on.

It is for these reasons that there can be no *general* answer to the question "What should I do?" except "Do what is *appropriate* (not "right") under the specific circumstances." Fairly careful readers of the *Analects* will note that Confucius sometimes gives a different answer to the same question asked by one of his disciples. But *very* careful readers of the text will also note that it is *different* disciples who ask the question, and the Master gives an answer appropriate for each questioner. To do this is neither dissembling, nor wrong. For example, your roommate asks you to read and comment on a paper she has just written for a course. You are not impressed with it. What do you say? Well, if your roommate is fairly intelligent, but having troubles at home right now, is experiencing her identity crisis, and is thinking of quitting school, your answer might run something like "There are problems with this paper, but you have a really good potential thesis here, and argument there, which you can develop along thus-and-such lines. And when you've done so, I'll be happy to read it again." But now suppose that your roommate is different. He has just received a few *A*s on exams he didn't really study for, and while he is basically a good person, is showing signs of arrogance and pomposity; in which case you might well be inclined to say "This paper is junk from start to finish. Why did you have me waste my time reading it?"

For a Confucian, these differing responses are not at all either inconsistent or hypocritical, but are both altogether appropriate responses with respect to the second Confucian moral question: "With whom did you do it?" The third question, "When?" is equally significant, because the benefactor–beneficiary relationships are not static. Having just failed an examination yourself, you schedule an appointment with your instructor to go over it, your basic question being "How can I improve next time?" But upon arriving at the appointed time, you find that your instructor—who does not drive—has just learned that his wife has had a heart attack, and been taken to the emergency room at the hospital. Not at all surprisingly, you do not ask your original question, but instead say "Please let me drive you to the hospital."

All of these little examples appear simple, everyday, common-sensical at best, perhaps even trivial when compared to these moral issues focused on in the West: abortion, euthanasia, draft resistance, suicide, and so forth. But . . . they are the basic "stuff" of our human interactions, and Confucius seems to be telling us that if we learn to get the little things right on a day-in and day-out basis, the "big" things will take care of themselves.

And we start out on the path of getting the little things right by focusing on our first, most important, and lifelong role: that of son or daughter. . . .

We did not ask to come into this world, we did not choose to be offspring, but we nevertheless have manifold responsibilities toward our parents; we are responsible for their well-being even though we have not freely chosen to assume those responsibilities. . . .

Confucius insists that we cannot merely rest content with seeing to the material needs of our parents: filial piety is "something much more than that." We must not only meet our familial obligations, we must have the proper attitude toward them, we must *want* to meet our responsibilities; we must have feelings appropriate to the situation. This is why Confucius "could not bear to see the rituals of mourning conducted purely formally, without genuine grief." This point is brought home forcefully when it is seen that our obligations to our parents do not cease when they die; we must continue to show respect for them, and honor their memory. Only then will we know and show the extent of our true filiality.

By cultivating filial piety in our relational roles to our parents—as both beneficiaries and benefactors—we are on the way (better: the Confucian Way) to achieving *ren,* which is the highest excellence, or virtue, for Confucius. . . . Usually translated as "goodness," or "benevolence," it is perhaps best captured in English by "authoritativeness," which signifies both having to do with authoring, and authority. On the one hand, *ren* is easy, because we are human. On the other hand, it can be difficult to achieve in practice owing to our more basic—i.e., biological—desires. But once we set out on the path of *ren,* it is with us forever. . . .

In order to achieve ren one must submit to *li.* This term has been variously translated as "rituals," "rites," "etiquette," "ceremony," "mores," "customs," "propriety," and "worship." . . . "Rituals" and "rites" are the two most common translations, and are acceptable so long as it is appreciated that the *li* are not only to be thought of in terms of a solemn high mass, wedding, bar mitzvah, or funeral; the *li* pertain equally to our manner of greeting, leave-taking, sharing food, and most other everyday interpersonal activities as well.

It is through rituals, custom, and tradition that one's roles are properly effected. There are customary rituals, large and small, by means of which we interact with our parents, grandparents, relatives, young children, neighbors, officials, friends. These rituals are different for the different people with whom we are relating, and they may differ across time as well (we wouldn't hug friends we saw every day, but probably would if we hadn't seen them for some time). It is through the rituals that we express our filial piety toward our parents, respect for elders, care and affection for the young, and love and friendship for lovers and friends. We cannot simply "go through the motions" of performing the rituals, for this would show both a lack of concern for the other(s), and a lack of sincerity as well. It is through rituals, properly performed, that our true attitudes and feelings shine forth, and we more nearly approach *ren.*

Consider meeting someone for the first time. Your right hand automatically is raised, as is theirs; then you clasp it. Your clasp can be such that your hand feels like a dead fish, or you can show off your strength by attempting to crack the other's knuckles, and in either case you can utter a flat "How do you do?" Or you can present a warm hand, squeezing only an appropriate amount; perhaps you will put your left hand over the handshake, after which you say "I'm very pleased to meet you," looking at the other directly. In short, it is not the case that when we've seen one introduction we've seen them all.

Rituals, and the proper performance thereof, have been largely neglected in developing theories of the right and the good in the Western philosophical tradition. Worse, the contemporary West is virtually anti-ritualistic. Rituals are seen as purely formal, empty, dead weights of the past, and detrimental to the full expression of individuality.

They are, however, absolutely central in Confucianism, and without an understanding of their potential for enriching human life, the *Analects* cannot come alive for the modern reader. We can only become fully human, for Confucius, by learning to restrain our impulses to accord with the prescriptions of rituals. Rituals are the templates within which we interact with our fellows: there are proper (customary) ways of being a father, a sister, a neighbor, a student, a teacher. These ways are constrained by rituals, but once mastered, are liberating, are the vehicle by means of which we express our uniqueness.

But unless we have guidelines (the rituals) our behaviors can only be random. (Listen to Beethoven's Fifth Symphony, first as conducted by Toscanini, then by Bernstein, then by Rostropovich; is it not easy to distinguish them despite the severe constraints imposed on them all by the score?) There are many ways to be a good parent, teacher, friend, etc.; if Confucian selves aren't autonomous, they are certainly not automatons either.

So, then, it is through ritual that we cultivate and enhance our authoritativeness, but this can only be done as we become full participants in the rituals, expressing our feelings thereby, and thereby in turn investing them—and consequently ourselves—with significance. If someone you know is getting married, the ritual tradition dictates the giving of a gift. But if you merely purchase the first thing you see—or worse, have someone else buy it for you—you may be "going through the ritual," but are not participating in it, and it will thus be largely devoid of meaning. You must, first, *want* to buy the betrothed a gift (evidenced even in the modern Western expression "It's the thought that counts"), but in order to be a full participant in the ritual, and express yourself relationally, you must devote the time and effort to secure a gift that is appropriate for that person. This is what Confucius is telling us when he says "Ritual, ritual! Is it no more than giving gifts of jade and silk?"

It must also be noted that for Confucius, the significance of rituals is not confined to our interpersonal relations, rituals can also serve as the glue of a society. A people who accept and follow ritual prescriptions will not need much in the way of laws or punishments to achieve harmony, and no government that fails to submit to rituals will long endure; indeed, he even suggests that rituals can be sufficient for regulating a society. And true rulers, having a full measure of authoritativeness and submitting to ritual, will rule by personal example, not coercion; their formal duties are minimal.

Excepting the sages and sage kings, Confucius gives his highest praise to the *jun zi*, usually rendered as "Gentleman," which can be highly misleading. The *jun zi* have traveled a goodly distance along the Confucian way, and live a goodly number of roles. Benefactors to many, they are still beneficiaries of others like themselves. While still capable of anger in the presence of wrongdoing, they are in their persons tranquil. They know many rituals (and much music) and perform all of their roles not only with skill, but with grace, dignity, and beauty, and they take delight in the performances. Still filial toward parents and elders, they now endeavor to take "All under heaven"—i.e., the world—as their province. Always proper in the conduct of their roles, that conduct is not forced, but rather effortless, spontaneous, creative.

Thus the best way to understand Confucius' concept of the *jun zi* is to render the term as "exemplary person." Having learned, submitted to, and mastered the rituals of the past, the *jun zi* re-authorizes them by making them his or her own, thus becoming their author, who can speak with authority in the present. The *jun zi* fully exemplify authoritativeness, and are content with it, no longer worrying about wealth, fame, or glory.

Against the background of the authoritative person as an ideal, we can appreciate that even though Confucianism is highly particularistic in defining our conduct in specific relational roles, it nevertheless bespeaks a universalistic vision. The one exception to the lack of general principles ... is the negative formulation of the Golden Rule: "Do not do unto others as you would not have them do unto you."

But more than that, it should be clear that Confucius had a strong sense of, empathy with, and concept of humanity writ large. All of the specific human relations of which we are a part, interacting with the dead as well as the living, will be mediated by the *li*, i.e., the rituals, customs, and traditions we come to share as our inextricably linked histories unfold, and by fulfilling the obligations defined by these relationships, we are, for Confucius, following the human way (*dao*).

It is a comprehensive way. By the manner in which we interact with others our lives will clearly have a moral dimension infusing *all,* not just some, of our conduct. By the ways in which this ethical interpersonal conduct is effected, with reciprocity, and governed by courtesy, respect, affection, custom, ritual, and tradition, our lives will also have an aesthetic dimension for ourselves and others. And by specifically meeting our defining traditional obligations to our parents, elders, and ancestors on the one hand, and to our contemporaries and descendants on the other, Confucius proffers an uncommon, but nevertheless spiritually authentic form of transcendence, a human capacity to go beyond the specific spatiotemporal circumstances in which we live, giving our personhood the sense of humanity shared in common and thereby a strong sense of continuity with what has gone before and what will come later. In the cosmic sense, Confucius never addresses the question of the meaning of life; he probably wouldn't even have understood it. But his vision of what it is to be a human being provided for everyone to find meaning *in* life, a not inconsiderable accomplishment. . . .

Study Questions

1. According to Rosemont, how does a Confucian differentiate between a relational and an autonomous self?
2. What is meant by *ren*?
3. How do rituals acquire meaning?
4. Does performing rituals play a significant part in your own life?

Part VII

⊠

Moral Problems

A.   Morality and The Law

Crito

PLATO

The *Crito,* probably written about the time of the *Defence of Socrates,* relates a conversation Socrates has in prison while awaiting death. His lifelong friend Crito urges Socrates to run away, assuring him that his rescue can be arranged. Socrates refuses to try to escape, arguing that he is morally obligated to submit to the sentence of the Court, for he accepts its authority and does not wish to bring the system of laws into disrepute.

A much-discussed issue is whether the view Socrates adopts in the *Crito* coheres with the opinions he espouses in his *Defence.* As our translator, David Gallop, explains the apparent inconsistency:

> To some readers the positions adopted by Socrates in the two works have seemed utterly opposed. In the *Defence* he comes across as a champion of intellectual liberty, an individualist bravely defying the conservative Athenian establishment; whereas in the *Crito* he appears to be advocating the most abject submission of the citizen to state authority.

Gallop believes the supposed conflict is illusory, and many commentators agree. Yet they have not reached consensus as to how the reconciliation is to be achieved. I have a suggestion to offer but urge that you proceed now to the *Crito* and return here after finishing it.

The notes are the translator's. The Index of Names he prepared can be found at the end of the *Defence of Socrates* in Part 1.

In my view the key to recognizing the consistency of Socrates' position is found near the end of the dialogue, where a distinction is drawn, in essence, between unjust laws and unjust application of just laws. Socrates believes his fellow citizens decided his case wrongly, but he accepts the fairness of the laws under which he was tried and convicted. If he believed the laws themselves were unfair, he would break them. As he says in his *Defence,* were a law to be passed banning the study of philosophy, he would disobey it. But he will not evade his death sentence, for he "has been treated unjustly not by us Laws, but by human beings. . . ."

Whether you accept this analysis, you can see why the life of Socrates has so fascinated subsequent generations. He embodies the spirit of philosophical inquiry and the ideal of intellectual integrity.

SOCRATES: Why have you come at this hour, Crito? It's still very early, isn't it?

CRITO: Yes, very.

SOCRATES: About what time?

CRITO: Just before daybreak.

SOCRATES: I'm surprised the prison-warder was willing to answer the door.

CRITO: He knows me by now, Socrates, because I come and go here so often; and besides, I've done him a small favour.

SOCRATES: Have you just arrived, or have you been here for a while?

CRITO: For quite a while.

SOCRATES: Then why didn't you wake me up right away instead of sitting by me in silence?

CRITO: Well *of course* I didn't wake you, Socrates! I only wish I weren't so sleepless and wretched myself. I've been marvelling all this time as I saw how peacefully you were sleeping, and I deliberately kept from waking you, so that you could pass the time as peacefully as possible. I've often admired your disposition in the past, in fact all your life; but more than ever in your present plight, you bear it so easily and patiently.

SOCRATES: Well, Crito, it really would be tiresome for a man of my age to get upset if the time has come when he must end his life.

CRITO: And yet others of your age, Socrates, are overtaken by similar troubles, but their age brings them no relief from being upset at the fate which faces them.

SOCRATES: That's true. But tell me, why *have* you come so early?

CRITO: I bring painful news, Socrates—not painful for you, I suppose, but painful and hard for me and all your friends—and hardest of all for me to bear, I think.

SOCRATES: What news is that? Is it that the ship has come back from Delos,[1] the one on whose return I must die?

CRITO: Well no, it hasn't arrived yet, but I think it will get here today, judging from reports of people who've come from Sunium,[2] where they disembarked. That makes it obvious that it will get here today; and so tomorrow, Socrates, you will have to end your life.

SOCRATES: Well, may that be for the best, Crito. If it so please the gods, so be it. All the same, I don't think it will get here today.

CRITO: What makes you think that?

SOCRATES: I'll tell you. You see, I am to die on the day after the ship arrives, am I not?

CRITO: At least that's what the authorities say.

SOCRATES: Then I don't think it will get here on the day that is just dawning, but on the next one. I infer that from a certain dream I had in the night—a short time ago, so it may be just as well that you didn't wake me.

CRITO: And what was your dream?

SOCRATES: I dreamt that a lovely, handsome woman approached me, robed in white. She called me and said: "Socrates,

Thou shalt reach fertile Phthia upon the third day."[3]

CRITO: What a curious dream, Socrates.

SOCRATES: Yet its meaning is clear, I think, Crito.

CRITO: All too clear, it would seem. But please, Socrates, my dear friend, there is still time to take my advice, and make your escape—because if you die, I shall suffer more than one misfortune: not only shall I lose such a friend as I'll never find again, but it will look to many people, who hardly know you or me, as if I'd abandoned you—since I could have rescued you if I'd been willing to put up the money. And yet what could be more shameful than a reputation for valuing money more highly than friends? Most people won't believe that it was you who refused to leave this place yourself, despite our urging you to do so.

SOCRATES: But why should we care so much, my good Crito, about what most people believe? All the most capable people, whom we should take more seriously, will think the matter has been handled exactly as it has been.

CRITO: Yet surely, Socrates, you can see that one must heed popular opinion too. Your present plight shows by itself that the populace can inflict not the least of evils, but just about the worst, if someone has been slandered in their presence.

SOCRATES: Ah Crito, if only the populace *could* inflict the worst of evils! Then they would also be capable of providing the greatest of goods, and a fine thing that would be. But the fact is that they can do neither: they are unable to give anyone understanding or lack of it, no matter what they do.

CRITO: Well, if you say so. But tell me this, Socrates: can it be that you are worried for me and your other friends, in case the blackmailers[4] give us trouble, if you escape, for having smuggled you out of here? Are you worried that we might be forced to forfeit all our property as well, or pay heavy fines, or even incur some further penalty? If you're afraid of anything like that, put it out of your mind. In rescuing you we are surely justified in taking that risk, or even worse if need be. Come on, listen to me and do as I say.

SOCRATES: Yes, those risks do worry me, Crito—amongst many others.

CRITO: Then put those fears aside—because no great sum is needed to pay people who are willing to rescue you and get you out of here. Besides, you can surely see that those blackmailers are cheap, and it wouldn't take much to buy them off. My own means are available to you and would be ample, I'm sure. Then again, even if—out of concern on my behalf—you think you shouldn't be spending my money, there are visitors here who are ready to spend theirs. One of them, Simmias from Thebes, has actually brought enough money for this very purpose, while Cebes and quite a number of others are also prepared to contribute. So, as I say, you shouldn't hesitate to save yourself on account of those fears.

And don't let it trouble you, as you were saying in court, that you wouldn't know what to do with yourself if you went into exile. There will be people to welcome you anywhere else you may go: if you want to go to Thessaly,[5] I have friends there who will make much of you and give you safe refuge, so that no one from anywhere in Thessaly will trouble you.

Next, Socrates, I don't think that what you propose—giving yourself up, when you could be rescued—is even just. You are actually hastening to bring upon yourself just the sorts of thing which your enemies would hasten to bring upon you—indeed, they have done so—in their wish to destroy you.

What's more, I think you're betraying those sons of yours. You will be deserting them, if you go off when you could be raising and educating them: as far as you're concerned, they will fare as best they may. In all likelihood, they'll meet the sort of fate which usually befalls orphans once they've lost their parents. Surely, one should either not have children at all, or else see the toil and trouble of their upbringing and education through to the end; yet you seem to me to prefer the easiest path. One should rather choose the path that a good and resolute man would choose, particularly if one professes to cultivate goodness all one's life. Frankly, I'm ashamed for you and for us, your friends: it may appear that this whole predicament of yours has been handled with a certain feebleness on our part. What with the bringing of your case to court when that could have been avoided, the actual conduct of the trial, and now, to crown it all, this absurd outcome of the business, it may seem that the problem has eluded us through some fault or feebleness on our part—in that we failed to save you, and you failed to save yourself, when that was quite possible and feasible, if we had been any use at all.

Make sure, Socrates, that all this doesn't turn out badly, and a disgrace to you as well as us. Come now, form a plan—or rather, don't even plan, because the time for that is past, and only a single plan remains. Everything needs to be carried out during the coming night; and if we go on waiting around, it won't be possible or feasible any longer. Come on, Socrates, do all you can to take my advice, and do exactly what I say.

SOCRATES: My dear Crito, your zeal will be invaluable if it should have right on its side; but otherwise, the greater it is, the harder it makes matters. We must therefore consider whether or not the course you urge should be followed—because it is in my nature, not just now for the first time but always, to follow nothing within me but the principle which appears to me, upon reflection, to be best.

I cannot now reject the very principles that I previously adopted, just because this fate has overtaken me; rather, they appear to me much the same as ever, and I respect and honour the same ones that I did before. If we cannot find better ones to maintain in the present situation, you can be sure that I won't agree with you—not even if the power of the populace threatens us, like children, with more bogeymen than it does now, by visiting us with imprisonment, execution, or confiscation of property.

What, then, is the most reasonable way to consider the matter? Suppose we first take up the point you make about what people will think. Was it always an acceptable principle that one should pay heed to some opinions but not to others, or was it not? Or was it acceptable before I had to die, while now it is exposed as an idle assertion made for the sake of talk, when it is really childish nonsense? For my part, Crito, I'm eager to look into this together with you, to see whether the principle is to be viewed any differently, or in the same way, now that I'm in this position, and whether we should disregard or follow it.

As I recall, the following principle always used to be affirmed by people who thought they were talking sense: the principle, as I was just saying, that one should have a high regard for some opinions held by human beings, but not for others. Come now, Crito: don't you think that was a good principle? I ask because you are not, in all foreseeable likelihood, going to die tomorrow, and my present trouble shouldn't impair your judgement. Consider, then: don't you think it a good principle, that one shouldn't respect all human opinions, but only some and not others; or, again, that one shouldn't respect everyone's opinions, but those of some people, and not those of others? What do you say? Isn't that a good principle?

CRITO: It is.

SOCRATES: And one should respect the good ones, but not the bad ones?

CRITO: Yes.

SOCRATES: And good ones are those of people with understanding, whereas bad ones are those of people without it?

CRITO: Of course.

SOCRATES: Now then, once again, how were such points established? When a man is in training, and concentrating upon that, does he pay heed to the praise or censure or opinion of each and every man, or only to those of the individual who happens to be his doctor or trainer?

CRITO: Only to that individual's.

SOCRATES: Then he should fear the censures, and welcome the praises of that individual, but not those of most people.

CRITO: Obviously.

SOCRATES: So he must base his actions and exercises, his eating and drinking, upon the opinion of the individual, the expert supervisor, rather than upon everyone else's.

CRITO: True.

SOCRATES: Very well. If he disobeys that individual and disregards his opinion and his praises, but respects those of most people, who are ignorant, he'll suffer harm, won't he?

CRITO: Of course.

SOCRATES: And what is that harm? What does it affect? What element within the disobedient man?

CRITO: Obviously, it affects his body, because that's what it spoils.

SOCRATES: A good answer. And in other fields too, Crito—we needn't go through them all, but they surely include matters of just and unjust, honourable and dishonourable, good and bad, the subjects of our present deliberation—is it the opinion of most people that we should follow and fear, or is it that of the individual authority—assuming that some expert exists who should be respected and feared above all others? If we don't follow that person, won't we corrupt and impair the element which (as we agreed) is made better by what is just, but is spoilt by what is unjust? Or is there nothing in all that?

CRITO: I accept it myself, Socrates.

SOCRATES: Well now, if we spoil the part of us that is improved by what is healthy but corrupted by what is unhealthy, because it is not expert opinion that we are following, are our lives worth living once it has been corrupted? The part in question is, of course, the body, isn't it?

CRITO: Yes.

SOCRATES: And are our lives worth living with a poor or corrupted body?

CRITO: Definitely not.

SOCRATES: Well then, are they worth living if the element which is impaired by what is unjust and benefited by what is just has been corrupted? Or do we consider the element to which justice or injustice belongs, whichever part of us it is, to be of less value than the body?

CRITO: By no means.

SOCRATES: On the contrary, it is more precious?

CRITO: Far more.

SOCRATES: Then, my good friend, we shouldn't care all that much about what the populace will say of us, but about what the expert on matters of justice and injustice will say, the individual authority, or Truth. In the first place, then, your proposal that we should care about popular opinion regarding just, honourable, or good actions, and their opposites, is mistaken.

"Even so," someone might say, "the populace has the power to put us to death."

CRITO: *That's* certainly clear enough; one might say that, Socrates.

SOCRATES: You're right. But the principle we've rehearsed, my dear friend, still remains as true as it was before—for me at any rate. And now consider this further one, to see whether or not it still holds good for us. We should attach the highest value, shouldn't we, not to living, but to living well?

CRITO: Why yes, that still holds.

SOCRATES: And living well is the same as living honourably or justly? Does that still hold or not?

CRITO: Yes, it does.

SOCRATES: Then in the light of those admissions, we must ask the following question: is it just, or is it not, for me to try to get out of here, when Athenian authorities are unwilling to release me? Then, if it does seem just, let us attempt it; but if it doesn't, let us abandon the idea.

As for the questions you raise about expenses and reputation and bringing up children, I suspect they are the concerns of those who cheerfully put people to death, and would bring them back to life if they could, without any intelligence, namely, the populace. For us, however, because our principle so demands, there is no other question to ask except the one we just raised: shall we be acting justly—we who are rescued as well as the rescuers themselves—if we pay money and do favours to those who would get me out of here? Or shall we in truth be acting unjustly if we do all those things? And if it is clear that we shall be acting unjustly in taking that course, then the question whether we shall have to die through standing firm and holding our peace, or suffer in any other way, ought not to weigh with us in comparison with acting unjustly.

CRITO: I think that's finely *said*, Socrates; but do please consider what we should *do*.

SOCRATES: Let's examine that question together, dear friend; and if you have objections to anything I say, please raise them, and I'll listen to you—otherwise, good fellow, it's time to stop telling me, again and again, that I should leave here against the will of Athens. You see, I set great store upon persuading you as to my course of action, and not acting against your will. Come now, just consider whether you find the starting-point of our inquiry acceptable, and try to answer my questions according to your real beliefs.

CRITO: All right, I'll try.

SOCRATES: Do we maintain that people should on no account whatever do injustice willingly? Or may it be done in some circumstances but not in others? Is acting unjustly in no way good or honourable, as we frequently agreed in the past? Or have all those former agreements been jettisoned during these last few days? Can it be, Crito, that men of our age have long failed to notice, as we earnestly conversed with each other, that we ourselves were no better than children? Or is what we then used to say true above all else? Whether most people say so or not, and whether we must be treated more harshly or more leniently than at present, isn't it a fact, all the same, that acting unjustly is utterly bad and shameful for the agent? Yes or no?

CRITO: Yes.

SOCRATES: So one must not act unjustly at all.

CRITO: Absolutely not.

SOCRATES: Then, even if one is unjustly treated, one should not return injustice, as most people believe—given that one should act not unjustly at all.

CRITO: Apparently not.

SOCRATES: Well now, Crito, should one ever ill-treat anybody or not?

CRITO: Surely not, Socrates.

SOCRATES: And again, when one suffers ill-treatment, is it just to return it, as most people maintain, or isn't it?

CRITO: It is not just at all.

SOCRATES: Because there's no difference, I take it, between ill-treating people and treating them unjustly.

CRITO: Correct.

SOCRATES: Then one shouldn't return injustice or ill-treatment to any human being, no matter how one may be treated by that person. And in making those admissions, Crito, watch out that you're not agreeing to anything contrary to your real beliefs. I say that, because I realize that the belief is held by few people, and always will be. Those who hold it share no common counsel with those who don't; but each group is bound to regard the other with contempt when they observe one another's decisions. You too, therefore, should consider very carefully whether you share that belief with me, and whether we may begin our deliberations from the following premise: neither doing nor returning injustice is ever right, nor should one who is ill-treated defend himself by retaliation. Do you agree? Or do you dissent and not share my belief in that premise? I've long been of that opinion myself, and I still am now; but if you've formed any different view, say so, and explain it. If you stand by our former view, however, then listen to my next point.

CRITO: Well, I do stand by it and share that view, so go ahead.

SOCRATES: All right, I'll make my next point—or rather, ask a question. Should the things one agrees with someone else be done, provided they are just, or should one cheat?

CRITO: They should be done.

SOCRATES: Then consider what follows. If we leave this place without having persuaded our city, are we or are we not ill-treating certain people, indeed people whom we ought least of all to be ill-treating? And would we be abiding by the things we agreed, those things being just, or not?

CRITO: I can't answer your question, Socrates, because I don't understand it.

SOCRATES: Well, look at it this way. Suppose we were on the point of running away from here, or whatever else one should call it. Then the Laws, or the State of Athens, might come and confront us, and they might speak as follows:

"Please tell us, Socrates, what do you have in mind? With this action you are attempting, do you intend anything short of destroying us, the Laws and the city as a whole, to the best of your ability? Do you think that a city can still exist without being overturned, if the legal judgments rendered within it possess no force, but are nullified or invalidated by individuals?"

What shall we say, Crito, in answer to that and other such questions? Because somebody, particularly a legal advocate,[6] might say a great deal on behalf of the law that is being invalidated here, the one requiring that judgments, once rendered, shall have authority. Shall we tell them: "Yes, that is our intention, because the city was treating us unjustly, by not judging our case correctly"? Is that to be our answer, or what?

CRITO: Indeed it is, Socrates.

SOCRATES: And what if the Laws say: "And was that also part of the agreement between you and us, Socrates? Or did you agree to abide by whatever judgments the city rendered?"

Then, if we were surprised by their words, perhaps they might say: "Don't be surprised at what we are saying, Socrates, but answer us, seeing that you like to use question-and-answer. What complaint, pray, do you have against the city and ourselves, that you should now attempt to destroy us? In the first place, was it not we who gave you birth? Did your father not marry your mother and beget you under our auspices? So will you inform those of us here who regulate marriages whether you have any criticism of them as poorly framed?"

"No, I have none," I should say.

"Well then, what of the laws dealing with children's upbringing and education, under which you were educated yourself? Did those of us Laws who are in charge of that area not give proper direction, when they required your father to educate you in the arts and physical training?"[7]

"They did," I should say.

"Very good. In view of your birth, upbringing, and education, can you deny, first, that you belong to us as our offspring and slave, as your forebears also did? And if so, do you imagine that you are on equal terms with us in regard to what is just, and that whatever treatment we may accord to you, it is just for you to do the same thing back to us? You weren't on equal terms with your father, or your master (assuming you had one), making it just for you to return the treatment you received—answering back when you were scolded, or striking back when you were struck, or doing many other things of the same sort.

Will you then have licence against your fatherland and its Laws, if we try to destroy you, in the belief that that is just? Will you try to destroy us in return, to the best of your ability? And will you claim that in doing so you are acting justly, you who are genuinely exercised about goodness? Or are you, in your wisdom, unaware that, in comparison with your mother and father and all your other forebears, your fatherland is more precious and venerable, more sacred and held in higher esteem among gods, as well as among human beings who have any sense; and that you should revere your fatherland, deferring to it and appeasing it when it is angry, more than your own father? You must either persuade it, or else do whatever it commands; and if it ordains that you must submit to certain treatment, then you must hold your peace and submit to it: whether that means being beaten or put in bonds, or whether it leads you into war to be wounded or killed, you must act accordingly, and that is what is just; you must neither give way nor retreat, nor leave your position; rather, in warfare, in court, and everywhere else, you must do whatever your city or fatherland commands, or else persuade it as to what is truly just; and if it is sinful to use violence against your mother or father, it is far more so to use it against your fatherland."

What shall we say to that, Crito? That the Laws are right or not?

CRITO: I think they are.

SOCRATES: "Consider then, Socrates," the Laws might go on, "whether the following is also true: in your present undertaking you are not proposing to treat us justly. We gave you birth, upbringing, and education, and a share in all the benefits we could provide for you along with all your fellow citizens. Nevertheless, we proclaim, by the formal granting of permission, that any Athenian who wishes, once he has been admitted to adult status,[8] and has observed the conduct of city business and ourselves, the Laws, may—if he is dissatisfied with us—go wherever he pleases and take his property. Not one of us Laws hinders or forbids that: whether any of you wishes to emigrate to a colony, or to go and live as an alien elsewhere, he may go wherever he pleases and keep his property, if we and the city fail to satisfy him.

"We do say, however, that if any of you remains here after he has observed the system by which we dispense justice and otherwise manage our city, then he has agreed with us by his conduct to obey whatever orders we give him. And thus we claim that anyone who fails to obey is guilty on three counts: he disobeys us as his parents; he disobeys those who nurtured him; and after agreeing to obey us he neither obeys nor persuades us if we are doing anything amiss, even though we offer him a choice, and do not harshly insist that he must do whatever we command. Instead, we give him two options: he must either persuade us or else do as we say; yet he does neither. Those are the charges, Socrates, to which we say you too will be liable if you carry out your intention; and among Athenians, you will be not the least liable, but one of the most."

And if I were to say, "How so?" perhaps they could fairly reproach me, observing that I am actually among those Athenians who have made that agreement with them most emphatically.

"Socrates," they would say, "we have every indication that you were content with us, as well as with our city, because you would never have stayed home here, more than is normal for all other Athenians, unless you were abnormally content. You never left our city for a festival—except once to go to the Isthmus[9]—nor did you go elsewhere for other purposes, apart from military service. You never travelled abroad, as other people do; nor were you eager for acquaintance with a different city or different laws: we and our city sufficed for you. Thus, you emphatically opted for us, and agreed to be a citizen on our terms. In particular, you fathered children in our city, which would suggest that you were content with it.

"Moreover, during your actual trial it was open to you, had you wished, to propose exile as your penalty; thus, what you are now attempting to do without the city's consent, you could then have done with it. On that occasion, you kept priding yourself that it would not trouble you if you had to die: you would choose death ahead of exile, so you said. Yet now you dishonour those words, and show no regard for us, the Laws, in your effort to destroy us. You are acting as the meanest slave would act, by trying to run away in spite of those compacts and agreements you made with us, whereby you agreed to be a citizen on our terms.

"First, then, answer us this question: are we right in claiming that you agreed, by your conduct if not verbally, that you would be a citizen on our terms? Or is that untrue?"

What shall we say in reply to that, Crito? Mustn't we agree?

CRITO: We must, Socrates.

SOCRATES: "Then what does your action amount to," they would say, "except breaking the compacts and agreements you made with us? By your own admission, you were not coerced or tricked into making them, or forced to reach a decision in a short time: you had seventy years in which it was open to you to leave if you were not happy with us, or if you thought those agreements unfair. Yet you preferred neither Lacedaemon nor Crete[10]—places you often say are well governed—nor any other Greek or foreign city: in fact, you went abroad less often than the lame and the blind or other cripples. Obviously, then, amongst Athenians you were exceptionally content with our city and with us, its Laws—because who would care for a city apart from its laws? Won't you, then, abide by your agreements now? Yes you will, if you listen to us, Socrates; and then at least you won't make yourself an object of derision by leaving the city.

"Just consider: if you break those agreements, and commit any of those offences, what good will you do yourself or those friends of yours? Your friends, pretty obviously, will risk being exiled themselves, as well as being disenfranchised or losing their property. As for you, first of all, if you go to one of the nearest cities, Thebes or Megara[11]—they are both well governed—you will arrive as an enemy of their political systems, Socrates: all who are concerned for their own cities will look askance at you, regarding you as a subverter of laws. You will also confirm your jurors in their judgment, making them think they decided your case correctly: any subverter of laws, presumably, might well be thought to be a corrupter of young, unthinking people.

"Will you, then, avoid the best-governed cities and the most respectable of men? And if so, will your life be worth living? Or will you associate with those people, and be shameless enough to converse with them? And what will you say to them, Socrates? The things you used to say here, that goodness and justice are most precious to mankind, along with institutions and laws? Don't you think that the predicament of Socrates will cut an ugly figure? Surely you must.

"Or will you take leave of those spots, and go to stay with those friends of Crito's up in Thessaly? That, of course, is a region of the utmost disorder and licence; so perhaps they would enjoy hearing from you about your comical escape from gaol, when you dressed up in some outfit, wore a leather jerkin or some other runaway's garb, and altered your appearance. Will no one observe that you, an old man with probably only a short time left to live, had the nerve to cling so greedily to life by violating the most important laws? Perhaps not, so long as you don't trouble anyone. Otherwise, Socrates, you will hear a great deal to your own discredit. You will live as every person's toady and lackey; and what will you be doing—apart from living it up in Thessaly, as if you had travelled all the way to Thessaly to have dinner? As for those principles of yours about justice and goodness in general—tell us, where will they be then?

"Well then, is it for your children's sake that you wish to live, in order to bring them up and give them an education? How so? Will you bring them up and educate them by taking them off to Thessaly and making foreigners of them, so that they may gain that advantage too? Or if, instead of that, they are brought up here, will they be better brought up and educated just because you are alive, if you are not with them? Yes, you may say, because those friends of yours will take care of them. Then will they take care of them if you travel to Thessaly, but not take care of them if you travel to Hades? Surely if those professing to be your friends are of any use at all, you must believe that they will.

"No, Socrates, listen to us, your own nurturers: do not place a higher value upon children, upon life, or upon anything else, than upon what is just, so that when you leave for Hades, this may be your whole defence before the authorities there: to take that course seems neither better nor more just or holy, for you or for any of your friends here in this world. Nor will it be better for you when you reach the next. As things stand, you will leave this world (if you do) as one who has been treated unjustly not by us Laws, but by human beings; whereas if you go into exile, thereby shamefully returning injustice for injustice and ill-treatment for ill-treatment, breaking the agreements and compacts you made with us, and inflicting harm upon the people you should least harm—yourself, your friends, your fatherland, and ourselves—then we shall be angry with you in your lifetime; and our brother Laws in Hades will not receive you kindly there, knowing that you tried, to the best of your ability, to destroy us too. Come then, do not let Crito persuade you to take his advice rather than ours."

That, Crito, my dear comrade, is what I seem to hear them saying, I do assure you. I am like the Corybantic revellers[12] who think they are still hearing the music of pipes: the sound of those arguments is ringing loudly in my head, and makes me unable to hear the others. As far as these present thoughts of mine go, then, you may be sure that if you object to them, you will plead in vain. None the less, if you think you will do any good, speak up.

CRITO: No, Socrates, I've nothing to say.

SOCRATES: Then let it be, Crito, and let us act accordingly, because that is the direction in which God is guiding us.

NOTES

1. The small island of Delos was sacred to the god Apollo. A mission sailed there annually from Athens to commemorate her deliverance by Theseus from servitude to King Minos of Crete. No executions could be carried out in Athens until the sacred ship returned.

2. The headland at the south-eastern extremity of Attica, about 50 kilometres from Athens. The winds were unfavourable at the time; so the ship may have been taking shelter at Sunium when the travellers left it there.

3. In Homer's *Iliad* (ix. 363) Achilles says, "on the third day I may return to fertile Phthia," meaning that he can get home in three days.

4. Athens had no public prosecutors. Prosecutions were undertaken by private citizens, who sometimes threatened legal action for personal, political, or financial gain.

5. The region of northern Greece, lying 200–300 kilometres north-west of Attica.

6. It was customary in Athens to appoint a public advocate to defend laws which it was proposed to abrogate.

7. The standard components of traditional Athenian education.

8. Admission to Athenian citizenship was not automatic, but required formal registration by males at the age of 17 or 18, with proof of age and parental citizenship.

9. The Isthmus was the strip of land linking the Peloponnese with the rest of Greece. Socrates may have attended the Isthmian Games, which were held every two years at Corinth.

10. Lacedaemon was the official name for the territory of Sparta. Sparta and Crete were both authoritarian and "closed" societies, which forbade their citizens to live abroad.

11. Thebes was the chief city in Boeotia, the region lying to the north-west of Attica; Megara was on the Isthmus. Both lay within easy reach of Athens.

12. The Corybantes performed orgiastic rites and dances to the sound of pipe and drum music. Their music sometimes induced a state of frenzy in emotionally disordered people, which was followed by a deep sleep from which the patients awoke cured.

Study Questions

1. According to Socrates, must one heed popular opinion about moral matters?
2. If you reside in a country, do you implicitly agree to abide by its laws?
3. Does Socrates accept the fairness of the laws under which he was tried and convicted?
4. Do you believe Socrates would have been wrong to escape?

Letter from a Birmingham Jail

MARTIN LUTHER KING, JR.

A democracy may pass an unjust law. If citizens of that democracy believe the law is unjust, are they entitled to violate it? Doing so would not be in accord with the principle of majority rule, which is the procedure by which a democracy is supposed to function. But to act in accord with an unjust law would be to act unjustly. Can we find a satisfactory way out of this dilemma?

In 1963 Dr. Martin Luther King, Jr., was imprisoned in Birmingham, Alabama, for participating in a civil rights demonstration. While in jail he writes a letter justifying his actions. He explains that because he believes that the laws enforcing racial

From James M. Washington, ed., *A Testament of Hope: The Essential Writings of Martin Luther King, Jr.* Copyright © 1963 by Martin Luther King, Jr. Renewed © 1991 by Coretta Scott King. Reprinted by arrangement with The Heirs to the Estate of Martin Luther King, Jr., c/o Writers House as agent for the proprietor New York, NY.

segregation are unjust, he refuses to act as the government requires but willingly accepts the legal punishment for his actions, thus indicating his respect for democratic procedure. He insists that such civil disobedience be nonviolent, that all laws except the unjust ones be obeyed, and that breaking of the law be resorted to only when fundamental moral principles are at stake.

In 1964 he was awarded the Nobel Peace Prize. In 1968 he was assassinated.

My dear Fellow Clergymen,

While confined here in the Birmingham city jail, I came across your recent statement calling our present activities "unwise and untimely." Seldom, if ever, do I pause to answer criticism of my work and ideas. If I sought to answer all of the criticisms that cross my desk, my secretaries would be engaged in little else in the course of the day, and I would have no time for constructive work. But since I feel that you are men of genuine good will and your criticisms are sincerely set forth, I would like to answer your statement in what I hope will be patient and reasonable terms.

I think I should give the reason for my being in Birmingham, since you have been influenced by the argument of "outsiders coming in."

I have the honor of serving as president of the Southern Christian Leadership Conference, an organization operating in every southern state, with headquarters in Atlanta, Georgia. We have some eighty-five affiliate organizations all across the South—one being the Alabama Christian Movement for Human Rights. Whenever necessary and possible we share staff, educational and financial resources with our affiliates. Several months ago our local affiliate here in Birmingham invited us to be on call to engage in a nonviolent direct-action program if such were deemed necessary. We readily consented and when the hour came we lived up to our promises. So I am here, along with several members of my staff, because we were invited here. I am here because I have basic organizational ties here.

Beyond this, I am in Birmingham because injustice is here. Just as the eighth century prophets left their little villages and carried their "thus saith the Lord" far beyond the boundaries of their hometowns; and just as the Apostle Paul left his little village of Tarsus and carried the gospel of Jesus Christ to practically every hamlet and city of the Graeco-Roman world, I too am compelled to carry the gospel of freedom beyond my particular hometown. Like Paul, I must constantly respond to the Macedonian call for aid.

Moreover, I am cognizant of the interrelatedness of all communities and states. I cannot sit idly by in Atlanta and not be concerned about what happens in Birmingham. Injustice anywhere is a threat to justice anywhere. We are caught in an inescapable network of mutuality, tied in a single garment of destiny. Whatever affects one directly affects all indirectly. Never again can we afford to live with the narrow, provincial "outside agitator" idea. Anyone who lives in the United States can never be considered an outsider anywhere in this country.

You deplore the demonstrations that are presently taking place in Birmingham. But I am sorry that your statement did not express a similar concern for the conditions that brought the demonstrations into being. I am sure that each of you would want to go beyond the superficial social analyst who looks merely at effects, and does not grapple with underlying causes. I would not hesitate to say that it is unfortunate that so-called demonstrations are taking place in Birmingham at this time, but I would say in more emphatic terms that it is even more unfortunate that the white power structure of this city left the Negro community with no other alternative.

In any nonviolent campaign there are four basic steps: (1) collection of the facts to determine whether injustices are alive, (2) negotiation, (3) self-purification, and (4) direct action. We have gone through all of these steps in Birmingham. There can be no gainsaying of the fact that racial injustice engulfs this community.

Birmingham is probably the most thoroughly segregated city in the United States. Its ugly record of police brutality is known in every section of this country. Its unjust treatment of Negroes in the courts is a notorious reality. There have been more unsolved bombings of Negro homes and churches in Birmingham than any city in this nation. These are the hard, brutal and unbelievable facts. On the basis of these conditions Negro leaders sought to negotiate with the city fathers. But the political leaders consistently refused to engage in good faith negotiation.

Then came the opportunity last September to talk with some of the leaders of the economic community. In these negotiating sessions certain promises were made by the merchants—such as the promise to remove the humiliating racial signs from the stores. On the basis of these promises Rev. Shuttlesworth and the leaders of the Alabama Christian Movement for Human Rights agreed to call a moratorium on any type of demonstrations. As the weeks and months unfolded we realized that we were the victims of a broken promise. The signs remained. Like so many experiences of the past we were confronted with blasted hopes, and the dark shadow of a deep disappointment settled upon us. So we had no alternative except that of preparing for direct action, whereby we would present our very bodies as a means of laying our case before the conscience of the local and national community. We were not unmindful of the difficulties involved. So we decided to go through a process of self-purification. We started having workshops on nonviolence and repeatedly asked ourselves the questions, "Are you able to accept blows without retaliating?" "Are you able to

endure the ordeals of jail?" We decided to set our direct-action program around the Easter season, realizing that with the exception of Christmas, this was the largest shopping period of the year. Knowing that a strong economic withdrawal program would be the by-product of direct action, we felt that this was the best time to bring pressure on the merchants for the needed changes. Then it occurred to us that the March election was ahead and so we speedily decided to postpone action until after election day. When we discovered that Mr. Connor was in the run-off, we decided again to postpone action so that the demonstrations could not be used to cloud the issues. At this time we agreed to begin our nonviolent witness the day after the run-off.

This reveals that we did not move irresponsibly into direct action. We too wanted to see Mr. Connor defeated; so we went through postponement after postponement to aid in this community need. After this we felt that direct action could be delayed no longer.

You may well ask, "Why direct action? Why sit-ins, marches, etc.? Isn't negotiation a better path?" You are exactly right in your call for negotiation. Indeed, this is the purpose of direct action. Nonviolent direct action seeks to create such a crisis and establish such creative tension that a community that has constantly refused to negotiate is forced to confront the issue. It seeks so to dramatize the issue that it can no longer be ignored. I just referred to the creation of tension as a part of the work of the nonviolent resister. This may sound rather shocking. But I must confess that I am not afraid of the word tension. I have earnestly worked and preached against violent tension, but there is a type of constructive nonviolent tension that is necessary for growth. Just as Socrates felt that it was necessary to create a tension in the mind so that individuals could rise from the bondage of myths and half-truths to the unfettered realm of creative analysis and objective appraisal, we must see the need of having nonviolent gadflies to create the kind of tension in society that will help men to rise from the dark depths of prejudice and racism to the majestic heights of understanding and brotherhood. So the purpose of the direct action is to create a situation so crisis-packed that it will inevitably open the door to negotiation. We, therefore, concur with you in your call for negotiation. Too long has our beloved Southland been bogged down in the tragic attempt to live in monologue rather than dialogue.

One of the basic points in your statement is that our acts are untimely. Some have asked, "Why didn't you give the new administration time to act?" The only answer that I can give to this inquiry is that the new administration must be prodded about as much as the outgoing one before it acts. We will be sadly mistaken if we feel that the election of Mr. Boutwell will bring the millennium to Birmingham. While Mr. Boutwell is much more articulate and gentle than Mr. Connor, they are both segregationists, dedicated to the task of maintaining the status quo. The hope I see in Mr. Boutwell is that he will be reasonable enough to see the futility of massive resistance to desegregation. But he will not see this without pressure from the devotees of civil rights. My friends, I must say to you that we have not made a single gain in civil rights without determined legal and nonviolent pressure. History is the long and tragic story of the fact that privileged groups seldom give up their privileges voluntarily. Individuals may see the moral light and voluntarily give up their unjust posture; but as Reinhold Niebuhr has reminded us, groups are more immoral than individuals.

We know through painful experience that freedom is never voluntarily given by the oppressor; it must be demanded by the oppressed. Frankly, I have never yet engaged in a direct action movement that was "well-timed," according to the timetable of those who have not suffered unduly from the disease of segregation. For years now I have heard the words "Wait!" It rings in the ear of every Negro with a piercing familiarity. This "Wait" has almost always meant "Never." It has been a tranquilizing thalidomide, relieving the emotional stress for a moment, only to give birth to an ill-formed infant of frustration. We must come to see with the distinguished jurist of yesterday that "justice too long delayed is justice denied." We have waited for more than 340 years for our constitutional and God-given rights. The nations of Asia and Africa are moving with jet-like speed toward the goal of political independence, and we still creep at horse and buggy pace toward the gaining of a cup of coffee at the lunch counter. I guess it is easy for those who have never felt the stinging darts of segregation to say, "Wait." But when you have seen vicious mobs lynch your mothers and fathers at will and drown your sisters and brothers at whim; when you have seen hatefilled policemen curse, kick, brutalize and even kill your black brothers and sisters with impunity; when you see the vast majority of your twenty million Negro brothers smothering in an airtight cage of poverty in the midst of an affluent society; when you suddenly find your tongue twisted and your speech stammering as you seek to explain to your six-year-old daughter why she can't go to the public amusement park that has just been advertised on television, and see tears welling up in her little eyes when she is told that Funtown is closed to colored children, and see the depressing clouds of inferiority begin to form in her little mental sky, and see her begin to distort her little personality by unconsciously developing a bitterness toward white people; when you have to concoct an answer for a five-year-old son asking in agonizing pathos: "Daddy, why do white people treat colored people so mean?"; when you take a crosscountry drive and find it necessary to sleep night after night in the uncomfortable corners of your automobile because no motel will accept you; when you are humiliated day in and day out by nagging signs reading "white" and "colored"; when your first name becomes "nigger" and your middle name becomes "boy" (however old you are) and your last name becomes "John," and when your wife and mother are never given the respected title "Mrs."; when you are harried by day and haunted by night by the fact that you are a Negro, living constantly at tiptoe stance never quite knowing what to expect next, and plagued with inner fears and outer resentments; when you are forever fighting a degenerating sense of "nobodiness"; then you will understand why we find it difficult to wait. There comes a time when the cup of endurance runs over, and men are no longer willing to be plunged into an abyss of injustice where they experience the blackness of corroding despair. I hope, sirs, you can understand our legitimate and unavoidable impatience.

You express a great deal of anxiety over our willingness to break laws. This is certainly a legitimate concern. Since we so diligently urge people to obey the Supreme Court's decision of 1954 outlawing segregation in the public schools, it is rather strange and paradoxical to find us consciously breaking laws. One may well ask, "How can you advocate breaking some laws and obeying others?" The answer is found in the fact that there are two types of laws: there are *just* and there are *unjust* laws. I would agree with Saint Augustine that "An unjust law is no law at all."

Now what is the difference between the two? How does one determine when a law is just or unjust? A just law is a man-made code that squares with the moral law or the law of God. An unjust law is a code that is out of harmony with the moral law. To put it in the terms of Saint Thomas Aquinas, an unjust law is a human law that is not rooted in eternal and natural law. Any law that uplifts human personality is just. Any law that degrades human personality is unjust. All segregation statutes are unjust because segregation distorts the soul and damages the personality. It gives the segregator a false sense of superiority, and the segregated a false sense of inferiority. To use the words of Martin Buber, the great Jewish philosopher, segregation substitutes an "I-it" relationship for the "I-thou" relationship, and ends up relegating persons to the status of things. So segregation is

not only politically, economically and sociologically unsound, but it is morally wrong and sinful. Paul Tillich has said that sin is separation. Isn't segregation an existential expression of man's tragic separation, an expression of his awful estangement, his terrible sinfulness? So I can urge men to disobey segregation ordinances because they are morally wrong.

Let us turn to a more concrete example of just and unjust laws. An unjust law is a code that a majority inflicts on a minority that is not binding on itself. This is difference made legal. On the other hand a just law is a code that a majority compels a minority to follow that it is willing to follow itself. This is sameness made legal.

Let me give another explanation. An unjust law is a code inflicted upon a minority which that minority had no part in enacting or creating because they did not have the unhampered right to vote. Who can say that the legislature of Alabama which set up the segregation laws was democratically elected? Throughout the state of Alabama all types of conniving methods are used to prevent Negroes from becoming registered voters and there are some counties without a single Negro registered to vote despite the fact that the Negro constitutes a majority of the population. Can any law set up in such a state be considered democratically structured?

These are just a few examples of unjust and just laws. There are some instances when a law is just on its face and unjust in its application. For instance, I was arrested Friday on a charge of parading without permit. Now there is nothing wrong with an ordinance which requires a permit for a parade, but when the ordinance is used to preserve segregation and to deny citizens the First Amendment privilege of peaceful assembly and peaceful protest, then it becomes unjust.

I hope you can see the distinction I am trying to point out. In no sense do I advocate evading or defying the law as the rabid segregationist would do. This would lead to anarchy. One who breaks an unjust law must do it *openly, lovingly* (not hatefully as the white mothers did in New Orleans when they were seen on television screaming, "nigger, nigger, nigger"), and with a willingness to accept the penalty. I submit that an individual who breaks a law that conscience tells him is unjust, and willingly accepts the penalty by staying in jail to arouse the conscience of the community over its injustice, is in reality expressing the very highest respect for law.

Of course, there is nothing new about this kind of civil disobedience. It was seen sublimely in the refusal of Shadrach, Meshach and Abednego to obey the laws of Nebuchadnezzar because a higher moral law was involved. It was practiced superbly by the early Christians who were willing to face hungry lions and the excruciating pain of chopping blocks, before submitting to certain unjust laws of the Roman Empire. To a degree academic freedom is a reality today because Socrates practiced civil disobedience.

We can never forget that everything Hitler did in Germany was "legal" and everything the Hungarian freedom fighters did in Hungary was "illegal." It was "illegal" to aid and comfort a Jew in Hitler's Germany. But I am sure that if I had lived in Germany during that time I would have aided and comforted my Jewish brothers even though it was illegal. If I lived in a Communist country today where certain principles dear to the Christian faith are suppressed, I believe I would openly advocate disobeying these anti-religious laws. I must make two honest confessions to you, my Christian and Jewish brothers. First, I must confess that over the last few years I have been gravely disappointed with the white moderate. I have almost reached the regrettable conclusion that the Negro's great stumbling block in the stride toward freedom is not the White Citizen's Counciler or the Ku Klux Klanner, but the white moderate who is more devoted to "order" than to justice; who prefers a negative peace which is the absence of tension to a positive peace which is the presence of justice; who constantly says, "I agree with you in the goal you seek, but I can't agree with your methods of direct action"; who paternalistically feels that he can set the timetable for another man's freedom; who lives by the myth of time and who constantly advised the Negro to wait until a "more convenient season." Shallow understanding from people of good will is more frustrating than absolute misunderstanding from people of ill will. Lukewarm acceptance is much more bewildering than outright rejection.

I had hoped that the white moderate would understand that law and order exist for the purpose of establishing justice, and that when they fail to do this they become dangerously structured dams that block the flow of social progress. I had hoped that the white moderate would understand that the present tension of the South is merely a necessary phase of the transition from an obnoxious negative peace, where the Negro passively accepted his unjust plight, to a substance-filled positive peace, where all men will respect the dignity and worth of human personality. Actually, we who engage in nonviolent direct action are not the creators of tension. We merely bring to the surface the hidden tension that is already alive. We bring it out in the open where it can be seen and dealt with. Like a boil that can never be cured as long as it is covered up but must be opened with all its pus-flowing ugliness to the natural medicines of air and light, injustice must likewise be exposed, with all of the tension its exposing creates, to the light of human conscience and the air of national opinion before it can be cured.

In your statement you asserted that our actions, even though peaceful, must be condemned because they precipitate violence. But can this assertion be logically made? Isn't this like condemning the robbed man because his possession of money precipitated the evil act of robbery? Isn't this like condemning Socrates because his unswerving commitment to truth and his philosophical delvings precipitated the misguided popular mind to make him drink the hemlock? Isn't this like condemning Jesus because His unique God-consciousness and never-ceasing devotion to his will precipitated the evil act of crucifixion? We must come to see, as federal courts have consistently affirmed, that it is immoral to urge an individual to withdraw his efforts to gain his basic constitutional rights because the quest precipitates violence. Society must protect the robbed and punish the robber.

I had also hoped that the white moderate would reject the myth of time. I received a letter this morning from a white brother in Texas which said: "All Christians know that the colored people will receive equal rights eventually, but it is possible that you are in too great of a religious hurry. It has taken Christianity almost two thousand years to accomplish what it has. The teachings of Christ take time to come to earth." All that is said here grows out of a tragic misconception of time. It is the strangely irrational notion that there is something in the very flow of time that will inevitably cure all ills. Actually time is neutral. It can be used either destructively or constructively. I am coming to feel that the people of ill will have used time much more effectively than the people of good will. We will have to repent in this generation not merely for the vitriolic words and actions of the bad people, but for the appalling silence of the good people. We must come to see that human progress never rolls in on wheels of inevitability. It comes through the tireless efforts and persistent work of men willing to be co-workers with God, and without this hard work time itself becomes an ally of the forces of social stagnation. We must use time creatively, and forever realize that the time is always ripe to do right. Now is the time to make real the promise of democracy, and transform our pending national elegy into a creative psalm of brotherhood. Now is the time to lift our national policy from the quicksand of racial injustice to the solid rock of human dignity.

You spoke of our activity in Birmingham as extreme. At first I was rather disappointed that fellow clergymen would see my nonviolent efforts as those of the extremist. I started thinking about the fact that I stand in the middle of two opposing forces in the Negro community. One is a force of complacency made up of Negroes who, as a result of long years of oppression, have been so completely drained of self-respect and a sense of "somebodiness" that they have adjusted to segregation, and, of a few Negroes in the middle class who, because of a degree of academic and economic security, and because at points they profit by segregation, have unconsciously become insensitive to the problems of the masses. The other force is one of bitterness and hatred, and comes perilously close to advocating violence. It is expressed in the various black nationalist groups that are springing up over the nation, the largest and best known being Elijah Muhammad's Muslim movement. This movement is nourished by the contemporary frustration over the continued existence of racial discrimination. It is made up of people who have lost faith in America, who have absolutely repudiated Christianity, and who have concluded that the white man is an incurable "devil." I have tried to stand between these two forces, saying that we need not follow the "donothingism" of the complacent or the hatred and despair of the black nationalist. There is the more excellent way of love and nonviolent protest. I'm grateful to God that, through the Negro church, the dimension of nonviolence entered our struggle. If this philosophy had not emerged, I am convinced that by now many streets of the South would be flowing with floods of blood. And I am further convinced that if our white brothers dismiss as "rabble-rousers" and "outside agitators" those of us who are working through the channels of nonviolent direct action and refuse to support our nonviolent efforts, millions of Negroes, out of frustration and despair, will seek solace and security in black nationalist ideologies, a development that will lead inevitably to a frightening racial nightmare.

Oppressed people cannot remain oppressed forever. The urge for freedom will eventually come. This is what happened to the American Negro. Something within has reminded him of his birthright of freedom; something without has reminded him that he can gain it. Consciously and unconsciously, he has been swept in by what the Germans call the *Zeitgeist,* and with his black brothers of Africa, and his brown and yellow brothers of Asia, South America and the Caribbean, he is moving with a sense of cosmic urgency toward the promised land of racial justice. Recognizing this vital urge that has engulfed the Negro community, one should readily understand public demonstrations. The Negro has many pent-up resentments and latent frustrations. He has to get them out. So let him march sometime; let him have his prayer pilgrimages to the city hall; understand why he must have sit-ins and freedom rides. If his repressed emotions do not come out in these nonviolent ways, they will come out in ominous expressions of violence. This is not a threat; it is a fact of history. So I have not said to my people "get rid of your discontent." But I have tried to say that this normal and healthy discontent can be channelized through the creative outlet of nonviolent direct action. Now this approach is being dismissed as extremist. I must admit that I was initially disappointed in being so categorized.

But as I continued to think about the matter I gradually gained a bit of satisfaction from being considered an extremist. Was not Jesus an extremist in love—"Love your enemies, bless them that curse you, pray for them that despitefully use you." Was not Amos an extremist for justice—"Let justice roll down like waters and righteousness like a mighty stream." Was not Paul an extremist for the gospel of Jesus Christ—"I bear in my body the marks of the Lord Jesus." Was not Martin Luther an extremist—"Here I stand; I can do none other so help me God." Was not John Bunyan an extremist—"I will stay in jail to the end of my days before I make a butchery of my conscience." Was not Abraham Lincoln an extremist—"This nation cannot survive half slave and half free." Was not Thomas Jefferson an extremist—"We hold these truths to be self-evident, that all men are created equal." So the question is not whether we will be extremist but what kind of extremist will we be. Will we be extremists for hate or will we be extremists for love? Will we be extremists for the preservation of injustice—or will we be extremists for the cause of justice? In that dramatic scene on Calvary's hill, three men were crucified. We must not forget that all three were crucified for the same crime—the crime of extremism. Two were extremists for immorality, and thusly fell below their environment. The other, Jesus Christ, was an extremist for love, truth and goodness, and thereby rose above his environment. So, after all, maybe the South, the nation and the world are in dire need of creative extremists.

I had hoped that the white moderate would see this. Maybe I was too optimistic. Maybe I expected too much. I guess I should have realized that few members of a race that has oppressed another race can understand or appreciate the deep groans and passionate yearnings of those that have been oppressed and still fewer have the vision to see that injustice must be rooted out by strong, persistent and determined action. I am thankful, however, that some of our white brothers have grasped the meaning of this social revolution and committed themselves to it. They are still all too small in quantity, but they are big in quality. Some like Ralph McGill, Lillian Smith, Harry Golden and James Dabbs have written about our struggle in eloquent, prophetic and understanding terms. Others have marched with us down nameless streets of the South. They have languished in filthy roach-infested jails, suffering the abuse and brutality of angry policemen who see them as "dirty nigger-lovers." They, unlike so many of their moderate brothers and sisters, have recognized the urgency of the moment and sensed the need for powerful "action" antidotes to combat the disease of segregation.

Let me rush on to mention my other disappointment. I have been so greatly disappointed with the white church and its leadership. Of course, there are some notable exceptions. I am not unmindful of the fact that each of you has taken some significant stands on this issue. I commend you, Rev. Stallings, for your Christian stance on this past Sunday, in welcoming Negroes to your worship service on a nonsegregated basis. I commend the Catholic leaders of this state for integrating Springhill College several years ago.

But despite these notable exceptions I must honestly reiterate that I have been disappointed with the church. I do not say that as one of the negative critics who can always find something wrong with the church. I say it as a minister of the gospel, who loves the church; who was nurtured in its bosom; who has been sustained by its spiritual blessings and who will remain true to it as long as the cord of life shall lengthen.

I had the strange feeling when I was suddenly catapulted into the leadership of the bus protest in Montgomery several years ago that we would have the support of the white church. I felt that the white ministers, priests and rabbis of the South would be some of our strongest allies. Instead, some have been outright opponents, refusing to understand the freedom movement and misrepresenting its leaders; all too many others have been more cautious than courageous and have remained silent behind the anesthetizing security of the stained-glass windows.

In spite of my shattered dreams of the past, I came to Birmingham with the hope that the white religious leadership of this community would see the justice of our cause, and with deep moral concern, serve as the channel through which our just grievances would get to the power structure. I had hoped that each of you would understand. But again I have been disappointed. I have heard numerous religious leaders of the South call upon their worshippers to comply with a desegregation decision because it is the *law,* but I have longed to hear white ministers say, "Follow this decree because integration is morally *right* and the Negro is your brother." In the midst of blatant injustices

inflicted upon the Negro, I have watched white churches stand on the sideline and merely mouth pious irrelevancies and sanctimonious trivialities. In the midst of a mighty struggle to rid our nation of racial and economic injustice, I have heard so many ministers say, "Those are social issues with which the gospel has no real concern," and I have watched so many churches commit themselves to a completely otherworldly religion which made a strange distinction between body and soul, the sacred and the secular.

So here we are moving toward the exit of the twentieth century with a religious community largely adjusted to the status quo, standing as a taillight behind other community agencies rather than a headlight leading men to higher levels of justice.

I have traveled the length and breadth of Alabama, Mississippi and all the other southern states. On sweltering summer days and crisp autumn mornings I have looked at her beautiful churches with their lofty spires pointing heavenward. I have beheld the impressive outlay of her massive religious education buildings. Over and over again I have found myself asking: "What kind of people worship here? Who is their God? Where were their voices when the lips of Governor Barnett dripped with words of interposition and nullification? Where were they when Governor Wallace gave the clarion call for defiance and hatred? Where were their voices of support when tired, bruised and weary Negro men and women decided to rise from the dark dungeons of complacency to the bright hills of creative protest?"

Yes, these questions are still in my mind. In deep disappointment, I have wept over the laxity of the church. But be assured that my tears have been tears of love. There can be no deep disappointment where there is not deep love. Yes, I love the church; I love her sacred walls. How could I do otherwise? I am in a rather unique position of being the son, the grandson and the great-grandson of preachers. Yes, I see the church as the body of Christ. But, oh! How we have blemished and scarred that body through social neglect and fear of being nonconformists.

There was a time when the church was very powerful. It was during that period when the early Christians rejoiced when they were deemed worthy to suffer for what they believed. In those days the church was not merely a thermometer that recorded the ideas and principles of popular opinion; it was a thermostat that transformed the mores of society. Wherever the early Christians entered a town the power structure got disturbed and immediately sought to convict them for being "disturbers of the peace" and "outside agitators." But they went on with the conviction that they were "a colony of heaven," and had to obey God rather than man. They were small in number but big in commitment. They were too God-intoxicated to be "astronomically intimidated." They brought an end to such ancient evils as infanticide and gladiatorial contest.

Things are different now. The contemporary church is often a weak, ineffectual voice with an uncertain sound. It is so often the arch-supporter of the status quo. Far from being disturbed by the presence of the church, the power structure of the average community is consoled by the church's silent and often vocal sanction of things as they are.

But the judgment of God is upon the church as never before. If the church of today does not recapture the sacrificial spirit of the early church, it will lose its authentic ring, forfeit the loyalty of millions, and be dismissed as an irrelevant social club with no meaning for the twentieth century. I am meeting young people every day whose disappointment with the church has risen to outright disgust.

Maybe again, I have been too optimistic. Is organized religion too inextricably bound to the status quo to save our nation and the world? Maybe I must turn my faith to the inner spiritual church, the church within the church, as the true *ecclesia* and the hope of the world. But again I am thankful to God that some noble souls from the ranks of organized religion have broken loose from the paralyzing chains of conformity and joined us as active partners in the struggle for freedom. They have left their secure congregations and walked the streets of Albany, Georgia, with us. They have gone through the highways of the South on tortuous rides for freedom. Yes, they have gone to jail with us. Some have been kicked out of their churches, and lost support of their bishops and fellow ministers. But they have gone with the faith that right defeated is stronger than evil triumphant. These men have been the leaven in the lump of the race. Their witness has been the spiritual salt that has preserved the true meaning of the gospel in these troubled times. They have carved a tunnel of hope through the dark mountain of disappointment.

I hope the church as a whole will meet the challenge of this decisive hour. But even if the church does not come to the aid of justice, I have no despair about the future. I have no fear about the outcome of our struggle in Birmingham, even if our motives are presently misunderstood. We will reach the goal of freedom in Birmingham and all over the nation, because the goal of America is freedom. Abused and scorned though we may be, our destiny is tied up with the destiny of America. Before the Pilgrims landed at Plymouth we were here. Before the pen of Jefferson etched across the pages of history the majestic words of the Declaration of Independence, we were here. For more than two centuries our foreparents labored in this country without wages; they made cotton king; and they built the homes of their masters in the midst of brutal injustice and shameful humiliation—and yet out of a bottomless vitality they continued to thrive and develop. If the inexpressible cruelties of slavery could not stop us, the opposition we now face will surely fail. We will win our freedom because the sacred heritage of our nation and the eternal will of God are embodied in our echoing demands.

I must close now. But before closing I am impelled to mention one other point in your statement that troubled me profoundly. You warmly commended the Birmingham police force for keeping "order" and "preventing violence." I don't believe you would have so warmly commended the police force if you had seen its angry violent dogs literally biting six unarmed, nonviolent Negroes. I don't believe you would so quickly commend the policemen if you would observe their ugly and inhuman treatment of Negroes here in the city jail; if you would watch them push and curse old Negro women and young Negro girls; if you would see them slap and kick old Negro men and young boys; if you will observe them, as they did on two occasions, refuse to give us food because we wanted to sing our grace together. I'm sorry that I can't join you in your praise for the police department.

It is true that they have been rather disciplined in their public handling of the demonstrators. In this sense they have been rather publicly "nonviolent." But for what purpose? To preserve the evil system of segregation. Over the last few years I have consistently preached that nonviolence demands that the means we use must be as pure as the ends we seek. So I have tried to make it clear that it is wrong to use immoral means to attain moral ends. But now I must affirm that it is just as wrong, or even more so, to use moral means to preserve immoral ends. Maybe Mr. Connor and his policemen have been rather publicly nonviolent, as Chief Pritchett was in Albany, Georgia, but they have used the moral means of nonviolence to maintain the immoral end of flagrant racial injustice. T. S. Eliot has said that there is no greater treason than to do the right deed for the wrong reason.

I wish you had commended the Negro sit-inners and demonstrators of Birmingham for their sublime courage, their willingness to suffer and their amazing discipline in the midst of the most inhuman provocation. One day the South will recognize its real heroes. They will be the James Merediths, courageously and with a majestic sense of purpose facing jeering and hostile mobs and the agonizing loneliness that characterizes the life of the pioneer. They will be old, oppressed, battered Negro women, symbolized in a seventy-two-year-old woman of Montgomery, Alabama, who rose up with a sense of dignity and with her people decided not to ride the segregated buses, and responded to one who inquired about her tiredness with ungrammatical profundity: "My feet is tired, but my soul is rested." They will be the young high school and college students, young ministers of the gospel and a host of their elders courageously and nonviolently sitting-in at lunch counters and willingly going to jail for conscience's sake. One day the South will know that when these disinherited children of God sat down at lunch counters they were in reality standing up for the best in the American dream and the most sacred values in our Judeo-Christian heritage, and thusly, carrying our whole nation back to those great walls of democracy which were dug deep by the Founding Fathers in the formulation of the Constitution and the Declaration of Independence.

Never before have I written a letter this long (or should I say a book?). I'm afraid that it is much too long to take your precious time. I can assure you that it would have been much shorter if I had been writing from a comfortable desk, but what else is there to do when you are alone for days in the dull monotony of a narrow jail cell other than write long letters, think strange thoughts, and pray long prayers?

If I have said anything in this letter that is an overstatement of the truth and is indicative of an unreasonable impatience, I beg you to forgive me. If I have said anything in this letter that is an understatement of the truth and is indicative of my having a patience that makes me patient with anything less than brotherhood, I beg God to forgive me.

I hope this letter finds you strong in the faith. I also hope that circumstances will soon make it possible for me to meet each of you, not as an integrationist or a civil rights leader, but as a fellow clergyman and a Christian brother. Let us all hope that the dark clouds of racial prejudice will soon pass away and the deep fog of misunderstanding will be lifted from our fear-drenched communities and in some not too distant tomorrow the radiant stars of love and brotherhood will shine over our great nation with all of their scintillating beauty.

Yours for the cause of Peace and Brotherhood, Martin Luther King, Jr.

Study Questions

1. What is civil disobedience?
2. How does civil disobedience differ from mere lawbreaking?
3. Is every unjust law an appropriate target for civil disobedience?
4. What is the connection, if any, between Dr. King's religious commitments and his political actions?

B. Abortion

A Defense of Abortion

JUDITH JARVIS THOMSON

Consider the following argument:

1. A fetus is an innocent human being.

2. Killing an innocent human being is always wrong.

3. Therefore killing a fetus is always wrong.

This argument is valid because the premises imply the conclusion. But is the argument sound? In other words, are both its premises true?

Premise (1) is open to question, for arguably the earliest embryo is not a human person. Yet some believe it is and may defend their view on religious grounds. In any case you might suppose that if premise (1) were granted, then the conclusion of the argument would follow, because premise (2) may appear uncontroversial. Much philosophical discussion, however, has hypothesized that premise (1) is true and nevertheless denied the argument's conclusion by claiming that premise (2) is false.

On what grounds, if any, can premise (2) be rejected? That question lies at the heart of the following essay by Judith Jarvis Thomson, who is

From Judith Jarvis Thomson, "A Defense of Abortion," *Philosophy & Public Affairs* 1 (1971). Reprinted by permission of Blackwell Publishers.

Professor Emerita of Philosophy at the Massachusetts Institute of Technology. Thomson argues that even if the human fetus is a person, abortion remains morally permissible in a variety of cases in which the mother's life is not threatened.

Most opposition to abortion relies on the premise that the fetus is a human being, a person, from the moment of conception. The premise is argued for, but, as I think, not well. Take, for example, the most common argument. We are asked to notice that the development of a human being from conception through birth into childhood is continuous; then it is said that to draw a line, to choose a point in this development and say "before this point the thing is not a person, after this point it is a person" is to make an arbitrary choice, a choice for which in the nature of things no good reason can be given. It is concluded that the fetus is, or anyway that we had better say it is, a person from the moment of conception. But this conclusion does not follow. Similar things might be said about the development of an acorn into an oak tree, and it does not follow that acorns are oak trees, or that we had better say they are. Arguments of this form are sometimes called "slippery slope arguments"— the phrase is perhaps self-explanatory—and it is dismaying that opponents of abortion rely on them so heavily and uncritically.

I am inclined to agree, however, that the prospects for "drawing a line" in the development of the fetus look dim. I am inclined to think also that we shall probably have to agree that the fetus has already become a human person well before birth. Indeed, it comes as a surprise when one first learns how early in its life it begins to acquire human characteristics. By the tenth week, for example, it already has a face, arms and legs, fingers and toes; it has internal organs, and brain activity is detectable. On the other hand, I think that the premise is false, that the fetus is not a person from the moment of conception. A newly fertilized ovum, a newly implanted clump of cells, is no more a person than an acorn is an oak tree. But I shall not discuss any of this. For it seems to me to be of great interest to ask what happens if, for the sake of argument, we allow the premise. How, precisely, are we supposed to get from there to the conclusion that abortion is morally impermissible? Opponents of abortion commonly spend most of their time establishing that the fetus is a person, and hardly any time explaining the step from there to the impermissibility of abortion. Perhaps they think the step too simple and obvious to require much comment. Or perhaps instead they are simply being economical in argument. Many of those who defend abortion rely on the premise that the fetus is not a person, but only a bit of tissue that will become a person at birth; and why pay out more arguments than you have to? Whatever the explanation, I suggest that the step they take is neither easy nor obvious, that it calls for closer examination than it is commonly given, and that when we do give it this closer examination we shall feel inclined to reject it.

I propose, then, that we grant that the fetus is a person from the moment of conception. How does the argument go from here? Something like this, I take it. Every person has a right to life. So the fetus has a right to life. No doubt the mother has a right to decide what shall happen in and to her body; everyone would grant that. But surely a person's right to life is stronger and more stringent than the mother's right to decide what happens in and to her body, and so outweighs it. So the fetus may not be killed; an abortion may not be performed.

It sounds plausible. But now let me ask you to imagine this. You wake up in the morning and find yourself back to back in bed with an unconscious violinist. A famous unconscious violinist. He has been found to have a fatal kidney ailment, and the Society of Music Lovers has canvassed all the available medical records and found that you alone have the right blood type to help. They have therefore kidnapped you, and last night the violinist's circulatory system was plugged into yours, so that your kidneys can be used to extract poisons from his blood as well as your own. The director of the hospital now tells you, "Look, we're sorry the Society of Music Lovers did this to you—we would never have permitted it if we had known. But still, they did it, and the violinist now is plugged into you. To unplug you would be to kill him. But never mind, it's only for nine months. By then he will have recovered from his ailment, and can safely be unplugged from you." Is it morally incumbent on you to accede to this situation? No doubt it would be very nice of you if you did, a great kindness. But do you *have* to accede to it? What if it were not nine months, but nine years? Or longer still? What if the director of the hospital says, "Tough luck, I agree, but you've now got to stay in bed, with the violinist plugged into you, for the rest of your life. Because remember this. All persons have a right to life, and violinists are persons. Granted you have a right to decide what happens in and to your body, but a person's right to life outweighs your right to decide what happens in and to your body. So you cannot ever be unplugged from him." I imagine you would regard this as outrageous, which suggests that something really is wrong with that plausible-sounding argument I mentioned a moment ago.

In this case, of course, you were kidnapped; you didn't volunteer for the operation that plugged the violinist into your kidneys. Can those who oppose abortion on the ground I mentioned make an exception for a pregnancy due to rape? Certainly. They can say that persons have a right to life only if they didn't come into existence because of rape; or they can say that all persons have a right to life, but that some have less of a right to life than others, in particular, that those who came into existence because of rape have less. But these statements have a rather unpleasant sound. Surely the

question of whether you have a right to life at all, or how much of it you have, shouldn't turn on the question of whether or not you are the product of a rape. And in fact the people who oppose abortion on the ground I mentioned do not make this distinction, and hence do not make an exception in case of rape.

Nor do they make an exception for a case in which the mother has to spend the nine months of her pregnancy in bed. They would agree that would be a great pity, and hard on the mother; but all the same, all persons have a right to life, the fetus is a person, and so on. I suspect, in fact, that they would not make an exception for a case in which, miraculously enough, the pregnancy went on for nine years, or even the rest of the mother's life.

Some won't even make an exception for a case in which continuation of the pregnancy is likely to shorten the mother's life; they regard abortion as impermissible even to save the mother's life. Such cases are nowadays very rare, and many opponents of abortion do not accept this extreme view. All the same, it is a good place to begin: a number of points of interest come out in respect to it.

1. Let us call the view that abortion is impermissible even to save the mother's life "the extreme view." I want to suggest first that it does not issue from the argument I mentioned earlier without the addition of some fairly powerful premises. Suppose a woman has become pregnant, and now learns that she has a cardiac condition such that she will die if she carries the baby to term. What may be done for her? The fetus, being a person, has a right to life, but as the mother is a person too, so has she a right to life. Presumably they have an equal right to life. How is it supposed to come out that an abortion may not be performed? If mother and child have an equal right to life, shouldn't we perhaps flip a coin? Or should we add to the mother's right to life her right to decide what happens in and to her body, which everybody seems to be ready to grant—the sum of her rights now outweighing the fetus' right to life?

The most familiar argument here is the following. We are told that performing the abortion would be directly killing[1] the child, whereas doing nothing would not be killing the mother, but only letting her die. Moreover, in killing the child, one would be killing an innocent person, for the child has committed no crime, and is not aiming at his mother's death. And then there are a variety of ways in which this might be continued. (1) But as directly killing an innocent person is always and absolutely impermissible, an abortion may not be performed. Or, (2) as directly killing an innocent person is murder, and murder is always and absolutely impermissible, an abortion may not be performed. Or, (3) as one's duty to refrain from directly killing an innocent person is more stringent than one's duty to keep a person from dying, an abortion may not be performed. Or, (4) if one's only options are directly killing an innocent person or letting a person die, one must prefer letting the person die, and thus an abortion may not be performed.

Some people seem to have thought that these are not further premises which must be added if the conclusion is to be reached, but that they follow from the very fact that an innocent person has a right to life. But this seems to me to be a mistake, and perhaps the simplest way to show this is to bring out that while we must certainly grant that innocent persons have a right to life, the theses in (1) through (4) are all false. Take (2), for example. If directly killing an innocent person is murder, and thus is impermissible, then the mother's directly killing the innocent person inside her is murder, and thus is impermissible. But it cannot seriously be thought to be murder if the mother performs an abortion on herself to save her life. It cannot seriously be said that she *must* refrain, that she *must* sit passively by and wait for her death. Let us look again at the case of you and the violinist. There you are, in bed with the violinist, and the director of the hospital says to you, "It's all most distressing, and I deeply sympathize, but you see

this is putting an additional strain on your kidneys, and you'll be dead within the month. But you *have* to stay where you are all the same. Because unplugging you would be directly killing an innocent violinist, and that's murder, and that's impermissible." If anything in the world is true, it is that you do not commit murder, you do not do what is impermissible, if you reach around to your back and unplug yourself from that violinist to save your life. . . .

I should perhaps stop to say explicitly that I am not claiming that people have a right to do anything whatever to save their lives. I think, rather, that there are drastic limits to the right of self-defense. If someone threatens you with death unless you torture someone else to death, I think you have not the right, even to save your life, to do so. But the case under consideration here is very different. In our case there are only two people involved, one whose life is threatened, and one who threatens it. Both are innocent: the one who is threatened is not threatened because of any fault, the one who threatens does not threaten because of any fault. For this reason we may feel that we bystanders cannot intervene. But the person threatened can.

In sum, a woman surely can defend her life against the threat to it posed by the unborn child, even if doing so involves its death. And this shows not merely that the theses in (1) through (4) are false; it shows also that the extreme view of abortion is false, and so we need not canvass any other possible ways of arriving at it from the argument I mentioned at the outset.

2. The extreme view could of course be weakened to say that while abortion is permissible to save the mother's life, it may not be performed by a third party, but only by the mother herself. But this cannot be right either. For what we have to keep in mind is that the mother and the unborn child are not like two tenants in a small house which has, by an unfortunate mistake, been rented to both: the mother *owns* the house. The fact that she does adds to the offensiveness of deducing that the mother can do nothing

from the supposition that third parties can do nothing. But it does more than this: it casts a bright light on the supposition that third parties can do nothing. Certainly it lets us see that a third party who says "I cannot choose between you" is fooling himself if he thinks this is impartiality. If Jones has found and fastened on a certain coat, which he needs to keep him from freezing, but which Smith also needs to keep him from freezing, then it is not impartiality that says "I cannot choose between you" when Smith owns the coat. Women have said again and again "This body is *my* body!" and they have reason to feel angry, reason to feel that it has been like shouting into the wind. . . .

3. Where the mother's life is not at stake, the argument I mentioned at the outset seems to have a much stronger pull. "Everyone has a right to life, so the unborn person has a right to life." And isn't the child's right to life weightier than anything other than the mother's own right to life, which she might put forward as ground for an abortion?

This argument treats the right to life as if it were unproblematic. It is not, and this seems to me to be precisely the source of the mistake.

For we should now, at long last, ask what it comes to, to have a right to life. In some views having a right to life includes having a right to be given at least the bare minimum one needs for continued life. But suppose that what in fact *is* the bare minimum a man needs for continued life is something he has no right at all to be given? If I am sick unto death, and the only thing that will save my life is the touch of Henry Fonda's cool hand on my fevered brow, then all the same, I have no right to be given the touch of Henry Fonda's cool hand on my fevered brow. It would be frightfully nice of him to fly in from the West Coast to provide it. It would be less nice, though no doubt well meant, if my friends flew out to the West Coast and carried Henry Fonda back with them. But I have no right at all against anybody that he should do this for me. Or again, to return to the story I told earlier, the

fact that for continued life that violinist needs the continued use of your kidneys does not establish that he has a right to be given the continued use of your kidneys. He certainly has no right against you that *you* should give him continued use of your kidneys. For nobody has any right to use your kidneys unless you give him such a right; and nobody has the right against you that you shall give him this right—if you do allow him to go on using your kidneys, this is a kindness on your part, and not something he can claim from you as his due. Nor has he any right against anybody else that *they* should give him continued use of your kidneys. Certainly he had no right against the Society of Music Lovers that they should plug him into you in the first place. And if you now start to unplug yourself, having learned that you will otherwise have to spend nine years in bed with him, there is nobody in the world who must try to prevent you, in order to see to it that he is given something he has a right to be given.

Some people are rather stricter about the right to life. In their view, it does not include the right to be given anything, but amounts to, and only to, the right not to be killed by anybody. But here a related difficulty arises. If everybody is to refrain from killing that violinist, then everybody must refrain from doing a great many different sorts of things. Everybody must refrain from slitting his throat, everybody must refrain from shooting him—and everybody must refrain from unplugging you from him. But does he have a right against everybody that they shall refrain from unplugging you from him? To refrain from doing this is to allow him to continue to use your kidneys. It could be argued that he has a right against us that *we* should allow him to continue to use your kidneys. That is, while he had no right against us that we should give him the use of your kidneys, it might be argued that he anyway has a right against us that we shall not now intervene and deprive him of the use of your kidneys. I shall come back to third-party interventions later. But certainly the violinist has no right against you that *you* shall allow him to continue to use your kidneys. As I said, if you do allow him to use them, it is a kindness on your part, and not something you owe him.

The difficulty I point to here is not peculiar to the right to life. It reappears in connection with all the other natural rights; and it is something which an adequate account of rights must deal with. For present purposes it is enough just to draw attention to it. But I would stress that I am not arguing that people do not have a right to life—quite to the contrary, it seems to me that the primary control we must place on the acceptability of an account of rights is that it should turn out in that account to be a truth that all persons have a right to life. I am arguing only that having a right to life does not guarantee having either a right to be given the use of or a right to be allowed continued use of another person's body—even if one needs it for life itself. So the right to life will not serve the opponents of abortion in the very simple and clear way in which they seem to have thought it would.

4. There is another way to bring out the difficulty. In the most ordinary sort of case, to deprive someone of what he has a right to is to treat him unjustly. Suppose a boy and his small brother are jointly given a box of chocolates for Christmas. If the older boy takes the box and refuses to give his brother any of the chocolates, he is unjust to him, for the brother has been given a right to half of them. But suppose that, having learned that otherwise it means nine years in bed with that violinist, you unplug yourself from him. You surely are not being unjust to him, for you gave him no right to use your kidneys, and no one else can have given him any such right. But we have to notice that in unplugging yourself, you are killing him; and violinists, like everybody else, have a right to life, and thus in the view we were considering just now, the right not to be killed. So here you do what he supposedly has a right you shall not do, but you do not act unjustly to him in doing it.

The emendation which may be made at this point is this: the right to life consists not in the right not to be killed, but rather in the right not to be killed unjustly. This runs a risk of circularity, but never mind: it would enable us to square the fact that the violinist has a right to life with the fact that you do not act unjustly toward him in unplugging yourself, thereby killing him. For if you do not kill him unjustly, you do not violate his right to life, and so it is no wonder you do him no injustice.

But if this emendation is accepted, the gap in the argument against abortion stares us plainly in the face: it is by no means enough to show that the fetus is a person, and to remind us that all persons have a right to life—we need to be shown also that killing the fetus violates its right to life, i.e., that abortion is unjust killing. And is it?

I suppose we may take it as a datum that in a case of pregnancy due to rape the mother has not given the unborn person a right to the use of her body for food and shelter. Indeed, in what pregnancy could it be supposed that the mother has given the unborn person such a right? It is not as if there were unborn persons drifting about the world, to whom a woman who wants a child says "I invite you in."

But it might be argued that there are other ways one can have acquired a right to the use of another person's body than by having been invited to use it by that person. Suppose a woman voluntarily indulges in intercourse, knowing of the chance it will issue in pregnancy, and then she does become pregnant; is she not in part responsible for the presence, in fact the very existence, of the unborn person inside her? No doubt she did not invite it in. But doesn't her partial responsibility for its being there itself give it a right to the use of her body? If so, then her aborting it would be more like the boy's taking away the chocolates, and less like your unplugging yourself from the violinist—doing so would be depriving it of what it does have a right to, and thus would be doing it an injustice.

And then, too, it might be asked whether or not she can kill it even to save her own life: If she voluntarily called it into existence, how can she now kill it, even in self-defense?

The first thing to be said about this is that it is something new. Opponents of abortion have been so concerned to make out the independence of the fetus, in order to establish that it has a right to life, just as its mother does, that they have tended to overlook the possible support they might gain from making out that the fetus is *dependent* on the mother, in order to establish that she has a special kind of responsibility for it, a responsibility that gives it rights against her which are not possessed by any independent person—such as an ailing violinist who is a stranger to her.

On the other hand, this argument would give the unborn person a right to its mother's body only if her pregnancy resulted from a voluntary act, undertaken in full knowledge of the chance a pregnancy might result from it. It would leave out entirely the unborn person whose existence is due to rape. Pending the availability of some further argument, then, we would be left with the conclusion that unborn persons whose existence is due to rape have no right to the use of their mothers' bodies, and thus that aborting them is not depriving them of anything they have a right to and hence is not unjust killing.

And we should also notice that it is not at all plain that this argument really does go even as far as it purports to. For there are cases and cases, and the details make a difference. If the room is stuffy, and I therefore open a window to air it, and a burglar climbs in, it would be absurd to say, "Ah, now he can stay, she's given him a right to the use of her house—for she is partially responsible for his presence there, having voluntarily done what enabled him to get in, in full knowledge that there are such things as burglars, and that burglars burgle." It would be still more absurd to say this if I had had bars installed outside my windows, precisely to prevent burglars

from getting in, and a burglar got in only because of a defect in the bars. It remains equally absurd if we imagine it is not a burglar who climbs in, but an innocent person who blunders or falls in. Again, suppose it were like this: people-seeds drift about in the air like pollen, and if you open your windows, one may drift in and take root in your carpets or upholstery. You don't want children, so you fix up your windows with fine mesh screens, the very best you can buy. As can happen, however, and on very, very rare occasions does happen, one of the screens is defective; and a seed drifts in and takes root. Does the person-plant who now develops have a right to the use of your house? Surely not—despite the fact that you voluntarily opened your windows, you knowingly kept carpets and upholstered furniture, and you knew that screens were sometimes defective. Someone may argue that you are responsible for its rooting, that it does have a right to your house, because after all you *could* have lived out your life with bare floors and furniture, or with sealed windows and doors. But this won't do—for by the same token anyone can avoid a pregnancy due to rape by having a hysterectomy, or anyway by never leaving home without a (reliable!) army.

It seems to me that the argument we are looking at can establish at most that there are *some* cases in which the unborn person has a right to the use of its mother's body, and therefore *some* cases in which abortion is unjust killing. There is room for much discussion and argument as to precisely which, if any. But I think we should sidestep this issue and leave it open, for at any rate the argument certainly does not establish that all abortion is unjust killing.

5. There is room for yet another argument here, however. We surely must all grant that there may be cases in which it would be morally indecent to detach a person from your body at the cost of his life. Suppose you learn that what the violinist needs is not nine years of your life, but only one hour: all you need do to save his life is to spend one hour in that bed with him.

Suppose also that letting him use your kidneys for that one hour would not affect your health in the slightest. Admittedly you were kidnapped. Admittedly you did not give anyone permission to plug him into you. Nevertheless it seems to me plain you *ought* to allow him to use your kidneys for that hour—it would be indecent to refuse.

Again, suppose pregnancy lasted only an hour, and constituted no threat to life or health. And suppose that a woman becomes pregnant as a result of rape. Admittedly she did not voluntarily do anything to bring about the existence of a child. Admittedly she did nothing at all which would give the unborn person a right to the use of her body. All the same it might well be said, as in the newly emended violinist story, that she *ought* to allow it to remain for that hour—that it would be indecent of her to refuse. . . .

8. My argument will be found unsatisfactory on two counts by many of those who want to regard abortion as morally permissible. First, while I do argue that abortion is not impermissible, I do not argue that it is always permissible. There may well be cases in which carrying the child to term requires only Minimally Decent Samaritanism of the mother, and this is a standard we must not fall below. I am inclined to think it a merit of my account precisely that it does *not* give a general yes or a general no. It allows for and supports our sense that, for example, a sick and desperately frightened fourteen-year-old schoolgirl, pregnant due to rape, may *of course* choose abortion, and that any law which rules this out is an insane law. And it also allows for and supports our sense that in other cases resort to abortion is even positively indecent. It would be indecent in the woman to request an abortion, and indecent in a doctor to perform it, if she is in her seventh month, and wants the abortion just to avoid the nuisance of postponing a trip abroad. The very fact that the arguments I have been drawing attention to treat all cases of abortion, or even all cases of abortion in which the mother's life is not at stake, as morally on a par ought to have made them suspect at the outset.

Secondly, while I am arguing for the permissibility of abortion in some cases, I am not arguing for the right to secure the death of the unborn child. It is easy to confuse these two things in that up to a certain point in the life of the fetus it is not able to survive outside the mother's body; hence removing it from her body guarantees its death. But they are importantly different. I have argued that you are not morally required to spend nine months in bed, sustaining the life of that violinist; but to say this is by no means to say that if, when you unplug yourself, there is a miracle and he survives, you then have a right to turn round and slit his throat. You may detach yourself even if this costs him his life; you have no right to be guaranteed his death, by some other means, if unplugging yourself does not kill him. There are some people who will feel dissatisfied by this feature of my argument. A woman may be utterly devastated by the thought of a child, a bit of herself, put out for adoption and never seen or heard of again. She may therefore want not merely that the child be detached from her, but more, that it die. Some opponents of abortion are inclined to regard this as beneath contempt—thereby showing insensitivity to what is surely a powerful source of despair. All the same, I agree that the desire for the child's death is not one which anybody may gratify, should it turn out to be possible to detach the child alive.

At this place, however, it should be remembered that we have only been pretending throughout that the fetus is a human being from the moment of conception. A very early abortion is surely not the killing of a person, and so is not dealt with by anything I have said here.

NOTE

1. The term "direct" in the arguments I refer to is a technical one. Roughly, what is meant by "direct killing" is either killing as an end in itself, or killing as a means of some end, for example, the end of saving someone else's life.

Study Questions

1. What are the main points Thomson seeks to make by the example of the unconscious violinist?
2. Does the morality of aborting a fetus depend on the conditions surrounding its conception?
3. If abortion is murder, who is the murderer and what is the appropriate punishment?
4. If the abortion controversy is described as a debate between those who believe in a right to life and those who affirm a woman's right to choose, on which side is Thomson?

Why Abortion Is Immoral

DON MARQUIS

Don Marquis, who is Professor of Philosophy at the University of Kansas, disagrees with the position on abortion defended by Judith Jarvis Thomson. He argues that, with rare exceptions, abortion is immoral. Note that he does not base his reasoning on the claim that the fetus is a person but rather on the view that the fetus has a valuable future.

The view that abortion is, with rare exceptions, seriously immoral has received little support in the recent philosophical literature. No doubt most philosophers affiliated with secular institutions of higher education believe that the anti-abortion position is either a symptom of irrational religious dogma or a conclusion generated by seriously confused philosophical argument. The purpose of this essay is to undermine this general belief. This essay sets out an argument that purports to show, as well as any argument in ethics can show, that abortion is, except possibly in rare cases, seriously immoral, that it is in the same moral category as killing an innocent adult human being. . . .

I

A sketch of standard anti-abortion and pro-choice arguments exhibits how those arguments possess certain symmetries that explain why partisans of those positions are so convinced of the correctness of their own positions, why they are not successful in convincing their opponents, and why, to others, this issue seems to be unresolvable. An analysis of the nature of this standoff suggests a strategy for surmounting it.

Consider the way a typical anti-abortionist argues. She will argue or assert that life is present from the moment of conception or that

From Don Marquis, "Why Abortion Is Immoral," *The Journal of Philosophy*, 86 (1989). Reprinted with the permission of the author and the journal.

fetuses look like babies or that fetuses possess a characteristic such as a genetic code that is both necessary and sufficient for being human. Anti-abortionists seem to believe that (1) the truth of all of these claims is quite obvious, and (2) establishing any of these claims is sufficient to show that abortion is morally akin to murder.

A standard pro-choice strategy exhibits similarities. The pro-choicer will argue or assert that fetuses are not persons or that fetuses are not rational agents or that fetuses are not social beings. Pro-choicers seem to believe that (1) the truth of any of these claims is quite obvious, and (2) establishing any of these claims is sufficient to show that an abortion is not a wrongful killing.

In fact, both the pro-choice and the anti-abortion claims do seem to be true, although the "it looks like a baby" claim is more difficult to establish the earlier the pregnancy. We seem to have a standoff. How can it be resolved?

As everyone who has taken a bit of logic knows, if any of these arguments concerning abortion is a good argument, it requires not only some claim characterizing fetuses, but also some general moral principle that ties a characteristic of fetuses to having or not having the right to life or to some other moral characteristic that will generate the obligation or the lack of obligation not to end the life of a fetus. Accordingly, the arguments of the anti-abortionist and the pro-choicer need a bit of filling in to be regarded as adequate.

Note what each partisan will say. The anti-abortionist will claim that her position is supported by such generally accepted moral principles as "It is always prima facie seriously wrong to take a human life" or "It is always prima facie seriously wrong to end the life of a baby." Since these are generally accepted moral principles, her position is certainly not obviously wrong. The pro-choicer will claim that her position is supported by such plausible moral principles as "Being a person is what gives an individual intrinsic moral worth" or "It is only seriously prima facie wrong to take

the life of a member of the human community." Since these are generally accepted moral principles, the pro-choice position is certainly not obviously wrong. Unfortunately, we have again arrived at a standoff.

Now, how might one deal with this standoff? The standard approach is to try to show how the moral principles of one's opponent lose their plausibility under analysis. It is easy to see how this is possible. On the one hand, the anti-abortionist will defend a moral principle concerning the wrongness of killing which tends to be broad in scope in order that even fetuses at an early stage of pregnancy will fall under it. The problem with broad principles is that they often embrace too much. In this particular instance, the principle "It is always prima facie wrong to take a human life" seems to entail that it is wrong to end the existence of a living human cancer-cell culture, on the grounds that the culture is both living and human. Therefore, it seems that the anti-abortionist's favored principle is too broad.

On the other hand, the pro-choicer wants to find a moral principle concerning the wrongness of killing which tends to be narrow in scope in order that fetuses will *not* fall under it. The problem with narrow principles is that they often do not embrace enough. Hence, the needed principles such as "It is prima facie seriously wrong to kill only persons" or "It is prima facie wrong to kill only rational agents" do not explain why it is wrong to kill infants or young children or the severely retarded or even perhaps the severely mentally ill. Therefore, we seem again to have a standoff. The anti-abortionist charges, not unreasonably, that pro-choice principles concerning killing are too narrow to be acceptable; the pro-choicer charges, not unreasonably, that anti-abortionist principles concerning killing are too broad to be acceptable. . . .

All this suggests that a necessary condition of resolving the abortion controversy is a more theoretical account of the wrongness of killing. After all, if we merely believe, but do not understand, why killing adult human beings such as ourselves is wrong, how could we conceivably show that abortion is either immoral or permissible?

II

In order to develop such an account, we can start from the following unproblematic assumption concerning our own case: it is wrong to kill *us*. Why is it wrong? Some answers can be easily eliminated. It might be said that what makes killing us wrong is that a killing brutalizes the one who kills. But the brutalization consists of being inured to the performance of an act that is hideously immoral; hence, the brutalization does not explain the immorality. It might be said that what makes killing us wrong is the great loss others would experience due to our absence. Although such hubris is understandable, such an explanation does not account for the wrongness of killing hermits, or those whose lives are relatively independent and whose friends find it easy to make new friends.

A more obvious answer is better. What primarily makes killing wrong is neither its effect on the murderer nor its effect on the victim's friends and relatives, but its effect on the victim. The loss of one's life is one of the greatest losses one can suffer. The loss of one's life deprives one of all the experiences, activities, projects, and enjoyments that would otherwise have constituted one's future. Therefore, killing someone is wrong, primarily because the killing inflicts (one of) the greatest possible losses on the victim. To describe this as the loss of life can be misleading, however. The change in my biological state does not by itself make killing me wrong. The effect of the loss of my biological life is the loss to me of all those activities, projects, experiences, and enjoyments which would otherwise have constituted my future personal life. These activities, projects, experiences, and enjoyments are either valuable for their own sakes or are means to something else that is valuable for its own sake. Some parts of my future are not valued by me now, but will come

to be valued by me as I grow older and as my values and capacities change. When I am killed, I am deprived both of what I now value which would have been part of my future personal life, but also what I would come to value. Therefore, when I die, I am deprived of all of the value of my future. Inflicting this loss on me is ultimately what makes killing me wrong. This being the case, it would seem that what makes killing *any* adult human being prima facie seriously wrong is the loss of his or her future.[1]

How should this rudimentary theory of the wrongness of killing be evaluated? It cannot be faulted for deriving an "ought" from an "is," for it does not. The analysis assumes that killing me (or you, reader) is prima facie seriously wrong. The point of the analysis is to establish which natural property ultimately explains the wrongness of the killing, given that it is wrong. A natural property will ultimately explain the wrongness of killing, only if (1) the explanation fits with our intuitions about the matter and (2) there is no other natural property that provides the basis for a better explanation of the wrongness of killing. This analysis rests on the intuition that what makes killing a particular human or animal wrong is what it does to that particular human or animal. What makes killing wrong is some natural effect or other of the killing. Some would deny this. For instance, a divine-command theorist in ethics would deny it. Surely this denial is, however, one of those features of divine-command theory which renders it so implausible.

The claim that what makes killing wrong is the loss of the victim's future is directly supported by two considerations. In the first place, this theory explains why we regard killing as one of the worst of crimes. Killing is especially wrong, because it deprives the victim of more than perhaps any other crime. In the second place, people with AIDS or cancer who know they are dying believe, of course, that dying is a very bad thing for them. They believe that the loss of a future to them that they would otherwise have experienced is what makes their premature death a very bad thing for them. A better theory of the wrongness of killing would require a different natural property associated with killing which better fits with the attitudes of the dying. What could it be?

The view that what makes killing wrong is the loss to the victim of the value of the victim's future gains additional support when some of its implications are examined. In the first place, it is incompatible with the view that it is wrong to kill only beings who are biologically human. It is possible that there exists a different species from another planet whose members have a future like ours. Since having a future like that is what makes killing someone wrong, this theory entails that it would be wrong to kill members of such a species. Hence, this theory is opposed to the claim that only life that is biologically human has great moral worth, a claim which many anti-abortionists have seemed to adopt. This opposition, which this theory has in common with personhood theories, seems to be a merit of the theory.

In the second place, the claim that the loss of one's future is the wrong-making feature of one's being killed entails the possibility that the futures of some actual nonhuman mammals on our own planet are sufficiently like ours that it is seriously wrong to kill them also. Whether some animals do have the same right to life as human beings depends on adding to the account of the wrongness of killing some additional account of just what it is about my future or the futures of other adult human beings which makes it wrong to kill us. No such additional account will be offered in this essay. Undoubtedly, the provision of such an account would be a very difficult matter. Undoubtedly, any such account would be quite controversial. Hence, it surely should not reflect badly on this sketch of an elementary theory of the wrongness of killing that it is indeterminate with respect to some very difficult issues regarding animal rights.

In the third place, the claim that the loss of one's future is the wrong-making feature of one's being killed does not entail, as sanctity of human life theories do, that active euthanasia is wrong. Persons who are severely and incurably ill, who face a future of pain and despair, and who wish to die will not have suffered a loss if they are killed. It is, strictly speaking, the value of a human's future which makes killing wrong in this theory. This being so, killing does not necessarily wrong some persons who are sick and dying. Of course, there may be other reasons for a prohibition of active euthanasia, but that is another matter. Sanctity-of-human-life theories seem to hold that active euthanasia is seriously wrong even in an individual case where there seems to be good reason for it independently of public policy considerations. This consequence is most implausible, and it is a plus for the claim that the loss of a future of value is what makes killing wrong that it does not share this consequence.

In the fourth place, the account of the wrongness of killing defended in this essay does straightforwardly entail that it is prima facie seriously wrong to kill children and infants, for we do presume that they have futures of value. Since we do believe that it is wrong to kill defenseless little babies, it is important that a theory of the wrongness of killing easily account for this. Personhood theories of the wrongness of killing, on the other hand, cannot straightforwardly account for the wrongness of killing infants and young children. Hence, such theories must add special ad hoc accounts of the wrongness of killing the young. The plausibility of such ad hoc theories seems to be a function of how desperately one wants such theories to work. The claim that the primary wrong-making feature of a killing is the loss to the victim of the value of its future accounts for the wrongness of killing young children and infants directly; it makes the wrongness of such acts as obvious as we actually think it is. This is a further merit of this theory. Accordingly, it seems that this value of a future-like-ours theory of the wrongness of killing shares strengths of both sanctity-of-life and personhood accounts while avoiding weaknesses of both. In addition, it meshes with a central intuition concerning what makes killing wrong.

The claim that the primary wrong-making feature of a killing is the loss to the victim of the value of its future has obvious consequences for the ethics of abortion. The future of a standard fetus includes a set of experiences, projects, activities, and such which are identical with the futures of adult human beings and are identical with the futures of young children. Since the reason that is sufficient to explain why it is wrong to kill human beings after the time of birth is a reason that also applies to fetuses, it follows that abortion is prima facie seriously morally wrong.

This argument does not rely on the invalid inference that, since it is wrong to kill persons, it is wrong to kill potential persons also. The category that is morally central to this analysis is the category of having a valuable future like ours; it is not the category of personhood. The argument to the conclusion that abortion is prima facie seriously morally wrong proceeded independently of the notion of person or potential person or any equivalent. Someone may wish to start with this analysis in terms of the value of a human future, conclude that abortion is, except perhaps in rare circumstances, seriously morally wrong, infer that fetuses have the right to life, and then call fetuses "persons" as a result of their having the right to life. Clearly, in this case, the category of person is being used to state the *conclusion* of the analysis rather than to generate the *argument* of the analysis. . . .

Of course, this value of a future-like-ours argument, if sound, shows only that abortion is prima facie wrong, not that it is wrong in any and all circumstances. Since the loss of the future to a standard fetus, if killed, is, however, at least as great a loss as the loss of the future to a standard adult human being who is killed, abortion, like ordinary killing, could be justified only by the most compelling reasons. The loss of one's life is almost the greatest misfortune that can happen to one. Presumably abortion could be justified in some circumstances, only if the loss consequent on failing to abort would be at least as great. Accordingly, morally permissible abortions will be rare indeed unless, perhaps, they occur so early in pregnancy that a fetus is not yet definitely an individual. Hence, this argument should be taken as showing that abortion is presumptively very seriously wrong, where the presumption is very strong—as strong as the presumption that killing another adult human being is wrong.

NOTE

1. I have been most influenced on this matter by Jonathan Glover, *Causing Death and Saving Lives* (New York: Penguin, 1977), chap. 3; and Robert Young, "What Is So Wrong with Killing People?" *Philosophy* LIV, 210 (1979), 518–28.

Study Questions

1. Is the loss of one's future as devastating for a fetus as for a child?
2. Does Marquis's argument that abortion is immoral depend on religious considerations?
3. Does Marquis accept the argument that because killing persons is wrong, killing potential persons is also wrong?
4. According to Marquis, in what circumstances is abortion not wrong?

Virtue Theory and Abortion

ROSALIND HURSTHOUSE

Rosalind Hursthouse is Professor of Philosophy at the University of Auckland in New Zealand. She demonstrates how virtue theory can be applied to the issue of abortion. The term "deontological" that she uses refers to an ethical theory, such as Kant's, based on fulfilling duties, as opposed to a consequentialist theory, such as utilitarianism, that appeals to achieving good states of affairs.

The sort of ethical theory derived from Aristotle, variously described as virtue ethics, virtue-based ethics, or neo-Aristotelianism, is becoming better known, and is now quite widely recognized as at least a possible rival to deontological and utilitarian theories. . . . I aim to deepen that understanding . . . by illustrating what the theory looks like when it is applied to a particular issue, in this case, abortion. . . .

As everyone knows, the morality of abortion is commonly discussed in relation to just two considerations: first, and predominantly, the status of the fetus and whether or not it is the sort of thing that may or may not be innocuously or justifiably killed; and second, and less predominantly (when, that is, the discussion concerns the *morality* of abortion rather than the question of permissible legislation in a just society), women's rights. If one thinks within this familiar framework, one may well be puzzled about what virtue theory, as such, could contribute. Some people assume the discussion will be conducted solely in terms of what the virtuous agent would or would not do. . . . Others assume that only justice, or at most justice and charity, will be applied to the issue, generating a discussion very similar to Judith Jarvis Thomson's.[1]

Now if this is the way the virtue theorist's discussion of abortion is imagined to be, no wonder people think little of it. It seems obvious in advance that in any such discussion there must be either a great deal of extremely tendentious application of the virtue terms *just, charitable,* and so on or a lot of rhetorical appeal to "this is what only the virtuous agent knows." But these are caricatures; they fail to appreciate the way in which virtue theory quite transforms the discussion of abortion by dismissing the two familiar dominating considerations as, in a way, fundamentally irrelevant. In what way or ways, I hope to make both clear and plausible.

Let us first consider women's rights. Let me emphasize again that we are discussing the *morality* of abortion, not the rights and wrongs of laws prohibiting or permitting it. If we suppose that women do have a moral right to do as they choose with their own bodies, or, more particularly, to terminate their pregnancies, then it may well follow that a *law* forbidding abortion would be unjust. Indeed, even if they have no such right, such a law might be, as things stand at the moment, unjust, or impractical, or inhumane: on this issue I have nothing to say in this article. But, putting all questions about the justice or injustice of laws to one side, and supposing only

From *Philosophy & Public Affairs,* 20 (1991), by permission of Blackwell Publishing.

that women have such a moral right, *nothing* follows from this supposition about the morality of abortion, according to virtue theory, once it is noted (quite generally, not with particular reference to abortion) that in exercising a moral right I can do something cruel, or callous, or selfish, light-minded, self-righteous, stupid, inconsiderate, disloyal, dishonest—that is act viciously.[2] Love and friendship do not survive their parties constantly insisting on their rights, nor do people live well when they think that getting what they have a right to is of preeminent importance; they harm others, and they harm themselves. So whether women have a moral right to terminate their pregnancies is irrelevant within virtue theory, for it is irrelevant to the question "In having an abortion in these circumstances, would the agent be acting virtuously or viciously or neither?"

What about the consideration of the status of the fetus—what can virtue theory say about that? One might say that this issue is not in the province of *any* moral theory; it is a metaphysical question, and an extremely difficult one at that. Must virtue theory then wait upon metaphysics to come up with the answer?

At first sight it might seem so. For virtue is said to involve knowledge, and part of this knowledge consists in having the *right* attitude to things. "Right" here does not just mean "morally right" or "proper" or "nice" in the modern sense; it means "accurate, true." One cannot have the right or correct attitude to something if the attitude is based on or involves false beliefs. And this suggests that if the status of the fetus is relevant to the rightness or wrongness of abortion, its status must be known, as a truth, to the fully wise and virtuous person.

But the sort of wisdom that the fully virtuous person has is not supposed to be recondite; it does not call for fancy philosophical sophistication, and it does not depend upon, let alone wait upon, the discoveries of academic philosophers.[3] And this entails the following, rather startling, conclusion: that the status of the fetus—that issue over which so much ink has been spilt—is,

according to virtue theory, simply not relevant to the rightness or wrongness of abortion (within, that is, a secular morality).

Or rather, since that is clearly too radical a conclusion, it is in a sense relevant, but only in the sense that the familiar biological facts are relevant. By "the familiar biological facts" I mean the facts that most human societies are and have been familiar with—that, standardly (but not invariably), pregnancy occurs as the result of sexual intercourse, that it lasts about nine months, during which time the fetus grows and develops, that standardly it terminates in the birth of a living baby, and that this is how we all come to be.

It might be thought that this distinction—between the familiar biological facts and the status of the fetus—is a distinction without a difference. But this is not so. To attach relevance to the status of the fetus, in the sense in which virtue theory claims it is not relevant, is to be gripped by the conviction that we must go beyond the familiar biological facts, deriving some sort of conclusion from them, such as that the fetus has rights, or is not a person, or something similar. It is also to believe that this exhausts the relevance of the familiar biological facts, that all they are relevant to is the status of the fetus and whether or not it is the sort of thing that may or may not be killed.

These convictions, I suspect, are rooted in the desire to solve the problem of abortion by getting it to fall under some general rule such as "You ought not to kill anything with the right to life but may kill anything else." But they have resulted in what should surely strike any nonphilosopher as a most bizarre aspect of nearly all the current philosophical literature on abortion, namely, that, far from treating abortion as a unique moral problem, markedly unlike any other, nearly everything written on the status of the fetus and its bearing on the abortion issue would be consistent with the human reproductive facts' (to say nothing of family life) being totally different from what they are. Imagine that you are an alien extraterrestrial anthropologist who does not know that the human race is roughly 50 percent female and 50 percent male, or that our only (natural) form of reproduction involves heterosexual intercourse, viviparous birth, and the female's (and only the female's) being pregnant for nine months, or that females are capable of childbearing from late childhood to late middle age, or that childbearing is painful, dangerous, and emotionally charged—do you think you would pick up these facts from the hundreds of articles written on the status of the fetus? I am quite sure you would not. And that, I think, shows that the current philosophical literature on abortion has got badly out of touch with reality.

Now if we are using virtue theory, our first question is not "What do the familiar biological facts show—what can be derived from them about the status of the fetus?" but "How do these facts figure in the practical reasoning, actions and passions, thoughts and reactions, of the virtuous and the nonvirtuous? What is the mark of having the right attitude to these facts and what manifests having the wrong attitude to them?" This immediately makes essentially relevant not only all the facts about human reproduction I mentioned above, but a whole range of facts about our emotions in relation to them as well. I mean such facts as that human parents, both male and female, tend to care passionately about their offspring, and that family relationships are among the deepest and strongest in our lives—and, significantly, among the longest-lasting.

These facts make it obvious that pregnancy is not just one among many other physical conditions; and hence that anyone who genuinely believes that an abortion is comparable to a haircut or an appendectomy is mistaken.[4] The fact that the premature termination of a pregnancy is, in some sense, the cutting off of a new human life, and thereby, like the procreation of a new human life, connects with all our thoughts about human life and death, parenthood, and family relationships, must make it a serious matter. To disregard this fact about it, to think of abortion as nothing but the killing of something that does

not matter, or as nothing but the exercise of some right or rights one has, or as the incidental means to some desirable state of affairs, is to do something callous and light-minded, the sort of thing that no virtuous and wise person would do. It is to have the wrong attitude not only to fetuses, but more generally to human life and death, parenthood, and family relationships.

Although I say that the facts make this obvious, I know that this is one of my tendentious points. In partial support of it I note that even the most dedicated proponents of the view that deliberate abortion is just like an appendectomy or haircut rarely hold the same view of spontaneous abortion, that is, miscarriage. It is not so tendentious of me to claim that to react to people's grief over miscarriage by saying, or even thinking, "What a fuss about nothing!" would be callous and light-minded, whereas to try to laugh someone out of grief over an appendectomy scar or a botched haircut would not be. It is hard to give this point due prominence within act-centered theories, for the inconsistency is an inconsistency in attitude about the seriousness of loss of life, not in beliefs about which acts are right or wrong. Moreover, an act-centered theorist may say, "Well, there is nothing wrong with *thinking* 'What a fuss about nothing!' as long as you do not say it and hurt the person who is grieving. And besides, we cannot be held responsible for our thoughts, only for the intentional actions they give rise to." But the character traits that virtue theory emphasizes are not simply dispositions to intentional actions, but a seamless disposition to certain actions and passions, thoughts and reactions.

To say that the cutting off of a human life is always a matter of some seriousness, at any stage, is not to deny the relevance of gradual fetal development. Notwithstanding the well-worn point that clear boundary lines cannot be drawn, our emotions and attitudes regarding the fetus do change as it develops, and again when it is born, and indeed further as the baby grows. Abortion for shallow reasons in the later stages is much more shocking than abortion for the same reasons in the early stages in a way that matches the fact that deep grief over miscarriage in the later stages is more appropriate than it is over miscarriage in the earlier stages (when, that is, the grief is solely about the loss of *this* child, not about, as might be the case, the loss of one's only hope of having a child or of having one's husband's child). Imagine (or recall) a woman who already has children; she had not intended to have more, but finds herself unexpectedly pregnant. Though contrary to her plans, the pregnancy, once established as a fact, is welcomed—and then she loses the embryo almost immediately. If this were bemoaned as a tragedy, it would, I think, be a misapplication of the concept of what is tragic. But it may still properly be mourned as a loss. The grief is expressed in such terms as "I shall always wonder how she or he would have turned out" or "When I look at the others, I shall think, 'How different their lives would have been if this other one had been part of them.'" It would, I take it, be callous and light-minded to say, or think, "Well, she has already *got* four children; what's the problem?"; it would be neither, nor arrogantly intrusive in the case of a close friend, to try to correct prolonged mourning by saying, "I know it's sad, but it's not a tragedy; rejoice in the ones you have." The application of *tragic* becomes more appropriate as the fetus grows, for the mere fact that one has lived with it for longer, conscious of its existence, makes a difference. To shrug off an early abortion is understandable just because it is very hard to be fully conscious of the fetus's existence in the early stages and hence hard to appreciate that an early abortion is the destruction of life. It is particularly hard for the young and inexperienced to appreciate this, because appreciation of it usually comes only with experience.

I do not mean "with the experience of having an abortion" (though that may be part of it) but, quite generally, "with the experience of life." Many women who have borne children contrast their later pregnancies with their first successful one, saying that in the later ones they were conscious of a new life growing in them from very early on. And, more generally, as one reaches the age at which the next generation is coming up close behind one, the counterfactuals "If I, or she, had had an abortion, Alice, or Bob, would not have been born" acquire a significant application, which casts a new light on the conditionals "If I or Alice have an abortion then some Caroline or Bill will not be born."

The fact that pregnancy is not just one among many physical conditions does not mean that one can never regard it in that light without manifesting a vice. When women are in very poor physical health, or worn out from childbearing, or forced to do very physically demanding jobs, then they cannot be described as self-indulgent, callous, irresponsible, or light-minded if they seek abortions mainly with a view to avoiding pregnancy as the physical condition that it is. To go through with a pregnancy when one is utterly exhausted, or when one's job consists of crawling along tunnels hauling coal, as many women in the nineteenth century were obliged to do, is perhaps heroic, but people who do not achieve heroism are not necessarily vicious. That they can view the pregnancy only as eight months of misery, followed by hours if not days of agony and exhaustion, and abortion only as the blessed escape from this prospect, is entirely understandable and does not manifest any lack of serious respect for human life or a shallow attitude to motherhood. What it does show is that something is terribly amiss in the conditions of their lives, which make it so hard to recognize pregnancy and childbearing as the good that they can be.

In relation to this last point I should draw attention to the way in which virtue theory has a sort of built-in indexicality. Philosophers arguing against anything remotely resembling a belief in the sanctity of life (which the above claims clearly embody) frequently appeal to the existence of other communities in which abortion and infanticide are practiced. We should not automatically assume that it is impossible that some other communities could be morally inferior to our own; maybe some are, or have been, precisely insofar as their members are, typically, callous or light-minded or unjust. But in communities in which life is a great deal tougher for everyone than it is in ours, having the right attitude to human life and death, parenthood, and family relationships might well manifest itself in ways that are unlike ours. When it is essential to survival that most members of the community fend for themselves at a very young age or work during most of their waking hours, selective abortion or infanticide might be practiced either as a form of genuine euthanasia or for the sake of the community and not, I think, be thought callous or light-minded. But this does not make everything all right; as before, it shows that there is something amiss with the conditions of their lives, which are making it impossible for them to live really well.

The foregoing discussion, insofar as it emphasizes the right attitude to human life and death, parallels to a certain extent those standard discussions of abortion that concentrate on it solely as an issue of killing. But it does not, as those discussions do, gloss over the fact, emphasized by those who discuss the morality of abortion in terms of women's rights, that abortion, wildly unlike any other form of killing, is the termination of a pregnancy, which is a condition of a woman's body and results in *her* having a child if it is not aborted. This fact is given due recognition not by appeal to women's rights but by emphasizing the relevance of the familiar biological and psychological facts and their connection with having the right attitude to parenthood and family relationships. But it may well be thought that failing to bring in women's rights still leaves some important aspects of the problem of abortion untouched.

Speaking in terms of women's rights, people sometimes say things like, "Well, it's her life you're talking about too, you know; she's got a right to her own life, her own happiness." And the discussion stops there. But in the context of virtue theory, given that we are particularly concerned with what constitutes a good human life, with what true happiness or *eudaimonia* is, this is no place to stop. We go on to ask, "And is this life of hers a good one? Is she living well?"

If we are to go on to talk about good human lives, in the context of abortion, we have to bring in our thoughts about the value of love and family life, and our proper emotional development through a natural life cycle. The familiar facts support the view that parenthood in general, and motherhood and childbearing in particular, are intrinsically worthwhile, are among the things that can be correctly thought to be partially constitutive of a flourishing human life.[5] If this is right, then a woman who opts for not being a mother (at all, or again, or now) by opting for abortion may thereby be manifesting a flawed grasp of what her life should be, and be about—a grasp that is childish, or grossly materialistic, or short-sighted, or shallow.

I said *"may* thereby"; this *need* not be so. Consider, for instance, a woman who has already had several children and fears that to have another will seriously affect her capacity to be a good mother to the ones she has—she does not show a lack of appreciation of the intrinsic value of being a parent by opting for abortion. Nor does a woman who has been a good mother and is approaching the age at which she may be looking forward to being a good grandmother. Nor does a woman who discovers that her pregnancy may well kill her, and opts for abortion and adoption. Nor, necessarily, does a woman who has decided to lead a life centered around some other worthwhile activity or activities with which motherhood would compete.

People who are childless by choice are sometimes described as "irresponsible," or "selfish," or "refusing to grow up," or "not knowing what life is about." But one can hold that having children is intrinsically worthwhile without endorsing this, for we are, after all, in the happy position of there being more worthwhile things to do than can be fitted into one lifetime. Parenthood, and motherhood in particular, even if granted to be intrinsically worthwhile, undoubtedly take up a lot of one's adult life, leaving no room for some other worthwhile pursuits.

But some women who choose abortion rather than have their first child, and some men who encourage their partners to choose abortion, are not avoiding parenthood for the sake of other worthwhile pursuits, but for the worthless one of "having a good time," or for the pursuit of some false vision of the ideals of freedom or self-realization. And some others who say "I am not ready for parenthood yet" are making some sort of mistake about the extent to which one can manipulate the circumstances of one's life so as to make it fulfill some dream that one has. Perhaps one's dream is to have two perfect children, a girl and a boy, within a perfect marriage, in financially secure circumstances, with an interesting job of one's own. But to care too much about that dream, to demand of life that it give it to one and act accordingly, may be both greedy and foolish, and is to run the risk of missing out on happiness entirely. Not only may fate make the dream impossible, or destroy it, but one's own attachment to it may make it impossible. Good marriages, and the most promising children, can be destroyed by just one adult's excessive demand for perfection.

Once again, this is not to deny that girls may quite properly say "I am not ready for motherhood yet," especially in our society, and, far from manifesting irresponsibility or light-mindedness, show an appropriate modesty or humility, or a fearfulness that does not amount to cowardice. However, even when the decision to have an abortion is the right decision—one that does not itself fall under a vice-related term and thereby one that the perfectly virtuous could recommend—it does not follow that there is no sense in which having the abortion is wrong, or guilt inappropriate. For, by virtue of the fact that a human life has been cut short, some evil has probably been brought about,[6] and that circumstances make the decision to bring about some evil the right decision will be a ground for guilt if getting into those circumstances in the first place itself manifested a flaw in character.

What "gets one into those circumstances" in the case of abortion is, except in the case of rape,

one's sexual activity and one's choices, or the lack of them, about one's sexual partner and about contraception. The virtuous woman (which here of course does not mean simply "chaste woman" but "woman with the virtues") has such character traits as strength, independence, resoluteness, decisiveness, self-confidence, responsibility, serious-mindedness, and self-determination—and no one, I think, could deny that many women become pregnant in circumstances in which they cannot welcome or cannot face the thought of having *this* child precisely because they lack one or some of these character traits. So even in the cases where the decision to have an abortion is the right one, it can still be the reflection of a moral failing—not because the decision itself is weak or cowardly or irresolute or irresponsible or light-minded, but because lack of the requisite opposite of these failings landed one in the circumstances in the first place. Hence the common universalized claim that guilt and remorse are never appropriate emotions about an abortion is denied. They may be appropriate, and appropriately inculcated, even when the decision was the right one.

Another motivation for bringing women's rights into the discussion may be to attempt to correct the implication, carried by the killing-centered approach, that insofar as abortion is wrong, it is a wrong that only women do, or at least (given the preponderance of male doctors) that only women instigate. I do not myself believe that we can thus escape the fact that nature bears harder on women than it does on men,[7] but virtue theory can certainly correct many of the injustices that the emphasis on women's rights is rightly concerned about. With very little amendment, everything that has been said above applies to boys and men too. Although the abortion decision is, in a natural sense, the woman's decision, proper to her, boys and men are often party to it, for well or ill, and even when they are not, they are bound to have been party to the circumstances that brought it up. No less than girls and women, boys and men can, in their actions, manifest self-centeredness, callousness, and light-mindedness about life and parenthood in relation to abortion. They can be self-centered or courageous about the possibility of disability in their offspring; they need to reflect on their sexual activity and their choices, or the lack of them, about their sexual partner and contraception; they need to grow up and take responsibility for their own actions and life in relation to fatherhood. If it is true, as I maintain, that insofar as motherhood is intrinsically worthwhile, being a mother is an important purpose in women's lives, being a father (rather than a mere generator) is an important purpose in men's lives as well, and it is adolescent of men to turn a blind eye to this and pretend that they have many more important things to do.

Much more might be said, but I shall end the actual discussion of the problem of abortion here, and conclude by highlighting what I take to be its significant features. . . .

The discussion does not proceed simply by our trying to answer the question "Would a perfectly virtuous agent ever have an abortion and, if so, when?"; virtue theory is not limited to considering "Would Socrates have had an abortion if he were a raped, pregnant fifteen-year-old?" nor automatically stumped when we are considering circumstances into which no virtuous agent would have got herself. Instead, much of the discussion proceeds in the virtue- and vice-related terms whose application, in several cases, yields practical conclusions . . . These terms are difficult to apply correctly, and anyone might challenge my application of any one of them. So, for example, I have claimed that some abortions, done for certain reasons, would be callous or light-minded; that others might indicate an appropriate modesty or humility; that others would reflect a greedy and foolish attitude to what one could expect out of life. Any of these examples may be disputed, but what is at issue is, should these difficult terms be there, or should the discussion be couched in terms that all clever adolescents can apply correctly? . . .

Proceeding as it does in the virtue- and vice-related terms, the discussion thereby, inevitably,

also contains claims about what is worthwhile, serious and important, good and evil, in our lives. So, for example, I claimed that parenthood is intrinsically worthwhile, and that having a good time was a worthless end (in life, not on individual occasions); that losing a fetus is always a serious matter (albeit not a tragedy in itself in the first trimester) whereas acquiring an appendectomy scar is a trivial one; that (human) death is an evil. Once again, these are difficult matters, and anyone might challenge any one of my claims. But what is at issue is, as before, should those difficult claims be there or can one reach practical conclusions about real moral issues that are in no way determined by premises about such matters? . . .

The discussion also thereby, inevitably, contains claims about what life is like (e.g., my claim that love and friendship do not survive their parties' constantly insisting on their rights; or the claim that to demand perfection of life is to run the risk of missing out on happiness entirely). What is at issue is, should those disputable claims be there, or is our knowledge (or are our false opinions) about what life is like irrelevant to our understanding of real moral issues? . . .

Naturally, my own view is that all these concepts should be there in any discussion of real moral issues and that virtue theory, which uses all of them, is the right theory to apply to them. I do not pretend to have shown this. I realize that proponents of rival theories may say that, now that they have understood how virtue theory uses the range of concepts it draws on, they are more convinced than ever that such concepts should not figure in an adequate normative theory, because they are sectarian, or vague or too particular, or improperly anthropocentric. . . . Or, finding many of the details of the discussion appropriate, they may agree that many, perhaps even all, of the concepts should figure, but argue that virtue theory gives an inaccurate account of the way the concepts fit together (and indeed of the concepts themselves) and that another theory provides a better account; that would be interesting to see.

NOTES

1. Judith Jarvis Thomson, "A Defense of Abortion," *Philosophy & Public Affairs* 1, no. 1 (Fall 1971): 47–66. One could indeed regard this article as proto-virtue theory (no doubt to the surprise of the author) if the concepts of callousness and kindness were allowed more weight.

2. One possible qualification: if one ties the concept of justice very closely to rights, then if women do have a moral right to terminate their pregnancies it *may* follow that in doing so they do not act unjustly. (Cf. Thomson, "A Defense of Abortion.") But it is debatable whether even that much follows.

3. This is an assumption of virtue theory, and I do not attempt to defend it here. An adequate discussion of it would require a separate article, since, although most moral philosophers would be chary of claiming that intellectual sophistication is a necessary condition of moral wisdom or virtue, most of us, from Plato onward, tend to write as if this were so. Sorting out which claims about moral knowledge are committed to this kind of elitism and which can, albeit with difficulty, be reconciled with the idea that moral knowledge can be acquired by anyone who really wants it would be a major task.

4. Mary Anne Warren, in "On the Moral and Legal Status of Abortion," *Monist* 57 (1973), sec. 1, says of the opponents of restrictive laws governing abortion that "their conviction (for the most part) is that abortion is not a *morally* serious and extremely unfortunate, even though sometimes justified, act, comparable to killing in self-defense or to letting the violinist die, but rather is closer to being a *morally neutral* act, like cutting one's hair" (italics mine). I would like to think that no one *genuinely* believes this. But certainly in discussion, particularly when arguing against restrictive laws or the suggestion that remorse over abortion might be appropriate, I have found that some people *say* they believe it . . . Those who allow that it is morally serious, and far from morally neutral, have to argue against restrictive laws, or the appropriateness of remorse, on a very different ground from that laid down by the premise "The fetus is just part of the woman's body (and she has a right to determine what happens to her body and should not feel guilt about anything she does to it)."

5. I take this as a premise here, but argue for it in some detail in my *Beginning Lives* (Oxford: Basil Blackwell, 1987). In this connection I also discuss adoption and the sense in which it may be regarded as "second best," and the difficult question of whether the good of parenthood may properly be sought, or indeed bought, by surrogacy.

6. I say "some evil has probably been brought about" on the ground that (human) life is (usually) a good and hence (human) death usually an evil. The exceptions would be (*a*) where death is actually a good or a benefit, because the baby that would come to be if the life were not cut short would be better off dead than alive, and (*b*) where death, though not a good, is not an evil either, because the life that would be led (e.g., in a state of permanent coma) would not be a good.

7. I discuss this point at greater length in *Beginning Lives*.

Study Questions

1. According to Hursthouse, do women's rights have anything to do with the morality of abortion?
2. According to Hursthouse, is the status of the fetus relevant to the rightness or wrongness of abortion?
3. What connections does Hursthouse draw between good human lives and a decision about abortion?
4. Can a correct moral decision result in some evil?

C.   World Hunger

Famine, Affluence, and Morality

PETER SINGER

What obligations do we have toward those around the globe who are suffering from a lack of food, shelter, or medical care? Does morality permit us to purchase luxuries for ourselves, our families, and our friends instead of providing needed resources to other people who are suffering in unfortunate circumstances? Peter Singer, who is Ira W. DeCamp Professor of Bioethics at the University Center for Human Values at Princeton University, argues that if we can prevent something bad without thereby sacrificing anything of comparable worth, we ought to do so.

As I write this, in November 1971, people are dying in East Bengal from lack of food, shelter, and medical care. The suffering and death that are occurring there now are not inevitable, not unavoidable in any fatalistic sense of the term. Constant poverty, a cyclone, and a civil war have turned at least nine million people into destitute refugees; nevertheless, it is not beyond the capacity of the richer nations to give enough assistance to reduce any further suffering to very small proportions. The decisions and actions of human beings can prevent this kind of suffering. Unfortunately, human beings have not made the necessary decisions. At the individual level, people have, with very few exceptions, not responded to the situation in any significant way. Generally speaking, people have not given large sums to relief funds; they have not written to their parliamentary representatives demanding increased government assistance; they have not demonstrated in the streets, held symbolic fasts, or done anything else directed toward providing the refugees with the means to satisfy their essential needs. At the government level, no government has given the sort of massive aid that would enable the refugees to survive for more than a few days. Britain, for instance, has given rather more than most countries. It has, to date, given £14,750,000. For comparative purposes, Britain's share of the nonrecoverable development costs of the Anglo-French Concorde project is already in excess of £275,000,000, and on present estimates will reach £400,000,000. The implication is that the British government values a supersonic transport more than thirty times as highly as it values the lives of the nine million refugees. Australia is another country which, on a per capita basis, is well up in the "aid to Bengal" table. Australia's aid, however, amounts to less than one-twelfth of the cost of Sydney's new opera house. The total amount given, from all sources, now stands at about £65,000,000. The estimated cost of keeping the refugees alive for one year is £464,000,000. Most of the refugees have now been in the camps for more than six months. The World Bank has said that India needs a minimum of £300,000,000 in assistance from other countries before the end of the year. It seems obvious that assistance on this scale will not be forthcoming. India will be forced to choose between letting the refugees starve or diverting funds from her own development program, which will mean that more of her own people will starve in the future.[1]

These are the essential facts about the present situation in Bengal. So far as it concerns us here, there is nothing unique about this situation except its magnitude. The Bengal emergency is just the latest and most acute of a series of major emergencies in various parts of the world, arising both from natural and from man-made causes. There are also many parts of the world in which people die from malnutrition and lack of food independent of any special emergency. I take Bengal as my example only because it is the present concern, and because the size of the problem has ensured that it has been given adequate publicity. Neither individuals nor governments can claim to be unaware of what is happening there.

What are the moral implications of a situation like this? In what follows, I shall argue that the way people in relatively affluent countries react to a situation like that in Bengal cannot be justified; indeed, the whole way we look at moral issues—our moral conceptual scheme—needs to be altered, and with it, the way of life that has come to be taken for granted in our society.

In arguing for this conclusion I will not, of course, claim to be morally neutral. I shall, however, try to argue for the moral position that I take, so that anyone who accepts certain assumptions, to be made explicit, will, I hope, accept my conclusion.

I begin with the assumption that suffering and death from lack of food, shelter, and medical care are bad. I think most people will agree about this, although one may reach the same view by different routes. I shall not argue for this view. People can hold all sorts of eccentric positions, and perhaps from some of them it would not follow that death by starvation is in

itself bad. It is difficult, perhaps impossible, to refute such positions, and so for brevity I will henceforth take this assumption as accepted. Those who disagree need read no further.

My next point is this: if it is in our power to prevent something bad from happening, without thereby sacrificing anything of comparable moral importance, we ought, morally, to do it. By "without sacrificing anything of comparable moral importance" I mean without causing anything else comparably bad to happen, or doing something that is wrong in itself, or failing to promote some moral good, comparable in significance to the bad thing that we can prevent. This principle seems almost as uncontroversial as the last one. It requires us only to prevent what is bad, and not to promote what is good, and it requires this of us only when we can do it without sacrificing anything that is, from the moral point of view, comparably important. I could even, as far as the application of my argument to the Bengal emergency is concerned, qualify the point so as to make it: if it is in our power to prevent something very bad from happening, without thereby sacrificing anything morally significant, we ought, morally, to do it. An application of this principle would be as follows: if I am walking past a shallow pond and see a child drowning in it, I ought to wade in and pull the child out. This will mean getting my clothes muddy, but this is insignificant, while the death of the child would presumably be a very bad thing.

The uncontroversial appearance of the principle just stated is deceptive. If it were acted upon, even in its qualified form, our lives, our society, and our world would be fundamentally changed. For the principle takes, firstly, no account of proximity or distance. It makes no moral difference whether the person I can help is a neighbor's child ten yards from me or a Bengali whose name I shall never know, ten thousand miles away. Secondly, the principle makes no distinction between cases in which I am the only person who could possibly do anything and cases in which I am just one among millions in the same position.

I do not think I need to say much in defense of the refusal to take proximity and distance into account. The fact that a person is physically near to us, so that we have personal contact with him, may make it more likely that we *shall* assist him, but this does not show that we *ought* to help him rather than another who happens to be further away. If we accept any principle of impartiality, universalizability, equality, or whatever, we cannot discriminate against someone merely because he is far away from us (or we are far away from him). Admittedly, it is possible that we are in a better position to judge what needs to be done to help a person near to us than one far away, and perhaps also to provide the assistance we judge to be necessary. If this were the case, it would be a reason for helping those near to us first. This may once have been a justification for being more concerned with the poor in one's own town than with famine victims in India. Unfortunately for those who like to keep their moral responsibilities limited, instant communication and swift transportation have changed the situation. From the moral point of view, the development of the world into a "global village" has made an important, though still unrecognized, difference to our moral situation. Expert observers and supervisors, sent out by famine relief organizations or permanently stationed in the famine-prone areas, can direct our aid to a refugee in Bengal almost as effectively as we could get it to someone in our own block. There would seem, therefore, to be no possible justification for discriminating on geographical grounds.

There may be a greater need to defend the second implication of my principle—that the fact that there are millions of other people in the same position, in respect to the Bengali refugees, as I am, does not make the situation significantly different from a situation in which I am the only person who can prevent something very bad from occurring. Again, of course, I admit that there is a psychological difference between the cases; one feels less guilty about doing nothing if one can point to others, similarly placed, who have also done nothing. Yet this can make no real difference to our moral obligations. Should I consider that I am less obliged to pull the drowning child out of the pond if on looking around I see other people, no further away than I am, who have also noticed the child but are doing nothing? One has only to ask this question to see the absurdity of the view that numbers lessen obligation. It is a view that is an ideal excuse for inactivity; unfortunately most of the major evils—poverty, overpopulation, pollution—are problems in which everyone is almost equally involved.

The view that numbers do make a difference can be made plausible if stated in this way: if everyone in circumstances like mine gave £5 to the Bengal Relief Fund, there would be enough to provide food, shelter, and medical care for the refugees; there is no reason why I should give more than anyone else in the same circumstances as I am; therefore I have no obligation to give more than £5. Each premise in this argument is true, and the argument looks sound. It may convince us, unless we notice that it is based on a hypothetical premise, although the conclusion is not stated hypothetically. The argument would be sound if the conclusion were: if everyone in circumstances like mine were to give £5, I would have no obligation to give more than £5. If the conclusion were so stated, however, it would be obvious that the argument has no bearing on a situation in which it is not the case that everyone else gives £5. This, of course, is the actual situation. It is more or less certain that not everyone in circumstances like mine will give £5. So there will not be enough to provide the needed food, shelter, and medical care. Therefore by giving more than £5 I will prevent more suffering than I would if I gave just £5.

It might be thought that this argument has an absurd consequence. Since the situation appears to be that very few people are likely to give substantial amounts, it follows that I and everyone else in similar circumstances ought to give as much as possible, that is, at least up to the point at which by giving more one would begin to cause serious suffering for oneself and one's dependents—perhaps even beyond this point to the point of marginal utility, at which by giving more one would cause oneself and one's dependents as much suffering as one would prevent in Bengal. If everyone does this, however, there will be more than can be used for the benefit of the refugees, and some of the sacrifice will have been unnecessary. Thus, if everyone does what he ought to do, the result will not be as good as it would be if everyone did a little less than he ought to do, or if only some do all that they ought to do.

The paradox here arises only if we assume that the actions in question—sending money to the relief funds—are performed more or less simultaneously, and are also unexpected. For if it is to be expected that everyone is going to contribute something, then clearly each is not obliged to give as much as he would have been obliged to had others not been giving too. And if everyone is not acting more or less simultaneously, then those giving later will know how much more is needed, and will have no obligation to give more than is necessary to reach this amount. To say this is not to deny the principle that people in the same circumstances have the same obligations, but to point out that the fact that others have given, or may be expected to give, is a relevant circumstance: those giving after it has become known that many others are giving and those giving before are not in the same circumstances. So the seemingly absurd consequence of the principle I have put forward can occur only if people are in error about the actual circumstances—that is, if they think they are giving when others are not, but in fact they are giving when others are. The result of everyone doing what he really ought to do cannot be worse than the result of everyone doing less than he ought to do, although the result of everyone doing what he reasonably believes he ought to do could be.

If my argument so far has been sound, neither our distance from a preventable evil nor the number of other people who, in respect to that evil, are in the same situation as we are, lessens our obligation to mitigate or prevent that evil. I shall therefore take as established the principle I asserted earlier. As I have already said, I need to assert it only in its qualified form: if it is in our power to prevent something very bad from happening, without thereby sacrificing anything else morally significant, we ought, morally, to do it.

The outcome of this argument is that our traditional moral categories are upset. The traditional distinction between duty and charity cannot be drawn, or at least, not in the place we normally draw it. Giving money to the Bengal Relief Fund is regarded as an act of charity in our society. The bodies which collect money are known as "charities." These organizations see themselves in this way—if you send them a check, you will be thanked for your "generosity." Because giving money is regarded as an act of charity, it is not thought that there is anything wrong with not giving. The charitable man may be praised, but the man who is not charitable is not condemned. People do not feel in any way ashamed or guilty about spending money on new clothes or a new car instead of giving it to famine relief. (Indeed, the alternative does not occur to them.) This way of looking at the matter cannot be justified. When we buy new clothes not to keep ourselves warm but to look "well-dressed" we are not providing for any important need. We would not be sacrificing anything significant if we were to continue to wear our old clothes, and give the money to famine relief. By doing so, we would be preventing another person from starving. It follows from what I have said earlier that we ought to give money away, rather than spend it on clothes which we do not need to keep us warm. To do so is not charitable, or generous. Nor is it the kind of act which philosophers and theologians have called "supererogatory"—an act which it would be good to do, but not wrong not to do. On the contrary, we ought to give the money away, and it is wrong not to do so.

I am not maintaining that there are no acts which are charitable, or that there are no acts which it would be good to do but not wrong not to do. It may be possible to redraw the distinction between duty and charity in some other place. All I am arguing here is that the present way of drawing the distinction, which makes it an act of charity for a man living at the level of affluence which most people in the "developed nations" enjoy to give money to save someone else from starvation, cannot be supported. It is beyond the scope of my argument to consider whether the distinction should be redrawn or abolished altogether. There would be many other possible ways of drawing the distinction—for instance, one might decide that it is good to make other people as happy as possible, but not wrong not to do so.

Despite the limited nature of the revision in our moral conceptual scheme which I am proposing, the revision would, given the extent of both affluence and famine in the world today, have radical implications. These implications may lead to further objections, distinct from those I have already considered. I shall discuss two of these.

One objection to the position I have taken might be simply that it is too drastic a revision of our moral scheme. People do not ordinarily judge in the way I have suggested they should. Most people reserve their moral condemnation for those who violate some moral norm, such as the norm against taking another person's property. They do not condemn those who indulge in luxury instead of giving to famine relief. But given that I did not set out to present a morally neutral description of the way people make moral judgments, the way people do in fact judge has nothing to do with the validity of my conclusion. My conclusion follows from the principle which I advanced earlier, and unless that principle is rejected, or the arguments shown to be unsound, I think the conclusion must stand, however strange it appears. . . .

The second objection to my attack on the present distinction between duty and charity is one which has from time to time been made against utilitarianism. It follows from some forms of utilitarian theory that we all ought, morally, to be working full time to increase the balance of happiness over misery. The position I have taken here would not lead to this conclusion in all circumstances, for if there were no bad occurrences that we could prevent without sacrificing something of comparable moral importance, my argument would have no application. Given the present conditions in many parts of the world, however, it does follow from my argument that we ought, morally, to be working full time to relieve great suffering of the sort that occurs as a result of famine or other disasters. Of course, mitigating circumstances can be adduced—for instance, that if we wear ourselves out through overwork, we shall be less effective than we would otherwise have been. Nevertheless, when all considerations of this sort have been taken into account, the conclusion remains: we ought to be preventing as much suffering as we can without sacrificing something else of comparable moral importance. This conclusion is one which we may be reluctant to face. I cannot see, though, why it should be regarded as a criticism of the position for which I have argued, rather than a criticism of our ordinary standards of behavior. Since most people are self-interested to some degree, very few of us are likely to do everything that we ought to do. It would, however, hardly be honest to take this as evidence that it is not the case that we ought to do it. . . .

The conclusion reached earlier [raises] the question of just how much we all ought to be giving away. One possibility, which has already been mentioned, is that we ought to give until we reach the level of marginal utility—that is, the level at which, by giving more, I would cause as much suffering to myself or my dependents as I would relieve by my gift. This would mean, of course, that one would reduce oneself to very near the material circumstances of a Bengali refugee. It will be recalled that earlier I put forward both a strong and a moderate version of the principle of preventing bad occurrences. The strong version, which required us to prevent bad things from happening unless in doing so we would be sacrificing something of a comparable moral significance, does seem to require reducing ourselves to the level of marginal utility. I should also say that the strong version seems to me to be the correct one. I proposed the more moderate version—that we should prevent bad occurrences unless, to do so, we had to sacrifice something morally significant—only in order to show that even on this surely undeniable principle a great change in our way of life is required. On the more moderate principle, it may not follow that we ought to reduce ourselves to the level of marginal utility, for one might hold that to reduce oneself and one's family to this level is to cause something significantly bad to happen. Whether this is so I shall not discuss, since, as I have said, I can see no good reason for holding the moderate version of the principle rather than the strong version. Even if we accepted the principle only in its moderate form, however, it should be clear that we would have to give away enough to ensure that the consumer society, dependent as it is on people spending on trivia rather than giving to famine relief, would slow down and perhaps disappear entirely. There are several reasons why this would be desirable in itself. The value and necessity of economic growth are now being questioned not only by conservationists, but by economists as well.[2] There is no doubt, too, that the consumer society has had a distorting effect on the goals and purposes of its members. Yet looking at the matter purely from the point of view of overseas aid, there must be a limit to the extent to which we should deliberately slow down our economy; for it might be the case that if we gave away, say, forty percent of our Gross National Product, we would slow down the economy so much that in absolute terms we would be giving less than if we gave twenty-five percent of the much larger GNP that we would

have if we limited our contribution to this smaller percentage.

I mention this only as an indication of the sort of factor that one would have to take into account in working out an ideal. Since Western societies generally consider one percent of the GNP an acceptable level for overseas aid, the matter is entirely academic. Nor does it affect the question of how much an individual should give in a society in which very few are giving substantial amounts.

It is sometimes said, though less often now than it used to be, that philosophers have no special role to play in public affairs, since most public issues depend primarily on an assessment of facts. On questions of fact, it is said, philosophers as such have no special expertise, and so it has been possible to engage in philosophy without committing oneself to any position on major public issues. No doubt there are some issues of social policy and foreign policy about which it can truly be said that a really expert assessment of the facts is required before taking sides or acting, but the issue of famine is surely not one of these. The facts about the existence of suffering are beyond dispute. Nor, I think, is it disputed that we can do something about it, either through orthodox methods of famine relief or through population control or both. This is therefore an issue on which philosophers are competent to take a position. The issue is one which faces everyone who has more money than he needs to support himself and his dependents, or who is in a position to take some sort of political action. These categories must include practically every teacher and student of philosophy in the universities of the Western world. If philosophy is to deal with matters that are relevant to both teachers and students, this is an issue that philosophers should discuss.

Discussion, though, is not enough. What is the point of relating philosophy to public (and personal) affairs if we do not take our conclusions seriously? In this instance, taking our conclusion seriously means acting upon it. The philosopher will not find it any easier than anyone else to alter his attitudes and way of life to the extent that, if I am right, is involved in doing everything that we ought to be doing. At the very least, though, one can make a start. The philosopher who does so will have to sacrifice some of the benefits of the consumer society, but he can find compensation in the satisfaction of a way of life in which theory and practice, if not yet in harmony, are at least coming together.

NOTES

1. There was also a third possibility; that India would go to war to enable the refugees to return to their lands. Since I wrote this paper, India has taken this way out. The situation is no longer that described above, but this does not affect my argument, as the next paragraph indicates.

2. See, for instance, John Kenneth Galbraith, *The New Industrial State* (Boston, 1967); and E. J. Mishan, *The Costs of Economic Growth* (London, 1967).

Study Questions

1. If you can prevent something bad from happening at a comparatively small cost to yourself, are you obligated to do so?
2. Are you acting immorally by buying a luxury car while others are starving?
3. Are you acting immorally by paying college tuition for your own children while other children have no opportunity for any schooling at all?
4. Do we have a moral obligation to try to alleviate extreme poverty in our own country before attempting to do so in other countries?

World Hunger and Moral Obligation: The Case Against Singer

JOHN ARTHUR

John Arthur (1946–2007) was Professor of Philosophy at Binghamton University of the State University of New York. He believes that Singer has ignored our right to control the earnings for which we labored and that, therefore, we are not morally required to use our financial resources as Singer would suggest.

If you agreed with Singer, does Arthur's reasoning lead you to change your view? If you disagreed with Singer, are Arthur's criticisms the same as yours?

INTRODUCTION

My guess is that everyone who reads these words is wealthy by comparison with the poorest millions of people on our planet. Not only do we have plenty of money for food, clothing, housing, and other necessities, but a fair amount is left over for far less important purchases like phonograph records, fancy clothes, trips, intoxicants, movies, and so on. And what's more we don't usually give a thought to whether or not we ought to spend our money on such luxuries rather than to give it to those who need it more; we just assume it's ours to do with as we please.

Peter Singer, "Famine, Affluence, and Morality" argues that our assumption is wrong, that we should not buy luxuries when others are in severe need. But [is he] correct? . . .

He first argues that two general moral principles are widely accepted, and then that those principles imply an obligation to eliminate starvation.

The first principle is simply that "suffering and death from lack of food, shelter and medical care are bad." Some may be inclined to think that the mere existence of such an evil in itself places an obligation on others, but that is, of course, the problem which Singer addresses. I take it that he is not begging the question in this obvious way and will argue from the existence of evil to the obligation of others to eliminate it. But how, exactly, does he establish this? The second principle, he thinks, shows the connection, but it is here that controversy arises.

This principle, which I will call the greater moral evil rule, is as follows:

> If it is in our power to prevent something bad from happening, without thereby sacrificing anything of comparable moral importance, we ought, morally, to do it.[1]

In other words, people are entitled to keep their earnings only if there is no way for them to prevent a greater evil by giving them away. Providing others with food, clothing, and housing would generally be of more importance than buying luxuries, so the greater moral evil rule now requires substantial redistribution of wealth.

Certainly there are few, if any, of us who live by that rule, although that hardly shows we are *justified* in our way of life; we often fail to live up to our own standards. Why does Singer think our shared morality requires that we follow the greater moral evil rule? What arguments does he give for it?

He begins with an analogy. Suppose you came across a child drowning in a shallow pond. Certainly we feel it would be wrong not to help. Even if saving the child meant we must dirty our clothes, we would emphasize that those clothes are not of comparable significance to the child's life. The greater moral evil rule thus seems a natural way of capturing why we think it would be wrong not to help.

But the argument for the greater moral evil rule is not limited to Singer's claim that it explains our feelings about the drowning child or that it appears "uncontroversial." Moral equality also enters the picture. Besides the Jeffersonian idea that we share certain rights equally, most of us are also attracted to another type of equality, namely that like amounts of suffering (or happiness) are of equal significance, no matter who is experiencing them. I cannot reasonably say that, while my pain is no more severe than yours, I am somehow special and it's more important that mine be alleviated. Objectivity requires us to admit the opposite, that no one has a unique status which warrants such special pleading. So equality demands equal consideration of interests as well as respect for certain rights.

But if we fail to give to famine relief and instead purchase a new car when the old one will do, or buy fancy clothes for a friend when his or her old ones are perfectly good, are we not assuming that the relatively minor enjoyment we or our friends may get is as important as another person's life? And that is a form of prejudice; we are acting as if people were not equal in the sense that their interests deserve equal consideration.

We are giving special consideration to ourselves or to our group, rather like a racist does. Equal consideration of interests thus leads naturally to the greater moral evil rule.

RIGHTS AND DESERT

Equality, in the sense of giving equal consideration to equally serious needs, is part of our moral code. And so we are led, quite rightly I think, to the conclusion that we should prevent harm to others if in doing so we do not sacrifice anything of comparable moral importance. But there is also another side to the coin, one which Singer ignore[s]. . . . This can be expressed rather awkwardly by the notion of entitlements. These fall into two broad categories, rights and desert. A few examples will show what I mean.

All of us could help others by giving away or allowing others to use our bodies. While your life may be shortened by the loss of a kidney or less enjoyable if lived with only one eye, those costs are probably not comparable to the loss experienced by a person who will die without any kidney or who is totally blind. We can even imagine persons who will actually be harmed in some way by your not granting sexual favors to them. Perhaps the absence of a sexual partner would cause psychological harm or even rape. Now suppose that you can prevent this evil without sacrificing anything of comparable importance. Obviously such relations may not be pleasant, but according to the greater moral evil rule that is not enough; to be justified in refusing, you must show that the unpleasantness you would experience is of equal importance to the harm you are preventing. Otherwise, the rule says you must consent.

If anything is clear, however, it is that our code does not *require* such heroism; you are entitled to keep your second eye and kidney and not bestow sexual favors on anyone who may be harmed without them. The reason for this is often expressed in terms of rights; it's your body, you have a right to it, and that weighs against whatever duty you have to help. To sacrifice a kidney for a stranger is to do more than is required, it's heroic.

Moral rights are normally divided into two categories. Negative rights are rights of noninterference. The right to life, for example, is a right not to be killed. Property rights, the right to privacy, and the right to exercise religious freedom are also negative, requiring only that people leave others alone and not interfere.

Positive rights, however, are rights of recipience. By not putting their children up for adoption, parents give them various positive rights, including rights to be fed, clothed, and housed. If I agree to share in a business venture, my promise creates a right of recipience, so that when I back out of the deal, I've violated your right.

Negative rights also differ from positive in that the former are natural; the ones you have depend on what you are. If lower animals lack rights to life or liberty it is because there is a relevant difference between them and us. But the positive rights you may have are not natural; they arise because others have promised, agreed, or contracted to give you something.

Normally, then, a duty to help a stranger in need is not the result of a right he has. Such a right would be positive, and since no contract or promise was made, no such right exists. An exception to this would be a lifeguard who contracts to watch out for someone's children. The parent whose child drowns would in this case be doubly wronged. First, the lifeguard should not have cruelly or thoughtlessly ignored the child's interests, and second, he ought not to have violated the rights of the parents that he helped. Here, unlike Singer's case, we can say there are rights at stake. Other bystanders also act wrongly by cruelly ignoring the child, but unlike the lifeguard they do not violate anybody's rights. Moral rights are one factor to be weighed, but we also have other obligations; I am not claiming that rights are all we need to consider. That view, like the greater moral evil rule, trades simplicity for accuracy. In fact, our code expects us to help people in need as well as to respect negative and positive rights. But we are also entitled to invoke our own rights as justification for not giving to distant strangers or when the cost to us is substantial, as when we give up an eye or kidney. . . .

Desert is a second form of entitlement. Suppose, for example, an industrious farmer manages through hard work to produce a surplus of food for the winter while a lazy neighbor spends his summer fishing. Must our industrious farmer ignore his hard work and give the surplus away because his neighbor or his family will suffer? What again seems clear is that we have more than one factor to weigh. Not only should we compare the consequences of his keeping it with his giving it away; we also should weigh the fact that one farmer deserves the food, he earned it through his hard work. Perhaps his deserving the product of his labor is outweighed by the greater need of his lazy neighbor, or perhaps it isn't, but being outweighed is in any case not the same as weighing nothing!

Desert can be negative, too. The fact that the Nazi war criminal did what he did means he deserves punishment, that we have a reason to send him to jail. Other considerations, for example the fact that nobody will be deterred by his suffering, or that he is old and harmless, may weigh against punishment and so we may let him go; but again that does not mean he doesn't still deserve to be punished.

Our moral code gives weight to both the greater moral evil principle and entitlements. The former emphasizes equality, claiming that from an objective point of view all comparable suffering, whoever its victim, is equally significant. It encourages us to take an impartial look at all the various effects of our actions; it is thus forward-looking. When we consider matters of entitlement, however, our attention is directed to the past. Whether we have rights to money, property, eyes, or whatever, depends on how we came to possess them. If they were acquired by theft rather than from birth or through gift exchange, then the right is suspect. Desert, like rights, is also backward-looking, emphasizing past effort or past transgressions which now warrant reward or punishment.

Our commonly shared morality thus requires that we ignore neither consequences nor entitlements, neither the future results of our action nor relevant events in the past. It encourages people to help others in need, especially when it's a friend or someone we are close to geographically, and when the cost is not significant. But it also gives weight to rights and desert, so that we are not usually obligated to give to strangers. . . .

But unless we are moral relativists, the mere fact that entitlements are an important part of our moral code does not in itself justify such a role. Singer . . . can perhaps best be seen as a moral reformer advocating the rejection of rules which provide for distribution according to rights and desert. Certainly the fact that in the past our moral code condemned suicide and racial mixing while condoning slavery should not convince us that a more enlightened moral code, one which we would want to support, would take such positions. Rules which define acceptable behavior are continually changing, and we must allow for the replacement of inferior ones.

Why should we not view entitlements as examples of inferior rules we are better off without? What could justify our practice of evaluating actions by looking backward to rights and desert instead of just to their consequences? One answer is that more fundamental values than rights and desert are at stake, namely fairness, justice, and respect. Failure to reward those who earn good grades or promotions is wrong because it's *unfair;* ignoring past guilt shows a lack of regard for *justice;* and failure to respect rights to life, privacy, or religious choice suggests a lack of *respect for other persons.*

Some people may be persuaded by those remarks, feeling that entitlements are now on an acceptably firm foundation. But an advocate of equality may well want to question why fairness, justice, and respect for persons should matter.

But since it is no more obvious that preventing suffering matters than that fairness, respect, and justice do, we again seem to have reached an impasse. . . .

The lesson to be learned here is a general one: The moral code it is rational for us to support must be practical; it must actually work. This means, among other things, that it must be able to gain the support of almost everyone.

But the code must be practical in other respects as well. . . . [It] is wrong to ignore the possibilities of altruism, but it is also important that a code not assume people are more unselfish than they are. Rules that would work only for angels are not the ones it is rational to support for humans. Second, an ideal code cannot assume we are more objective than we are; we often tend to rationalize when our own interests are at stake, and a rational person will also keep that in mind when choosing a moral code. Finally, it is not rational to support a code which assumes we have perfect knowledge. We are often mistaken about the consequences of what we do, and a workable code must take that into account as well. . . .

It seems to me, then, that a reasonable code would require people to help when there is no substantial cost to themselves, that is, when

what they are sacrificing would not mean *significant* reduction in their own or their families' level of happiness. Since most people's savings accounts and nearly everybody's second kidney are not insignificant, entitlements would in those cases outweigh another's need. But if what is at stake is trivial, as dirtying one's clothes would normally be, then an ideal moral code would not allow rights to override the greater evil that can be prevented. Despite our code's unclear and sometimes schizophrenic posture, it seems to me that these judgments are not that different from our current moral attitudes. We tend to blame people who waste money on trivia when they could help others in need, yet not to expect people to make large sacrifices to distant strangers. An ideal moral code thus might not be a great deal different from our own.

NOTE

1. Singer also offers a "weak" version of this principle which, it seems to me, is *too* weak. It requires giving aid only if the gift is of *no* moral significance to the giver. But since even minor embarrassment or small amounts of happiness are not completely without moral importance, this weak principle implies little or no obligation to aid, even to the drowning child.

Study Questions

1. How do positive rights differ from negative rights?
2. Does Arthur believe residents of wealthy countries ought to be charitable?
3. How might residents of a poor country respond to Arthur?
4. How might he reply to them?

D.   Terrorism

Terrorism

MICHAEL WALZER

Michael Walzer is Professor of Social Science at the Institute for Advanced Study in Princeton, New Jersey. He considers the moral justification for terrorism and finds such activity not permissible.

The word "terrorism" is used most often to describe revolutionary violence. That is a small victory for the champions of order, among whom the uses of terror are by no means unknown. The systematic terrorizing of whole populations is a strategy of both conventional and guerrilla war, and of established governments as well as radical movements. Its purpose is to destroy the morale of a nation or a class, to undercut its solidarity; its method is the random murder of innocent people. Randomness is the crucial feature of terrorist activity. If one wishes fear to spread and intensify over time, it is not desirable to kill specific people identified in some particular way with a regime, a party, or a policy. Death must come by chance to individual Frenchmen, or Germans, to Irish Protestants, or Jews, simply because they are Frenchmen or Germans, Protestants or Jews, or until they feel themselves fatally exposed and demand that their governments negotiate for their safety.

In war, terrorism is a way of avoiding engagement with the enemy army. It represents an extreme form of the strategy of the "indirect approach."[1] It is so indirect that many soldiers have refused to call it war at all. This is a matter as much of professional pride as of moral judgment. Consider the statement of a British admiral in World War II, protesting the terror bombing of German cities: "We are a hopelessly unmilitary nation to imagine that we [can] win the war by bombing German women and children instead of defeating their army and navy."[2] The key word here is unmilitary. The admiral rightly sees terrorism as a civilian strategy. One might say that it represents the continuation of war by political means. Terrorizing ordinary men and women is first of all the work of domestic tyranny, as Aristotle wrote: "The first aim and end [of tyrants] is to break the spirit of their subjects."[3] The British described the "aim and end" of terror bombing in the same way: what they sought was the destruction of civilian morale.

Tyrants taught the method to soldiers, and soldiers to modern revolutionaries. That is a crude history; I offer it only in order to make a more precise historical point: that terrorism in the strict sense, the random murder of innocent people, emerged as a strategy of revolutionary struggle only in the period after World War II, that is, only after it had become a feature of conventional war. In both cases, in war and revolution, a kind of warrior honor stood in the way of this development, especially among professional officers and "professional revolutionaries." The increasing use of terror by far left and ultranationalist movements represents the breakdown of a political code first worked out in the second half of the nineteenth century and roughly analogous to the laws of war worked out at the same time. Adherence to this code did not prevent revolutionary militants from being called terrorists, but in fact the violence they committed bore little resemblance to contemporary terrorism. It was not random murder but assassination, and it involved the drawing of a line that we will have little difficulty recognizing as the political parallel of the line that marks off combatants from noncombatants.

THE RUSSIAN POPULISTS, THE IRA, AND THE STERN GANG

I can best describe the revolutionary "code of honor" by giving some examples of so-called terrorists who acted or tried to act in accordance with its norms. I have chosen three historical cases. The first will be readily recognizable, for Albert Camus made it the basis of his play *The Just Assassins*.

1. In the early twentieth century, a group of Russian revolutionaries decided to kill a Tsarist official, the Grand Duke Sergei, a man personally involved in the repression of radical activity. They planned to blow him up in his carriage, and on the appointed day one of their number was in place along the Grand Duke's usual route. As the carriage drew near, the young revolutionary, a bomb hidden under his coat, noticed that his victim was not alone; on his lap he held two small children. The would-be assassin looked, hesitated, then walked quickly away. He would wait for another occasion. Camus has one of his comrades say, accepting this decision, "Even in destruction, there's a right way and a wrong way—and there are limits."[4]

2. During the years 1938–39, the Irish Republican Army waged a bombing campaign in Britain. In the course of this campaign, a republican militant was ordered to carry a pre-set time bomb to a Coventry power station. He traveled by bicycle, the bomb in his basket, took a wrong turn, and got lost in a maze of streets. As the time for the explosion drew near, he panicked, dropped his bike, and ran off. The bomb exploded, killing five passersby. No one in the IRA (as it was then) thought this a victory for the cause; the men immediately involved were horrified. The campaign had been carefully planned, according to a recent historian, so as to avoid the killing of innocent bystanders.[5]

3. In November 1944, Lord Moyne, British Minister of State in the Middle East, was assassinated in Cairo by two members of the Stern Gang, a right-wing Zionist group. The two assassins were caught, minutes later, by an Egyptian policeman. One of them described the capture at his trial: "We were being followed by the constable on his motorcycle. My comrade was behind me. I saw the constable approach him . . . I would have been able to kill the constable easily, but I contented myself with . . . shooting several times into the air. I saw my comrade fall off his bicycle. The constable was almost upon him. Again, I could have eliminated the constable with a single bullet, but I did not. Then I was caught."[6]

What is common to these cases is a moral distinction, drawn by the "terrorists," between people who can and people who cannot be killed. The first category is not composed of men and women bearing arms, immediately threatening by virtue of their military training and commitment. It is composed instead of officials, the political agents of regimes thought to be oppressive. Such people, of course, are protected by the war convention and by positive international law. Characteristically (and not foolishly), lawyers have frowned on assassination, and political officials have been assigned to the class of nonmilitary persons, who are never the legitimate objects of attack.[7] But this assignment only partially represents our common moral judgments. For we judge the assassin by his victim, and when the victim is Hitler-like in character, we are likely to praise the assassin's work, though we still do not call him a soldier. The second category is less problematic: ordinary citizens, not engaged in political harming—that is, in administering or enforcing laws thought to be unjust—are immune from attack whether or not they support those laws. Thus the aristocratic children, the Coventry pedestrians, even the Egyptian policeman (who had nothing to do with British imperialism in Palestine)—these people are like civilians in wartime. They are innocent politically as civilians are innocent militarily. It is precisely these people, however, that contemporary terrorists try to kill.

The war convention and the political code are structurally similar, and the distinction between officials and citizens parallels that between soldiers and civilians (though the two are not the same). What lies behind them both, I think, and lends them plausibility, is the moral difference between aiming and not aiming—or, more accurately, between aiming at particular people because of things they have done or are doing, and aiming at whole groups of people, indiscriminately, because of who they are. The first kind of aiming is appropriate to a limited struggle directed against regimes and policies. The second reaches beyond all limits; it is infinitely threatening to whole peoples, whose individual members are systematically exposed to violent death at any and every moment in the course of their (largely innocuous) lives. A bomb planted on a streetcorner, hidden in a bus station, thrown into a cafe or pub—this is aimless killing, except that the victims are likely to share what they cannot avoid, a collective identity. Since some of these victims must be immune from attack (unless liability follows from original sin), any code that directs and controls the fire of political militants is going to be at least minimally appealing. It is so much of an advance over the willful randomness of terrorist attacks. One might even feel easier about killing officials than about killing soldiers, since the state rarely conscripts its political, as it does

its military agents; they have chosen officialdom as a career.

Soldiers and officials are, however, different in another respect. The threatening character of the soldier's activities is a matter of fact; the unjust or oppressive character of the official's activities is a matter of political judgment. For this reason, the political code has never attained the same status as the war convention. Nor can assassins claim any rights, even on the basis of the strictest adherence to its principles. In the eyes of those of us whose judgments of oppression and injustice differ from their own, political assassins are simply murderers, exactly like the killers of ordinary citizens. The case is not the same with soldiers, who are not judged politically at all and who are called murderers only when they kill noncombatants. Political killing imposes risks quite unlike those of combat, risks whose character is best revealed by the fact that there is no such thing as benevolent quarantine for the duration of the political struggle. Thus the young Russian revolutionary, who eventually killed the Grand Duke, was tried and executed for murder, as were the Stern Gang assassins of Lord Moyne. All three were treated exactly like the IRA militants, also captured, who were held responsible for the deaths of ordinary citizens. That treatment seems to me appropriate, even if we share the political judgments of the men involved and defend their resort to violence. On the other hand, even if we do not share their judgments, these men are entitled to a kind of moral respect not due to terrorists, because they set limits to their actions.

THE VIETCONG ASSASSINATION CAMPAIGN

The precise limits are hard to define, as in the case of noncombatant immunity. But we can perhaps move toward a definition by looking at a guerrilla war in which officials were attacked on a large scale. Beginning at some point in the late 1950s, the NLF waged a campaign aimed at destroying the governmental structure of the South Vietnamese countryside. Between 1960 and 1965, some 7,500 village and district officials were assassinated by Vietcong militants. An American student of the Vietcong, describing these officials as the "natural leaders" of the Vietnamese society, argues that "by any definition this NLF action . . . amounts to genocide."[8] This assumes that all Vietnam's natural leaders were government officials (but then, who was leading the NLF?) and hence that government officials were literally indispensable to national existence. Since these assumptions are not remotely plausible, it has to be said that "by any definition" the killing of leaders is not the same as the destruction of entire peoples. Terrorism may foreshadow genocide, but assassination does not.

On the other hand, the NLF campaign did press against the limits of the notion of officialdom as I have been using it. The Front tended to include among officials anyone who was paid by the government, even if the work he was doing—as a public health officer, for example—had nothing to do with the particular policies the NLF opposed.[9] And it tended to assimilate into officialdom people like priests and landowners who used their nongovernmental authority in specific ways on behalf of the government. They did not kill anyone, apparently, just because he was a priest or a landowner; the assassination campaign was planned with considerable attention to the details of individual action, and a concerted effort was made "to ensure that there were no unexplained killings."[10] Still, the range of vulnerability was widened in disturbing ways.

One might argue, I suppose, that any official is by definition engaged in the political efforts of the (putatively) unjust regime, just as any soldier, whether he is actually fighting or not, is engaged in the war effort. But the variety of activities sponsored and paid for by the modern state is extraordinary, and it seems intemperate and extravagant to make all such activities into occasions for assassination. Assuming that the regime is in fact oppressive, one should look for agents of oppression and not simply for government agents. As for private persons, they seem to me immune entirely. They are subject, of course, to the conventional forms of social and political pressure (which are conventionally intensified in guerrilla wars) but not to political violence. Here the case is the same with citizens as with civilians: if their support for the government or the war were allowable as a reason for killing them, the line that marks off immune from vulnerable persons would quickly disappear. It is worth stressing that political assassins generally don't want that line to disappear; they have reasons for taking careful aim and avoiding indiscriminate murder. "We were told," a Vietcong guerrilla reported to his American captors, "that in Singapore the rebels on certain days would dynamite every 67th streetcar . . . the next day it might be every 30th, and so on; but that this hardened the hearts of the people against the rebels because so many people died needlessly."[11]

I have avoided noticing until now that most political militants don't regard themselves as assassins at all but rather as executioners. They are engaged, or so they regularly claim, in a revolutionary version of vigilante justice. This suggests another reason for killing only some officials and not others, but it is entirely a self-description. Vigilantes in the usual sense apply conventional conceptions of criminality, though in a rough and ready way. Revolutionaries champion a new conception, about which there is unlikely to be wide agreement. They hold that officials are vulnerable because or insofar as they are actually guilty of "crimes against the people." The more impersonal truth is that they are vulnerable, or more vulnerable than ordinary citizens, simply because their activities are open to such descriptions. The exercise of political power is a dangerous business. Saying this, I do not mean to defend assassination. It is most often a vile politics, as vigilante justice is most often a bad kind of law enforcement; its agents are usually gangsters, and sometimes madmen, in political dress. And yet "just assassinations" are at least possible, and men and women who aim at that kind of killing and renounce every other kind need to be marked off from those who kill at random—not as doers of justice, necessarily, for one can disagree about that, but as revolutionaries with honor. They do not want the revolution, as one of Camus' characters says, "to be loathed by the whole human race."

However the political code is specified, terrorism is the deliberate violation of its norms. For ordinary citizens are killed and no defense is offered—none could be offered—in terms of their individual activities. The names and occupations of the dead are not known in advance; they are killed simply to deliver a message of fear to others like themselves. What is the content of the message? I suppose it could be anything at all; but in practice terrorism, because it is directed against entire peoples or classes, tends to communicate the most extreme and brutal intentions—above all, the tyrannical repression, removal, or mass murder of the population under attack. Hence contemporary terrorist campaigns are most often focused on people whose national existence has been radically devalued: the Protestants of Northern Ireland, the Jews of Israel, and so on. The campaign announces the devaluation. That is why the people under attack are so unlikely to believe that compromise is possible with their enemies. In war, terrorism is associated with the demand for unconditional surrender and, in similar fashion, tends to rule out any sort of compromise settlement.

In its modern manifestations, terror is the totalitarian form of war and politics. It shatters the war convention and the political code. It breaks across moral limits beyond which no further limitation seems possible, for within the categories of civilian and citizen, there isn't any smaller group for which immunity might be claimed (except children; but I don't think children can be called "immune" if their parents are attacked

and killed). Terrorists anyway make no such claim; they kill anybody. Despite this, terrorism has been defended, not only by the terrorists themselves, but also by philosophical apologists writing on their behalf. The political defenses mostly parallel those that are offered whenever soldiers attack civilians. They represent one or another version of the argument from military necessity. It is said, for example, that there is no alternative to terrorist activity if oppressed peoples are to be liberated. And it is said, further, that this has always been so: terrorism is the only means and so it is the ordinary means of destroying oppressive regimes and founding new nations.[12] The cases I have already worked through suggest the falsity of these assertions. Those who make them, I think, have lost their grip on the historical past; they suffer from a malign forgetfulness, erasing all moral distinctions along with the men and women who painfully worked them out.

NOTES

1. But Liddell Hart, the foremost strategist of the "indirect approach," has consistently opposed terrorist tactics: see, for example, *Strategy* (2nd rev. ed., New York, 1974), pp. 349–50 (on terror bombing).

2. Rear Admiral L. H. K. Hamilton, quoted in Irving, *Destruction of Convoy PQ 17,* p. 44.

3. *Politics,* trans. Ernest Barker (Oxford, 1948), p. 288 (1314a).

4. *The Just Assassins,* in *Caligula and Three Other Plays,* trans. Stuart Gilbert (New York, 1958), p. 258. The actual historical incident is described in Roland Gaucher, *The Terrorists: From Tsarist Russia to the OAS* (London, 1965), pp. 49, 50 n.

5. J. Bowyer Bell, *The Secret Army: A History of the IRA* (Cambridge, MA, 1974), pp. 161–62.

6. Gerold Frank, *The Deed* (New York, 1963), pp. 248–49.

7. James E. Bond, *The Rules of Riot: Internal Conflict and the Law of War* (Princeton, 1974), pp. 89–90.

8. Douglas Pike, *Viet Cong* (Cambridge, MA, 1968), p. 248.

9. Jeffrey Race, *War Comes to Long An* (Berkeley, 1972), p. 83, which suggests that it was precisely the *best* public health officers, teachers, and so on who were attacked—because they constituted a possible anti-communist leadership.

10. Pike, p. 250.

11. Pike, p. 251.

12. The argument, I suppose, goes back to Machiavelli, though most of his descriptions of the necessary violence of founders and reformers have to do with the killing of particular people, members of the old ruling class: see *The Prince,* ch. VIII, and *Discourses,* I:9, for examples.

Study Questions

1. What is terrorism?
2. In a war should a moral distinction be drawn between people who can legitimately be killed and those who cannot?
3. Is assassination ever morally justifiable?
4. Do soldiers differ from political officials as appropriate targets of attack?

Is Terrorism Distinctively Wrong?

LIONEL K. MCPHERSON

Lionel K. McPherson is Associate Professor of Philosophy at Tufts University. He argues that terrorism, like war, can be justifiable despite the harm it does to noncombatants.

Many people, including philosophers, believe that terrorism is necessarily and egregiously wrong. I will call this "the dominant view." The dominant view maintains that terrorism is akin to murder. This forecloses the possibility that terrorism, under any circumstances, could be morally permissible—murder, by definition, is wrongful killing. The unqualified wrongness of terrorism is thus part of this understanding of terrorism.

I will criticize the dominant view. . . .

I will define "terrorism" as the deliberate use of force against ordinary noncombatants, which can be expected to cause wider fear among them, for political ends. . . .

Moral evaluation of terrorism might begin with the question of what makes terrorism wrong. A better opening question, I believe, is whether [the] use of force that leads to casualties among ordinary noncombatants is morally objectionable. The latter question prompts [a] comparison of terrorism and conventional war.

Judging by practice and common versions of just war theory, the answer is plainly no. The journalist Chris Hedges reports these facts: "Between 1900 and 1990, 43 million soldiers died in wars. During the same period, 62 million civilians were killed. . . . In the wars of the 1990s, civilian deaths constituted between 75 and 90 percent of all war deaths."[1] Such numbers may seem counterintuitive. More noncombatants than combatants have died in war, by a sizable margin, and the margin has only grown in an era of the most advanced weapons technology. We must conclude that war generally is highly dangerous for noncombatants. I will characterize this as the brute reality of war for noncombatants. This reality cannot be attributed simply to the conduct of war departing from the laws of war.

There is an ambiguity in the data I have cited: they do not clearly support the claim that most noncombatants who died in these wars were killed by military actions, for example, through the use of bombs, artillery, and land mines. Many noncombatant deaths in war have been the result of displacement and the lack of shelter, [the] inability to get food, and the spread of disease. At the same time, modern warfare is marked by a nontrivial number of noncombatant deaths that are the direct result of military actions. The ratio of war to "war-related" noncombatant casualties and the distribution of moral responsibility for these casualties will not be at issue here. I proceed on the assumption that evaluating the ethics of war involves recognizing that war, directly or indirectly, leads to a great many noncombatant casualties. Modern warfare and widespread harm to noncombatants are virtually inextricable. . . .

Immediately doubtful is the popular notion that terrorism is distinctively wrong because of the fear it usually spreads among ordinary noncombatants. Recall that my nonmoral definition of terrorism includes a fear effects clause which descriptively distinguishes terrorism from other forms of political violence. However, this does not morally distinguish terrorism and conventional war. The brute reality of war for noncombatants indicates that in general they have more to fear from conventional war than (nonstate) terrorism, particularly since (nonstate) terrorists rarely have had the capacity to employ violence on a mass scale.[2] Noncombatants in states that are military powers might have more to fear from terrorism than conventional war, since these states are relatively unlikely to be conventionally attacked. But surely this situational advantage that does not extend more broadly to noncombatants cannot ground the claim that terrorism is distinctively wrong.

The laws of war recognize a principle that prohibits disproportionate or excessive use of force, with an emphasis on noncombatants. For example, Article 51 (5) (b) of the 1977 Geneva Protocol I rules out use of force "which may be expected to cause incidental loss of civilian life, injury to civilians, damage to civilian objects, or a combination thereof, which would be excessive in relation to the concrete and direct military advantage anticipated."[3] Standard just war theory considers this the proportionality principle. Proponents of the dominant view might take the proportionality principle to illuminate an essential moral difference between conventional war and terrorism. They might claim that, unlike proper combatants, terrorists do not care about disproportionate harm to noncombatants. But the full impact of this charge is not easily sustained for two reasons.

The first reason is that terrorists could have some concern about disproportionate harm to noncombatants. This point is most salient when proportionality is understood in instrumental terms of whether violence is gratuitous, namely, in exceeding what is minimally necessary to achieve particular military or political goals, despite the availability of an alternative course of action that would be less harmful and no less efficacious. Terrorists may possess a normative if flawed sensibility that disapproves of instrumentally gratuitous violence, for the harm done would serve no strategic purpose. So the plausible charge is that terrorists reject the proportionality principle as conventionally construed (since it implicitly rules out deliberate use of force against noncombatants), not that they lack all concern for disproportionate harm to noncombatants.

The second reason is that the proportionality principle requires rather modest due care for noncombatants. Force may be used against them, provided that the incidental, or collateral, harm to them is not excessive when measured against the expected military gains. According to one legal scholar, "the interpretation by the United States and its allies of their legal obligations concerning the prevention of collateral casualties and the concept of proportionality comprehends prohibiting only two types of attacks: first, those that intentionally target civilians; and second, those that involve negligent behavior in ascertaining the nature of a target or the conduct of the attack itself.[4] Such an interpretation seems accurately to reflect the principle's leniency. Indeed, the U.S. general and military theorist James M. Dubik argues that commanders have a special moral duty "not to waste lives of their soldiers" in balancing the responsibility to ensure that due care is afforded to noncombatants.[5] A commander may give priority to limiting risk of harm to his own combatants, for their sake, at the expense of noncombatants on the other side.

We find, then, that the proportionality principle does not express a commitment to minimizing noncombatant casualties. The principle more modestly would reduce noncombatant casualties in requiring that they be worth military interests. Perhaps my reading appears too narrow. A prominent reason for thinking that terrorism is distinctively wrong is that terrorists, unlike combatants who comply with the laws of war, do not acknowledge the moral significance of bearing burdens in order to reduce noncombatant casualties for the sake of noncombatants themselves. To reply that terrorists might well be motivated to reduce noncombatant casualties on strategic grounds, for example, to avoid eroding sympathy for their political goals, would miss the point. Basic respect for the lives

of noncombatants seems evidenced instead by a willingness to bear burdens in order to reduce harm to them. Terrorists, the objection goes, do not have this respect for noncombatant lives, which is a major source of the sense that terrorism is distinctively wrong as compared to conventional war.

There are difficulties with this objection. It suggests that the laws of war are imbued with a certain moral character, namely, fundamental moral concern for noncombatants. These laws, though, are part of the war convention, adopted by states and codified in international law for reasons that seem largely to reflect their shared interests, at least in the long run.[6] We do not have to be political realists to see this. Given that noncombatants are vulnerable enough on all sides and no state generally has much to gain by harming them, states usually are prudent to accept mutually a principle that seeks to reduce noncombatant casualties. States usually are also prudent to comply with the laws of war, since this compliance is a benchmark of moral and political respectability on the world stage. Simply put, states, like terrorists, would seem contingently motivated to accept the proportionality principle on broadly strategic grounds.

Now the objection might go that, even if a realist analysis of the proportionality principle's place in the war convention is correct, this is no barrier to states' recognizing that the principle has independent, nonprudential moral standing. But the same can be true for terrorists. Familiar characterizations of them as "evil" or unconstrained by moral boundaries are an unreliable indication of moral indifference to harming noncombatants. As Virginia Held observes, "Terrorists often believe, whether mistakenly or not, that violence is the only course of action open to them that can advance their political objectives."[7] When terrorism is seen by its agents as a means of last resort, this provides some evidence that they acknowledge the moral significance of bearing burdens out of respect for the lives of noncombatants. Such agents will not have employed terrorism earlier, despite their grievances.

A model case is the African National Congress (ANC) in its struggle against apartheid in South Africa. Nelson Mandela, during the 1964 trial that produced his sentence of life imprisonment, summed up the ANC's position as follows:

(a) It was a mass political organization with a political function to fulfill. Its members had joined on the express policy of nonviolence.

(b) Because of all this, it could not and would not undertake violence. This must be stressed.

(c) On the other hand, in view of this situation I have described, ANC was prepared to depart from its fifty-year-old policy of nonviolence. . . . There is sabotage, there is guerrilla warfare, there is terrorism, and there is open revolution. We chose to adopt the first method and to exhaust it before taking any other decision.[8]

Mandela was implying that violence, including terrorism, became an option "only when all else had failed, when all channels of peaceful protest had been barred to us," which led the ANC to conclude that "to continue preaching peace and nonviolence at a time when the government met our peaceful demands with force" would be "unrealistic and wrong."[9] By the 1980s, at the height of government repression, the ANC did resort to acts of terrorism before reaffirming its earlier position on controlled violence that does not target civilians.[10] The case of the ANC demonstrates that those who employ terrorism can have and sometimes have had fundamental moral concern for noncombatants. Such moral concern, however, is overriding neither for terrorists nor for proper combatants. . . .

I have argued that terrorism is not distinctively wrong as compared to conventional war in the following respects. Both types of political violence may be waged for just or unjust causes. Both types employ use of force against noncombatants, with conventional war usually causing them many more casualties. War and terrorism

hence can be expected to produce fear widely among noncombatants where force is used. . . .

If we believe that war can be justifiable on grounds of just cause and the unavailability of less harmful means, despite the harm it does to noncombatants, we must take seriously whether these same grounds could ever justify terrorism. The failures of the dominant view of terrorism should lead us to adopt either a more critical attitude toward conventional war or a less condemnatory attitude toward terrorism.

NOTES

1. Chris Hedges, *What Every Person Should Know about War* (New York: Free Press, 2003), p. 7.

2. I add the qualification "nonstate" since states have employed tactics (e.g., firebombing of cities) and weapons (e.g., chemical, biological, and nuclear) that could count as terrorist.

3. Adam Roberts and Richard Guelff, eds., *Documents on the Laws of War*, 3rd ed. (Oxford: Oxford University Press, 1982), p. 489. Also see, e.g., Michael Walzer, *Just and Unjust Wars* (New York: Basic Books, 1977), pp. 145–46.

4. Judith Gail Gardam, "Proportionality and Force in International Law," *American Journal of International Law* 87 (1993): pp. 391–413, 410. To be clear, Gardam is not endorsing this interpretation. For a critical assessment of standard treatments of proportionality and an alternative approach, see Lionel K. McPherson, "Excessive Force in War: A 'Golden Rule' Test," *Theoretical Inquiries in Law* 7 (2005): pp. 81–95.

5. James M. Dubik, *Philosophy & Public Affairs* 11 (1982): pp. 354–71, 368. Dubik is responding to Walzer's more demanding requirement that combatants must accept greater costs to themselves for the sake of minimizing harm to noncombatants. See Walzer, *Just and Unjust Wars*, p. 155.

6. For criticism of the war convention as a source of moral obligation, see Lionel K. McPherson, "The Limits of the War Convention," *Philosophy and Social Criticism* 31 (2005): pp. 147–63.

7. Virginia Held, "Terrorism and War," *Journal of Ethics* 8 (2004): pp. 59–75, 69.

8. Nelson Mandela, "I Am Prepared to Die," in *Mandela, Tambo, and the African National Congress:*

The Struggle against Apartheid, 1948–1990: A Documentary Survey, ed. Sheridan Johns and R. Hunt Davis Jr. (New York: Oxford University Press, 1991), pp. 115–33, 121.

   9. Ibid., p. 120.

10. Sheridan Johns and R. Hunt Davis, "Conclusion: Mandela, Tambo, and the ANC in the 1990s," in their *Mandela, Tambo, and the African National Congress,* pp. 309–17, 312.

Study Questions

1. Can modern warfare be waged without harm to noncombatants?
2. Do noncombatants have more to fear from war or from terrorism?
3. Might terrorists acknowledge the moral value of the lives of noncombatants?
4. Can terrorism be used on behalf of a just cause?

E.   ANIMAL RIGHTS

The Case for Animal Rights

TOM REGAN

Tom Regan, whose work we read previously, here develops the case for animal rights. He calls for the abolition of animal agriculture, commercial and sport hunting, and the use of animals in scientific research.

We begin by asking how the moral status of animals has been understood by thinkers who deny that animals have rights. Then we test the mettle of their ideas by seeing how well they stand up under the heat of fair criticism. If we start our thinking in this way, we soon find that some people believe that we have no duties directly to animals, that we owe nothing to them, that we can do nothing that wrongs them. Rather, we can do wrong acts that involve animals, and so we have duties regarding them, though none to them. Such views may be called indirect duty views. By way of illustration: suppose your neighbour kicks your dog. Then your neighbour has done something wrong. But not to your dog. The wrong that has been done is a wrong to you. After all, it is wrong to upset people, and your neighbour's kicking your dog upsets you. So you are the one who is wronged, not your dog. Or again: by kicking your dog your neighbour damages another person's property. And since it is wrong to damage another person's property, your neighbour has done something wrong—to you, of course, not to your dog. Your neighbour no more wrongs your dog than your car would be wronged if the windshield were smashed. Your neighbour's duties involving your dog are indirect duties to you. More generally, all of our duties regarding animals are indirect duties to one another—to humanity.

How could someone try to justify such a view? Someone might say that your dog doesn't feel anything and so isn't hurt by your neighbour's kick, doesn't care about pain since none is felt, is as unaware of anything as is your windshield. Someone might say this, but no rational person will, since, among other considerations, such a view will commit anyone who holds it to the position that no human being feels pain either—that human beings also don't care about what happens to them. A second possibility is that though both humans and your dog are hurt when kicked, it is only human pain that matters. But, again, no rational person can believe this. Pain is pain wherever it occurs. If your neighbour's causing you pain is wrong because of the pain that is caused, we cannot rationally ignore or dismiss the moral relevance of the pain that your dog feels.

Philosophers who hold indirect duty views—and many still do—have come to understand that they must avoid the two defects just noted: that is, both the view that animals don't feel anything as well as the idea that only human pain can be morally relevant. Among such thinkers the sort of view now favoured is one or other form of what is called *contractarianism*.

Here, very crudely, is the root idea: morality consists of a set of rules that individuals voluntarily agree to abide by, as we do when we sign a contract (hence the name contractarianism). Those who understand and accept the terms of the contract are covered directly; they have rights created and recognized by, and protected in, the contract. And these contractors can also have protection spelled out for others who, though they lack the ability to understand morality and so cannot sign the contract themselves, are loved or cherished by those who can. Thus young children, for example, are unable to sign contracts and lack rights. But they are protected by the contract nonetheless because of the sentimental interests of others, most notably their parents. So we have, then, duties involving these children, duties regarding them, but no duties to them. Our duties in their case are indirect duties to other human beings, usually their parents.

As for animals, since they cannot understand contracts, they obviously cannot sign; and since they cannot sign, they have no rights. Like children, however, some animals are the objects of the sentimental interest of others. You, for example, love your dog or cat. So those animals that enough people care about (companion animals, whales, baby seals, the American bald eagle), though they lack rights themselves, will be protected because of the sentimental interests of people. I have, then, according to contractariansim, no duty directly to your dog or any other animal, not even the duty not to cause them pain or suffering; my duty not to hurt them is a duty I have to those people who care about what happens to them. As for other animals, where no or little sentimental interest is present—in the case of farm animals, for example, or laboratory rats—what duties we have grow weaker and weaker, perhaps to vanishing point. The pain and death they endure, though real, are not wrong if no one cares about them.

When it comes to the moral status of animals, contractarianism could be a hard view to refute if it were an adequate theoretical approach to the moral status of human beings. It is not adequate in this latter respect, however, which makes the question of its adequacy in the former case, regarding animals, utterly moot. For consider: morality, according to the (crude) contractarian position before us, consists of rules that people agree to abide by. What people? Well, enough to make a difference—enough, that is, *collectively* to have the power to enforce the rules that are drawn up in the contract. That is very well and good for the signatories but not so good for anyone who is not asked to sign. And there is nothing in contractarianism of the sort we are discussing that guarantees or requires that everyone will have a chance to participate equally in framing the rules of morality. The result is that this approach to ethics could sanction the most blatant forms of social, economic, moral, and political injustice, ranging from a repressive caste system to systematic racial or sexual discrimination. Might, according to this theory, does make right. Let those who are the victims of injustice suffer as they will. It matters not so long as no one else—no contractor, or too few of them—cares about it. Such a theory takes one's moral breath away . . . as if, for example, there would be nothing wrong with apartheid in South Africa if few white South Africans were upset by it. A theory with so little to recommend it at the level of the ethics of our treatment of our fellow humans cannot have anything more to recommend it when it comes to the ethics of how we treat our fellow animals.

The version of contractarianism just examined is, as I have noted, a crude variety, and in fairness to those of a contractarian persuasion it must be noted that much more refined, subtle, and ingenious varieties are possible. For example, John Rawls, in his *A Theory of Justice,* sets forth a version of contractarianism that forces contractors to ignore the accidental features of being a human being—for example, whether one is white or black, male or female, a genius or of modest intellect. Only by ignoring such features, Rawls believes, can we ensure that the principles of justice that contractors would agree upon are not based on bias or prejudice. Despite the improvement a view such as Rawls's represents over the cruder forms of contractarianism, it remains deficient: it systematically denies that we have direct duties to those human beings who do not have a sense of justice—young children, for instance, and many mentally retarded humans. And yet it seems reasonably certain that, were we to torture a young child or a retarded elder, we would be doing something that wronged him or her, not something that would be wrong if (and only if) other humans with a sense of justice were upset. And since this is true in the case of these humans, we cannot rationally deny the same in the case of animals.

Indirect duty views, then, including the best among them, fail to command our rational assent. Whatever ethical theory we should accept rationally, therefore, it must at least recognize that we have some duties directly to animals, just as we have some duties directly to each other. The next two theories I'll sketch attempt to meet this requirement.

The first I call the cruelty-kindness view. Simply stated, this says that we have a direct duty to be kind to animals and a direct duty not to be cruel to them. Despite the familiar, reassuring ring of these ideas, I do not believe that this view offers an adequate theory. To make this clearer, consider kindness. A kind person acts from a certain kind of motive—compassion or concern, for example. And that is a virtue. But there is no guarantee that a kind act is a right act. If I am a generous racist, for example, I will be inclined to act kindly towards members of my own race, favouring their interests above those of others. My kindness would be real and, so far as it goes, good. But I trust it is too obvious to require argument that my kind acts may not be above moral reproach—may, in fact, be positively wrong because rooted in injustice. So kindness, notwithstanding its status as a virtue to be encouraged, simply will not carry the weight of a theory of right action.

Cruelty fares no better. People or their acts are cruel if they display either a lack of sympathy for or, worse, the presence of enjoyment in another's suffering. Cruelty in all its guises is a bad thing, a tragic human failing. But just as a person's being motivated by kindness does not guarantee that he or she does what is right, so the absence of cruelty does not ensure that he or she avoids doing what is wrong. Many people who perform abortions, for example, are not cruel, sadistic people. But that fact alone does not settle the terribly difficult question of the morality of abortion. The case is no different when we examine the ethics of our treatment of animals. So, yes, let us be for kindness and against cruelty. But let us not suppose that being for the one and against the other answers questions about moral right and wrong.

Some people think that the theory we are looking for is utilitarianism. A utilitarian accepts two moral principles. The first is that of equality: everyone's interests count, and similar interests must be counted as having similar weight or importance. White or black, American or Iranian, human or animal—everyone's pain or frustration matter, and matter just as much as the equivalent pain or frustration of anyone else. The second principle a utilitarian accepts is that of utility: do the act that will bring about the best balance between satisfaction and frustration for everyone affected by the outcome.

As a utilitarian, then, here is how I am to approach the task of deciding what I morally ought to do: I must ask who will be affected if I choose to do one thing rather than another, how much each individual will be affected, and where the best results are most likely to lie—which option, in other words, is most likely to bring about the best results, the best balance between satisfaction and frustration. That option, whatever it may be, is the one I ought to choose. That is where my moral duty lies.

The great appeal of utilitarianism rests with its uncompromising *egalitarianism*: everyone's interests count and count as much as the like interests of everyone else. The kind of odious discrimination that some forms of contractarianism can justify—discrimination based on race or sex, for example—seems disallowed in principle by utilitarianism, as is speciesism, systematic discrimination based on species membership.

The equality we find in utilitarianism, however, is not the sort an advocate of animal or human rights should have in mind. Utilitarianism has no room for the equal moral rights of different individuals because it has no room for their equal inherent value or worth. What has value for the utilitarian is the satisfaction of an individual's interests, not the individual whose interests they are. A universe in which you satisfy your desire for

water, food, and warmth is, other things being equal, better than a universe in which these desires are frustrated. And the same is true in the case of an animal with similar desires. But neither you nor the animal have any value in your own right. Only your feelings do.

Here is an analogy to help make the philosophical point clearer: a cup contains different liquids, sometimes sweet, sometimes bitter, sometimes a mix of the two. What has value are the liquids: the sweeter the better, the bitterer the worse. The cup, the container, has no value. It is what goes into it, not what they go into, that has value. For the utilitarian you and I are like the cup; we have no value as individuals and thus no equal value. What has value is what goes into us, what we serve as receptacles for; our feelings of satisfaction have positive value, our feelings of frustration negative value.

Serious problems arise for utilitarianism when we remind ourselves that it enjoins us to bring about the best consequences. What does this mean? It doesn't mean the best consequences for me alone, or for my family or friends, or any other person taken individually. No, what we must do is, roughly, as follows: we must add up (somehow!) the separate satisfactions and frustrations of everyone likely to be affected by our choice, the satisfactions in one column, the frustrations in the other. We must total each column for each of the options before us. That is what it means to say the theory is aggregative. And then we must choose that option which is most likely to bring about the best balance of totalled satisfactions over totalled frustrations. Whatever act would lead to this outcome is the one we ought morally to perform—it is where our moral duty lies. And that act quite clearly might not be the same one that would bring about the best results for me personally, or for my family or friends, or for a lab animal. The best aggregated consequences for everyone concerned are not necessarily the best for each individual.

That utilitarianism is an aggregative theory— different individuals' satisfactions or frustrations are added, or summed, or totalled—is the key objection to this theory. My Aunt Bea is old, inactive, a cranky, sour person, though not physically ill. She prefers to go on living. She is also rather rich. I could make a fortune if I could get my hands on her money, money she intends to give me in any event, after she dies, but which she refuses to give me now. In order to avoid a huge tax bite, I plan to donate a handsome sum of my profits to a local children's hospital. Many, many children will benefit from my generosity, and much joy will be brought to their parents, relatives, and friends. If I don't get the money rather soon, all these ambitions will come to naught. The once-in-a-lifetime opportunity to make a real killing will be gone. Why, then, not kill my Aunt Bea? Oh, of course I *might* get caught. But I'm no fool and, besides, her doctor can be counted on to cooperate (he has an eye for the same investment and I happen to know a good deal about his shady past). The deed can be done . . . professionally, shall we say. There is *very* little chance of getting caught. And as for my conscience being guilt-ridden, I am a resourceful sort of fellow and will take more than sufficient comfort—as I lie on the beach at Acapulco—in contemplating the joy and health I have brought to so many others.

Suppose Aunt Bea is killed and the rest of the story comes out as told. Would I have done anything wrong? Anything immoral? One would have thought that I had. Not according to utilitarianism. Since what I have done has brought about the best balance between totalled satisfaction and frustration for all those affected by the outcome, my action is not wrong. Indeed, in killing Aunt Bea the physician and I did what duty required.

This same kind of argument can be repeated in all sorts of cases, illustrating, time after time, how the utilitarian's position leads to results that impartial people find morally callous. It *is* wrong to kill my Aunt Bea in the name of bringing about the best results for others. A good end does not justify an evil means. Any adequate moral theory will have to explain why this is so.

Utilitarianism fails in this respect and so cannot be the theory we seek.

What to do? Where to begin anew? The place to begin, I think, is with the utilitarian's view of the value of the individual—or, rather, lack of value. In its place, suppose we consider that you and I, for example, do have value as individuals—what we'll call *inherent value*. To say we have such value is to say that we are something more than, something different from, mere receptacles. Moreover, to ensure that we do not pave the way for such injustices as slavery or sexual discrimination, we must believe that all who have inherent value have it equally, regardless of their sex, race, religion, birthplace, and so on. Similarly to be discarded as irrelevant are one's talents or skills, intelligence and wealth, personality or pathology, whether one is loved and admired or despised and loathed. The genius and the retarded child, the prince and the pauper, the brain surgeon and the fruit vendor, Mother Teresa and the most unscrupulous used-car salesman—all have inherent value, all possess it equally, and all have an equal right to be treated with respect, to be treated in ways that do not reduce them to the status of things, as if they existed as resources for others. My value as an individual is independent of my usefulness to you. Yours is not dependent on your usefulness to me. For either of us to treat the other in ways that fail to show respect for the other's independent value is to act immorally, to violate the individual's rights.

Some of the rational virtues of this view—what I call the rights view—should be evident. Unlike (crude) contractarianism, for example, the rights view *in principle* denies the moral tolerability of any and all forms of racial, sexual, or social discrimination; and unlike utilitarianism, this view *in principle* denies that we can justify good results by using evil means that violate an individual's rights—denies, for example, that it could be moral to kill my Aunt Bea to harvest beneficial consequences for others. That would be to sanction the disrespectful treatment of the individual in the name of the social good, something the rights view will not—categorically will not—ever allow.

The rights view, I believe, is rationally the most satisfactory moral theory. It surpasses all other theories in the degree to which it illuminates and explains the foundation of our duties to one another—the domain of human morality. On this score it has the best reasons, the best arguments, on its side. Of course, if it were possible to show that only human beings are included within its scope, then a person like myself, who believes in animal rights, would be obliged to look elsewhere.

But attempts to limit its scope to humans only can be shown to be rationally defective. Animals, it is true, lack many of the abilities humans possess. They can't read, do higher mathematics, build a bookcase, or make *baba ghanoush*. Neither can many human beings, however, and yet we don't (and shouldn't) say that they (these humans) therefore have less inherent value, less of a right to be treated with respect, than do others. It is the *similarities* between those human beings who most clearly, most noncontroversially have such value (the people reading this, for example), not our differences, that matter most. And the really crucial, the basic similarity is simply this: we are each of us the experiencing subject of a life, a conscious creature having an individual welfare that has importance to us whatever our usefulness to others. We want and prefer things, believe and feel things, recall and expect things. And all these dimensions of our life, including our pleasure and pain, our enjoyment and suffering, our satisfaction and frustration, our continued existence or our untimely death—all make a difference to the quality of our life as lived, as experienced, by us as individuals. As the same is true of those animals that concern us (the ones that are eaten and trapped, for example), they too must be viewed as the experiencing subjects of a life, with inherent value of their own.

Some there are who resist the idea that animals have inherent value. "Only humans have such value," they profess. How might this narrow view be defended? Shall we say that only humans have the requisite intelligence, or autonomy, or reason? But there are many, many humans who fail to meet these standards and yet are reasonably viewed as having value above and beyond their usefulness to others. Shall we claim that only humans belong to the right species, the species *Homo sapiens*? But this is blatant speciesism. Will it be said, then, that all—and only—humans have immortal souls? Then our opponents have their work cut out for them. I am myself not ill-disposed to the proposition that there are immortal souls. Personally, I profoundly hope I have one. But I would not want to rest my position on a controversial ethical issue on the even more controversial question about who or what has an immortal soul. That is to dig one's hole deeper, not to climb out. Rationally, it is better to resolve moral issues without making more controversial assumptions than are needed. The question of who has inherent value is such a question, one that is resolved more rationally without the introduction of the idea of immortal souls than by its use.

Well, perhaps some will say that animals have some inherent value, only less than we have. Once again, however, attempts to defend this view can be shown to lack rational justification. What could be the basis of our having more inherent value than animals? Their lack of reason, or autonomy, or intellect? Only if we are willing to make the same judgement in the case of humans who are similarly deficient. But it is not true that such humans—the retarded child, for example, or the mentally deranged—have less inherent value than you or I. Neither, then, can we rationally sustain the view that animals like them in being the experiencing subjects of a life have less inherent value. *All* who have inherent value have it *equally,* whether they be human animals or not.

Inherent value, then, belongs equally to those who are the experiencing subjects of a life. Whether it belongs to others—to rocks and rivers, trees and glaciers, for example—we do not know and may never know. But neither do we need to know, if we are to make the case for animal rights. We do not need to know, for example, how many people are eligible to vote in the next presidential election before we can know whether I am. Similarly, we do not need to know how many individuals have inherent value before we can know that some do. When it comes to the case for animal rights, then, what we need to know is whether the animals that, in our culture, are routinely eaten, hunted, and used in our laboratories, for example, are like us in being subjects of a life. And we do know this. We do know that many—literally, billions and billions—of these animals are the subjects of a life in the sense explained and so have inherent value if we do. And since, in order to arrive at the best theory of our duties to one another, we must recognize our equal inherent value as individuals, reason—not sentiment, not emotion—reason compels us to recognize the equal inherent value of these animals and, with this, their equal right to be treated with respect.

That, *very* roughly, is the shape and feel of the case for animal rights. Most of the details of the supporting argument are missing. They are to be found in the book to which I alluded earlier. Here, the details go begging, and I must, in closing, limit myself to four final points.

The first is how the theory that underlies the case for animal rights shows that the animal rights movement is a part of, not antagonistic to, the human rights movement. The theory that rationally grounds the rights of animals also grounds the rights of humans. Thus those involved in the animal rights movement are partners in the struggle to secure respect for human rights—the rights of women, for example, or minorities, or workers. The animal rights movement is cut from the same moral cloth as these.

Second, having set out the broad outlines of the rights view, I can now say why its implications for farming and science, among other fields, are both clear and uncompromising. In the case of the use of animals in science, the rights view is categorically abolitionist. Lab animals are not our tasters; we are not their kings. Because these animals are treated routinely, systematically as if their value were reducible to their usefulness to others, they are routinely, systematically treated with a lack of respect, and thus are their rights routinely, systematically violated. This is just as true when they are used in trivial, duplicative, unnecessary, or unwise research as it is when they are used in studies that hold out real promise of human benefits. We can't justify harming or killing a human being (my Aunt Bea, for example) just for these sorts of reason. Neither can we do so even in the case of so lowly a creature as a laboratory rat. It is not just refinement or reduction that is called for, not just larger, cleaner cages, not just more generous use of anaesthetic or the elimination of multiple surgery, not just tidying up the system. It is complete replacement. The best we can do when it comes to using animals in science is—not to use them. That is where our duty lies, according to the rights view.

As for commercial animal agriculture, the rights view takes a similar abolitionist position. The fundamental moral wrong here is not that animals are kept in stressful close confinement or in isolation, or that their pain and suffering, their needs and preferences are ignored or discounted. All these *are* wrong, or course, but they are not the fundamental wrong. They are symptoms and effects of the deeper systematic wrong that allows these animals to be viewed and treated as lacking independent value, as resources for us—as, indeed, a renewable resource. Giving farm animals more space, more natural environments, more companions does not right the fundamental wrong, any more than giving lab animals more anaesthesia or bigger, cleaner cages would right the fundamental wrong in their case. Nothing less than the total dissolution of commercial animal agriculture will do this, just as, for similar reasons I won't develop at length here, morality requires nothing less than the total elimination of hunting and trapping for commercial and sporting ends. The rights view's implications, then, as I have said, are clear and uncompromising.

My last two points are about philosophy, my profession. It is, most obviously, no substitute for political action. The words I have written here and in other places by themselves don't change a thing. It is what we do with the thoughts that the words express—our acts, our deeds—that changes things. All that philosophy can do, and all I have attempted, is to offer a vision of what our deeds should aim at. And the why. But not the how.

Finally, I am reminded of my thoughtful critic, the one I mentioned earlier, who chastised me for being too cerebral. Well, cerebral I have been: indirect duty views, utilitarianism, contractarianism—hardly the stuff deep passions are made of. I am also reminded, however, of the image another friend once set before me—the image of the ballerina as expressive of disciplined passion. Long hours of sweat and toil, of loneliness and practice, of doubt and fatigue: those are the discipline of her craft. But the passion is there too, the fierce drive to excel, to speak through her body, to do it right, to pierce our minds. That is the image of philosophy I would leave with you, not "too cerebral" but *disciplined passion*. Of the discipline enough has been seen. As for the passion: there are times, and these not infrequent, when tears come to my eyes when I see, or read, or hear of the wretched plight of animals in the hands of humans. Their pain, their suffering, their loneliness, their innocence, their death. Anger. Rage. Pity. Sorrow. Disgust. The whole creation groans under the weight of the evil we humans visit upon these mute, powerless creatures. It *is* our hearts, not just our heads, that call for an end to it all, that demand of us that we overcome, for them, the habits and forces behind their systematic oppression. All great movements, it is written, go through three stages: ridicule, discussion, adoption. It is the realization of this third stage, adoption, that requires both our passion and our discipline, our hearts and our heads. The fate of animals is in our hands. God grant we are equal to the task.

Study Questions

1. What does Regan mean by "inherent value"?
2. Why does he believe that limiting inherent value to human beings is a mistake?
3. Does a lion that eats a zebra violate the zebra's right to life?
4. Under what circumstances, if any, are zoos morally acceptable?

Speaking of Animal Rights

MARY ANNE WARREN

Mary Anne Warren (1942–2010) was Professor of Philosophy at San Francisco State University. She maintains that animals have rights but not identical in strength to those of persons. She argues that practicality precludes our treating all animals as our moral equals.

Mary Anne Warren, "Difficulties with the Strong Rights Position," from *Between the Species* 2, No. 4 (Fall 1987). Reprinted by permission.

Tom Regan has produced what is perhaps the definitive defense of the view that the basic moral rights of at least some non-human animals are in no way inferior to our own. In *The Case for Animal Rights,* he argues that all normal mammals over a year of age have the same basic moral rights.[1] Non-human mammals have essentially the same right not to be harmed or killed as we do. I shall call this "the strong animal rights position," although it is weaker than the claims made by some animal liberationists in that it ascribes rights to only some sentient animals.[2]

I will argue that Regan's case for the strong animal rights position is unpersuasive and that this position entails consequences which a reasonable person cannot accept. I do not deny that some non-human animals have moral rights; indeed, I would extend the scope of the rights claim to include all sentient animals, that is, all those capable of having experiences, including experiences of pleasure or satisfaction and pain, suffering, or frustration.[3] However, I do not think that the moral rights of most non-human animals are identical in strength to those of persons.[4] The rights of most non-human animals may be overridden in circumstances which would not justify overriding the rights of persons. There are, for instance, compelling realities which sometimes require that we kill animals for reasons which could not justify the killing of persons. I will call this view "the weak animal rights" position, even though it ascribes rights to a wider range of animals than does the strong animal rights position.

I will begin by summarizing Regan's case for the strong animal rights position and noting two problems with it. Next, I will explore some consequences of the strong animal rights position which I think are unacceptable. Finally, I will outline the case for the weak animal rights position.

REGAN'S CASE

Regan's argument moves through three stages. First, he argues that normal, mature mammals are not only sentient but have other mental capacities as well. These include the capacities for emotion, memory, belief, desire, the use of general concepts, intentional action, a sense of the future, and some degree of self-awareness. Creatures with such capacities are said to be subjects-of-a-life. They are not only alive in the biological sense but have a psychological identity over time and an existence which can go better or worse for them. Thus, they can be harmed or benefited. These are plausible claims, and well defended. One of the strongest parts of the book is the rebuttal of philosophers, such as R. G. Frey, who object to the application of such mentalistic terms to creatures that do not use a human-style language.[5] The second and third stages of the argument are more problematic.

In the second stage, Regan argues that subjects-of-a-life have inherent value. His concept of inherent value grows out of his opposition to utilitarianism. Utilitarian moral theory, he says, treats individuals as "mere receptacles" for morally significant value, in that harm to one individual may be justified by the production of a greater net benefit to other individuals. In opposition to this, he holds that subjects-of-a-life have a value independent of both the value they may place upon their lives or experiences and the value others may place upon them.

Inherent value, Regan argues, does not come in degrees. To hold that some individuals have more inherent value than others is to adopt a "perfectionist" theory, i.e., one which assigns different moral worth to individuals according to how well they are thought to exemplify some virtue(s), such as intelligence or moral autonomy. Perfectionist theories have been used, at least since the time of Aristotle, to rationalize such injustices as slavery and male domination, as well as the unrestrained exploitation of animals. Regan argues that if we reject these injustices, then we must also reject perfectionism and conclude that all subjects-of-a-life have equal inherent value. Moral agents have no more inherent value than moral patients, i.e., subjects-of-a-life who are not morally responsible for their actions.

In the third phase of the argument, Regan uses the thesis of equal inherent value to derive strong moral rights for all subjects-of-a-life. This thesis underlies the Respect Principle, which forbids us to treat beings who have inherent value as mere receptacles, i.e., mere means to the production of the greatest overall good. This principle, in turn, underlies the Harm Principle, which says that we have a direct prima facie duty not to harm beings who have inherent value. Together, these principles give rise to moral rights. Rights are defined as valid claims, claims to certain goods and against certain beings, i.e., moral agents. Moral rights generate duties not only to refrain from inflicting harm upon beings with inherent value but also to come to their aid when they are threatened by other moral agents. Rights are not absolute but may be overridden in certain circumstances. Just what these circumstances are we will consider later. But first, let's look at some difficulties in the theory as thus far presented.

THE MYSTERY OF INHERENT VALUE

Inherent value is a key concept in Regan's theory. It is the bridge between the plausible claim that all normal, mature mammals— human or otherwise—are subjects-of-a-life and the more debatable claim that they all have basic moral rights of the same strength. But it is a highly obscure concept, and its obscurity makes it ill-suited to play this crucial role.

Inherent value is defined almost entirely in negative terms. It is not dependent upon the value which either the inherently valuable individual or anyone else may place upon that individual's life or experiences. It is not (necessarily) a function of sentience or any other mental capacity, because, Regan says, some entities which are not sentient (e.g., trees, rivers, or rocks) may, nevertheless, have inherent value. . . . It cannot

attach to anything other than an individual; species, ecosystems, and the like cannot have inherent value.

These are some of the things which inherent value is not. But what is it? Unfortunately, we are not told. Inherent value appears as a mysterious non-natural property which we must take on faith. Regan says that it is a *postulate* that subjects-of-a-life have inherent value, a postulate justified by the fact that it avoids certain absurdities which he thinks follow from a purely utilitarian theory. . . . But why is the postulate that *subjects-of-a-life* have inherent value? If the inherent value of a being is completely independent of the value that it or anyone else places upon its experiences, then why does the fact that it has certain sorts of experiences constitute evidence that it has inherent value? If the reason is that subjects-of-a-life have an existence which can go better or worse for them, then why isn't the appropriate conclusion that all sentient beings have inherent value, since they would all seem to meet that condition? Sentient but mentally unsophisticated beings may have a less extensive range of possible satisfactions and frustrations, but why should it follow that they have—or may have— no inherent value at all?

In the absence of a positive account of inherent value, it is also difficult to grasp the connection between being inherently valuable and having moral rights. Intuitively, it seems that value is one thing, and rights are another. It does not seem incoherent to say that some things (e.g., mountains, rivers, redwood trees) are inherently valuable and yet are not the sorts of things which can have moral rights. Nor does it seem incoherent to ascribe inherent value to some things which are not individuals, e.g., plant or animal species, though it may well be incoherent to ascribe moral rights to such things.

In short, the concept of inherent value seems to create at least as many problems as it solves. If inherent value is based on some natural property, then why not try to identify that property and explain its moral significance, without appealing to inherent value? And if it is not based on any natural property, then why should we believe in it? That it may enable us to avoid some of the problems faced by the utilitarian is not a sufficient reason, if it creates other problems which are just as serious.

IS THERE A SHARP LINE?

Perhaps the most serious problems are those that arise when we try to apply the strong animal rights position to animals other than normal, mature mammals. Regan's theory requires us to divide all living things into two categories: those which have the same inherent value and the same basic moral rights that we do, and those which have no inherent value and presumably no moral rights. But wherever we try to draw the line, such a sharp division is implausible.

It would surely be arbitrary to draw such a sharp line between normal, mature mammals and all other living things. Some birds (e.g., crows, magpies, parrots, mynahs) appear to be just as mentally sophisticated as most mammals and thus are equally strong candidates for inclusion under the subject-of-a-life criterion. Regan is not in fact advocating that we draw the line here. His claim is only that normal mature mammals are clear cases, while other cases are less clear. Yet, on his theory, there must be such a sharp line *somewhere,* since there are no degrees of inherent value. But why should we believe that there is a sharp line between creatures that are subjects-of-a-life and creatures that are not? Isn't it more likely that "subjecthood" comes in degrees, that some creatures have only a little self-awareness, and only a little capacity to anticipate the future, while some have a little more, and some a good deal more?

Should we, for instance, regard fish, amphibians, and reptiles as subjects-of-a-life? A simple yes-or-no answer seems inadequate. On the one hand, some of their behavior is difficult to explain without the assumption that they have sensations, beliefs, desires, emotions, and memories; on the other hand, they do not seem to exhibit very much self-awareness or very much conscious anticipation of future events. Do they have enough mental sophistication to count as subjects-of-a-life? Exactly how much is enough?

It is still more unclear what we should say about insects, spiders, octopi, and other invertebrate animals which have brains and sensory organs but whose minds (if they have minds) are even more alien to us than those of fish or reptiles. Such creatures are probably sentient. Some people doubt that they can feel pain, since they lack certain neurological structures which are crucial to the processing of pain impulses in vertebrate animals. But this argument is inconclusive, since their nervous systems might process pain in ways different from ours. When injured, they sometimes act as if they are in pain. On evolutionary grounds, it seems unlikely that highly mobile creatures with complex sensory systems would not have developed a capacity for pain (and pleasure), since such a capacity has obvious survival value. It must, however, be admitted that we do not *know* whether spiders can feel pain (or something very like it), let alone whether they have emotions, memories, beliefs, desires, self-awareness, or a sense of the future.

Even more mysterious are the mental capacities (if any) of mobile microfauna. The brisk and efficient way that paramecia move about in their incessant search for food *might* indicate some kind of sentience, in spite of their lack of eyes, ears, brains, and other organs associated with sentience in more complex organisms. It is conceivable— though not very probable—that they, too, are subjects-of-a-life.

The existence of a few unclear cases need not pose a serious problem for a moral theory, but in this case, the unclear cases constitute most of those with which an adequate theory of animal rights would need to deal. The subject-of-a-life criterion can provide us with little or no moral guidance in our interactions with the vast majority of animals. That might be acceptable if it could be supplemented with additional principles which would provide such guidance. However, the radical dualism of the theory precludes supplementing it in this way. We are forced to say that either a spider has the same right to life as you and I do, or it has no right to life whatever—and that only the gods know which of these alternatives is true.

Regan's suggestion for dealing with such unclear cases is to apply the "benefit of the doubt" principle. That is, when dealing with beings that may or may not be subjects-of-a-life, we should act as if they are.[6] But if we try to apply this principle to the entire range of doubtful cases, we will find ourselves with moral obligations which we cannot possibly fulfill. In many climates, it is virtually impossible to live without swatting mosquitoes and exterminating cockroaches, and not all of us can afford to hire someone to sweep the path before we walk, in order to make sure that we do not step on ants. Thus, we are still faced with the daunting task of drawing a sharp line somewhere on the continuum of life forms— this time, a line demarcating the limits of the benefit of the doubt principle.

The weak animal rights theory provides a more plausible way of dealing with this range of cases, in that it allows the rights of animals of different kinds to vary in strength. . . .

WHY ARE ANIMAL RIGHTS WEAKER THAN HUMAN RIGHTS?

How can we justify regarding the rights of persons as generally stronger than those of sentient beings which are not persons? There are a plethora of bad justifications, based on religious premises or false or unprovable claims about the differences between human and non-human nature. But there is one difference which has a clear moral relevance: people are at least sometimes capable of being moved to action or inaction by the force of reasoned argument. Rationality rests upon other mental capacities, notably those which Regan cites as criteria for being a subject-of-a-life. We share these capacities with many other animals. But it is not just because we are subjects-of-a-life that we are both

able and morally compelled to recognize one another as beings with equal basic moral rights. It is also because we are able to "listen to reason" in order to settle our conflicts and cooperate in shared projects. This capacity, unlike the others, may require something like a human language.

Why is rationality morally relevant? It does not make us "better" than other animals or more "perfect." It does not even automatically make us more intelligent. (Bad reasoning reduces our effective intelligence rather than increasing it.) But it is morally relevant insofar as it provides greater possibilities for cooperation and for the nonviolent resolution of problems. It also makes us more dangerous than non-rational beings can ever be. Because we are potentially more dangerous and less predictable than wolves, we need an articulated system of morality to regulate our conduct. Any human morality, to be workable in the long run, must recognize the equal moral status of all persons, whether through the postulate of equal basic moral rights or in some other way. The recognition of the moral equality of other persons is the price we must each pay for their recognition of our moral equality. Without this mutual recognition of moral equality, human society can exist only in a state of chronic and bitter conflict. The war between the sexes will persist so long as there is sexism and male domination; racial conflict will never be eliminated so long as there are racist laws and practices. But, to the extent that we achieve a mutual recognition of equality, we can hope to live together, perhaps as peacefully as wolves, achieving (in part) through explicit moral principles what they do not seem to need explicit moral principles to achieve.

Why not extend this recognition of moral equality to other creatures, even though they cannot do the same for us? The answer is that we cannot. Because we cannot reason with most non-human animals, we cannot always solve the problems which they may cause without harming them—although we are always obligated to try. We cannot negotiate a treaty with the feral cats and foxes, requiring them to stop preying on endangered native species in return for suitable concessions on our part.

> If rats invade our houses . . . we cannot reason with them, hoping to persuade them of the injustice they do us. We can only attempt to get rid of them.[7]

Aristotle was not wrong in claiming that the capacity to alter one's behavior on the basis of reasoned argument is relevant to the full moral status which he accorded to free men. Of course, he was wrong in his other premise, that women and slaves by their nature cannot reason well enough to function as autonomous moral agents. Had that premise been true, so would his conclusion that women and slaves are not quite the moral equals of free men. In the case of most non-human animals, the corresponding premise is true. If, on the other hand, there are animals with whom we can (learn to) reason, then we are obligated to do this and to regard them as our moral equals.

Thus, to distinguish between the rights of persons and those of most other animals on the grounds that only people can alter their behavior on the basis of reasoned argument does not commit us to a perfectionist theory of the sort Aristotle endorsed. There is no excuse for refusing to recognize the moral equality of some people on the grounds that we don't regard them as quite as rational as we are, since it is perfectly clear that most people can reason well enough to determine how to act so as to respect the basic rights of others (if they choose to), and that is enough for moral equality.

But what about people who are clearly not rational? It is often argued that sophisticated mental capacities such as rationality cannot be essential for the possession of equal basic moral rights, since nearly everyone agrees that human infants and mentally incompetent persons have such rights, even though they may lack those sophisticated mental capacities. But this argument is inconclusive, because there are powerful practical and emotional reasons for protecting non-rational human beings, reasons which are absent in the case of most non-human animals. Infancy and mental incompetence are human conditions which all of us either have experienced or are likely to experience at some time. We also protect babies and mentally incompetent people because we care for them. We don't normally care for animals in the same way, and when we do—e.g., in the case of much-loved pets—we may regard them as having special rights by virtue of their relationship to us. We protect them not only for their sake but also for our own, lest we be hurt by harm done to them. Regan holds that such "side-effects" are irrelevant to moral rights, and perhaps they are. But in ordinary usage, there is no sharp line between moral rights and those moral protections which are not rights. The extension of strong moral protections to infants and the mentally impaired in no way proves that non-human animals have the same basic moral rights as people.

WHY SPEAK OF "ANIMAL RIGHTS" AT ALL?

If, as I have argued, reality precludes our treating all animals as our moral equals, then why should we still ascribe rights to them? Everyone agrees that animals are entitled to some protection against human abuse, but why speak of animal *rights* if we are not prepared to accept most animals as our moral equals? The weak animal rights position may seem an unstable compromise between the bold claim that animals have the same basic moral rights that we do and the more common view that animals have no rights at all.

It is probably impossible to either prove or disprove the thesis that animals have moral rights by producing an analysis of the concept of a moral right and checking to see if some or all animals satisfy the conditions for having rights. The concept of a moral right is complex, and it is not clear which of its strands are essential. Paradigm rights holders, i.e., mature and mentally competent persons, are *both* rational and morally autonomous beings and sentient subjects-of-a-life. Opponents of animal rights claim that rationality and moral autonomy are essential for the possession of rights, while defenders of animal rights claim that they are not. The ordinary concept of a moral right is probably not precise enough to enable us to determine who is right on purely definitional grounds.

If logical analysis will not answer the question of whether animals have moral rights, practical considerations may, nevertheless, incline us to say that they do. The most plausible alternative to the view that animals have moral rights is that, while they do not have *rights,* we are, nevertheless, obligated not to be cruel to them. Regan argues persuasively that the injunction to avoid being cruel to animals is inadequate to express our obligations towards animals, because it focuses on the mental states of those who cause animal suffering, rather than on the harm done to the animals themselves. . . . Cruelty is inflicting pain or suffering and either taking pleasure in that pain or suffering or being more or less indifferent to it. Thus, to express the demand for the decent treatment of animals in terms of the rejection of cruelty is to invite the too easy response that those who subject animals to suffering are not being cruel because they regret the suffering they cause but sincerely believe that what they do is justified. The injunction to avoid cruelty is also inadequate in that it does not preclude the killing of animals— for any reason, however trivial—so long as it is done relatively painlessly.

The inadequacy of the anti-cruelty view provides one practical reason for speaking of animal rights. Another practical reason is that this is an age in which nearly all significant moral claims tend to be expressed in terms of rights. Thus, the denial that animals have rights, however carefully qualified, is likely to be taken to mean that we may do whatever we like to them, provided that we do not violate any human rights. In such a context, speaking of the rights of animals may be the only way to persuade many people to take seriously protests against the abuse of animals.

Why not extend this line of argument and speak of the rights of trees, mountains, oceans, or anything else which we may wish to see protected from destruction? Some environmentalists have not hesitated to speak in this way, and, given the importance of protecting such elements of the natural world, they cannot be blamed for using this rhetorical device. But, I would argue that moral rights can meaningfully be ascribed only to entities which have some capacity for sentience. This is because moral rights are protections designed to protect rights holders from harms or to provide them with benefits which matter *to them.* Only beings capable of sentience can be harmed or benefited in ways which matter to them, for only such beings can like or dislike what happens to them or prefer some conditions to others. Thus, sentient animals, unlike mountains, rivers, or species, are at least logically possible candidates for moral rights. This fact, together with the need to end current abuses of animals—e.g., in scientific research . . . — provides a plausible case for speaking of animal rights.

CONCLUSION

I have argued that Regan's case for ascribing strong moral rights to all normal, mature mammals is unpersuasive because (1) it rests upon the obscure concept of inherent value, which is defined only in negative terms, and (2) it seems to preclude any plausible answer to questions about the moral status of the vast majority of sentient animals . . .

The weak animal rights theory asserts that (1) any creature whose natural mode of life includes the pursuit of certain satisfactions has the right not to be forced to exist without the opportunity to pursue those satisfactions; (2) that any creature which is capable of pain, suffering, or frustration has the right that such experiences not be deliberately inflicted upon it without some compelling reason; and (3) that no sentient being should be killed without good reason. However, moral rights are not an all-or-nothing affair. The strength of the reasons required to override the rights of a non-human organism varies, depending upon—among other things—the probability that it is sentient and (if it is clearly sentient) its probable degree of mental sophistication.

NOTES

1. Tom Regan, *The Case for Animal Rights* (Berkeley: University of California Press, 1983). All page references are to this edition.

2. For instance, Peter Singer, although he does not like to speak of rights, includes all sentient beings under the protection of his basic utilitarian principle of equal respect for like interests. (Animal Liberation [New York: Avon Books, 1975], p. 3.)

3. The capacity for sentience, like all of the mental capacities mentioned in what follows, is a disposition. Dispositions do not disappear whenever they are not currently manifested. Thus, sleeping or temporarily unconscious persons or non-human animals are still sentient in the relevant sense (i.e., still capable of sentience), so long as they still have the neurological mechanisms necessary for the occurrence of experiences.

4. It is possible, perhaps probable that some non-human animals—such as cetaceans and anthropoid apes—should be regarded as persons. If so, then the weak animal rights position holds that these animals have the same basic moral rights as human persons.

5. See R. G. Frey, *Interests and Rights: The Case Against Animals* (Oxford: Oxford University Press, 1980).

6. See, for instance, p. 319, where Regan appeals to the benefit of the doubt principle when dealing with infanticide and late-term abortion.

7. Bonnie Steinbock, "Speciesism and the Idea of Equality," *Philosophy* 53 (1978): 253.

Study Questions

1. How does Warren distinguish the strong animal rights position and the weak one?
2. Do all human beings deserve the same rights?
3. Do all nonhuman animals deserve the same rights?
4. According to Warren, why do mountains not have rights?

F.   THE ENVIRONMENT

We Are What We Eat

TOM REGAN

In the next selection Tom Regan, Professor Emeritus of Philosophy at North Carolina State University, considers a variety of moral issues related to our environment. How do our actions affect the earth and the other creatures with whom we share it?

From Tom Regan, ed., *New Introductory Essays in Environmental Ethics.* Copyright © 1984. Reprinted by permission of the author.

The concerns of environmental ethics might begin with the food on our plate. If "we are what we eat," that food should tell us a good deal about what we are, both individually and as a nation. Those of us who live in the United States are blessed with abundant food supplies and, thanks to modern transportation systems, agricultural innovations, and competitive retail stores, we are able to select what we eat from a wide variety of tasty foods available throughout the year at low cost—at least the costs are low when compared with prices elsewhere! Popular national wisdom has it that we are the best fed, as well as the best dressed and housed, people in the world. Are we? And at what costs to the environment and others with whom we share it?

Some of the worries about our food concern the methods used to produce it. Modern agriculture is increasingly monocultural and chemically intensive. It is monocultural because a particular crop, say wheat or corn, soybeans or barley, is grown on the same land year after year; crops are not rotated, nor is acreage allowed to lie fallow so that the earth might renew itself. It is chemically intensive because of extensive use of fertilizers, herbicides, nematicides, pesticides, and the like. Though this form of agriculture has doubtless produced many benefits, it also leaves many serious questions in its wake.

One concerns pesticide residue in the food itself. At present there are approximately 400 different pesticides in agricultural use. Three different government agencies—the Environmental Protection Agency (EPA), the United States Department of Agricultural (USDA), and the Food and Drug Administration (FDA)—are charged with insuring that pesticide residue in food, including pesticides known to be carcinogens, do not exceed the "tolerance levels" set by the government. Some critics of government policies and efficiency are skeptical, however, perhaps none more so than Lewis Regenstein who, in his recent book *America the Poisoned*, states that

> a review of the government's policy in setting and enforcing tolerance levels of toxic pesticides

leads to the inescapable conclusions that the program exists primarily to insure the public that it is being protected from harmful chemical residues. In fact, the program, as currently administered, does little to minimize or even monitor the amount of poisons in our food, and serves the interests of the users and producers of pesticides rather than those of the public.[1]

If Regenstein is right, the food we eat could be poisoning us to death.

In addition to pesticide residue in our food serious worries also arise concerning the contamination of our water supplies from runoffs of pesticides and other chemicals commonly used in agriculture. Almost 50 percent of Americans use water from underground reservoirs, and approximately 40 percent of the water used in farm irrigation systems comes from this source. The purity of this water, which does not pass through filtration systems, is seriously jeopardized by the presence of toxic chemicals, including those employed as agricultural pesticides. Dibromochloropropane (DBCP), for example, widely used as a pesticide in California before it was banned in 1977, was found in half the irrigation and drinking wells surveyed in the San Joaquin Valley *two years later*. DBCP is a known carcinogen. Even water that comes from above-ground sources (lakes, rivers, streams, and the like) and that passes through municipal filtration systems is not always free from toxic chemicals, including pesticide residue from agricultural use perhaps hundreds of miles away. "The drinking water of every major American city," writes Regenstein, "contains dozens of cancer-causing chemicals and other toxins,"[2] a number of which can be traced to the chemically intensive methods used to produce the food on our plate.

Pesticides, of course, and the other chemicals essential to monocultural agriculture do not occur in nature but are the products of the petrochemical industry. The food on our plate is, therefore, causally related to that industry and, in this respect, is indirectly related to the pollution caused by petrochemical plants. That pollution, critics like Regenstein claim, besides adversely affecting the quality of the water we drink and the food we eat, also impacts detrimentally, directly and indirectly, on the quality of the air we breathe. Directly, quality is affected by petrochemical plants by way of their release into the air of toxic substances, some of which are causally implicated in increased incidences of respiratory diseases, such as emphysema and bronchitis, as well as a variety of cancers, especially lung cancer. Indirectly, the petrochemical industry, pesticides, and the food on our plate are a party to a decline in air quality because industry runs on electrical power that is frequently generated by methods that are themselves detrimental to the quality of the air we breathe.

The phenomenon known as acid rain illustrates the tangled web of cause and effect. The chemistry seems fairly simple. Sulphur oxides and nitrogen oxides emitted into the air form acids when they combine with water vapor. These acids in turn fall to the earth when it rains or snows with the result that both land and water acidity increase. The acidity of rain falling in some parts of the United States, for example, is estimated by an EPA study to have increased fiftyfold in the last twenty-five years and is sometimes over 100 times more acidic than normal rainfall. Though estimates vary, perhaps as much as 80 percent of the sulphur emissions that are the first link in the chain of events that culminate in acid rain result from human activities. Along with the increase in the acidity of rain there is a predictable increase in the incidence of acute and chronic respiratory ailments, and there are also serious reasons to question the continued fertility of the earth itself. Even the products of human creation—buildings, monuments, and the like—are not immune to acid rain. To cite just one example: In 1883 Cleopatra's Needle, a granite obelisk, after spending some thirty-five centuries in the Egyptian desert, was placed in New York City's Central Park. Exposed to the scorching sun, to wind, to sand, the obelisk

withstood the rigors of its desert environment for 3,500 years—better than it has its New York home, where in just 100 years it has lost several inches of its granite, in part because of the chemical fallout of acid rain. Human creations, our *urban* environment, not just nature and our bodies, can feel the bite of the acid rain.

Older coal-burning power plants along the Ohio River are among the principal causes of acid rain. But pollution travels, and the areas most affected by acid rain are across state and even national boundaries. "Dead" lakes—absent any plant or aquatic life—are found throughout the northeastern United States and southeastern Canada. A thousand lakes "dead" in Wisconsin, perhaps 10,000 endangered. There are "dead" lakes in Colorado and California, and in other countries, such as Sweden, which has lost approximately 15,000 lakes. Some experts predict that 50,000 or more lakes in Canada and the United States will "die" in the next fifteen years, all as a result of acid rain. How long the surrounding vegetation can withstand this onslaught and what the long-term effects for the earth's fertility will be is anyone's guess. Might the food on our plate turn out to be causally linked with forces which, if allowed to continue, will threaten the very possibility of growing food in the future?

The mention of the future takes us a step beyond concerns we are likely to have about our own health. Barring a catastrophic nuclear war, we will not be the last generation on this earth; an indefinite number of future generations will come after us. The effects of those practices we allow at present, including the effects of pesticides in the food chain and the petrochemical industry's contamination of the air, are likely to be here after we are gone. "Dead" lakes are likely to be here, and so is drinking water that is hazardous to anyone's health. The underground sources of water, mentioned earlier, move beneath the surface of the earth at a snail's pace. Some of the water we drink from these sources today fell as rain over a hundred years ago, and

today's rain, absorbed into underground aqui-
fers, may not resurface until the twenty-second
century. With the increase in acid rain attributable to human activities, including the power
plants that produce the energy to fuel the petrochemical plants that produce the pesticides
that are used to produce the food on our plate,
and even ignoring, if we may, the many other
sources of chemical contamination of the
earth's water supplies, are we doing what we
should with respect to generations yet unborn?
Would we be doing it if, instead of relying on
power from coal we rely instead on nuclear
plants, given the serious problems *for them,* our
descendants, posed by storing nuclear wastes?
The food on our plate that we eat today—does
it include a message from future persons, condemning us for a failure of moral will and vision
to act now to protect the vital interests of generations yet to come?

Except for descendants of the Marquis de
Sade, few people are likely to look with enthusiasm on pollution of any kind. It is, as some have
said, a *public evils* problem: *public* because pollution travels and, in doing so, harms, or puts at
risk of harm, people in general (the "public at
large"); *evil* because the effects of pollution on
those who are exposed are either actually or potentially harmful. Few of us, then, are likely to
be in favor of pollution as such, since this is tantamount to harming, or putting at risk of harm,
people in general (perhaps even ourself!). If we
consider matters from a political point of view
(not "political" in the sense of this or that
actual political party, but theoretically—from,
that is, the point of view of those who aspire to
say what is *the best* political arrangement under
which persons can live), how should we deal
with this public evils problem? To choose
among the options is a daunting challenge.
Some political theories will allow a lot of pollution; some might disallow any at all; in between
these two extremes are subtly differing conceptions of the ideal state and their respective policies regarding pollution. That there is pollution

in America at all, and that the history of the
food on our plate involves the use of pesticides
and other chemicals that everyone must agree
can pollute and that some claim *do* pollute, tells
us something about the political arrangements
under which we in fact live. Should we tolerate
pollutants? Should we be less concerned than
we are? Or should we restrict their presence,
possibly to the extent of banning them altogether? When we think about the food we eat,
can we rationally avoid asking these questions?
And once they are asked, can we rationally
refuse to expend the effort to answer them as
best we can?

Unless we happen to be one of the estimated
20 to 25 million people who are practicing vegetarians in the United States, that food on our
plate is likely to include meat. Part of the national wisdom about Americans being "the best
fed people in the world" includes our access to
flesh foods—chicken, steak, ham, ribs, burgers,
hot dogs, and the like. Not a few critics of the
farm animal industry have argued that, from the
point of view of our individual health, we would
be better off if we ate no or far less meat. A
major part of the health risk, so these critics
claim, again involves chemicals. Like other
forms of contemporary agriculture, farm animal
agriculture tends to be chemically intensive,
only the food sources receiving the chemicals in
this case are not carrots and wheat but are hogs
and chickens, cows and turkeys. Raised in close
confinement systems or what are called "factory
farms," farm animals increasingly live indoors in
dense populations or in cages or stalls. These
animals are fed a veritable diet of chemicals from
birth to death—growth stimulants, for example, and drugs to prevent or control the outbreak of contagious diseases. Residues of these
chemicals collect and are stored in various tis-
sues and organs in the animals' bodies. Some
are toxic and again pose serious health questions
when consumed by humans. Others, such as an-
tibiotics, could lose their restorative properties
for people who, in consuming animal flesh or

products, also consume unsuspected quantities of these "wonder drugs." That meat on our plate—perhaps there is more to it than meets the eye? . . .

Moral questions about the treatment of animals are by no means restricted to farm or other domesticated varieties. Wild animals also fall within the scope of moral inquiry, a point given sharp focus by the concern many people have in preserving endangered species. That concern often is selective, with a few exotic, mysterious, or symbolic species favored over others (including many species of plants) that are equally endangered. For Americans, the bald eagle gets a resounding "yes!," the snail darter, a politically vociferous "no!" Whatever we might or should say about the selectivity of concern about endangered species, a variety of causes—including, not surprisingly, the chemical contamination of the air, water, and earth to which, as has been noted, the food on our plate is related—place a large number of species at risk. Another, perhaps subtler relationship between our food and endangered species involves the destruction of their natural habitat. One pattern of destruction repeats itself on a global scale. Cities and their populations grow, pushing ever farther out from the center. Former agricultural lands are converted to residential and other urban uses, and wild areas, formerly home to delicately balanced systems of life (ecosystems), are cleared or plowed under to make room for new farms only to have urban growth encroach on agricultural lands again, and so on, and so on. Wild species caught in the spiral of urban expansion are threatened. Some hang on. Others do not.

The pressures of urban growth, then, are a principal contributing cause of endangering species. If this were a case of one good thing winning out over another, we could rest content that a kind of cosmic justice prevails. But there are problems on both sides of the contest as so described. Most of us live in an urban environment—a city or town of one size or another, or the outskirts (the "burbs"). Quite apart from the impact of urban growth on endangered

species, how big is too big? Is there, that is, a limit to the size of the urban environment beyond which it is no longer *good for us* to live there? If there is (and many critics of urban and suburban sprawl think so), then we cannot automatically assume that urban growth is "a good thing." Nor can we breezily dismiss questions about what in our urban environments is worth saving when, as we often must, we have to choose between preservation and redevelopment. If there is a limit to how much outward growth of our urban centers we should allow, there are also important questions about which, if any, of our urban landmarks and neighborhoods we should preserve.

The idea that the survival of a species is itself "a good thing" poses fundamental questions of its own. To a large extent the industrial, technological, and agricultural development that has led to and now underlies the variety of foods available to us has proceeded on the tacit assumption that *human interests* are the measure of all things valuable—at least things of the earth. "Anthropocentrism" is the name usually given to this vision of value. To consider seriously that the continued existence of a species is "a good thing" is to force ourselves to question the credentials of anthropocentrism. Is it possible that *species themselves* have a kind of value that is not reducible to the degree to which they serve human interests? Many would deny this. Value, they say, is to be fixed in economic terms, measured by the yardstick of human satisfaction as determined by what we would be willing to pay for that satisfaction. The value of a car, a house, a coat is set by how much we would be willing to pay for it or, if we already are the owner, by how much we would be willing to take in exchange. To speak of "the value of endangered species," then, in such a view, is a roundabout way of referring to how much we would be willing to pay to have them survive. To establish the amount we would be willing to pay might be difficult but, so proponents of an economic theory of value believe, not impossible. *Species as such* have no value, given an economic theory of value, but neither does anything else, neither truth, nor beauty, nor (noneconomic) goodness.

Many people, including many concerned to protect endangered species, reject economic theories of value. Even among those who are of one voice in rejecting such theories, however, serious and possibly divisive questions remain. In what can the (supposed) value of species as such consist, and how does the value of a species, assuming that it has one, correspond to or depart from the value of individual members, assuming that each member has some kind of (noneconomic) value? Or again, if species as such have value that is independent of human interests, including human economic interests, is it possible that we owe it to species themselves to protect them against human agents and forces which, if they were allowed to operate, would bring about the extinction of these species? If, for example, people in certain localities, responding to population pressures, are destroying the natural habitat of the last known representatives of an endangered species—ought we to halt this human encroachment, not in the name of human interests but for the sake of the value of species themselves? Ought we perhaps to do this *no matter what* the costs to the humans most directly involved, those who need new agricultural land to feed the new mouths which otherwise are likely to go hungry? To dismiss this question out of hand is to run the risk of accepting anthropocentrism uncritically.

The food on our plate is, one might say, a symbol of our predecessors' "conquest of nature," a conquest made possible by the widespread acceptance of anthropocentrism. That food, then, should remind us of our debts to them. But it should also occasion our critical curiosity as we assess the anthropocentric moral vision they have passed down to us. To do so, in its way, is to pay the finest tribute to our predecessors, since one ideal they bequeathed to us (one needs only to think of those true revolutionaries, America's Founding Fathers) *is* to be curious, to question the received opinions and common practices of the day. Those opinions and practices operative today are, metaphorically speaking, part of what we eat when we eat as we do. If we are what we eat, then divining the food on our plate does promise to tell us a good deal about what we are, as individuals and as a nation. And perhaps a good deal more about what we can and should be.

NOTES

1. Lewis Regenstein, *America the Poisoned* (Washington, DC: Acropolis Books, 1982) p. 86.
2. Ibid., p. 182.

Study Questions

1. What does Regan mean by "We are what we eat"?
2. What is a public evils problem?
3. What is meant by anthropocentrism?
4. What is valuable about the survival of a species?

Philosophical Problems for Environmentalism

ELLIOTT SOBER

Elliott Sober is Professor of Philosophy at the University of Wisconsin–Madison. In this essay he explores possible bases for the values implicit in the environmental movement.

I. INTRODUCTION

A number of philosophers have recognized that the environmental movement, whatever its practical political effectiveness, faces considerable theoretical difficulties in justification.[1] It has been recognized that traditional moral theories do not provide natural underpinnings for policy objectives and this has led some to skepticism about the claims of environmentalists, and others to the view that a revolutionary reassessment of ethical norms is needed. In this chapter, I will try to summarize the difficulties that confront a philosophical defense of environmentalism. I also will suggest a way of making sense of some environmental concerns that does not require the wholesale jettisoning of certain familiar moral judgments.

Preserving an endangered species or ecosystem poses no special conceptual problem when the instrumental value of that species or ecosystem is known. When we have reason to think that some natural object represents a resource to us, we obviously ought to take that fact into account in deciding what to do. A variety of potential uses may be under discussion, including food supply, medical applications, recreational use, and so on. As with any complex decision, it may be difficult even to agree on how to compare the competing values that

may be involved. Willingness to pay in dollars is a familiar least common denominator, although it poses a number of problems. But here we have nothing that is specifically a problem for environmentalism.

The problem for environmentalism stems from the idea that species and ecosystems ought to be preserved for reasons additional to their known value as resources for human use. The feeling is that even when we cannot say what nutritional, medicinal, or recreational benefit the preservation provides, there still is a value in preservation. It is the search for a rationale for this feeling that constitutes the main conceptual problem for environmentalism.

The problem is especially difficult in view of the holistic (as opposed to individualistic) character of the things being assigned value. Put simply, what is special about environmentalism is that it values the preservation of species, communities, or ecosystems, rather than the individual organisms of which they are composed. "Animal liberationists" have urged that we should take the suffering of sentient animals into account in ethical deliberation.[2] Such beasts are not mere things to be used as cruelly as we like no matter how trivial the benefit we derive. But in "widening the ethical circle," we are simply including in the community more individual organisms whose costs and benefits

From Bryan G. Norton, ed., *The Preservation of Species,* 1986 by Princeton University Press, 1988 paperback edition. Reprinted by permission of Princeton University Press.

we compare. Animal liberationists are extending an old and familiar ethical doctrine—namely, utilitarianism—to take account of the welfare of other individuals. Although the practical consequences of this point of view may be revolutionary, the theoretical perspective is not at all novel. If suffering is bad, then it is bad for any individual who suffers.[3] Animal liberationists merely remind us of the consequences of familiar principles.

But trees, mountains, and salt marshes do not suffer. They do not experience pleasure and pain, because, evidently, they do not have experiences at all. The same is true of species. Granted, individual organisms may have mental states; but the species—taken to be a population of organisms connected by certain sorts of interactions (preeminently, that of exchanging genetic material in reproduction)—does not. Or put more carefully, we might say that the only sense in which species have experiences is that their member organisms do: the attribution at the population level, if true, is true simply in virtue of its being true at the individual level. Here is a case where reductionism is correct.

So perhaps it is true in this reductive sense that some species experience pain. But the values that environmentalists attach to preserving species do not reduce to any value of preserving organisms. It is in this sense that environmentalists espouse a holistic value system. Environmentalists care about entities that by no stretch of the imagination have experiences (e.g., mountains). What is more, their position does not force them to care if individual organisms suffer pain, so long as the species is preserved. Steel traps may outrage an animal liberationist because of the suffering they inflict, but an environmentalist aiming just at the preservation of a balanced ecosystem might see here no cause for complaint. Similarly, environmentalists think that the distinction between wild and domesticated organisms is important, in that it is the preservation of "natural" (i.e., not created by the "artificial interference" of human beings) objects that matters, whereas animal liberationists see the main problem in terms of the

suffering of any organism—domesticated or not. And finally, environmentalists and animal liberationists diverge on what might be called the $n + m$ question. If two species—say blue and sperm whales—have roughly comparable capacities for experiencing pain, an animal liberationist might tend to think of the preservation of a sperm whale as wholly on an ethical par with the preservation of a blue whale. The fact that one organism is part of an endangered species while the other is not does not make the rare individual more intrinsically important. But for an environmentalist, this holistic property—membership in an endangered species—makes all the difference in the world: a world with n sperm and m blue whales is far better than a world with $n + m$ sperm and 0 blue whales. Here we have a stark contrast between an ethic in which it is the life situation of individuals that matters, and an ethic in which the stability and diversity of populations of individuals are what matter.[4]

Both animal liberationists and environmentalists wish to broaden our ethical horizons—to make us realize that it is not just human welfare that counts. But they do this in very different, often conflicting, ways. It is no accident that at the level of practical politics the two points of view increasingly find themselves at loggerheads. This practical conflict is the expression of a deep theoretical divide.

II. THE IGNORANCE ARGUMENT

"Although we might not now know what use a particular endangered species might be to us, allowing it to go extinct forever closes off the possibility of discovering and exploiting a future use." According to this point of view, our ignorance of value is turned into a reason for action. The scenario envisaged in this environmentalist argument is not without precedent; who could have guessed that penicillin would be good for something other than turning out cheese? But there is a fatal defect in such arguments, which we might summarize with the phrase *out of nothing, nothing comes:* rational decisions require assumptions about what is true and what is valuable (in decision-theoretic jargon, the inputs must be probabilities and utilities). If you are completely ignorant of values, then you are incapable of making a rational decision, either for or against preserving some species. The fact that you do not know the value of a species, by itself, cannot count as a reason for wanting one thing rather than another to happen to it.

And there are so many species. How many geese that lay golden eggs are there apt to be in that number? It is hard to assign probabilities and utilities precisely here, but an analogy will perhaps reveal the problem confronting this environmentalist argument. Most of us willingly fly on airplanes, when safer (but less convenient) alternative forms of transportation are available. Is this rational? Suppose it were argued that there is a small probability that the next flight you take will crash. This would be very bad for you. Is it not crazy for you to risk this, given that the only gain to you is that you can reduce your travel time by a few hours (by not going by train, say)? Those of us who not only fly, but congratulate ourselves for being rational in doing so, reject this argument. We are prepared to accept a small chance of a great disaster in return for the high probability of a rather modest benefit. If this is rational, no wonder that we might consistently be willing to allow a species to go extinct in order to build a hydroelectric plant.

That the argument from ignorance is no argument at all can be seen from another angle. If we literally do not know what consequences the extinction of this or that species may bring, then we should take seriously the possibility that the extinction may be beneficial as well as the possibility that it may be deleterious. It may sound deep to insist that we preserve endangered species precisely because we do not know why they are valuable. But ignorance on a scale like this cannot provide the basis for any rational action.

Rather than invoke some unspecified future benefit, an environmentalist may argue that the species in question plays a crucial role in stabilizing the ecosystem of which it is a part. This will undoubtedly be true for carefully chosen species and ecosystems, but one should not generalize this argument into a global claim to the effect that *every* species is crucial to a balanced ecosystem. Although ecologists used to agree that the complexity of an ecosystem stabilizes it, this hypothesis has been subject to a number of criticisms and qualifications, both from a theoretical and an empirical perspective.[5] And for certain kinds of species (those which occupy a rather small area and whose normal population is small) we can argue that extinction would probably not disrupt the community. However fragile the biosphere may be, the extreme view that everything is crucial is almost certainly not true.

But, of course, environmentalists are often concerned by the fact that extinctions are occurring now at a rate much higher than in earlier times. It is mass extinction that threatens the biosphere, they say, and this claim avoids the spurious assertion that communities are so fragile that even one extinction will cause a crash. However, if the point is to avoid a mass extinction of species, how does this provide a rationale for preserving a species of the kind just described, of which we rationally believe that its passing will not destabilize the ecosystem? And, more generally, if mass extinction is known to be a danger to us, how does this translate into a value for preserving any particular species? Notice that we have now passed beyond the confines of the argument from ignorance; we are taking as a premise the idea that mass extinction would be a catastrophe (since it would destroy the ecosystem on which we depend). But how should that premise affect our valuing the California condor, the blue whale, or the snail darter?

III. THE SLIPPERY SLOPE ARGUMENT

Environmentalists sometimes find themselves asked to explain why each species matters so much to them, when there are, after all, so many. We may know of special reasons for valuing particular species, but how can we justify thinking that each and every species is important? "Each extinction impoverishes the biosphere" is often the answer given, but it really fails to resolve the issue. Granted, each extinction impoverishes, but it only impoverishes a little bit. So if it is the *wholesale* impoverishment of the biosphere that matters, one would apparently have to concede that each extinction matters a little, but only a little. But environmentalists may be loathe to concede this, for if they concede that each species matters only a little, they seem to be inviting the wholesale impoverishment that would be an unambiguous disaster. So they dig in their heels and insist that each species matters a lot. But to take this line, one must find some other rationale than the idea that mass extinction would be a great harm. Some of these alternative rationales we will examine later. For now, let us take a closer look at the train of thought involved here.

Slippery slopes are curious things: if you take even one step onto them, you inevitably slide all the way to the bottom. So if you want to avoid finding yourself at the bottom, you must avoid stepping onto them at all. To mix metaphors, stepping onto a slippery slope is to invite being nickeled and dimed to death.

Slippery slope arguments have played a powerful role in a number of recent ethical debates. One often hears people defend the legitimacy of abortions by arguing that since it is permissible to abort a single-celled fertilized egg, it must be permissible to abort a foetus of any age, since there is no place to draw the line from 0 to 9 months. Antiabortionists, on the other hand, sometimes argue in the other direction: since infanticide of newborns is not permissible, abortion at any earlier time is also not allowed, since there is no place to draw the line. Although these two arguments reach opposite conclusions about the permissibility of abortions, they agree on the following idea: since there is no principled place to draw the line on the continuum from newly fertilized egg to foetus gone to term, one must treat all these cases in the same way. Either abortion is always permitted or it never is, since there is no place to draw the line. Both sides run their favorite slippery slope arguments, but try to precipitate slides in opposite directions.

Starting with 10 million extant species, and valuing overall diversity, the environmentalist does not want to grant that each species matters only a little. For having granted this, commercial expansion and other causes will reduce the tally to 9,999,999. And then the argument is repeated, with each species valued only a little, and diversity declines another notch. And so we are well on our way to a considerably impoverished biosphere, a little at a time. Better to reject the starting premise—namely, that each species matters only a little—so that the slippery slope can be avoided.

Slippery slopes should hold no terror for environmentalists, because it is often a mistake to demand that a line be drawn. Let me illustrate by an example. What is the difference between being bald and not? Presumably, the difference concerns the number of hairs you have on your head. But what is the precise number of hairs marking the boundary between baldness and not being bald? There is no such number. Yet, it would be a fallacy to conclude that there is no difference between baldness and hairiness. The fact that you cannot draw a line does not force you to say that the two alleged categories collapse into one. In the abortion case, this means that even if there is no precise point in foetal development that involves some discontinuous, qualitative change, one is still not obliged to think of newly fertilised eggs and foetuses gone to term as morally on a par. Since the biological differences are ones of degree, not kind, one may want to adopt the position that the moral differences are likewise matters of degree. This may lead to the view that a woman should have a better reason for having an abortion, the more developed her foetus is. Of course, this position does not logically follow from the idea that there is no place to draw the line; my point is just that differences in degree do not demolish the possibility of there being real moral differences.

In the environmental case, if one places a value on diversity, then each species becomes more valuable as the overall diversity declines. If we begin with 10 million species, each may matter little, but as extinctions continue, the remaining ones matter more and more. According to this outlook, a better and better reason would be demanded for allowing yet another species to go extinct. Perhaps certain sorts of economic development would justify the extinction of a species at one time. But granting this does not oblige one to conclude that the same sort of decision would have to be made further down the road. This means that one can value diversity without being obliged to take the somewhat exaggerated position that each species, no matter how many there are, is terribly precious in virtue of its contribution to that diversity.

Yet, one can understand that environmentalists might be reluctant to concede this point. They may fear that if one now allows that most species contribute only a little to overall diversity, one will set in motion a political process that cannot correct itself later. The worry is that even when the overall diversity has been drastically reduced, our ecological sensitivities will have been so coarsened that we will no longer be in a position to realize (or to implement policies fostering) the preciousness of what is left. This fear may be quite justified, but it is important to realize that it does not conflict with what was argued above. The political utility of making an argument should not be confused with the argument's soundness.

The fact that you are on a slippery slope, by itself, does not tell you whether you are near the beginning, in the middle, or at the end. If species diversity is a matter of degree, where do we currently find ourselves—on the verge of catastrophe, well on our way in that direction, or at some distance from a global crash? Environmentalists often urge that we are fast approaching a precipice; if we are, then the reduction in diversity that every succeeding extinction engenders should be all we need to justify species preservation.

Sometimes, however, environmentalists advance a kind of argument not predicated on the idea of fast approaching doom. The goal is to show that there is something wrong with allowing a species to go extinct (or with causing it to go extinct), even if overall diversity is not affected much. I now turn to one argument of this kind.

IV. APPEALS TO WHAT IS NATURAL

I noted earlier that environmentalists and animal liberationists disagree over the significance of the distinction between wild and domesticated animals. Since both types of organisms can experience pain, animal liberationists will think of each as meriting ethical consideration. But environmentalists will typically not put wild and domesticated organisms on a par. Environmentalists typically are interested in preserving what is natural, be it a species living in the wild or a wilderness ecosystem. If a kind of domesticated chicken were threatened with extinction, I doubt that environmental groups would be up in arms. And if certain unique types of human environments—say urban slums in the United States—were "endangered," it is similarly unlikely that environmentalists would view this process as a deplorable impoverishment of the biosphere.

The environmentalist's lack of concern for humanly created organisms and environments may be practical rather than principled. It may be that at the level of values, no such bifurcation is legitimate, but that from the point of view of practical political action, it makes sense to put one's energies into saving items that exist in the wild. This subject has not been discussed much in the literature, so it is hard to tell. But I sense that the distinction between wild and domesticated has a certain theoretical importance to many environmentalists. They perhaps think that the difference is that we created domesticated organisms which would otherwise not exist, and so are entitled to use them solely for our own interests. But we did not create wild organisms and environments, so it is the height of presumption to expropriate them for our benefit. A more fitting posture would be one of "stewardship": we have come on the scene and found a treasure not of our making. Given this, we ought to preserve this treasure in its natural state.

I do not wish to contest the appropriateness of "stewardship." It is the dichotomy between artificial (domesticated) and natural (wild) that strikes me as wrong-headed. I want to suggest that to the degree that "natural" means anything biologically, it means very little ethically. And, conversely, to the degree that "natural" is understood as a normative concept, it has very little to do with biology.

Environmentalists often express regret that we human beings find it so hard to remember that we are part of nature—one species among many others—rather than something standing outside of nature. I will not consider here whether this attitude is cause for complaint; the important point is that seeing us as part of nature rules out the environmentalist's use of the distinction between artificial-domesticated and natural-wild described above. *If we are part of nature, then everything we do is part of nature, and is natural in that primary sense.* When we domesticate organisms and bring them into a state of dependence on us, this is simply an example of one species exerting a selection pressure on another. If one calls this "unnatural," one might just as well say the same of parasitism or symbiosis (compare human domestication of animals and plants and "slave-making" in the social insects).

The concept of naturalness is subject to the same abuses as the concept of normalcy. *Normal* can mean *usual* or it can mean *desirable*. Although only the total pessimist will think that the two concepts are mutually exclusive, it is generally recognized that the mere fact that

something is common does not by itself count as a reason for thinking that it is desirable. This distinction is quite familiar now in popular discussions of mental health, for example. Yet, when it comes to environmental issues, the concept of naturalness continues to live a double life. The destruction of wilderness areas by increased industrialization is bad because it is unnatural. And it is unnatural because it involves transforming a natural into an artificial habitat. Or one might hear that although extinction is a natural process, the kind of mass extinction currently being precipitated by our species is unprecedented, and so is unnatural. Environmentalists should look elsewhere for a defense of their policies, lest conservation simply become a variant of uncritical conservatism in which the axiom "Whatever is, is right" is modified to read "Whatever is (before human beings come on the scene), is right."

This conflation of the biological with the normative sense of "natural" sometimes comes to the fore when environmentalists attack animal liberationists for naive do-goodism. Callicott writes:

> ... the value commitments of the humane movement seem at bottom to betray a world-denying or rather a life-loathing philosophy. The natural world as actually constituted is one in which one being lives at the expense of others. Each organism, in Darwin's metaphor, struggles to maintain its own organic integrity. ... To live is to be anxious about life, to feel pain and pleasure in a fitting mixture, and sooner or later to die. That is the way the system works. *If nature as a whole is good, then pain and death are also good.* Environmental ethics in general require people to play fair in the natural system. The neo-Benthamites have in a sense taken the uncourageous approach. People have attempted to exempt themselves from the life death reciprocities of natural processes and from ecological limitations in the name of a prophylactic ethic of maximizing rewards (pleasure) and minimizing unwelcome information (pain). To be fair, the humane moralists seem to suggest that we should

attempt to project the same values into the nonhuman animal world and to widen the charmed circle—no matter that it would be biologically unrealistic to do so or biologically ruinous if, per impossible, such an environmental ethic were implemented.

There is another approach. Rather than imposing our alienation from nature and natural processes and cycles of life on other animals, we human beings could reaffirm our participation in nature by accepting life as it is given without a sugar coating. . . .[6]

On the same page, Callicott quotes with approval Shepard's remark that "the humanitarian's projection onto nature of illegal murder and the rights of civilized people to safety not only misses the point but is exactly contrary to fundamental ecological reality: the structure of nature is a sequence of killings."[7]

Thinking that what is found in nature is beyond ethical defect has not always been popular. Darwin wrote:

. . . That there is much suffering in the world no one disputes.

Some have attempted to explain this in reference to man by imagining that it serves for his moral improvement. But the number of men in the world is as nothing compared with that of all other sentient beings, and these often suffer greatly without any moral improvement. A being so powerful and so full of knowledge as a God who could create the universe, is to our finite minds omnipotent and omniscient, and it revolts our understanding to suppose that his benevolence is not unbounded, for what advantage can there be in the sufferings of millions of the lower animals throughout almost endless time?

This very old argument from the existence of suffering against the existence of an intelligent first cause seems to me a strong one; whereas, as just remarked, the presence of much suffering agrees well with the view that all organic beings have been developed through variation and natural selection.[8]

Darwin apparently viewed the quantity of pain found in nature as a melancholy and sobering consequence of the struggle for existence. But once we adopt the Panglossian attitude that this is the best of all possible worlds ("there is just the right amount of pain," etc.), a failure to identify what is natural with what is good can only seem "world-denying," "life-loathing," "in a sense uncourageous," and "contrary to fundamental ecological reality."

Earlier in his essay, Callicott expresses distress that animal liberationists fail to draw a sharp distinction "between the very different plights (and rights) of wild and domestic animals."[9] Domestic animals are creations of man, he says. "They are living artifacts, but artifacts nevertheless. . . . There is thus something profoundly incoherent (and insensitive as well) in the complaint of some animal liberationists that the 'natural behavior' of chickens and bobby calves is cruelly frustrated on factory farms. It would make almost as much sense to speak of the natural behavior of tables and chairs."[10] Here again we see teleology playing a decisive role: wild organisms do not have the natural function of serving human ends, but domesticated animals do. Cheetahs in zoos are crimes against what is natural; veal calves in boxes are not.

The idea of "natural tendency" played a decisive role in pre-Darwinian biological thinking. Aristotle's entire science—both his physics and his biology—is articulated in terms of specifying the natural tendencies of kinds of objects and the interfering forces that can prevent an object from achieving its intended state. Heavy objects in the sublunar sphere have location at the center of the earth as their natural state; each tends to go there, but is prevented from doing so. Organisms likewise are conceptualized in terms of this natural state model:

. . . [for] any living thing that has reached its normal development and which is unmutilated, and whose mode of generation is not spontaneous, the most natural act is the production of another like itself, an animal producing an animal, a plant a plant. . . .[11]

But many interfering forces are possible, and in fact the occurrence of "monsters" is anything but uncommon. According to Aristotle, mules (sterile hybrids) count as deviations from the natural state. In fact, females are monsters as well, since the natural tendency of sexual reproduction is for the offspring to perfectly resemble the father, who, according to Aristotle, provides the "genetic instructions" (to put the idea anachronistically) while the female provides only the matter.

What has happened to the natural state model in modern science? In physics, the idea of describing what a class of objects will do in the absence of "interference" lives on: Newton specified this "zero-force state" as rest or uniform motion, and in general relativity, this state is understood in terms of motion along geodesics. But one of the most profound achievements of Darwinian biology has been the jettisoning of this kind of model. It isn't just that Aristotle was wrong in his detailed claims about mules and women; the whole structure of the natural state model has been discarded. Population biology is not conceptualized in terms of positing some characteristic that all members of a species would have in common, were interfering forces absent. Variation is not thought of as a deflection from the natural state of uniformity. Rather, variation is taken to be a fundamental property in its own right. Nor, at the level of individual biology, does the natural state model find an application. Developmental theory is not articulated by specifying a natural tendency and a set of interfering forces. The main conceptual tool for describing the various developmental pathways open to a genotype is the norm of reaction. The norm of reaction of a genotype within a range of environments will describe what phenotype the genotype will produce in a given environment. Thus, the norm of reaction for a corn plant genotype might describe how its height is influenced by the amount of moisture in the soil. The norm of reaction is entirely silent on which phenotype is the "natural" one. The idea that a corn plant might have some "natural height," which can be, augmented or diminished by "interfering forces" is entirely alien to post-Darwinian biology.

The fact that the concepts of natural state and interfering force have lapsed from biological thought does not prevent environmentalists from inventing them anew. Perhaps these concepts can be provided with some sort of normative content; after all, the normative idea of "human rights" may make sense even if it is not a theoretical underpinning of any empirical science. But environmentalists should not assume that they can rely on some previously articulated scientific conception of "natural."

V. APPEALS TO NEEDS AND INTERESTS

The version of utilitarianism considered earlier (according to which something merits ethical consideration if it can experience pleasure and/or pain) leaves the environmentalist in the lurch. But there is an alternative to Bentham's hedonistic utilitarianism that has been thought by some to be a foundation for environmentalism. Preference utilitarianism says that an object's having interests, needs, or preferences gives it ethical status. This doctrine is at the core of Stone's affirmative answer to the title question of his book *Should Trees Have Standing?*[12] "Natural objects can communicate their wants (needs) to us, and in ways that are not terribly ambiguous. . . . The lawn tells me that it wants water by a certain dryness of the blades and soil—immediately obvious to the touch—the appearance of bald spots, yellowing, and a lack of springiness after being walked on." And if plants can do this, presumably so can mountain ranges, and endangered species. Preference utilitarianism may thereby seem to grant intrinsic ethical importance to precisely the sorts of objects about which environmentalists have expressed concern.

The problems with this perspective have been detailed by Sagoff.[13] If one does not require of an object that it have a mind for it to have wants or needs, what is required for the possession of these ethically relevant properties? Suppose one says that an object needs something if it will cease to exist if it does not get it. Then species, plants, and mountain ranges have needs, but only in the sense that automobiles, garbage dumps, and buildings do too. If everything has needs, the advice to take needs into account in ethical deliberation is empty, unless it is supplemented by some technique for weighing and comparing the needs of different objects. A corporation will go bankrupt unless a highway is built. But the swamp will cease to exist if the highway is built. Perhaps one should take into account all relevant needs, but the question is how to do this in the event that needs conflict.

Although the concept of need can be provided with a permissive, all-inclusive definition, it is less easy to see how to do this with the concept of want. Why think that a mountain range "wants" to retain its unspoiled appearance, rather than house a new amusement park?[14] Needs are not at issue here, since in either case, the mountain continues to exist. One might be tempted to think that natural objects like mountains and species have "natural tendencies," and that the concept of want should be liberalized so as to mean that natural objects "want" to persist in their natural states. This Aristotelian view, as I argued in the previous section, simply makes no sense. Granted, a commercially undeveloped mountain will persist in this state, unless it is commercially developed. But it is equally true that a commercially untouched hill will become commercially developed, unless something causes this not to happen. I see no hope for extending the concept of wants to the full range of objects valued by environmentalists.

The same problems emerge when we try to apply the concepts of needs and wants to species. A species may need various resources, in the sense that these are necessary for its continued existence. But what do species want? Do they want to remain stable in numbers, neither growing nor shrinking? Or since most species

have gone extinct, perhaps what species really want is to go extinct, and it is human meddlesomeness that frustrates this natural tendency? Preference utilitarianism is no more likely than hedonistic utilitarianism to secure autonomous ethical status for endangered species.

Ehrenfeld describes a related distortion that has been inflicted on the diversity/stability hypothesis in theoretical ecology.[15] If it were true that increasing the diversity of an ecosystem causes it to be more stable, this might encourage the Aristotelian idea that ecosystems have a natural tendency to increase their diversity. The full realization of this tendency—the natural state that is the goal of ecosystems—is the "climax" or "mature" community. Extinction diminishes diversity, so it frustrates ecosystems from attaining their goal. Since the hypothesis that diversity causes stability is now considered controversial (to say the least), this line of thinking will not be very tempting. But even if the diversity/stability hypothesis were true, it would not permit the environmentalist to conclude that ecosystems have an interest in retaining their diversity.

Darwinism has not banished the idea that parts of the natural world are goal-directed systems, but has furnished this idea with a natural mechanism. We properly conceive of organisms (or genes, sometimes) as being in the business of maximizing their chances of survival and reproduction. We describe characteristics as adaptations—as devices that exist for the furtherance of these ends. Natural selection makes this perspective intelligible. But Darwinism is a profoundly individualistic doctrine. Darwinism rejects the idea that species, communities, and ecosystems have adaptations that exist for their own benefit. These higher-level entities are not conceptualized as goal-directed systems; what properties of organization they possess are viewed as artifacts of processes operating at lower levels of organization. An environmentalism based on the idea that the ecosystem is directed toward stability and diversity must find its foundation elsewhere.

VI. GRANTING WHOLES AUTONOMOUS VALUE

A number of environmentalists have asserted that environmental values cannot be grounded in values based on regard for individual welfare. Aldo Leopold wrote in *A Sand County Almanac* that "a thing is right when it tends to preserve the integrity, stability, and beauty of the biotic community. It is wrong when it tends otherwise."[16] Callicott develops this idea at some length, and ascribes to ethical environmentalism the view that "the preciousness of individual deer, *as of any other specimen,* is inversely proportional to the population of the species."[17] In his *Desert Solitaire,* Edward Abbey notes that he would sooner shoot a man than a snake.[18] And Garrett Hardin asserts that human beings injured in wilderness areas ought not to be rescued: making great and spectacular efforts to save the life of an individual "makes sense only when there is a shortage of people. I have not lately heard that there is a shortage of people."[19] The point of view suggested by these quotations is quite clear. It isn't that preserving the integrity of ecosystems has autonomous value, to be taken into account just as the quite distinct value of individual human welfare is. Rather, the idea is that the only value is the holistic one of maintaining ecological balance and diversity. Here we have a view that is just as monolithic as the most single-minded individualism; the difference is that the unit of value is thought to exist at a higher level of organization.

It is hard to know what to say to someone who would save a mosquito, just because it is rare, rather than a human being, if there were a choice. In ethics, as in any other subject, rationally persuading another person requires the existence of shared assumptions. If this monolithic environmentalist view is based on the notion that ecosystems have needs and interests, and that these take total precedence over the rights and interests of individual human beings, then the discussion of the previous sections is relevant. And even supposing that these higher-level entities have needs and wants, what reason is there to suppose that these matter and that the wants and needs of individuals matter not at all? But if this source of defense is jettisoned, and it is merely asserted that only ecosystems have value, with no substantive defense being offered, one must begin by requesting an argument: *why* is ecosystem stability and diversity the only value?

Some environmentalists have seen the individualist bias of utilitarianism as being harmful in ways additional to its impact on our perception of ecological values. Thus, Callicott writes:

> On the level of social organization, the interests of society may not always coincide with the sum of the interests of its parts. Discipline, sacrifice, and individual restraint are often necessary in the social sphere to maintain social integrity as within the bodily organism. A society, indeed, is particularly vulnerable to disintegration when its members become preoccupied totally with their own particular interest, and ignore those distinct and independent interests of the community as a whole. One example, unfortunately, our own society, is altogether too close at hand to be examined with strict academic detachment. The United States seems to pursue uncritically a social policy of reductive utilitarianism, aimed at promoting the happiness of all its members severally. Each special interest accordingly clamors more loudly to be satisfied while the community as a whole becomes noticeably more and more infirm economically, environmentally, and politically.[20]

Callicott apparently sees the emergence of individualism and alienation from nature as two aspects of the same process. He values "the symbiotic relationship of Stone Age man to the natural environment" and regrets that "civilization has insulated and alienated us from the rigors and challenges of the natural environment. The hidden agenda of the humane ethic," he says, "is the imposition of the anti-natural prophylactic ethos of comfort and soft pleasure on an even wider scale. The land ethic, on the other hand, requires a shrinkage, if at all possible, of the domestic sphere; it rejoices in a recrudescence of the wilderness and a renaissance of tribal cultural experience."[21]

Callicott is right that "strict academic detachment" is difficult here. The reader will have to decide whether the United States currently suffers from too much or too little regard "for the happiness of all its members severally" and whether we should feel nostalgia or pity in contemplating what the Stone Age experience of nature was like.

VII. THE DEMARCATION PROBLEM

Perhaps the most fundamental theoretical problem confronting an environmentalist who wishes to claim that species and ecosystems have autonomous value is what I will call the *problem of demarcation*. Every ethical theory must provide principles that describe which objects matter for their own sakes and which do not. Besides marking the boundary between these two classes by enumerating a set of ethically relevant properties, an ethical theory must say why the properties named, rather than others, are the ones that count. Thus, for example, hedonistic utilitarianism cites the capacity to experience pleasure and/or pain as the decisive criterion; preference utilitarianism cites the having of preferences (or wants, or interests) as the decisive property. And a Kantian ethical theory will include an individual in the ethical community only if it is capable of rational reflection and autonomy. Not that justifying these various proposed solutions to the demarcation problem is easy; indeed, since this issue is so fundamental, it will be very difficult to justify one proposal as opposed to another. Still, a substantive ethical theory is obliged to try.

Environmentalists, wishing to avoid the allegedly distorting perspective of individualism, frequently want to claim autonomous value for wholes. This may take the form of a monolithic doctrine according to which the only thing that matters is the stability of the ecosystem. Or it may embody a pluralistic outlook according to which ecosystem stability and species preservation have an importance additional to the welfare of individual organisms. But an environmentalist theory shares with all ethical theories an interest in not saying that everything has autonomous value. The reason this position is proscribed is that it makes the adjudication of ethical conflict very difficult indeed. (In addition, it is radically implausible, but we can set that objection to one side.)

Environmentalists, as we have seen, may think of natural objects, like mountains, species, and ecosystems, as mattering for their own sake, but of artificial objects, like highway systems and domesticated animals, as having only instrumental value. If a mountain and a highway are both made of rock, it seems unlikely that the difference between them arises from the fact that mountains have wants, interests, and preferences, but highway systems do not. But perhaps the place to look for the relevant difference is not in their present physical composition, but in the historical fact of how each came into existence. Mountains were created by natural processes, whereas highways are humanly constructed. But once we realize that organisms construct their environments in nature, this contrast begins to cloud. Organisms do not passively reside in an environment whose properties are independently determined. Organisms transform their environments by physically interacting with them. An anthill is an artifact just as a highway is. Granted, a difference obtains at the level of whether conscious deliberation played a role, but can one take seriously the view that artifacts produced by conscious planning are thereby *less* valuable than ones that arise without the intervention of mentality.[22] As we have noted before, although environmentalists often accuse their critics of failing to think in a biologically realistic way, their use of the distinction between "natural" and "artificial" is just the sort of idea that stands in need of a more realistic biological perspective.

My suspicion is that the distinction between natural and artificial is not the crucial one. On the contrary, certain features of environmental concerns imply that natural objects are exactly on a par with certain artificial ones. Here the intended comparison is not between mountains and highways, but between mountains and works of art. My goal in what follows is not to sketch a substantive conception of what determines the value of objects in these two domains, but to motivate an analogy.

For both natural objects and works of art, our values extend beyond the concerns we have for experiencing pleasure. Most of us value seeing an original painting more than we value seeing a copy, even when we could not tell the difference. When we experience works of art, often what we value is not just the kinds of experiences we have, but, in addition, the connections we usually have with certain real objects. Routley and Routley have made an analogous point about valuing the wilderness experience: a "wilderness experience machine" that caused certain sorts of hallucinations would be no substitute for actually going into the wild.[23] Nor is this fact about our valuation limited to such aesthetic and environmentalist contexts. We love various people in our lives. If a molecule-for-molecule replica of a beloved person were created, you would not love that individual, but would continue to love the individual to whom you actually were historically related. Here again, our attachments are to objects and people as they really are, and not just to the experiences that they facilitate.

Another parallel between environmentalist concerns and aesthetic values concerns the issue of context. Although environmentalists often stress the importance of preserving endangered species, they would not be completely satisfied if an endangered species were preserved by putting a number of specimens in a zoo or in a humanly constructed preserve. What is taken to be important is preserving the species in its natural habitat. This leads to the more holistic position that preserving ecosystems, and not simply preserving certain member species, is of primary importance. Aesthetic concerns often lead in the same direction. It was not merely saving a fresco or an altar piece that motivated art historians after the most recent flood in Florence. Rather, they wanted to save these works of art in their original ("natural") settings. Not just the painting, but the church that housed it; not just the church, but the city itself. The idea of objects residing in a "fitting" environment plays a powerful role in both domains.

Environmentalism and aesthetics both see value in rarity. Of two whales, why should one be more worthy of aid than another, just because one belongs to an endangered species? Here we have the $n + m$ question mentioned in Section I. As an ethical concern, rarity is difficult to understand. Perhaps this is because our ethical ideas concerning justice and equity (note the word) are saturated with individualism. But in the context of aesthetics, the concept of rarity is far from alien. A work of art may have enhanced value simply because there are very few other works by the same artist, or from the same historical period, or in the same style. It isn't that the price of the item may go up with rarity; I am talking about aesthetic value, not monetary worth. Viewed as valuable aesthetic objects, rare organisms may be valuable because they are rare.

A disanalogy may suggest itself. It may be objected that works of art are of instrumental value only, but that species and ecosystems have intrinsic value. Perhaps it is true, as claimed before, that our attachment to works of art, to nature, and to our loved ones extends beyond the experiences they allow us to have. But it may be argued that what is valuable in the aesthetic case is always the relation of a valuer to a valued object.[24] When we experience a work of art, the value is not simply in the experience, but in the composite fact that we and the work of art are related in certain ways. This immediately suggests that if there were no valuers in the world, nothing would have value, since such relational facts could no longer obtain. So, to adapt Routley and Routley's "last man argument," it would seem that if an ecological crisis precipitated a collapse of the world system, the last human being (whom we may assume for the purposes of this example to be the last valuer) could set about destroying all works of art, and there would be nothing wrong in this.[25] That is, if aesthetic objects are valuable only in so far as valuers can stand in certain relations to them, then when valuers disappear, so does the possibility of aesthetic value. This would deny, in one sense, that aesthetic objects are intrinsically valuable: it isn't they, in themselves, but rather the relational facts that they are part of, that are valuable.

In contrast, it has been claimed that the "last man" would be wrong to destroy natural objects such as mountains, salt marshes, and species. (So as to avoid confusing the issue by bringing in the welfare of individual organisms, Routley and Routley imagine that destruction and mass extinctions can be caused painlessly, so that there would be nothing wrong about this undertaking from the point of view of the nonhuman organisms involved.) If the last man ought to preserve these natural objects, then these objects appear to have a kind of autonomous value; their value would extend beyond their possible relations to valuers. If all this were true, we would have here a contrast between aesthetic and natural objects, one that implies that natural objects are more valuable than works of art.

Routley and Routley advance the last man argument as if it were decisive in showing that environmental objects such as mountains and salt marshes have autonomous value. I find the example more puzzling than decisive. But, in the present context, we do not have to decide whether Routley and Routley are right. We only have to decide whether this imagined situation brings out any relevant difference between aesthetic and environmental values. Were the last man to look up on a certain hillside, he would see a striking rock formation next to the ruins of a Greek temple. Long ago the temple was built from some of the very rocks that still stud the slope. Both promontory and temple have a history, and both have been transformed by the biotic and the abiotic environments. I myself find it impossible to advise the last man that the peak matters more than the temple. I do not see a relevant difference. Environmentalists, if they hold that the solution to the problem of demarcation is to be found in the distinction between natural and artificial, will have to find such a distinction. But if environmental values are aesthetic, no difference need be discovered.

Environmentalists may be reluctant to classify their concern as aesthetic. Perhaps they will feel that aesthetic concerns are frivolous. Perhaps they will feel that the aesthetic regard for artifacts that has been made possible by culture is antithetical to a proper regard for wilderness. But such contrasts are illusory. Concern for environmental values does not require a stripping away of the perspective afforded by civilization; to value the wild, one does not have to "become wild" oneself (whatever that may mean). Rather, it is the material comforts of civilization that make possible a serious concern for both aesthetic and environmental values. These are concerns that can become pressing in developed nations in part because the populations of those countries now enjoy a certain substantial level of prosperity. It would be the height of condescension to expect a nation experiencing hunger and chronic disease to be inordinately concerned with the autonomous value of ecosystems or with creating and preserving works of art. Such values are not frivolous, but they can become important to us only after certain fundamental human needs are satisfied. Instead of radically jettisoning individualist ethics, environmentalists may find a more hospitable home for their values in a category of value that has existed all along.

NOTES

1. Mark Sagoff, "On Preserving the Natural Environment," *Yale Law Review* 84 (1974): 205–38; J. Baird Callicott, "Animal Liberation: A Triangular Affair," *Environmental Ethics* 2 (1980): 311–38; and Bryan Norton, "Environmental Ethics and Nonhuman Rights," *Environmental Ethics* 4 (1982): 17–36.

2. Peter Singer, *Animal Liberation* (New York: Random House, 1975), has elaborated a position of this sort.

3. Occasionally, it has been argued that utilitarianism is not just *insufficient* to justify the principles of environmentalism but is actually mistaken in holding that pain is intrinsically bad. Callicott writes: "I herewith declare in all soberness that I see nothing wrong with pain. It is a marvelous method, honed by the evolutionary process, of conveying important organic information. I think it was the late Alan Watts who somewhere remarks that upon being asked if he did not think there was too much pain in the world replied, 'No, I think there's just enough'" ("A Triangular Affair," p. 333). Setting to one side the remark attributed to Watts, I should point out that pain can be intrinsically bad and still have some good consequences. The point of calling pain intrinsically bad is to say that one essential aspect of experiencing it is negative.

4. A parallel with a quite different moral problem will perhaps make it clearer how the environmentalist's holism conflicts with some fundamental ethical ideas. When we consider the rights of individuals to receive compensation for harm, we generally expect that the individuals compensated must be one and the same as the individuals harmed. This expectation runs counter to the way an affirmative action program might be set up, if individuals were to receive compensation simply for being members of groups that have suffered certain kinds of discrimination, whether or not they themselves were victims of discrimination. I do not raise this example to suggest that a holistic conception according to which groups have entitlements is beyond consideration. Rather, my point is to exhibit a case in which a rather common ethical idea is individualistic rather than holistic.

5. David Ehrenfeld, "The Conservation of Non-Resources," *American Scientist* 64 (1976): 648–56. For a theoretical discussion see Robert M. May, *Stability and Complexity in Model Ecosystems* (Princeton: Princeton University Press, 1973).

6. Callicott, "A Triangular Affair," pp. 333–34 (my emphasis).

7. Paul Shepard, "Animal Rights and Human Rites." *North American Review* (Winter 1974): 35–41.

8. Charles Darwin, *The Autobiography of Charles Darwin* (London: Collins, 1876, 1958), p. 90.

9. Callicott, "A Triangular Affair," p. 330.

10. Callicott, "A Triangular Affair," p. 330.

11. Aristotle, *De Anima*, 415a26.

12. Christopher Stone, *Should Trees Have Standing?* (Los Altos, Calif.: William Kaufmann, 1972), p. 24.

13. Sagoff, "Natural Environment," pp. 220–24.

14. The example is Sagoff's, "Natural Environment," pp. 220–24.

15. Ehrenfeld, "The Conservation of Non-Resources," pp. 651–52.

16. Aldo Leopold, *A Sand County Almanac* (New York: Oxford University Press, 1949), pp. 224–25.

17. Callicott, "A Triangular Affair," p. 326 (emphasis mine).

18. Edward Abbey, *Desert Solitaire* (New York: Ballantine Books, 1968), p. 20.

19. Garrett Hardin, "The Economics of Wilderness," *Natural History* 78 (1969): 176.

20. Callicott, "A Triangular Affair," p. 323.

21. Callicott, "A Triangular Affair," p. 335.

22. Here we would have an inversion, not just a rejection, of a familiar Marxian doctrine—the labor theory of value.

23. Richard Routley and Val Routley, "Human Chauvinism and Environmental Ethics," *Environmental Philosophy, Monograph Series 2*, edited by D. S. Mannison, M. A. McRobbie, and R. Routley (Philosophy Department, Australian National University, 1980), p. 154.

24. Donald H. Regan, "Duties of Preservation," *The Preservation of Species,* ed. B. Norton (Princeton: Princeton University Press, 1986), pp. 195–220.

25. Routley and Routley, "Human Chauvinism," pp. 121–22.

Study Questions

1. What is a "slippery slope argument"?
2. According to Sober, what is the moral significance of the distinction between wild and domesticated animals?
3. According to Sober, what is "the demarcation problem"?
4. Do you find any relevant differences between aesthetic and environmental values?

Part VIII

Social Theory

The Republic

PLATO

Social and political philosophy focuses on ethical issues related to the structure of society and the practices of government. Our first reading is from Plato's *Republic*, a remarkable work that offers a unified account of central issues in metaphysics, epistemology, philosophy of mind, ethics, political philosophy, philosophy of art, and philosophy of education. Due to that book's length, which is more than half as long as this entire collection, space permits only the reprinting of relatively short segments, thereby necessarily omitting crucial materials.

For our purposes, however, I have chosen to highlight Plato's defense of a nondemocratic system of government, directed by a small group of philosopher-kings, both men and women, chosen on the basis of their natural aptitudes and specially educated for their roles. A community exhibits justice if the experts rule, supported by those in the military force, while workers and merchants attend to their own trades and businesses.

Note the parable toward the end of the selection in which Plato compares the working of a democratic society to the situation aboard a ship on which the sailors argue over the control of the helm, while none of them has ever learned navigation. And if someone on board happens to possess the needed skills, that person's qualifications are disregarded on the grounds that steering a ship requires no special competence. Plato was no friend of democracy, the system of government that put to death his beloved teacher, Socrates.

This excerpt ends with one of the most famous passages in the history of philosophy, the parable of the cave. This story is intended to reveal why those with knowledge are reviled by others, yet should be compelled to rule so as to promote the good of all. Never has democracy been challenged in a more compelling fashion, and developing a satisfactory response surely tests one's philosophical powers.

In the scenes that follow, Socrates is the first speaker and converses with Glaucon and Adeimantus, Plato's brothers, who are representative of the Athenian aristocracy.

[S]uppose we imagine a state coming into being before our eyes. We might then be able to watch the growth of justice or of injustice within it. . . .

Don't waste any more time.

My notion is, said I, that a state comes into existence because no individual is self-sufficing; we all have many needs. But perhaps you can suggest some different origin for the foundation of a community?

No, I agree with you.

So, having all these needs, we call in one another's help to satisfy our various requirements; and when we have collected a number of helpers and associates to live together in one place, we call that settlement a state.

Yes.

So if one man gives another what he has to give in exchange for what he can get, it is because each finds that to do so is for his own advantage.

Certainly.

Very well, said I. Now let us build up our imaginary state from the beginning. Apparently, it will owe its existence to our needs, the first and greatest need being the provision of food to keep us alive. Next we shall want a house; and thirdly, such things as clothing.

True.

How will our state be able to supply all these demands? We shall need at least one man to be a farmer, another a builder, and a third a weaver. Will that do, or shall we add a shoemaker and one or two more to provide for our personal wants?

By all means.

The minimum state, then, will consist of four or five men.

Apparently.

Now here is a further point. Is each one of them to bring the product of his work into a common stock? Should our one farmer, for example, provide food enough for four people and spend the whole of his working time in producing corn, so as to share with the rest; or should he take no notice of them and spend only a quarter of his time on growing just enough corn for himself, and divide the other three-quarters between building his house, weaving his clothes, and making his shoes, so as to save the trouble of sharing with others and attend himself to all his own concerns?

The first plan might be the easier, replied Adeimantus.

That may very well be so, said I; for, as you spoke, it occurred to me, for one thing, that no two people are born exactly alike. There are innate differences which fit them for different occupations.

I agree.

And will a man do better working at many trades, or keeping to one only?

Keeping to one.

And there is another point: obviously work may be ruined, if you let the right time go by. The workman must wait upon the work; it will not wait upon his leisure and allow itself to be done in a spare moment. So the conclusion is that more things will be produced and the work be more easily and better done, when every man is set free from all other occupations to do, at the right time, the one thing for which he is naturally fitted.

That is certainly true.

We shall need more than four citizens, then, to supply all those necessaries we mentioned. You see, Adeimantus, if the farmer is to have a good plough and spade and other tools, he will not make them himself. No more will the builder and weaver and shoemaker make all the many implements they need. So quite a number of carpenters and smiths and other craftsmen must be enlisted. Our miniature state is beginning to grow.

It is.

Still, it will not be very large, even when we have added cowherds and shepherds to provide the farmers with oxen for the plough, and the builders as well as the farmers with draught-animals, and the weavers and shoemakers with wool and leather.

No; but it will not be so very small either.

And yet, again, it will be next to impossible to plant our city in a territory where it will need no imports. So there will have to be still another set of people, to fetch what it needs from other countries.

There will.

Moreover, if these agents take with them nothing that those other countries require in exchange, they will return as empty-handed as they went. So, besides everything wanted for consumption at home, we must produce enough goods of the right kind for the foreigners whom we depend on to supply us. That will mean increasing the number of farmers and craftsmen.

Yes.

And then, there are these agents who are to import and export all kinds of goods—merchants, as we call them. We must have them; and if they are to do business overseas, we shall need quite a number of ship-owners and others who know about that branch of trading.

We shall.

Again, in the city itself how are the various sets of producers to exchange their products? That was our object, you will remember, in forming a community and so laying the foundation of our state.

Obviously, they must buy and sell.

That will mean having a market-place, and a currency to serve as a token for purposes of exchange.

Certainly.

Now suppose a farmer, or an artisan, brings some of his produce to market at a time when no one is there who wants to exchange with him. Is he to sit there idle, when he might be at work?

No, he replied; there are people who have seen an opening here for their services. In well-ordered communities they are generally men not strong enough to be of use in any other occupation. They have to stay where they are in the marketplace and take goods for money from those who want to sell, and money for goods from those who want to buy.

That, then, is the reason why our city must include a class of shopkeepers—so we call these people who sit still in the market-place to buy and sell, in contrast with merchants who travel to other countries.

Quite so.

There are also the services of yet another class, who have the physical strength for heavy work, though on intellectual grounds they are hardly worth including in our society—hired labourers, as we call them, because they sell the use of their strength for wages. They will go to make up our population.

Yes.

Well, Adeimantus, has our state now grown to its full size?

Perhaps.

Then, where in it shall we find justice or injustice? If they have come in with one of the elements we have been considering, can you say with which one?

I have no idea, Socrates; unless it be somewhere in their dealings with one another.

You may be right, I answered. Anyhow, it is a question which we shall have to face.

Let us begin, then, with a picture of our citizens' manner of life, with the provision we have made for them. They will be producing corn and wine, and making clothes and shoes. When they have built their houses, they will mostly work without their coats or shoes in summer, and in winter be well shod and clothed. For their food, they will prepare flour and barley-meal for kneading and baking, and set out a grand spread of loaves and cakes on rushes or fresh leaves. Then they will lie on beds of myrtle-boughs and bryony and make merry with their children, drinking their wine after the feast with garlands on their heads and singing the praises of the gods. So they will live pleasantly together; and a prudent fear of poverty or war will keep them from begetting children beyond their means.

Here Glaucon interrupted me: You seem to expect your citizens to feast on dry bread.

True, I said; I forgot that they will have something to give it a relish, salt, no doubt, and olives, and cheese, and country stews of roots and vegetables. And for dessert we will give them figs and peas and beans; and they shall roast myrtle-berries and acorns at the fire, while they sip their wine. Leading such a healthy life in peace, they will naturally come to a good old age, and leave their children to live after them in the same manner.

That is just the sort of provender you would supply, Socrates, if you were founding a community of pigs.

Well, how are they to live, then, Glaucon?

With the ordinary comforts. Let them lie on couches and dine off tables on such dishes and sweets as we have nowadays.

Ah, I see, said I; we are to study the growth, not just of a state, but of a luxurious one. Well, there may be no harm in that; the consideration of luxury may help us to discover how justice and injustice take root in society. The community I have described seems to me the ideal one, in sound health as it were: but if you want to see one suffering from inflammation, there is nothing to hinder us. So some people, it seems, will not be satisfied to live in this simple way; they must have couches and tables and furniture of all sorts; and delicacies too, perfumes, unguents, courtesans, sweetmeats, all in plentiful variety. And besides, we must not limit ourselves now to those bare necessaries of house and clothes and shoes; we shall have to set going the arts of embroidery and painting, and collect rich materials, like gold and ivory.

Yes.

Then we must once more enlarge our community. The healthy one will not be big enough now; it must be swollen up with a whole multitude of callings not ministering to any bare necessity: hunters and fishermen, for instance; artists in sculpture, painting, and music; poets with their attendant train of professional reciters, actors, dancers, producers; and makers of all sorts of household gear, including everything for women's adornment. And we shall want more servants: children's nurses and attendants, ladies' maids, barbers, cooks and confectioners. And then swineherds—there was no need for them in our original state, but we shall want them now; and a great quantity of sheep and cattle too, if people are going to live on meat.

Of course.

And with this manner of life physicians will be in much greater request.

No doubt.

The country, too, which was large enough to support the original inhabitants, will now be too small. If we are to have enough pasture and plough land, we shall have to cut off a slice of our neighbours' territory; and if they too are not content with necessaries, but give themselves up to getting unlimited wealth, they will want a slice of ours.

That is inevitable, Socrates.

So the next thing will be, Glaucon, that we shall be at war.

No doubt.

We need not say yet whether war does good or harm, but only that we have discovered its origin in desires which are the most fruitful source of evils both to individuals and to states.

Quite true.

This will mean a considerable addition to our community—a whole army, to go out to battle with any invader, in defence of all this property and of the citizens we have been describing.

Why so? Can't they defend themselves?

Not if the principle was right, which we all accepted in framing our society. You remember we agreed that no one man can practise many trades or arts satisfactorily.

True.

Well, is not the conduct of war an art, quite as important as shoemaking?

Yes.

But we would not allow our shoemaker to try to be also a farmer or weaver or builder, because we wanted our shoes well made. We gave each man one trade, for which he was naturally fitted; he would do good work, if he confined himself to that all his life, never letting the right moment slip by. Now in no form of work is efficiency so important as in war; and fighting is not so easy a business that a man can follow another trade, such as farming or shoemaking, and also be an efficient soldier. Why, even a game like draughts or dice must be studied from childhood; no one can become a fine player in his spare moments. Just taking up a shield or other weapon will not make a man capable of fighting that very day in any sort of warfare, any more than taking up a tool or implement of some kind will make a man a craftsman or an athlete, if he does not understand its use and has never been properly trained to handle it.

No; if that were so, tools would indeed be worth having.

These guardians of our state, then, inasmuch as their work is the most important of all, will need the most complete freedom from other occupations and the greatest amount of skill and practice.

I quite agree.

And also a native aptitude for their calling.

Certainly.

So it is our business to define, if we can, the natural gifts that fit men to be guardians of a commonwealth, and to select them accordingly. It will certainly be a formidable task; but we must grapple with it to the best of our power.

Yes.

Don't you think then, said I, that, for the purpose of keeping guard, a young man should have much the same temperament and qualities as a well-bred watchdog? I mean, for instance, that both must have quick senses to detect an enemy, swiftness in pursuing him, and strength, if they have to fight when they have caught him.

Yes, they will need all those qualities.

And also courage, if they are to fight well.

Of course.

And courage, in dog or horse or any other creature, implies a spirited disposition. You must have noticed that a high spirit is unconquerable. Every soul possessed of it is fearless and indomitable in the face of any danger.

Yes, I have noticed that.

So now we know what physical qualities our Guardian must have, and also that he must be of a spirited temper.

Yes.

Then, Glaucon, how are men of that natural disposition to be kept from behaving pugnaciously to one another and to the rest of their countrymen?

It is not at all easy to see.

And yet they must be gentle to their own people and dangerous only to enemies; otherwise they will destroy themselves without waiting till others destroy them.

True.

What are we to do, then? If gentleness and a high temper are contraries, where shall we find a character to combine them? Both are necessary to make a good Guardian, but it seems they are incompatible. So we shall never have a good Guardian.

It looks like it.

Here I was perplexed, but on thinking over what we had been saying, I remarked that we deserved to be puzzled, because we had not followed up the comparison we had just drawn.

What do you mean? he asked.

We never noticed that, after all, there are natures in which these contraries are combined. They are to be found in animals, and not least in the kind we compared to our Guardian. Well-bred dogs, as you know, are by instinct perfectly gentle to people whom they know and are accustomed to, and fierce to strangers. So the combination of qualities we require for our Guardian is, after all, possible and not against nature.

Evidently.

Do you further agree that, besides this spirited temper, he must have a philosophical element in his nature?

I don't see what you mean.

This is another trait you will see in the dog. It is really remarkable how the creature gets angry at the mere sight of a stranger and welcomes anyone he knows, though he may never have been treated unkindly by the one or kindly by the other. Did that never strike you as curious?

I had not thought of it before; but that certainly is how a dog behaves.

Well, but that shows a fine instinct, which is philosophic in the true sense.

How so?

Because the only mark by which he distinguishes a friendly and an unfriendly face is that he knows the one and does not know the other; and if a creature makes that the test of what it finds congenial or otherwise, how can you deny that it has a passion for knowledge and understanding?

Of course, I cannot.

And that passion is the same thing as philosophy—the love of wisdom.[1]

Yes.

Shall we boldly say, then, that the same is true of human beings? If a man is to be gentle towards his own people whom he knows, he must have an instinctive love of wisdom and understanding.

Agreed.

So the nature required to make a really noble Guardian of our commonwealth will be swift and strong, spirited, and philosophic.

Quite so. . . .

[W]hat is the next point to be settled? Is it not the question, which of these Guardians are to be rulers and which are to obey?

No doubt.

Well, it is obvious that the elder must have authority over the young, and that the rulers must be the best.

Yes.

And as among farmers the best are those with a natural turn for farming, so, if we want the best among our Guardians, we must take those naturally fitted to watch over a commonwealth. They must have the right sort of intelligence and ability; and also they must look upon the commonwealth as their special concern—the sort of concern that is felt for something so closely bound up with oneself that its interests and fortunes, for good or ill, are held to be identical with one's own.

Exactly.

So the kind of men we must choose from among the Guardians will be those who, when we look at the whole course of their lives, are found to be full of zeal to do whatever they believe is for the good of the commonwealth and never willing to act against its interest.

Yes, they will be the men we want. . . .

We shall have to watch them from earliest childhood and set them tasks in which they would be most likely to forget or to be beguiled out of this duty. We shall then choose only those whose memory holds firm and who are proof against delusion.

Yes.

We must also subject them to ordeals of toil and pain and watch for the same qualities there. And we must observe them when exposed to the test of yet a third kind of bewitchment. As people lead colts up to alarming noises to see whether they are timid, so these young men must be brought into terrifying situations and then into scenes of pleasure, which will put them to severer proof than gold tried in the furnace. If we find one bearing himself well in all these trials and resisting every enchantment, a true guardian of himself, preserving always that perfect rhythm and harmony of being which he has acquired from his training in music and poetry, such a one will be of the greatest service to the commonwealth as well as to himself. Whenever we find one who has come unscathed through every test in childhood, youth, and manhood, we shall set him as a Ruler to watch over the commonwealth; he will be honoured in life, and after death receive the highest tribute of funeral rites and other memorials. All who do not reach this standard we must reject. And that, I think, my dear Glaucon, may be taken as an outline of the way in which we shall select Guardians to be set in authority as Rulers.

I am very much of your mind.

These, then, may properly be called Guardians in the fullest sense, who will ensure that neither foes without shall have the power, nor friends within the wish, to do harm. Those young men whom up to now we have been speaking of as Guardians, will be better described as Auxiliaries, who will enforce the decisions of the Rulers.

I agree.

Now, said I, can we devise . . . a single bold flight of invention, which we may induce the community in general, and if possible the Rulers themselves, to accept?

What kind of fiction? . . .

Well, here it is; though I hardly know how to find the courage or the words to express it. I shall try to convince, first the Rulers and the soldiers,[2] and then the whole community, that all that nurture and education which we gave them was only something they seemed to experience as it were in a dream. In reality they were the whole time down inside the earth, being moulded and fostered while their arms and all their equipment were being fashioned also; and at last, when they were complete, the earth sent them up from her womb into the light of day. So now they must think of the land they dwell in as a mother and nurse, whom they must take thought for and defend against any attack, and of their fellow citizens as brothers born of the same soil.

You might well be bashful about coming out with your fiction.

No doubt; but still you must hear the rest of the story. It is true, we shall tell our people in this fable, that all of you in this land are brothers; but the god who fashioned you mixed gold in the composition of those among you who are fit to rule, so that they are of the most precious quality; and he put silver in the Auxiliaries, and iron and brass in the farmers and craftsmen. Now, since you are all of one stock, although your children will generally be like their parents, sometimes a golden parent may have a silver child or a silver parent a golden one, and so on with all the other combinations. So the first and chief injunction laid by heaven upon the Rulers is that, among all the things of which they must show themselves good guardians, there is none that needs to be so carefully watched as the mixture of metals in the souls of the children. If a child of their own is born with an alloy of iron or brass, they must, without the smallest pity, assign him the station proper to his nature and thrust him out among the craftsmen or the farmers. If, on the contrary, these classes produce a child with gold or silver in his composition, they will promote him, according to his value, to be a Guardian or an Auxiliary. They will appeal to a prophecy that

ruin will come upon the state when it passes into the keeping of a man of iron or brass. Such is the story; can you think of any device to make them believe it?

Not in the first generation; but their sons and descendants might believe it, and finally the rest of mankind.

Well, said I, even so it might have a good effect in making them care more for the commonwealth and for one another; for I think I see what you mean. . . .

Listen, then, and judge whether I am right. You remember how, when we first began to establish our commonwealth and several times since, we have laid down, as a universal principle, that everyone ought to perform the one function in the community for which his nature best suited him. Well, I believe that that principle, or some form of it, is justice.

We certainly laid that down.

Yes, and surely we have often heard people say that justice means minding one's own business and not meddling with other men's concerns; and we have often said so ourselves.

We have. . . .

Again, do you agree with me that no great harm would be done to the community by a general interchange of most forms of work, the carpenter and the cobbler exchanging their positions and their tools and taking on each other's jobs, or even the same man undertaking both?

Yes, there would not be much harm in that.

But I think you will also agree that another kind of interchange would be disastrous. Suppose, for instance, someone whom nature designed to be an artisan or tradesman should be emboldened by some advantage, such as wealth or command of votes or bodily strength, to try to enter the order of fighting men; or some member of that order should aspire, beyond his merits, to a seat in the council-chamber of the Guardians. Such interference and exchange of social positions and tools, or the attempt to combine all these forms of work in the same person, would be fatal to the commonwealth.

Most certainly.

Where there are three orders, then, any plurality of functions or shifting from one order to another is not merely utterly harmful to the community, but one might fairly call it the extreme of wrongdoing. And you will agree that to do the greatest of wrongs to one's own community is injustice.

Surely.

This, then, is injustice. And, conversely, let us repeat that when each order—tradesman, Auxiliary, Guardian—keeps to its own proper business in the commonwealth and does its own work, that is justice and what makes a just society.

I entirely agree. . . .

Then our next attempt, it seems, must be to point out what defect in the working of existing states prevents them from being so organized, and what is the least change that would effect a transformation into this type of government—a single change if possible, or perhaps two; at any rate let us make the changes as few and insignificant as may be.

By all means.

Well, there is one change which, as I believe we can show, would bring about this revolution—not a small change, certainly, nor an easy one, but possible.

What is it? . . .

Unless either philosophers become kings in their countries or those who are now called kings and rulers come to be sufficiently inspired with a genuine desire for wisdom; unless, that is to say, political power and philosophy meet together, while the many natures who now go their several ways in the one or the other direction are forcibly debarred from doing so, there can be no rest from troubles, my dear Glaucon, for states, nor yet, as I believe, for all mankind; nor can this commonwealth which we have imagined ever till then see the light of day and grow to its full stature. . . .

Here Adeimantus interposed. . . . [A]s a matter of plain fact, the votaries of philosophy, when they carry on the study too long, instead of taking it up in youth as a part of general culture and then dropping it, almost always become . . . utterly worthless; while even the most respectable are so far the worse for this pursuit you are praising as to become useless to society.

Well, I replied, do you think that charge is untrue?

I do not know, he answered; I should like to hear your opinion.

You shall; I think it is true.

Then how can it be right to say that there will be no rest from trouble until states are ruled by these philosophers whom we are now admitting to be of no use to them?

That is a question which needs to be answered by means of a parable. . . .

Imagine this state of affairs on board a ship or a number of ships. The master is bigger and burlier than any of the crew, but a little deaf and short-sighted and no less deficient in seamanship. The sailors are quarrelling over the control of the helm; each thinks he ought to be steering the vessel, though he has never learnt navigation and cannot point to any teacher under whom he has served his apprenticeship; what is more, they assert that navigation is a thing that cannot be taught at all, and are ready to tear in pieces anyone who says it can. Meanwhile they besiege the master himself, begging him urgently to trust them with the helm; and sometimes, when others have been more successful in gaining his ear, they kill them or throw them overboard, and, after somehow stupefying the worthy master with strong drink or an opiate, take control of the ship, make free with its stores, and turn the voyage, as might be expected of such a crew, into a drunken carousal. Besides all this, they cry up as a skilled navigator and master of seamanship anyone clever enough to lend a hand in persuading or forcing the master to set them in command. Every other kind of man they condemn as useless. They do not understand that the genuine navigator can only make himself fit to command a ship by studying the seasons of the year, sky, stars, and winds, and all that belongs to his craft; and they have no idea that, along with the science of navigation, it is possible for him to gain, by instruction or practice, the skill to keep control of the helm whether some of them like it or not. If a ship were managed in that way, would not those on board be likely to call the expert in navigation a mere stargazer, who spent his time in idle talk and was useless to them?

They would indeed.

I think you understand what I mean and do not need to have my parable interpreted in order to see how it illustrates the attitude of existing states towards the true philosopher.

Quite so.

Use it, then, to enlighten that critic whom you spoke of as astonished that philosophers are not held in honour by their country. You may try, in the first place, to convince him that it would be far more astonishing if they were; and you may tell him further that he is right in calling the best sort of philosophers useless to the public; but for that he must rather blame those who make no use of them. It is not in the natural course of things for the pilot to beg the crew to take his orders, any more than for the wise to wait on the doorsteps of the rich; the author of that epigram[3] was mistaken. What is natural is that the sick man, whether rich or poor, should wait at the door of the physician, and that all who need to be governed should seek out the man who can govern them; it is not for him to beg them to accept his rule, if there is really any help in him. But our present rulers may fairly be compared to the sailors in our parable, and the useless visionaries, as the politicians call them, to the real masters of navigation.

Quite true.

Under these conditions, the noblest of pursuits can hardly be thought much of by men whose own way of life runs counter to it. . . .

But what do you mean by the highest kind of knowledge and with what is it concerned? You cannot hope to escape that question. . . .

First we must come to an understanding. Let me remind you of the distinction we drew earlier and have often drawn on other occasions, between the multiplicity of things that we call good or beautiful or whatever it may be and, on the other hand, Goodness itself or Beauty itself and so on. Corresponding to each of these sets of many things, we postulate a single Form or real essence, as we call it.

Yes, that is so.

Further, the many things, we say, can be seen, but are not objects of rational thought; whereas the Forms are objects of thought, but invisible.

Yes, certainly.

And we see things with our eyesight, just as we hear sounds with our ears and, to speak generally, perceive any sensible thing with our sense-faculties.

Of course.

Have you noticed, then, that the artificer who designed the senses has been exceptionally lavish of his materials in making the eyes able to see and their objects visible?

That never occurred to me.

Well, look at it in this way. Hearing and sound do not stand in need of any third thing, without which the ear will not hear nor sound be heard; and I think the same is true of most, not to say all, of the other senses. Can you think of one that does require anything of the sort?

No, I cannot.

But there is this need in the case of sight and its objects. You may have the power of vision in your eyes and try to use it, and colour may be there in the objects; but sight will see nothing and the colours will remain invisible in the absence of a third thing peculiarly constituted to serve this very purpose.

By which you mean—?

Naturally I mean what you call light; and if light is a thing of value, the sense of sight and the power of being visible are linked together by a very precious bond, such as unites no other sense with its object.

No one could say that light is not a precious thing.

And of all the divinities in the skies[4] is there one whose light, above all the rest, is responsible for making our eyes see perfectly and making objects perfectly visible?

There can be no two opinions: of course you mean the Sun.

And how is sight related to this deity? Neither sight nor the eye which contains it is the Sun, but of all the sense-organs it is the most sun-like; and further, the power it possesses is dispensed by the Sun, like a stream flooding the eye. And again, the Sun is not vision, but it is the cause of vision and also is seen by the vision it causes.

Yes.

It was the Sun, then, that I meant when I spoke of that offspring which the Good has created in the visible world, to stand there in the same relation to vision and visible things as that which the Good itself bears in the intelligible world to intelligence and to intelligible objects.

How is that? You must explain further.

You know what happens when the colours of things are no longer irradiated by the daylight, but only by the fainter luminaries of the night: when you look at them, the eyes are dim and seem almost blind, as if there were no unclouded vision in them. But when you look at things on which the Sun is shining, the same eyes see distinctly and it becomes evident that they do contain the power of vision.

Certainly.

Apply this comparison, then, to the soul. When its gaze is fixed upon an object irradiated by truth and reality, the soul gains understanding and knowledge and is manifestly in possession of intelligence. But when it looks towards that twilight world of things that come into existence and pass away, its sight is dim and it has only opinions and beliefs which shift to and fro, and now it seems like a thing that has no intelligence.

That is true.

This, then, which gives to the objects of knowledge their truth and to him who knows them his power of knowing, is the Form or essential nature of Goodness. It is the cause of knowledge and truth; and so, while you may think of it as an object of knowledge, you will do well to regard it as something beyond truth and knowledge and, precious as these both are, of still higher worth. And, just as in our analogy light and vision were to be thought of as like the Sun, but not identical with it, so here both knowledge and truth are to be regarded as like the Good, but to identify either with the Good is wrong. The Good must hold a yet higher place of honour.

You are giving it a position of extraordinary splendour, if it is the source of knowledge and truth and itself surpasses them in worth. You surely cannot mean that it is pleasure.

Heaven forbid, I exclaimed. But I want to follow up our analogy still further. You will agree that the Sun not only makes the things we see visible, but also brings them into existence and gives them growth and nourishment; yet he is not the same thing as existence. And so with the objects of knowledge: these derive from the Good not only their power of being known, but their very being and reality; and Goodness is not the same thing as being, but even beyond being, surpassing it in dignity and power.

Glaucon exclaimed with some amusement at my exalting Goodness in such extravagant terms.

It is your fault, I replied; you forced me to say what I think.

Yes, and you must not stop there. At any rate, complete your comparison with the Sun, if there is any more to be said.

There is a great deal more, I answered.

Let us hear it, then; don't leave anything out.

I am afraid much must be left unspoken. However, I will not, if I can help it, leave out anything that can be said on this occasion.

Please do not.

Conceive, then, that there are these two powers I speak of, the Good reigning over the domain of all that is intelligible, the Sun over the visible world—or the heaven as I might call it; only you would think I was showing off my skill in etymology. At any rate you have these two orders of things clearly before your mind: the visible and the intelligible?

I have.

Now take a line divided into two unequal parts, one to represent the visible order, the other the intelligible; and divide each part again in the same proportion, symbolizing degrees of comparative clearness or obscurity. Then (A) one of the two sections in the visible world will stand for images. By images I mean first *shadows*, and then *reflections in water* or in close-grained, polished surfaces, and everything of that kind, if you understand.

Yes, I understand.

Let the second section (B) stand for the *actual things* of which the first are likenesses, the living creatures about us and all the works of nature or of human hands.

So be it.

Will you also take the proportion in which the visible world has been divided as corresponding to degrees of reality and truth, so that the likeness shall stand to the original in the same ratio as the sphere of appearances and belief to the sphere of knowledge?

Certainly.

Now consider how we are to divide the part which stands for the intelligible world. There are two sections. In the first (C) the mind uses as images those actual things which themselves had images in the visible world; and it is compelled to pursue its inquiry by starting from assumptions and travelling, not up to a principle, but down to a conclusion. In the second (D) the mind moves in the other direction, from an assumption up towards a principle which is not hypothetical; and it makes no use of the images employed in the other section, but only of Forms, and conducts its inquiry solely by their means.

I don't quite understand what you mean.

Then we will try again; what I have just said will help you to understand. (C) You know, of course, how students of subjects like geometry and arithmetic begin by postulating odd and even numbers, or the various figures and the three kinds of angle, and other such data in each subject. These data they take as known; and,

having adopted them as assumptions, they do not feel called upon to give any account of them to themselves or to anyone else, but treat them as self-evident. Then, starting from these assumptions, they go on until they arrive, by a series of consistent steps, at all the conclusions they set out to investigate.

Yes, I know that.

You also know how they make use of visible figures and discourse about them, though what they really have in mind is the originals of which these figures are images: they are not reasoning, for instance, about this particular square and diagonal which they have drawn, but about *the* Square and *the* Diagonal; and so in all cases. The diagrams they draw and the models they make are actual things, which may have their shadows or images in water; but now they serve in their turn as images, while the student is seeking to behold those realities which only thought can apprehend.

True.

This, then, is the class of things that I spoke of as intelligible, but with two qualifications: first, that the mind, in studying them, is compelled to employ assumptions, and, because it cannot rise above these, does not travel upwards to a first principle; and second, that it uses as images those actual things which have images of their own in the section below them and which, in comparison with those shadows and reflections, are reputed to be more palpable and valued accordingly.

I understand: you mean the subject-matter of geometry and of the kindred arts.

(D) Then by the second section of the intelligible world you may understand me to mean all that unaided reasoning apprehends by the power of dialectic, when it treats its assumptions, not as first principles, but as *hypotheses* in the literal sense, things "laid down" like a flight of steps up which it may mount all the way to something that is not hypothetical, the first principle of all; and having grasped this, may turn back and, holding on to the consequences which depend upon it, descend at last to a conclusion, never making use of any sensible object, but only of Forms, moving through Forms from one to another, and ending with Forms.

I understand, he said, though not perfectly; for the procedure you describe sounds like an enormous undertaking. But I see that you mean to distinguish the field of intelligible reality studied by dialectic as having a greater certainty and truth than the subject-matter of the "arts," as they are called, which treat their assumptions as first principles. The students of these arts are, it is true, compelled to exercise thought in contemplating objects which the senses cannot perceive; but because they start from assumptions without going back to a first principle, you do not regard them as gaining true understanding about those objects, although the objects themselves, when connected with a first principle, are intelligible. And I think you would call the state of mind of the students of geometry and other such arts, not intelligence, but thinking, as being something between intelligence and mere acceptance of appearances.

You have understood me quite well enough, I replied. And now you may take, as corresponding to the four sections, these four states of mind: *intelligence* for the highest, *thinking* for the second, *belief* for the third, and for the last *imagining*. These you may arrange as the terms in a proportion, assigning to each a degree of clearness and certainty corresponding to the measure in which their objects possess truth and reality.

I understand and agree with you. I will arrange them as you say.

Next, said I, here is a parable to illustrate the degrees in which our nature may be enlightened or unenlightened. Imagine the condition of men living in a sort of cavernous chamber underground, with an entrance open to the light and a long passage all down the cave.[5] Here they have been from childhood, chained by the leg and also by the neck, so that they cannot move and can see only what is in front of them, because the chains will not let them turn their heads. At some distance higher up is the light of a fire burning behind them; and between the prisoners and the fire is a track[6] with a parapet built along it, like the screen at a puppet-show, which hides the performers while they show their puppets over the top.

I see, said he.

Now behind this parapet imagine persons carrying along various artificial objects, including figures of men and animals in wood or stone or other materials, which project above the parapet. Naturally, some of these persons will be talking, others silent.[7]

It is a strange picture, he said, and a strange sort of prisoners.

Like ourselves, I replied; for in the first place prisoners so confined would have seen nothing of themselves or of one another, except the shadows thrown by the fire-light on the wall of the Cave facing them, would they?

Not if all their lives they had been prevented from moving their heads.

And they would have seen as little of the objects carried past.

Of course.

Now, if they could talk to one another, would they not suppose that their words referred only to those passing shadows which they saw?[8]

Necessarily.

And suppose their prison had an echo from the wall facing them? When one of the people crossing behind them spoke, they could only suppose that the sound came from the shadow passing before their eyes.

No doubt.

In every way, then, such prisoners would recognize as reality nothing but the shadows of those artificial objects.

Inevitably.

Now consider what would happen if their release from the chains and the healing of their unwisdom should come about in this way. Suppose one of them set free and forced suddenly to stand up, turn his head, and walk with eyes lifted to the light; all these movements would be painful, and he would be too dazzled to make out the objects whose shadows he had been used to see. What do you think he would say, if someone told him that what he had formerly seen was meaningless illusion, but now, being somewhat nearer to reality and turned towards more real objects, he was getting a truer view? Suppose further that he were shown the various objects being carried by and were made to say, in reply to questions, what each of them was. Would he not be perplexed and believe the objects now shown him to be not so real as what he formerly saw?

Yes, not nearly so real.

And if he were forced to look at the fire-light itself, would not his eyes ache, so that he would try to escape and turn back to the things which he could see distinctly, convinced that they really were clearer than these other objects now being shown to him?

Yes.

And suppose someone were to drag him away forcibly up the steep and rugged ascent and not let him go until he had hauled him out into the sunlight, would he not suffer pain and vexation at such treatment, and, when he had come out into the light, find his eyes so full of its radiance that he could not see a single one of the things that he was now told were real?

Certainly he would not see them all at once.

He would need, then, to grow accustomed before he could see things in that upper world. At first it would be easiest to make out shadows, and then the images of men and things reflected in water, and later on the things themselves. After that, it would be easier to watch the heavenly bodies and the sky itself by night, looking at the light of the moon and stars rather than the Sun and the Sun's light in the day-time.

Yes, surely.

Last of all, he would be able to look at the Sun and contemplate its nature, not as it appears when reflected in water or any alien medium, but as it is in itself in its own domain.

No doubt.

And now he would begin to draw the conclusion that it is the Sun that produces the seasons and the course of the year and controls everything in the visible world, and moreover is in a way the cause of all that he and his companions used to see.

Clearly he would come at last to that conclusion.

Then if he called to mind his fellow prisoners and what passed for wisdom in his former dwelling-place, he would surely think himself happy in the change and be sorry for them. They may have had a practice of honouring and commending one another, with prizes for the man who had the keenest eye for the passing shadows and the best memory for the order in which they followed or accompanied one another, so that he could make a good guess as to which was going to come next. Would our released prisoner be likely to covet those prizes or to envy the men exalted to honour and power in the Cave? Would he not feel like Homer's Achilles, that he would far sooner "be on earth as a hired servant in the house of a landless man" or endure anything rather than go back to his old beliefs and live in the old way?

Yes, he would prefer any fate to such a life.

Now imagine what would happen if he went down again to take his former seat in the Cave. Coming suddenly out of the sunlight, his eyes would be filled with darkness. He might be required once more to deliver his opinion on those shadows, in competition with the prisoners who had never been released, while his eyesight was still dim and unsteady; and it might take some time to become used to the darkness. They would laugh at him and say that he had gone up only to come back with his sight ruined; it was worth no one's while even to attempt the ascent. If they could lay hands on the man who was trying to set them free and lead them up, they would kill him.[9]

Yes, they would.

Every feature in this parable, my dear Glaucon, is meant to fit our earlier analysis. The prison dwelling corresponds to the region revealed to us through the sense of sight, and the fire-light within it to the power of the Sun. The ascent to see the things in the upper world you may take as standing for the upward journey of the soul into the region of the intelligible; then you will be in possession of what I surmise, since that is what you wish to be told. Heaven knows whether it is true; but this, at any rate, is how it appears to me. In the world of knowledge, the last thing to be perceived and only with great difficulty is the essential Form of Goodness. Once it is perceived, the conclusion must follow that, for all things, this is the cause of whatever is right and good; in the visible world it gives birth to light and to the lord of light, while it is itself sovereign in the intelligible world and the parent of intelligence and truth. Without having had a vision of this Form no one can act with wisdom, either in his own life or in matters of state.

So far as I can understand, I share your belief.

Then you may also agree that it is no wonder if those who have reached this height are reluctant to manage the affairs of men. Their souls long to spend all their time in that upper world—naturally enough, if here once more our parable holds true. Nor, again, is it at all strange that one who comes from the contemplation of divine things to the miseries of human life should appear awkward and ridiculous when, with eyes still dazed and not yet accustomed to the darkness, he is compelled, in a law-court or elsewhere, to dispute about the shadows of justice or the images that cast those shadows, and to wrangle over the notions of what is right in the minds of men who have never beheld Justice itself.

It is not at all strange. . . .

It is for us, then, as founders of a commonwealth, to bring compulsion to bear on the noblest natures. They . . . must not be allowed, as they now are, to remain on the heights, refusing to come down again to the prisoners or to take any part in their labours and rewards, however much or little these may be worth.

Shall we not be doing them an injustice, if we force on them a worse life than they might have?

You have forgotten again, my friend, that the law is not concerned to make any one class specially happy, but to ensure the welfare of the commonwealth as a whole. By persuasion or constraint it will unite the citizens in harmony, making them share whatever benefits each class can contribute to the common good; and its purpose in forming men of that spirit was not that each should be left to go his own way, but that they should be instrumental in binding the community into one.

True, I had forgotten.

You will see, then, Glaucon, that there will be no real injustice in compelling our philosophers to watch over and care for the other citizens. We can fairly tell them that their compeers in other states may quite reasonably refuse to collaborate: there they have sprung up, like a self-sown plant, in despite of their country's institutions; no one has fostered their growth, and they cannot be expected to show gratitude for a care they have never received. "But," we shall say, "it is not so with you. We have brought you into existence for your country's sake as well as for your own, to be like leaders and king-bees in a hive; you have been better and more thoroughly educated than those others and hence you are more capable of playing your part both as men of thought and as men of action. You must go down, then, each in his turn, to live with the rest and let your eyes grow accustomed to the darkness. You will then see a thousand times better than those who live there always; you will recognize every image for what it is and know what it represents, because you have seen justice, beauty, and goodness in their reality; and so you and we shall find life in our commonwealth no mere dream, as it is in most existing states, where men live fighting one another about shadows and quarrelling for power, as if that were a great prize; whereas in truth government can be at its best and free from dissension only where the destined rulers are least desirous of holding office."

Quite true.

Then will our pupils refuse to listen and to take their turns at sharing in the work of the community, though they may live together for most of their time in a purer air?

No; it is a fair demand, and they are fair-minded men. No doubt, unlike any ruler of the present day, they will think of holding power as an unavoidable necessity.

Yes, my friend; for the truth is that you can have a well-governed society only if you can discover for your future rulers a better way of life than being in office; then only will power be in the hands of men who are rich, not in gold, but in the wealth that brings happiness, a good and wise life. All goes wrong when, starved for lack of anything good in their own lives, men turn to public affairs hoping to snatch from thence the happiness they hunger for. They set about fighting for power, and this internecine conflict ruins them and their country. The life of true philosophy is the only one that looks down upon offices of state; and access to power must be confined to men who are not in love with it; otherwise rivals will start fighting. So whom else can you compel to undertake the guardianship of the commonwealth, if not those who, besides understanding best the principles of government, enjoy a nobler life than the politician's and look for rewards of a different kind?

There is indeed no other choice.

Notes

1. The ascription of a philosophic element to dogs is not seriously meant. We might regard man's love of knowledge as rooted in an instinct of curiosity to be found in animals; but curiosity has no connexion with gentleness, and for Plato reason is an independent faculty, existing only in man and not developed from any animal instinct.

2. Note that the Guardians themselves are to accept this allegory, if possible. It is not "propaganda" foisted on the masses by the Rulers.

3. Simonides was asked by Hiero's queen whether it was better to be wise (a man of genius) or rich. He replied: Rich; for the wise are to be found at the court of the rich.

4. Plato held that the heavenly bodies are immortal living creatures, i.e, gods.

5. The *length* of the "way in" (*eisodos*) to the chamber where the prisoners sit is an essential feature, explaining why no daylight reaches them.

6. The track crosses the passage into the cave at right angles, and is *above* the parapet built along it.

7. A modern Plato would compare his Cave to an underground cinema, where the audience watch the play of shadows thrown by the film passing before a light at their backs. The film itself is only an image of "real" things and events in the world outside the cinema. For the film Plato has to substitute the clumsier apparatus of a procession of artificial objects carried on their heads by persons who are merely part of the machinery, providing for the movement of the objects and the sounds whose echo the prisoners hear. The parapet prevents these persons' shadows from being cast on the wall of the Cave.

8. . . . The prisoners, having seen nothing but shadows, cannot think their words refer to the objects carried past behind their backs. For them shadows (images) are the only realities.

9. An allusion to the fate of Socrates.

Study Questions

1. How do you defend a system of government in which those who know much about public issues have no more say in the decision process than those who know little?
2. What is the fable of the metals, and does it strengthen or weaken Plato's case against democracy?
3. Do you believe that the parable of the state of affairs on board a ship misrepresents democracy?
4. Do you agree with Plato that the best rulers are found among those not seeking to rule?

Leviathan

THOMAS HOBBES

Thomas Hobbes (1588–1679) was an English philosopher who played a crucial role in the history of social thought. He developed a moral and political theory that views justice and other ethical ideals as resting on an implied agreement among individuals to relinquish the right to do whatever they please in exchange for all others limiting their rights in a similar manner, thus achieving security for all.

OF THE NATURAL CONDITION OF MANKIND AS CONCERNING THEIR FELICITY, AND MISERY

Nature hath made men so equal, in the faculties of body, and mind; as that though there be found one man sometimes manifestly stronger in body, or of quicker mind than another; yet when all is reckoned together, the difference between man, and man, is not so considerable, as that one man can thereupon claim to himself any benefit, to which another may not pretend, as well as he. For as to the strength of body, the weakest has strength enough to kill the strongest, either by secret machination, or by confederacy with others, that are in the same danger as himself.

And as to the faculties of the mind, (setting aside the arts grounded upon words, and especially that skill of proceeding upon general, and infallible rules, called science; which very few have, and but in few things; as being not a native faculty, born with us; nor attained, (as prudence,) while we look after someone else,) I find yet a greater equality amongst men, than that of strength. For prudence, is but experience; which equal time, equally bestows on all men, in those things they equally apply themselves unto. That which may perhaps make such equality incredible, is but a vain conceit of one's own wisdom, which almost all men think they have in a greater degree, than the vulgar; that is, than all men but themselves, and a few others, whom by fame, or for concurring with themselves, they approve. For such is the nature of men, that howsoever they may acknowledge many others to be more witty, or more eloquent, or more learned; yet they will hardly believe there be many so wise as themselves: For they see their own wit at hand, and other men's at a distance. But this proveth rather that men are in that point equal, than unequal. For there is not ordinarily a greater sign of the equal distribution of any thing, than that every man is contented with his share.

From this equality of ability, ariseth equality of hope in the attaining of our ends. And therefore if any two men desire the same thing, which nevertheless they cannot both enjoy, they become enemies; and in the way to their end, (which is principally their own conservation, and sometimes their delectation only,) endeavour to destroy, or subdue one another. And from hence it comes to pass, that where an invader hath no more to fear, than another man's single power; if one plant, sow, build, or possess

From Thomas Hobbes, *Leviathan* (1651).

a convenient seat, others may probably be expected to come prepared with forces united, to dispossess, and deprive him, not only of the fruit of his labour, but also of his life, or liberty. And the invader again is in the like danger of another.

And from this diffidence of one another, there is no way for any man to secure himself, so reasonable, as anticipation; that is, by force, or wiles, to master the persons of all men he can, so long, till he see no other power great enough to endanger him: and this is no more than his own conservation requireth, and is generally allowed. Also because there be some, that taking pleasure in contemplating their own power in the acts of conquest, which they pursue farther than their security requires; if others, that otherwise would be glad to be at ease within modest bounds, should not by invasion increase their power, they would not be able, long time, by standing only on their defence, to subsist. And by consequence, such augmentation of dominion over men, being necessary to a man's conservation, it ought to be allowed him.

Again, men have no pleasure, (but on the contrary a great deal of grief) in keeping company, where there is no power able to over-awe them all. For every man looketh that his companion should value him, at the same rate he sets upon himself: and upon all signs of contempt, or undervaluing, naturally endeavours, as far as he dares (which amongst them that have no common power to keep them in quiet, is far enough to make them destroy each other,) to extort a greater value from his contemners, by damage; and from others, by the example.

So that in the nature of man, we find three principal causes of quarrel. First, competition; secondly, diffidence; thirdly, glory.

The first, maketh man invade for gain; the second, for safety; and the third, for reputation. The first use violence, to make themselves masters of other men's persons, wives, children, and cattle; the second, to defend them; the third for trifles, as a word, a smile, a different opinion, and any other sign of undervalue, either direct in their persons, or by reflection in their kindred, their friends, their nation, their profession, or their name.

Hereby it is manifest, that during the time men live without a common power to keep them all in awe, they are in that condition which is called war; and such a war, as is of every man, against every man. For WAR, consisteth not in battle only, or the act of fighting; but in a tract of time, wherein the will to contend by battle is sufficiently known: and therefore the notion of *time*, is to be considered in the nature of war; as it is in the nature of weather. For as the nature of foul weather, lieth not in a shower or two of rain; but in an inclination thereto of many days together: so the nature of war, consisteth not in actual fighting; but in the known disposition thereto, during all the time there is no assurance to the contrary. All other time is PEACE.

Whatsoever therefore is consequent to a time of war, where every man is enemy to every man; the same is consequent to the time, wherein men live without other security, than what their own strength, and their own invention shall furnish them withal. In such condition, there is no place for industry; because the fruit thereof is uncertain: and consequently no culture of the earth; no navigation, nor use of the commodities that may be imported by sea; no commodious building; no instruments of moving, and removing such things as require much force; no knowledge of the face of the earth; no account of time; no arts; no letters; no society; and which is worst of all, continual fear, and danger of violent death; and the life of man, solitary, poor, nasty, brutish, and short.

It may seem strange to some man, that has not well weighed these things; that nature should thus dissociate, and render men apt to invade, and destroy one another: and he may therefore, not trusting to this inference, made from the passions, desire perhaps to have the same confirmed by experience. Let him therefore consider with himself, when taking a journey, he arms himself, and seeks to go well accompanied; when going to sleep, he locks his doors; when even in his house he locks his chests; and this when he knows there be laws, and public officers, armed, to revenge all injuries shall be done him; what opinion he has of his fellow subjects, when he rides armed; of his fellow citizens, when he locks his doors; and of his children, and servants, when he locks his chests. Does he not there as much accuse mankind by his actions, as I do by my words? But neither of us accuse man's nature in it. The desires, and other passions of man, are in themselves no sin. No more are the actions, that proceed from those passions, till they know a law that forbids them: which till laws be made they cannot know: nor can any law be made, till they have agreed upon the person that shall make it.

It may peradventure be thought, there was never such a time, nor condition of war as this; and I believe it was never generally so, over all the world: but there are many places, where they live so now. For the savage people in many places of *America*, except the government of small families, the concord whereof dependeth on natural lust, have no government at all: and live at this day in that brutish manner, as I said before. Howsoever, it may be perceived what manner of life there would be, where there were no common power to fear; by the manner of life, which men that have formerly lived under a peacefull government, use to degenerate into, in a civil war.

But though there had never been any time, wherein particular men were in a condition of war one against another; yet in all times, kings, and persons of sovereign authority, because of their independency, are in continual jealousies, and in the state and posture of gladiators; having their weapons pointing, and their eyes fixed on one another; that is, their forts, garrisons, and guns upon the frontiers of their kingdoms; and continual spies upon their neighbours; which is a posture of war. But because they uphold thereby; the industry of their subjects; there does not follow from it, that misery, which accompanies the liberty of particular men.

To this war of every man against every man, this also is consequent; that nothing can be unjust. The notions of right and wrong, justice and injustice have there no place. Where there is no common power, there is no law: where no law, no injustice. Force, and fraud, are in war the two cardinal virtues. Justice, and injustice are none of the faculties neither of the body, nor mind. If they were, they might be in a man that were alone in the world, as well as his senses, and passions. They are qualities, that relate to men in society, not in solitude. It is consequent also to the same condition, that there be no propriety, no dominion, no *mine* and *thine* distinct; but only that to be every man's, that he can get; and for so long, as he can keep it. And thus much for the ill condition which many by mere nature is actually placed in; though with a possibility to come out of it, consisting partly in the passions, partly in his reason.

The passions that incline men to peace, are fear of death; desire of such things as are necessary to commodious living; and a hope by their industry to obtain them. And reason suggesteth convenient articles of peace, upon which men may be drawn to agreement. These articles, are they, which otherwise are called the Laws of Nature: whereof I shall speak more particularly, in the two following chapters.

OF THE FIRST AND SECOND NATURAL LAWS, AND OF CONTRACTS

The RIGHT OF NATURE, which writers commonly call *jus naturale*, is the liberty each man hath, to use his own power, as he will himself, for the preservation of his own nature; that is to say, of his own life; and consequently, of doing any thing, which in his own judgment, and reason, he shall conceive to be the aptest means thereunto.

By LIBERTY, is understood, according to the proper signification of the word, the absence of external impediments: which impediments, may oft take away part of a man's power to do what he would; but cannot hinder him from using the power left him, according as his judgment, and reason shall dictate to him.

A LAW OF NATURE, (*lex naturalis*,) is a precept, or general rule, found out by reason, by which a man is forbidden to do that, which is destructive of his life, or taketh away the means of preserving the same; and to omit that, by which he thinketh it may be best preserved. For though they that speak of this subject, use to confound *jus*, and *lex*, *right* and *law*; yet they ought to be distinguished; because RIGHT, consisteth in liberty to do, or to forbear; whereas LAW, determineth, and bindeth to one of them: so that law, and right, differ as much, as obligation, and liberty, which in one and the same matter are inconsistent.

And because the condition of man, (as hath been declared in the precedent chapter) is a condition of war of every one against every one; in which case every one is governed by his own reason; and there is nothing he can make use of, that may not be a help unto him, in preserving his life against his enemies, it followeth, that in such a condition, every man has a right to every thing: even to one another's body. And therefore, as long as this natural right of every man to every thing endureth, there can be no security to any man, (how strong or wise soever he be,) of living out the time, which nature ordinarily alloweth men to live. And consequently it is a precept, or general rule of reason, *that every man, ought to endeavour peace, as far as he has hope of obtaining it; and when he cannot obtain it, that he may seek, and use, all helps, and advantages of war*. The first branch of which rule, containeth the first, and fundamental law of nature; which is, *to seek peace, and follow it*. The second, the sum of the right of nature; which is, *by all means we can, to defend ourselves*.

From this fundamental law of nature, by which men are commanded to endeavor peace, is derived this second law; *that a man be willing, when others are so too, as farforth, as for peace, and defence of himself he shall think it necessary, to lay down this right to all things; and be contented with so much liberty against other men, as he would allow other men against himself*. For as long as every man holdeth this right, of doing any thing he liketh; so long are all men in the condition of war. But if other men will not lay down their right, as well as he; then there is no reason for any one, to divest himself of his: for that were to expose himself to prey, (which no man is bound to) rather than to dispose himself to peace. This is that law of the Gospel, *whatsoever you require that others should do for you, that do ye to them*. . . .

OF OTHER LAWS OF NATURE

From that law of nature, by which we are obliged to transfer to another, such rights, as being retained, hinder the peace of mankind, there followeth a third; which is this, *that men perform their covenants made*: without which, covenants are in vain, and but empty words; and the right of all men to all things remaining, we are still in the condition of war.

And in this law of nature, consisteth the fountain and original of JUSTICE. For where no covenant hath preceded, there hath no right been transferred, and every man has right to every thing; and consequently, no action can be unjust. But when a covenant is made, then to break it is *unjust;* and the definition of INJUSTICE, is no other than *the not performance of covenant*. And whatsoever is not unjust, is *just*.

But because covenants of mutual trust, where there is fear of not performance on either part, (as hath been said in the former chapter,) are invalid; though the original of justice be the making of covenants; yet injustice actually there can be none, till the cause of such fear be taken away; which while men are in the natural condition of war, cannot be done. Therefore before the names of just, and unjust can have place, there must be some coercive power, to compel men equally to the performance of their covenants, by the terror of some punishment, greater than the benefit they expect by the breach of their convenant; and to make good that propriety, which by mutual contract men acquire, in recompense of the universal right they abandon: and such power there is none before the erection of a commonwealth. And this is also to be gathered out of the ordinary definition of justice in the Schools: for they say, that *justice is the constant will of giving to every man his own*. And therefore where there is no *own*, that is, no propriety, there is no injustice; and where there is no coercive power erected, that is, where there is no commonwealth, there is no propriety; all men having right to all things: therefore where there is no commonwealth, there nothing is unjust. So that the nature of justice, consisteth in keeping of valid covenants: but the validity of covenants begins not but with the constitution of a civil power, sufficient to compel men to keep them: and then it is also that propriety begins. . . .

The fool hath said in his heart, there is no such thing as justice; and sometimes also with his tongue; seriously alleging, that every man's conservation, and contentment, being committed to his own care, there could be no reason, why every man might not do what he thought conduced thereunto: and therefore also to make, or not make: keep, or not keep covenants, was not against reason, when it conduced to one's benefit. He does not therein deny, that there be covenants; and that they are sometimes broken, sometimes kept; and that such breach of them may be called injustice, and the observance of them justice: but he questioneth, whether injustice, taking away the fear of God, (for the same fool hath said in his heart there is no God,) may not sometimes stand with that reason, which dictateth to every man his own good; and particularly then, when it conduceth to such a benefit, as shall put a man in a condition, to neglect not only the dispraise, and reviling, but also the power of other men. . . . This specious reasoning is nevertheless false.

For the question is not of promises mutual, where there is no security of performance on either side; as when there is no civil power erected over the parties promising; for such promises are no covenants: but either where one of the parties has performed already; or where there is a power to make him perform; there is the question whether it be against reason, that is against the benefit of the other to perform, or not. And I say it is not against reason. For the manifestation whereof, we are to consider; first, that when a man doth a thing, which notwithstanding any thing can be foreseen, and reckoned on, tendeth to his own destruction, howsoever some accident which he could not expect, arriving may turn it to his benefit; yet such events do not make it reasonably or wisely done. Secondly, that in a condition of war, wherein every man to every man, for want of a common power to keep them all in awe, is an enemy, there is no man can hope by his own strength, or wit, to defend himself from destruction, without the help of confederates; where every one expects the same defence by the confederation, that any one else does: and therefore he which declares he thinks it reason to deceive those that help him, can in reason expect no other means of safety, than what can be had from his own single power. He therefore that breaketh his covenant, and consequently declareth that he thinks he may with reason do so, cannot be received into any society, that unite themselves for peace and defence, but by the error of them that receive him; nor when he is received, be retained in it, without seeing the danger of their error; which errors a man cannot reasonably reckon upon as the means of his security: and therefore if he be left, or cast out of society, he perisheth; and if he live in society, it is by the errors of other men, which he could not foresee, nor reckon upon; and consequently against the reason of his preservation; and so, as all men that contribute not to his destruction, forbear him only out of ignorance of what is good for themselves.

Study Questions

Study Questions

1. Without government to enforce laws, would life be, as Hobbes says, "nasty, brutish, and short"?
2. What does Hobbes mean by "the right of nature"?
3. What does he mean by a "law of nature"?
4. Why are we obliged to keep our agreements?

On Liberty

JOHN STUART MILL

Bring to your mind an opinion so outrageous that it would be repudiated by any sensible person. Now suppose that stating this opinion openly would be an affront to the vast majority of listeners. Under such circumstances, why shouldn't the representatives of the people be empowered to pass a law banning the public expression of this foolishness, thus ensuring that no one is offended by it or tempted to repeat it?

One answer might be that the First Amendment to the Constitution of the United States prohibits any law abridging the freedom of speech. But if an opinion is wrongheaded and repugnant, why does it merit protection?

The most celebrated and eloquent reply is provided in John Stuart Mill's classic work, *On Liberty*. It is dedicated to his wife, Harriet Taylor, "the inspirer, and in part the author, of all that is best in my writings."

Most surprisingly, Mill defends an individual's free speech by appealing not to the kindheartedness of the majority but to its own welfare. Yet how can the interest of the majority be served by allowing blatantly false views to be expressed? Let us consider Mill's argument.

CHAPTER I

Introductory

The object of this essay is to assert one very simple principle, as entitled to govern absolutely the dealings of society with the individual in the way of compulsion and control, whether the means used be physical force in the form of legal penalties or the moral coercion of public opinion. That principle is that the sole end for which mankind are warranted, individually or collectively, in interfering with the liberty of action of any of their number is self-protection. That the only purpose for which power can be rightfully exercised over any member of a civilized community, against his will, is to prevent

From *On Liberty* by John Stuart Mill (1859).

harm to others. His own good, either physical or moral, is not a sufficient warrant. He cannot rightfully be compelled to do or forbear because it will be better for him to do so, because it will make him happier, because, in the opinions of others, to do so would be wise or even right. These are good reasons for remonstrating with him, or reasoning with him, or persuading him, or entreating him, but not for compelling him or visiting him with any evil in case he do otherwise. To justify that, the conduct from which it is desired to deter him must be calculated to produce evil to someone else. The only part of the conduct of anyone for which he is amenable to society is that which concerns others. In the part which merely concerns himself, his independence is, of right, absolute. Over himself, over his own body and mind, the individual is sovereign. . . .

This, then, is the appropriate region of human liberty. It comprises, first, the inward domain of consciousness, demanding liberty of conscience in the most comprehensive sense, liberty of thought and feeling, absolute freedom of opinion and sentiment on all subjects, practical or speculative, scientific, moral, or theological. The liberty of expressing and publishing opinions may seem to fall under a different principle, since it belongs to that part of the conduct of an individual which concerns other people, but, being almost of as much importance as the liberty of thought itself and resting in great part on the same reasons, is practically inseparable from it. Secondly, the principle requires liberty of tastes and pursuits, of framing the plan of our life to suit our own character, of doing as we like, subject to such consequences as may follow, without impediment from our fellow creatures, so long as what we do does not harm them, even though they should think our conduct foolish, perverse, or wrong. Thirdly, from this liberty of each individual follows the liberty, within the same limits, of combination among individuals; freedom to unite for any purpose not involving harm to others: the persons combining being supposed to be of full age and not forced or deceived.

No society in which these liberties are not, on the whole, respected is free, whatever may be its form of government; and none is completely free in which they do not exist absolute and unqualified. The only freedom which deserves the name is that of pursuing our own good in our own way, so long as we do not attempt to deprive others of theirs or impede their efforts to obtain it. Each is the proper guardian of his own health, whether bodily *or* mental and spiritual. Mankind are greater gainers by suffering each other to live as seems good to themselves than by compelling each to live as seems good to the rest. . . .

It will be convenient for the argument if, instead of at once entering upon the general thesis, we confine ourselves in the first instance to a single branch of it on which the principle here stated is, if not fully, yet to a certain point, recognized by the current opinions. This one branch is the Liberty of Thought, from which it is impossible to separate the cognate liberty of speaking and of writing. Although these liberties, to some considerable amount, form part of the political morality of all countries which profess religious toleration and free institutions, the grounds, both philosophical and practical, on which they rest are perhaps not so familiar to the general mind, nor so thoroughly appreciated by many, even of the leaders of opinion, as might have been expected. . . .

CHAPTER II

Of the Liberty of Thought and Discussion

The time, it is to be hoped, is gone by when any defense would be necessary of the "liberty of the press" as one of the securities against corrupt or tyrannical government. No argument, we may suppose, can now be needed against permitting a legislature or an executive, not identified in interest with the people, to prescribe opinions to them and determine what doctrines or what arguments they shall be allowed to hear. . . . Let us suppose, therefore, that the government is entirely at one with the people, and never thinks of exerting any power of coercion unless in agreement with what it conceives to be their voice. But I deny the right of the people to exercise such coercion, either by themselves or by their government. The power itself is illegitimate. The best government has no more title to it than the worst. It is as noxious, or more noxious, when exerted in accordance with public opinion than when in opposition to it. If all mankind minus one were of one opinion, and only one person were of the contrary opinion, mankind would be no more justified in silencing that one person than he, if he had the power, would be justified in silencing mankind. Were an opinion a personal possession of no value except to the owner, if to be obstructed in the enjoyment of it were simply a private injury, it would make some difference whether the injury was inflicted only on a few persons or on many. But the peculiar evil of silencing the expression of an opinion is that it is robbing the human race, posterity as well as the existing generation—those who dissent from the opinion, still more than those who hold it. If the opinion is right, they are deprived of the opportunity of exchanging error for truth; if wrong, they lose, what is almost as great a benefit, the clearer perception and livelier impression of truth produced by its collision with error.

It is necessary to consider separately these two hypotheses, each of which has a distinct branch of the argument corresponding to it. We can never be sure that the opinion we are endeavoring to stifle is a false opinion; and if we were sure, stifling it would be an evil still.

First, the opinion which it is attempted to suppress by authority may possibly be true. Those who desire to suppress it, of course, deny its truth; but they are not infallible. They have no authority to decide the question for all mankind and exclude every other person from the means of judging. To refuse a hearing to an opinion because they are sure that it is false is to assume that *their* certainty is the same thing as *absolute* certainty. All silencing of discussion is an assumption of infallibility. Its condemnation may be allowed to rest on this common argument, not the worse for being common.

Unfortunately for the good sense of mankind, the fact of their fallibility is far from carrying the weight in their practical judgment which is always allowed to it in theory; for while everyone well knows himself to be fallible, few think it necessary to take any precautions against their own fallibility, or admit the supposition that any opinion of which they feel very certain may be one of the examples of the error to which they acknowledge themselves to be liable. Absolute princes, or others who are accustomed to unlimited deference, usually feel this complete confidence in their own opinions on nearly all subjects. People more happily situated, who sometimes hear their opinions disputed and are not wholly unused to be set right when they are wrong, place the same unbounded reliance only on such of their opinions as are shared by all who surround them, or to whom they habitually defer; for in proportion to a man's want of confidence in his own solitary judgment does he usually repose, with implicit trust, on the infallibility of "the world" in general. And the world, to each individual, means the part of it with which he comes in contact: his party, his sect, his church, his class of society; the man may be called, by comparison, almost liberal and large-minded to whom it means anything so comprehensive as his own country or his own age. Nor is his faith in this collective authority at all shaken by his being aware that other ages, countries, sects, churches, classes, and parties have thought, and even now think, the exact reverse. He devolves upon his own world the responsibility of being in the right against the dissentient worlds of other people; and it never troubles him that mere accident has decided which of these numerous worlds is the object of his reliance, and that the same causes which make him a churchman in London would have made him a Buddhist or a Confucian in Peking. Yet it is as evident in itself, as any amount of argument can make it, that ages are no more infallible than individuals—every age having held many opinions which subsequent ages have deemed not only false but absurd; and it is as certain that many opinions, now general, will be rejected by future ages, as it is that many, once general, are rejected by the present.

The objection likely to be made to this argument would probably take some such form as the following. There is no greater assumption of infallibility in forbidding the propagation of error than in any other thing which is done by public authority on its own judgment and responsibility. Judgment is given to men that they may use it. Because it may be used erroneously, are men to be told that they ought not to use it at all? To prohibit what they think pernicious is not claiming exemption from error, but fulfilling the duty incumbent on them, although fallible, of acting on their conscientious conviction. If we were never to act on our opinions, because those opinions may be wrong, we should leave all our interests uncared for, and all our duties unperformed. An objection which applies to all conduct can be no valid objection to any conduct in particular. It is the duty of governments, and of individuals, to form the truest opinions they can; to form them carefully, and never impose them upon others unless they are quite sure of being right. But when they are sure (such reasoners may say), it is not conscientiousness but cowardice to shrink from acting on their opinions and allow doctrines which they honestly think dangerous to the welfare of mankind, either in this life or in another, to be scattered abroad without restraint, because other people, in less enlightened times, have persecuted opinions now believed to be true. Let us take care, it may be said, not to make the same mistake; but governments and nations have made mistakes in other things which are not denied to be fit subjects for the exercise of authority: they have laid on bad taxes, made unjust wars. Ought we therefore to lay on no taxes and, under whatever provocation, make no wars? Men and governments must act to the best of their ability. There is no such thing as absolute certainty, but there is assurance sufficient for the purposes of human life. We may, and must, assume our opinion to be true for the guidance of our own conduct; and it is assuming no more when we forbid bad men to pervert society by the propagation of opinions which we regard as false and pernicious.

I answer, that it is assuming very much more. There is the greatest difference between presuming an opinion to be true because, with every opportunity for contesting it, it has not been refuted, and assuming its truth for the purpose of not permitting its refutation. Complete liberty of contradicting and disproving our opinion is the very condition which justifies us in assuming its truth for purposes of action; and on no other terms can a being with human faculties have any rational assurance of being right.

When we consider either the history of opinion or the ordinary conduct of human life, to what is it to be ascribed that the one and the other are no worse than they are? Not certainly to the inherent force of the human understanding, for on any matter not self-evident there are ninety-nine persons totally incapable of judging of it for one who is capable; and the capacity of the hundredth person is only comparative, for the majority of the eminent men of every past generation held many opinions now known to be erroneous, and did or approved numerous things which no one will now justify. Why is it, then, that there is on the whole a preponderance among mankind of rational opinions and rational conduct? If there really is this preponderance—which there must be unless human affairs are, and have always been, in an almost desperate state—it is owing to a quality of the human mind, the source of everything respectable in man either as an intellectual or as a moral being, namely, that his errors are corrigible. He is capable of rectifying his mistakes by discussion and experience. Not by experience alone. There must be discussion to show how experience is to be interpreted. Wrong opinions and practices gradually yield to fact and argument; but facts and arguments, to produce any effect on the mind, must be brought before it. Very few facts are able to tell their own story, without comments to bring out their meaning. The whole strength and value, then, of human judgment depending on the one property, that it can be set right when it is wrong, reliance can be placed on it only when the means of setting it right are kept constantly at hand. In the case of any person whose judgment is really deserving of confidence, how has it become so? Because he has kept his mind open to criticism of his opinions and conduct. Because it has been his practice to listen to all that could be said against him; to profit by as much of it as was just, and to expound to himself, and upon occasion to others, the fallacy of what was fallacious. Because he has felt that the only way in which a human being can make some approach to knowing the whole of a subject is by hearing what can be said about it by persons of every variety of opinion, and studying all modes in which it can be looked at by every character of mind. No wise man ever acquired his wisdom in any mode but this; nor is it in the nature of human intellect to become wise in any other manner. The steady habit of correcting and completing his own opinion by collating it with those of others, so far from causing doubt and hesitation in carrying it into practice, is the only stable foundation for a just reliance on it; for, being cognizant of all that can, at least obviously, be said against him, and having taken up his position against all gainsayers—knowing that he has sought for objections and difficulties instead of avoiding them, and has shut out no light which can be thrown upon the subject from any quarter—he has a right to think his judgment better than that of any person, or any multitude, who have not gone through a similar process. . . .

In order more fully to illustrate the mischief of denying a hearing to opinions because we, in our own judgment, have condemned them, it will be desirable to fix down the discussion to a concrete case; and I choose, by preference, the cases which are least favorable to me—in which the argument against freedom of opinion, both on the score of truth and on that of utility, is considered the strongest. Let the opinions impugned be the belief in a God and in a future state, or any of the commonly received doctrines of morality. To fight the battle on such ground gives a great advantage to an unfair antagonist, since he will be sure to say (and many who have no desire to be unfair will say it internally), Are these the doctrines which you do not deem sufficiently certain to be taken under the protection of law? Is the belief in a God one of the opinions to feel sure of which you hold to be assuming infallibility? But I must be permitted to observe that it is not the feeling sure of a doctrine (be it what it may) which I call an assumption of infallibility. It is the undertaking to decide that question *for others*, without allowing them to hear what can be said on the contrary side. And I denounce and reprobate this pretension not the less if put forth on the side of my most solemn convictions. However positive anyone's persuasion may be, not only of the falsity but of the pernicious consequences—not only of the pernicious consequences, but (to adopt expressions which I altogether condemn) the immorality and impiety of an opinion—yet if, in pursuance of that private judgment, though backed by the public judgment of his country or his contemporaries, he prevents the opinion from being heard in its defense, he assumes infallibility. And so far from the assumption being less objectionable or less dangerous because the opinion is called immoral or impious, this is the case of all others in which it is most fatal. These are exactly the occasions on which the men of one generation commit those dreadful mistakes which excite the astonishment and horror of posterity. It is among such that we find the instances memorable in history, when the arm of the law has been employed to root out the best men and the noblest doctrines; with deplorable success as to the men, though some of the doctrines have survived to be (as if in mockery) invoked in defense of similar conduct toward those who dissent from *them*, or from their received interpretation.

Mankind can hardly be too often reminded that there was once a man called Socrates, between whom and the legal authorities and public opinion of his time there took place a memorable collision. Born in an age and country abounding in individual greatness, this man has been handed down to us by those who best knew both him and the age as the most virtuous man in it. . . . This acknowledged master of all the eminent thinkers who have since lived—whose fame, still growing after more than two thousand years, all but outweighs the whole remainder of the names which make his native city illustrious—was put to death by his countrymen, after a judicial conviction, for impiety and immorality. Impiety, in denying the gods recognized by the State; indeed, his accuser asserted (see the *Apologia*) that he believed in no gods at all. Immorality, in being, by his doctrines and instructions, a "corruptor of youth." Of these charges the tribunal, there is every ground for believing, honestly found him guilty, and condemned the man who probably of all then born had deserved best of mankind to be put to death as a criminal.

To pass from this to the only other instance of judicial iniquity, the mention of which, after the condemnation of Socrates, would not be an anticlimax: the event which took place on Calvary rather more than eighteen hundred years ago. The man who left on the memory of those who witnessed his life and conversation such an impression of his moral grandeur that eighteen subsequent centuries have done homage to him as the Almighty in person, was ignominiously put to death, as what? As a blasphemer. Men did not merely mistake their benefactor, they mistook him for the exact contrary of what he was and treated him as that prodigy of impiety which they themselves are now held to be for their treatment of him. The feelings with which mankind now regard these lamentable transactions, especially the later of the two, render them extremely unjust in their judgment of the unhappy actors. . . . Orthodox Christians who are tempted to think that those who stoned to death the first martyrs must have been worse men than they themselves are ought to remember that one of those persecutors was Saint Paul. . . .

Let us now pass to the second division of the argument, and dismissing the supposition that any of the received opinions may be false, let us assume them to be true and examine into the worth of the manner in which they are likely to be held when their truth is not freely and openly canvassed. However unwillingly a person who has a strong opinion may admit the possibility that his opinion may be false, he ought to be moved by the consideration that, however true it may be, if it is not fully, frequently, and fearlessly discussed, it will be held as a dead dogma, not a living truth.

There is a class of persons (happily not quite so numerous as formerly) who think it enough if a person assents undoubtingly to what they think true, though he has no knowledge whatever of the grounds of the opinion and could not make a tenable defense of it against the most superficial objections. Such persons, if they can once get their creed taught from authority, naturally think that no good, and some harm, comes of its being allowed to be questioned. Where their influence prevails, they make it nearly impossible for the received opinion to be rejected wisely and considerately, though it may still be rejected rashly and ignorantly; for to shut out discussion entirely is seldom possible, and when it once gets in, beliefs not grounded on conviction are apt to give way before the slightest semblance of an argument. Waiving, however, this possibility—assuming that the true opinion abides in the mind, but abides as a prejudice, a belief independent of, and proof against, argument—this is not the way in which truth ought to be held by a rational being. This is not knowing the truth. Truth, thus held, is but one superstition the more, accidentally clinging to the words which enunciate a truth.

If the intellect and judgment of mankind ought to be cultivated, a thing which Protestants at least do not deny, on what can these faculties be more appropriately exercised by anyone than on the things which concern him so much that it is considered necessary for him to hold opinions on them? If the cultivation of the understanding consists in one thing more than in another, it is surely in learning the grounds of one's own opinions. Whatever people believe, on subjects on which it is of the first importance to believe rightly, they ought to be able to defend against at least the common objections. But, someone may say, "Let them be *taught* the grounds of their opinions. It does not follow that opinions must be merely parroted because they are never heard controverted. Persons who learn geometry do not simply commit the theorems to memory, but understand and learn likewise the demonstrations; and it would be absurd to say that they remain ignorant of the grounds of geometrical truths because they never hear anyone deny and attempt to disprove them." Undoubtedly: and such teaching suffices on a subject like mathematics, where there is nothing at all to be said on the wrong side of the question. The peculiarity of the evidence of mathematical truths is that all the argument is on one side. There are no objections, and no answers to objections. But on every subject on which difference of opinion is possible, the truth depends on a balance to be struck between two sets of conflicting reasons. Even in natural philosophy, there is always some other explanation possible of the same facts; some geocentric theory instead of heliocentric, some phlogiston instead of oxygen; and it has to be shown why that other theory cannot be the true one; and until this is shown, and until we know how it is shown, we do not understand the grounds of our opinion. But when we turn to subjects infinitely more complicated, to morals, religion, politics, social relations, and the business of life, three-fourths of the arguments for every disputed opinion consist in dispelling the appearances which favor some opinion different from it. The greatest orator, save one, of antiquity, has left it on record that he always studied his adversary's case with as great, if not still

greater, intensity than even his own. What Cicero practiced as the means of forensic success requires to be imitated by all who study any subject in order to arrive at the truth. He who knows only his own side of the case knows little of that. His reasons may be good, and no one may have been able to refute them. But if he is equally unable to refute the reasons on the opposite side, if he does not so much as know what they are, he has no ground for preferring either opinion. The rational position for him would be suspension of judgment, and unless he contents himself with that, he is either led by authority or adopts, like the generality of the world, the side to which he feels most inclination. Nor is it enough that he should hear the arguments of adversaries from his own teachers, presented as they state them, and accompanied by what they offer as refutations. That is not the way to do justice to the arguments or bring them into real contact with his own mind. He must be able to hear them from persons who actually believe them, who defend them in earnest and do their very utmost for them. He must know them in their most plausible and persuasive form; he must feel the whole force of the difficulty which the true view of the subject has to encounter and dispose of, else he will never really possess himself of the portion of truth which meets and removes that difficulty. Ninety-nine in a hundred of what are called educated men are in this condition, even of those who can argue fluently for their opinions. Their conclusion may be true, but it might be false for anything they know; they have never thrown themselves into the mental position of those who think differently from them, and considered what such persons may have to say; and, consequently, they do not, in any proper sense of the word, know the doctrine which they themselves profess. . . .

We have now recognized the necessity to the mental well-being of mankind (on which all their other well-being depends) of freedom of opinion, and freedom of the expression of opinion, on four distinct grounds, which we will now briefly recapitulate:

First, if any opinion is compelled to silence, that opinion may, for aught we can certainly know, be true. To deny this is to assume our own infallibility.

Secondly, though the silenced opinion be an error, it may, and very commonly does, contain a portion of truth; and since the general or prevailing opinion on any subject is rarely or never the whole truth, it is only by the collision of adverse opinions that the remainder of the truth has any chance of being supplied.

Thirdly, even if the received opinion be not only true, but the whole truth; unless it is suffered to be, and actually is, vigorously and earnestly contested, it will, by most of those who receive it, be held in the manner of a prejudice, with little comprehension or feeling of its rational grounds. And not only this, but, fourthly, the meaning of the doctrine itself will be in danger of being lost or enfeebled, and deprived of its vital effect on the character and conduct: the dogma becoming a mere formal profession, inefficacious for good, but cumbering the ground and preventing the growth of any real and heartfelt conviction from reason or personal experience.

Study Questions

1. According to Mill, if we are certain that an opinion is false, would stifling it still be wrong?
2. How does Mill defend his claim that "He who knows only his own side of the case knows little of that"?
3. Do we learn more from listening to those with whom we disagree than from those with whom we agree?
4. How would Mill react to the suggestion that a speaker with views demeaning some members of the student body should be banned from speaking at a university campus?

Economic and Philosophic Manuscripts of 1844

KARL MARX

Karl Marx (1818–1883), who was born in Prussia and earned a doctorate in philosophy, became the founder of revolutionary communism. He considers the key to understanding the social order to be the conflict between those who own property and those who work for them. In his view labor produces wonderful things, but only for owners. He sees workers as estranged or alienated from the products of their work. The cure, he believes, lies in the creation of a new economic system based on common control of production.

From *Economic and Philosophic Manuscripts of 1844,* translated by Martin Milligan.

Do not let us go back to a fictitious primordial condition as the political economist does, when he tries to explain. Such a primordial condition explains nothing; it merely pushes the question away into a gray nebulous distance. . . .

We proceed from an economic fact *of the present.* The worker becomes all the poorer the more wealth he produces, the more his production increases in power and size. The worker becomes an ever cheaper commodity the more commodities he creates. With the *increasing value* of the world of things proceeds in direct proportion the *devaluation* of the world of men. Labor produces not only commodities: it produces itself and the worker as a *commodity*—and this in the same general proportion in which it produces commodities.

This fact expresses merely that the object which labor produces—labor's product—confronts it as *something alien*, as a *power independent* of the producer. The product of labor is labor which has been embodied in an object, which has become material: it is the objectification of labor. Labor's realization is its objectification. In the sphere of political economy this realization of labor appears as loss of *realization* for the workers; objectification as loss of the *object* and *bondage to it*; appropriation as *estrangement*, as *alienation*.

So much does labor's realization appear as loss of realization that the worker loses realization to the point of starving to death. So much does objectification appear as loss of the object that the worker is robbed of the objects most necessary not only for his life but for his work. Indeed, labor itself becomes an object which he can obtain only with the greatest effort and with the most irregular interruptions. So much does the appropriation of the object appear as estrangement that the more objects the worker produces the less he can possess and the more he falls under the sway of his product, capital.

All these consequences result from the fact that the worker is related to the *product of his labor* as to an *alien* object. For on this premise it is clear that the more the worker spends himself, the more powerful becomes the alien world of objects which he creates over and against himself—his inner world— the poorer he himself— becomes, the less belongs to him as his own. It is the same in religion. The more man puts into God, the less he retains in himself. The worker puts his life into the object; but now his life no longer belongs to him but to the object. Hence, the greater this activity, the greater is the worker's lack of objects. Whatever the product of his labor is, he is not. Therefore the greater this product, the less is he himself. The *alienation* of the worker in his product means not only that his labor becomes an object, an *external* existence, but that it exists *outside* him, independently, as something alien to him, and that it becomes a power on its own confronting him. It means that the life which he has conferred on the object confronts him as something hostile and alien.

Let us now look more closely at the *objectification*, at the production of the worker; and in it as the *estrangement*, the *loss of* the object, of his product.

The worker can create nothing without *nature*, without the *sensuous external world*. It is the material on which his labor is realized, in which it is active, from which and by means of which it produces.

But just as nature provides labor with the *means of life* in the sense that labor cannot live without objects on which to operate, on the other hand, it also provides the *means of life* in the more restricted sense, i.e., the means for the physical subsistence of the *worker* himself.

Thus the more the worker by his labor *appropriates* the external world, hence sensuous nature, the more he deprives himself of *means of life* in double manner: first, in that the sensuous external world more and more ceases to be an object belonging to his labor—to be his labor's *means of life*; and secondly, in that it more and more ceases to be *means of life* in the immediate sense, means for the physical subsistence of the worker.

In both respects, therefore, the worker becomes a slave of his object, first, in that he receives an *object of labor*, i.e., in that he receives *work;* and secondly, in that he receives *means of subsistence.* Therefore, it enables him to exist, first, as a *worker,* and, second as a *physical subject.* The height of this bondage is that it is only as a *worker* that he continues to maintain himself as a *physical subject,* and that is only as a *physical subject* that he is a *worker.*

(The laws of political economy express the estrangement of the worker in his object thus: the more the worker produces, the less he has to consume; the more values he creates, the more valueless, the more unworthy he becomes; the better formed his product, the more deformed becomes the worker; the more civilized his object, the more barbarous becomes the worker; the more powerful labor becomes, the more powerless becomes the worker; the more ingenious labor becomes, the less ingenious becomes the worker and the more he becomes nature's bondsman.)

Political economy conceals the estrangement inherent in the nature of labor by not considering the direct relationship between the worker (labor) *and production.* It is true that labor produces for the rich wonderful things—but for the worker it produces privation. It produces palaces—but for the worker, hovels. It produces beauty—but for the worker, deformity. It replaces labor by machines, but it throws a section of the workers back to a barbarous type of labor, and turns the other workers into machines. It produces intelligence—but for the worker stupidity, cretinism. . . .

Till now we have been considering the estrangement, the alienation of the worker only in one of its aspects, i.e., the worker's *relationship to the products of his labor.* But the estrangement is manifested not only in the result but in the *act of production,* within the *producing activity,* itself. How would the worker come to face the product of his activity as a stranger, were it not that in the very act of production he was estranging himself from himself? The product is after all but the summary of the activity, of production. If then the product of labor is alienation, production itself must be active alienation, the alienation of activity, the activity of alienation. In the estrangement of the object of labor

is merely summarized the estrangement, the alienation, in the activity of labor itself.

What, then, constitutes the alienation of labor?

First, the fact that labor is *external* to the worker, i.e., it does not belong to his essential being; that in his work, therefore, he does not affirm himself but denies himself, does not feel content but unhappy, does not develop freely his physical and mental energy but mortifies his body and ruins his mind. The worker therefore only feels himself outside his work, and in his work feels outside himself. He is at home when he is not working, and when he is working he is not at home. His labor is therefore not voluntary, but coerced; it is *forced labor.* It is therefore not the satisfaction of a need; it is merely a *means* to satisfy needs external to it. Its alien character emerges clearly in the fact that as soon as no physical or other compulsion exists, labor is shunned like the plague. External labor, labor in which man alienates himself, is a labor of self-sacrifice, of mortification. Lastly, the external character of labor for the worker appears in the fact that it is not his own, but someone else's, that it does not belong to him, that in it he belongs, not to himself, but to another. Just as in religion the spontaneous activity of the human imagination, of the human brain and the human heart, operates independently of the individual—that is, operates on him as an alien, divine or diabolical activity—so is the worker's activity not his spontaneous activity. It belongs to another; it is the loss of his self. . . .

We took our departure from a fact of political economy—the estrangement of the worker and his production. We have formulated this fact in conceptual terms as *estranged, alienated* labor. We have analyzed this concept—hence analyzing merely a fact of political economy.

Let us now see, further, how the concept of estranged, alienated labor must express and present itself in real life.

If the product of labor is alien to me, if it confronts me as an alien power, to whom, then, does it belong?

If my own activity does not belong to me, if it is an alien, a coerced activity, to whom, then, does it belong? . . .

The *alien* being, to whom labor and the product of labor belongs, in whose service labor is done and for whose benefit the product of labor is provided, can only be *man* himself.

If the product of labor does not belong to the worker, if it confronts him as an alien power, then this can only be because it belongs to some *other man than the worker.* If the worker's activity is a torment to him, to another it must be *delight* and his life's joy. . . .

Through *estranged, alienated* labor, then, the worker produces the relationship to this labor of a man alien to labor and standing outside it. The relationship of the worker to labor creates the relation to it of the capitalist (or whatever one chooses to call the master of labor). *Private property* is thus the product, the result, the necessary consequence, of *alienated labor,* of the external relation of the worker to nature and to himself.

Private property thus results by analysis from the concept of *alienated labor,* of *alienated man,* of estranged labor, of estranged life, of estranged man.

True, it is as a result of the *movement of private property* that we have obtained the concept of *alienated labor (of alienated life)* from political economy. But on analysis of this concept it becomes clear that though private property appears to be the source, the cause of alienated labor, it is rather its consequence, just as the gods are *originally* not the cause but the effect of man's intellectual confusion. Later this relationship becomes reciprocal.

Only at the last culmination of the development of private property does this, its secret, appear again, namely, that on the one hand it is the *product* of alienated labor, and that on the other it is the *means* by which labor alienates itself, the *realization of this alienation.*

Study Questions

1. According to Marx, why does the worker become all the poorer the more wealth he produces?
2. What does Marx mean by "alienation"?
3. According to Marx, does labor produce beauty?
4. Explain Marx's view of private property.

Democracy

JOHN DEWEY

John Dewey (1859–1952) was the foremost American philosopher of the first half of the twentieth century. Born and bred in Burlington, Vermont, his life and thought reflected the commitment to social equality he found exemplified in the life of his

From *The Collected Works of John Dewey, Later Works,* vol. 11. Copyright © 1986 by the Center for Dewey Studies. Reprinted by permission of the publisher, Southern Illinois University Press.

boyhood New England community. He spent most of his career as Professor of Philosophy at Columbia University.

Reprinted here is the text of a talk he delivered in 1937 to a meeting of educational administrators. It offers, in brief, his account of democracy.

[D]emocracy is much broader than a special political form, a method of conducting government, of making laws and carrying on governmental administration by means of popular suffrage and elected officers. It is that of course. But it is something broader and deeper than that.

The political and governmental phase of democracy is a means, the best means so far found, for realizing ends that lie in the wide domain of human relationships and the development of human personality. It is, as we often say, though perhaps without appreciating all that is involved in the saying, a way of life, social and individual. The key-note of democracy as a way of life may be expressed, it seems to me, as the necessity for the participation of every mature human being in formation of the values that regulate the living of men together—which is necessary from the standpoint of both the general social welfare and the full development of human beings as individuals.

Universal suffrage, recurring elections, responsibility of those who are in political power to the voters, and the other factors of democratic government are means that have been found expedient for realizing democracy as the truly human way of living. They are not a final end and a final value. They are to be judged on the basis of their contribution to an end. It is a form of idolatry to erect means into the end which they serve. Democratic political forms are simply the best means that human wit has devised up to a special time in history. But they rest back upon the idea that no man or limited set of men is wise enough or good enough to rule others without their consent; the positive meaning of this statement is that all those who are affected by social institutions must have a share in producing and managing them. The two facts that each one is influenced in what he does and enjoys and in what he becomes by the institutions under which he lives, and that therefore he shall have, in a democracy, a voice in shaping them, are the passive and active sides of the same fact.

The development of political democracy came about through substitution of the method of mutual consultation and voluntary agreement for the method of subordination of the many to the few enforced from above. Social arrangements which involve fixed subordination are maintained by coercion. The coercion need not be physical. There have existed, for short periods, benevolent despotisms. But coercion of some sort there has been; perhaps economic, certainly psychological and moral. The very fact of exclusion from participation is a subtle form of suppression. It gives individuals no opportunity to reflect and decide upon what is good for them. Others who are supposed to be wiser and who in any case have more power decide the question for them and also decide the methods and means by which subjects may arrive at the enjoyment of what is good for them. This form of coercion and suppression is more subtle and more effective than is overt intimidation and restraint. When it is habitual and embodied in social institutions, it seems the normal and natural state of affairs. The mass usually become unaware that they have a claim to a development of their own powers. Their experience is so restricted that they are not conscious of restriction. It is part of the democratic conception that they as individuals are not the only sufferers, but that the whole social body is deprived of the potential resources that should be at its service. The individuals of the submerged mass may not be very wise. But there is one thing they are wiser about than anybody else can be, and that is where the shoe pinches, the troubles they suffer from.

The foundation of democracy is faith in the capacities of human nature; faith in human intelligence, and in the power of pooled and cooperative experience. It is not belief that these things are complete but that if given a show they will grow and be able to generate progressively the knowledge and wisdom needed to guide collective action. Every autocratic and authoritarian scheme of social action rests on a belief that the needed intelligence is confined to a superior few who because of inherent natural gifts are endowed with the ability and the right to control the conduct of others; laying down principles and rules and directing the ways in which they are carried out. It would be foolish to deny that much can be said for this point of view. It is that which controlled human relations in social groups for much the greater part of human history. The democratic faith has emerged very, very recently in the history of mankind. Even where democracies now exist, men's minds and feelings are still permeated with ideas about leadership imposed from above, ideas that developed in the long early history of mankind. After democratic political institutions were nominally established, beliefs and ways of looking at life and of acting that originated when men and women were externally controlled and subjected to arbitrary power, persisted in the family, the church, business and the school, and experience shows that as long as they persist there, political democracy is not secure.

Belief in equality is an element of the democratic credo. It is not, however, belief in equality of natural endowments. Those who proclaimed the idea of equality did not suppose they were enunciating a psychological doctrine, but a legal and political one. All individuals are entitled to equality of treatment by law and in its administration. Each one is affected equally in quality if not in quantity by the institutions under which he lives and has an equal right to express his judgment, although the weight of his judgment may not be equal in amount when it enters into the pooled result to that of others. In short, each one is equally an individual and entitled to equal opportunity of development of his own capacities, be they large or small in range. Moreover, each has needs of his own, as significant to him as those of others are to them. The very fact of natural and psychological inequality is all the more reason for establishment by law of equality of opportunity, since otherwise the former becomes a means of oppression of the less gifted.

While what we call intelligence be distributed in unequal amounts, it is the democratic faith that it is sufficiently general so that each individual has something to contribute whose value can be assessed only as it enters into the final pooled intelligence constituted by the contributions of all. Every authoritarian scheme, on the contrary assumes that its value may be assessed by some *prior* principle, if not of family and birth or race and color or possession of material wealth, then by the position and rank a person occupies in the existing social scheme. The democratic faith in equality is the faith that each individual shall have the chance and opportunity to contribute whatever he is capable of contributing, and that the value of his contribution be decided by its place and function in the organized total of similar contributions—not on the basis of prior status of any kind whatever.

I have emphasized in what precedes the importance of the effective release of intelligence in connection with personal experience in the democratic way of living. I have done so purposely because democracy is so often and so naturally associated in our minds with freedom of *action*, forgetting the importance of freed intelligence which is necessary to direct and to warrant freedom of action. Unless freedom of individual action has intelligence and informed conviction back of it, its manifestation is almost sure to result in confusion and disorder. The democratic idea of freedom is not the right of each individual to *do* as he pleases, even if it be qualified by adding "provided he does not interfere with the same freedom on the part of others." While the idea is not always, not often enough, expressed in words, the basic freedom is that of freedom of *mind* and of whatever degree of freedom of action and experience is necessary to produce freedom of intelligence. The modes of freedom guaranteed in the Bill of Rights are all of this nature: Freedom of belief and conscience, of expression of opinion, of assembly for discussion and conference, of the press as an organ of communication. They are guaranteed because without them individuals are not free to develop and society is deprived of what they might contribute. . . .

There is some kind of government, of control, wherever affairs that concern a number of persons who act together are engaged in. It is a superficial view that holds government is located in Washington and Albany. There is government in the family, in business, in the church, in every social group. There are regulations, due to custom if not to enactment, that settle how individuals in a group act in connection with one another.

It is a disputed question of theory and practice just how far a democratic political government should go in control of the conditions of action within special groups. At the present time, for example, there are those who think the federal and state governments leave too much freedom of independent action to industrial and financial groups and there are others who think the Government is going altogether too far at the present time. I do not need to discuss this phase of the problem much less to try to settle it. But it must be pointed out that if the methods of regulation and administration in vogue in the conduct of secondary social groups are non-democratic, whether directly or indirectly or both, there is bound to be an unfavorable reaction back into the habits of feeling, thought and action of citizenship in the broadest sense of that word. The way in which

any organized social interest is controlled necessarily plays an important part in forming the dispositions and tastes, the attitudes, interests, purposes and desires, of those engaged in carrying on the activities of the group. For illustration, I do not need to do more than point to the moral, emotional, and intellectual effect upon both employers and laborers of the existing industrial system. Just what the effects specifically are is a matter about which we know very little. But I suppose that every one who reflects upon the subject admits that it is impossible that the ways in which activities are carried on for the greater part of the waking hours of the day; and the way in which the shares of individuals are involved in the management of affairs in such a matter as gaining a livelihood and attaining material and social security, can only be a highly important factor in shaping personal dispositions; in short, forming character and intelligence.

In the broad and final sense all institutions are educational in the sense that they operate to form the attitudes, dispositions, abilities, and disabilities that constitute a concrete personality. The principle applies with special force to the school. For it is the main business of the family and the school to influence directly the formation and growth of attitudes and dispositions, emotional, intellectual and moral. Whether this educative process is carried on in a predominantly democratic or non-democratic way becomes therefore a question of transcendent importance not only for education itself but for its final effect upon all the interests and activities of a society that is committed to the democratic way of life. . . .

[T]here are certain corollaries which clarify the meaning of the issue. Absence of participation tends to produce lack of interest and concern on the part of those shut out. The result is a corresponding lack of effective responsibility. Automatically and unconsciously, if not consciously, the feeling develops, "this is none of our affair; it is the business of those at the top; let that particular set of Georges do what needs to be done." The countries in which autocratic government prevails are just those in which there is least public spirit and the greatest indifference to matters of general as distinct from personal concern. . . . Where there is little power, there is correspondingly little sense of positive responsibility—It is enough to do what one is told to do sufficiently well to escape flagrant unfavorable notice. About larger matters a spirit of passivity is engendered. . . .

[I]t still is also true that incapacity to assume the responsibilities involved in having a voice in shaping policies is bred and increased by conditions in which that responsibility is denied. I suppose there has never been an autocrat, big or little, who did not justify his conduct on the ground of the unfitness of his subjects to take part in government. . . . But, as was said earlier, habitual exclusion has the effect of reducing a sense of responsibility for what is done and its consequences. What the argument for democracy implies is that the best way to produce initiative and constructive power is to exercise it. Power, as well as interest, comes by use and practice. . . .

The fundamental beliefs and practices of democracy are now challenged as they never have been before. In some nations they are more than challenged. They are ruthlessly and systematically destroyed. Everywhere there are waves of criticism and doubt as to whether democracy can meet pressing problems of order and security. The causes for the destruction of political democracy in countries where it was nominally established are complex. But of one thing I think we may be sure. Wherever it has fallen it was too exclusively political in nature. It had not become part of the bone and blood of the people in daily conduct of its life. Democratic forms were limited to Parliament, elections, and combats between parties. What is happening proves conclusively, I think, that unless democratic habits of thought and action are part of the fiber of a people, political democracy is insecure. It cannot stand in isolation. It must be buttressed by the presence of democratic methods in all social relationships. The relations that exist in educational institutions are second only in importance in this respect to those which exist in industry and business, perhaps not even to them. . . .

I can think of nothing so important in this country at present as a rethinking of the whole problem of democracy and its implications. Neither the rethinking nor the action it should produce can be brought into being in a day or year. The democratic idea itself demands that the thinking and activity proceed cooperatively.

Study Questions

1. Why does Dewey believe that democracy is much broader than a method of electing officials?
2. According to Dewey, about what are individuals wiser than anyone else can be?
3. According to Dewey, what is the foundation of democracy?
4. How does Dewey connect democracy and education?

A Theory of Justice

JOHN RAWLS

Under what conditions could a society be properly described as just? An influential answer to this question has been developed by John Rawls (1921–2002), who was Professor of Philosophy at Harvard University. He contends that the fairest way to distribute goods is in accord with principles that everyone would accept, regardless of the abilities they happen to possess, or the social or economic circumstances in which they find themselves.

THE MAIN IDEA OF THE THEORY OF JUSTICE

. . . [T]he principles of justice . . . are the principles that free and rational persons concerned to further their own interests would accept in an initial position of equality. . . .

[T]he original position of equality corresponds to the state of nature in the traditional theory of the social contract. This original position is not, of course, thought of as an actual historical state of affairs, much less as a primitive condition of culture. It is understood as a purely hypothetical situation. . . . Among the essential features of this situation is that no one knows his place in society, his class position or social status, nor does any one know his fortune in the distribution of natural assets and abilities, his intelligence, strength, and the like. I shall even assume that the parties do not know their conceptions of the good or their special psychological propensities. The principles of justice are chosen behind a veil of ignorance. This ensures that no one is advantaged or disadvantaged in the choice of principles by the outcome of natural chance or the contingency of social circumstances. Since all are similarly situated and no one is able to design principles to favor his particular condition, the principles of justice are the result of a fair agreement or bargain. For given the circumstances of the original position, the symmetry of everyone's relations to each other, this initial situation is fair between individuals as moral persons, that is, as rational beings with their own ends and capable, I shall assume, of a sense of justice. The original position is, one might say, the appropriate initial status quo, and thus the fundamental agreements reached in it are fair. This explains the propriety of the name "justice as fairness": it conveys the idea that the principles of justice are agreed to in an initial situation that is fair. . . .

I shall maintain . . . that the persons in the initial situation would choose two . . . principles: the first requires equality in the assignment of basic rights and duties, while the second holds that social and economic inequalities, for example inequalities of wealth and authority, are just only if they result in compensating benefits for everyone, and in particular for the least advantaged members of society. These principles rule out justifying institutions on the grounds that the hardships of some are offset by a greater good in the aggregate. It may be expedient but it is not just that some should have less in order that others may prosper. But there is no injustice in the greater benefits earned by a few provided that the situation of persons not so fortunate is thereby improved. The intuitive idea is that since everyone's well-being depends upon a scheme of cooperation without which no one could have a satisfactory life, the division of advantages should be such as to draw forth the willing cooperation of everyone taking part in it, including those less well situated. The two principles mentioned seem to be a fair basis on which those better endowed, or more fortunate in their social position, neither of which we can be said to deserve, could expect the willing cooperation of others when some workable scheme is a necessary condition of the welfare of all. Once we decide to look for a conception of justice that prevents the use of the accidents of natural endowment and the contingencies of social circumstance as counters in a quest of political and economic advantage, we are led to these principles. They express the result of leaving aside those aspects of the social world that seem arbitrary from a moral point of view. . . .

THE ORIGINAL POSITION AND JUSTIFICATION

. . . One should not be misled . . . by the somewhat unusual conditions which characterize the original position. The idea here is simply to make vivid to ourselves the restrictions that it seems reasonable to impose on arguments for principles of justice, and therefore on these principles themselves. Thus it seems reasonable and generally acceptable that no one should be advantaged or disadvantaged by natural fortune or social circumstances in the choice of principles. It also seems widely agreed that it should be impossible to tailor principles to the circumstances of one's own case. We should insure further that

particular inclinations and aspirations, and persons' conceptions of their good, do not affect the principles adopted. The aim is to rule out those principles that it would be rational to propose for acceptance, however little the chance of success, only if one knew certain things that are irrelevant from the standpoint of justice. For example, if a man knew that he was wealthy, he might find it rational to advance the principle that various taxes for welfare measures be counted unjust; if he knew that he was poor, he would most likely propose the contrary principle. To represent the desired restrictions one imagines a situation in which everyone is deprived of this sort of information. One excludes the knowledge of those contingencies which sets men at odds and allows them to be guided by their prejudices. In this manner the veil of ignorance is arrived at in a natural way. This concept should cause no difficulty if we keep in mind the constraints on arguments that it is meant to express. At any time we can enter the original position, so to speak, simply by following a certain procedure, namely, by arguing for principles of justice in accordance with these restrictions.

It seems reasonable to suppose that the parties in the original position are equal. That is, all have the same rights in the procedure for choosing principles; each can make proposals, submit reasons for their acceptance, and so on. Obviously the purpose of these conditions is to represent equality between human beings as moral persons, as creatures having a conception of their good and capable of a sense of justice. The basis of equality is taken to be similarity in these two respects. Systems of ends are not ranked in value; and each man is presumed to have the requisite ability to understand and to act upon whatever principles are adopted. Together with the veil of ignorance, these conditions define the principles of justice as those which rational persons concerned to advance their interests would consent to as equals when none are known to be advantaged or disadvantaged by social and natural contingencies. . . .

TWO PRINCIPLES OF JUSTICE

I shall now state in a provisional form the two principles of justice that I believe would be chosen in the original position. . . .

The first statement of the two principles reads as follows.

First: each person is to have an equal right to the most extensive scheme of equal basic liberties compatible with a similar scheme of liberties for others.

Second: social and economic inequalities are to be arranged so that they are both (a) reasonably expected to be to everyone's advantage, and (b) attached to positions and offices open to all. . . .

These principles primarily apply . . . to the basic structure of society and govern the assignment of rights and duties and regulate the distribution of social and economic advantages. . . . [I]t is essential to observe that the basic liberties are given by a list of such liberties. Important among these are political liberty (the right to vote and to hold public office) and freedom of speech and assembly; liberty of conscience and freedom of thought; freedom of the person, which includes freedom from psychological oppression and physical assault and dismemberment (integrity of the person); the right to hold personal property and freedom from arbitrary arrest and seizure as defined by the concept of the rule of law. These liberties are to be equal by the first principle.

The second principle applies . . . to the distribution of income and wealth and to the design of organizations that make use of differences in authority and responsibility. While the distributions of wealth and income need not be equal, it must be to everyone's advantage, and at the same time, positions of authority and responsibility must be accessible to all. One applies the second principle by holding positions open, and then, subject to this constraint, arranges social and economic inequalities so that everyone benefits.

These principles are to be arranged in a serial order with the first principle prior to the second. This ordering means that infringements of the basic equal liberties protected by the first principle cannot be justified, or compensated for, by greater social and economic advantages. . . .

[I]n regard to the second principle, the distribution of wealth and income, and positions of authority and responsibility, are to be consistent with both the basic liberties and equality of opportunity. . . .

[T]hese principles are a special case of a more general conception of justice that can be expressed as follows.

> All social values—liberty and opportunity, income and wealth, and the social bases of self-respect—are to be distributed equally unless an unequal distribution of any, or all, of these values is to everyone's advantage.
>
> Injustice, then, is simply inequalities that are not to the benefit of all. . . .

THE VEIL OF IGNORANCE

. . . The notion of the veil of ignorance raises several difficulties. Some may object that the exclusion of nearly all particular information makes it difficult to grasp what is meant by the original position. Thus it may be helpful to observe that one or more persons can at any time enter this position, or perhaps better, simulate the deliberations of this hypothetical situation, simply by reasoning in accordance with the appropriate restrictions. . . .

It may be protested that the condition of the veil of ignorance is irrational. Surely, some may object, principles should be chosen in the light of all the knowledge available. There are various replies to this contention. . . . To begin with, it is clear that since the differences among the parties are unknown to them, and everyone is equally rational and similarly situated, each is convinced by the same arguments. Therefore, we can view the agreement in the original position from the standpoint of one person selected at random. If anyone after due reflection prefers a conception of justice to another, then they all do, and a unanimous agreement can be reached. We can, to make the circumstances more vivid, imagine that the parties are required to communicate with each other through a referee as intermediary, and that he is to announce which alternatives have been suggested and the reasons offered in their support. He forbids the attempt to form coalitions, and he informs the parties when they have come to an understanding. But such a referee is actually superfluous, assuming that the deliberations of the parties must be similar.

Thus there follows the very important consequence that the parties have no basis for bargaining in the usual sense. No one knows his situation in society nor his natural assets, and therefore no one is in a position to tailor principles to his advantage. We might imagine that one of the contractees threatens to hold out unless the others agree to principles favorable to him. But how does he know which principles are especially in his interests? The same holds for the formation of coalitions: if a group were to decide to band together to the disadvantage of the others, they would not know how to favor themselves in the choice of principles. Even if they could get everyone to agree to their proposal, they would have no assurance that it was to their advantage, since they cannot identify themselves either by name or description. . . .

The restrictions on particular information in the original position are, then, of fundamental importance. Without them we would not be able to work out any definite theory of justice at all. We would have to be content with a vague formula stating that justice is what would be agreed to without being able to say much, if anything, about the substance of the agreement itself . . . The veil of ignorance makes possible a unanimous choice of a particular conception of justice. Without these limitations on knowledge the bargaining problem of the original position would be hopelessly complicated.

Study Questions

1. What is "the original position"?
2. What is "the veil of ignorance"?
3. According to Rawls, what are the two principles of justice?
4. Do you agree with Rawls that these two principles would be chosen in the original position?

Distributive Justice

ROBERT NOZICK

Robert Nozick (1938–2002) was Professor of Philosophy at Harvard University. Nozick argues that in treating all goods as though they were unowned and distributing them in accord with some preferred scheme, we ignore the source of these goods in the labor and ingenuity of the people who created them. As he sees it, past history plays a crucial role in determining entitlements. If I acquired property appropriately, through my own efforts or by a legal exchange with its rightful owner, then I should not have the property taken away from me in order to satisfy someone's conception of justice.

The term "distributive justice" is not a neutral one. Hearing the term "distribution," most people presume that some thing or mechanism uses some principle or criterion to give out a supply of things. Into this process of distributing shares some error may have crept. So it is an open question, at least, whether *re*distribution should take place; whether we should do again what has already been done once, though poorly. However, we are not in the position of children who have been given portions of pie by someone who now makes last minute adjustments to rectify careless cutting. There is no *central* distribution, no person or group entitled to control all the resources, jointly deciding how they are to be doled out. What each person gets, he gets from others who give to him in exchange for something, or as a gift. In a free society, diverse persons control different resources, and new holdings arise out of the voluntary exchanges and actions of persons. There is no more a distributing or distribution of shares than there is a distributing of mates in a society in which persons choose whom they shall marry. The total result is the product of many individual decisions which the different individuals involved are entitled to make. . . . We shall speak of people's holdings; a principle of justice in holdings describes (part of) what justice tells us (requires) about holdings. . . .

THE ENTITLEMENT THEORY

The subject of justice in holdings consists of three major topics. The first is the *original acquisition of holdings,* the appropriation of unheld things. This includes the issues of how unheld things may come to be held, the process, or processes, by which unheld things may come to be held, the things that may come to be held by these processes, the extent of what comes to be held by a particular process, and so on. We shall refer to the complicated truth about this topic, which we shall not formulate here, as the principle of justice in acquisition. The second topic concerns the *transfer of holdings* from one person to another. By what processes may a person transfer holdings to another? How may a person acquire a holding from another who holds it? Under this topic come general descriptions of voluntary exchange, and gift and (on the other hand) fraud, as well as reference to particular conventional details fixed upon in a given society. The complicated truth about this subject (with placeholders for conventional details) we shall call the principle of justice in transfer. (And we shall suppose it also includes principles governing how a person may divest himself of a holding, passing it into an unheld state.)

If the world were wholly just, the following inductive definition would exhaustively cover the subject of justice in holdings.

1. A person who acquires a holding in accordance with the principle of justice in acquisition is entitled to that holding.

2. A person who acquires a holding in accordance with the principle of justice in transfer, from someone else entitled to the holding, is entitled to the holding.

3. No one is entitled to a holding except by (repeated) applications of 1 and 2.

The complete principle of distributive justice would say simply that a distribution is just if everyone is entitled to the holdings they possess under the distribution.

A distribution is just if it arises from another just distribution by legitimate means. The legitimate means of moving from one distribution to another are specified by the principle of justice in transfer. The legitimate first "moves" are specified by the principle of justice in acquisition. Whatever arises from a just situation by just steps is itself just. The means of change specified by the principle of justice in transfer preserve justice. As correct rules of inference are truth-preserving, and any conclusion deduced via repeated application of such rules from only true premises is itself true, so the means of transition from one situation to another specified by the principle of justice in transfer are justice-preserving, and any situation actually arising from repeated transitions in accordance with the principle from a just situation is itself just. The parallel between justice-preserving transformations and truth-preserving transformations illuminates where it fails as well as where it holds. That a conclusion could have been deduced by truth-preserving means from premises that are true suffices to show its truth. That from a just situation a situation *could* have arisen via justice-preserving means does *not* suffice to show its justice. The fact that a thief's victims voluntarily *could* have presented him with gifts does not entitle the thief to his ill-gotten gains. Justice in holdings is historical; it depends upon what actually has happened. We shall return to this point later.

Not all actual situations are generated in accordance with the two principles of justice in holdings: the principle of justice in acquisition and the principle of justice in transfer. Some people steal from others, or defraud them, or enslave them, seizing their product and preventing them from living as they choose, or forcibly exclude others from competing in exchanges. None of these are permissible modes of transition from one situation to another. And some persons acquire holdings by means not sanctioned by the principle of justice in acquisition. The existence of past injustice (previous violations of the first two principles of justice in holdings) raises the third major topic under justice in holdings: the rectification of injustice in holdings. If past injustice has shaped present holdings in various ways, some identifiable and some not, what now, if anything, ought to be done to rectify these injustices? What obligations do the performers of injustice have toward those whose position is worse than it would have been had the injustice not been done?

The general outlines of the theory of justice in holdings are that the holdings of a person are just if he is entitled to them by the principles of justice in acquisition and transfer, or by the principle of rectification of injustice (as specified by the first two principles). If each person's holdings are just, then the total set (distribution) of holdings is just. To turn these general outlines into a specific theory we would have to specify the details of each of the three principles of justice in holdings: the principle of acquisition of holdings, the principle of transfer of holdings, and the principle of rectification of violations of the first two principles. I shall not attempt that task here. . . .

HOW LIBERTY UPSETS PATTERNS

It is not clear how those holding alternative conceptions of distributive justice can reject the entitlement conceptions of justice in holdings. For suppose a distribution favored by one of these nonentitlement conceptions is realized. Let us suppose it is your favorite one and let us call this distribution D_1; perhaps everyone has an equal share, perhaps shares vary in accordance with some dimension you treasure. Now suppose that Wilt Chamberlain is greatly in demand by basketball teams, being a great gate attraction. (Also suppose contracts run only for a year, with players being free agents.) He signs the following sort of contract with a team: In each home game, twenty-five cents from the price of each ticket of admission goes to him. (We ignore the question of whether he is "gouging" the owners, letting them look out for themselves.) The season starts, and people cheerfully attend his team's games; they buy their tickets, each time dropping a separate twenty-five cents of their admission price into a special box with Chamberlain's name on it. They are excited about seeing him play; it is worth the total admission price to them. Let us suppose that in one season one million persons attend his home games, and Wilt Chamberlain winds up with $250,000, a much larger sum than the average income and larger even than anyone else has. Is he entitled to this income? Is this new distribution D_2 unjust? If so, why? There is *no* question about whether each of the people was entitled to the control over the resources they held in D_1; because that was the distribution (your favorite) that (for the purposes of argument) we assumed was acceptable. Each of these persons *chose* to give twenty-five cents of their money to Chamberlain. They could have spent it on going to the movies, or on candy bars, or on copies of *Dissent* magazine, or on *Monthly Review*. But they all, at least one million of them, converged on giving it to Wilt Chamberlain in exchange for watching him play basketball. If D_1 was a just distribution, and people voluntarily moved from it to D_2, transferring parts of their shares they were given under D_1 (what was it for if not to do something with?), isn't D_2 also just? If the people were entitled to dispose of the resources to which they were entitled (under D_1), didn't this include their being entitled to give it to, or exchange it with, Wilt Chamberlain? Can anyone else complain on grounds of justice? Each other person already has his legitimate share under D_1. Under D_1, there is nothing that anyone has that anyone else has a claim of justice against. After someone transfers something to Wilt Chamberlain, third parties *still* have their legitimate shares; *their* shares are not changed. By what process could such a transfer among two persons give rise to a legitimate claim of distributive justice on a portion of what was transferred, by a third party who had no claim of justice on any holding of the others *before* the transfer? . . .

The general point illustrated by the Wilt Chamberlain example . . . is that no end-state principle[1] or distributional patterned principle of justice[2] can be continuously realized without continuous interference with people's lives. Any favored pattern would be transformed into one unfavored by the principle, by people choosing to act in various ways; for example, by people exchanging goods and services with other people, or giving things to other people, things the transferrers are entitled to under the favored distributional pattern. To maintain a pattern one must either continually interfere to stop people from transferring resources as they wish to, or continually (or periodically) interfere to take from some persons resources that others for some reason chose to transfer to them. (But if some time limit is to be set on how long people may keep resources others voluntarily transfer to them, why let them keep these resources for *any* period of time? Why not have immediate confiscation?) It might be objected that all persons voluntarily will choose to refrain from actions which would upset the pattern. This presupposes unrealistically (1) that all will most want to maintain the pattern (are those who don't, to be "reeducated" or forced to undergo "self-criticism"?), (2) that each can gather enough information about his own actions and the ongoing activities of others to discover which of his actions will upset the pattern, and (3) that diverse and far-flung persons can coordinate their actions to dovetail into the pattern. Compare the manner in which the market is neutral among persons' desires, as it reflects and transmits widely scattered information via prices, and coordinates persons' activities.

NOTES

1. [An "end-state principle" requires that goods be distributed to promote a certain structure of holdings, such as maximizing utility or achieving equality.—S.M.C.]

2. [A "patterned principle" requires that goods be distributed in accord with some feature of persons, such as need or desert.]

Study Questions

1. What does Nozick mean by "justice in acquisition"?
2. What does Nozick mean by "justice in transfer"?
3. What is the general point illustrated by the Wilt Chamberlain example?
4. How is the Wilt Chamberlain example supposed to undermine a theory of justice such as Rawls proposed?

Non-contractual Society: A Feminist View

VIRGINIA HELD

Virginia Held, whose work we read previously, next explores how the relations suitable for mothering persons and children might be used as a social model. Instead of thinking of human relations as a contract between rationally self-interested individuals, she envisions society as a group of persons tied together by ongoing relations of caring and trust.

Contemporary society is in the grip of contractual thinking. Realities are interpreted in contractual terms, and goals are formulated in terms of rational contracts. The leading current conceptions of rationality begin with assumptions that human beings are independent, self-interested or mutually disinterested, individuals; they then typically argue that it is often rational for human beings to enter into contractual relationships with each other. . . .

To see contractual relations between self-interested or mutually disinterested individuals as constituting a paradigm of human relations is to take a certain historically specific conception of "economic man" as representative of humanity.

And it is, many feminists are beginning to agree, to overlook or to discount in very fundamental ways the experience of women.

I will try in this paper to look at society from a thoroughly different point of view than that of economic man. I will take the point of view of women, and especially of mothers, as the basis for trying to rethink society and its possible goals. Certainly there is no single point of view of women; the perspectives of women are potentially as diverse as those of men. But since the perspectives of women have all been to a large extent discounted, across the spectrum, I will not try to deal here with diversity among such views, but rather to give voice to one possible feminist outlook. . . .

Since it is the practice of mothering with which I will be concerned in what follows, rather than with women in the biological sense. I will use the term "mothering person" rather than "mother." A "mothering person" can be male or female. . . .

From *Science, Morality, and Feminist Theory*, ed. Marsha Hanen and Kai Nielsen, *Canadian Journal of Philosophy*, Supplementary Volume 13. Calgary: University of Calgary Press, 1987. Reprinted by permission of the publisher with a minor revision by the author.

WOMEN AND FAMILY

A first point to note in trying to imagine society from the point of view of women is that the contractual model was hardly ever applied, as either description or ideal, to women or to relations within the family. The family was imagined to be "outside" the polis and "outside" the market in a "private" domain. This private domain was contrasted with the public domain, and with what, by the time of Hobbes and Locke, was thought of as the contractual domain of citizen and state and tradesman and market. Although women have always worked, and although both women and children were later pressed into work in factories, they were still thought of as outside the domain in which the contractual models of "equal men" were developed. Women were not expected to demand equal rights either in the public domain or at home. Women were not expected to be "economic men." And children were simply excluded from the realm of what was being interpreted in contractual terms as distinctively human.

Women have . . . been thought to be closer to nature than men, to be enmeshed in a biological function involving processes more like those in which other animals are involved than like the rational contracting of distinctively human "economic man." The total or relative exclusion of women from the domain of voluntary contracting has then been thought to be either inevitable or appropriate.

The view that women are more governed by biology than are men is still prevalent. It is as questionable as many other traditional misinterpretations of women's experience. Human mothering is an extremely different activity from the mothering engaged in by other animals. It is as different from the mothering of other animals as is the work and speech of men different from the "work" and "speech" of other animals. Since humans are also animals, one should not exaggerate the differences between humans and other animals. But to whatever extent it is appropriate to recognize a difference between "man" and other animals, so would it be appropriate to recognize a comparable difference between human mothering and the mothering of other animals.

Human mothering shapes language and culture, and forms human social personhood. Human mothering develops morality, it does not merely transmit techniques of survival; impressive as the latter can be, they do not have built into them the aims of morality. Human mothering teaches consideration for others based on moral concern; it does not merely follow and bring the child to follow instinctive tendency. Human mothering creates autonomous persons; it does not merely propagate a species. It can be fully as creative an activity as most other human activities; to create *new* persons, and new types of *persons,* is surely as creative as to make new objects, products, or institutions. Human mothering is no more "natural" than any other human activity. It may include many dull and repetitive tasks, as does farming, industrial production, banking, and work in a laboratory. But degree of dullness has nothing to do with degree of "naturalness." In sum, human mothering is as different from animal mothering as humans are from animals. . . .

FAMILY AND SOCIETY

In recent years, many feminists have demanded that the principles of justice and freedom and equality on which it is claimed that democracy rests be extended to women and the family. They have demanded that women be treated as equals in the polity, in the workplace, and, finally, at home. They have demanded, in short, to be accorded full rights to enter freely the contractual relations of modern society. They have asked that these be extended to take in the family.

But some feminists are now considering whether the arguments should perhaps, instead, run the other way. Instead of importing into the household principles derived from the marketplace, perhaps we should export to the wider society the relations suitable for mothering persons and children. This approach suggests that just as relations between persons within the family should be based on concern and caring, rather than on contracts based on self-interest, so various relations in the wider society should be characterized by more care and concern and openness and trust and human feeling than are the contractual bargains that have developed so far in political and economic life, or even than are aspired to in contractarian prescriptions. Then, the household instead of the marketplace might provide a model for society. Of course what we would mean by the household would not be the patriarchal household which was, before the rise of contractual thinking, also thought of as a model of society. We would now mean the relations between children and mothering persons *without* the patriarch. We would take our conception of the *post*-patriarchal family as a model. . . .

THE MOTHER/CHILD RELATION

Let us examine in more detail the relation between mothering person and child. A first aspect of the relation that we can note is the extent to which it is not voluntary and, for this reason among others, not contractual. The ties that bind child and mothering persons are affectional and solicitous on the one hand, and emotional and dependent on the other. The degree to which bearing and caring for children has been voluntary for most mothers throughout most of history has been extremely limited; it is still quite limited for most mothering persons. The relation *should* be voluntary for the mothering person but it cannot possibly be voluntary for the young child, and it can only become, gradually, slightly more voluntary.

A woman can have decided voluntarily to have a child, but once that decision has been made, she will never again be unaffected by the fact that she has brought this particular child

into existence. And even if the decision to have a child is voluntary, the decision to have this particular child, for either parent, cannot be. Technological developments can continue to reduce the uncertainties of childbirth, but unpredictable aspects are likely to remain great for most parents. Unlike that contract where buyer and seller can know what is being exchanged, and which is void if the participants cannot know what they are agreeing to, a parent cannot know what a particular child will be like. And children are totally unable to choose their parents and, for many years, any of their caretakers.

The recognition of how limited are the aspects of voluntariness in the relation between child and mothering person may help us to gain a closer approximation to reality in our understanding of most human relations, especially at a global level, than we can gain from imagining the purely voluntary trades entered into by rational economic contractors to be characteristic of human relations in other domains.

Society may impose certain reciprocal obligations: on parents to care for children when the children are young, and on children to care for parents when the parents are old. But if there is any element of a bargain in the relation between mothering person and child, it is very different from the bargain supposedly characteristic of the marketplace. If a parent thinks, "I'll take care of you now so you'll take care of me when I'm old," it must be based, unlike the contracts of political and economic bargains, on enormous trust and on a virtual absence of enforcement. And few mothering persons have any such exchange in mind when they engage in the activities of mothering. At least the bargain would only be resorted to when the callousness or poverty of the society made the plight of the old person desperate. This is demonstrated in survey after survey: old persons certainly hope not to have to be a burden on their children. And they prefer social arrangements that will allow them to refuse to cash in on any such bargain. So the intention and goal of mothering is to give of one's care without obtaining a return of a self-interested kind. The emotional satisfaction of a mothering person is a satisfaction in the well-being and happiness of another human being, and a satisfaction in the health of the relation between the two persons, not the gain that results from an egoistic bargain. The motive behind the activity of mothering is thus entirely different from that behind a market transaction. And so is, perhaps even more clearly, the motive behind the child's project of growth and development.

A second aspect of the contrast between market relations and relations between mothering person and child is found in the qualities of permanence and non-replaceability. The market makes of everything, even human labor and artistic expression and sexual desire, a commodity to be bought and sold, with one unit of economic value replaceable by any other of equivalent value. To the extent that political life reflects these aspects of the market, politicians are replaceable and political influence is bought and sold. Though rights may be thought of as outside the economic market, in contractual thinking they are seen as inside the wider market of the social contract, and can be traded against each other. But the ties between parents and children are permanent ties, however strained or slack they become at times. And no person within a family should be a commodity to any other. Although various persons may participate in mothering a given child, and a given person may mother many children, still no child and no mothering person is to the other a merely replaceable commodity. The extent to which more of our attitudes, for instance toward our society's cultural productions, should be thought of in these terms rather than in the terms of the marketplace, should be considered.

A third aspect of the relation between mothering person and child that may be of interest is the insight it provides for our notions of equality. It shows us unmistakably that equality is not equivalent to having equal legal rights. All feminists are committed to equality and to equal rights in contexts where rights are what are appropriately at issue. But in many contexts, concerns other than rights are more salient and appropriate. And the equality that is at issue in the relation between child and mothering person is the equal consideration of persons, not a legal or contractual notion of equal rights.

Parents and children should not have equal rights in the sense that what they are entitled to decide or to do or to have should be the same. A family of several small children, an adult or two, and an aged parent should not, for instance, make its decisions by majority vote in most cases. But every member of a family is worthy of equal respect and consideration. Each person in a family is as important as a person as every other.

Sometimes the interests of children have been thought in some sense to count for more, justifying "sacrificing for the children." Certainly, the interests of mothers have often counted for less than those of either fathers or children. Increasingly, we may come to think that the interests of all should count equally, but we should recognize that this claim is appropriately invoked only if the issue should be thought of as one of interest. Often, it should not. Much of the time we can see that calculations of interest, and of equal interests, are as out of place as are determinations of equal rights. Both the rights and the interests of individuals seen as separate entities, and equality between them all, should not exhaust our moral concerns. The flourishing of shared joy, of mutual affection, of bonds of trust and hope between mothering persons and children can illustrate this as clearly as anything can. Harmony, love, and cooperation cannot be broken down into individual benefits or burdens. They are goals we ought to share and relations *between* persons. And although the degree of their intensity may be different, many and various relations *between* persons are important also at the level of communities or societies. We can consider, of a society, whether the relations between its members are trusting and mutually supportive, or suspicious and hostile. To focus only on contractual relations and the gains and losses of individuals obscures these often more important relational aspects of societies.

A fourth important feature of the relation between child and mothering person is that we obviously do not fulfil our obligations by merely leaving people alone. If one leaves an infant alone he will starve. If one leaves a two-year old alone she will rapidly harm herself. The whole tradition that sees respecting others as constituted by non-interference with them is most effectively shown up as inadequate. It assumes that people can fend for themselves and provide through their own initiatives and efforts what they need. This Robinson Crusoe image of "economic man" is false for almost everyone, but it is totally and obviously false in the case of infants and children, and recognizing this can be salutary. It can lead us to see very vividly how unsatisfactory are those prevalent political views according to which we fulfil our obligations merely by refraining from interference. We ought to acknowledge that our fellow citizens, and fellow inhabitants of the globe, have moral rights to what they need to live—to the food, shelter, and medical care that are the necessary conditions of living and growing—and that when the resources exist for honoring such rights there are few excuses for not doing so. Such rights are not rights to be left to starve unimpeded. Seeing how unsatisfactory rights merely to be left alone are as an interpretation of the rights of children may help us to recognize a similar truth about other persons. And the arguments—though appropriately in a different form—can be repeated for interests as distinct from rights.

A fifth interesting feature of the relation between mothering person and child is the very different view it provides of privacy. We come to see that to be in a position where others are *not* making demands on us is a rare luxury, not a normal state. To be a mothering person is to be subjected to the continual demands and needs of others. And to be a child is to be subjected to the continual demands and expectations of others. Both mothering persons and children need to extricate themselves from the thick and heavy social fabric in which they are entwined in order to enjoy any pockets of privacy at all.

Here the picture we form of our individuality and the concept we form of a "self" is entirely different from the one we get if we start with the self-sufficient individual of the "state of nature." If we begin with the picture of rational contractor entering into agreements with others, the "natural" condition is seen as one of individuality and privacy, and the problem is the building of society and government. From the point of view of the relation between mothering person and child, on the other hand, the problem is the reverse. The starting condition is an enveloping tie, and the problem is individuating oneself. The task is to carve out a gradually increasing measure of privacy in ways appropriate to a constantly shifting independency. For the child, the problem is to become gradually more interdependent. For the mothering person, the problem is to free oneself from an all-consuming involvement. For both, the progression is from society to greater individuality rather than from self-sufficient individuality to contractual ties. . . .

A sixth aspect of the relation between child and mothering person which is noteworthy is the very different view of power it provides. We are accustomed to thinking of power as something that can be wielded by one person over another, as a means by which one person can bend another to his will. An ideal has been to equalize power so that agreements can be forged and conflicts defused. But consider now the very different view of power in the relation between mothering person and child. The superior power of the mothering person over the child is relatively useless for most of what the mothering person aims to achieve in bringing up the child. The mothering person seeks to *empower* the child to act responsibly, she neither wants to "wield" power nor to defend herself against the power "wielded" by the child. The relative powerlessness of the child is largely irrelevant to most of the project of growing up. When the child is physically weakest, as in infancy and illness, the child can "command" the greatest amount of attention and care from the mother-ing person because of the seriousness of the child's needs.

The mothering person's stance is characteris-tically one of caring, of being vulnerable to the needs and pains of the child, and of fearing the loss of the child before the child is ready for in-dependence. It is not characteristically a stance of domination. The child's project is one of de-veloping, of gaining ever greater control over his or her own life, of relying on the mothering person rather than of submitting to superior strength. Of course the relation may in a degen-erate form be one of domination and submis-sion, but this only indicates that the relation is not what it should be. . . . The power of a moth-ering person to empower others, to foster trans-formative growth, is a different sort of power than that of a stronger sword or dominant will. And the power of a child to call forth tenderness and care is perhaps more different still.

MODELS FOR SOCIETY

The relation between child and mothering person seems especially worth exploring to see what implications and insights it might suggest for a transformed society.

There are good reasons to believe that a soci-ety resting on no more than bargains between self-interested or mutually disinterested individ-uals will not be able to withstand the forces of egoism and dissolution pulling such societies apart. Although there may be some limited do-mains in which rational contracts are the appro-priate form of social relations, as a foundation for the fundamental ties which ought to bind human beings together, they are clearly inade-quate. Perhaps we can learn from a non-patriarchal household better than from further searching in the marketplace what the sources might be for justifiable trust, cooperation, and caring.

Many persons can imagine human society on the model of "economic man," society built on a contract between rationally self-interested persons, because these are the theories they have been brought up with. But they cannot imagine society resembling a group of persons tied together by on-going relations of caring and trust between persons in positions such as those of mothers and children where, as adults, we would sometimes be one and sometimes the other. Suppose now we ask: in the relation be-tween mothering person and child, who are the contractors? Where is the rational self-interest? The model of "economic man" makes no sense in this context. Anyone in the social contract tradition who has noticed the relation of child and mothering person at all has supposed it to belong to some domain outside the realm of the "free market" and outside the "public" realm of politics and the law. Such theorists have supposed the context of mothering to be of much less significance for human history and of much less relevance for moral theory than the realms of trade and government, or they have imagined mothers and children as some-how outside human society altogether in a region labelled "nature," and engaged wholly in "reproduction." But mothering is at the heart of human society.

If the dynamic relation between child and mothering person is taken as the primary social relation, then it is the model of "economic man" that can be seen to be deficient as a model for society and morality, and unsuitable for all but a special context. A domain such as law, if built on no more than contractual foundations, can then be recognized as one limited domain among others; law protects some moral rights when people are too immoral or weak to respect them without the force of law. But it is hardly a majes-tic edifice that can serve as a model for morality. Neither can the domain of politics, if built on no more than self-interest or mutual disinterest, provide us with a model with which to under-stand and improve society and morality. And neither, even more clearly, can the market itself.

When we explore the implications of these speculations we may come to realize that instead of seeing the family as an anomalous island in a sea of rational contracts composing economic and political and social life, perhaps it is instead "economic man" who belongs on a relatively small island surrounded by social ties of a less hostile, cold, and precarious kind.

Study Questions

1. What does Held mean by "contractual thinking"?
2. According to Held, what are the distinctive features of the relation between mothering person and child?
3. According to Held, in what specific ways might the relation between mothering person and child provide a model for society?
4. Does envisioning society as Held proposes suggest support for any particular governmental policies?

Part IX

⊠

Social Problems

A.   Education

What Is a Liberal Education?

SIDNEY HOOK

The welfare of a democratic community depends on the understanding and capability of its citizenry. But what knowledge, skills, and values do we all require to enable us to make a success of our experiment in self-government? That is the question addressed in our next essay, which is written by Sidney Hook (1902–1989), who was Professor of Philosophy at New York University.

What, concretely, should the modern man know in order to live intelligently in the world today? What should we require that he learn of subject matters and skills in his educational career in order that he may acquire maturity in feeling, in judgment, in action? Can we indicate the minimum indispensables of a liberal education in the modern world? This approach recognizes that no subject per se is inherently liberal at all times and places. But it also recognizes that within a given age in a given culture, the enlightenment and maturity, the freedom and power, which liberal education aims to impart, is more likely to be achieved by mastery of some subject matters and skills than by others. In short, principles must bear fruit in specific programs in specific times. In what follows I shall speak of studies rather than of conventional courses.

1. The liberally educated person should be intellectually at home in the world of physical nature. He should know something about the earth he inhabits and its place in the solar system, about the solar system and its relation to the cosmos. He should know something about mechanics, heat, light, electricity, and magnetism as the universal forces that condition anything he is or may become. He should be just as intimately acquainted with the nature of man as a biological species, his evolution, and the discoveries of experimental genetics. He should know something about the structure of his own body and mind, and the cycle of birth, growth, learning, and decline. To have even a glimmer of understanding of these things, he must go beyond the level of primary description and acquire some grasp of the principles that explain what he observes. Where an intelligent grasp of principles requires a knowledge of mathematics, its fundamental ideas should be presented in such a way that students carry away the sense of mathematics not only as a tool for the solution of problems but as a study of types of order, system, and language.

Such knowledge is important to the individual *not* merely because of its intrinsic fascination. Every subject from numismatics to Sanskrit possesses an intrinsic interest to those who are curious about it. It is important because it helps make everyday experience more intelligible; because it furnishes a continuous exemplification of scientific method in action; because our world is literally being remade by the consequences and applications of science; because the fate of nations and the vocations of men depend upon the use of this knowledge; and because it provides the instruments to reduce our vast helplessness and dependence in an uncertain world.

Such knowledge is no less important because it bears upon the formation of *rational belief* about the place of man in the universe. Whatever views a man professes today about God, human freedom, Cosmic Purpose, and personal survival, he cannot reasonably hold them in ignorance of the scientific account of the world and man.

These are some of the reasons why the study of the natural sciences, and the elementary mathematical notions they involve, should be *required* of everyone. Making such study required imposes a heavy obligation and a difficult task of pedagogical discovery upon those who teach it. It is commonly recognized that the sciences today are taught as if all students enrolled in science courses were preparing to be professional scientists. Most of them are not. Naturally they seek to escape a study whose wider and larger uses they do not see because many of their teachers do not see it. Here is not the place to canvass and evaluate the attempts being made to organize instruction in the sciences. The best experience seems to show that one science should not be taken as the exemplar of all, but that the basic subject matter of astronomy, physics, chemistry, geology, in one group, and biology and psychology in another, should be covered. For when only one science is taught it tends to be treated professionally. Similarly, the best experience indicates that instruction should be interdepartmental—any competent teacher from one of these fields in either group should be able to teach all of them in the group, instead of having a succession of different teachers each representing his own field. This usually destroys both the continuity and the cumulative effect of the teaching as a whole.

2. Every student should be required to become intelligently aware of how the society in which he lives functions, of the great forces molding contemporary civilization, and of the crucial problems of our age which await decision. The studies most appropriate to this awareness have been conventionally separated into history, economics, government, sociology, social psychology, and anthropology. This separation is an intellectual scandal. For it is impossible to have an adequate grasp of the problems of government without a knowledge of economics, and vice versa. Except for some special domains of professional interest, the same is true for the other subjects as well.

The place of the social studies, properly integrated around problems and issues, is fundamental in the curriculum of modern education. It is one of the dividing points between the major conflicting schools of educational thought. The question of its justification must be sharply distinguished from discussion of the relative merits of this or that mode of approach to the social studies.

The knowledge and insight that the social studies can give are necessary for every student because no matter what his specialized pursuits may later be, the extent to which he can follow them, and the "contextual" developments within these fields, depend upon the total social situation of which they are in some sense a part. An engineer today whose knowledge is restricted only to technical matters of engineering, or a physician whose competence extends only to the subject matter of traditional medical training, is ill-prepared to plan intelligently for a life-career or to understand the basic problems that face his profession. He is often unable to cope adequately with those specific problems in his own domain that involve, as so many problems of social and personal health do, economic and psychological difficulties. No matter what an individual's vocation, the conditions of his effective functioning depend upon pervasive social tendencies which set the occasions for the application of knowledge, provide the opportunities of employment, and not seldom determine even the direction of research.

More important, the whole presupposition of the theory of democracy is that the electorate will be able to make intelligent decisions on the issues before it. These issues are basically political, social, and economic. Their specific character changes from year to year. But their generic form, and the character of the basic problems, do not. Nor, most essential of all, do the proper intellectual habits of meeting them change. It is undeniably true that the world we live in is one marked by greater changes, because of the impact of technology, than ever before. This does not necessitate changing the curriculum daily to catch up with today's newspapers, nor does it justify a concentration on presumably eternal problems as if these problems had significance independent of cultural place–time. The fact that we are living in a world where the rate of cultural change is greater than at any time in the past, together with its ramifications, may itself become a central consideration for analysis. . . .

3. Everyone recognizes a distinction between knowledge and wisdom. This distinction is not clarified by making a mystery of wisdom and speaking of it as if it were begotten by divine inspiration while knowledge had a more lowly source. Wisdom is a kind of knowledge. It is knowledge of the nature, career, and consequences of *human values*. Since these cannot be separated from the human organism and the social scene, the moral ways of man cannot be understood without knowledge of the ways of things and institutions.

To study social affairs without an analysis of policies is to lose oneself in factual minutiae that lack interest and relevance. But knowledge of values is a prerequisite of the intelligent determination of policy. Philosophy, most broadly viewed, is the critical survey of existence from the standpoint of value. This points to the twofold role of philosophy in the curriculum of the college.

The world of physical nature may be studied without reference to human values. But history, art, literature, and particularly the social studies involve problems of value at every turn. A social philosophy whose implications are worked out is a series of proposals that something be *done* in the world. It includes a set of *plans* to conserve or change aspects of social life. Today the community is arrayed under different banners without a clear understanding of the basic issues involved. In the press of controversy, the ideals and values at the heart of every social philosophy are widely affirmed as articles of blind faith. They are partisan commitments justified only by the emotional security they give to believers. They spread by contagion, unchecked by critical safeguards; yet the future of civilization largely depends upon them and how they are held. It is therefore requisite that their study be made an integral part of the liberal arts curriculum. Systematic and critical instruction should be given in the great maps of life—the ways to heaven, hell, and earth—which are being unrolled in the world today.

Ideals and philosophies of life are not parts of the world of nature; but it is a pernicious illusion to imagine that they cannot be studied "scientifically." Their historical origins, their concatenation of doctrine, their controlling assumptions, their means, methods, and consequences in practice, can and should be investigated in a scientific spirit. There are certain social philosophies that would forbid such an investigation for fear of not being able to survive it; but it is one of the great merits of the democratic way of life and one of its strongest claims for acceptance that it can withstand analysis of this sort. It is incumbent upon the liberal arts college to provide for close study of the dominant social and political philosophies, ranging from one end of the color spectrum to the other. Proper study will disclose that these philosophies cannot be narrowly considered in their own terms. They involve an examination of the great ways of life—of the great visions of philosophy which come into play whenever we try to arrange our values in a preference scale in order to choose the better between conflicting goods. Philosophy is best taught when the issues of moral choice arise naturally out of the problems of social life. The effective integration of concrete materials from history, literature, and social studies can easily be achieved within a philosophical perspective.

4. Instruction in the natural, social, and technological forces shaping the world, and in the dominant conflicting ideals in behalf of which these forces are to be controlled, goes a long way. But not far enough. Far more important than knowledge is the method by which it is reached, and the ability to recognize when it constitutes *evidence* and when not; and more important than any particular ideal is the way in which it is held, and the capacity to evaluate it in relation to other ideals. From first to last, in season and out, our educational institutions, especially on the college level, must emphasize *methods* of analysis. They must build up in students a critical sense of evidence, relevance, and validity against which the multitudinous seas of propaganda will wash in vain. They must strengthen the powers of independent reflection, which will enable students to confront the claims of ideals and values by their alternatives and the relative costs of achieving them. . . .

The field of language, of inference and argument, is a broad field but a definite one in which specific training can be given to all students. How to read intelligently, how to recognize good from bad reasoning, how to evaluate evidence, how to distinguish between a definition and a hypothesis and between a hypothesis and a resolution, can be taught in such a way as to build up permanent habits of logic in action. The result of thorough training in "semantic" analysis—using that term in its broadest sense without invidious distinctions between different schools—is an intellectual sophistication without which a man may be learned but not intelligent.

Judging by past and present curricular achievements in developing students with intellectual sophistication and maturity, our colleges must be pronounced, in the main, dismal failures. The main reason for the failure is the absence of serious effort, except in a few institutions, to realize this goal. The necessity of the task is not even recognized. This failure is not only intellectually reprehensible; it is socially dangerous. For the natural susceptibility of youth to enthusiasms, its tendency to glorify action, and its limited experience make it easy recruiting material for all sorts of demagogic movements which flatter its strength and impatience. Recent history furnishes many illustrations of how, in the absence of strong critical sense, youthful strength can lead to cruelty, and youthful impatience to folly. It is true that people who are incapable of thinking cannot be taught how to think, and that the incapacity for thought is not restricted to those who learn. But the first cannot be judged without being exposed to the processes of critical instruction, and the second should be eliminated from the ranks of the teachers. There is considerable evidence to show that students who are capable of completing high school can be so taught that they are aware of *whether* they are thinking or not. There is hope that, with better pedagogic skill and inspiration, they may become capable of grasping the main thought of *what* they are reading or hearing in non-technical fields—of developing a sense of *what validly follows from what,* an accompanying sensitiveness to the dominant types of fallacies, and a habit of weighing evidence for conclusions advanced.

My own experience has led me to the conclusion that this is *not* accomplished by courses in formal logic which, when given in a rigorous and elegant way, accomplish little more than courses in pure mathematics. There is an approach to the study of logic that on an elementary level is much more successful in achieving the ends described above than the traditional course in formal logic. This plunges the student into an analysis of language material around him. By constant use of concrete illustrations drawn from all fields, but especially the fields of politics and social study, insight is developed into the logical principles of definition, the structure of analogies, dilemmas, types of fallacies and the reasons *why* they are fallacies, the criteria of good hypotheses, and related topics. Such training may legitimately be required of all students. Although philosophers are usually best able to give it, any teacher who combines logical capacity with pedagogic skill can make this study a stimulating experience.

5. There is less controversy about the desirability of the study of composition and literature than about any other subject in the traditional or modern curriculum. It is appreciated that among the essentials of clear thought are good language habits and that, except in the higher strata of philosophic discourse, tortuous obscurities of expression are more likely to be an indication of plain confusion than of stuttering profundity. It is also widely recognized that nothing can take the place of literature in developing the imagination, and in imparting a sense of the inexhaustible richness of human personality. The questions that arise at this point are not of justification, but of method, technique, and scope of comprehensiveness.

If good language habits are to be acquired *only* in order to acquire facility in thinking, little can be said for the conventional courses in English composition. Students cannot acquire facility in clear expression in the space of a year, by developing sundry themes from varied sources, under the tutelage of instructors whose training and interest may not qualify them for sustained critical thought. Clear thinking is best controlled by those who are at home in the field in which thinking is done. If language instruction is to be motivated only by the desire to strengthen the power of organizing ideas in written discourse, it should be left to properly trained instructors in other disciplines.

But there are other justifications for teaching students English composition. The first is that there are certain rules of intelligent reading that are essential to—if they do not constitute—understanding. These rules are very elementary. By themselves they do not tell us how to understand a poem, a mathematical demonstration, a scientific text, or a religious prayer—all of which require special skills. But they make it easier for the student to uncover the nature of the "argument"—what is being said, what is being assumed, what is being presented as evidence—in any piece of prose that is not a narrative or simply informational in content. In a sense these rules are integral to the study of logic in action, but in such an introductory way that they are usually not considered part of logical study which begins its work after basic meanings have been established, or in independence of the meaning of logical symbols.

Another reason for teaching English composition independently is its uses in learning how to write. "Effective writing" is not necessarily the same thing as logical writing. The purpose for which we write determines whether our writing is effective. And there are many situations in which we write not to convince or to prove but to explain, arouse, confess, challenge, or assuage. To write *interestingly* may sometimes be just as important as to write soundly because getting a hearing and keeping attention may depend upon it. How much of the skills of writing can be taught is difficult to say. That it is worth making the effort to teach these skills is indisputable.

The place of language in the curriculum involves not merely our native language but *foreign* languages. Vocational considerations aside, should knowledge of a foreign language be required, and why? . . .

The main reason why students should be requested to learn another language is that it is the most effective medium by which, when properly taught, they can acquire a sensitivity to language, to the subtle tones, undertones, and overtones of words, and to the licit ambiguities of imaginative discourse. No one who has not translated prose or poetry from one language to another can appreciate both the unique richness and the unique limitations of his own language. This is particularly true where the life of the emotions is concerned; and it is particularly important that it should be realized. For the appreciation of emotions, perhaps even their recognition in certain cases, depends upon their linguistic identification. The spectrum of human emotions is much more dense than the words by which we render them. Knowledge of different languages, and the attempts made to communicate back and forth between them in our own minds, broaden and diversify our own feelings. They multiply points of view, and liberate us from the prejudice that words—*our* words—are the natural signs of things and events. The genius of a culture is exemplified in a preeminent way in the characteristic idioms of its language. In learning another language we enable ourselves to appreciate both the cultural similarities and differences of the Western world. . . .

The place of literature in the curriculum is justified by so many considerations that it is secure against all criticism. Here, too, what is at issue is not whether literature—Greek, Latin, English, European, American—should be read and studied in the schools but what should be read, when, and by what methods. These are details, important details—but outside the scope of our inquiry.

Something should be said about the unique opportunity which the teaching of literature provides, not only in giving delight by heightening perception of the formal values of literary craftsmanship, but in giving insight into people. The opposite of a liberal education, William James somewhere suggests, is a literal education. A literal education is one which equips a person to read formulas and equations, straightforward prose, doggerel verse, and advertising signs. It does not equip one to read the language of metaphor, of paradox, of indirect analogy, of serious fancy in which the emotions and passions and half-believed ideas of human beings express themselves. To read great literature is to read men—their fears and motives, their needs and hopes. Every great novelist is a *Menschenkenner* who opens the hearts of others to us and helps us to read our own hearts as well. The intelligent study of literature should never directly aim to strengthen morals and improve manners. For its natural consequences are a delicacy of perception and an emotional tact that are defeated by preaching and didactic teaching.

A liberal education will impart an awareness of the amazing and precious complexity of human relationships. Since those relationships are violated more often out of insensitiveness than out of deliberate intent, whatever increases sensitiveness of perception and understanding humanizes life. Literature in all its forms is the great humanizing medium of life. It must therefore be representative of life; not only of past life but of our own; not only of our own culture but of different cultures.

6. An unfailing mark of philistinism in education is reference to the study of art and music as "the frills and fads" of schooling. Insofar as those who speak this way are not tone-deaf or color-blind, they are themselves products of a narrow education, unaware of the profound experiences which are uniquely bound up with the trained perception of color and form. There is no reason to believe that the capacity for the appreciation of art and music shows a markedly different curve of distribution from what is observable in the measurement of capacity of drawing inferences or recalling relevant information. A sufficient justification for making some study of art and music required in modern education is that it provides an unfailing source of delight in personal experience, a certain grace in living, and a variety of dimensions of meaning by which to interpret the world around us. This is a sufficient justification: there are others, quite subsidiary, related to the themes, the occasions, the history and backgrounds of the works studied. Perhaps one should add—although this expresses only a reasonable hope—that a community whose citizens have developed tastes would

not tolerate the stridency, the ugliness and squalor which assault us in our factories, our cities, and our countryside.

One of the reasons why the study of art and music has not received as much attention as it should by educators, particularly on the college level, is that instruction in these subjects often suffers from two opposite defects. Sometimes courses in art and music are given as if all students enrolled in them were planning a career as practicing artists or as professional *teachers* of the arts. Sometimes they are given as hours for passive enjoyment or relaxation in which the teacher does the performing or talking and in which there is no call upon the students to make an intelligent response.

The key-stress in courses in art and music should be *discrimination* and *interpretation,* rather than appreciation and cultivation. The latter can take care of themselves, when the student has learned to discriminate and interpret intelligently.

Briefly summarized: the answer to the question *What should we teach?* is selected materials from the fields of mathematics and the natural sciences; social studies, including history; language and literature; philosophy and logic; art and music. The knowledge imparted by such study should be acquired in such a way as to strengthen the skills of reading and writing, of thinking and imaginative interpretation, of criticism and evaluation.

Study Questions

1. What does Hook mean by "a liberal education"?
2. According to Hook, what are the chief components of a liberal education?
3. Would a democratic society be more likely to prosper if its citizens had received a liberal education?
4. How could a faculty ensure that each student who is graduated has mastered the essentials of a liberal education?

Discipline and Punish

MICHEL FOUCAULT

Michel Foucault (1926–1984) was a French philosopher and historian of ideas. He had a special interest in how reason can be used as an instrument of power. In this selection he draws an analogy between military organization and the structure of schools, in which teachers dominate the learning process and use exercises to enforce control.

Discipline and Punish by Michel Foucault. English Translation copyright © 1977 by Alan Sheridan (New York: Pantheon). Originally published in French as *Surveiller et Punir.* Copyright © 1975 by Editions Gallimard. Reprinted by permission of Georges Borchardt, Inc. for Editions Gallimard. The ellipses are the author's.

In 1667, the edict that set up the manufactory of the Gobelins[1] envisaged the organization of a school. Sixty scholarship children were to be chosen by the superintendent of royal buildings, entrusted for a time to a master whose task it would be to provide them with "upbringing and instruction," then apprenticed to the various master tapestry makers of the manufactory (who by virtue of this fact received compensation deducted from the pupils' scholarships); after six years' apprenticeship, four years of service and a qualifying examination, they were given the right to "set up and run a shop" in any town of the kingdom. We find here the characteristics of guild apprenticeship: the relation of dependence on the master that is both individual and total; the statutory duration of the training, which is concluded by a qualifying examination, but which is not broken down according to a precise programme; an overall exchange between the master who must give his knowledge and the apprentice who must offer his services, his assistance and often some payment. The form of domestic service is mixed with a transference of knowledge. In 1737, an edict organized a school of drawing for the apprentices of the Gobelins; it was not intended to replace the training given by the master workers, but to complement it. It involved a quite different arrangement of time. Two hours a day, except on Sundays and feast days, the pupils met in the school. A roll-call was taken, from a list on the wall; the absentees were noted down in a register. The school was divided into three classes. The first for those who had no notion of drawing; they were made to copy models, which were more or less difficult according to the abilities of each pupil. The second "for those who already have some principles," or who had passed through the first class; they had to reproduce pictures "at sight, without tracing," but considering only the drawing. In the third class, they learnt colouring and pastel drawing, and were introduced to the theory and practice of dyeing. The pupils performed individual tasks at regular intervals; each of these exercises, signed with the name of its author and date of execution, was handed in to the teacher; the best were rewarded; assembled together at the end of the year and compared, they made it possible to establish the progress, the present ability and the relative place of each pupil; it was then decided which of them could pass into the next class. A general book, kept by the teachers and their assistants, recorded from day to day the behaviour of the pupils and everything that happened in the school; it was periodically shown to an inspector (Gerspach, 1892).

The Gobelins school is only one example of an important phenomenon: the development, in the classical period, of a new technique for taking charge of the time of individual existences; for regulating the relations of time, bodies and forces; for assuring an accumulation of duration; and for turning to ever-increased profit or use the movement of passing time. How can one capitalize the time of individuals, accumulate it in each of them, in their bodies, in their forces or in their abilities, in a way that is susceptible of use and control? How can one organize profitable durations? The disciplines, which analyse space, break up and rearrange activities, must also be understood as machinery for adding up and capitalizing time. This was done in four ways, which emerge most clearly in military organization.

1. Divide duration into successive or parallel segments, each of which must end at a specific time. For example, isolate the period of training and the period of practice; do not mix the instruction of recruits and the exercise of veterans; open separate military schools for the armed service (in 1764, the creation of the École Militaire in Paris, in 1776 the creation of twelve schools in the provinces); recruit professional soldiers at the youngest possible age, take children, "have them adopted by the nation, and brought up in special schools" (Servan, J., 456); teach in turn posture, marching, the handling of weapons, shooting, and do not pass to another activity until the first has been completely mastered: "One of the principal mistakes is to

show a soldier every exercise at once" ("Regle-
ment de 1743 . . . "); in short, break down time
into separate and adjusted threads. 2. Organize
these threads according to an analytical plan—
successions of elements as simple as possible,
combining according to increasing complexity.
This presupposes that instruction should abandon the principle of analogical repetition. In the
sixteenth century, military exercise consisted
above all in copying all or part of the action, and
of generally increasing the soldier's skill or
strength; in the eighteenth century, the instruction of the "manual" followed the principle of
the "elementary" and not of the "exemplary":
simple gestures—the position of the fingers, the
bend of the leg, the movement of the arms—
basic elements for useful actions that also provide a general training in strength, skill, docility.
3. Finalize these temporal segments, decide on
how long each will last and conclude it with an
examination, which will have the triple function
of showing whether the subject has reached the
level required, of guaranteeing that each subject
undergoes the same apprenticeship and of dif-
ferentiating the abilities of each individual.
When the sergeants, corporals, etc. "entrusted
with the task of instructing the others, are of
the opinion that a particular soldier is ready to
pass into the first class, they will present him
first to the officers of their company, who will
carefully examine him; if they do not find him
sufficiently practised, they will refuse to admit
him; if, on the other hand, the man presented
seems to them to be ready, the said officers will
themselves propose him to the commanding officer of the regiment, who will see him if he
thinks it necessary, and will have him examined
by the senior officers. The slightest mistakes will
be enough to have him rejected, and no one will
be able to pass from the second class to the first
until he has undergone this first examination"
(*Instruction par l'exercice de l'infanterie*, 14 mai
1754). 4. Draw up series of series; lay down for
each individual, according to his level, his se-
niority, his rank, the exercises that are suited to
him; common exercises have a differing role and

each difference involves specific exercises. At the
end of each series, others begin, branch off and
subdivide in turn. Thus each individual is caught
up in a temporal series which specifically defines
his level or his rank. It is a disciplinary polyph-
ony of exercises: "Soldiers of the second class
will be exercised every morning by sergeants,
corporals, *anspessades*, lance-corporals. . . . The
lance-corporals will be exercised every Sunday
by the head of the section . . .; the corporals and
anspessades will be exercised every Tuesday afternoon by the sergeants and their company and
these in turn on the afternoons of every second,
twelfth and twenty-second day of each month
by senior officers" (*Instruction . . .*).

It is this disciplinary time that was gradually
imposed on pedagogical practice—specializing
the time of training and detaching it from the
adult time, from the time of mastery; arranging
different stages, separated from one another by
graded examinations; drawing up programmes,
each of which must take place during a particular
stage and which involves exercises of increasing
difficulty; qualifying individuals according to the
way in which they progress through these series.
For the "initiatory" time of traditional training
(an overall time, supervised by the master alone,
authorized by a single examination), disciplinary
time had substituted its multiple and progressive
series. A whole analytical pedagogy was being
formed, meticulous in its detail (it broke down
the subject being taught into its simplest elements, it hierarchized each stage of development
into small steps) and also very precocious in its
history (it largely anticipated the genetic analyses
of the *idéologues*, whose technical model it appears to have been). At the beginning of the eighteenth century, Demia suggested a division of the
process of learning to read into seven levels: the
first for those who are beginning to learn the letters, the second for those who are learning to
spell, the third for those who are learning to join
syllables together to make words, the fourth for
those who are reading Latin in sentences or from
punctuation to punctuation, the fifth for those
who are beginning to read French, the sixth for

the best readers, the seventh for those who can read manuscripts. But, where there are a great many pupils, further subdivisions would have to be introduced; the first class would comprise four streams: one for those who are learning the "simple letters" a second for those who are learning the "mixed" letters; a third for those who are learning the abbreviated letters (*â*, *ê* . . .); a fourth for those who are learning the double letters (*ff, ss, tt, st*). The second class would be divided into three streams: for those who "count each letter aloud before spelling the syllable, *D.O., DO*"; for those "who spell the most difficult syllables, such as *bant, brand, spinx,*" etc. (Demia, 19–20). Each stage in the combinatory of elements must be inscribed within a great temporal series, which is both a natural progress of the mind and a code for educative procedures.

The "seriation" of successive activities makes possible a whole investment of duration by power: the possibility of a detailed control and a regular intervention (of differentiation, correction, punishment, elimination) in each moment of time; the possibility of characterizing, and therefore of using individuals according to the level in the series that they are moving through; the possibility of accumulating time and activity, of rediscovering them, totalized and usable in a final result, which is the ultimate capacity of an individual. Temporal dispersal is brought together to produce a profit, thus mastering a duration that would otherwise elude one's grasp. Power is articulated directly onto time; it assures its control and guarantees its use.

The disciplinary methods reveal a linear time whose moments are integrated, one upon another, and which is orientated towards a terminal, stable point; in short, an "evolutive" time. But it must be recalled that, at the same moment, the administrative and economic techniques of control reveal a social time of a serial, orientated, cumulative type: the discovery of an evolution in terms of "progress." The disciplinary techniques reveal individual series: the discovery of an evolution in terms of "genesis." These two great "discoveries" of

the eighteenth century—the progress of societies and the geneses of individuals—were perhaps correlative with the new techniques of power, and more specifically, with a new way of administering time and making it useful, by segmentation, seriation, synthesis and totalization. A macro- and a micro-physics of power made possible, not the invention of history (it had long had no need of that), but the integration of a temporal, unitary, continuous, cumulative dimension in the exercise of controls and the practice of dominations. "Evolutive" historicity, as it was then constituted—and so profoundly that it is still self-evident for many today—is bound up with a mode of functioning of power. No doubt it is as if the "history-remembering" of the chronicles, genealogies, exploits, reigns and deeds had long been linked to a modality of power. With the new techniques of subjection, the "dynamics" of continuous evolutions tends to replace the "dynastics" of solemn events.

In any case, the small temporal continuum of individuality-genesis certainly seems to be, like the individuality-cell or the individuality-organism, an effect and an object of discipline. And, at the centre of this seriation of time, one finds a procedure that is, for it, what the drawing up of "tables" was for the distribution of individuals and cellular segmentation, or, again, what *"manoeuvre"* was for the economy of activities and organic control. This procedure is "exercise." Exercise is that technique by which one imposes on the body tasks that are both repetitive and different, but always graduated. By bending behaviour towards a terminal state, exercise makes possible a perpetual characterization of the individual either in relation to this term, in relation to other individuals, or in relation to a type of itinerary. It thus assures, in the form of continuity and constraint, a growth, an observation, a qualification. Before adopting this strictly disciplinary form, exercise had a long history: it is to be found in military, religious and university practices either as initiation ritual, preparatory ceremony, theatrical rehearsal or examination. Its linear, continuously progressive organization, its genetic development in time were, at least in the army and the school, introduced at a later date—and were no doubt of religious origin. In any case, the idea of an educational "programme" that would follow the child to the end of his schooling and which would involve from year to year, month to month, exercises of increasing complexity, first appeared, it seems, in a religious group, the Brothers of the Common Life (cf. Meir, 160 ff). Strongly inspired by Ruysbroek and Rhenish mysticism, they transposed certain of the spiritual techniques to education—and to the education not only of clerks, but also of magistrates and merchants: the theme of a perfection towards which the exemplary master guides the pupil became with them that of an authoritarian perfection of the pupils by the teacher; the ever-increasing rigorous exercises that the ascetic life proposed became tasks of increasing complexity that marked the gradual acquisition of knowledge and good behaviour; the striving of the whole community towards salvation became the collective, permanent competition of individuals being classified in relation to one another. Perhaps it was these procedures of community life and salvation that were the first nucleus of methods intended to produce individually characterized, but collectively useful aptitudes. In its mystical or ascetic form, exercise was a way of ordering earthly time for the conquest of salvation. It was gradually, in the history of the West, to change direction while preserving certain of its characteristics; it served to economize the time of life, to accumulate it in a useful form and to exercise power over men through the mediation of time arranged in this way. Exercise, having become an element in the political technology of the body and of duration, does not culminate in a beyond, but tends towards a subjection that has never reached its limit.

References

Demia, C., *Règlement pour les écoles de la ville de Lyon,* 1716.

Gerspach, E., *La Manufacture des Gobelins,* 1892.

Meir, G. Codina, *Aux sources de la pédagogie des Jésuites,* 1968.

"Règlement de 1743 pour l' infanterie prussienne," Arsenal, M.S. 4076.

Servan, J., *Le Soldat citoyen,* 1780.

Note

1. [A French family of dyers who also manufactured tapestry.—S.M.C.]

Study Questions

1. According to Foucault, in what ways is education treated as guild apprenticeship?
2. Is time management crucial to schools?
3. Are schools akin to military organizations?
4. Is self-discipline a form of discipline?

B. Affirmative Action

Proportional Representation

CELIA WOLF-DEVINE

Affirmative action has been a divisive issue in the United States for over fifty years. In one version, which I call "procedural affirmative action," the policy is noncontroversial, calling for the enactment of policies, such as open posting of employment opportunities, that aim to eradicate blatant discrimination. Yet another version of affirmative acton, which I call "preferential affirmative action," is highly controversial. It requires that steps be put in place to enhance inclusion of members of a particular race, sex, or ethnicity.

Note that preferential affirmative action has been defended on three grounds: (1) to offset past discrimination; (2) to counteract present unfairness; and (3) to achieve future equality. The first is often referred to as "compensation," the second "a level playing field," and the third "diversity." All three might be appropriate goals, but each requires a different justification and may call for a different remedy.

Even the concept of preference is ambiguous. Does it imply (1) showing preference among equally qualified candidates, (2) preferring a strong candidate to an even stronger one, (3) preferring a merely qualified candidate to a strongly qualified one, or (4) preferring a candidate who doesn't meet traditional qualifications because the qualifications themselves are suspect?

The authors of the next three selections defend different sides in the affirmative action debate. First, Celia Wolf-Devine, Professor Emerita of Philosophy at Stonehill College, argues that numbers alone do not prove discrimination.

I begin by asking a question, an affirmative answer to which seems presupposed by the current debate on affirmative action:[1] Is there necessarily something wrong if there is a low percentage of African Americans or women or Hispanics, et cetera, in the field of college teaching relative to their proportion in the population at large? Why is this a goal we should aim at? I do not mean to deny that women and racial and ethnic minorities have been victims of discrimination in academia (although this is by no means limited to blacks, Asians, Hispanics, and Native Americans—consider, for example, Polish, Lebanese, or Portuguese Americans) or that some discrimination still persists. Such discrimination is bad and should be eliminated; in fact, we ought to put more resources into enforcing antidiscrimination laws. My argument

Reprinted with minor omissions from *Affirmative Action and the University: A Philosophical Inquiry,* ed. Steven M. Cahn (Philadelphia: Temple University Press, 1993), by permission of the publisher.

here is that there is no reason to believe that proportional representation of minorities and women among the professoriate is a requirement of justice or that a situation where such proportional representation obtained would necessarily be better than one in which it did not.[2]

Arguments that might be advanced in favor of the claim that something is wrong if women and minorities are not proportionally represented fall into two general categories: those that take the existence of such statistical disparities to be evidence of discrimination or injustice, and those based on the value of diversity. These two types of arguments differ in that those based on the need for diversity would not prove that universities are required as a matter of justice to appoint more women and minorities, but merely that it would be educationally desirable were they to do so. But if it could be shown that the lack of proportional representation of minority groups among the professoriate either itself constituted an injustice or provided adequate evidence of the existence of ongoing injustice, then the case for involvement of the federal government to correct this becomes stronger.[3]

IS PROPORTIONAL REPRESENTATION A REQUIREMENT OF JUSTICE?

Does the lack of proportional representation of women and minorities among the professoriate constitute an injustice? Or is it necessarily evidence of discrimination or injustice of any sort? It would be evidence of injustice or discrimination only if it is reasonable to believe that, in the absence of discrimination and injustice, women and all racial and ethnic minorities would be proportionately represented in college teaching (and other professions). But *is* it reasonable to believe this?

The important issue here philosophically is where we place the burden of proof. Should we assume that the statistics reflect some sort of

discrimination or injustice unless we have evidence to the contrary? But why put the burden of proof here? While it is legitimate to put the burden of proof on the employer in cases where the proportion of women and minorities hired is radically lower than their proportion *in the applicant pool,* the case is totally different when we are comparing the proportion of women and minorities in the professoriate with their proportion in the population as a whole.

Looking first at racial and ethnic groups, there is no prima facie reason to suppose that members of different racial and ethnic minorities would be equally likely to want to go into the professoriate and, on the contrary, many reasons to expect that they would not. To the extent that ethnic and racial groups form at least partially self-contained communities (and they do), members of one community will value different sorts of character traits, encourage the acquisition of different skills, and have different ideas about what sorts of jobs carry the most prestige.[4] Most arguments in favor of affirmative action in fact suppose that racial and ethnic groups differ in these sorts of ways; if they did not, then bringing in a wider variety of such groups would not contribute to diversity.

In one culture, scientists might be particularly respected, while in another being a media personality might be viewed as the height of success. Sometimes traditional patterns in a culture predispose members toward certain professions, as the great respect for Torah scholars in Jewish culture fits very naturally with aspirations for careers as scholars or lawyers. Cultures that are highly verbal might be expected to produce more teachers than others. In addition, of course, as some members of a community go into a particular field, others aspire to go into it also since they already know something about it from their friends and relatives and have contacts in the field.[5]

So even if equal percentages of the members of all racial and ethnic groups might desire some sort of prestigious job, there is no reason to suppose that all of them would regard the same jobs as prestigious. Or to put the point more bluntly, not everyone would regard being a professor as prestigious. And there are special reasons why college teaching might be less attractive than other professions to those (for example, blacks and Hispanics) who are trying to struggle out of poverty. Due to its low salaries relative to the amount of training required, college teaching has long tended to attract people brought up in relatively secure financial conditions, plus a few other individuals who feel a strong calling to the intellectual life.

To put the dialogue about affirmative action in academia in the proper perspective, we need to keep in mind some background facts. Certainly there are some prestigious research institutions where professors make excellent salaries, and in business or technical fields professors can often make good money consulting and exercise some power in the larger society. But the salary of the average academic has not kept pace with salaries in other fields; nonacademics I meet are universally shocked to learn how little professors are paid. An associate professor I know is forced to teach an extra night course each term, to teach both summer sessions, and on top of that to sell suits at a men's store during the Christmas season in order to be able to support a wife and two children and to meet mortgage payments on a house in an area that is adequate but by no means fancy.

In addition, the social status of professors (particularly in the humanities) has declined significantly from what it was in the 1950s and 1960s. (And if affirmative action is stronger in academia than elsewhere, this might lower the status of professors still more, since they would be perceived as being appointed because of their sex or race.) These problems, together with a widespread loss of a sense of purpose among academics, have led to a lot of demoralization among faculty. Ambitious young members of minority groups may quite reasonably prefer careers in law, politics, industry, or the media. Indeed, the problem of how to attract bright young people of *any* racial or ethnic group into

college teaching is becoming increasingly severe. Even students who feel strongly drawn to the intellectual life are often deterred from pursuing academic careers by poor salaries and by what they hear about academic politics.

If I am right, then, one important reason why racial and ethnic minorities are not proportionately represented in the professoriate is because those who are in a position to acquire the credentials are going into other professions. Bright, ambitious members of such groups who have B.A.s often find careers in other areas more attractive than college teaching. This is partly a function of their cultures, which may not accord high prestige to professors relative to other professions, and partly a result of low salaries and demoralization among many (although certainly not all) professors. And in order to attract them into the professoriate, it is essential to begin by improving the situation of those already in the field in a number of ways (and not just salary, although that is important). We should then make it clear to minority members that they are genuinely welcome in academia and will receive fair consideration.

Another reason why racial and ethnic minorities are not proportionally represented in the professoriate is because large numbers of them have been deeply scarred by poverty (and often racism) and do not enter college. They are therefore not even in the running for becoming college teachers or for pursuing most careers with high status and pay. The difficulties involved in remedying this situation are massive, and the universities can play only a limited role. Universities could, for example, set up tutorial programs aimed at helping disadvantaged students (and staffed by faculty and student volunteers). Or they could offer scholarships for college and graduate school to talented disadvantaged students or have need-blind admissions if they can afford to do so. Since such programs are costly, government assistance would probably be necessary.

The big question that arises at this point is to what extent such remedial programs should be directed at racial and ethnic minorities. At this point I believe another background fact becomes relevant—one that is too often overlooked by supporters of affirmative action. During the Reagan years, American society underwent a marked polarization between rich and poor. We have, in fact, the most extreme polarization of any industrialized country (measured by the gap between the wealth of the upper fifth of society and that of the lower fifth). And it is arguable that affirmative action has contributed to this polarization (at least it has done nothing to prevent it), since those women and blacks who were in a position to take advantage of it (i.e., those who had suffered less discrimination) did so, leaving the really poor no better off and simply displacing other groups and pushing them down into poverty.[6]

The problem of the widening gap of rich and poor should be confronted directly, rather than gearing remedial programs too closely to race and ethnic group (as affirmative action does). In addition to making people more rather than less race conscious and generating resentments along racial and ethnic lines, such programs are not radical enough, because they lead people to think that by appointing middle-class blacks, Hispanics, or Asians that they have thereby really helped the poor.

The poor need direct assistance, and it is not only minority members who are poor. There are enormous numbers of white poor, particularly in rural areas of the South. Many ethnic groups are impoverished and have suffered discrimination at least as severe as that against Hispanics and Asians. The children of single mothers of all races and ethnic groups have been pushed down into severe poverty, and many blue-collar workers have been impoverished (e.g., small farmers or residents of the Minnesota Iron Range). Programs targeted at the economically disadvantaged should perhaps be supplemented by special compensatory programs aimed at blacks and Native Americans (since most Hispanics and Asians are recent immigrants, compensatory arguments do not carry the same force in their case). I do not here take a position on this thorny

issue, except to say that not all scholarships and special assistance programs should be earmarked for such groups, but a significant proportion should be awarded on the basis of merit and financial need alone.

The more poor people are brought up into the middle class, the more of them will obtain B.A.s and be in a position to consider college teaching as a career. We will still need to improve the situation of the professoriate if we are to be able to attract good Ph.D. candidates. But at least more people will have a chance to enter the profession, especially if graduate school scholarships are available to talented students who need them. The poor who are not upwardly mobile (e.g., the retired, the chronically ill, the mentally retarded, etc.) will still need direct financial and medical assistance.

The situation of women in academia is somewhat different from that of ethnic and racial minorities, in that they are closer to being proportionally represented, at least in the humanities, although they tend still to be absent from some scientific and technical fields and from the most prestigious positions. Does this prove they are being discriminated against? Certainly in some cases they have been and still are discriminated against (especially in promotion and pay), and these abuses should be corrected. But here also the statistics alone do not establish discrimination. Their own choices to spend more time with their children may account for their failure to advance as far or as quickly as their male colleagues and for the fact that they hold part-time positions more frequently. Certainly not all women make these sorts of choices, but enough do to affect the statistics. (It could, of course, be argued to be unjust that women take on a larger share of child care, but we should beware of paternalistically telling people what choices they ought to make.)

In order to establish the presence of injustice or discrimination, we need to know more about the actual preferences of the women in question, and not just adopt a bureaucratic approach of trying to get the numbers to come out right.

Suppose an academic couple who wish to combine career and family decide between themselves that he will work full time and she will work part time in order to spend time with the children. Then suppose that due to affirmative action he is unable to get a full-time job and she is forced to take full-time work to support the family. The statistics may look better, but both people are less happy than they would have been without affirmative action.

Proportional representation of women and of blacks, Hispanics, Native Americans, and Asians in the professoriate, then, is not a requirement of justice, and a situation where such proportional representation is present is not necessarily more just than one where it is not—for example, if it was obtained by overriding the preferences of those concerned without some reason other than a desire to get the statistics to come out right.[7] Furthermore, a society where such proportional representation was present along with a vast and unbridgeable gap between rich and poor would be less just than one with a more equitable distribution of wealth and opportunities for advancement but which lacked proportional representation of women and minorities in some professions.

PROMOTING DIVERSITY

Affirmative action is often defended as a means to greater diversity on college faculties, and a faculty that does not have proportional representation of women and minorities is regarded as not diverse enough. Diversity, unfortunately, has become something of a buzzword these days, and it is necessary to give thought to what sorts of diversity should be promoted and why. And this requires some reflection about what the purposes of the university are. Diversity of opinion is not enough, but neither is diversity of methodology. Not all methodologies deserve representation. Consider, for example, astrology, or the systematic vilification of one's opponents.

If one agrees that encouraging intelligent dialogue about important issues is one of the purposes of the university (and I do), then this has at least some implications for the sort of diversity we want. If dialogue is of central importance, then it is desirable to have intellectual diversity. But limitless intellectual diversity is not good; the value of diversity must be weighed against the value of community. Certainly, there can be communities that are too ingrown and homogenous. If a psychology department appoints only behaviorists, then students are deprived of exposure to other quite legitimate traditions of thought within their discipline. And the same is true if an economics department appoints only followers of Milton Friedman, or a philosophy department appoints only Thomists or only phenomenologists. But on the other hand, too much diversity leads to the breakdown of communication between groups. If this occurs, faculty become unable to talk with each other and work within totally different conceptual frameworks, making no attempts to respond to positions other than their own. Students, then, tend to become hopelessly confused, give up even trying to develop coherent beliefs of their own, and retreat into just giving each professor what he or she wants. Maintaining community is, thus, just as important for education as introducing intellectual diversity.

Suppose, then, we are agreed that intellectual diversity, per se, is not simply a good to be maximized (and in real life, no one, not even the defenders of affirmative action, believes in the value of limitless diversity); we then must specify what sorts of diversity will contribute to stimulating intelligent dialogue and learning on college campuses. And I see no reason why proportional representation of groups now officially recognized as protected minorities should be expected to produce the right sort of diversity. First of all, diversity of skin color is quite consistent with total ideological conformity and therefore need not conduce to dialogue at all.

Furthermore, as people like Stephen Carter have been pointing out lately, we ought not to suppose that because a person is black or Hispanic that he or she will have some particular set of beliefs or espouse a particular methodology.[8] This expectation is a form of racial stereotyping and as such is demeaning to the person. Pressures toward ideological conformity among members of minority groups are increased by this sort of dishonest attempt to smuggle in one's ideological agendas under the guise of affirmative action. A Hispanic who is a Republican is no less a Hispanic, and a woman who is not a feminist is no less a woman.

There is, then, no good reason to suppose that proportional representation of the minority groups now officially recognized will yield the right sort of intellectual diversity. And the same sorts of arguments developed above could be applied to cultural diversity as well as to intellectual diversity. People from the same cultural background share common prereflective attitudes, patterns of feeling and imagination, ways of talking, and styles of behavior. But although it is educationally valuable for students to be exposed to people from different cultures, limitless cultural diversity is not a good thing (for the same reasons that limitless intellectual diversity is not), and skin color is not a reliable guide to culture. An enormous amount of cultural diversity exists, for example, among blacks and Hispanics. Poor rural Southern blacks, for example, may be culturally more similar to poor rural Southern whites than they are to Northern middle-class urban blacks.

In short, one cannot generate the right sort of diversity (intellectual or cultural) by simply pursuing neatly measurable goals like proportional representation of women, blacks, Hispanics, Asians, and Native Americans. In addition, the sort of diversity needed at a given school will itself be a function of a number of factors, such as the character of the faculty already there, the student body, and the sorts of vocations for which students are preparing. A school preparing students for careers in international business or diplomacy might find that the sort of diversity introduced by appointing foreign nationals to their faculty is particularly valuable, for example. These sorts of judgments involve a great many complex considerations and cannot be made mechanically by trying to get statistics to meet some target percentages (comforting though it would be if things were so simple).

NOTES

1. By affirmative action, I mean preferential treatment and not just things like announcing openings and encouraging women and minorities to apply. And tie-breaking affirmative action might, I believe, be justified in some cases on the basis of the role model argument. The reason the role model argument does not support preferential appointments in order to attain proportional representation is that a minority member can only function as a model for excellence if he or she is perceived as having been appointed because of qualifications rather than race or sex. One really good minority faculty member is a more effective and inspiring role model than ten mediocre ones.

2. Note, again, that I am speaking of proportional representation relative to their percentage in the population at large.

3. I do not consider here compensatory arguments. That institutions should make compensation to individuals they have discriminated against is self-evident, but problems arise when those receiving compensation are not the persons who were wronged. For example, how are older women who have suffered discrimination in any way made whole from their injury by the appointment of younger women unrelated to them? In any case, there is no clear way compensatory arguments could tell us what proportion of minority groups should be on university faculties. How can we tell what proportion of Hispanics would have become professors in the absence of discrimination? Or, in the absence of slavery, that the number of blacks teaching in American universities would be no higher than it is now. An additional problem with compensatory arguments is that, like redistributive arguments, they treat teaching appointments as plums to be distributed instead of as focusing on the responsibilities that such positions involve.

4. Perhaps instead of conceptualizing society as a pyramid with one top, we should think of it as a group

of hills with many different peaks; people may choose different paths to wealth, power, and prestige.

5. This is called the "cousinhood advantage." While in academia it operates in favor of WASPs and Jews, this is not the case everywhere. Although building contractors frequently make very good money, a WASP would be at a great disadvantage in this field in many parts of the country where the building trades are heavily dominated by certain ethnic groups.

6. See Kevin Phillips, *The Politics of Rich and Poor* (New York: Random House, 1990), pp. 18, 203, 207.

7. People should, I believe, be free to enter the occupation of their choice (subject, of course, to certain broad constraints based on the common good—such as that if everyone wanted to be lawyers and no one wanted to grow crops, some adjustments would be necessary) and make other career decisions as they see fit, even though we might think (rightly even) that it would be better for them to choose otherwise.

8. Stephen Carter, *Reflections of an Affirmative Action Baby* (New York: Basic Books, 1991).

Study Questions

1. If few women or members of a racial, religious, or ethnic group enter a particular profession, does that circumstance prove that the members of that profession are guilty of discrimination?
2. What does Wolf-Devine mean by "intellectual diversity"?
3. Which types of diversity are most important?
4. How would we know when diversity of a particular sort has been achieved?

Facing Facts and Responsibilities

KAREN HANSON

Karen Hanson is Professor of Philosophy at the University of Minnesota. She defends preferential treatment for women and minority group men, while admitting that such a system may contain flaws that need correction.

. . . [O]ne of the continuing intellectual problems in the debates about affirmative action is determining where the burden of proof should lie. If women and minority group men are not employed in academia in numbers and at levels proportional to their numbers in qualified applicant pools, are we entitled to assume the likelihood of unfair hiring and promotion practices and to insist that opponents of affirmative action prove opportunities really are equal for all? Or should we suppose that all racial and gender biases must be identifiable, so that, absent any specification of a problematic practice, we are entitled to rely on the fairness of sex-blind and race-blind employment procedures? If we admit that there has been racial and sexual injustice in the past, and we want to give some special treatment to those who have been disadvantaged, is it reasonable to extend this special treatment to all members of a racial group and to all women? Or should we proceed to attend immediately to disadvantage, formulating race- and sex-neutral policies that respond more directly to the specific disadvantages that are the ground of our concern? Although I grant that no general formula can be given concerning where, in discussion of actual circumstances and proposed policies, the burden of proof must lie, it seems to me that we should be inclined to doubt equality of opportunity and inclined to think race and sex are relevant categories to attempted amelioration. This inclination may be more widely shared if we begin our discussion of affirmative action only after open reflection on a couple of very basic, very general, very simple questions: Do we think our society, as a whole, has eliminated all traces of racism and sexism? And do we take the academy—and ourselves, as members of the academy—to be isolated from, or insulated against, the practices and institutions of the larger society?

I do not think we can responsibly deny that racism and sexism are still very much a part of American life; and, once we admit that, it becomes difficult to insist that we must always begin in a race-neutral and sex-neutral fashion as we try to attend to the "disadvantages" of some members of our society. An important part of the evidence of continuing racism and sexism is economic, but we must not reduce these problems to their economic markers and associated deprivations. An African American boy whose parents can afford to send him to a fine private prep school will still be exposed, throughout his life, to vicious racial epithets. As a young man, even after he has completed college and graduate school and has begun a promising professional career, he may not be able to jog in old clothes through an affluent white neighborhood without attracting undue attention and unpleasant suspicion. A young girl's interest in science may be encouraged and supported by her family, and they may, when the time comes, pay her tuition to, say, MIT. But she will grow up in a society rife with special contests for women only—those, for example, where young women parade about in swimsuits and evening gowns, seeking appearance points from their judges, and where, perhaps in quirky response to feminist criticism, more points can be earned for the appearance of "poise." She will notice, with or without rueful hilarity, that the events themselves are now often dubbed "scholarship pageants." And however our young woman finances her years at MIT, she may still be reasonably reluctant, as her male colleagues are not, to walk alone to the library at night. . . .

Thus . . . I find untenable the suggestion that we can address the injustices of racism and sexism without taking special account of race and sex. Ethnicity and gender play important roles in the social experience of every American, and racism and sexism are special, distinctive difficulties for all women and all members of some minority groups, whether or not there is, in an individual case, economic deprivation as well. This of course does not mean that every African American male and every woman has suffered more or had to overcome more in life than any white male. It does mean, however, that it is inappropriate to insist on a common category of generic "disadvantages" in our initial consideration of and responses to the problems of racism and sexism. The distinctiveness of racism and sexism also suggests that it may simply be a red herring to note, in these discussions, that many white men have had to suffer and overcome economic and other disadvantages. There are indeed other structural injustices in our society—as well as plain individual misfortunes—and perhaps there should be, from the academy, an institutional response to these problems. But if the topic on the table is racism and sexism, and the question being pursued is whether the academy should use any form of affirmative action to attack *these* injustices, we do not show that it should not by noting that the world may already contain other injustices as well.

The adversion to other injustices would not be irrelevant if it could be shown that all forms of affirmative action must exacerbate these other standing problems. It is, however, exceedingly unlikely that such a demonstration could ever be made. What unbreakable link could there possibly be between attempting to improve the lot of women and minority group men and positively worsening the condition of, say, economically exploited white males? That these groups may sometimes be pitted against one another is one thing. It would be quite a different matter to show that in all social and economic arrangements these groups' fortunes must be inversely related. In fact, the usual worry about other injustices is rather different. The concern is that affirmative action may generate new injustices. White males, especially young white males, may suddenly be deprived of equal opportunity and fair treatment; and women and minority group males may be freshly stigmatized by being treated once again in terms of group identity and as if they were in need of special allowances, help, or protection. Raising these possibilities of injustice opens wider questions about the conditions for equal opportunity and about the nature of fair treatment, and we may once again be barred from progress by disagreements about the appropriate location of the burden of proof.

While I do not deny that there could be policies of preferential treatment for women and minorities that would be unjust to white men and harmful to the academy, and I do not deny there could be affirmative action procedures that would treat white men unfairly, it seems to me that we should be able, in each such case, to identify precisely the elements we judge unjust, harmful, or unfair. (Are white men's applications being solicited but never read or taken seriously? Are men with demonstrably superior qualifications being passed over in favor of

women and minority group males lacking even minimal credentials?) We do not, however, need such specific worries to feel intellectually respectable anxiety about the extent to which our employment and promotion practices provide fair opportunity for women and racial minorities. To arouse that anxiety we should, I suggest, ask ourselves the second of my two very general questions: Is the academy—and are we, as members of the academy—untouched by the sexism and racism pervading the surrounding society?

What could be the ground of the requisite confidence that we—and all our colleagues on hiring and promotion committees—have escaped the pernicious social influences that maintain racism and sexism? We might want to insist that our disciplinary training and our allegiance to a meritocratic academy force judgments free of racist and sexist taints. But the fact that the academy has in the past undeniably practiced unfair discrimination and the fact that many academic disciplines have in the past undeniably supplied specious theoretical underpinnings for racism and sexism should give us pause. Are the social and economic pressures on the academy—and the psychological pressures on its inhabitants—entirely different from those at play in the larger society?

The academy's reaction to the infusion of women and minorities into its ranks has not been dissimilar to the reaction to integration elsewhere in the world of work. There has been, from some quarters, a begrudging attitude and a diffuse sense that white males are being denied fair treatment and equal opportunity. Does anything beyond an unwarranted sense of entitlement stand behind this sense? . . .

A bit of distemper should be expected. If a pie once enjoyed by our group alone now must be shared with individuals from groups formerly denied a piece, then unless we can make a bigger pie, some of us are going to get less than before or none at all. Even if we are now making an equitable distribution, if the field of distribution has been enlarged, the expectations of individuals in the group with a once exclusive claim will have to be lowered. Is this all that has happened with extant policies of affirmative action? Perhaps not, but when we have seen the morally indefensible resistance to integration in various other segments of the work world, can we simply assume that all academic uneasiness is a product of sound reasoning?

Whether or not we are willing to entertain the idea of an academic parallel to the meanly self-interested opposition to integration in other sections of society, we should attend not only to the similarities between the academy and other institutions but also to the articulation of our own institution with others. Even if we cherish some ideal of an ivory tower, we must recognize that the denizens of the tower in fact live in ordinary communities and in ordinary families; that work done in the tower affects the nation and the world; that the tower and its staff are visible to those outside it. Even if we could be certain that the hiring and promotion procedures within academia were fair and untinged by racism and sexism, if conditions outside the tower clearly tend to impede participation by women and minority group males, should we rest content that we have done our bit for equal opportunity? . . . Our institutional self-reflection cannot be undertaken from a perspective wholly within our institution, and our reflection on society is not from a point outside our society. Facing the fact that the professoriate is mainly white and male, we may show some proper respect for individual autonomy when we explain this profile by alluding to the "different choices" made and "alternative career paths" taken by women and minority group males. But it is a shallow morality and a faulty analysis that portrays these "different choices" as made, the "alternative paths" as taken, in circumstances unrelated to the legacy and the continuing existence of racism and sexism.

Insofar as we want to end racism and sexism and insofar as we value academia and believe in the social and personal importance of our enterprise, we should want to see a fair proportion of women and minority group males participating in our profession. It is not just the content of our courses and our research results but also the structure of our institution that teaches lessons to our students and to the wider society. Until recently, one of the lessons we taught was that higher education is conducted mostly by white men, that the professionals who are equipped to train our society's professionals are mostly white men, that the keepers and extenders of a significant portion of our society's intellectual tradition and activity are mostly white men. When an argument for affirmative action adverts to the value of diversity within academia, the rationale need not be only the assumption that women and minority group men are likely to bring fresh and different perspectives to the academy's search for truth. The idea may also be that our society now has a stale perspective *on* women and minority group males and that the visible faculty diversity encouraged by policies of affirmative action could be properly edifying.

The haste with which opponents of affirmative action contend that what will be visible is a stigma on all women and minority faculty, the quick assurance that affirmative action hiring will brand as inferior the women and minority males thus hired, should provoke a further moment of institutional and personal self-reflection. If we have granted that members of these groups are, in our society, already stigmatized by sexism and racism, what, exactly, do we think will be added by our proposed procedures? Are we sure that we are, in our claims about stigmatization, doing more than expressing our resolve not to see women and minority males as full members of the academy? For most of the life of American higher education, white men have been hired to the faculty not through the fairest and most open procedures but through friendships and old school ties. Prestigious all-male colleges have had special "legacy" admissions, and family connections have meant more than individual merit. Did these practices ever stigmatize all white males? Did they even cast general doubt on the competence of the specific white males who were their specific beneficiaries?

I raise these questions not to suggest that we should, for the sake of a crude balance, replace one flawed system with another. I suggest instead that, as we take up the issue of whether there are genuine flaws in various policies of affirmative action, as we consider the need for affirmative action at all, we ask ourselves again: Are we sure that we—in our individual consciousnesses and judgments and in the academy as a whole—have left behind the unfairness of a racist, sexist past?

Study Questions

1. What does Hanson mean by "the burden of proof"?
2. Do preferential appointments help to overcome prejudice?
3. Who else besides women and minority group men suffer from what Hanson refers to as "structural injustices in our society"?
4. Would Hanson approve passing over candidates for faculty positions with "demonstrably superior qualifications" in favor of others who are unanimously believed to lack such qualifications?

What Good Am I?

LAURENCE THOMAS

Laurence Thomas is Professor of Philosophy and of Political Science at Syracuse University. He explains why he believes in the importance of appointing women and members of minorities to college and university faculties. He suggests that their absence results from the insincerity of those who talk about equality but fail to act in accord with this ideal.

What good am I as a black professor? The raging debate over affirmative action surely invites me to ask this searching question of myself, just as it must invite those belonging to other so-called suspect categories to ask it of themselves. If knowledge is color blind, why should it matter whether the face in front of the classroom is a European white, a Hispanic, an Asian, and so on? Why should it matter whether the person is female or male?

One of the most well-known arguments for affirmative action is the role-model argument. It is also the argument that I think is the least satisfactory—not because women and minorities do not need role models—everyone does—but because as the argument is often presented, it comes dangerously close to implying that about the only thing a black, for instance, can teach a white is how not to be a racist. Well, I think better of myself than that. And I hope that all women and minorities feel the same about themsleves. . . .

But even if the role-model argument were acceptable in some version or the other, affirmative action would still seem unsavory, as the implicit assumption about those hired as affirmative action appointments is that they are less qualified than those who are not. For, so the argument goes, the practice would be unnecessary if, in the first place, affirmative action appointees were the most qualified for the position, since they would be hired by virtue of their merits. I call this the counterfactual argument from qualifications.

Now, while I do not want to say much about it, this argument has always struck me as extremely odd. In a morally perfect world, it is no doubt true that if women and minorities were the most qualified they would be hired by virtue of their merits. But this truth tells me nothing about how things are in this world. It does not show that biases built up over decades and centuries do not operate in the favor of, say, white males over nonwhite males. It is as if one argued against feeding the starving simply on the grounds that in a morally perfect world starvation would not exist. Perhaps it would not. But this is no argument against feeding the starving now.

It would be one thing if those who advance the counterfactual argument from qualifications addressed the issue of built-up biases that operate against women and minorities. Then I could perhaps suppose that they are arguing in good faith. But for them to ignore these built-up biases in the name of an ideal world is sheer hypocrisy. It is to confuse what the ideal should be with the steps that should be taken to get there. Sometimes the steps are very simple or, in any case, purely procedural: instead of *A,* do *B*; or

perform a series of well-defined steps that guarantee the outcome. Not so with nonbiased hiring, however, since what is involved is a change in attitude and feelings—not even merely a change in belief. After all, it is possible to believe something quite sincerely and yet not have the emotional wherewithal to act in accordance with that belief. . . .

The philosophical debate over affirmative action has stalled . . . because so many who oppose it, and some who do not, are unwilling to acknowledge the fact that sincere belief in equality does not entail a corresponding change in attitude and feelings in day-to-day interactions with women and minorities. Specifically, sincere belief does not eradicate residual and, thus, unintentional sexist and racist attitudes.[1] So, joviality among minorities may be taken by whites as the absence of intellectual depth or sincerity on the part of those minorities, since such behavior is presumed to be uncommon among high-minded intellectual whites. Similarly, it is a liability for academic women to be too fashionable in their attire, since fashionably attired women are often taken by men as aiming to be seductive.

Lest there be any misunderstanding, nothing I have said entails that unqualified women and minorities should be hired. I take it to be obvious, though, that whether someone is the best qualified is often a judgment call. On the other hand, what I have as much as said is that there are built-up biases in the hiring process that disfavor women and minorities and need to be corrected. I think of it as rather on the order of correcting for unfavorable moral headwinds. It is possible to be committed to gender and racial equality and yet live a life in which residual, and thus unintentional, sexism and racism operate to varying degrees of explicitness.

I want to return now to the question with which I began this essay: What good am I as a black professor? I want to answer this question because, insofar as our aim is a just society, I think it is extremely important to see the way in which it does matter that the person in front of the class is not always a white male, notwithstanding the truth that knowledge, itself, is color blind.

Teaching is not just about transmitting knowledge. If it were, then students could simply read books and professors could simply pass out tapes or lecture notes. Like it or not, teachers are the object of intense emotions and feelings on the part of students [who are] solicitous of faculty approval and affirmation. Thus, teaching is very much about intellectual affirmation; and there can be no such affirmation of the student by the mentor in the absence of deep trust between them, be the setting elementary or graduate school. Without this trust, a mentor's praise will ring empty; constructive criticism will seem mean spirited; and advice will be poorly received, if sought after at all. A student needs to be confident that he can make a mistake before the professor without being regarded as stupid in the professor's eyes and that the professor is interested in seeing beyond his weaknesses to his strengths. Otherwise, the student's interactions with the professor will be plagued by uncertainty; and that uncertainty will fuel the self-doubts of the student.

Now, the position that I should like to defend, however, is not that only women can trust women, only minorities can trust minorities, and only whites can trust whites. That surely is not what we want. Still, it must be acknowledged, first of all, that racism and sexism have very often been a bar to such trust between mentor and student, when the professor has been a white male and the student has been either a woman or a member of a minority group. Of course, trust between mentor and student is not easy to come by in any case. This, though, is compatible with women and minorities having even greater problems if the professor is a white male.

Sometimes a woman professor will be necessary if a woman student is to feel the trust of a mentor that makes intellectual affirmation possible; sometimes a minority professor will be necessary for a minority student; indeed, sometimes a white professor will be necessary for a white student. (Suppose the white student is from a very sexist and racist part of the United States, and it takes a white professor to undo the student's biases.)

Significantly, though, in an academy where there is gender and racial diversity among the faculty, that diversity alone gives a woman or minority student the hope that intellectual affirmation is possible. This is so even if the student's mentor should turn out to be a white male. For part of what secures our conviction that we are living in a just society is not merely that we experience justice, but that we see justice around us. A diverse faculty serves precisely this end in terms of women and minority students believing that it is possible for them to have an intellectually affirming mentor relationship with a faculty member regardless of the faculty's gender or race.

Naturally, there are some women and minority students who will achieve no matter what the environment. Harriet Jacobs and Frederick Douglass were slaves who went on to accomplish more than many of us will who have never seen the chains of slavery. Neither, though, would have thought their success a reason to leave slavery intact. Likewise, the fact that there are some women and minorities who will prevail in spite of the obstacles is no reason to leave the status quo in place.

There is another part of the argument. Where there is intellectual affirmation, there is also gratitude. When a student finds that affirmation in a faculty member, a bond is formed, anchored in the student's gratitude, that can weather almost anything. Without such ties there could be no "ole boy" network—a factor that is not about racism, but a kind of social interaction running its emotional course. When women and minority faculty play an intellectually affirming role in the lives of white male students, such faculty undermine a nonracist and nonsexist pattern of emotional feelings that has unwittingly served the sexist and racist end of passing the intellectual mantle from white male to white male. For what we want, surely, is not just blacks passing the mantle to blacks, women to women, and white males to white males, but a world in which it is possible for all to see one another as proper recipients of the intellectual mantle. Nothing serves this end better than the gratitude between mentor and student that often enough ranges over differences between gender and race or both.

Ideally, my discussion of trust, intellectual affirmation, and gratitude should have been supplemented with a discussion of nonverbal behavior. For it seems to me that what has been ignored . . . is the way in which judgments are communicated not simply by what is said but by a vast array of nonverbal behavior. Again, a verbal and sincere commitment to equality, without the relevant change in emotions and feelings, will invariably leave nonverbal behavior intact. Mere voice intonation and flow of speech can be a dead giveaway that the listener does not expect much of substance to come from the speaker. Anyone who doubts this should just remind her- or himself that it is a commonplace to remark to someone over the phone that he sounds tired or "down" or distracted, where the basis for this judgment, obviously, can only be how the individual sounds. One can get the clear sense that one called at the wrong time just by the way in which the other person responds or gets involved in the conversation. So, ironically, there is a sense in which it can be easier to convince ourselves that we are committed to gender and racial equality than it is to convince a woman or a minority person, for the latter see and experience our nonverbal behavior in a way that we ourselves do not. Specifically, it so often happens that a woman or minority can see that a person's nonverbal behavior belies their verbal support of gender and racial equality in faculty hiring—an interruption here, or an all-too-quick dismissal of a remark there. And this is to say nothing of the ways in which the oppressor often seems to know better than the victim how the victim is affected by the oppression that permeates her or his life, an arrogance that is communicated in myriad ways. This is not the place,

though, to address the topic of social justice and nonverbal behavior.[2]

Before moving on let me consider an objection to my view. No doubt some will balk at the very idea of women and minority faculty intellectually affirming white male students. But this is just so much nonsense on the part of those [who are] balking. For I have drawn attention to a most powerful force in the lives of all individuals, namely, trust and gratitude; and I have indicated that just as these feelings have unwittingly served racist and sexist ends, they can serve ends that are morally laudable. Furthermore, I have rejected the idea, often implicit in the role-model argument, that women and minority faculty are only good for their own kind. What is more, the position I have advocated is not one of subservience in the least, as I have spoken of an affirming role that underwrites an often unshakable debt of gratitude.

So, to return to the question with which I began this essay: I matter as a black professor and so do women and minority faculty generally, because collectively, if not in each individual case, we represent the hope, sometimes in a very personal way, that the university is an environment where the trust that gives rise to intellectual affirmation and the accompanying gratitude is possible for all, and between all peoples. Nothing short of the reality of diversity can permanently anchor this hope for ourselves and posterity. . . .

I do not advocate the representation of given viewpoints or the position that the ethnic and gender composition of faculty members should be proportional to their numbers in society. The former is absurd because it is a mistake to insist that points of view are either gender- or color-coded. The latter is absurd because it would actually entail getting rid of some faculty, since the percentage of Jews in the academy far exceeds their percentage in the population. If one day this should come to be true of blacks or Hispanics, they in turn would be fair game. . . .

[T]he continued absence of any diversity whatsoever draws attention to itself. My earlier remarks about nonverbal behavior taken in conjunction with my observations about trust, affirmation, and gratitude are especially apropos here. The complete absence of diversity tells departments more about themselves than no doubt they are prepared to acknowledge.

I would like to conclude with a concrete illustration of the way in which trust and gratitude can make a difference in the academy. As everyone knows, being cited affirmatively is an important indication of professional success. Now, who gets cited is not just a matter of what is true and good. On the contrary, students generally cite the works of their mentors and the work of others introduced to them by their mentors; and, on the other hand, mentors generally cite the work of those students of theirs for whom they have provided considerable intellectual affirmation. Sexism and racism have often been obstacles to faculty believing that women and minorities can be proper objects of full intellectual affirmation. It has also contributed to the absence of women and minority faculty which, in turn, has made it well-nigh impossible for white male students to feel an intellectual debt of gratitude to women and minority faculty. Their presence in the academy cannot help but bring about a change with regard to so simple a matter as patterns of citation, the professional ripple effect of which will be significant beyond many of our wildest dreams.

If social justice were just a matter of saying or writing the correct words, then equality would have long ago been a *fait accompli* in the academy. For I barely know anyone who is a faculty member who has not bemoaned the absence of minorities and women in the academy, albeit to varying degrees. So, I conclude with a very direct question: Is it really possible that so many faculty could be so concerned that women and minorities should flourish in the academy, and yet so few do? You will have to forgive me for not believing that it is. For as any good Kantian knows, one cannot consistently will an end without also willing the means to that end. Onora O'Neill writes, "Willing, after all, is not just a matter of wishing that something were the case, but involves committing oneself to doing something to bring that situation about when opportunity is there and recognized. Kant expressed this point by insisting that rationality requires that whoever wills some end wills the necessary means insofar as these are available."[3] If Kant is right, then much hand-wringing talk about social equality for women and minorities can only be judged insincere.

Notes

1. For a most illuminating discussion along this line, see Adrian M. S. Piper's very important essay, "Higher-Order Discrimination," in Owen Flanagan and Amelie Oksenberg Rorty, eds., *Identity, Character, and Morality: Essays in Moral Psychology* (Cambridge, MA: MIT Press, 1990).

2. For an attempt, see my "Moral Deference," *Philosophical Forum* 24, no. 1–3 (1992–1993): pp. 233–50.

3. Onora O'Neill, *Constructions of Reason: Explorations of Kant's Practical Philosophy* (Cambridge University Press, 1989), p. 90.

Study Questions

1. What is the role-model argument?
2. What does Thomas mean by "unintentional sexist and racist attitudes"?
3. According to Thomas, does an effective mentor need to be of the same race or sex as the student?
4. Do Thomas's arguments in favor of appointing women and minorities also imply the importance of adding members of any other specific groups to the faculty?

C.   Sexism, Racism, and Rights

Sexism

MARILYN FRYE

Marilyn Frye is Professor Emerita of Philosophy at Michigan State University. She argues that sex-identification intrudes into every moment of our lives and discourse. Thus to resist sexism requires undermining social and political structures and revising ourselves.

The first philosophical project I undertook as a feminist was that of trying to say carefully and persuasively what sexism is, and what it is for someone, some institution or some act to be sexist. This project was pressed on me with considerable urgency because, like most women coming to a feminist perception of themselves and the world, I was seeing sexism everywhere and trying to make it perceptible to others. I would point out, complain and criticize, but most frequently my friends and colleagues would not see that what I declared to be sexist was sexist, or at all objectionable.

As the critic and as the initiator of the topic, I was the one on whom the burden of proof fell—it was I who had to explain and convince. Teaching philosophy had already taught me that people cannot be persuaded of things they are not ready to be persuaded of; there are certain complexes of will and prior experience which will inevitably block persuasion, no matter the merits of the case presented. I knew that even if I could explain fully and clearly what I was saying when I called something sexist, I would not necessarily be able to convince various others of the correctness of this claim. But what

troubled me enormously was that I could not explain it in any way which satisfied *me*. It is this sort of moral and intellectual frustration which, in my case at least, always generates philosophy.

The following was the product of my first attempt to state clearly and explicitly what sexism is:

> The term 'sexist' in its core and perhaps most fundamental meaning is a term which characterizes anything whatever which creates, constitutes, promotes or exploits any irrelevant or impertinent marking of the distinction between the sexes.[1]

When I composed this statement, I was thinking of the myriads of instances in which persons of the two sexes are treated differently, or behave differently, but where nothing in the real differences between females and males justifies or explains the difference of treatment or behavior. I was thinking, for instance, of the tracking of boys into Shop and girls into Home Ec, where one can see nothing about boys or girls considered in themselves which seems to connect essentially with the distinction between wrenches and eggbeaters. I was thinking also of sex discrimination in employment—cases where someone otherwise apparently qualified for a job is not hired because she is a woman. But when I tried to put this definition of 'sexist' to use, it did not stand the test.

Consider this case: If a company is hiring a supervisor who will supervise a group of male workers who have always worked for male supervisors, it can scarcely be denied that the sex of a candidate for the job is relevant to the candidate's prospects of moving smoothly and successfully into an effective working relationship with the supervisees (though the point is usually exaggerated by those looking for excuses not to hire women). Relevance is an intrasystematic thing. The patterns of behavior, attitude and custom within which a process goes on determine what is relevant to what in matters of describing, predicting or evaluating. In the case at hand, the workers' attitudes and the surrounding customs of the culture make a difference to how they interact with their supervisor and, in particular, *make* the sex of the supervisor a relevant factor in predicting how things will work out. So then, if the company hires a man, in preference to a more experienced and knowledgeable woman, can we explain our objection to the decision by saying it involved distinguishing on the basis of sex when sex is irrelevant to the ability to do the job? No: sex is relevant here.

So, what did I mean to say about 'sexist'? I was thinking that in a case of a candidate for a supervisory job, the reproductive capacity of the candidate has nothing to do with that person's knowing what needs to be done and being able to give properly timed, clear and correct directions. What I was picturing was a situation purified of all sexist perception and reaction. But, of course. *If* the whole context were not sexist, sex would not be an issue in such a job situation; indeed, it might go entirely unnoticed. It is precisely the fact that the sex of the candidate *is* relevant that is the salient symptom of the sexism of the situation.

I had failed, in that first essay, fully to grasp or understand that the locus of sexism is primarily in the system or framework, not in the particular act. It is not accurate to say that what is going on in cases of sexism is that distinctions are made on the basis of sex when sex is irrelevant; what is wrong in cases of sexism is, in the first place, that sex *is* relevant; and then that the making of distinctions on the basis of sex reinforces the patterns which make it relevant.

In sexist cultural/economic systems, sex is always relevant. To understand what sexism is, then, we have to step back and take a larger view.

Sex-identification intrudes into every moment of our lives and discourse, no matter what the supposedly primary focus or topic of the moment is. Elaborate, systematic, ubiquitous and redundant marking of a distinction between two sexes of humans and most animals is customary and obligatory. One *never* can ignore it.

Examples of sex-marking behavior patterns abound. A couple enters a restaurant; the headwaiter or hostess addresses the man and does not address the woman. The physician addresses the man by surname and honorific (Mr. Baxter, Rev. Jones) and addresses the woman by given name (Nancy, Gloria). You congratulate your friend—a hug, a slap on the back, shaking hands, kissing; one of the things which determines which of these you do is your friend's sex. In everything one does one has two complete repertoires of behavior, one for interactions with women and one for interactions with men. Greeting, storytelling, ordergiving and order-receiving, negotiating, gesturing deference or dominance, encouraging, challenging, asking for information: one does all of these things differently depending upon whether the relevant others are male or female.

That this is so has been confirmed in sociological and socio-linguistic research,[2] but it is just as easily confirmed in one's own experience. To discover the differences in how you greet a woman and how you greet a man, for instance, just observe yourself, paying attention to the following sorts of things: frequency and duration of eye contact, frequency and type of touch, tone and pitch of voice, physical distance maintained between bodies, how and whether you smile, use of slang or swear words, whether your body dips into a shadow curtsy or bow. That I have two repertoires for handling introductions to people was vividly confirmed for me when a student introduced me to his friend, Pat, and I really could not tell what sex Pat was. For a moment I was stopped cold, completely incapable of action. I felt myself helplessly caught between two paths—the one I would take if Pat were female and the one I would take if Pat were male. Of course the paralysis does not last. One is rescued by one's ingenuity and good will; one can invent a way to behave as one says "How do you do?" to a human being. But the habitual ways are not for humans: they are one way for women and another for men.

Interlaced through all our behavior is our speaking—our linguistic behavior. Third person singular pronouns mark the sex of their referents. The same is true for a huge range of the nouns we use to refer to people ('guy', 'boy', 'lady', 'salesman', etc., and all the terms which covertly indicate the sex of the referent, like 'pilot', 'nurse', etc.), and the majority of given proper names ('Bob', 'Gwen', etc.). In speaking, one constantly marks the sexes of those one speaks about.

The frequency with which our behavior marks the sexes of those we interact with cannot be exaggerated. The phenomenon is absolutely pervasive and deeply entrenched in all the patterns of behavior which are habitual, customary, acceptable, tolerable and intelligible. One can invent ways of behaving in one situation or another which are not sex-marking, which do not vary with the sexes of the persons involved, but if one were to succeed in removing sex-marking from one's behavior altogether, one's behavior would be so odd as to precipitate immediate crises of intelligibility and strenuous moral, religious or aesthetic objections from others. Everything one did would seem strange. And this is a matter of no small moment. We are a gregarious species. Our lives depend on our abilities to interact with

others in relations of work, of exchange and of sympathy. What one cannot do without seeming excessively odd or unintelligible, one cannot do without severe disturbance to patterns of interaction upon which one's life depends. Sex-marking behavior is not optional; it is as obligatory as it is pervasive. . . .

The pressure on each of us to guess or determine the sex of everybody else both generates and is exhibited in a great pressure on each of us to *inform* everybody all the time of our sex. For, if you strip humans of most of their cultural trappings, it is not always that easy to tell without close inspection which are female, which are male. The tangible and visible physical differences between the sexes are not particularly sharp or numerous. Individual variation along the physical dimensions we think of as associated with maleness and femaleness are great, and the differences between the sexes could easily be obscured by bodily decoration, hair removal and the like. One of the shocks, when one does mistake someone's sex, is the discovery of how easily one can be misled. We could not ensure that we could identify people by their sex virtually any time and anywhere under any conditions if they did not announce themselves, did not *tell* us in one way or another.

We do not, in fact, announce our sexes "in one way or another." We announce them in a thousand ways. We deck ourselves from head to toe with garments and decorations which serve like badges and buttons to announce our sexes. For every type of occasion there are distinct clothes, gear and accessories, hairdos, cosmetics and scents, labeled as "ladies'" or "men's" and labeling us as females or males, and most of the time most of us choose, use, wear or bear the paraphernalia associated with our sex. It goes below the skin as well. There are different styles of gait, gesture, posture, speech, humor, taste and even of perception, interest and attention that we learn as we grow up to be women or to be men and that label and announce us as women or as men. It begins early in life: even infants in arms are color coded.

That we wear and bear signs of our sexes, and that this is compulsory, is made clearest in the relatively rare cases when we do not do so, or not enough. Responses ranging from critical to indignant to hostile meet mothers whose small children are not immediately sex-identifiable, and hippies used to be accosted on the streets (by otherwise reserved and polite people) with criticisms and accusations when their clothing and style gave off mixed and contradictory sex-announcements. Anyone in any kind of job placement service and any Success Manual will tell you that you cannot expect to get or keep a job if your clothing or personal style is ambiguous in its announcement of your sex. You don't go to a job interview wearing the other sex's shoes and socks. . . .

Along with all the making, marking and announcing of sex-distinction goes a strong and visceral feeling or attitude to the effect that sex-distinction is the most important thing in the world: that it would be the end of the world if it were not maintained, clear and sharp and rigid; that a sex-dualism which is rooted in the nature of the beast is absolutely crucial and fundamental to all aspects of human life, human society and human economy. Where feminism is perceived as a project of blurring this distinction, antifeminist rhetoric is vivid with the dread that the world will end if the feminists have their way.[3] Some feminists' insistence that the feminist goal is *not* a "unisex" society is defensive in a way that suggests they too believe that culture or civilization would not survive blurring the distinction. I think that one of the sources of the prevalence and profundity of this conviction and dread is our immersion in the very behavior patterns I have been discussing.

It is a general and obvious principle of information theory that when it is very, very important that certain information be conveyed, the suitable strategy is redundancy. If a message *must* get through, one sends it repeatedly and by as many means or media as one has at one's command. On the other end, as a receiver of information, if one receives the same information over and over, conveyed by every medium one knows, another message comes through as well, and implicitly: the message that this information is very, very important. The enormous frequency with which information about people's sexes is conveyed conveys implicitly the message that this topic is enormously important. I suspect that this is the single topic on which we most frequently receive information from others throughout our entire lives. If I am right, it would go part way to explaining why we end up with an almost irresistible impression, unarticulated, that the matter of people's sexes is the most important and most fundamental topic in the world.

We exchange sex-identification information, along with the implicit message that it is very important, in a variety of circumstances in which there really is no concrete or experientially obvious point in having the information. There are reasons, as this discussion has shown, why you should want to know whether the person filling your water glass or your tooth is male or female and why that person wants to know what you are, but those reasons are woven invisibly into the fabric of social structure and they do not have to do with the bare mechanics of things being filled. Furthermore, the same culture which drives us to this constant information exchange also simultaneously enforces a strong blanket rule requiring that the simplest and most nearly definitive physical manifestations of sex difference be hidden from view in all but the most private and intimate circumstances. The double message of sex-distinction and its preeminent importance is conveyed, in fact, in part *by* devices which systematically and deliberately cover up and hide from view the few physical things which do (to a fair extent) distinguish two sexes of humans. The messages are overwhelmingly dissociated from the concrete facts they supposedly pertain to, and from matrices of concrete and sensible reasons and consequences.

Small children's minds must be hopelessly boggled by all this. We know our own sexes, and learn to think it a matter of first importance that one is a girl or a boy so early that we do not re-member not knowing—long before physical dif-ferences in our young bodies could make more than the most trivial practical differences. A friend of mine whose appearance and style have a little bit about them that is gender-ambiguous walked past a mother and child, and heard the child ask the mother, "Is she a man or a woman?" The struggle to divine some connection between social behavior and physical sex, and the high priority of it all, seem painfully obvious here.

If one is made to feel that a thing is of prime importance, but common sensory experience does not connect it with things of obvious con-crete and practical importance, then there is mystery, and with that a strong tendency to the construction of mystical or metaphysical con-ceptions of its importance. If it is important, but not of mundane importance, it must be of tran-scendent importance. All the more so if it is *very* important.

This matter of our sexes must be very pro-found indeed if it must, on pain of shame and ostracism, be covered up and must, on pain of shame and ostracism, be boldly advertised by every means and medium one can devise.

There is one more point about redundancy that is worth making here. If there is one thing more effective in making one believe a thing than receiving the message repetitively, it is re-hearsing it repetitively. Advertisers, preachers, teachers, all of us in the brainwashing profes-sions, make use of this apparently physical fact of human psychology routinely. The redun-dancy of sex-marking and sex-announcing serves not only to make the topic seem transcendently important, but to make the sex-duality it adver-tises seem transcendently and unquestionably *true*. . . .

Sex-marking and sex-announcing are equally compulsory for males and females; but that is as far as equality goes in this matter. The meaning and import of this behavior is profoundly differ-ent for women and for men.

Whatever features an individual male person has which tend to his social and economic disadvantage (his age, race, class, height, etc.), one feature which never tends to his disadvan-tage in the society at large is his maleness. The case for females is the mirror image of this. Whatever features an individual female person has which tend to her social and economic ad-vantage (her age, race, etc.), one feature which always tends to her disadvantage is her female-ness. Therefore, when a male's sex-category is the thing about him that gets first and most re-peated notice, the thing about him that is being framed and emphasized and given primacy is a feature which in general is an asset to him. When a female's sex-category is the thing about her that gets first and most repeated notice, the thing about her that is being framed and empha-sized and given primacy is a feature which in general is a liability to her. Manifestations of this divergence in the meaning and consequences of sex-announcement can be very concrete.

Walking down the street in the evening in a town or city exposes one to some risk of assault. For males the risk is less; for females the risk is greater. If one announces oneself male, one is presumed by potential assailants to be more rather than less likely to defend oneself or be able to evade the assault and, if the male-announcement is strong and unambiguous, to be a noncandidate for sexual assault. If one an-nounces oneself female, one is presumed by po-tential assailants to be less rather than more likely to defend oneself or to evade the assault and, if the female-announcement is strong and unambiguous, to be a prime candidate for sexual assault. Both the man and the woman "an-nounce" their sex through style of gait, cloth-ing, hair style, etc., but they are not equally or identically affected by announcing their sex. The male's announcement tends toward his pro-tection or safety, and the female's announce-ment tends toward her victimization. It could not be more immediate or concrete; the mean-ing of the sex-identification could not be more different.

The sex-marking behavioral repertoires are such that in the behavior of almost all people of both sexes addressing or responding to males (especially within their own culture/race) generally is done in a manner which suggests basic respect, while addressing or responding to females is done in a manner that suggests the females' inferiority (condescending tones, presumptions of ignorance, overfamiliarity, sexual aggression, etc.). So, when one approaches an ordinary well-socialized person in such cultures, if one is male, one's own behavioral announcement of maleness tends to evoke supportive and beneficial response and if one is female, one's own behavioral announcement of femaleness tends to evoke degrading and detrimental response.

The details of the sex-announcing behaviors also contribute to the reduction of women and the elevation of men. The case is most obvious in the matter of clothing. As feminists have been saying for two hundred years or so, ladies' clothing is generally restrictive, binding, burdening and frail; it threatens to fall apart and/or to uncover something that is supposed to be covered if you bend, reach, kick, punch or run. It typically does not protect effectively against hazards in the environment, nor permit the wearer to protect herself against the hazards of the human environment. Men's clothing is generally the opposite of all this—sturdy, suitably protective, permitting movement and locomotion. The details of feminine manners and postures also serve to bind and restrict. To be feminine is to take up little space, to defer to others, to be silent or affirming of others, etc. It is not necessary here to survey all this, for it has been done many times and in illuminating detail in feminist writings. My point here is that though both men and women must behave in sex-announcing ways, the behavior which announces femaleness is in itself both physically and socially binding and limiting as the behavior which announces maleness is not.

The sex-correlated variations in our behavior tend systematically to the benefit of males and the detriment of females. The male, announcing his sex in sex-identifying behavior and dress, is both announcing and acting on his membership in a dominant caste—dominant within his subculture and to a fair extent across subcultures as well. The female, announcing her sex, is both announcing and acting on her membership in the subordinated caste. She is obliged to inform others constantly and in every sort of situation that she is to be treated as inferior, without authority, assaultable. She cannot move or speak within the usual cultural norms without engaging in self-deprecation. The male cannot move or speak without engaging in self-aggrandizement. Constant sex-identification both defines and maintains the caste boundary without which there could not be a dominance-subordination structure.

The forces which make us mark and announce sexes are among the forces which constitute the oppression of women, and they are central and essential to the maintenance of that system.

Oppression is a system of interrelated barriers and forces which reduce, immobilize and mold people who belong to a certain group, and effect their subordination to another group (individually to individuals of the other group, and as a group, to that group). Such a system could not exist were not the groups, the categories of persons, well defined. Logically, it presupposes that there are two distinct categories. Practically, they must be not only distinct but relatively easily identifiable; the barriers and forces could not be suitably located and applied if there were often much doubt as to which individuals were to be contained and reduced, which were to dominate.

It is extremely costly to subordinate a large group of people simply by applications of material force, as is indicated by the costs of maximum security prisons and of military supression of nationalist movements. For subordination to be permanent and cost effective, it is necessary to create conditions such that the subordinated group acquiesces to some extent in the subordination. Probably one of the most efficient ways to secure acquiescence is to convince the people that their subordination is inevitable. The mechanisms by which the subordinate and dominant categories are defined can contribute greatly to popular belief in the inevitability of the dominance/subordination structure.

For efficient subordination, what's wanted is that the structure not appear to be a cultural artifact kept in place by human decision or custom, but that it appear *natural*—that it appear to be a quite direct consequence of facts about the beast which are beyond the scope of human manipulation or revision. It must seem natural that individuals of the one category are dominated by individuals of the other and that as groups, the one dominates the other.[4] To make this seem natural, it will help if it seems to all concerned that members of the two groups are *very* different from each other, and this appearance is enhanced if it can be made to appear that within each group, the members are very like one another. In other words, the appearance of the naturalness of the dominance of men and the subordination of women is supported by anything which supports the appearance that men are very like other men and very unlike women, and that women are very like other women and very unlike men. All behavior which encourages the appearance that humans are biologically sharply sex-dimorphic encourages the acquiescence of women (and, to the extent it needs encouragement, of men) in women's subordination.

That we are trained to behave so differently as women and as men, and to behave so differently toward women and toward men, itself contributes mightily to the appearance of extreme natural dimorphism, but also, the *ways* we act as women and as men, and the *ways* we act toward women and toward men, mold our bodies and our minds to the shapes of subordination and dominance. We do become what we practice being.

Throughout this essay I have seemed to beg the question at hand. Should I not be trying to prove that there are few and insignificant differences between females and males, if that is

what I believe, rather than assuming it? What I have been doing is offering observations which suggest that if one thinks there are biologically deep differences between women and men which cause and justify divisions of labor and responsibility such as we see in the modern patriarchal family and male-dominated workplace, one may *not* have arrived at this belief because of direct experience of unmolested physical evidence, but because our customs serve to construct that appearance; and I suggest that these customs are artifacts of culture which exist to support a morally and scientifically insupportable system of dominance and subordination.[5]

But also, in the end, I do not want to claim simply that there are not socially significant biologically-grounded differences between human females and males. Things are much more complex than that.

Enculturation and socialization are, I think, misunderstood if one pictures them as processes which apply layers of cultural gloss over a biological substratum. It is with that picture in mind that one asks whether this or that aspect of behavior is due to "nature" or "nurture." One means, does it emanate from the biological substratum or does it come from some layer of the shellac? A variant on this wrong picture is the picture according to which enculturation or socialization is something mental or psychological, as opposed to something physical or biological. Then one can think of attitudes and habits of perception, for instance, as "learned" versus "biologically determined." And again, one can ask such things as whether men's aggressiveness is learned or biologically determined, and if the former is asserted, one can think in terms of changing them while if the latter is asserted, one must give up all thought of reform.

My observations and experience suggest another way of looking at this. I see enormous social pressure on us all to act feminine or act masculine (and not both), so I am inclined to think that if we were to break the habits of culture which generate that pressure, people would not act particularly masculine or feminine. The fact that there are such penalties threatened for deviations from these patterns strongly suggests that the patterns would not be there but for the threats. This leads, I think, to a skeptical conclusion: we do not know whether human behavior patterns would be dimorphic along lines of chromosomal sex if we were not threatened and bullied; nor do we know, if we assume that they would be dimorphous, *what* they would be, that is, *what* constellations of traits and tendencies would fall out along that genetic line. And these questions are odd anyway, for there is no question of humans growing up *without* culture, so we don't know what other cultural variables we might imagine to be at work in a culture in which the familiar training to masculinity and femininity were not going on.

On the other hand, as one goes about in the world, and in particular as one tries out strategies meant to alter the behaviors which constitute and support male dominance, one often has extremely convincing experiences of the *inflexibility* of people in this respect, of a resistance to change which seems to run much, much deeper than willingness or willfulness in the face of arguments and evidence. As feminist activists, many of us have felt this most particularly in the case of men, and it has sometimes seemed that the relative flexibility and adaptability of women and the relative rigidity of men are so widespread within each group respectively, and so often and convincingly encountered, that they must be biologically given. And one watches men and women on the streets, and their bodies seem so different—one hardly can avoid thinking there are vast and profound differences between women and men without giving up the hard won confidence in one's powers of perception.

The first remedy here is to lift one's eyes from a single culture, class and race. If the bodies of Asian women set them apart so sharply from Asian men, see how different they are also from Black women; if white men all look alike and very different from white women,

it helps to note that Black men don't look so like white men.

The second remedy is to think about the subjective experience we have of our *habits*. If one habitually twists a lock of one's hair whenever one is reading and has tried to break this habit, one knows how "bodily" it is; but that does not convince one it is genetically determined. People who drive to work every day often take the same route every day, and if they mean to take another route one day in order to do an errand on the way, they may find themselves at work, conveyed along the habitual route, without having revised the decision to do the errand. The habit of taking that course is mapped into one's body; it is not a matter of a decision—a mental event—that is repeated each day upon a daily rejudgment of the reasonableness of the course. It is also not genetic. We are animals. Learning is physical, bodily. There is not a separate, nonmaterial "control room" where socialization, enculturation and habit formation take place and where, since it is nonmaterial, change is independent of bodies and easier than in bodies.

Socialization molds our bodies; enculturation forms our skeletons, our musculature, our central nervous systems. By the time we are gendered adults, masculinity and femininity *are* "biological." They are structural and material features of how our bodies are. My experience suggests that they are changeable just as one would expect bodies to be—slowly, through constant practice and deliberate regimens designed to remap and rebuild nerve and tissue. This is how many of us *have* changed when we chose to change from "women" as culturally defined to "women" as we define ourselves. Both the sources of the changes and the resistances to them are bodily—are among the possibilities of our animal natures, whatever those may be.

But now "biological" does not mean "genetically determined" or "inevitable." It just means "of the animal."

It is no accident that feminism has often focused on our bodies. Rape, battering, reproductive self-determination, health, nutrition, self-defense, athletics, financial independence (control of the means of feeding and sheltering ourselves). And it is no accident that with varying degrees of conscious intention, feminists have tried to create separate spaces where women could exist somewhat sheltered from the prevailing winds of patriarchal culture and try to stand up straight for once. One needs space to *practice* an erect posture; one cannot just will it to happen. To retrain one's body one needs physical freedom from what are, in the last analysis, physical forces misshaping it to the contours of the subordinate.

The cultural and economic structures which create and enforce elaborate and rigid patterns of sex-marking and sex-announcing behavior, that is, create gender as we know it, mold us as dominators and subordinates (I do not say "mold our minds" or "mold our personalities"). They construct two classes of animals, the masculine and the feminine, where another constellation of forces might have constructed three or five categories, and not necessarily hierarchically related. Or such a spectrum of sorts that we would not experience them as "sorts" at all.

The term 'sexist' characterizes cultural and economic structures which create and enforce the elaborate and rigid patterns of sex-marking and sex-announcing which divide the species, along lines of sex, into dominators and subordinates. Individual acts and practices are sexist which reinforce and support those structures, either as culture or as shapes taken on by the enculturated animals. Resistance to sexism is that which undermines those structures by social and political action and by projects of reconstruction and revision of ourselves.

Notes

1. "Male Chauvinism—A Conceptual Analysis," *Philosophy and Sex,* edited by Robert Baker and Frederick Elliston (Prometheus Books, Buffalo, New York, 1975), p. 66. The inadequacies of such an account of sexism are reflected in the inadequacies of a standard legal interpretation of what sex discrimination is as it is analyzed by Catharine A. MacKinnon in *Sexual Harassment of Working Women* (Yale University Press, New Haven and London, 1979), cf. Chapters 5 and 6. See also my review of this book, "Courting Gender Justice," *New Women's Times Feminist Review,* No. 17, September–October 1981, pp. 10–11.

2. See, for example, such works as *Body Politics: Power, Sex and Nonverbal Communication,* by Nancy Henley (Prentice-Hall, Englewood Cliffs, New Jersey, 1977); *Language and Sex: Difference and Dominance,* edited by Barrie Thorne and Nancy Henley (Newbury House Publishers, Rowley, Massachusetts, 1975); and *Gender and Nonverbal Behavior,* edited by Clara Mayo and Nancy M. Henley (Springer-Verlag, New York, 1981).

3. See, for example, *Sexual Suicide,* by George F. Gilder (Quadrangle, New York, 1979). For an eloquent example of the Victorian version of this anxiety and the world view which underlies it, see "The Emancipation of Women," by Frederic Harrison in *Fortnightly Review,* CCXCVII, October 1, 1891, as quoted in a talk given by Sandra Siegel at the Berkshire Conference on Women's History, April 1981, entitled "Historiography, 'Decadence,' and the Legend of 'Separate Spheres' in Late Victorian England," which connects Victorian conceptions of civilization and the separateness and differentness of women and men.

4. See "Feminist Leaders Can't Walk on Water," by Lorraine Masterson, *Quest: A Feminist Quarterly* (Volume II, Number 4, Spring, 1976), especially pp. 35–36 where the author refers to Paulo Freire's *Pedagogy of the Oppressed* and speaks to the special case of women's belief that our subordination is inevitable because rooted in biology.

5. Cf., the early and powerful article by Naomi Weisstein, "Psychology Constructs the Female," in *Woman in Sexist Society: Studies in Power and Powerlessness,* edited by Vivian Gornick and Barbara K. Moran (Basic Books, Inc., New York, 1971). Weisstein documents clearly that neither laypersons nor psychologists are the least bit dependable as observers of sex-correlated traits of people, and that theories of sex-difference based on "clinical experience" and based on primate studies are scientifically worthless.

Study Questions

1. What does Frye mean by "sexism"?
2. Is sexism as widespread as Frye maintains?
3. What actions can be taken to combat sexism?
4. Do Frye's observations about sexism also apply to racism and religious prejudice?

Fives Faces of Oppression

IRIS MARION YOUNG

Iris Marion Young (1949–2006) was Professor of Political Science at the University of Chicago. She explores the concept of oppression and argues that various groups in American society have been subject to exploitation, marginalization, powerlessness, cultural imperialism, and violence.

Politics is partly a struggle over the language people use to describe social and political experience. Most people in the United States would not use the term "oppression" to name injustice in this society. For a minority of Americans, on the other hand—such as socialists, radical feminists, American Indian activists, black activists, gay and lesbian activists, and others identifying with new left social movements of the 1960s and '70s—oppression is a central category of political discourse. Speaking the political language in which oppression is a central word involves adopting a whole mode of analyzing and evaluating social structures and practices that is quite incommensurate with the language of liberal individualism that dominates political discourse in the United States.

Consequently, those of us who identify with at least one of the movements I have named have a major political project: we must persuade people that the discourse of oppression makes sense of much of our social experience. We are ill prepared for this task, however, if we have no clear account of the meaning of the concept of oppression. While we commonly find the term used in the diverse philosophical and theoretical literature spawned by radical social movements in the United States, we find little direct discussion of the meaning of the concept of oppression as used by these movements.

In this chapter I offer some explication of the concept as I understand its use by new social movements in the United States since the 1960s. I offer you an explication of this concept, an unfolding of its meaning. I do not think the concept of oppression can be strictly defined, that is, corralled within one clear boundary. There is no attribute or set of attributes that all oppressed people have in common.

From Iris Marion Young, "Five Faces of Oppression," *The Philosophical Forum,* 6 (1988). Reprinted by permission of John Wiley & Sons.

In the following account of oppression I reflect on the situation and experience of those groups said by new left social movements to be oppressed in U.S. society: at least women, blacks, Chicanos, Puerto Ricans, and most other Spanish-speaking Americans, Native Americans, Jews, lesbians, gay men, Arabs, Asians, old people, working-class people, poor people, and physically or mentally disabled people.

Obviously, these groups are not oppressed to the same degree or in the same ways. In the most general sense, all oppressed people share some inhibition of their ability to develop and exercise their capacities and express their needs, thoughts, and feelings. Nevertheless, reflection on the concrete uses of the term "oppression" in radical political discourse convinces me that the term refers to several distinct structures or situations. I label these with five disparate categories: exploitation, marginality, powerlessness, cultural imperialism, and violence. . . .

EXPLOITATION

The central function of Marx's theory of exploitation is to explain how class structure can exist in the absence of legally and normatively sanctioned class distinctions. In precapitalist societies domination is overt and carried on through direct political means. In both slave society and feudal society the right to appropriate the product of the labor of others partly defines class privilege, and these societies legitimate class distinctions with ideologies of natural superiority and inferiority.

Capitalist society, on the other hand, removes traditional juridically enforced class distinctions and promotes a belief in the legal freedom of persons. Workers freely contract with employers, receive a wage, and no formal mechanisms of law or custom force them to work for that employer or any employer. Thus, the mystery of capitalism arises: when everyone is formally free, how can there be class domination? Why does there continue to be class distinction between the wealthy, who own the means of production, and the mass of people, who work for them? The theory of exploitation answers this question.

Profit, the basis of capitalist power and wealth, is a mystery if we assume that in the market goods exchange at their values. Marx's use of the labor theory of value, however, dispels this mystery. Every commodity's value is a function of the labor time necessary for the production of labor power. Labor power is the one commodity that in the process of being consumed produces new value. Profit then comes from the difference between the actual labor and the value of that capacity to labor that the capitalist purchases and puts to work. The owner of capital appropriates this surplus value, which accounts for the possibility of realizing a profit. . . .

The central insight expressed with the concept of exploitation, then, is that domination occurs through a steady process of the transfer of the results of the labor of some people to benefit others. The injustice of class division does not consist only in the fact that some people have great wealth while most people have little and some are severely deprived.[1] The theory of exploitation shows that this relation of power and inequality is produced and reproduced through a systematic process in which the energies of the have-nots are continuously expended to maintain and augment the power, status, and wealth of the haves.

Many writers have cogently argued that the Marxian concept of exploitation is too narrow to encompass all forms of domination and oppression.[2] In particular, by confining itself to examining class domination and oppression, the Marxist concept of exploitation does not contribute to an understanding of such group oppressions as sexism and racism. The question, then, is whether the concept of exploitation can be broadened to include other ways that the labor and energy expenditure of one group benefits another, thus reproducing a relation of domination between them.

Feminists have had little difficulty showing that women's oppression consists partly in a systematic and unreciprocated transfer of powers from women to men. Women's oppression consists not merely in an inequality of status, power, and wealth resulting from men's excluding women from privileged activities. The freedom, power, status, and self-realization of men is possible precisely because women work for them. Gender exploitation has two aspects, transfer of the fruits of material labor to men, and the transfer of nurturing and sexual energies to men.

Christine Delphy, for example, theorizes marriage as a class relation in which women's labor benefits men without comparable remuneration.[3] She makes it clear that the exploitation consists not in the sort of work that women do in the home, for it might be various kinds of tasks, but the fact that they perform tasks for someone else on whom they are dependent. Thus, for example, in most systems of agricultural production in the world, men take to market goods women have produced, and more often than not men receive the status and often the entire income from this labor.

With the concept of sex-affective production, Ann Ferguson identifies another form of the transfer of women's energies to men.[4] Women provide men and children with emotional care and provide men with sexual satisfaction, and as a class receive little of either from men.[5] The gender socialization of women makes us tend to be more attentive to interactive dynamics than men, and makes women good at providing empathy and support for people's feelings and at smoothing over interactive tensions. Both men and women look to women as nurturers of their personal lives, and women frequently complain that when they look to men for emotional support they do not receive it.[6] The norms of heterosexuality, moreover, are oriented around male pleasure, and consequently many women receive little satisfaction from their sexual interaction with men.[7]

Most feminist theories of gender exploitation have concentrated on the institutional structure of the patriarchal family. Recently, however, feminists have begun to theorize relations of gender exploitation enacted in the contemporary workplace and through the state. Carol Brown argues that as men have removed themselves from responsibility for children, many women have become dependent on the state for subsistence as they continue to bear nearly total responsibility for child rearing.[8] This creates a new system of the exploitation of women's domestic labor mediated by those state institutions, which she calls public patriarchy.

In twentieth-century capitalist economies, the workplaces that women have been entering in increasing numbers serve as another important site of gender exploitation. David Alexander argues that most typically feminine jobs have gender tasks involving sexual labor, nurturing, caring for a person's body, or smoothing over relations through personality.[9] In these ways, women's energies are expended in workplaces that enhance the status of, please, or comfort others, usually men; and these gender-based labors of waitresses, clerical workers, nurses, and other caretakers often go unnoticed and undercompensated.

To summarize, women are exploited in the Marxian sense to the degree that they are wage workers. Some have argued that women's domestic labor is also a form of capitalist class exploitation insofar as it is labor covered by the wages a family receives. As a class, however, women undergo specific forms of gender exploitation—ways the energies and power of women are expended, often unnoticed and unacknowledged, usually to benefit men by releasing them for more important and creative work, enhancing their status or the environment around them, or providing men with sexual or emotional service.

Race is a structure of oppression at least as basic as class or gender. Are there, then, racially specific forms of exploitation? This is different from the question of whether racial groups are subjected to intense capitalist exploitation. Racial groups in the United States, especially blacks and Latinos, are oppressed through capitalist superexploitation resulting from a segmented labor market that tends to reserve skilled, high-paying, unionized jobs for whites. There is wide disagreement about whether such superexploitation benefits whites as a group or only benefits the capitalist class, and I do not intend to resolve that dispute here.[10]

However one answers the question about capitalist superexploitation of racial groups, is it also possible to conceptualize a form of exploitation that is racially specific on analogy with the gender-specific forms I have discussed? The category of *menial* labor might provide an opening for such conceptualization. In its derivation "menial" means the labor of servants. Wherever there is racism, including the United States today, there is the assumption, more or less enforced, that members of the oppressed racial groups are or ought to be servants of those, or some of those, in the privileged group. In white racist societies this generally means that many white people have dark- or yellow-skinned domestic servants, and in the United States today there remains significant race structuring of private household service.

In the United States today much service labor has gone public: anybody can have servants if they go to a good hotel, a good restaurant, or hire a cleaning service. Servants often attend the daily—and nightly—activities of business executives, government officials, and other high-status professionals. In our society there remains strong cultural pressure to fill servant jobs—like bell hop, porter, chamber maid, bus boy, and so on—with black and Latin workers. These jobs entail a transfer of energies whereby the servers enhance the status of the served, to place them in an aristocracy—the rule of the best.

Menial labor today refers to more than service, however; it refers to any servile, unskilled, low-paying work lacking in autonomy, and in which a person is subject to orders from several people. Menial work tends to be auxiliary work, instrumental to another person's work, in which that other person receives primary recognition for doing the job. Laborers on a construction site, for example, are at the beck and call of welders, electricians, carpenters, and other skilled workers, who receive recognition for the job done. In the history of the United States, explicit racial discrimination reserved menial work for blacks, Chicanos, American Indians, and Chinese, and menial work still tends to be linked to black and Latino workers.[11] I offer this category of menial labor as a form of racially specific exploitation, only as a proposal, however, that needs discussion.

MARGINALIZATION

Increasingly in the United States, racial oppression occurs more in the form of marginalization than exploitation. Marginals are people the system of labor markets cannot or will not employ. Not only in Third World capitalist countries, but also in most Western capitalist societies, there is a growing underclass of people permanently confined to lives of social marginality, the majority of whom are racially marked—blacks or Indians in Latin America, blacks, East Indians, Eastern Europeans, or North Africans in Europe.

Marginalization is by no means the fate only of racially marked groups, however. In the United States a shamefully large proportion of the population is marginal: old people, and increasingly people who are not very old but get laid off from their jobs and cannot find new work; young people, especially black or Latino, who cannot find first or second jobs; many single mothers and their children; other people involuntarily unemployed; many mentally or physically disabled people; and American Indians, especially those on reservations.

Marginalization is perhaps the most dangerous form of oppression. A whole category of people is expelled from useful participation in social life, then potentially subject to severe material deprivation and even extermination. The material deprivation marginalization often causes certainly is unjust, especially in a society in which others have plenty. Contemporary advanced capitalist societies in principle have acknowledged the injustice of material deprivation caused by marginalization, and have taken some steps to address it by providing welfare payments and services. The continuance of this welfare state is by no means assured, and in most welfare-state societies, especially the United States, benefits are not sufficient to eliminate large-scale suffering and deprivation.

Material deprivation, which can be addressed by redistributive social policies, is not, however, the extent of the harm caused by marginalization. Two categories of injustice beyond distribution are associated with marginality in advanced capitalist societies. The provision of welfare itself produces new injustice when it deprives dependent persons of rights and freedoms that others have. If justice requires that every person have the opportunity to develop and exercise his or her capacities, finally, then marginalization is unjust primarily because it blocks such opportunity to exercise capacities in socially defined and recognized ways.

Liberalism traditionally asserts the right of all rational autonomous agents to equal citizenship. Early bourgeois liberalism made explicit that citizenship excluded all those whose reason was questionable or not fully developed and all those not independent.[12] Thus, poor people, women, the mad and the feeble-minded, and children were explicitly excluded from citizenship, and many of these were housed in institutions modeled on the modern prison: poor houses, insane asylums, schools.

In our own society the exclusion of dependent persons from equal citizenship rights is only barely hidden beneath the surface. Because they are dependent on bureaucratic institutions for support or services, old people, poor people, and mentally or physically disabled people are subject to patronizing, punitive, demeaning, and arbitrary treatment by the policies and people associated with welfare bureaucracies. Being a dependent in this society implies being legitimately subject to often arbitrary and invasive authority of social service providers and other public and private bureaucrats, who enforce rules with which the marginal must comply, and otherwise exercise power over the conditions of his or her life. In meeting needs of the marginalized, with the aid of social scientific disciplines, the welfare agencies also construct the needs themselves. Medical and social service professionals know what is good for those they serve, and the marginals and dependents themselves do not have the right to claim to know what is good for them.[13] Dependency thus implies in this society, as it has in all liberal societies, a sufficient condition to suspend rights to privacy, respect, and individual choice.

Although dependency thus produces conditions of injustice in our society, dependency in itself should not and need not be oppressive. We cannot imagine a society in which some people would not need to be dependent on others at least some of the time: children, sick people, women recovering from childbirth, old people who have become frail, and depressed or otherwise emotionally needy persons have the moral right to be dependent on others for subsistence and support.

An important contribution of feminist moral theory has consisted in questioning the deeply held assumption that moral agency and full citizenship require that a person be autonomous and independent. Feminists have exposed such an assumption as inappropriately individualistic and derived from a specifically male experience of social relations, valuing competition and solitary achievement.[14] Female experience of social relations, arising both from women's typical domestic care responsibilities and from the kinds of paid work that many women do, tends to recognize dependence as a basic human condition. Whereas in the autonomy model a just society would as much as possible give people the opportunity to be independent, the feminist model instead envisions justice as according respect and decision-making participation to those who are dependent as well as those who are independent.[15] Dependence should not be a reason to be deprived of choice and respect, and much of the oppression many marginals experience would diminish if a less individualistic model of rights prevailed.

Marginalization does not cease to be oppressive when one has shelter and food. Many old people, for example, have sufficient means to live comfortably but remain oppressed in their marginal status. Even if marginals were provided a comfortable material life within institutions that respected their freedom and dignity, injustices of marginality would remain in the form of uselessness, boredom, and lack of self-respect. Most of this society's productive and recognized activities take place in contexts of organized social cooperation, and social structures and processes that close persons out of participation in such social cooperation are unjust.

The fact of marginalization raises basic structural issues of justice. In particular, we must consider what is just about a connection between participation in productive activities of social cooperation, on the one hand, and acquisition of the means of consumption, on the other. As marginalization is increasing, with no sign of abatement, some social policy analysts have introduced the idea of a "social wage" as a socially provided, guaranteed income not tied to the wage system. Restructuring activities of production and service provision to ensure that everyone able and willing has socially recognized work to do, moreover, also implies organization of socially productive activity at least partly outside of a wage system.[16]

POWERLESSNESS

As I have indicated, the Marxian idea of class is important because it helps reveal the structure of exploitation: that some people have their power and wealth because they profit from the labor of others. For this reason I reject the claim of some that a traditional class exploitation model fails to capture the structure of contemporary society. It is still the case that the labor of most people in the society augments the power of a few; whatever their differences from nonprofessional workers, most professional workers share with them not being members of the capitalist class.

An adequate conception of oppression, however, cannot ignore the experience of social division colloquially referred to as the difference between the "middle class" and the "working class," a division structured by the social division of labor between professionals and nonprofessionals. Rather than expanding or revising the Marxian concept of class to take account of this experience, as some writers do, I suggest that we follow Weber and describe this as a difference in *status* rather than class.[17] Being a professional entails occupying a status position that nonprofessionals lack, creating a condition of oppression that nonprofessionals suffer. I shall call this kind of oppression "powerlessness."

The absence of genuine democracy in the United States means that most people do not participate in making decisions that regularly affect the conditions of their lives and actions. In this sense most people lack significant power. Powerlessness, however, describes the lives of people who have little or no work autonomy, exercise little creativity or judgment in their work, have no technical expertise or authority, express themselves awkwardly, especially in public or bureaucratic settings, and do not command respect. Powerlessness names the oppressive situations Sennet and Cobb describe in their famous study of working class men.[18]

The clearest way for me to think of this powerless status is negatively: the powerless lack the status and sense of self that professionals tend to have. There are three aspects of status privilege that professionals have, the lack of which produces oppression for nonprofessionals.

First, acquiring and practicing a profession has an expansive, progressive character. Being professional usually requires a college education and learning a specialized knowledge that entails working with symbols and concepts. In acquiring one's profession, a person experiences progress in learning the necessary expertise, and usually when one begins practicing one enters a career, that is, a working life of growth or progress in professional development. The life of the nonprofessional by comparison is powerless in the sense that it lacks this orientation toward the progressive development of one's capacities.

Second, while most professionals have supervisors and do not have power to affect many decisions or the action of very many people, most nevertheless have considerable day-to-day work autonomy. Professionals usually have some authority over others, moreover, either over workers they supervise or over auxiliaries or clients. Nonprofessionals, on the other hand, lack autonomy, and both in their working lives and in their consumer-client lives, they often stand under the authority of professionals.

Though having its material basis in a division of labor between mental and manual work, the group division between middle class and working class designates not a division only in working life, but also in nearly all aspects of social life. Professionals and nonprofessionals belong to different cultures in the United States. The two groups tend to live in segregated neighborhoods or even different towns, not least because of the actions and decisions of real estate people. They tend to have different tastes in food, decor, clothes, music, and vacations. Members of the two groups socialize for the most part with others in the same status group. While there is some intergroup mobility between generations, for the most part the children of professionals become professionals and the children of nonprofessionals do not.

Thus, third, the privileges of the professional extend beyond the workplace to elevate a whole way of life, which consists in being "respectable." To treat someone with respect is to be prepared to listen to what they have to say or to do what they request because they have some authority, expertise, or influence.

The norms of respectability in our society are associated specifically with professional culture. Professional dress, speech, tastes, and demeanor all connote respectability. Generally professionals expect and receive respect from others. In restaurants, banks, hotels, real estate offices, and many other such public places, professionals typically receive more respectful treatment than nonprofessionals. For this reason nonprofessionals seeking a loan or a job, or to buy a house or a car, will often try to look "professional" and "respectable" in these settings. The privilege of this professional respectability starkly appears in the dynamics of racism and sexism. In daily interchange women and men of color must prove their respectability. At first they are often not treated by strangers with respectful distance or deference. Once people discover that this woman or that Puerto Rican man is a college teacher or a business executive, however, people often behave more respectfully toward her or him. Working-class white men, on the other hand, are often treated with respect until their working class status is revealed.

CULTURAL IMPERIALISM

Exploitation, marginality, and powerlessness all refer to relations of power and oppression that occur by virtue of the social division of labor: who works for whom, who does not work, and how the content of work in one position is defined in relation to others. These three categories refer to the structural and institutional relations that delimit people's material lives, including but not limited to the resources they have access to, the concrete opportunity they have or do not have to develop and exercise capacities in involving, socially recognized ways that enhance rather than diminish their lives. These kinds of oppression are a matter of concrete power in relation to others, who benefits from whom, and who is dispensable.

Recent theorists of movements of group liberation, especially feminists and black liberation theorists, have also given prominence to a rather different experience of oppression, which I shall call cultural imperialism.[19] This is the experience of existing in a society whose dominant meanings render the particular perspectives and point of view of one's own group invisible at the same time as they stereotype one's group and mark it out as "other."

Cultural imperialism consists in the universalization of one group's experience and culture and its establishment as the norm. Some groups have exclusive or primary access to what Nancy Fraser calls the means of interpretation and communication in a society.[20] As a result, the dominant cultural products of the society, that is, those most widely disseminated, express the experience, values, goals, and achievements of the groups that produce them. The cultural products also express their perspective on and interpretation of events and elements in the society, including the other groups in the society, insofar as they are noticed at all. Often without noticing they do so, the dominant groups project their own experience as representative of humanity as such.

An encounter with groups different from the dominant group, however, challenges its claim to universality. The dominant group saves its position by bringing the other group under the measure of its dominant norms. Consequently, the difference of women from men, Native Americans or Africans from Europeans, Jews from Christians, homosexuals from heterosexuals, or workers from professionals becomes reconstructed as deviance and inferiority. The dominant groups and their cultural expressions are the normal, the universal, and thereby unremarkable. Since the dominant group's cultural expressions are the only expressions that receive wide dissemination, the dominant groups construct the differences that some groups exhibit as lack and negation in relation to the norms, and those groups become marked out as "other."

Victims of cultural imperialism experience a paradoxical oppression in that they are both marked out by stereotypes and rendered invisible. As remarkable, deviant beings, the culturally dominated are stamped with an essence. In contrast, the privileged are indefinable because

they are individual; each is whatever he or she wants to be, they are what they do, and by their doings they are judged. The stereotype marks and defines the culturally dominated, confines them to a nature that is usually attached in some way to their bodies, and thus that cannot easily be denied. These stereotypes so permeate the society that they are not noticed as contestable. Just as everyone knows that the earth goes around the sun, so everyone knows that gay people are promiscuous, that Indians are alcoholics, and that women are good with children.

Those living under cultural imperialism find themselves defined from the outside, positioned, and placed by a system of dominant meanings they experience as arising from elsewhere, from those with whom they do not identify and who do not identify with them. The dominant culture's stereotyped, marked, and inferiorized images of the group must be internalized by group members at least to the degree that they are forced to react to behaviors of others that express or are influenced by those images. This creates for the culturally oppressed the experience that W. E. B. DuBois called "double consciousness." "This sense of always looking at one's self through the eyes of others, of measuring one's soul by the tape of a world that looks on in amused contempt and pity."[21] This consciousness is double because the oppressed subject refuses to coincide with these devalued, objectified, stereotyped visions of herself or himself. The subject desires recognition as human, capable of activity, full of hope and possibility, but receives from the dominant culture only the judgment that he or she is different, marked, or inferior.

People in culturally oppressed groups often maintain a sense of positive subjectivity because they can affirm and recognize one another as sharing similar experiences and perspectives on social life. The group defined by the dominant culture as deviant, as a stereotyped other, *is* culturally different from the dominant group because the status of otherness creates specific experiences not shared by the dominant group and because culturally oppressed groups also are often socially segregated and occupy specific positions in the social division of labor. They express their specific group experiences and interpretations of the world to one another, developing and perpetuating their own culture. Double consciousness, then, occurs because one finds one's being defined by two cultures: a dominant and a subordinate culture.

Cultural imperialism involves the paradox of experiencing oneself as invisible at the same time that one is marked out and noticed as different. The perspectives of other groups dominate the culture without their noticing it as a perspective, and their cultural expressions are widely disseminated. These dominant cultural expressions often simply pay no attention to the existence and experience of those other groups, only to mention or refer to them in stereotyped or marginalized ways. This, then, is the injustice of cultural imperialism: that the oppressed group's experience and interpretation of social life finds no expression that touches the dominant culture, while that same culture imposes on the oppressed group its experience and interpretations of social life.

VIOLENCE

Finally, many groups suffer the oppression of systematic and legitimized violence. The members of some groups live with the fear of random, unprovoked attacks on their persons or property, which have no motive but to damage, humiliate, or destroy them. In U.S. society women, blacks, Asians, Arabs, gay men, and lesbians live under such threats of violence, and in at least some regions Jews, Puerto Ricans, Chicanos, and other Spanish-speaking Americans must fear such violence as well. Violation may also take the form of name-calling or petty harassment intended to degrade or humiliate, and always signals an underlying threat of physical attack.

Such violence is systematic because it is directed at any member of the group simply because he or she is a member of that group. Any woman, for example, has reason to fear rape. The violence to which these oppressed groups are subject, moreover, is usually legitimate in the sense that most people regard it as unsurprising, and so it usually goes unpunished. Police beatings or killings of black youths, for example, are rarely publicized, rarely provoke moral outrage on the part of most white people, and rarely receive punishment.

An important aspect of the kind of random but systematic violence I am referring to here is its utter irrationality. Xenophobic violence is different from the violence of state or ruling-class repression. Repressive violence has a rational, though evil, motive: rulers use it as a coercive tool to maintain their power. Many accounts of racist, sexist, or homophobic violence try to explain it as motivated by a desire to maintain group privilege or domination. I agree that fear of violence functions to help keep these oppressed groups subordinate. I think the causes of such violence must be traced to unconscious structures of identity formation that project onto some groups the fluid, bodily aspect of the subject that threatens the rigid unity of that identity.

CONCLUSION

The five faces of oppression that I have explicated here function as criteria of oppression, not as a full theoretical account of oppression. With them we can tell whether a group is oppressed, according to objective social structures and behaviors. Being subject to any one of these five conditions is sufficient for calling a group oppressed. Most of the groups I listed earlier as oppressed in U.S. society experience more than one of these forms, and some experience all five.

Nearly all, if not all, groups said by contemporary social movements to be oppressed in our society suffer cultural imperialism. Which other oppressions are experienced by which groups, however, is quite variable. Working-class people are exploited and powerless, for example, but if employed and white do not experience marginalization and violence. Gay men, on the other hand, are not *qua* gay exploited or powerless, but they experience severe cultural imperialism and violence. Similarly, Jews and Arabs as groups are victims of cultural imperialism and violence, though many members of these groups also suffer exploitation or powerlessness. Old people are oppressed by marginalization and cultural imperialism, and this is also true of physically or mentally disabled people. As a group women are subject to gender-based exploitation, powerlessness, cultural imperialism, and violence. Racism in the United States associates blacks and Latinos with marginalization, even though many members of these groups escape that condition; members of these groups often suffer all five forms of oppression.

With these criteria I have specifically avoided defining structures and kinds of oppression according to the groups oppressed: racism, classism, sexism, heterosexism, ageism. The forms of group oppression these terms name are not homologous, and the five criteria can help describe how and why not. The five criteria also help show that while no group oppression is reducible to or explained by any other group oppression, the oppression of one group is not a closed system with its own attributes, but overlaps with the oppression of other groups. With these criteria, moreover, we can claim that one group is more oppressed than another, insofar as it is subject to more of these five conditions, without thereby theoretically privileging a particular form of oppression or one oppressed group.

Are there any connections among these five forms of oppression? Why are particular groups subject to various combinations of them? The answers to these questions are beyond the scope of this chapter. My project here is analytical and descriptive, not explanatory. Answering these questions is important to the theoretical project of understanding oppression. I believe they cannot be answered by an *a priori* account, however, but require a specific explanatory account of the connections among forms of oppression for each social context and for each group.

NOTES

1. Alan Buchanan, *Marx and Justice.* (Totowa, N.J.: Rowman and Allenheld, 1980), 44–49; Nancy Holmstrom, "Exploitation," *Canadian Journal of Philosophy,* VII, no. 2 (1977):353–69.

2. Anthony Giddens, *A Contemporary Critique of Historical Materialism* (Berkeley: University of California Press, 1981), 242; Arthur Brittan and Mary Maynard, *Sexism, Racism and Oppression* (Oxford: Basil Blackwell, 1984), 93; Raymond Murphy, "Exploitation or Exclusion?" *Sociology* 19, no. 2 (May, 1985):225–43; Herbert Gintis and Samuel Bowles, *Capitalism and Democracy* (New York: Basic Books, 1986).

3. Christine Delphy, *Close to Home: A Materialist Analysis of Women's Oppression* (Amherst: University of Massachusetts Press, 1984).

4. See her "Women as a New Revolutionary Class" in *Between Labor and Capital,* ed. Pat Walker (Boston: South End Press, 1979) and "On Conceiving Motherhood and Sexuality: A Feminist Materialist Approach" in *Mothering: Essays in Feminist Theory,* ed. Joyce Trebilco (Totowa, N.J.: Rowman and Allenheld, 1984).

5. Cf. Brittan and Maynard, *Sexism,* 142–48.

6. Barbara Easton, "Feminism and the Contemporary Family," *Socialist Review* 39 (May/June 1978):11–36.

7. Rhonda Gottlieb, "The Political Economy of Sexuality," *Review of Radical Political Economy* 16, no. 1 (1984): 143–65.

8. Carol Brown, "Mothers, Fathers and Children: From Private to Public Patriarchy" in *Women and Revolution,* ed. Lydia Sargent (Boston: South End Press, 1981), 239–68; cf. Ellen Boris and Peter Bardaglio, "The Transformation of Patriarchy: The Historic Role of the State" in *Families, Politics and Public Policy,* ed. Irene Diamond (New York: Longman, 1983), 79–93; Kathy Ferguson, *The Feminist Case Against Bureaucracy* (Philadelphia: Temple University Press, 1984).

9. David Alexander, "Gendered Job Traits and Women's Occupations" (Ph.D. Dissertation, University of Massachusetts, 1987).

10. Michael Reich, *Racial Inequality* (Princeton, N.J.: Princeton University Press, 1981).

11. Al Symanski, "The Structure of Race," *Review of Radical Political Economy* 17, no. 4 (1985):106–20.

12. Gintis and Bowles, 1986.

13. Nancy Fraser, "Women, Welfare, and the Politics of Need Interpretation," *Hypatia: A Journal of Feminist Philosophy* 2, no. 1 (Winter, 1987):103–22; Ferguson, *The Feminist Case,* 1984, Chapter 4.

14. Carol Gilligan, *In a Different Voice* (Cambridge, Harvard University Press, 1982); Marilyn Friedman, "Care and Context in Moral Reasoning" in *Moral Dilemmas: Philosophical and Psychological Issues in the Development of Moral Reasoning,* ed. Carol Harding (Chicago: Precedent, 1985).

15. Virginia Held, "A Non-Contractual Society" (paper given at Conference on Feminist Moral, Legal and Political Theory, University of Cincinnati, November, 1986).

16. Claus Offe, *Disorganized Capitalism: Contemporary Transformation of Work and Politics* (Cambridge: M.I.T. Press, 1986), Chapters 1–3.

17. Max Weber, "Classes, Status Groups and Parties" in *Weber: Selections in Translation,* ed. W. G. Runciman (Cambridge: Cambridge University Press, 1978), 43–64; David Beetham, *Max Weber and the Theory of Modern Politics* (Oxford: Polity Press, 1985), 79–82.

18. Richard Sennet and Jonathan Cobb, *The Hidden Injuries of Class* (New York: Vintage Books, 1972).

19. Maria C. Lugones and Elizabeth V. Spelman, "Have We Got a Theory for You! Feminist Theory, Cultural Imperialism and the Demand for 'The Woman's Voice,'" *Women's Studies International Forum* 6, no. 6 (1983):573–81.

20. Nancy Fraser, "Social Movements vs. Disciplinary Bureaucracies: The Discourses of Social Needs," CHS Occasional Paper #8 (Center for Humanistic Studies, University of Minnesota, 1987), 1–37.

21. W. E. B. DuBois, *The Souls of Black Folks* (New York: Signet, 1903, 1969).

Study Questions

1. What does Young mean by "oppression"?
2. How do the five types of oppression differ from each other?
3. According to Young, which groups in the United States are not oppressed?
4. Are any groups in the United States oppressed but not mentioned by Young?

Globalizing Human Rights

KWAME ANTHONY APPIAH

Kwama Anthony Appiah is Professor of Philosophy and of Law at New York University. In the next selection he explores the nature of human rights. He views them not as grounded in metaphysical consensus but as a language for deliberation among those from different societies.

Human rights as they actually exist are, above all, creatures of something like law: they are the results of agreements promulgated by states, agreements that set rule-governed constraints on the actions of states and individuals, sometimes requiring action, sometimes forbidding it. They are used by officials to justify actions both within and across states, and they are called upon by citizens of many states claiming protection from abuse. The wide diversity of people who call upon them includes, to be sure, a substantial diversity of opinion on matters metaphysical—on religion in particular—and even if there is a single truth to be had about these matters, it is not one that we shall all come to soon.

The major advantage of instruments that are not framed as the working out of a metaphysical tradition is, obviously, that people from different metaphysical traditions can accept them. The major disadvantage is that without some grounding—metaphysical or not—it is hard to see why they should have any power or effect. The mere making of declarations that one should behave this way or that does not in general lead people to act in conformity with them, especially in the absence of mechanisms of enforcement. Granted the fact that they are so weakly philosophically grounded, there is a puzzle about what gives human rights instruments their power.

As Michael Ignatieff has observed in a thoughtful discussion of the matter, "human rights has gone global by going local." People around the world, working in different religious and juridical traditions, have nevertheless found reasons to support various human rights instruments because those instruments embody protections that they both want and need. "Human rights is the only universally available moral vernacular that validates the claims of women and children against the oppression they experience in patriarchal and tribal societies; it is the only vernacular that enables dependent persons to perceive themselves as moral agents and to act against practices—arranged marriages, purdah, civic disenfranchisement, genital mutilation,

domestic slavery, and so on—that are ratified by the weight and authority of their cultures," Ignatieff writes. "These agents seek out human rights protection precisely because it legitimizes their protests against oppression."[1] The moral individualism of human-rights discourse, as he insists, is what enables it to play this role, and so we cannot say that the notion of human rights is metaphysically *naked*; but it is, or should be, scantily clad, conceptually speaking. Certainly, we do not need to agree that we are all created in the image of God, or that we have natural rights that flow from our human essence, to agree that we do not want to be tortured by government officials, that we do not want to be subjected to arbitrary arrest, or have our lives, families, and property forfeited.

Still, it must be acknowledged that talk of human rights has long had a tendency to overflow its banks. You could see this tendency even in the Universal Declaration of Human Rights (UDHR), which the United Nations proclaimed in 1948, and it has been much in evidence since. The concern here is not that human rights are a Western parochialism; much of the UDHR is devoted to repudiating "traditional" Western values, including various forms of discrimination. No doubt some human-rights claims will be rejected, especially outside the nations of the developed world, when they are controversial, presuming too "thick" a conception of the human good. But sometimes we go wrong, too, when we use the glory term "human rights" to refer to objectives that aren't remotely controversial. Everybody can agree that it's a bad thing to starve to death. But (as I shall suggest in a moment) there's good reason to use "human rights" to designate something like side-constraints or conditions on the achievement of social goods, rather than those goods in themselves.[2] By contrast, the UDHR noticeably helps itself to both. To say, with the UDHR, that everyone has a right to education (to be compulsory through elementary school), and that higher education shall be equally available to all, according to merit, and that everyone has the right to ample food, clothing, medical care, and social services is to say—what? That these are terribly important things. And so they are. To say these things shouldn't be called rights isn't to say they're less important than rights; often they're *more* important. But they aren't things that an impoverished state, however well meaning, can simply provide. Unlike, say, a prohibition on torture, their realization depends on resources, not just on political will; they cannot simply be decreed. To think of human rights as side-constraints, as Robert Nozick did, is to say that if you have a right to X, then no one may deprive you of it. "Individuals have rights," he says, on the first page of *Anarchy, State and Utopia*, "and there are things no person or group may do to them (without violating their rights)." Side-constraints, then, are boundaries that it is always morally wrong to cross. We may pursue all sorts of goals, both moral and personal, but, on this view, we may do so only in ways that avoid violating the rights of others. Criticism of this idea has focused on Nozick's view that the constraints in question are infinitely stringent; for him, they are boundaries we must respect no matter what. And it is, indeed, more plausible to suppose that human rights may sometimes be abridged not only because there are circumstances where rights conflict and we must chose between them, but also because sufficiently substantial considerations of cost may sometimes be enough to outweigh a right. Take something as seemingly fundamental as freedom of expression ("through any media and regardless of frontiers," in the rhetoric of the UDHR). Suppose that abridging your freedom of expression significantly reduced the chances of an outbreak of rioting that would cause much damage to life and property. Here rights conflict. Or suppose that the problem is only that, because many people would be gravely offended, protecting your speech in these circumstances would be extraordinarily expensive. Here a right conflicts with considerations of cost.[3] Still, once we conceive of human rights as constraints on the pursuit of social ends, we

should not include among them demands that states cannot meet. That is why negative rights to do something—where other people have the obligation not to hinder me if I do choose to do it—are so prominent in the basic human rights instruments: abstaining from action is almost always possible.

Now human rights are rights you have not just against states but against all other people: my right to life is not a right only against the government. So in committing ourselves to human rights in international law, we are requiring states not just to respect them, but also to attempt to enforce respect for these rights on the part of those they govern. Even if the right in question is a negative right, protecting it will require more of a state than that it abstain from infringing it itself. And this can already take states beyond the realm of what they have the resources to do. In a society in which marriages are thought of as arrangements between families, where the choice or even the consent of the woman is not required, merely passing a law requiring that marriages require consent will not protect the rights of women. And many governments may rightly judge that they simply do not have the legitimacy to enforce such a law (they may not be able, for example, to get their police to take it seriously); and, even if they can, the financial costs of effective enforcement might leave them unable to carry out their other obligations.

You could extend the claims of human rights beyond the realm of negative rights. You could say, for example, that states ought affirmatively to guarantee certain basic needs—for nutrition and for nurture in infancy, say—either by requiring others to provide them (as when we require parents to sustain their children) or by providing them themselves (as when governments guarantee a minimum level of welfare, so long as they have the resources to do so). But such extensions increase the risk, already present, as we saw, in the case of negative rights, that we will be announcing that people have an entitlement that cannot in fact be met; which amounts, in effect, to declaring that a state has a duty to do what it cannot in fact do. Such pronouncements not only offend against the fundamental moral requirement that "ought implies can"; in doing so, they discredit the regime of human rights.

None of this is to deny the importance of international agreements establishing (or, if you like, recording) norms other than human rights: the World Health Organization and UNAIDS make declarations and policies for combating AIDS; UNESCO selects World Heritage Properties and nations pay money into the World Heritage Fund to provide resources for their protection; UNICEF promotes breastfeeding and clean water; and there are many international accounting conventions and Internet protocols that are sustained directly neither by governments nor by intergovernmental organizations. Who could be against any of this? All I am insisting is that not every good needs to be explained in the language of human rights, a language that makes most sense if it is kept within bounds.

Mission creep is not the only thing that bedevils talk of human rights. Consider the problem of indeterminacy. The predicate "arbitrary"—as when one seeks to prohibit arbitrary arrest, or arbitrary interference with privacy, family, home—typically gets a vigorous workout in the formal language of human rights, but what counts as "arbitrary" is irreducibly a matter of judgment. And so it is with what constitutes "degrading" treatment; in various patriarchal societies, measures that we might consider part of the subjugation of women are justified, sincerely, as measures to protect women's dignity. (Many members of these societies would hold that the woman whose genitals have not been properly "feminized" by surgery, or whose visage can be gazed upon without barrier by lascivious men, has been subjected to degrading treatment.) Such practices are frequently "thickly" embedded, fraught with social significances. . . . [D]ifferent societies evince greater agreement about the bad than about the good; but . . . people think of their acts "under

descriptions," and public actors seldom intend (or, at any rate, admit they intend) opprobrious deeds under opprobrious descriptions.

In raising these few perplexities, I have taken only a brief glimpse into a vast and crowded armory. On the subject of rights, you will find a great deal of conceptual ammunition for any position you wish to take. The basic dilemma is a familiar one. A conception of rights that's highly determinate in its application may not be thin enough to win widespread agreement; a conception of rights that's thin enough to win widespread agreement risks indeterminacy or impotence.

And yet the impressive thing about human rights, it seems to me, is how effectively they have functioned despite all their manifest limitations and obscurities. Yes, the promulgation of human rights, by international institutions, hardly guarantees assent—and even assent hardly guarantees anything in particular. The miracle is how well we've done without such guarantees. The substance of these rights will indeed always be contested and interpreted; but that doesn't mean they aren't useful instruments for drawing attention to the many ways in which people are brutal to one another. Like Ignatieff, I prefer to see human rights as a language for deliberation, or argument, or some other form of conversation.

And it is conversation, not mere conversion, that we should seek; we must be open to the prospect of gaining insight from our interlocutors. Let me take one example out of many. As Joseph Chan and others have remarked, the Confucian tradition holds it important that children take care of their elderly parents; from this perspective, the elderly would seem to have a right to our care similar to the claim that young children have on our nurture.[4] Certainly, in the wake of what happened in Paris during a recent heat wave that coincided with *le grand depart*—when thousands of elderly residents died alone in their apartments (some of whose children, according to news reports, declined to cut short their holidays to collect the bodies)—one wonders whether our "Western" attitude toward the care of the elderly isn't in need of reform. Now I have already expressed skepticism about the extension of such positive rights—which the right to care from your children surely is—so I offer this not as an example of a proposal I endorse, but as an example of a place where the flow of insight seems to be not from Us to Them, but in Our direction.

Though we've often been served notice that other societies, or their self-appointed spokesmen, resist talk of human rights—mistrusting them as a distinctively Western imposition, as excessively "individualist"—we should also be alert to the ways in which human rights, especially in their thinner conceptions, have managed to root themselves in a wide variety of social contexts. In effect, the reason why we do not need to ground human rights in any particular metaphysics is that many of them are already grounded in many metaphysics and can already derive sustenance from those many sources. A simple example, which I've used before, comes from the traditions of Asante, where I grew up. Free Asante citizens—both men and women—in the period before the state was conquered by Britain as well as since, are preoccupied with notions of personal dignity, with respect and self-respect. Treating others with the respect that is their due is central to Asante social life, as is a reciprocal anxiety about loss of respect, shame, and disgrace. Just as European liberalism—and democratic sentiment—grew by extending to every man and (then) woman the dignity that feudal society offered only to the aristocracy, and thus presupposes, in some sense, aspects of that feudal understanding of dignity, so modern Ghanaian thinking about politics depends, in part, on the prior grasp of concepts such as *animuonyam* (respect). Well-known Akan proverbs make it clear that, in the past, respect was precisely not something that belonged to everybody: *Agya Kra ne Agya Kwakyerēmē, emu biara mu nni animuonyam.* (Father Soul and Father Slave Kyerēmē, neither is respected; that is, whatever you call him, a slave is still a slave.)

But just as *dignitas,* which was once, by definition, the property of an elite, has grown into human dignity, which is the property of every man and woman, so *animuonyam* can be the basis of the respect for all others that lies at the heart of a commitment to human rights. . . .

When it comes to those cases where the different traditions part, a richer metaphysical grounding would not help us. For when someone argues—in the name of Confucian values or Maoism or Hinduism or Islam—that the human-rights tradition is overly individualist and so certain individual rights have a lesser weight than community interests, the return to first principles will simply take us from one terrain of disagreement to another where there seems no reason to expect greater hope of resolution.

Cass Sunstein has defended what he calls "incompletely theorized agreements" in the context of American constitutional law.[5] I would like to defend a similar freedom from the demand for high doctrine in the development of the internal practices of human-rights law. We should be able to defend our treaties by arguing that they offer people protections against governments that most of their citizens desire, and that are important enough that they also want other peoples, through their governments, to help sustain them. Once we seek to defend these rights in this pragmatic way, we can appeal to a highly diverse set of arguments: perhaps some rights—to freedom of expression, for example—are not only necessary for dignity and the maintenance of respect but also helpful in the development of economies and the stabilization of polities. And all of these are things that are wanted by most people everywhere. Sunstein's account of "incompletely theorized agreement" goes together with a proposal for a certain kind of judicial modesty: and, as I say, we do not go wrong if we resist designating everything we should devoutly hope for a "fundamental human right."

To make this pragmatic point—to argue for basic rights in a way that is receptive to a metaphysical ecumenism, responsive to the moral vocabularies we find on the ground—is not to hold, as some have suggested, that the foundation of the legitimacy of human rights is the consent of a majority of our species. After all, our most fundamental rights restrain majorities, and their consent to the system that embodies those restraints does not entail their consent to the rights themselves—otherwise there would be no need of them. (As Louis Menand has memorably observed, "Coercion is natural; freedom is artificial.")[6] If consent is an empirical notion, then most Americans do not consent to many rights that they actually have: for example, their right to marry even if they are condemned for capital crimes. The remarkable currency that human-rights discourse has gained around the world demonstrates that it speaks to people in a diversity of positions and traditions; this chord of resonating agreement explains why we can find global support for the human rights system. One reason for articulating these ideas in international documents, which are widely circulated and advertised, is just to draw attention to that core of agreement, however narrow, and to help to give it practical force. We needn't be unduly troubled by the fact that metaphysical debate is unlikely to yield consensus, because human rights can, and therefore should, be sustained without metaphysical consensus.

NOTES

1. Michael Ignatieff, *Human Rights as Politics and Idolatry* (Princeton: Princeton University Press, 2001), 7, 68.

2. See L. W. Sumner's fine discussion in "The Analysis of Rights," in *The Moral Foundation of Rights* (Oxford: Clarendon Press, 1987), especially 15–31.

3. In most respects, the United States has a singularly expansive free-expression regime, and yet even here, freedom of expression is tightly corseted, and legitimately so. The First Amendment does not protect a contract killer's verbal contract; it does not protect a fraudulent or defamatory claim; it does not protect expression that is a means of pursuing a tortious or criminal action. Then there's a matter of venue—of *where* this right is to be enjoyed. A student cannot say whatever he wants whenever he wants in a classroom; an employee has no First Amendment rights to expression in a private-sector workplace; a shopper at Macy's cannot display a placard touting the prices at Bloomingdale's. Even in places that look more like a "public forum," you'll find that signage is limited by zoning restrictions and the like. So this freedom, while real and important, doesn't fully apply in the places where you spend much of your life.

4. See Joseph Chan, "A Confucian Perspective on Human Rights for Contemporary China," in *The East Asian Challenge for Human Rights,* ed. Joanne R. Bauer and Daniel A. Bell (Cambridge: Cambridge University Press, 1999), 212–37; and Joseph Chan, "The Asian Challenge to Universal Human Rights: A Philosophical Appraisal," in *Human Rights and International Relations in the Asia-Pacific Region,* ed. James T. H. Tang (New York: St. Martin's Press, 1995). . . .

5. Cass R. Sunstein, "Incompletely Theorized Agreements," *Harvard Law Review* 108 (1995): 1733–72.

6. He continues, "Freedoms are socially engineered spaces where parties engaged in specified pursuits enjoy protection from parties who would otherwise naturally seek to interfere in those pursuits. One person's freedom is therefore always another person's restriction: we would not have even the concept of freedom if the reality of coercion were not already present." Louis Menand, "The Limits of Academic Freedom," in *The Future of Academic Freedom* (Chicago: University of Chicago Press, 1996), 1.

Study Questions

1. What are human rights?
2. Do human rights ever conflict?
3. What does Appiah mean by "talk of human rights has long had a tendency to overflow its banks?"
4. According to Appiah, why do human rights need not be grounded in any particular metaphysics?

Part X

⊠

Ultimate Questions

Phaedo

PLATO

The *Phaedo,* one of Plato's greatest and most complex works, is set in the Athenian prison on the day of Socrates's death. The discussion focuses on Plato's attempts to prove the immortality of the soul. Near the end of the dialogue, Socrates utters his last thoughts, drinks poison, and dies. This scene, reprinted here, has had an enormous impact on the conscience of countless succeeding generations.

When he'd spoken, Crito said: "Very well, Socrates: what instructions have you for these others or for me, about your children or about anything else? What could we do, that would be of most service to you?"

"What I'm always telling you, Crito," said he, "and nothing very new: if you take care for yourselves, your actions will be of service to me and mine, and to yourselves too, whatever they may be, even if you make no promises now; but if you take no care for yourselves, and are unwilling to pursue your lives along the tracks, as it were, marked by our present and earlier discussions, then even if you make many firm promises at this time, you'll do no good at all."

"Then we'll strive to do as you say," he said; "but in what fashion are we to bury you?"

"However you wish," said he: "provided you catch me, that is, and I don't get away from you." And with this he laughed quietly, looked towards us and said: "Friends, I can't persuade Crito that I am Socrates here, the one who is now conversing and arranging each of the things being discussed; but he imagines I'm that dead body he'll see in a little while, so he goes and asks how he's to bury me! But as for the great case I've been arguing all this time, that when I drink the poison,[1] I shall no longer remain with you, but

shall go off and depart for some happy state of the blessed, this, I think, I'm putting to him in vain, while comforting you and myself alike. So please stand surety for me with Crito, the opposite surety to that which he stood for me with the judges: his guarantee was that I *would* stay behind, whereas you must guarantee that, when I die, I shall *not* stay behind, but shall go off and depart; then Crito will bear it more easily, and when he sees the burning or interment of my body, he won't be distressed for me, as if I were suffering dreadful things, and won't say at the funeral that it is Socrates they are laying out or bearing to the grave or interring. Because you can be sure, my dear Crito, that misuse of words is not only troublesome in itself, but actually has a bad effect on the soul. Rather, you should have confidence, and say you are burying my body; and bury it however you please, and think most proper."

After saying this, he rose and went into a room to take a bath, and Crito followed him but told us to wait. So we waited, talking among ourselves about what had been said and reviewing it, and then again dwelling on how great a misfortune had befallen us, literally thinking of it as if we were deprived of a father and would lead the rest of our life as orphans. After he'd bathed and his children had been brought to him—he had two

From *Phaedo,* translated by David Gallop. Copyright © 1975 by Oxford University Press. Reprinted by permission of the publisher. The notes are by Andrea Tschemplik and are used with her permission.

little sons and one big one—and those women of his household had come, he talked with them in Crito's presence, and gave certain directions as to his wishes; he then told the women and children to leave, and himself returned to us.

By now it was close to sunset, as he'd spent a long time inside. So he came and sat down, fresh from his bath, and there wasn't much talk after that. Then the prison official came in, stepped up to him and said: "Socrates, I shan't reproach you as I reproach others for being angry with me and cursing, whenever by order of the rulers I direct them to drink the poison. In your time here I've known you for the most generous and gentlest and best of men who have ever come to this place; and now especially, I feel sure it isn't with me that you're angry, but with others, because you know who are responsible. Well now, you know the message I've come to bring: good-bye, then, and try to bear the inevitable as easily as you can." And with this he turned away in tears, and went off.

Socrates looked up at him and said: "Good-bye to you too, and we'll do as you say." And to us he added: "What a civil man he is! Throughout my time here he's been to see me, and sometimes talked with me, and been the best of fellows; and now how generous of him to weep for me! But come on, Crito, let's obey him: let someone bring in the poison, if it has been prepared; if not, let the man prepare it."

Crito said: "But Socrates, I think the sun is still on the mountains and hasn't yet gone down. And besides, I know of others who've taken the draught long after the order had been given them, and after dining well and drinking plenty, and even in some cases enjoying themselves with those they fancied. Be in no hurry, then: there's still time left."

Socrates said: "It's reasonable for those you speak of to do those things—because they think they gain by doing them; for myself, it's reasonable not to do them; because I think I'll gain nothing by taking the draught a little later: I'll only earn my own ridicule by clinging to life, and being sparing when there's nothing more left. Go on now; do as I ask, and nothing else."

Hearing this, Crito nodded to the boy who was standing nearby. The boy went out, and after spending a long time away he returned, bringing the man who was going to administer the poison, and was carrying it ready-pounded in a cup. When he saw the man, Socrates said: "Well, my friend, you're an expert in these things: what must one do?"

"Simply drink it," he said, "and walk about till a heaviness comes over your legs; then lie down, and it will act of itself." And with this he held out the cup to Socrates.

He took it perfectly calmly, Echecrates, without a tremor, or any change of colour or countenance; but looking up at the man, and fixing him with his customary stare, he said: "What do you say to pouring someone a libation from this drink? Is it allowed or not?"

"We only prepare as much as we judge the proper dose, Socrates," he said.

"I understand," he said: "but at least one may pray to the gods, and so one should, that the removal from this world to the next will be a happy one; that is my own prayer: so may it be." With these words he pressed the cup to his lips, and drank it off with good humour and without the least distaste.

Till then most of us had been fairly well able to restrain our tears; but when we saw he was drinking, that he'd actually drunk it, we could do so no longer. In my own case, the tears came pouring out in spite of myself, so that I covered my face and wept for myself—not for him, no, but for my own misfortune in being deprived of such a man for a companion. Even before me, Crito had moved away, when he was unable to restrain his tears. And Apollodorus, who even earlier had been continuously in tears, now burst forth into such a storm of weeping and grieving, that he made everyone present break down except Socrates himself.

But Socrates said: "What a way to behave, my strange friends! Why, it was mainly for this reason that I sent the women away, so that they shouldn't make this sort of trouble; in fact, I've heard one should die in silence. Come now, calm yourselves and have strength."

When we heard this, we were ashamed and checked our tears. He walked about, and when he said that his legs felt heavy he lay down on his back—as the man told him—and then the man, this one who'd given him the poison, felt him, and after an interval examined his feet and legs; he then pinched his foot hard and asked if he could feel it, and Socrates said not.

After that he felt his shins once more; and moving upwards in this way, he showed us that he was becoming cold and numb. He went on feeling him, and said that when the coldness reached his heart, he would be gone.

By this time the coldness was somewhere in the region of his abdomen, when he uncovered his face—it had been covered over—and spoke; and this was in fact his last utterance: "Crito," he said, "we owe a cock to Asclepius: please pay the debt, and don't neglect it."[2]

"It shall be done," said Crito; "have you anything else to say?"

To this question he made no answer, but after a short interval he stirred, and when the man uncovered him his eyes were fixed; when he saw this, Crito closed his mouth and his eyes.

And that, Echecrates, was the end of our companion, a man who, among those of his time we knew, was—so we should say—the best, the wisest too, and the most just.

NOTES

1. The poison was hemlock, frequently used in ancient executions.
2. Asclepius was the hero or god of healing. A provocative, but disputed, interpretation of Socrates's final instruction is that he considers death the cure for life and, therefore, wishes to make an offering in gratitude to the god of health.

Study Questions

1. According to Socrates, how could Crito be of most service?
2. Why, according to Socrates, will he have to be caught in order to be buried?
3. What lessons can be drawn from the equanimity with which Socrates faced death?
4. According to Socrates, is death an evil?

Writings

EPICURUS

Epicurus (341–270 B.C.E.) was an influential Greek philosopher who founded a community in Athens called "the Garden," in which men and women as well as free persons and slaves participated on equal terms. He was a prolific author, but few of his writings survive.

From *Epicurus, The Extant Remains,* ed. and trans. Cyril Bailey. Copyright © 1926 Oxford University Press. Used by permission of Oxford University Press, Inc.

His system of thought, known as Epicureanism, stressed that the gods are detached from this world. Its fundamental structure is that of atoms in motion, although persons have free will as a result of uncaused swerves in the atoms. Our knowledge is derived from sense experience. The ultimate aim of philosophy is to provide a guide to living well, maximizing pleasures and minimizing pains, but accepting such pains as lead to greater pleasures, and rejecting such pleasures as lead to greater pains. The result is a life that avoids extravagance. The virtues, such as temperance or courage, are prized because they lead to a pleasant life. So do friendships, which are, therefore, to be cultivated. Death is not to be feared, because while we exist, death is not present; when death is present, we do not exist.

LETTER TO MENOECEUS

Let no one when young delay to study philosophy, nor when he is old grow weary of his study. For no one can come too early or too late to secure the health of his soul. And the man who says that the age for philosophy has either not yet come or has gone by is like the man who says that the age for happiness is not yet come to him, or has passed away. Wherefore both when young and old a man must study philosophy, that as he grows old he may be young in blessings through the grateful recollection of what has been, and that in youth he may be old as well, since he will know no fear of what is to come. We must then meditate on the things that make our happiness, seeing that when that is with us we have all, but when it is absent we do all to win it.

The things which I used unceasingly to commend to you, these do and practice, considering them to be the first principles of the good life. First of all believe that god is a being immortal and blessed, even as the common idea of a god is engraved on men's minds, and do not assign to him anything alien to his immortality or ill-suited to his blessedness: but believe about him everything that can uphold his blessedness and immortality. For gods there are, since the knowledge of them is by clear vision. But they are not such as the many believe them to be: for indeed they do not consistently represent them as they

believe them to be. And the impious man is not he who denies the gods of the many, but he who attaches to the gods the beliefs of the many. For the statements of the many about the gods are not conceptions derived from sensation, but false suppositions, according to which the greatest misfortunes befall the wicked and the greatest blessings the good by the gift of the gods. For men being accustomed always to their own virtues welcome those like themselves, but regard all that is not of their nature as alien.

Become accustomed to the belief that death is nothing to us. For all good and evil consists in sensation, but death is deprivation of sensation. And therefore a right understanding that death is nothing to us makes the mortality of life enjoyable, not because it adds to it an infinite span of time, but because it takes away the craving for immortality. For there is nothing terrible in life for the man who has truly comprehended that there is nothing terrible in not living. So that the man speaks but idly who says that he fears death not because it will be painful when it comes, but because it is painful in anticipation. For that which gives no trouble when it comes, is but an empty pain in anticipation. So death, the most terrifying of ills, is nothing to us, since so long as we exist, death is not with us; but when death comes, then we do not exist. It does not then concern either the living or the dead, since for the former it is not, and the latter are no more.

But the many at one moment shun death as the greatest of evils, at another yearn for it as a respite from the evils in life. But the wise man neither seeks to escape life nor fears the cessation of life, for neither does life offend him nor does the absence of life seem to be any evil. And just as with food he does not seek simply the larger share and nothing else, but rather the most pleasant, so he seeks to enjoy not the longest period of time, but the most pleasant.

And he who counsels the young man to live well, but the old man to make a good end, is foolish, not merely because of the desirability of life, but also because it is the same training which teaches to live well and to die well. Yet much worse still is the man who says it is good not to be born, but

once born make haste to pass the gates of Death.[1]

For if he says this from conviction why does he not pass away out of life? For it is open to him to do so, if he had firmly made up his mind to this. But if he speaks in jest, his words are idle among men who cannot receive them.

We must then bear in mind that the future is neither ours, nor yet wholly not ours, so that we may not altogether expect it as sure to come, nor abandon hope of it, as if it will certainly not come.

We must consider that of desires some are natural, others vain, and of the natural some are necessary and others merely natural; and of the necessary some are necessary for happiness, others for the repose of the body, and others for very life. The right understanding of these facts enables us to refer all choice and avoidance to the health of the body and the soul's freedom from disturbance, since this is the aim of the life of blessedness. For it is to obtain this end that we always act, namely, to avoid pain and fear. And when this is once secured for us, all the tempest of the soul is dispersed, since the living creature has not to wander as though in search of something that is missing, and to look for some other thing by which he can fulfil the good of the soul and the good of the body. For

it is then that we have need of pleasure, when we feel pain owing to the absence of pleasure; but when we do not feel pain, we no longer need pleasure. And for this cause we call pleasure the beginning and end of the blessed life. For we recognize pleasure as the first good innate in us, and from pleasure we begin every act of choice and avoidance, and to pleasure we return again, using the feeling as the standard by which we judge every good.

And since pleasure is the first good and natural to us, for this very reason we do not choose every pleasure, but sometimes we pass over many pleasures, when greater discomfort accrues to us as the result of them: and similarly we think many pains better than pleasures, since a greater pleasure comes to us when we have endured pains for a long time. Every pleasure then because of its natural kinship to us is good, yet not every pleasure is to be chosen: even as every pain also is an evil, yet not all are always of a nature to be avoided. Yet by a scale of comparison and by the consideration of advantages and disadvantages we must form our judgement on all these matters. For the good on certain occasions we treat as bad, and conversely the bad as good.

And again independence of desire we think a great good—not that we may at all times enjoy but a few things, but that, if we do not possess many, we may enjoy the few in the genuine persuasion that those have the sweetest pleasure in luxury who least need it, and that all that is natural is easy to be obtained, but that which is superfluous is hard. And so plain savours bring us a pleasure equal to a luxurious diet, when all the pain due to want is removed; and bread and water produce the highest pleasure, when one who needs them puts them to his lips. To grow accustomed therefore to a simple and not luxurious diet gives us health to the full, and makes a man alert for the needful employments of life, and when after long intervals we approach luxuries disposes us better towards them, and fits us to be fearless of fortune.

When, therefore, we maintain that pleasure is the end, we do not mean the pleasures of profligates and those that consist in sensuality, as is supposed by some who are either ignorant or disagree with us or do not understand, but freedom from pain in the body and from trouble in the mind. For it is not continuous drinkings and revellings, nor the satisfaction of lusts, nor the enjoyment of fish and other luxuries of the wealthy table, which produce a pleasant life, but sober reasoning, searching out the motives for all choice and avoidance, and banishing mere opinions, to which are due the greatest disturbance of the spirit.

Of all this the beginning and the greatest good is prudence. Wherefore prudence is a more precious thing even than philosophy: for from prudence are sprung all the other virtues, and it teaches us that it is not possible to live pleasantly without living prudently and honourably and justly, nor, again, to live a life of prudence, honour, and justice without living pleasantly. For the virtues are by nature bound up with the pleasant life, and the pleasant life is inseparable from them. For indeed who, think you, is a better man than he who holds reverent opinions concerning the gods, and is at all times free from fear of death, and has reasoned out the end ordained by nature? He understands that the limit of good things is easy to fulfil and easy to attain, whereas the course of ills is either short in time or slight in pain: he laughs at destiny, whom some have introduced as the mistress of all things. He thinks that with us lies the chief power in determining events, some of which happen by necessity and some by chance, and some are within our control; for while necessity cannot be called to account, he sees that chance is inconstant, but that which is in our control is subject to no master, and to it are naturally attached praise and blame. For, indeed, it were better to follow the myths about the gods than to become a slave to the destiny of the natural philosophers: for the former suggests a hope of placating the gods by worship, whereas the latter involves a necessity which knows no placation. As to chance, he does not regard it as a god as most men do (for in a god's acts there is no disorder), nor as an uncertain cause of all things for he does not believe that good and evil are given by chance to man for the framing of a blessed life, but that opportunities for great good and great evil are afforded by it. He therefore thinks it better to be unfortunate in reasonable action than to prosper in unreason. For it is better in a man's actions that what is well chosen should fail, rather than that what is ill chosen should be successful owing to chance.

Meditate therefore on these things and things akin to them night and day by yourself, and with a companion like to yourself, and never shall you be disturbed waking or asleep, but you shall live like a god among men. For a man who lives among immortal blessings is not like to a mortal being.

PRINCIPLE DOCTRINES

I. The blessed and immortal nature knows no trouble itself nor causes trouble to any other, so that it is never constrained by anger or favour. For all such things exist only in the weak.
II. Death is nothing to us: for that which is dissolved is without sensation; and that which lacks sensation is nothing to us.
III. The limit of quantity in pleasures is the removal of all that is painful. Wherever pleasure is present, as long as it is there, there is neither pain of body nor of mind, nor of both at once.
IV. Pain does not last continuously in the flesh, but the acutest pain is there for a very short time, and even that which just exceeds the pleasure in the flesh does not continue for many days at once. But chronic illnesses permit a predominance of pleasure over pain in the flesh.
V. It is not possible to live pleasantly without living prudently and honourably and justly, [nor again to live a life of prudence, honour, and justice] without living pleasantly. And the man who does not possess the pleasant life, is not living prudently and honourably and justly, and the man who does not possess the virtuous life, cannot possibly live pleasantly.

VI. To secure protection from men anything is a natural good, by which you may be able to attain this end.

VII. Some men wished to become famous and conspicuous, thinking that they would thus win for themselves safety from other men. Wherefore if the life of such men is safe, they have obtained the good which nature craves; but if it is not safe, they do not possess that for which they strove at first by the instinct of nature.

VIII. No pleasure is a bad thing in itself: but the means which produce some pleasures bring with them disturbances many times greater than the pleasures.

IX. If every pleasure could be intensified so that it lasted and influenced the whole organism or the most essential parts of our nature, pleasures would never differ from one another.

X. If the things that produce the pleasures of profligates could dispel the fears of the mind about the phenomena of the sky and death and its pains, and also teach the limits of desires and of pains, we should never have cause to blame them: for they would be filling themselves full with pleasures from every source and never have pain of body or mind, which is the evil of life.

XI. If we were not troubled by our suspicions of the phenomena of the sky and about death, fearing that it concerns us, and also by our failure to grasp the limits of pains and desires, we should have no need of natural science.

XII. A man cannot dispel his fear about the most important matters if he does not know what is the nature of the universe but suspects the truth of some mythical story. So that without natural science it is not possible to attain our pleasures unalloyed.

XIII. There is no profit in securing protection in relation to men, if things above and things beneath the earth and indeed all in the boundless universe remain matters of suspicion.

XIV. The most unalloyed source of protection from men, which is secured to some extent by a certain force of expulsion, is in fact the immunity which results from a quiet life and the retirement from the world.

XV. The wealth demanded by nature is both limited and easily procured; that demanded by idle imaginings stretches on to infinity.

XVI. In but few things chance hinders a wise man, but the greatest and most important matters reason has ordained and throughout the whole period of life does and will ordain.

XVII. The just man is most free from trouble, the unjust most full of trouble.

XVIII. The pleasure in the flesh is not increased, when once the pain due to want is removed, but is only varied: and the limit as regards pleasure in the mind is begotten by the reasoned understanding of these very pleasures and of the emotions akin to them, which used to cause the greatest fear to the mind.

XIX. Infinite time contains no greater pleasure than limited time, if one measures by reason the limits of pleasure.

XX. The flesh perceives the limits of pleasure as unlimited and unlimited time is required to supply it. But the mind, having attained a reasoned understanding of the ultimate good of the flesh and its limits and having dissipated the fears concerning the time to come, supplies us with the complete life, and we have no further need of infinite time: but neither does the mind shun pleasure, nor, when circumstances begin to bring about the departure from life, does it approach its end as though it fell short in any way of the best life.

XXI. He who has learned the limits of life knows that that which removes the pain due to want and makes the whole of life complete is easy to obtain; so that there is no need of actions which involve competition.

XXII. We must consider both the real purpose and all the evidence of direct perception, to which we always refer the conclusions of opinion; otherwise, all will be full of doubt and confusion.

XXIII. If you fight against all sensations, you will have no standard by which to judge even those of them which you say are false.

XXIV. If you reject any single sensation and fail to distinguish between the conclusion of opinion as to the appearance awaiting confirmation and that which is actually given by the sensation or feeling, or each intuitive apprehension of the mind, you will confound all other sensations as well with the same groundless opinion, so that you will reject every standard of judgement. And if among the mental images created by your opinion you affirm both that which awaits confirmation and that which does not, you will not escape error, since you will have preserved the whole cause of doubt in every judgement between what is right and what is wrong.

XXV. If on each occasion instead of referring your actions to the end of nature, you turn to some other nearer standard when you are making a choice or an avoidance, your actions will not be consistent with your principles.

XXVI. Of desires, all that do not lead to a sense of pain, if they are not satisfied, are not necessary, but involve a craving which is easily dispelled, when the object is hard to procure or they seem likely to produce harm.

XXVII. Of all the things which wisdom acquires to produce the blessedness of the complete life, far the greatest is the possession of friendship.

XXVIII. The same conviction which has given us confidence that there is nothing terrible that lasts for ever or even for long, has also seen the protection of friendship most fully completed in the limited evils of this life.

XXIX. Among desires some are natural and necessary, some natural but not necessary, and others neither natural nor necessary, but due to idle imagination.

XXX. Wherever in the case of desires which are physical, but do not lead to a sense of pain, if they are not fulfilled, the effort is intense, such pleasures are due to idle imagination, and it is not owing to their own nature that they fail to be dispelled, but owing to the empty imaginings of the man.

XXXI. The justice which arises from nature is a pledge of mutual advantage to restrain men from harming one another and save them from being harmed.

XXXII. For all living things which have not been able to make compacts not to harm one another or be harmed, nothing ever is either just or unjust; and likewise too for all tribes of men which have been unable or unwilling to make compacts not to harm or be harmed.

NOTE

1. [These words are attributed to the sixth-century B.C.E. Greek poet Theognis—S.M.C.]

Study Questions

1. According to Epicurus, why is death nothing to us?
2. Do you agree with Epicurus that scientific knowledge helps dispel fear?
3. Why, according to Epicurus, can you not fight against all sensations?
4. Do you agree with Epicurus that the pleasant life is a life of virtue?

Death

THOMAS NAGEL

Is death an evil? If so, why? These questions are explored here by Thomas Nagel, whose work we read previously. Note that he does not discuss the value that one person's life or death may have for others, but only the value it has for the person who is its subject.

If death is the unequivocal and permanent end of our existence, the question arises whether it is a bad thing to die.

There is conspicuous disagreement about the matter: some people think death is dreadful; others have no objection to death *per se,* though they hope their own will be neither premature nor painful. Those in the former category tend to think those in the latter are blind to the obvious, while the latter suppose the former to be prey to some sort of confusion. On the one hand it can be said that life is all we have and the loss of it is the greatest loss we can sustain. On the other hand it may be objected that death deprives this supposed loss of its subject, and that if we realize that death is not an unimaginable condition of the persisting person, but a mere blank, we will see that it can have no value whatever, positive or negative.

Since I want to leave aside the question whether we are, or might be, immortal in some form, I shall simply use the word "death" and its cognates in this discussion to mean *permanent* death, unsupplemented by any form of conscious survival. I want to ask whether death is in itself an evil; and how great an evil, and of what kind, it might be. The question should be of interest even to those who believe in some form of immortality, for one's attitude toward immortality must depend in part on one's attitude toward death.

If death is an evil at all, it cannot be because of its positive features, but only because of what it deprives us of. I shall try to deal with the difficulties surrounding the natural view that death is an evil because it brings to an end all the goods that life contains. We need not give an account of these goods here, except to observe that some of them, like perception, desire, activity, and thought, are so general as to be constitutive of human life. They are widely regarded as formidable benefits in themselves, despite the fact that they are conditions of misery as well as of happiness, and that a sufficient quantity of more particular evils can perhaps outweigh them. That is what is meant, I think, by the allegation that it is good simply to be alive, even if one is undergoing terrible experiences. The situation is roughly this: There are elements which, if added to one's experience, make life better; there are other elements which, if added to one's experience, make life worse. But what remains when these are set aside is not merely *neutral:* it is emphatically positive. Therefore life is worth living even when the bad elements of experience are plentiful, and the good ones too meager to outweigh the bad ones on their own. The additional positive weight is supplied by experience itself, rather than by any of its contents.

I shall not discuss the value that one person's life or death may have for others, or its objective value, but only the value it has for the person who is its subject. That seems to me the primary case, and the case which presents the greatest difficulties. Let me add only two observations. First, the value of life and its contents does not attach to mere organic survival: almost everyone would be indifferent (other things equal) between immediate death and immediate coma followed by death twenty years later without reawakening. And second, like most goods, this can be multiplied by time: more is better than less. The added quantities need not be temporally continuous (though continuity has its social advantages). People are attracted to the possibility of long-term suspended animation or freezing, followed by the resumption of conscious life, because they can regard it from within simply as a *continuation* of their present life. If these techniques are ever perfected, what from outside appeared as a dormant interval of three hundred years could be experienced by the subject as nothing more than a sharp discontinuity in the character of his experiences. I do not deny, of course, that this has its own disadvantages. Family and friends may have died in the meantime; the language may have changed; the comforts of social, geographical, and cultural familiarity would be lacking. Nevertheless these inconveniences would not obliterate the basic advantage of continued, though discontinuous, existence.

If we turn from what is good about life to what is bad about death, the case is completely different. Essentially, though there may be problems about their specification, what we find desirable in life are certain states, conditions, or types of activity. It is *being* alive, *doing* certain things, having certain experiences, that we consider good. But if death is an evil, it is the *loss of life*, rather than the state of being dead, or nonexistent, or unconscious, that is objectionable.[1] This asymmetry is important. If it is good to be alive,

that advantage can be attributed to a person at each point of his life. It is a good of which Bach had more than Schubert, simply because he lived longer. Death, however, is not an evil of which Shakespeare has so far received a larger portion than Proust. If death is a disadvantage, it is not easy to say when a man suffers it.

There are two other indications that we do not object to death merely because it involves long periods of nonexistence. First, as has been mentioned, most of us would not regard the *temporary* suspension of life, even for substantial intervals, as in itself a misfortune. If it ever happens that people can be frozen without reduction of the conscious lifespan, it will be inappropriate to pity those who are temporarily out of circulation. Second, none of us existed before we were born (or conceived), but few regard that as a misfortune. I shall have more to say about this later.

The point that death is not regarded as an unfortunate *state* enables us to refute a curious but very common suggestion about the origin of the fear of death. It is often said that those who object to death have made the mistake of trying to imagine what it is like to *be* dead. It is alleged that the failure to realize that this task is logically impossible (for the banal reason that there is nothing to imagine) leads to the conviction that death is a mysterious and therefore terrifying prospective *state*. But this diagnosis is evidently false, for it is just as impossible to imagine being totally unconscious as to imagine being dead (though it is easy enough to imagine oneself, from the outside, in either of those conditions). Yet people who are averse to death are not usually averse to unconsciousness (so long as it does not entail a substantial cut in the total duration of waking life).

If we are to make sense of the view that to die is bad, it must be on the ground that life is a good and death is the corresponding deprivation or loss, bad not because of any positive features but because of the desirability of what it removes. We must now turn to the serious difficulties which this hypothesis raises, difficulties about loss and privation in general, and about death in particular.

Essentially, there are three types of problem. First, doubt may be raised whether *anything can be bad for a man without being* positively unpleasant to him: specifically, it may be doubted that there are any evils which consist merely in the deprivation or absence of possible goods, and which do not depend on someone's *minding that deprivation*. Second, there are special difficulties, in the case of death, about how the supposed misfortune is to be assigned to a subject at all. There is doubt both as to *who* its subject is, and as to *when* he undergoes it. So long as a person exists, he has not yet died, and once he has died, he no longer exists; so there seems to be no time when death, if it is a misfortune, can be ascribed to its unfortunate subject. The third type of difficulty concerns the asymmetry, mentioned above, between our attitudes to posthumous and prenatal nonexistence. How can the former be bad if the latter is not?

It should be recognized that if these are valid objections to counting death as an evil, they will apply to many other supposed evils as well. The first type of objection is expressed in general form by the common remark that what you don't know can't hurt you. It means that even if a man is betrayed by his friends, ridiculed behind his back, and despised by people who treat him politely to his face, none of it can be counted as a misfortune for him so long as he does not suffer as a result. It means that a man is not injured if his wishes are ignored by the executor of his will, or if, after his death, the belief becomes current that all the literary works on which his fame rests were really written by his brother, who died in Mexico at the age of 28. It seems to me worth asking what assumptions about good and evil lead to these drastic restrictions.

All the questions have something to do with time. There certainly are goods and evils of a simple kind (including some pleasures and pains) which a person possesses at a given time simply in virtue of his condition at that time. But this is not true of all the things we regard as good or bad for a man. Often we need to know his history to tell whether something is a misfortune or not; this applies to ills like deterioration, deprivation, and damage. Sometimes his experiential *state* is relatively unimportant—as in the case of a man who wastes his life in the cheerful pursuit of a method of communicating with asparagus plants. Someone who holds that all goods and evils must be temporally assignable states of the person may of course try to bring difficult cases into line by pointing to the pleasure or pain that more complicated goods and evils cause. Loss, betrayal, deception, and ridicule are on this view bad because people suffer when they learn of them. But it should be asked how our ideas of human value would have to be constituted to accommodate these cases directly instead. One advantage of such an account might be that it would enable us to explain *why* the discovery of these misfortunes causes suffering—in a way that makes it reasonable. For the natural view is that the discovery of betrayal makes us unhappy because it is bad to be betrayed—not that betrayal is bad because its discovery makes us unhappy.

It therefore seems to me worth exploring the position that most good and ill fortune has as its subject a person identified by his history and his possibilities, rather than merely by his categorical state of the moment—and that while this subject can be exactly located in a sequence of places and times, the same is not necessarily true of the goods and ills that befall him.[2]

These ideas can be illustrated by an example of deprivation whose severity approaches that of death. Suppose an intelligent person receives a brain injury that reduces him to the mental condition of a contented infant, and that such desires as remain to him can be satisfied by a custodian, so that he is free from care. Such a development would be widely regarded as a severe misfortune, not only for his friends and relations, or for society, but also, and primarily, for the person himself. This does not mean that a contented infant is unfortunate. The intelligent adult who has been *reduced* to this condition is the subject of the misfortune. He is the one we pity, though of course he does not mind his condition—there is some doubt, in fact, whether he can be said to exist any longer.

The view that such a man has suffered a misfortune is open to the same objections which have been raised in regard to death. He does not mind his condition. It is in fact the same condition he was in at the age of three months, except that he is bigger. If we did not pity him then, why pity him now; in any case, who is there to pity? The intelligent adult has disappeared, and for a creature like the one before us, happiness consists in a full stomach and a dry diaper.

If these objections are invalid, it must be because they rest on a mistaken assumption about the temporal relation between the subject of a misfortune and the circumstances which constitute it. If, instead of concentrating exclusively on the oversized baby before us, we consider the person he was, and the person he *could* be now, then his reduction to this state and the cancellation of his natural adult development constitute a perfectly intelligible catastrophe.

This case should convince us that it is arbitrary to restrict the goods and evils that can befall a man to nonrelational properties ascribable to him at particular times. As it stands, that restriction excludes not only such cases of gross degeneration, but also a good deal of what is important about success and failure, and other features of a life that have the character of processes. I believe we can go further, however. There are goods and evils which are irreducibly relational; they are features of the relations between a person, with spatial and temporal boundaries of the usual sort, and circumstances which may not coincide with him either in space or in time. A man's life includes much that does not take place within the boundaries of his body and his mind, and what happens to him can include much that does not take place within the boundaries of his life. These boundaries are commonly crossed by the misfortunes of being deceived, or despised, or betrayed. (If this is correct, there is a simple account of what is wrong with breaking a deathbed promise. It is an injury to the dead man. For certain purposes it is possible to regard time as

just another type of distance.) The case of mental degeneration shows us an evil that depends on a contrast between the reality and the possible alternatives. A man is the subject of good and evil as much because he has hopes which may or may not be fulfilled, or possibilities which may or may not be realized, as because of his capacity to suffer and enjoy. If death is an evil, it must be accounted for in these terms, and the impossibility of locating it within life should not trouble us.

When a man dies we are left with his corpse, and while a corpse can suffer the kind of mishap that may occur to an article of furniture, it is not a suitable object for pity. The man, however, is. He has lost his life, and if he had not died, he would have continued to live it, and to possess whatever good there is in living. If we apply to death the account suggested for the case of dementia, we shall say that although the spatial and temporal locations of the individual who suffered the loss are clear enough, the misfortune itself cannot be so easily located. One must be content just to state that his life is over and there will never be any more of it. That *fact*, rather than his past or present condition, constitutes his misfortune, if it is one. Nevertheless if there is a loss, someone must suffer it, and *he* must have existence and specific spatial and temporal location even if the loss itself does not. The fact that Beethoven had no children may have been a cause of regret to him, or a sad thing for the world, but it cannot be described as a misfortune for the children that he never had. All of us, I believe, are fortunate to have been born. But unless good and ill can be assigned to an embryo, or even to an unconnected pair of gametes, it cannot be said that not to be born is a misfortune. (That is a factor to be considered in deciding whether abortion and contraception are akin to murder.)

This approach also provides a solution to the problem of temporal asymmetry, pointed out by Lucretius.[3] He observed that no one finds it disturbing to contemplate the eternity preceding his own birth, and he took this to show that it must be irrational to fear death, since death is simply the mirror image of the prior abyss. That is not true, however, and the difference between the two explains why it is reasonable to regard them differently. It is true that both the time before a man's birth and the time after his death are times when he does not exist. But the time after his death is time of which his death deprives him. It is time in which, had he not died then, he would be alive. Therefore any death entails the loss of *some* life that its victim would have led had he not died at that or any earlier point. We know perfectly well what it would be for him to have had it instead of losing it, and there is no difficulty in identifying the loser.

But we cannot say that the time prior to a man's birth is time in which he would have lived had he been born not then but earlier. For aside from the brief margin permitted by premature labor, he *could* not have been born earlier: anyone born substantially earlier than he was would have been someone else. Therefore the time prior to his birth is not time in which his subsequent birth prevents him from living. His birth, when it occurs, does not entail the loss to him of any life whatever.

The direction of time is crucial in assigning possibilities to people or other individuals. Distinct possible lives of a single person can diverge from a common beginning, but they cannot converge to a common conclusion from diverse beginnings. (The latter would represent not a set of different possible lives of one individual, but a set of distinct possible individuals, whose lives have identical conclusions.) Given an identifiable individual, countless possibilities for his continued existence are imaginable, and we can clearly conceive of what it would be for him to go on existing indefinitely. However inevitable it is that this will not come about, its possibility is still that of the continuation of a good for him, if life is the good we take it to be.[4]

We are left, therefore, with the question whether the nonrealization of this possibility is in every case a misfortune, or whether it depends on what can naturally be hoped for. This seems to me the most serious difficulty with the view that death is always an evil. Even if we can dispose of the objections against admitting misfortune that is not experienced, or cannot be assigned to a definite time in the person's life, we still have to set some limits on *how* possible a possibility must be for its nonrealization to be a misfortune (or good fortune, should the possibility be a bad one). The death of Keats at 24 is generally regarded as tragic; that of Tolstoy at 82 is not. Although they will both be dead for ever, Keats' death deprived him of many years of life which were allowed to Tolstoy; so in a clear sense Keats' loss was greater (though not in the sense standardly employed in mathematical comparison between infinite quantities). However, this does not prove that Tolstoy's loss was insignificant. Perhaps we record an objection only to evils which are gratuitously added to the inevitable; the fact that it is worse to die at 24 than at 82 does not imply that it is not a terrible thing to die at 82, or even at 806. The question is whether we can regard as a misfortune any limitation, like mortality, that is normal to the species. Blindness or near-blindness is not a misfortune for a mole, nor would it be for a man if that were the natural condition of the human race.

The trouble is that life familiarizes us with the goods of which death deprives us. We are already able to appreciate them, as a mole is not able to appreciate vision. If we put aside doubts about their status as goods and grant that their quantity is in part a function of their duration, the question remains whether death, no matter when it occurs, can be said to deprive its victim of what is in the relevant sense a possible continuation of life.

The situation is an ambiguous one. Observed from without, human beings obviously have a natural lifespan and cannot live much longer than a hundred years. A man's sense of his own experience, on the other hand, does not embody this idea of a natural limit. His existence defines for him an essentially open-ended possible future, containing the usual mixture of goods and evils that he has found so tolerable in the past. Having been gratuitously introduced to the world by a collection of natural, historical, and social accidents, he finds himself the subject of a *life,* with an indeterminate and not essentially limited future. Viewed in this way, death, no matter how inevitable, is an abrupt cancellation of indefinitely extensive possible goods. Normality seems to have nothing to do with it, for the fact that we will all inevitably die in a few score years cannot by itself imply that it would not be good to live longer. Suppose that we were all inevitably going to die in *agony*—physical agony lasting six months. Would inevitability make *that* prospect any less unpleasant? And why should it be different for a deprivation? If the normal lifespan were a thousand years, death at 80 would be a tragedy. As things are, it may just be a more widespread tragedy. If there is no limit to the amount of life that it would be good to have, then it may be that a bad end is in store for us all.

NOTES

1. It is sometimes suggested that what we really mind is the process of *dying.* But I should not really object to dying if it were not followed by death.

2. It is certainly not true in general of the things that can be said of him. For example, Abraham Lincoln was taller than Louis XIV. But when?

3. [Lucretius (c. 99–c. 55 B.C.E.) was a Roman poet and philosopher who wrote the epic poem *De rerum natura* (Of the nature of things), in which he expounds the philosophy of Epicurus.—S.M.C.]

4. I confess to being troubled by the above argument, on the ground that it is too sophisticated to explain the simple difference between our attitudes to prenatal and posthumous nonexistence. For this reason I suspect that something essential is omitted from the account of the badness of death by an analysis which treats it as a deprivation of possibilities. My suspicion is supported by the following suggestion of Robert Nozick. We could imagine discovering that people developed from individual spores that had existed indefinitely far in advance of their birth. In this fantasy, birth never occurs naturally more than a hundred years before the permanent end of the spore's existence. But then we discover a way to trigger the premature batching of these spores, and people are born who have thousands of years of active life before them. Given such a situation, it would be possible to imagine *oneself* having come into existence thousands of years previously. If we put aside the question whether this would really be the same person, even given the identity of the spore, then the consequence appears to be that a person's birth at a given time *could* deprive him of many earlier years of possible life. Now while it would be cause for regret that one had been deprived of all those possible years of life by being born too late, the feeling would differ from that which many people have about death. I conclude that something about the future *prospect* of permanent nothingness is not captured by the analysis in terms of denied possibilities. If so, then Lucretius' argument still awaits an answer. I suspect that it requires a general treatment of the difference between past and future in our attitudes toward our own lives. Our attitudes toward past and future pain are very different, for example. Derek Parfit's unpublished writings on this topic have revealed its difficulty to me.

Study Questions

1. If death is not an evil for a person who dies, is death, therefore, not an evil for anyone?
2. Do you agree with Nagel that a man who devotes himself to cheerful pursuit of a method of communicating with asparagus has wasted his life?
3. Would a life devoted to trying to communicate with beings from another galaxy be wasted?
4. Do you agree with Nagel that all of us are fortunate to have been born?

The Badness of Death

SHELLY KAGAN

Shelly Kagan is Professor of Philosophy at Yale University. He considers a puzzle raised by Lucretius, who asked why we should be concerned about not being alive after the time of our death, although we are unconcerned about not being alive before the time of our birth.

Let me turn to . . . a puzzle that we get from Lucretius, a Roman philosopher.[1] Lucretius was one of those who thought it a mistake to claim that death could be bad for us. He thinks we are confused when we find the prospect of our death upsetting. He recognizes, of course, that most of us *are* upset at the fact that we're going to die. We think death is bad for us. Why? In my own case, of course, it's because after my death I won't exist. . . . [A]fter my death it will be true that if only I were still alive, I could be enjoying the good things in life.

Fair enough, says Lucretius, but wait a minute. The time after I die isn't the *only* period during which I won't exist. It's not the only period in which it is true that if only I were alive, I could be enjoying the good things in life. There's *another* period of nonexistence: the period before my birth. To be sure, there will be an infinite period after my death in which I won't exist—and realizing that fills me with dismay. But be that all as it may, there was of course also an infinite period *before* I came into existence. Well, says Lucretius, if nonexistence is so bad—and by the deprivation account it seems that we want to say that it is—shouldn't I be upset at the fact that there was also this eternity of nonexistence before I was born?

But, Lucretius suggests, that's silly, right? Nobody is upset about the fact that there was an eternity of nonexistence *before* they were born. In which case, he concludes, it doesn't make any sense to be upset about the eternity of nonexistence *after* you die.

Lucretius doesn't offer this as a puzzle. Rather, he offers it as an argument that we should not be concerned about the fact that we're going to die. Unsurprisingly, however, most philosophers aren't willing to go with Lucretius all the way to this conclusion. They insist, instead, that there must be something wrong with this argument someplace. The challenge is to figure out just where the mistake is.

What are the options here? One possibility, of course, is to simply agree with Lucretius. There is nothing bad about the eternity of nonexistence before I was born. So, similarly, there is nothing bad about the eternity of nonexistence after I die. Despite what most of us think, death is not bad for me. That's certainly one possibility—completely agreeing with Lucretius.

A second possibility is to partly agree with Lucretius. Perhaps we really do need to treat these two eternities of nonexistence on a par; but instead of saying with Lucretius that there was nothing bad about the eternity of nonexistence before birth and so nothing bad about the eternity of nonexistence after death, maybe we should say, instead, that just as there is something bad about the eternity of nonexistence

From Shelly Kagan, *Death*, Yale University Press, 2012. Reprinted by permission of the publisher.

after we die, so too there must be something bad about the eternity of nonexistence before we were born! Maybe we should just stick with the deprivation account and not lose faith in it. The deprivation account tells us that it's bad for us that there's this period after we die, because if only we weren't dead then, we would still be able to enjoy the good things in life. So maybe we should say, similarly, that it *is* bad for us that there's this period before we come into existence. After all, if only we had existed then, we would have been able to enjoy the good things in life. So maybe Lucretius was right when he tells us that we have to treat both periods the same, but for all that he could be wrong in concluding that neither period is bad. Maybe we should think *both* periods are bad. That's a possibility, too.

What other possibilities are there? We might say that although Lucretius is right when he points out that there are two periods of nonexistence, not just one, nonetheless there is a justification for treating them differently. Perhaps there is an important difference between the two periods, a kind of asymmetry that explains why we should care about the one but not the other.

Most philosophers want to take this last way out. They say that there's something that explains why it makes sense, why it's reasonable, to care about the eternity of nonexistence after my death in a way that I don't care about the eternity of nonexistence before my birth. But then the puzzle, of course, is to point to a difference that would *justify* that kind of asymmetrical treatment of the two periods. It's easy to *say* that it's reasonable to treat the two periods differently; the philosophical challenge is to point to something that explains or justifies that asymmetrical treatment.

One very common response is to say something like this. Consider the period after my death. I'm no longer alive. I have *lost* my life. In contrast, during the period before my birth, although I'm not alive, I have not *lost* my life. I have never yet been alive. And, of course, you can't lose something you've never yet had. So

what's worse about the period after death is the fact that death involves *loss,* whereas prenatal nonexistence does *not* involve loss. And so (the argument goes), we can see why it's reasonable to care more about the period after death than the period before birth. The one involves loss, while the other does not.

This is, as I say, a very common response. But I am inclined to think that it can't be an adequate answer. It is true, of course, that the period after death involves loss while the period before birth does not. The very definition of "loss," after all, requires that in order to have lost something, it must be true that you don't have something that at an earlier time you did have. Given this definition, it follows trivially that the period after death involves loss, while the period before birth does not. After all, as we just observed, during the period before birth, although I do not *have* life, it is also true that I haven't had life previously. So I haven't *lost* anything.

Of course, there's another thing that's true about this prenatal period, to wit, I don't have life and I'm *going* to get it. So I don't yet have something that's going to come in the future. That's not true about the postlife period. After death I've *lost* life. But it's not true of this postdeath period that I don't have life and I'm going to get it in the future. So this period after death isn't quite like the period before birth: in the period after death, I am not in the state of not yet having something that I am going to get. That's an interesting difference.

As it happens, we don't have a name for this other kind of state—where you don't yet have something that you will get later. It is similar to loss, in one way, but it's not quite like loss. Let's call it "schmoss." When I have *lost* something, then, I don't have it, but I did have it earlier. And when I have *schmost* something, I don't have it yet, but I will get it later.

So here's the deal. During the period after death, there's a loss of life, but no schmoss of life. And during the period before birth, there's no loss of life, but there is a schmoss of life. And now, as philosophers, we need to ask: why do we care more about *loss* of life than *schmoss* of life? What is it about the fact that we don't have something that we used to have, that makes this worse than not having something that we're going to have?

It's easy to overlook the symmetry here, because we've got this nice word "loss," and we don't have the word "schmoss." But that's not really explaining anything, it's just pointing to the thing that needs explaining. Why do we care more about not having what once upon a time we did, than about not having what once upon a time we will? That's really quite puzzling.

Various proposals have been made to explain this difference in attitude toward the two periods of nonexistence. One of them comes from Thomas Nagel, a contemporary philosopher.[2] Nagel starts by pointing out how easy it is to imagine the possibility of living longer. Suppose I die at the age of eighty. Perhaps I will get hit by a car. Imagine, though, that if I didn't die then, I would have continued living until I was ninety or even one hundred. That certainly seems possible, even if in fact I am going to die at eighty. The fact that I am going to die at eighty is a *contingent* fact about me. It is not a necessary fact about me that I die at eighty. So it is an easy enough matter to imagine my living longer, by having my death come later. That's why it makes sense to get upset at the fact of my death coming when it does: I could have lived longer, by having death come later.

In contrast, Nagel notes, if I am going to be upset about my nonexistence before my birth, we have to imagine my being born earlier. We have to imagine my living longer by having my birth come sooner. Is this possible? I was born in 1954. Can I be upset about the fact that I was born in 1954 instead of, say, 1944?

Nagel thinks, however, that I shouldn't be upset about the fact that I wasn't born in 1944, because in fact it isn't *possible* for me to have an earlier birth. The date of my *death* is a contingent fact about me. But the date of my *birth* is not a contingent fact about me. Well, that's not

quite right. We could change the time of birth slightly, perhaps by having me delivered prematurely, or through Caesarean section, or what have you. Strictly speaking, of course, the crucial moment is the moment at which I come into *existence*. Let's suppose that this is the time when the egg and the sperm join. Nagel's thought is that this is not a contingent moment in my life story. That's an *essential* moment in my life story.

How could that be? Can't we easily imagine my parents having had sex ten years earlier? Sure we can. But remember, if they had had sex ten years earlier, it would have been a different egg and a different sperm coming together, so it wouldn't be *me*. It would be some sibling of mine that, as it happens, never got born. Obviously, there could have been some sibling of mine that came into existence in 1944, but *I* couldn't have come into existence in 1944. The person we are imagining with the earlier birth date wouldn't be *me*. What this means, Nagel suggests, is that although we can *say* the words "if only I had been born earlier," this isn't really pointing to a genuine metaphysical possibility. So there is no point in being upset at the nonexistence before you started to exist, because you couldn't have had a longer life by coming into existence earlier. (In contrast, as we have seen, you could have a longer life by going out of existence later.)

I must say, that's a pretty intriguing suggestion. But I think it can't be quite right. Or rather, it cannot be the complete story about how to answer Lucretius's puzzle. For in some cases, I think, we *can* easily imagine the possibility of having come into existence earlier. Suppose we've got a fertility clinic that has some sperm on hold and has some eggs on hold. Perhaps they keep them there frozen until they're ready to use them. And they thaw a pair out in, say, 2025. They fertilize the egg and eventually the person is born. That person, it seems to me, can correctly say that he could have come into existence earlier. He could look back and say that if only they had put the relevant sperm and egg together ten years earlier, he would have come into existence ten years earlier. It wouldn't be a sibling; it would have been *him*. After all, it would have been the very same sperm and the very same egg, resulting in the very same person. So if only they had combined the sperm and egg ten years earlier, he would have been born ten years earlier.

If that's right—and it does seem to me to be right—then Nagel is wrong in saying it's not possible to imagine being born earlier. In at least some cases it is. Yet, if we imagine somebody like this, somebody who's an offspring of this kind of fertility clinic, and we ask, "Would they be upset that they weren't born earlier?" it still seems as though most people would say, "No, of course not." So Nagel's solution to our puzzle doesn't seem to me to be an adequate one.

Here's another possible answer. This one comes from Fred Feldman, another contemporary philosopher.[3] If I say, "if only I would die later," what am I imagining? Suppose I will get hit by a car in 2034, when I am eighty. We can certainly imagine what would happen if I *didn't* get killed at that point. What do we imagine? Something like this, I suppose: instead of my living a "mere" eighty years, we imagine that I would live to be eighty-five or ninety, or more. We imagine a longer life. When we imagine my dying later, we imagine my having a longer life.

But what do I imagine when I say, "if only I had been born *earlier*"? According to Feldman, you don't actually imagine a longer life, you just *shift* the entire life and start it earlier. After all, suppose I ask you to imagine being born in 1800 instead of the year you were actually born. Nobody thinks, "Why, if I had been born in 1800, I'd still be alive. I would be more than two hundred years old!" Rather, you think, "If I had been born in 1800 I would have died in 1860, or 1870, or some such."

When we imagine being born earlier, we don't imagine a longer life, just an *earlier* life. And of course there is nothing about having a life that takes place earlier that makes it

particularly better, according to the deprivation account. So there is no point in bemoaning the fact that you weren't born earlier. But in contrast, when we imagine dying later, it's not as though we shift the life *forward*. We don't imagine being *born* later, keeping the life the same length. No, we imagine a *longer* life. And so, Feldman says, it's no wonder that you care about nonexistence after death in a way that you don't care about nonexistence before birth. When you imagine death coming later, you imagine a longer life, with more of the goods of life. But when you imagine birth coming earlier, you don't imagine more goods in your life, you just imagine them taking place at a different time.

That too is an interesting suggestion, and I imagine it is probably part of a complete answer to Lucretius. But I don't think it can be the complete story. Because we can in fact imagine cases where the person reasonably thinks that if only she had been born earlier she *would* have had a longer life.

Let's suppose that next week astronomers discover the horrible fact that there's an asteroid that's about to land on the Earth and wipe out all life. Suppose that it is going to crash into the Earth on January 1st of next year. Now imagine someone who is currently only thirty years old. It seems to me to be perfectly reasonable for such a person to think to herself that she has only had thirty years of life, and if only she had been born ten years earlier, she would have had forty years before she died, instead of thirty; if she had been born twenty years earlier, she would have had fifty years, instead of thirty. That all seems perfectly intelligible. So it does seem as though, if we work at it, we can think of cases where an earlier birth does result in a longer life and not merely a shifted life. In cases like this, it seems, we can imagine making life longer in the "pre-birth" direction rather than in the "postdeath" direction.

What does that show us? I am not sure. When I think about the asteroid example, I find myself thinking that maybe symmetry is the right way to go here after all. Maybe in a case like this, the relevant bit of prenatal nonexistence *is* just as bad as a corresponding bit of postmortem nonexistence. Maybe Feldman is right when he says that normally, when thinking about an earlier birth, we just shift the life, instead of lengthening it. But for all that, if we are careful to describe a case where an earlier birth would truly mean a longer life for me, maybe it really *is* bad that I didn't get started sooner. (Feldman would probably agree.)

Here's one more answer to Lucretius that's been proposed. This is by yet another contemporary philosopher, Derek Parfit.[4] Recall the fact that even though nonexistence before birth doesn't involve loss, it does involve schmoss. So it would be helpful if we had an explanation of why loss is worse than schmoss. Why should we care more about the former than the latter? Parfit's idea, in effect, is that this is not an arbitrary preference on our part. Rather, it's part of a quite general pattern we have of caring about the future in a way that we don't care about the past. This is a very deep fact about human caring. We are oriented toward the future and concerned about what will happen in it, in a way that we're not oriented toward and concerned about what happened in the past.

Parfit's got a very nice example to bring the point home. He asks you to imagine that you've got some medical condition that will kill you unless you have an operation. So you're going to have the operation. Unfortunately, in order to perform the operation, they can't have you anesthetized. You have to be awake, perhaps in order to tell the surgeon, "Yes, that's where it hurts." You've got to be awake during the operation, and it's a *very* painful operation. Furthermore, we can't give you painkiller, because then you won't be able to tell the surgeon where it hurts. In short, you need to be awake while you are, in effect, being tortured. Of course, it's still worth it, because this will cure your condition, and you can go on to have a nice long life. But during the operation itself, it is going to hurt like hell.

Since we can't give you painkillers and we can't put you out, all we can do is this: after the operation is over, we'll give you this very powerful medication, which will induce a very localized form of amnesia, destroying your very recent memories. You won't remember anything about the operation itself. And in particular, then, you won't ever have to revisit horrible memories of having been tortured. Any such memory will be completely destroyed. Indeed, *all* memories from the preceding twenty-four hours will be completely wiped out. In sum, you are going to have a horrendously painful operation, and you are going to be awake during it. But after the operation you will be given medication that will make you completely forget the pain of the operation, indeed forget everything about the entire day.

So you're in the hospital and you wake up and you ask yourself, "Have I had the operation yet or not?" And of course, you don't know. You certainly don't remember having had it. But that doesn't tell you anything. On the one hand, if you haven't had it yet, it is no wonder you have no memories of having had it. But on the other hand, even if you *have* had the operation, you would have been given the medication afterwards, so would have no memories of it now. So you ask the nurse, "Have I had the operation yet or not?" She answers, "I don't know. We have several patients like you on the floor today, some of whom have already had the procedure, and some of whom are scheduled to have it later today. I don't remember which group you are in. Let me go look at your file. I'll come back in a moment and I'll tell you." So she wanders off. She's going to come back in a minute or two. And as you are waiting for her to come back, you ask yourself, what do you want the answer to be? Do you care which group you're in? Do you prefer to be someone who has *already* had the operation? Someone who *hasn't* had it yet? Or are you indifferent?

Now, if you're like Parfit, and for that matter like me, then you're going to say that *of course* you care. I certainly want it to be the case that

I have *already* had the operation. I don't want to be someone who hasn't had the operation yet.

We might ask, how can that make any sense? You are going to have the operation sooner or later. At some point in your life history, that operation is going to have occurred. And so there's going to be the same amount of pain and torture at some point in your life, regardless of whether you're one of the people that had it yesterday or one of the people that are going to have it later today. But for all that, says Parfit, the fact of the matter is perfectly plain: we *do* care. We want the pain to be in the past. We don't want the pain to be in the future. We care more about what's happening in the future than about what's happened in the past.

That being the case, however, it is no surprise that we care about our nonexistence in the future in a way that we don't care about our nonexistence in the past. So perhaps that is the answer that we should give to Lucretius: the future matters in a way that the past does not.

That too is an intriguing suggestion. And it may well provide us with a convincing explanation of our asymmetrical attitudes. But we might still wonder whether it gives us any kind of *justification* for them. The fact that we've got this deep-seated asymmetrical attitude toward time doesn't in any way, as far as I can see, yet tell us whether or not that's a *justified* attitude. Maybe evolution built us to care about the future in a way that we don't care about the past, and this expresses itself in all sorts of places, including Parfit's hospital case and our attitude toward loss versus schmoss, and so forth and so on. But the fact that we've got this attitude doesn't yet show that it's a *rational* attitude.

How could we show that it's a rational attitude? Perhaps we would have to start doing some heavy-duty metaphysics (if what we have been doing so far isn't yet heavy-duty enough). Maybe we need to talk about the metaphysical difference between the past and the future. Intuitively, after all, the past is fixed, while the future is open, and time seems to have a direction, from past to future. Maybe somehow we could bring all these things in and explain why our attitude toward time is a reasonable one. I'm not going to go there. All I want to say is, it's not altogether obvious what the best answer to Lucretius's puzzle is. . . .

But for all that, it seems to me that . . . what's bad about death is that when you're dead, you're not experiencing the good things in life. Death is bad for you precisely because you don't have what life would bring you if only you hadn't died.

NOTES

1. Lucretius, *On the Nature of Things.*
2. Thomas Nagel, "Death," in *Mortal Questions* (Cambridge, 1979).
3. Fred Feldman, *Confrontations with the Reaper* (Oxford, 1992), pp. 154–156.
4. This example comes from Derek Parfit, *Reasons and Persons* (Oxford, 1984), pp. 165–166. I should note, however, that Parfit isn't here explicitly discussing Lucretius. I am simply applying some of his ideas to that puzzle. (Parfit's own discussion of the puzzle can be found in *Reasons and Persons,* pp. 174–177.)

Study Questions

1. Are you concerned about not being alive before the time of your birth?
2. Do you agree with Lucretius that we should be unconcerned about not being alive after the time of our death?
3. How do you assess Nagel's reply to Lucretius?
4. How do you assess Feldman's reply to Lucretius?

What The Buddha Taught

WALPOLA RAHULA

Walpola Rahula (1907–1997), a Buddhist monk, was a professor of history and literature of religions at Northwestern University. In our next selection, he seeks to explain the Buddhist goal of attaining *nirvana,* a term drawn from the Sanskrit word for "extinction." Nirvāna is the goal of life, a state of existence in which all that causes suffering is absent. It is attainable both in this life and beyond.

. . . [W]hat is Nirvāna? Volumes have been written in reply to this quite natural and simple question; they have, more and more, only confused the issue rather than clarified it. The only reasonable reply to give to the question is that it can never be answered completely and satisfactorily in words, because human language is too poor to express the real nature of the Absolute Truth or Ultimate Reality which is Nirvāna. Language is created and used by masses of human beings to express things and ideas experienced by their sense organs and their mind. A supramundane experience like that of the Absolute Truth is not of such a category. Therefore there cannot be words to express that experience, just as the fish had no words in his vocabulary to express the nature of the solid land. The tortoise told his friend the fish that he (the tortoise) just returned to the lake after a walk on the land. 'Of course' the fish said, 'You mean swimming.' The tortoise tried to explain that one couldn't swim on the land, that it was solid, and that one walked on it. But the fish insisted that there could be nothing like it, that it must be liquid like his lake, with waves, and that one must be able to dive and swim there.

Words are symbols representing things and ideas known to us; and these symbols do not and cannot convey the true nature of even ordinary things. Language is considered deceptive and misleading in the matter of understanding of the Truth. So . . . ignorant people get stuck in words like an elephant in the mud.

Nevertheless we cannot do without language. But if Nirvāna is to be expressed and explained in positive terms, we are likely immediately to grasp an idea associated with those terms, which may be quite the contrary. Therefore it is generally expressed in negative terms—a less dangerous mode perhaps. So it is often referred to by such negative terms as 'Extinction of Thirst', 'Uncompound', 'Unconditioned', 'Absence of desire', 'Cessation', 'Blowing out' or 'Extinction'. . . .

Because Nirvāna is thus expressed in negative terms, there are many who have got a wrong notion that it is negative, and expresses self-annihilation. Nirvāna is definitely no annihilation of self, because there is no self to annihilate. If at all, it is the annihilation of the illusion, of the false idea of self. . . .

A negative word need not necessarily indicate a negative state. The Pali or Sanskrit word for health is *ārogya,* a negative term, which literally means 'absence of illness'. But *ārogya* (health) does not represent a negative state. The word 'Immortal' (or its Sanskrit equivalent *Amrta* or

From Walpola Rahula, *What the Buddha Taught,* Grove Press, 1974. Reprinted by permission of the publisher.

Pali *Amata*), which also is a synonym for Nirvāna, is negative, but it does not denote a negative state. The negation of negative values is not negative. One of the well-known synonyms for Nirvāna is 'Freedom'. Nobody would say that freedom is negative. But even freedom has a negative side: freedom is always a liberation from something which is obstructive, which is evil, which is negative. But freedom is not negative. So Nirvāna . . . is freedom from all evil, freedom from craving, hatred and ignorance, freedom from all terms of duality, relativity, time and space.

We may get some idea of Nirvāna as Absolute Truth from the . . . extremely important discourse . . . delivered by the Buddha to Pukkusāti,[1] whom the Master found to be intelligent and earnest, in the quiet of the night in a potter's shed. The essence of the relevant portions of the sutta[2] is as follows:

A man is composed of six elements: solidity, fluidity, heat, motion, space and consciousness. He analyses them and finds that none of them is 'mine', or 'me'; or 'my self'. He understands how consciousness appears and disappears, how pleasant, unpleasant and neutral sensations appear and disappear. Through this knowledge his mind becomes detached. Then he finds within him a pure equanimity, which he can direct towards the attainment of any high spiritual state, and he knows that thus this pure equanimity will last for a long period. But then he thinks:

'If I focus this purified and cleansed equanimity on the Sphere of Infinite Space and develop a mind conforming thereto, that is a mental creation. If I focus this purified and cleansed equanimity on the Sphere of Infinite Consciousness . . . on the Sphere of Nothingness . . . or on the Sphere of Neither-perception nor Non-perception and develop a mind conforming thereto, that is a mental creation. Then he neither mentally creates nor wills continuity and becoming or annihilation. As he does not construct or does not will continuity and becoming or annihilation, he does not cling to anything in the world; as he does not cling, he is not anxious; as he is not anxious, he is completely calmed within. And he knows: 'Finished is birth, lived is pure life, what should be done is done, nothing more is left to be done.'

Now, when he experiences a pleasant, unpleasant or neutral sensation, he knows that it is impermanent, that it does not bind him, that it is not experienced with passion. Whatever may be the sensation, he experiences it without being bound to it. He knows that all those sensations will be pacified with the dissolution of the body, just as the flame of a lamp goes out when oil and wick give out.

'Therefore, O bhikkhu, a person so endowed is endowed with the absolute wisdom, for the knowledge of the extinction of all *dukkha*[3] is the absolute noble wisdom.

'This his deliverance, founded on Truth, is unshakable. O bhikkhu, that which is unreality is false; that which is reality Nibbāna, is Truth. Therefore, O bhikkhu, a person so endowed is endowed with this Absolute Truth. For, the Absolute Noble Truth is Nibbāna, which is Reality.'

Elsewhere the Buddha unequivocally uses the word Truth in place of Nibbāna: 'I will teach you the Truth and the Path leading to the Truth.' Here Truth definitely means Nirvāna.

Now, what is Absolute Truth? According to Buddhism, the Absolute Truth is that there is nothing absolute in the world, that everything is relative, conditioned and impermanent, and that there is no unchanging, everlasting, absolute substance like Self, Soul or *Ātman* within or without. This is the Absolute Truth. Truth is never negative, though there is a popular expression as negative truth. The realization of this Truth, i.e., to see things as they are without illusion or ignorance, is the extinction of craving 'thirst', and the cessation of *dukkha*, which is Nirvāna. . . .

People often ask: What is there after Nirvāna? This question cannot arise, because Nirvāna is the Ultimate Truth. If it is Ultimate, there can be nothing after it. If there is anything after

Nirvāṇa, then that will be the Ultimate Truth and not Nirvāṇa. A monk named Rādha put this question to the Buddha in a different form: 'For what purpose (or end) is Nirvāṇa?' This question presupposes something after Nirvāṇa, when it postulates some purpose or end for it. So the Buddha answered: 'O Rādha, this question could not catch its limit (i.e., it is beside the point). One lives the holy life with Nirvāṇa as its final plunge (into the Absolute Truth), as its goal, as its ultimate end.'

Some popular inaccurately phrased expressions like 'The Buddha entered into Nirvāṇa or Parinirvāṇa[4] after his death' have given rise to many imaginary speculations about Nirvāṇa. The moment you hear the phrase that 'the Buddha entered into Nirvāṇa or Parinirvāṇa', you take Nirvāṇa to be a state, or a realm, or a position in which there is some sort of existence, and try to imagine it in terms of the senses of the word 'existence' as it is known to you. This popular expression 'entered into Nirvāṇa' has no equivalent in the original texts. There is no such thing as 'entering into Nirvāṇa after death'. There is a word *parinibbuto* used to denote the death of the Buddha or an Arahant[5] who has realized Nirvāṇa, but it does not mean 'entering into Nirvāṇa'. *Parinibbuto* simply means 'fully passed away', 'fully blown out' or 'fully extinct', because the Buddha or an Arahant has no re-existence after his death. . . .

In almost all religions the *summum bonum* can be attained only after death. But Nirvāṇa can be realized in this very life; it is not necessary to wait till you die to 'attain' it.

He who has realized the Truth, Nirvāṇa, is the happiest being in the world. He is free from all 'complexes' and obsessions, the worries and troubles that torment others. His mental health is perfect. He does not repent the past, nor does he brood over the future. He lives fully in the present. Therefore he appreciates and enjoys things in the purest sense without self-projections. He is joyful, exultant, enjoying the pure life, his faculties pleased, free from anxiety, serene and

peaceful. As he is free from selfish desire, hatred, ignorance, conceit, pride, and all such 'defilements', he is pure and gentle, full of universal love, compassion, kindness, sympathy, understanding and tolerance. His service to others is of the purest, for he has no thought of self. He gains nothing, accumulates nothing, not even anything spiritual, because he is free from the illusion of Self, and the 'thirst' for becoming.

Nirvāṇa is beyond all terms of duality and relativity. It is therefore beyond our conceptions of good and evil, right and wrong, existence and non-existence. Even the word 'happiness' which is used to describe Nirvāṇa has an entirely different sense here. Sāriputta once said: 'O friend, Nirvāṇa is happiness! Nirvāṇa is happiness!' Then Udāyi asked: 'But, friend Sāriputta, what happiness can it be if there is no sensation?' Sāriputta's reply was highly philosophical and beyond ordinary comprehension: 'That there is no sensation itself is happiness'.

Nirvāṇa is beyond logic and reasoning. However much we may engage, often as a vain intellectual pastime, in highly speculative discussions regarding Nirvāṇa or Ultimate Truth or Reality, we shall never understand it that way. A child in the kindergarten should not quarrel about the theory of relativity. Instead, if he follows his studies patiently and diligently, one day he may understand it. Nirvāṇa is 'to be realized by the wise within themselves'. If we follow the Path patiently and with diligence, train and purify ourselves earnestly, and attain the necessary spiritual development, we may one day realize it within ourselves—without taxing ourselves with puzzling and high-sounding words.

NOTES

1. [A student of the Buddha.—S.M.C.]
2. [Sermon.]
3. [Suffering.]
4. [The final passing away of one who is free from rebirth.]
5. [One who is free from rebirth.]

Study Questions

Study Questions

1. Are some truths inexpressible?
2. According to the Buddha, can the truth be realized in this life?
3. According to the Buddha, what is the most noble wisdom?
4. According to the Buddha, how can the most noble wisdom be understood?

The Cessation of Suffering

CHRISTOPHER W. GOWANS

In the next selection Christopher W. Gowans, whose work we read previously, considers further philosophical perplexities that arise in seeking to explain the Buddhist concept of Nirvana-after-death. Does the notion cohere with the Buddhist not-self doctrine? Furthermore, is happiness possible if consciousness is extinguished?

In an important respect, stream-observers[1] are in a better position to evaluate the life of an *arahant*[2] who is still alive than they are to assess the state of an *arahant* who has died. We could observe a living *arahant* and judge whether he has a truly good life. However, we cannot directly observe the state of an *arahant* after death. From the Buddha's perspective, an unenlightened person cannot fully comprehend the worth of an *arahant*'s life before or after death. But he thought stream-observers could comprehend enough to conclude that it would be worthwhile to undertake the Eightfold Path.[3] We now need to consider whether or not the state of an *arahant* beyond this life is sufficiently coherent to make this preliminary assessment. There are several philosophical perplexities on the horizon.

The most important problem concerns what it means to say a person has attained *Nibbāna*-after-death.[4] Since *Nibbāna* as ultimate reality is beyond change and conditioning, the fact that a person attains *Nibbāna* cannot result in a change to *Nibbāna* itself: it does not change. Hence, a person's attainment of *Nibbāna*-after-death must involve a transformation within the person. But the Buddha regularly speaks as if a person in this life is nothing more than the aggregates,[5] and he says a person who attains *Nibbāna*-after-death abandons all the aggregates (in my terminology, the person is not a substance-self, and the process-self is completely dissolved with the attainment of *Nibbāna*-after-death). The consequence is that there does not seem to be anything left of a person who attains *Nibbāna*-after-death. However, there must be something left or attainment of *Nibbāna*-after-death would be annihilation—and this the Buddha denies.

There are four main responses to this problem. First, it may be contended that, despite what

From *Philosophy of the Buddha*, Routledge, 2003. Reprinted by permission of Taylor & Francis.

the Buddha says, *Nibbāna*-after-death really is annihilation of the person. Even if what he claims about *Nibbāna* as ultimate reality is correct, his overall position entails that attainment of *Nibbāna*-after-death could be nothing else but the complete cessation of the person. Second, it may be argued that, in spite of the Buddha's not-self doctrine, there surely is a self *in some sense* that permanently exists through this life and attains *Nibbāna*-after-death. If this attainment is not annihilation, then there must be a self that attains *Nibbāna*. Both of these interpretations attribute an unintended inconsistency to the Buddha's teaching. The remaining interpretations take a different approach. The third says the rational irresolvability of this problem is part of the Buddha's teaching. Though it is true from a rational standpoint that this is a problem, the Buddha acknowledges that his teaching concerning *Nibbāna* is 'unattainable by mere reasoning.' For one who is enlightened all will be clear, but for others nothing more can be said than this. The difficulty with this interpretation is that it seems to deprive stream-observers of a solid rationale for undertaking the Eightfold Path. It requires them to have considerable faith in the Buddha as a prelude to achieving enlightenment for themselves.

The fourth interpretation maintains that there is an aspect of the person that, like *Nibbāna* as ultimate reality, is beyond space and time, change and conditioning, and so on. Though any label misleads, it will be convenient to call this aspect of the person its *liberated dimension*. This dimension cannot be identified with the aggregates and it cannot be described as any kind of self: both the process-self and the substance-self presuppose categories that the liberated dimension is beyond. On this interpretation, it is the liberated dimension that persists in *Nibbāna*-after-death. If this were the case, the Buddha could consistently maintain both the not-self doctrine and the view that attainment of *Nibbāna* is not complete annihilation. But if both *Nibbāna* and the liberated dimension are beyond change and conditioning, what would it

mean for a person to attain *Nibbāna*? Attainment involves change, and both *Nibbāna* and the liberated dimension do not change. What would have to be said is that *Nibbāna* and the liberated dimension have always been united in the appropriate way (however union might be understood). This does not change. To attain *Nibbāna* means that the person dissolves all sense of selfhood as an illusion and thereby discovers the previously hidden fact that the liberated dimension and *Nibbāna* have always been united. Here an analogy may help. Suppose your living room window overlooks a beautiful mountain valley, but nothing can be seen because the window is too dirty. Cleaning the window enables you to see the valley. But this does not create the fact that your living room overlooks the valley. It merely reveals what was already the case. Similarly, on this interpretation, enlightenment creates no new reality, but by cleansing the person of the illusion of selfhood it reveals the fact that the liberated dimension has always been united with *Nibbāna*—and this ends suffering and brings the greatest bliss.

In support of this interpretation is the fact that a fundamental premise of the Buddha's teaching is that the person, though not a self, is capable of attaining the highest happiness of *Nibbāna*-after-death. This suggests that the Buddha was committed to this view or something close to it. On the other hand, he did not directly formulate the problem about the meaning of the attainment of *Nibbāna,* and he did not explicitly articulate this understanding of the person as a resolution of that problem (nor for any other reason). His primary instinct was to say little about *Nibbāna* and to focus on the means to its attainment. This interpretation could be defended only on the ground that it makes the best overall sense of the Buddha's teaching in comparison with the other three.

Two related perplexities should also be mentioned. They both are rooted in the fact that an *arahant* who attains *Nibbāna*-after-death has abandoned all the aggregates. First, one of the aggregates is consciousness (*viññāṇa*). Hence, it seems that an *arahant* who attains *Nibbāna*-after-death is not conscious. But what could it mean to attain *Nibbāna* without being conscious? Would this be any different than annihilation? It might be said that consciousness, as one of the aggregates, is inescapably tied up with the illusion of selfhood. For this reason, one who attains *Nibbāna* cannot be conscious in this sense. However, there might be another form of consciousness that involves no notion of selfhood and is present in one who attains *Nibbāna*. . . . Of course, we might wonder whether consciousness-without-selfhood is really possible. Perhaps animals have such consciousness. But it seems unlikely that our liberated dimension is akin to animal consciousness: animals are below humans in the Buddha's cosmology. In the end, the Buddha might respond in this way: the distinction between what is and is not conscious applies to the conditioned world of our experience, and since *Nibbāna* is beyond this world, in this respect nothing meaningful can be said about the *arahant* after death.

Second, another of the aggregates is feelings or sensations (*vedanā*). Attaining *Nibbāna* is said to be the highest happiness, but how is happiness possible in the absence of feelings? The Buddha has something to say in response to this question. The happiness of *Nibbāna*-after-death is not a matter of pleasant feelings, and it is immeasurably higher than any form of happiness available to the unenlightened in the cycle of rebirth. For example, we hear of a happiness that comes with 'the ending of perception and feeling' (G IV 281) and a 'delight apart from sensual pleasures' (M 610). Most people would probably acknowledge that happiness is not merely pleasant feelings (and the absence of painful ones). Much that is ordinarily associated with happiness, such as a fulfilling family life or a satisfying job, cannot plausibly be understood simply in terms of pleasant feelings. But it is another matter whether we can envision a form of happiness in the absence of *any* of the aggregates. The issue here is closely related to the last: it is hard to imagine a state we would consider the highest happiness without some form of consciousness. As before, the Buddha was less inclined to explain this than to encourage us to experience it for ourselves by following the Eightfold Path.

NOTES

1. [Those who are culturally part of the contemporary Western world and have no Buddhist upbringing.—S.M.C.]

2. [Fully enlightened ones; the Buddha's first followers.]

3. [The Noble Eightfold Path leading to the cessation of suffering: Right Understanding, Right Thought, Right Speech, Right Action, Right Livelihood, Right Effort, Right Mindfulness, Right Concentration.]

4. [See this book's previous selection by Christopher W. Gowans titled "The Buddha's Message."]

5. [Matter, Sensations, Perceptions, Mental Formations, Consciousness.]

Study Questions

1. What four responses does Gowans consider for explaining what is left of a person who attains Nirvana-after-death?

2. According to Gowans, how might the Buddha respond to the claim that consciousness without selfhood is not possible?

3. According to Gowans, how might the Buddha respond to the claim that happiness without feelings is not possible?

4. Are some questions best answered by experiences rather than words?

The Meaning of Life

RICHARD TAYLOR

Those who begin the study of philosophy often assume that the subject will focus on the meaning of life. This supposedly crucial topic, however, is rarely mentioned. Yet philosophers do occasionally consider the issue, as witness our next selection. Its author is Richard Taylor (1919-2003), who was Professor of Philosophy at the University of Rochester. He concludes that the meaning of life is not bestowed from without but comes from within us.

The question whether life has any meaning is difficult to interpret, and the more you concentrate your critical faculty on it the more it seems to elude you, or to evaporate as any intelligible question. You want to turn it aside, as a source of embarrassment, as something that, if it cannot be abolished, should at least be decently covered. And yet I think any reflective person recognizes that the question it raises is important, and that it ought to have a significant answer.

If the idea of meaningfulness is difficult to grasp in this context, so that we are unsure what sort of thing would amount to answering the question, the idea of meaninglessness is perhaps less so. If, then, we can bring before our minds a clear image of meaningless existence, then perhaps we can take a step toward coping with our original question by seeing to what extent our lives, as we actually find them, resemble that image, and draw such lessons as we are able to from the comparison.

MEANINGLESS EXISTENCE

A perfect image of meaninglessness, of the kind we are seeking, is found in the ancient myth of Sisyphus. Sisyphus, it will be remembered, betrayed divine secrets to mortals, and for this he was condemned by the gods to roll a stone to the top of a hill, the stone then immediately to roll back down, again to be pushed to the top by Sisyphus, to roll down once more, and so on again and again, *forever*. Now in this we have the picture of meaningless, pointless toil, of a meaningless existence that is absolutely *never* redeemed. It is not even redeemed by a death that, if it were to accomplish nothing more, would at least bring this idiotic cycle to a close. If we were invited to imagine Sisyphus struggling for a while and accomplishing nothing, perhaps eventually falling from exhaustion, so that we might suppose him then eventually turning to something having some sort of promise, then the meaninglessness of that chapter of his life would not be so stark. It would be a dark and dreadful dream, from which he eventually awakens to sunlight and reality. But he does not awaken, for there is nothing for him to awaken to. His repetitive toil is his life and reality, and it goes on forever, and it is without any meaning whatever. Nothing ever comes of what he is doing, except simply, more of the same. Not by one step, nor by a thousand, nor by ten thousand does he even expiate by the smallest token the sin against

From *Good and Evil*, revised edition, by Richard Taylor (Amherst, NY: Prometheus Books, 2000), pp. 319–334.

the gods that led him into this fate. Nothing comes of it, nothing at all.

This ancient myth has always enchanted people, for countless meanings can be read into it. Some of the ancients apparently thought it symbolized the perpetual rising and setting of the sun, and others the repetitious crashing of the waves upon the shore. Probably the commonest interpretation is that it symbolizes our eternal struggle and unquenchable spirit, our determination always to try once more in the face of overwhelming discouragement. This interpretation is further supported by that version of the myth according to which Sisyphus was commanded to roll the stone *over* the hill, so that it would finally roll down the other side, but was never quite able to make it.

I am not concerned with rendering or defending any interpretation of this myth, however. I have cited it only for the one element it does unmistakably contain, namely, that of a repetitious, cyclic activity that never comes to anything. We could contrive other images of this that would serve just as well, and no myth-makers are needed to supply the materials of it. Thus, we can imagine two persons transporting a stone—or even a precious gem, it does not matter—back and forth, relay style. One carries it to a near or distant point where it is received by the other; it is returned to its starting point, there to be recovered by the first, and the process is repeated over and over. Except in this relay nothing counts as winning, and nothing brings the contest to any close, each step only leads to a repetition of itself. Or we can imagine two groups of prisoners, one of them engaged in digging a prodigious hole in the ground that is no sooner finished than it is filled in again by the other group, the latter then digging a new hole that is at once filled in by the first group, and so on and on endlessly.

Now what stands out in all such pictures as oppressive and dejecting is not that the beings who enact these roles suffer any torture or pain, for it need not be assumed that they do. Nor is it that their labors are great, for they are no greater than the labors commonly undertaken by most people most of the time. According to the original myth, the stone is so large that Sisyphus never quite gets it to the top and must groan under every step, so that his enormous labor is all for nought. But this is not what appalls. It is not that his great struggle comes to nothing, but that his existence itself is without meaning. Even if we suppose, for example, that the stone is but a pebble that can be carried effortlessly, or that the holes dug by the prisoners are but small ones, not the slightest meaning is introduced into their lives. The stone that Sisyphus moves to the top of the hill, whether we think of it as large or small, still rolls back every time, and the process is repeated forever. Nothing comes of it, and the work is simply pointless. That is the element of the myth that I wish to capture.

Again, it is not the fact that the labors of Sisyphus continue forever that deprives them of meaning. It is, rather, the implication of this: that they come to nothing. The image would not be changed by our supposing him to push a different stone up every time, each to roll down again. But if we supposed that these stones, instead of rolling back to their places as if they had never been moved, were assembled at the top of the hill and there incorporated, say, in a beautiful and enduring temple, then the aspect of meaninglessness would disappear. His labors would then have a point, something would come of them all, and although one could perhaps still say it was not worth it, one could not say that the life of Sisyphus was devoid of meaning altogether. Meaningfulness would at least have made an appearance, and we could see what it was.

That point will need remembering. But in the meantime, let us note another way in which the image of meaninglessness can be altered by making only a very slight change. Let us suppose that the gods, while condemning Sisyphus to the fate just described, at the same time, as an afterthought, waxed perversely merciful by implanting in him a strange and irrational impulse;

namely, a compulsive impulse to roll stones. We may if we like, to make this more graphic, suppose they accomplish this by implanting in him some substance that has this effect on his character and drives. I call this perverse, because from our point of view there is clearly no reason why anyone should have a persistent and insatiable desire to do something so pointless as that. Nevertheless, suppose that is Sisyphus' condition. He has but one obsession, which is to roll stones, and it is an obsession that is only for the moment appeased by his rolling them—he no sooner gets a stone rolled to the top of the hill than he is restless to roll up another.

Now it can be seen why this little afterthought of the gods, which I called perverse, was also in fact merciful. For they have by this device managed to give Sisyphus precisely what he wants—by making him want precisely what they inflict on him. However it may appear to us, Sisyphus' fate now does not appear to him as a condemnation, but the very reverse. His one desire in life is to roll stones, and he is absolutely guaranteed its endless fulfillment. Where otherwise he might profoundly have wished surcease, and even welcomed the quiet of death to release him from endless boredom and meaninglessness, his life is now filled with mission and meaning, and he seems to himself to have been given an entry to heaven. Nor need he even fear death, for the gods have promised him an endless opportunity to indulge his single purpose, without concern or frustration. He will be able to roll stones *forever.*

What we need to mark most carefully at this point is that the picture with which we began has not really been changed in the least by adding this supposition. Exactly the same things happen as before. The only change is in Sisyphus' view of them. The picture before was the image of meaningless activity and existence. It was created precisely to be an image of that. It has not lost that meaninglessness, it has now gained not the least shred of meaningfulness. The stones still roll back as before, each phase of Sisyphus' life still exactly resembles all the others, the task is never completed, nothing comes of it, no temple ever begins to rise, and all this cycle of the same pointless thing over and over goes on forever in this picture as in the other. The *only* thing that has happened is this: Sisyphus has been reconciled to it, and indeed more, he has been led to embrace it. Not, however, by reason or persuasion, but by nothing more rational than the potency of a new substance in his veins.

THE MEANINGLESSNESS OF LIFE

I believe the foregoing provides a fairly clear content to the idea of meaninglessness and, through it, some hint of what meaningfulness, in this sense, might be. Meaninglessness is essentially endless pointlessness, and meaningfulness is therefore the opposite. Activity, and even long, drawn out and repetitive activity, has a meaning if it has some significant culmination, some more or less lasting end that can be considered to have been the direction and purpose of the activity. But the descriptions so far also provide something else; namely, the suggestion of how an existence that is objectively meaningless, in this sense, can nevertheless acquire a meaning for him whose existence it is.

Now let us ask: Which of these pictures does life in fact resemble? And let us not begin with our own lives, for here both our prejudices and wishes are great, but with the life in general that we share with the rest of creation. We shall find, I think, that it all has a certain pattern, and that this pattern is by now easily recognized.

We can begin anywhere, only saving human existence for our last consideration. We can, for example, begin with any animal. It does not matter where we begin, because the result is going to be exactly the same.

Thus, for example, there are caves in New Zealand, deep and dark, whose floors are quiet pools and whose walls and ceilings are covered with soft light. As you gaze in wonder in the stillness of these caves it seems that the Creator has reproduced there in microcosm the heavens themselves, until you scarcely remember the enclosing presence of the walls. As you look more closely, however, the scene is explained. Each dot of light identifies an ugly worm, whose luminous tail is meant to attract insects from the surrounding darkness. As from time to time one of these insects draws near it becomes entangled in a sticky thread lowered by the worm, and is eaten. This goes on month after month, the blind worm lying there in the barren stillness waiting to entrap an occasional bit of nourishment that will only sustain it to another bit of nourishment until. . . . Until what? What great thing awaits all this long and repetitious effort and makes it worthwhile? Really nothing. The larva just transforms itself finally to a tiny winged adult that lacks even mouth parts to feed and lives only a day or two. These adults, as soon as they have mated and laid eggs, are themselves caught in the threads and are devoured by the cannibalist worms, often without having ventured into the day, the only point to their existence having now been fulfilled. This has been going on for millions of years, and to no end other than that the same meaningless cycle may continue for another millions of years.

All living things present essentially the same spectacle. The larva of a certain cicada burrows in the darkness of the earth for seventeen years, through season after season, to emerge finally into the daylight for a brief flight, lay its eggs, and die—this all to repeat itself during the next seventeen years, and so on to eternity. We have already noted, in another connection, the struggles of fish, made only that others may do the same after them and that this cycle, having no other point than itself, may never cease. Some birds span an entire side of the globe each year and then return, only to insure that others may follow the same incredibly long path again and again. One is led to wonder what the point of it all is, with what great triumph this ceaseless effort, repeating itself through millions of years, might finally culminate, and why it should go on and on for so long, accomplishing nothing, getting nowhere. But then you realize that there is no point to it at all, that it really culminates in nothing, that each of these cycles, so filled with toil, is to be followed only by more of the same. The point of any living thing's life is, evidently, nothing but life itself.

This life of the world thus presents itself to our eyes as a vast machine, feeding on itself, running on and on forever to nothing. And we are part of that life. To be sure, we are not just the same, but the differences are not so great as we like to think; many are merely invented, and none really cancels the kind of meaninglessness that we found in Sisyphus and that we find all around, wherever anything lives. We are conscious of our activity. Our goals, whether in any significant sense we choose them or not, are things of which we are at least partly aware and can therefore in some sense appraise. More significantly, perhaps, we have a history, as other animals do not, such that each generation does not precisely resemble all those before. Still, if we can in imagination disengage our wills from our lives and disregard the deep interest we all have in our own existence, we shall find that they do not so little resemble the existence of Sisyphus. We toil after goals, most of them—indeed every single one of them—of transitory significance and, having gained one of them, we immediately set forth for the next, as if that one had never been, with this next one being essentially more of the same. Look at a busy street any day, and observe the throng going hither and thither. To what? Some office or shop, where the same things will be done today as were done yesterday, and are done now so they may be repeated tomorrow. And if we think that, unlike Sisyphus, these labors do have a point, that they culminate in something lasting and, independently of our own deep interests in them, very worthwhile, then we simply have not considered the thing closely enough. Most such effort is directed only to the establishment and perpetuation of home and family; that is, to the begetting of others who will follow in our steps to do more of the same. Everyone's life thus resembles one of Sisyphus's climbs to the summit of his hill, and each day of it one of his steps; the difference is that whereas Sisyphus himself returns to push the stone up again, we leave this to our children. We at one point imagined that the labors of Sisyphus finally culminated in the creation of a temple, but for this to make any difference it had to be a temple that would at least endure, adding beauty to the world for the remainder of time. Our achievements, even though they are often beautiful, are mostly bubbles; and those that do last, like the sand-swept pyramids, soon become mere curiosities while around them the rest of humankind continues its perpetual toting of rocks, only to see them roll down. Nations are built upon the bones of their founders and pioneers, but only to decay and crumble before long, their rubble then becoming the foundation for others directed to exactly the same fate. The picture of Sisyphus is the picture of existence of the individual man, great or unknown, of nations, of the human race, and of the very life of the world.

On a country road one sometimes comes upon the ruined hulks of a house and once extensive buildings, all in collapse and spread over with weeds. A curious eye can in imagination reconstruct from what is left a once warm and thriving life, filled with purpose. There was the hearth, where a family once talked, sang, and made plans; there were the rooms, where people loved, and babes were born to a rejoicing mother; there are the musty remains of a sofa, infested with bugs, once bought at a dear price to enhance an ever-growing comfort, beauty, and warmth. Every small piece of junk fills the mind with what once, not long ago, was utterly real, with children's voices, plans made, and enterprises embarked upon. That is how these stones of Sisyphus were rolled up, and that is how they became incorporated into a beautiful temple, and that temple is what now lies before you. Meanwhile other buildings, institutions, nations, and civilizations spring up all around, only to share the same fate before long. And if the question "What for?" is now asked, the answer is clear: so that just this may go on forever.

The two pictures—of Sisyphus and of our own lives, if we look at them from a distance—are in outline the same and convey to the mind the same image. It is not surprising, then, that we invent ways of denying it, our religions proclaiming a heaven that does not crumble, their hymnals and prayer books declaring a significance to life of which our eyes provide no hint whatever.[1] Even our philosophies portray some permanent and lasting good at which all may aim, from the changeless forms invented by Plato to the beatific vision of St. Thomas and the ideals of permanence contrived by the moderns. When these fail to convince, then earthly ideals such as universal justice and brotherhood are conjured up to take their places and give meaning to our seemingly endless pilgrimage, some final state that will be ushered in when the last obstacle is removed and the last stone pushed to the hilltop. No one believes, of course, that any such state will be final, or even wants it to be in case it means that human existence would then cease to be a struggle; but in the meantime such ideas serve a very real need.

THE MEANING OF LIFE

We noted that Sisyphus' existence would have meaning if there were some point to his labors, if his efforts ever culminated in something that was not just an occasion for fresh labors of the same kind. But that is precisely the meaning it lacks. And human existence resembles his in that respect. We do achieve things—we scale our towers and raise our stones to the hilltops—but every such accomplishment fades, providing only an occasion for renewed labors of the same kind.

But here we need to note something else that has been mentioned, but its significance not explored, and that is the state of mind and feeling with which such labors are undertaken. We noted that if Sisyphus had a keen and unappeasable desire to be doing just what he found himself doing, then, although his life would in no way be changed, it would nevertheless have a meaning for him. It would be an irrational one, no doubt, because the desire itself would be only the product of the substance in his veins, and not any that reason could discover, but a meaning nevertheless.

And would it not, in fact, be a meaning incomparably better than the other? For let us examine again the first kind of meaning it could have. Let us suppose that, without having any interest in rolling stones, as such, and finding this, in fact, a galling toil, Sisyphus did nevertheless have a deep interest in raising a temple, one that would be beautiful and lasting. And let us suppose he succeeded in this, that after ages of dreadful toil, all directed at this final result, he did at last complete his temple, such that now he could say his work was done, and he could rest and forever enjoy the result. Now what? What picture now presents itself to our minds? It is precisely the picture of infinite boredom! Of Sisyphus doing nothing ever again, but contemplating what he has already wrought and can no longer add anything to, and contemplating it for an eternity! Now in this picture we have a meaning for Sisyphus' existence, a point for his prodigious labor, because we have put it there; yet, at the same time, that which is really worthwhile seems to have slipped away entirely. Where before we were presented with the nightmare of eternal and pointless activity, we are now confronted with the hell of its eternal absence.

Our second picture, then, wherein we imagined Sisyphus to have had inflicted on him the irrational desire to be doing just what he found himself doing, should not have been dismissed so abruptly. The meaning that picture lacked was no meaning that he or anyone could crave, and the strange meaning it had was perhaps just what we were seeking.

At this point, then, we can reintroduce what has been until now, it is hoped, resolutely pushed aside in an effort to view our lives and human existence with objectivity; namely, our own wills, our deep interest in what we find ourselves doing. If we do this we find that our lives do indeed still resemble that of Sisyphus, but that the meaningfulness they thus lack is precisely the meaningfulness of infinite boredom. At the same time, the strange meaningfulness they possess is that of the inner compulsion to be doing just what we were put here to do, and to go on doing it forever. This is the nearest we may hope to get to heaven, but the redeeming side of that fact is that we do thereby avoid a genuine hell.

If the builders of a great and flourishing ancient civilization could somehow return now to see archaeologists unearthing the trivial remnants of what they had once accomplished with such effort—see the fragments of pots and vases, a few broken statues, and such tokens of another age and greatness—they could indeed ask themselves what the point of it all was, if this is all it finally came to. Yet, it did not seem so to them then, for it was just the building, and not what was finally built, that gave their life meaning. Similarly, if the builders of the ruined home and farm that I described a short while ago could be brought back to see what is left, they would have the same feelings. What we construct in our imaginations as we look over these decayed and rusting pieces would reconstruct itself in their very memories, and certainly with unspeakable sadness. The piece of a sled at our feet would revive in them a warm Christmas. And what rich memories would there be in the broken crib? And the weed-covered remains of a fence would reproduce the scene of a great herd of livestock, so laboriously built up over so many years. What was it all worth, if this is the final result? Yet, again, it did not seem so to them through those many years of struggle and toil, and they did not imagine they were building a Gibraltar. The things to which they bent their backs day after day, realizing one by one their ephemeral plans, were precisely the things in which their wills were deeply involved, precisely the things in which their interests lay, and there was no need then to ask questions. There is no more need of them now—the day was sufficient to itself, and so was the life.

This is surely the way to look at all of life—at one's own life, and each day and moment it contains; of the life of a nation; of the species; of the life of the world; and of everything that breathes. Even the glow worms I described, whose cycles of existence over the millions of years seem so pointless when looked at by us, will seem entirely different to us if we can somehow try to view their existence from within. Their endless activity, which gets nowhere, is just what it is their will to pursue. This is its whole justification and meaning. Nor would it be any salvation to the birds who span the globe every year, back and forth, to have a home made for them in a cage with plenty of food and protection, so that they would not have to migrate anymore. It would be their condemnation, for it is the doing that counts for them, and not what they hope to win by it. Flying these prodigious distances, never ending, is what it is in their veins to do, exactly as it was in Sisyphus's veins to roll stones, without end, after the gods had waxed merciful and implanted this in him.

You no sooner drew your first breath than you responded to the will that was in you to live. You no more ask whether it will be worthwhile, or whether anything of significance will come of it, than the worms and the birds. The point of living is simply to be living, in the manner that it is your nature to be living. You go through life building your castles, each of these beginning to fade into time as the next is begun; yet it would be no salvation to rest from all this. It would be a condemnation, and one that would in no way be redeemed were you able to gaze upon the things you have done, even if these were beautiful and absolutely permanent, as they never are. What counts is that you should be able to begin a new task, a new castle, a new bubble. It counts only because it is there to be done and you have the will to do it. The same will be the life of your children, and of theirs; and if the philosopher is apt to see in this a pattern similar to the unending cycles of the existence of Sisyphus, and to despair, then it is indeed because the meaning and point he is seeking is not there—but mercifully so. The meaning of life is from within us, it is not bestowed from without, and it far exceeds in both its beauty and permanence any heaven of which men have ever dreamed or yearned for.

NOTE

1. A popular Christian hymn, sung often at funerals and typical of many hymns, expresses this thought:

> *Swift to its close ebbs out life's little day;*
> *Earth's joys grow dim, its glories pass away;*
> *Change and decay in all around I see:*
> *O thou who changest not, abide with me.*

Study Questions

1. Can a life be enjoyed yet meaningless?
2. Can a life be immoral yet meaningful?
3. If you find meaning in a task, can you be mistaken?
4. If you don't find meaning in a task, can you be mistaken?

Meaning in Life

SUSAN WOLF

Susan Wolf is Professor of Philosophy at the University of North Carolina at Chapel Hill. She defends the view that not all lives are meaningful but only those in which a person actively engages in projects of worth. Thus, unlike Taylor, Wolf would not find meaning in the life of Sisyphus, even if his fondest desire was to roll stones up hills.

A meaningful life is, first of all, one that has within it the basis for an affirmative answer to the needs or longings that are characteristically described as needs for meaning. I have in mind, for example, the sort of questions people ask on their deathbeds, or simply in contemplation of their eventual deaths, about whether their lives have been (or are) worth living, whether they have had any point, and the sort of questions one asks when considering suicide and wondering whether one has any reason to go on. These questions are familiar from Russian novels and existentialist philosophy, if not from personal experience. Though they arise most poignantly in times of crisis and intense emotion, they also have their place in moments of calm reflection, when considering important life choices. Moreover, paradigms of what are taken to be meaningful and meaningless lives in our culture are readily available. Lives of great moral or intellectual accomplishment—Gandhi, Mother Teresa, Albert Einstein—come to mind as unquestionably meaningful lives (if any are); lives of waste and isolation—Thoreau's "lives of quiet desperation," typically anonymous to the rest of us, and the mythical figure of Sisyphus—represent meaninglessness.

To what general characteristics of meaningfulness do these images lead us and how do they provide an answer to the longings mentioned above? Roughly, I would say that meaningful lives are lives of active engagement in projects of worth. Of course, a good deal needs to be said in elaboration of this statement. Let me begin by discussing the two key phrases, "active engagement" and "projects of worth."

A person is actively engaged by something if she is gripped, excited, involved by it. Most obviously, we are actively engaged by the things and people about which and whom we are passionate. Opposites of active engagement are boredom and alienation. To be actively engaged in something is not always pleasant in the ordinary sense of the word. Activities in which people are actively engaged frequently involve stress, danger, exertion, or sorrow (consider, for example: writing a book, climbing a mountain, training for a marathon, caring for an ailing friend). However, there is something good about the feeling of engagement: one feels (typically without thinking about it) especially alive.

That a meaningful life must involve "projects of worth" will, I expect, be more controversial, for the phrase hints of a commitment to some sort of objective value. This is not accidental, for I believe that the idea of meaningfulness, and the concern that our lives possess it, are

From "Happiness and Meaning: Two Aspects of the Good Life," *Social Philosophy & Policy*, Vol. 24, 1997. Reprinted with the permission of Cambridge University Press.

conceptually linked to such a commitment.[1] Indeed, it is this linkage that I want to defend, for I have neither a philosophical theory of what objective value is nor a substantive theory about what has this sort of value. What is clear to me is that there can be no sense to the idea of meaningfulness without a distinction between more and less worthwhile ways to spend one's time, where the test of worth is at least partly independent of a subject's ungrounded preferences or enjoyment.

Consider first the longings or concerns about meaning that people have, their wondering whether their lives are meaningful, their vows to add more meaning to their lives. The sense of these concerns and resolves cannot fully be captured by an account in which what one does with one's life doesn't matter, as long as one enjoys or prefers it. Sometimes people have concerns about meaning despite their knowledge that their lives to date have been satisfying. Indeed, their enjoyment and "active engagement" with activities and values they now see as shallow seems only to heighten the sense of meaninglessness that comes to afflict them. Their sense that their lives so far have been meaningless cannot be a sense that their activities have not been chosen or fun. When they look for sources of meaning or ways to add meaning to their lives, they are searching for projects whose justifications lie elsewhere.

Second, we need an explanation for why certain sorts of activities and involvements come to mind as contributors to meaningfulness while others seem intuitively inappropriate. Think about what gives meaning to your own life and the lives of your friends and acquaintances. Among the things that tend to come up on such lists, I have already mentioned moral and intellectual accomplishments and the ongoing activities that lead to them. Relationships with friends and relatives are perhaps even more important for most of us. Aesthetic enterprises (both creative and appreciative), the cultivation of personal virtues, and religious practices frequently loom large. By contrast, it would be odd, if not bizarre, to think of crossword puzzles, sitcoms, or the kind of computer games to which I am fighting off addiction as providing meaning in our lives, though there is no question that they afford a sort of satisfaction and that they are the objects of choice. Some things, such as chocolate and aerobics class, I choose even at considerable cost to myself (it is irrelevant that these particular choices may be related); so I must find them worthwhile in a sense. But they are not the sorts of things that make life worth living.[2]

"Active engagement in projects of worth," I suggest, answers to the needs an account of meaningfulness in life must meet. If a person is or has been thus actively engaged, then she does have an answer to the question of whether her life is or has been worthwhile, whether it has or has had a point. When someone looks for ways to add meaning to her life, she is looking (though perhaps not under this description) for worthwhile projects about which she can get enthused. The account also explains why some activities and projects but not others come to mind as contributors to meaning in life. Some projects, or at any rate, particular acts, are worthwhile but too boring or mechanical to be sources of meaning. People do not get meaning from recycling or from writing checks to Oxfam and the ACLU. Other acts and activities, though highly pleasurable and deeply involving, like riding a roller coaster or meeting a movie star, do not seem to have the right kind of value to contribute to meaning.

Bernard Williams once distinguished categorical desires from the rest. Categorical desires give us reasons for living—they are not premised on the assumption that we will live. The sorts of things that give meaning to life tend to be objects of categorical desire. We desire them, at least so I would suggest, because we think them worthwhile. They are not worthwhile simply because we desire them or simply because they make our lives more pleasant.

Roughly, then, according to my proposal, a meaningful life must satisfy two criteria, suitably linked. First, there must be active engagement, and second, it must be engagement in (or with) projects of worth. A life is meaningless if it lacks active engagement with anything. A person who is bored or alienated from most of what she spends her life doing is one whose life can be said to lack meaning. Note that she may in fact be performing functions of worth. A housewife and mother, a doctor, or a busdriver may be competently doing a socially valuable job, but because she is not engaged by her work (or, as we are assuming, by anything else in her life), she has no categorical desires that give her a reason to live. At the same time, someone who is actively engaged may also live a meaningless life, if the objects of her involvement are utterly worthless. It is difficult to come up with examples of such lives that will be uncontroversial without being bizarre. But both bizarre and controversial examples have their place. In the bizarre category, we might consider pathological cases: someone whose sole passion in life is collecting rubber bands, or memorizing the dictionary, or making handwritten copies of *War and Peace*. Controversial cases will include the corporate lawyer who sacrifices her private life and health for success along the professional ladder, the devotee of a religious cult, or—an example offered by Wiggins[3]—the pig farmer who buys more land to grow more corn to feed more pigs to buy more land to grow more corn to feed more pigs.

We may summarize my proposal in terms of a slogan: "Meaning arises when subjective attraction meets objective attractiveness." The idea is that in a world in which some things are more worthwhile than others, meaning arises when a subject discovers or develops an affinity for one or typically several of the more worthwhile things and has and makes use of the opportunity to engage with it or them in a positive way.

NOTES

1. This point is made by David Wiggins in his brilliant but difficult essay "Truth, Invention, and the Meaning of Life," *Proceedings of the British Academy*, vol. 62 (1976).

2. Woody Allen appears to have a different view. His list of the things that make life worth living at the end of *Manhattan* includes, for example "the crabs at Sam Woo's," which would seem to be on the level of chocolates. On the other hand, the crabs' appearance on the list may be taken to show that he regards the dish as an accomplishment meriting aesthetic appreciation, where such appreciation is a worthy activity in itself; in this respect, the crabs might be akin to other items on his list such as the second movement of the *Jupiter Symphony*, Louis Armstrong's recording of "Potatohead Blues," and "those apples and pears of Cèzanne." Strictly speaking, the appreciation of great chocolate might also qualify as such an activity.

3. See Wiggins, "Truth, Invention, and the Meaning of Life," p. 342.

Study Questions

1. Based on the examples she provides, what does Wolf mean by "a project of worth"?
2. How would Wolf decide whether some activity was a project of worth?
3. In your view, are the lives of a college professor, a professional golfer, a janitor, and a hobo equally meaningful?
4. Would studying certain subjects add more meaning to life than studying other subjects?

Meaningful Lives?

CHRISTINE VITRANO

Christine Vitrano, who is Associate Professor of Philosophy at Brooklyn College of The City University of New York, considers the views of a meaningful life offered by both Richard Taylor and Susan Wolf. She finds neither convincing.

Richard Taylor and Susan Wolf offer contrasting visions of a meaningful life. I find each account partially persuasive, but neither entirely satisfactory.

For Wolf, a meaningful life is one in which you are actively engaged in projects of worth. To be engaged is to be "gripped, excited, involved."[1] If you find your life dreary, then it is not meaningful.

Enjoying activities, however, does not by itself render them meaningful; they also need to be worthwhile. As she says, "When someone looks for ways to add meaning to her life, she is looking . . . for worthwhile projects about which she can get enthused" and "whose justifications lie elsewhere," specifically in "objective value."

According to Wolf, worthwhile activities include "[r]elationships with friends and relatives . . . [a]esthetic enterprises (both creative and appreciative), the cultivation of personal virtues, and religious practices." Specific examples include "writing a book, climbing a mountain, training for a marathon." Among the activities that lack such worth are solving crossword puzzles, watching sitcoms, playing computer games, and eating chocolate, as well as "collecting rubber bands, or memorizing the dictionary, or making handwritten copies of *War and Peace*." Controversial cases are the paths of the "corporate lawyer who sacrifices her private life and

health for success along the professional ladder, the devotee of a religious cult, or . . . the pig farmer who buys more land to grow more corn to feed more pigs to buy more land to grow more corn to feed more pigs."

An obvious problem with Wolf's position is that by her own admission she has "neither a philosophical theory of what objective value is nor a substantive theory about what has that sort of value." She relies on supposedly shared intuitions regarding the worth of various activities, but to assume such agreement is unjustified. Some people appreciate an activity Wolf disparages, yet dismiss one she values highly. For example, spending thousands of hours training for a marathon strikes many as wearisome; they may be far more engaged by computer games. On the other hand, grappling with a New York Times Sunday Magazine crossword puzzle is a popular intellectual challenge, holding far more appeal for most than reading an article on metaethics, a subject Wolf finds fascinating.

She might respond to these observations by claiming that the problem with crossword puzzles lies not in their essential unimportance but in their use as mere pastimes. In other words, even those who enjoy solving them don't take them seriously.

This reply, however, only deepens Wolf's difficulty because the same activity could be judged as meaningful or meaningless depending on why a person engages in it. Consider, for instance, a physicist who does scientific research because of the enjoyment it brings but is devoted to chess problems for their intellectual challenge. For that scholar, pursuing physics would be meaningless, but composing and solving chess problems would be meaningful—hardly the conclusion Wolf is seeking.

Furthermore, suppose that in order to distract myself from the monotony of caring for my two children, I read an article on metaphysics. Why should the motive affect the worthiness of the activity?

Because Wolf's position is weakened by her commitment to an objective value that she cannot explain, we might drop that aspect of her position and accept Richard Taylor's view that a meaningful life is one that affords you long-term satisfaction, regardless of the activities you choose. Thus the life of Sisyphus would be meaningful if Sisyphus relished rolling stones up hills.

But why call such a life meaningful? Why not just describe it as pleasant, enjoyable, or happy?

Declaring it meaningful neither clarifies any issue nor solves any problem.

Taylor correctly claims that Sisyphus would be happy were he contented with his life, but meaningfulness means more than contentment. Wolf emphasizes that point but cannot say what more is required. Thus neither position is convincing.

In sum, we can appropriately characterize lives as long or short, moral or immoral, as well as successful or unsuccessful in various respects, including accumulating business profits, creating artistic works, or maintaining loving relationships. To ask whether a life is meaningful, however, is to pose a question that incorporates an enigmatic term. Searching for the right answer leads only to frustration.

NOTE

1. All quotations are from the preceding article by Susan Wolf.

Study Questions

1. What is Vitrano's objection to Wolf's account of a meaningful life?
2. What is Vitrano's objection to Taylor's account of a meaningful life?
3. Does Vitrano believe a life is either meaningful or meaningless?
4. Do you believe a life is either meaningful or meaningless?

Glossary

This collection of key terms with their meanings is drawn from *The Elements of Philosophy: Readings from Past and Present*, edited by Tamar Szabo Gendler (Yale University), Susanna Siegel (Harvard University), and Steven M. Cahn (City University of New York Graduate Center), published by Oxford University Press, 2008.

A priori/a posteriori (Latin)   Something can be known a priori if it can be known independently of—or prior to—experience; something can be known only a posteriori if it can be known only on the basis of—or posterior to—experience.

Ad hominem (Latin, "to the man")   Attacking the character or outlook of one's opponent, rather than replying to one's opponent's argument.

Analytic/synthetic   According to Immanuel Kant, who introduced the expression, an *analytic* proposition is one whose predicate is "contained in" its subject. Alternatively: an analytic proposition is one that can be transformed into a tautology merely by substituting synonymous terms for its constituent expressions. Statements such as "all bachelors are male" and "if something is a square then it is a rectangle" are often held to express true analytic propositions. A proposition is *synthetic* if it is not analytic. Statements such as "Kant was born on April 22" and "some apples are red" express synthetic propositions.

Argument/premise/conclusion   A set of considerations presented in support of some claim. The statement that one is trying to prove is called the *conclusion*; the statements that are meant to support that conclusion are called the *premises*. The premises and conclusion together form an *argument*.

Begging the question   Circular reasoning; taking as one of your assumptions that which you are seeking to establish.

Categorical/hypothetical imperative   A distinction made by Immanuel Kant between two sorts of imperatives, that is, commands that you have reason to obey. A *hypothetical imperative* is one that you have reason to obey only if (on the hypothesis that) you have some particular preexisting desire; for example, "get out of the kitchen" (. . . if you can't stand the heat). A categorical imperative is one that you have reason to obey categorically, regardless of your own inclinations, for example (according to Kant), "don't lie."

Ceteris paribus (Latin)   All other things being equal; with all other factors held constant.

Consequentialism/utilitarianism   The view that what makes an act right or wrong is the goodness or badness of the act's consequences; *utilitarianism* is a particular form of consequentialism that restricts its attention to consequences involving the welfare of sentient beings. Among the most famous advocates of utilitarianism is John Stuart Mill. Consequentialism/utilitarianism is often contrasted with deontology and virtue ethics. See also *deontology, virtue ethics*.

Consistent   A set of propositions is consistent if it does not entail a contradiction; a set of propositions is inconsistent otherwise. See also *contradiction*.

Contradiction   A proposition that is false by virtue of its form alone; a false but empty claim.

Counterexample   An example that shows the falsity of some theory or claim.

Deontology   An ethical view based on the notion of duty or rights. The most famous advocate of deontological ethics was Immanuel Kant. Deontology is often contrasted with consequentialism and virtue ethics. See also *consequentialism, virtue ethics*.

Determinism   The doctrine that every event has a cause and that if the cause occurs, the event must also occur.

Empiricism/rationalism   A distinction between two general philosophical outlooks. Whereas *empiricists* stress the role of sense experience in the acquisition of knowledge, *rationalists* stress the role of reason unaided by the senses.

Epiphenomenal/epiphenomenalism   A feature of a situation is *epiphenomenal* if it occurs as a side effect of the main phenomenon. In philosophy of mind, *epiphenomenalism* is

551

the view that mental events are caused by physical events but have no effects upon physical events.

Functionalism   In philosophy of mind, the view that mental states can be fully characterized by the role they play: by specifying what external conditions and other mental states typically cause them and what behaviors and other mental states they typically cause.

Identity theory of mind   The view that states and processes of the mind are identical to states and processes of the brain.

Intuitionism   The view that knowledge in a certain domain can be acquired through *intuition,* a process of direct nonsensory apprehension of the truth and falsity of certain claims.

Materialism   The view that everything that exists is composed entirely of matter, so that nothing nonmaterial exists. Materialism is often contrasted with *idealism* or *dualism*, and is roughly synonymous with *physicalism.*

Metaphysics   The branch of philosophy concerned with exploring the fundamental nature of reality.

Necessary/sufficient   If A is *necessary* for B, then it is not possible for B to hold without A holding. (This means that the absence of A guarantees the absence of B.) If A is *sufficient* for B, then if A holds, B must also hold. (This means that the absence of B guarantees the absence of A.) Being over thirty years old is necessary but not sufficient for being a senator (since all senators are over thirty, but there are people over thirty who are not senators); being a senator from Montana is sufficient but not necessary for being a senator (since all senators from Montana are senators, but there are senators who are not senators from Montana). Note that A is necessary for B if and only if B is sufficient for A. (Since being a senator from Montana is sufficient for being a senator, being a senator is necessary for being a senator from Montana.) Philosophers are often concerned with finding *necessary and sufficient* conditions for particular concepts. For example, being a rectangle with four equal sides is necessary and suf-

ficient for being a square; being an instance of justified true belief is (it might be thought) necessary and sufficient for being an instance of knowledge.

Physicalism   The view that everything that exists is entirely physical. Physicalism is often contrasted with *idealism*—the view that everything that exists is entirely nonphysical—and *dualism*—the view that some things that exist are physical and other things that exist are nonphysical. Physicalism is roughly synonymous with *materialism*—the view that everything that exists is made of matter.

Problem of evil   The challenge of reconciling the existence of a perfectly omniscient, omnipotent, and omnibenevolent deity with the manifest presence of evil in the world.

Qualia   The introspectively accessible felt qualities that are associated with an experience, such as the feeling of a pain or the smell of a rose. The singular of *qualia* is *quale.*

Sound/valid/entail   A deductive argument is *valid* if the premises *entail* the conclusion, so that it is not possible for the argument's premises to be true while the argument's conclusion is false; a deductive argument is *sound* if it is valid and all its premises are true. An argument that is not valid is *invalid*; an argument that is not sound is *unsound.* All invalid arguments are unsound, but not all unsound arguments are invalid.

Reductio ad absurdum   (Latin, "reduction to absurdity") A mode of reasoning that involves validly deriving a contradiction from a set of premises, thereby showing that at least one of the set's members must be rejected.

Tautology   A proposition that is true by virtue of its form alone; a true but empty claim.

Virtue ethics   An ethical view that gives a central role to the idea of virtuous character. The most famous advocate of virtue ethics is Aristotle. Virtue ethics is often contrasted with consequentialism and deontology. See also *consequentialism, deontology.*

Index